P9-CFK-132

Fighting Two Colonialisms
Women in Guinea-Bissau

by Stephanie Urdang

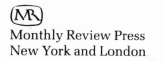

Monthly Review Press
New York and London

HQ
1818
.U69

Copyright © 1979 by Stephanie Urdang
All rights reserved

Library of Congress Cataloging in Publication Data
Urdang, Stephanie
    Fighting two colonialisms.
        1. Women—Guinea-Bissau.   2. Women's rights—
    Guinea-Bissau.   3. Guinea-Bissau—Colonial influence.
    I. Title.
    HQ1818.U69   301.41'2'096657   79-2329
    ISBN 0-85345-511-2
    ISBN 0-85345-524-4 paper

Monthly Review Press
62 West 14th Street, New York, N.Y. 10011
47 Red Lion Street, London WC1R 4PF

Manufactured in the United States of America

10 9 8 7 6 5 4 3 2 1

AUG 2 0 1987

Contents

Preface and Acknowledgments

I can pinpoint the exact evening that my particular interest in the role of women in Guinea-Bissau was aroused. Squashed in the corner of a friend's overcrowded car, I traveled through the cold and snowy streets of New York City one late February night in 1969, going home from a meeting. Amilcar Cabral was the speaker, and he talked about the revolution his people were fighting in Guinea-Bissau. I sat wrapped in emotions of elation and respect, still new to the reality of such struggles, inspired both by what was being achieved in the small African country and by the extraordinary man we had met. Around me, my equally excited friends discussed the impression that Cabral had made on them. "But we must admit he is a good politician," one voice declared. "He said just what we wanted to hear about women! No doubt he knows that this is a big issue in America at the moment." Her tone made it clear that she, at least, had not been taken in.

I felt stung. Among Cabral's many impressive traits were his uncompromising honesty and the clarity of his political position. Her words made no sense to me, and I retreated into my reverie— tinged with decided romanticism—and thought about what he had told us. During the informal meeting he had stressed the need for women to be liberated in the process of revolution, explaining that women were playing a fundamental role in the struggle. "Women and men are equal partners in our struggle," he had said. But the remarks of my skeptical friend echoed behind these words, making me determined to find out more.

Three years later, Cabral returned to New York, and once again he spoke to a small gathering of supporters. Once again he referred to the role of women. After the meeting a friend and I asked him for more specifics about women's participation. He responded by taking a fat envelope of photographs out of his brief case, and turning them over one by one, he pointed out the women. This woman is a political commissar for the south front. That woman teaches in a boarding school. Yet another is in charge of the radio broadcasts. Many are nurses, he said, many are health workers, others are in the army. His pride and pleasure in sharing this with us was obvious and convinced me further that he was not pandering to the American left. But fifteen minutes' conversation could not go beyond the superficial.

At the time the thought of visiting Guinea-Bissau and seeing the revolution for myself could not have been further from my mind. That idea was planted some nine months later when I attended the tenth anniversary of the Organization of African Unity in Addis Ababa in 1973. It was there that I was first invited to visit as a journalist by the head of the liberation movement (PAIGC) delegation.

A number of journalists (although few from the United States) traveled into the liberated zones of Guinea-Bissau during the war years and reported on the conditions they found there: the schools, the hospitals, the people's stores, the systems of local and regional government. Particularly they related the support of the people for the struggle, evidenced in numerous ways, and they confirmed PAIGC's claim that they controlled two-thirds of the country, a claim so hotly denied by the Portuguese government and its allies. If I went, I decided, I wanted to do more than add to these accounts. My idea was to write about the process of the revolution and its effect on the people of Guinea-Bissau, taking one aspect of the revolution and through it trying to elucidate the whole process. Both the memory of Cabral's emphasis on the equal role of women in his country and my own growing commitment to the women's movement turned my idea into intention. And it was for permission to do this that I asked in my written application sent on my return to the United States.

My interest in Guinea-Bissau, however, had a longer history than my identification with the women's movement. My opposition to the bitter oppression and brutality of the apartheid regime had made me decide to leave my country, South Africa, in 1967. After immigrating to the United States, I began to work with southern Africa liberation support groups, most particularly with the Southern Africa Committee in New York. Concerned by the chronic lack of information on the situation in southern Africa and U.S. involvement there, we began to publish *Southern Africa*, which over the years developed into a monthly news magazine and through which I was able to follow events on the subcontinent. (Although located in West Africa, Guinea-Bissau was included within the political boundaries of southern Africa because of its status as a Portuguese colony.)

But while my overall knowledge of the Guinea-Bissau revolution was fairly extensive by 1974, prior to my visit I had little concrete information about the role of women: a published interview here, a statement there, a comment in a speech of a leader. All these pointed to an active role for women, but for me the burning questions began with *how?* How does a liberation movement in one of the smallest, poorest, and least developed countries of the world put such a program into practice? How does the movement begin the process of change, given the attitudes firmly embedded in the minds of both men and women of Guinea-Bissau that are counter to the idea of an emancipated woman? How, on a day-to-day level, does this effect the lives of the people?

These were questions that could not be answered from a distance, and they led me to cable my acceptance of PAIGC's formal invitation, to fit myself out with surplus U.S. army uniforms and French canvas and rubber tropical boots, to walk miles each day through the icy streets of a New York winter in the hope of getting fit enough for the long marches through the hot and muggy forests of the liberated zones, and to finally set off for the headquarters of PAIGC in April 1974.

I was accompanied by more than my uniforms, my cameras and film, my small cassette tape recorder and tapes, and my new spiral notebooks: I took my own preconceptions of what I would find there. It may not be possible to go to another society without taking expectations colored by one's own experience, which in turn color the perceptions of the society. In my case I was traveling from a highly developed society to one of the most undeveloped; from the core of capitalism to a small revolutionary country that had more than a few lessons to offer the former. While preconceptions are inevitable, I hoped that I could be open enough to learn from what I saw and adjust as I went along.

By the time I arrived, the country had been proclaimed a state by the liberation movement but the war itself showed every sign of continuing well into the future. I anticipated that I would be observing a typical few weeks in a protracted war. I was wrong. While I was deep inside the country the fascist government of Caetano fell, and by the time I left negotiations for independence had begun.

I was a guest of PAIGC for two months, from mid-April to mid-June 1974, of which five weeks were spent in the liberated zones—three and a half weeks in the south front and ten days in the east. The rest of the time was spent in Boké, a border town in neighboring Guinea (Conakry)—the site of the PAIGC administrative center, Solidarity Hospital, and a nursing school—and in Conakry, where the movement's headquarters had been establish ed at the beginning of the struggle. Independence, which came in September the same year, allowed me to return to a totally liberated country, and for two and a half months, between June and August 1976, I traveled extensively throughout the country, beginning in Bissau, the capital.

In Guinea-Bissau I found what I had hoped to find: that the liberation of women is an explicit and integral part of the overall revolution. At the same time, it is considered a protracted struggle to be waged by the women themselves. As such, it would continue long after independence had been won. It was never implied that their liberation would conveniently materialize at that time, "because now everybody is free."

This is what this book is about: the way in which theory is put into practice so that it becomes a reality for both the women and the men, and the way in which the women themselves have taken up the fight against their own oppression. I have tried to convey the special conditions of Guinea-Bissau, so that the context of revolutionary practice can be better appreciated. Even at times when I disagreed with a particular method, I generally came to understand why it had been chosen consciously. I hope in telling of this story, women in different parts of the world will find aspects which are relevant and applicable to their own struggle. Most particularly, I hope that they will appreciate that without the basic principle of a total revolutionary process, true liberation for women cannot be acheived.

What follows are my own observations and my own understanding of the revolution in Guinea-Bissau. From this experience I personally learned lessons that had a profound impact on my view of the world and of revolution in general. For this I have much to thank the women of Guinea-Bissau, especially those who can be found in the pages of this book, who patiently showed me their revolution—in and out of war—and explained how and why they are doing what they are doing in the context of their own experience and social conditions.

I wish I could be confident that I have done justice to their revolution and their courage. For while the struggle is not romantic, it is certainly heroic.

May 1979

First and foremost I want to thank the many people in Guinea-Bissau who so patiently showed me their revolution and assisted this project in numerous ways. Particularly, I want to thank Teodora Ignacia Gomes, who spared no effort in her determination to have me understand their struggle. I must, however, take full credit for the misconceptions and misrepresentations.

It is hard to single out a few of the large number of friends who aided this project in different ways. The manuscript was read at various stages by Eve Hall, Hermione Harris, Janet Siskind, Jennifer Davis, and Brian. Their comments and criticisms were crucial in helping me shape this book into its present form. I especially value their input because of the sustained support and encouragement that came with it. Again, I must take responsibility for the failings. Thanks, too, for the same support and encouragement—essential to get and keep me going—to my "Friday night comrades," to Kered Boyd, and to Suzette Abbot, who also gave hours of her time to both print a number of my photographs and to teach me how to do them myself. I appreciate the care taken by Karen Judd, my editor at Monthly Review, which enabled the final rewrite to be surprisingly painless.

This project would not have been possible without the financial support I received from a number of sources. I want to express my sincere gratitude to the following:

The Louis M. Rabinowitz Foundation, whose grant enabled me to finish the book without having to expend precious time seeking a salary; Carol Bernstein Ferry and W. H. Ferry, whose generosity supported the major part of my expenses for both trips to Guinea-Bissau. Other assistance came from the Women's Division of the United Methodist Church, the Center for Social Action of the United Church of Christ, and Peter Weiss through the Fund for Tomorrow.

Introduction

It is easy to miss the Republic of Guinea-Bissau, when glancing casually over a map of Africa. But taking a closer look, it can be found on the west coast of that vast continent—a small wedge of a country, separating for a short distance the border between the two infinitely larger territories of Senegal to the north and the Republic of Guinea (Conakry)* to the south. Off its coast are a spattering of small islands, while the wedge itself is cracked by rivers that cover its surface. The jagged outline of Guinea-Bissau on the map lends itself to a caricature of the late-nineteenth-century "scramble for Africa": Portugal barely managing to grab a bite of the enormous West African pie, spilling crumbs in its haste, before France and Britain push their way in and greedily slice up the area between them.

Ninety years were to pass before Portugal had to give up even this portion of Africa. But this time it was the people who finally pushed: led by the African Party for the Independence of Guinea

---

*Guinea-Bissau is bordered by the Republic of Guinea, the ex-French colony, whose capital is Conakry. In order to avoid confusion I will refer to this country as Guinea (Conakry). However "Guinea" or "Guinean" used alone, refers to the Republic of Guinea-Bissau.

and Cape Verde (PAIGC), they pushed out the Portuguese in 1974, after fighting a guerrilla war for eleven and a half years. PAIGC was founded by Amilcar Cabral and a group of his comrades in Bissau, the capital, in the mid fifties, a time when negotiations for the independence of many of Africa's colonies were in progress. This period formed a prelude to the 1960s, which will be remembered as the decade of independence for most of Africa. But markedly absent in that burst of independence were the colonies of Portugal. Early efforts by PAIGC to negotiate independence for Guinea failed, and both independence and liberation had to be fought for—by protracted armed struggle.

The war began early in 1963, and ended in 1974, when Portugal recognized the independent Republic of Guinea-Bissau. Amilcar Cabral was not among those celebrating the small country's victory, however. He had been assassinated just one and a half years earlier in an unsuccessful effort by the colonialists to stem the PAIGC successes in winning the support of the people.

Cabral's contribution to the struggle lay not only in his exceptional leadership qualities, but in his theoretical formulations, firmly rooted in the African experience. It was these, as well as his ability to develop the strategies to transform theory into practice, that continued long after his death, and allowed the reverberations of the revolution to be felt far beyond the country's borders, from one end of Africa to the other, and throughout the third world.

Despite its size—only some 14,000 square miles—Guinea-Bissau now represents a significant new stream in African history and politics, due primarily to the nature of its liberation movement. For the first time in the history of sub-Saharan Africa a guerrilla movement forced a colonial power to withdraw. Moreover, that liberation movement, along with FRELIMO of Mozambique and MPLA of Angola*, was instrumental in the downfall of the fascist government of Portugal itself. Yet another dimension of this movement increased the importance of its revolution: its ideology. Armed struggle and defeat of the colo-

---

*The Popular Movement for the Liberation of Angola (MPLA) and the Front for the Liberation of Mozambique (FRELIMO) led the struggles against Portuguese colonialism in their respective countries. They share with PAIGC a similar ideology and practice, and all three have been closely related since their inception.

nialists was not the ultimate goal; rather, the overall perspective of the PAIGC embraced the need simultaneously to pick up arms and to build a new, nonexploitative society.

This dual goal required an intensive period of political mobilization, before and throughout the war, for Guinea's people, 95 percent of whom were peasants. The war of liberation thus enabled PAIGC to define its own terms for independence: a revolutionary society based on a socialist path of development. "Liberation of the people means the liberation of the productive forces of our country," explained Amilcar Cabral, "the liquidation of all kinds of imperialist or colonial domination in our country, and the taking of every measure to avoid any new exploitation of our people. We don't confuse exploitation with the color of one's skin. We want equality, social justice, and freedom."[1]

This book focuses on the way in which PAIGC ideology integrates the emancipation of women into the total revolution; the way it emphasizes the need for women to play an equal political, economic, and social role in both the armed struggle and the construction of the new society. Central to this is PAIGC's understanding that the liberation struggle must be waged by the women themselves. It is an analysis which grew out of the recognition that women suffer a dual oppression, expressed in Guinea-Bissau as the need for women to "fight against two colonialisms—the one of the Portuguese and the other of men."

What constitutes oppression? I think if a group, class, or nationality does not have control over its destiny, does not have the possibility to fulfill its potential, then it is oppressed. If a group, class, or nationality is dominated by another, then it is oppressed. The key to the perpetuation of such oppression is the ability of the oppressor to persuade the oppressed to cooperate in their servitude. This phenomenon is not confined to male-female relations, of course, but it remains a distinct and fundamental element in those relationships in any society. And, since oppression revolves around a calculated notion of the inferiority of the oppressed, which serves the oppressor's need to dominate and exploit, it is under capitalism that one finds this cultivated to the extreme; a marked feature of capitalism, being both male dominated and exploitative, is sexism.

This is not to suggest that socialist countries, or those in the process of building socialism, are not male dominated: women generally are as conspicuously absent in the high levels of government, and hence decision-making, as they are in capitalist societies. But in assessing the potential for change, it is necessary to look at the differences between the two systems, and the foundations upon which they rest.

The need to exploit workers is structurally inherent in capitalism, which relies on a vast reserve labor pool as a device to hold down wages. If one group becomes absorbed into the workforce— a particular group of immigrants, for instance—there must be others to fill the gap—migrants, say, or ethnic minorities. Because of women's subordinate social position in society, they are the most threatened or vulnerable workers within any such group, and they end up being paid the more miserable wages. Women thus form an exploited subgroup in any labor reserve, constant across particular ethnic or other groupings. Since it is convenient to capitalism to have this subgroup as a cheap labor reserve, capitalism will energetically resist equality for women. Equality would not only remove this cheap labor reserve from the market, it would challenge the capitalists' ability to control production by manipulating the workforce. Equality, moreover, is potentially destructive to the socioeconomic fabric of the patriarchal society by which capitalism is reproduced.

The revolutionary third world society that Guinea-Bissau envisions, by contrast, has no historically vested interest in sexism; it does not need divisions among the workers, it does not need unemployment. Rather, it needs the unified efforts of all, and egalitarianism, both economic and cultural, is not incompatible with its goals. Hence it is possible for women's emancipation to be national policy, encouraged by government and party as part of the overall process of social transformation. Women's organizations can be supported with government resources, and women can participate at all levels of government and party work and decision-making, for the very reason that their liberation is viewed as essential for the advancement of the society as a whole. This is by no means automatic to socialism, of course, or to Guinea-Bissau. The conditions there make the women's struggle possible, but a conscious commitment is needed, from both party and people, to counter the oppression of women as women and to overcome attitudes inherent in this form of oppression.

This commitment can be seen in the creativity with which the PAIGC has attacked problems that touched on the very core of the lives of the people. Its leaders did not stand back as moralistic observers, passing judgment on the social relations that exist among the people; they moved in partisan but sensitive ways to set in motion processes of change.

In Guinea-Bissau we can see the process of liberation develop— but the key word is "process." The oppression of women is not dissolving before our eyes, but slowly—"step by step," to use a favorite Guinean phrase—it is being overcome. The chapters that follow look at this process during two phases in the history of Guinea-Bissau's revolution: the first, the period of armed struggle, occupies the major portion of the book, while the second and transitional stage, the period immediately after independence, is discussed in less detail, having only just begun.

Early in the first stage, PAIGC showed a consciousness of the fact that women's liberation had to be fought on two fronts— from above and from below. Party pronouncements in themselves were insufficient: it was essential that women themselves take up the issue, so that liberation would be truly theirs. An essential element of this is that women raise their own demands. If they do not, it seems unlikely that the men or the top leadership of the state and party—almost totally male—will do it for them. From the outset this leadership stated clearly that women's liberation, like any freedom, is not given. It is a right, but it has to be taken. This is probably as much as can be expected. Women are just beginning to take men to task for their sexist attitudes. As they grow stronger, these same male leaders might be in for quite a shock. But their statements, that women make their own demands, while they give a certain legitimacy to women's actions that no doubt threaten men, can be uttered too easily. It is necessary to balance three elements: what the party or state proposes; how women respond to such proposals in order to strengthen and extend them; what the women themselves initiate and demand from their own experience. There is a limit, for instance, to the power of laws if women themselves do not challenge the men who can be sanctioned under them. On the other hand, all elements together will be necessary to engineer the profound structural changes needed to have an impact on the relations of production—a facet of the revolution that in the end may have the most far-reaching effect on the actual conditions of women's lives.

My trip to the liberated zones gave me a sense of the strides that were being made in changing the lives of peasant women— some 95 percent of the women in the country. I felt that the personal development of peasant women, due to conscious efforts to liberate their productive capacities, would continue to advance, that more and more girls would go to school, thereby securing the trend toward liberation for the coming generations, and that attitudes of both women and men would continue to change. But I sensed too that the next qualitative step forward for women could occur only when the sexual division of labor begins to change, when men are no longer "helping" women in their work, when the heavy burden of production is shifted to rest more equally on the shoulders of both men and women.

Evidence of the kind of fundamental obstacles to full liberation, as well as of the efforts of women and party to overcome them, can be seen in the changing customs considered oppressive to women, such as forced marriage, denial of divorce rights to women, and polygyny.* In Guinea-Bissau the labor of women provides the foundation for the economy. Women make up the bulk of the agricultural workforce, in a country in which agriculture is the mainstay of the economy. The customs defining their roles and rights were firmly embedded in the life of the people, and inextricably intertwined with the village economy. Such customs have survived not because they provided the basis for the most efficient economy, but because the economy which they supported was a viable one. And once viable, there was little internal demand for further adaptation. Polygyny was not

---

*Polygyny (as opposed to polygamy) refers to the practice in which a man marries more than one wife; polyandry to that where a woman marries more than one man. Polygamy refers to the custom in which either a man or a woman can marry more than one spouse. Although polygyny was the norm in Guinea-Bissau, when quoting sources that have used "polygamy," I have retained this term.

the only way that a man gained many workers for his land, but it was one way. The bride-price provided compensation for the worker that a father was about to lose through the marriage and thus fitted into the economic reality of village life. Divorce for women was out of the question in this context, as the whole system would founder if women were free to dissolve their marriages. Those who ran away had to leave their children behind. If they had no children, their families would have to return the bride-price.

These customs not only served to produce workers and the next generation of workers, they provided a system of social security for village life, an environment for mutual responsibility among the women. Women who were ill were looked after by other women. Children whose mother had died were cared for by her co-wives or husband's relatives. At harvesting time all the women pooled their labor to help each other bring in the harvest. Such customs, while restricting, enabled a particular economic system to work.

All of this makes it enormously difficult to bring these practices to an end. However strongly PAIGC felt about the destructive nature of the three customs, they could not, as Cabral was wont to say, pass a decree and outlaw them. Instead they began the process of political education directed toward the goal of total social transformation, the only way to remove the conditions which engendered oppressive social practices in the first place. The pace PAIGC set is well reflected in a comment of the commissioner of justice*: "We have to move, but we have to move slowly or the people will turn against us."

No simple task. For women, less willing to cooperate in their oppression, it has been relatively easier. The awareness that comes from oppression made many women quick to respond to the possibility of a life that did not bind them in prescribed ways. It was this awareness that prompted an old peasant woman to grab the arm of a visitor and say, "If you think that our society gave us the education to accept polygyny emotionally, you are wrong."

---

*In Guinea-Bissau the term *commisário* (commissioner) is used in place of "minister." This has been adopted to avoid the sense of overall authority which PAIGC feels is implied in the term "minister."

For men it was a totally different matter. They had everything to lose and, as far as they could see, little to gain. For a peasant boy growing up in a village both his social experience and his social expectations were determined by what he saw around him; the way he would choose his wife, the status he would gain through the inferior position of women as well as his status in relation to other men, the wealth he might accumulate, or the political power he might acquire. The pattern was set early and was acceptable to him. After all, it was all he knew, all he expected. And it was satisfying. The economy was organized in his best interests, with the consequence that women were reduced as low as men rose high.

With the political mobilization undertaken by PAIGC, all this was challenged. What started as a struggle to overthrow the brutal and oppressive colonialist regime quickly developed into a process of total social transformation, and men began to see that so long as they had a vested interest in maintaining the old social order, they would lose out. The social structure which had been the secure foundation of their everyday life must have suddenly seemed fragile. PAIGC supported women in challenging this older order, and women, in return, actively sought support from PAIGC.

The changes that occurred in the years that followed—and described in the body of this book—might look insignificant to an outside observer. But in this context, they are dramatic.

Dramatic, yet only the beginning. With independence came the urgent need to wrest an impoverished nation from a condition of almost total underdevelopment. What models did the leaders have? One might imagine they could look to those African states that had achieved independence a good ten to fifteen years earlier, but such examples tend to be negative, showing what *not* to do. Before considering the direction that PAIGC and the state are taking in their development programs, therefore, it may be useful to look briefly at the experience of neocolonial Africa, particularly as it relates to the effect of development on women.

Throughout Africa the new nations continued for the most part along the paths of development laid down by the colonizing powers, that is, directed primarily toward export production. At best, the new rulers were granted a small share in the wealth that kept flowing into Europe and the United States. This orientation has consequences for education, industrialization, and other aspects of development. For many this is a surprising realization. To most people, the concept of development connotes the idea of "improvement." "Modernization" should free the peasants from backbreaking toil. Education should help those unfortunates in illiterate societies to join the wide world. But it is becoming increasingly apparent that while "development" has benefited the elites of neocolonial countries, not to mention the capitalist investors, it has done little to improve the lives of the peasants— i.e., the majority of Africa's people. And, as is also becoming clear, development has done even less to improve the lot of the women, those most responsible for agricultural production.

Africa, in particular sub-Saharan Africa, continues to be dependent on the labor of women to feed the people. But it is not the women who have benefited from the training programs. Seldom have they had their heavy burden lightened by mechanized methods of production, or have they been educated for alternative work. Rather, they continue to work as their mothers and grandmothers before them, using time-honored, if generally inefficient, techniques to produce barely enough to feed their families. Despite women's greater role in agricultural production, it is the men who are placed in specially designed training programs and who apply their newly acquired skills to the production of cash crops rather than subsistence crops. These methods enable the male cultivators to increase their productivity and to gain access to cash. Women, on the other hand, continue to produce food to feed their husbands and children, get no cash rewards, and hence become even more dependent on the men as their society changes its role in the world market.

The new techniques, along with cash payment for their crops, serves to increase the gap in status between men and women. For instance, it is the women who continue to spread manure to fertilize their crops, just as they continue to carry loads on their heads as they make their way on foot over long distances. Nearby the men are quickly spreading chemical fertilizers, and when their field work is done can be seen riding bicycles and even trucks to transport their goods.

An important part of development is education. Most neo-colonial states have managed to improve upon the poor record of the colonial powers in providing schools, and along with schools have come new training programs. But the schoolrooms see far more boys than girls. The girls are needed at home to help their mothers with women's work, so that parents are less than eager to send them to school. This is compounded by the fact that girls are expected to marry young and to bring in a bride-price. What use then, a girl's parents will argue, is education to a daughter who will leave her father's village for her husband's village and so take the benefits of her education away with her? The investment made in her education will not help the parents when they grow old, as will the education of her brothers.

The percentage of girls in school has remained very low in the rural areas of Africa. Those who do go to school find a divided curriculum, with different subjects for girls and boys. This education and the assumptions of a girl's inferiority reinforce the attitudes that the girls take with them into the classroom from their homes, namely, that men are superior, have more initiative, and are expected to take on positions of responsibility and authority. Such attitudes continue to plague them when they leave school and try to enter the labor market.

Few women can be found in the growing industrial sector because jobs are being reserved for men. There is a widespread belief in many countries that industrialization must reach a certain level before "womanpower" can be utilized. Otherwise, women will be taking jobs away from men. But in fact, the planners need hardly worry. Without the education or political education that emphasizes the right for women to join the productive forces outside of the village, there are not large numbers of women waiting to push men out of their jobs. Women have been conditioned sufficiently not to venture too far outside the home. When they do enter the industrial sector, it is as lower paid workers, doing the most unskilled of work, filling vacancies left by the advancement of men. With insufficient education or training provided to equip them with the kind of skills needed to secure jobs in the modern sector, a pattern emerges in which men are becoming more qualified, while women lag further and further behind.

Those few women, particularly urban-born or -raised women, who do break into the more skilled professions tend to gravitate almost exclusively toward the two professions considered socially appropriate for respectable young ladies: nursing and teaching. The work of nurses—taking care of people—is regarded as an extension of women's role as mothers, while that of teaching keeps them in the school, in contact only with their pupils and the few other teachers. It does not bring them into the predominantly male life of the towns.[2]

The recurring lack of emphasis on the need for development programs to benefit women is linked to the poverty of these nations and to women's role in agricultural production. Subsistence agriculture based on women's unpaid labor feeds most of the people, but produces no visible income for the individual or the state. Cash crops, on the other hand, particularly such crops as cotton, coffee, or peanuts, can be exported to bring in foreign exchange. Any form of assistance that a government gives the cash-crop farmers—who are invariably male—is seen as an investment. Most governments want to be sure that this sector shows increasing returns, and so are willing to provide farmers with such incentives as seeds, mechanization, fertilizers, and loans for improvements. So long as women's work continues to feed the workers and their children, however badly, without outside incentives, many governments are happy to leave them to their own devices.

This depressing pattern can be traced through most of Africa, as one surveys the effects of the first few decades of independence from British and French rule. But while these manifestations of "development" are so widely prevalent, they are not inevitable. To look for more hopeful programs we must look away from the Senegals, the Ivory Coasts, the Kenyas of Africa, and toward such countries as Mozambique, Angola, and Guinea-Bissau, trying—or beginning to try—against huge odds to reconstruct their war-torn economies while improving rather than sacrificing the conditions of the masses of the people.

Since the percentage of peasants is particularly high in Guinea-Bissau, the battle to increase rural production is crucial. Growth has had to begin, however, from a devastatingly underdeveloped situation. When the Portuguese finally left, the PAIGC government inherited an economy that was one of the poorest in Africa, and peculiarly distorted by colonialism, having come to depend for its viability on infusions of cash from Lisbon. This relatively recent paradoxical situation stemmed from Portugal's last-ditch efforts to compete with the guerrillas, who in the latter years of the war set up an alternative economy, based on agricultural self-sufficiency, in the liberated zones. The Portuguese counterattack, which paid inflated salaries to Guineans connected with the administration even as the prices of basic commodities were set artificially low, drained the treasury. Meanwhile, whereas the movement had managed to feed its supporters in the liberated zones and even to export small quantities of rice, the colonialists, having lost most of the rural areas and hence both staple and export crops, had been forced to import rice to feed the half of the population they controlled. This left the new regime with still another credit problem, because the Portuguese had been paying fifteen escudos per kilo of rice and then reselling it for seven escudos, in response to competition from PAIGC.

Compounding the fiscal morass, independence also brought massive relocations of the population: refugees returned from Senegal and neighboring French Guinea; peasants who had fled to the towns to avoid the bombing returned to their old villages; and the people in the liberated zones, who to lessen the impact of the bombs had established their villages in fragments in the forests, moved back onto their own land. The priority of all these groups was to reestablish their homes, and agricultural production suffered a great setback as a result. Thus, in the first year of independence, PAIGC had to import 90 percent of the national food supply—and this without any way of earning foreign currency.

In every area then—education, justice, public works, communications, people's stores and town markets, health, housing, city and town government—new systems have to be developed. The bureaucracy inherited from the colonialists had to be dismantled and replaced with a government based on the ideology of PAIGC. As I was shown the difficulties confronting PAIGC, in every sector of the society I recalled words of Amilcar Cabral, which took on sharper meaning for me now that I could attach them to real conditions:

> Keep always in mind that people are not fighting for ideas, for things in anyone's head. They are fighting . . . for material benefits, to live better and in peace, to see their lives go forward, to guarantee the future of their children. National liberation, war on colonialism, building of peace and progress, independence—all that will remain meaningless for the people unless it brings a real improvement in conditions of life.[3]

On another occasion, speaking to a visitor to the liberated zones in 1967, Cabral identified who precisely should be the main beneficiaries of the fruits of progress:

> We shall put our whole priority on agriculture. That means more than cultivation. That means realizing what people can do, can actually do. That's a question of village democracy, of village schools, of village clinics, of village cooperation. . . . The general approach that we have is that all structural decisions are to be based on the needs and conditions of the peasantry, who are the vast majority of our people.[4]

In order to implement Cabral's vision, PAIGC now insists that even though it has the greatest concentration of population, the Bissau urban area should not be made the focus of development, draining the resources from the rural areas. Consequently, while the administration and the government have been centralized in the capital, the regions have been given considerable autonomy, and the development of the rural economy is seen as paramount. "We have seen how capitals have been developed in other parts of Africa," one leader told me, "to the detriment of the people. Where just kilometers outside of the towns people have never seen a car or hardly know that the government has become 'independent.' We must be able to learn from other people's mistakes."

The decentralization of the country and the deemphasis of the city of Bissau are now the subjects of policy speeches by members of the government. "What we want to do is to develop our country from the villages to the towns, not the other way round," Luiz Cabral, president of independent Guinea-Bissau said at independence. "We intend that our reconstruction shall continue to give primacy to the people of the villages. First and foremost, we also want them to see concrete gains from their struggle in their own villages, in the lives of their own families. For it is they who have fought hardest and suffered most during this long struggle."[5]

The liberation struggle now continues on a different front. The priority has shifted from winning a war to increasing agricultural production—not only to feed the people but to provide necessary capital for agricultural and industrial development. Despite the long, hard hours spent in the fields, Guinea-Bissau is still unable to produce enough to feed all of its people. While the problem has decreased considerably since that first post-independence year, the goal of reaching prewar production of 120,000 tons of raw rice (representing about 90,000 tons for internal consumption, the balance for export) has not yet been achieved. The year 1977 was projected as the one in which sufficient rice would be grown for domestic needs. But the vagaries of nature intervened and 1977 brought a severe drought. Despite this, rice imports did not exceed those of the previous year, but the goal of self-sufficiency had to be put forward a few years. This graphically illustrated the unavoidable risks involved in depending on agriculture in such an undeveloped situation. Such dependence may lessen in time, when systems of irrigation are extended throughout the country.

In the years immediately following independence three forms of agricultural production could be discerned: subsistence, state farms, and state supported cooperatives. The basic unit of production remained the village, much as it had been during the war. While collective work was seen as a future goal, the precise form it would take was not yet spelled out. Other innovations were instituted but were still very much in experimental and embryonic stages.

Today, while subsistence agriculture remains the work of women, PAIGC has begun transforming the traditional methods

of cultivation as well as providing impetus for increased production—in particular, by sharply increasing the price of rice
and peanuts. One of the ways that PAIGC's approach to change
stands out from that of their neocolonial neighbors lies in political mobilization. As in all work of PAIGC, political education is
seen as an essential part of the process of introducing new
techniques and an essential element in preparing the people for
future collectivization.

The introduction of small dams to supplement the natural
irrigation of the rice fields is an example. In each case a party
political worker would go to the proposed site and call meetings
of the villagers who worked the rice fields. The discussion
would not be limited to the benefits of dams to production, but
would stress the building of solidarity and unity among the
villages. Since dams were to be used by the different villages of
the district, the party worker stressed the need for collective
construction. Once the project was begun it would present a
concrete lesson in the advantages of such work.[6]

While collective work is seen as an eventual goal, movement
toward that goal has been slow. During the armed struggle
Cabral stressed the move to collective agriculture as fundamental.
He told a group of cadres:

> Regardless of their specific responsibilities, comrades everywhere
> in our organization should help our people to organize collective
> fields. This is a great experiment for our future, comrades. Those
> who do not yet understand this have not understood anything of
> our struggle, however much they have fought and however heroic
> they may have been.[7]

Cabral's concern notwithstanding, the way in which collective
fields will be organized has not yet been specified. PAIGC's
stated intention is to use the examples provided by dam construction as well as those provided on state farms and cooperatives
to demonstrate slowly to the peasants the value of collective
work. Their experience has shown that transformation will take
hold only when the peasants fully understand the need for
change in a particular area—be it picking up arms, relinquishing
polygyny, or working collectively. PAIGC leaders express hesi-

tation in rushing the process, referring to the fact that among the people's very recent memories of Portuguese colonialism is the practice of forced labor. Cautious about the risk of failure and intent on preserving people's support, PAIGC is approaching such problems of transformation "step by step."

Meanwhile the government is beginning to establish state farms, with the goal of one per region. The farms will be run by technical directors appointed by the government and staffed by paid workers from the locality. Both traditional and experimental crops will be grown, the proceeds from sale going directly to the government, which in turn covers the costs of wages and running the farm. By 1978 a number of state farms, still relatively small in size, were in operation.

The organization of the state-supported cooperatives differs from that of the farms, as workers are not paid but will generate their own incomes from the sale of crops; this money will also support the cost of the cooperative. In the initial stages, until the farms can be self-sufficient, the workers will be remunerated by the state. Cooperatives were still in the planning stages in 1978, with only one or two in operation. Similar cooperatives, however, have been set up for members of the national army. The end of the war meant a much smaller army was needed to defend the country, but because of extensive unemployment and the desire to build upon their political commitment, PAIGC soldiers were not simply demobilized. Instead they have the opportunity on state cooperatives not only to work productively but also to demonstrate the benefits of shared work to the population.

The emphasis of preparatory political work has meant that the government has been moving slowly in implementing technological changes, and economic problems have also hampered the process in both the agricultural and the industrial sectors. In the agricultural sector electrification projects, irrigation schemes, new techniques when viable (such as tractors) are being introduced with foreign aid. A number of schemes are getting off the ground, but most are still in the planning stages.

In the industrial sector the state has had little choice but to proceed slowly. It did not have the option of expanding existing industry in the hope of increasing exports. There *was* no industry, or as good as none, and the few factories that did exist were ill-suited to building a new society.* The new government has resisted the temptation to rush ahead and industrialize some more obvious resources, such as the considerable bauxite reserves left untouched by the Portuguese. Guinea-Bissau planners have avoided seeking an infusion of foreign finance capital to establish export-oriented industry, recognizing that although this may quickly produce profits and foreign exchange it also introduces new inequalities. The preference has been to seek foreign aid to assist in carefully planned industrial development that will support the policy of giving priority to the rural areas and agriculture. Projections include small factories in the rural areas rather than only in the towns. Some new factories will be tied into agriculture—a new fruit juice and preserve factory is one— while others are designed to produce goods that will reduce the need to import commodities. The commissioner of industry, Filinto Vaz Martins, explained the planning perspective to a visitor:

> Previously rice was the most important import article. But because production has increased strongly it does not play such an important role any longer. The third largest group of commodities that are imported are clothes and cloth. But we shall try to do something about that. Cotton in itself is cheap, but the finished cloth is very expensive. We will start by building a factory (for which Norway has promised us money), that can weave cloth from imported thread. In two years time, we will build a factory that can spin thread from imported raw cotton. Later we hope the development of agriculture will enable us to produce the cotton we need. There are good possibilities for growing cotton in Guinea-Bissau. Originally the peasants grew some cotton, but the

---

*The most prized of the Portuguese factories was the one producing beer, completed just before the end of the war. Employing seventy people, it had the capacity to supply a never-ending stream of beer to the 40,000 bored and disgruntled Portuguese troops stationed and fighting in the country. The only other factory dated back fifteen years, employed one hundred and forty people, and processed peanut oil, well below production capacity of the country. Besides these one might add the few small rice and peanut shellers, a number of saw mills, a few carpentry and furniture shops, a small brickmaking concern that supplied bricks for the shipyards, and one seamstress shop with twenty-seven sewing machines for shirts and other clothes.⁸

Portuguese forced them to grow groundnuts instead. In this way we hope gradually to eliminate clothes and cloth from our imports.

Agricultural tools and iron for construction work have also been important import commodities. We shall try to change this first by building a small foundry that can utilize the scrap that was left by the Portuguese. We have 20,000 tons of scrap iron from, e.g., cars that were left over the whole country as a result of the war. We will produce quite simple, non-automatic agricultural tools. And when the scrap has been used up, we will import raw iron which is not so expensive. In this way we can get a local technical development, and we only need to import cheap raw materials.[9]

A number of factories have been established and others have been planned, geared toward simultaneously promoting industrialization and saving foreign currency.* In addition, the establishment of fisheries is planned to produce fish for both internal consumption and export, as the coastal waters are particularly rich in fish.

The handling of bauxite exploitation provides an example of the party approach to industrialization. Bauxite is the only known mineral resource that the country has in any quantity, although there has been some exploration for offshore oil. The government is not hurrying to mine what promises in the future to be a good source of income, but has concentrated on developing a strategy for the entire region that surrounds the bauxite deposits. This includes the building of dams on a major river and the construction of a railroad to a planned coastal port. The dams will generate electricity for the production of semi-finished aluminum (the finished product will not be produced because of the excessive amounts of energy required) and provide irrigation for agricultural schemes. The railroad will carry not only bauxite but agricultural produce and passengers, and in this way stimulate development of that southern region of the country. As of 1978 only the first step had been taken, with the signing of an agreement for prospecting and general geological explorations with the Soviet Union.[11]

---

*These include a factory that will produce wooden tiles for export as well as coordinate the work of a number of saw mills and carpentry shops in various parts of the country (Guinea-Bissau has vast forests); the fruit juice and preserve factory; an import-substitution factory for foam mattresses; a major peanut- and rice-husking plant, the husks to be burnt for power which in turn will supply electricity for both a peanut oil and a soap factory.[10]

Other choices appear at this point, and from a distance, to be less wise. For instance, an agreement was signed recently with the French company Citroën for the establishment of an assembly plant, albeit a small one, that will produce between 250 and 500 cars annually, all restricted to internal use. This decision stimulated considerable debate in the government, critics questioning Citroën's motives and the benefit to the country. The view ultimately prevailed that the cars were needed and that local assembly would provide training and jobs for workers, while the Guineans would remain in control of any decision to expand.

The problem of reliance on foreign aid and grants is an extremely tricky one for any developing country with limited resources. Guinea-Bissau at present relies more heavily, per capita, on foreign aid than do most countries in Africa.*

Yet it can be argued that no country in such a fragile economic situation as Guinea-Bissau can afford to refuse aid because of a desire for economic independence. Indeed, such a stand could strangle growth and reverse the gains made so far in the revolution. For a small country such as Guinea-Bissau it might be more imperative to integrate itself into the modern world than it is for larger socialist countries, and this will require modernization. Yet a balance must be kept: too heavy reliance on foreign capital will most certainly mean the end of independence, as the history of neocolonial Africa has made clear.

So far the government has approached the problem somewhat pragmatically. It has spread its donors over many countries, both socialist and capitalist, to avoid heavy dependence on one or two countries, at the same time giving preference to aid agencies. Limited multinational investment has been accepted, and most aid comes in the form of grants, not loans, thus minimizing the need to cope with repayment and high interest rates at a later stage.[13] At the same time, aid has not always been accepted simply because it has been offered; in general it has been taken

---

*The largest amounts of aid and/or grants come from (and not necessarily in this order) the United Nations, the Soviet Union, Cuba, Sweden, the European Economic Community. Smaller donors include Portugal, Norway, Algeria, Holland, France, Brazil, the United States, Britain, East Germany, West Germany, Libya, China, Abu-Dhabi, Kuwait, and Italy.[12]

for projects designed by the Guineans themselves. As a result, a number of specific aid offers from foreign governments have been turned down.*

From the above discussion it is apparent that Guinea-Bissau is basing its development strategies on socialist principles, at least at this juncture. The state is controlled by a revolutionary party which has the support of the broad masses of the people; the state in turn controls the direction of the country's development, despite the present dependence on foreign aid; the surplus generated through the resources of the people is invested on behalf of all the people, rather than benefiting certain individuals.[14] However, while the programs and policies of the present can be evaluated, they cannot form guarantees for the future. Too many forces are at work, both internally and internationally, for such projections to be meaningful. What is certain is that unless socialism is achieved, the liberation of women cannot be realized. And so as we look for the trends and dynamics that edge the society in the direction of socialism we are looking at the same time for the potential for a successful struggle for women's liberation. How then do the development strategies described above relate to the role of women in the new society?

The development strategies of PAIGC began to take this aspect of the revolution into account from the onset, long before the country had won its independence. The party's stated goal of an equal society was more than rhetoric, and this goal was expressed in practice through numerous programs established in the liberated zones during the war.

While the village remained the basic economic unit in these areas—and hence women remained responsible for the major portion of agricultural work—political education and new programs focused on and gave impetus to the changing role of women in the society. At the same time men were encouraged to join more actively in all aspects of the work of production. This

---

*For instance, a Brazilian government offer of considerable funding and expertise to build schools and supply literacy teams was turned down. Instead, exiled Brazilian educator Paulo Freire was invited to help plan and advise on the literacy campaign, which has been established with the help of a number of Brazilian exiles and without special funding.

was more than practicing an ideal of equality; it was made essential by the need to compensate for the disruptions in food production that came from living in a war zone. In order to produce enough food all members of the society had to exert themselves to the fullest, accelerating the possibility of changes in the sexual division of labor. No foreign exchange to buy food from the outside was being earned by exports, and the gifts from friendly nations could not fill the breach. Besides, everything was carried in on foot, as this was the only means of transport. Soldiers in the army helped with production, working in the villages at various stages of the season while growing food for the army at the military bases. Their work in the fields provided an example to the men who remained in the villages.

Education for girls as well as boys was given high priority. Progress has been made in equalizing the numbers of girls and boys in school, although people continue to resist the idea of educating girls, and by the end of the war the ratio of girls to boys in school was at best one to three. There is one curriculum for all students, and both teachers and subject matter focus on eradicating attitudes that regard boys as superior to girls. When the students emerge at the other end of their schooling there is a much better chance that they will be equally equipped to enter the workforce, without being confined to sex-defined occupations, than there is anywhere else in Africa.

At the same time, the government is trying to reserve some jobs for women as the labor market begins to open. For example at SOCOTRAM, a state-owned project established in 1976 to produce wooden tiles for export, 40 percent of the several hundred jobs have been reserved for women. The new state has also begun to put into practice the view that women must be given equal treatment in employment, and must be encouraged to take their place in the paid workforce in order to contribute to the reconstruction of their society.

Because of this general emphasis, a visitor to Guinea-Bissau will find women at all levels of work outside the agricultural sector. While this is nowhere near the 50 percent mark, with a particularly low number in prominent government leadership, one does see a trend and a commitment to this goal voiced by both women and men at all levels of the government and party. Only time will tell whether the goals will be achieved. One exception is the field of nursing, which boasts close to a 50 percent representation by each sex, matching the situation elsewhere in Africa. While no doubt part of the rationale for this emanates from the belief that such occupations are suitable for young women, it has been a conscious decision by PAIGC to use this attitude in order to encourage women into the paid workforce. If parents are willing to allow their daughter to train as a nurse, but would be very disturbed if the party suggested she train as an engineer, then this can be used as a starting point. That it is not only seen as an end in itself is demonstrated, for instance, by the number of women political workers who began their careers as nurses.

Many of the changes that have been implemented successfully are primarily a result of the continuing and intensive campaigns of political mobilization undertaken by PAIGC. But in the long run, in order to ensure a more penetrating attack on women's oppression, more fundamental changes must be made in the economy, which now depends on unpaid agricultural labor of women to feed the people. Without such changes it will be more difficult to make a long-lasting break in the tight relationship between the customs of the people and the economic structures of the village. The village economy remains the basis on which the independent state stands, and it is the village economy which perpetuates the customs oppressive to women, not to mention maintains their unduly heavy workload.

In projecting the changes needed to ensure women's equal role in society, one of the party leaders, Teodora Gomes, spoke to me of the need to reorganize the village economy: "Women had to work at home, cooking, taking care of the children, and preparing everything for the men when they were working on the land, as well as work on the land themselves. They could do nothing but sleep at night and the next day work in the village and in the fields; sleep, work at home, and in the fields. They did not have the time or the opportunity to learn, to study, to do anything else.

"In the future the peasant woman will have a place to leave her children so she will be free from the constant care of babies and children. Agricultural technology will be introduced and this will give much freedom to women, and to men as well. They will organize cooperatives which will free women and men from the hard, endless work they have been doing. All the needs of the peasants will be met within the community. Besides working cooperatively, there will be child-care centers, schools, medical services, facilities for cultural entertainment. Women will have time to learn and study many things. Only at that time can the peasant women be free. Yes, only at that time."

To break the stranglehold on the village economy, therefore, it is necessary to devise a program to both increase productivity and phase out the unfair division of labor based on sex; otherwise men will continue to rely on more than one wife to provide sufficient food for the community. In the same way, the new willingness on the part of many fathers to allow their daughters free choice in marriage and to forego the bride-price will be hard to sustain. State farms and cooperatives represent such a program, but they have yet to be extended to the entire country. The problem of producing enough to eat, however, means that it is not possible to simply shift to cooperatives or collective farming without considerable prior preparation. For one thing, by concentrating on cash crops there is the danger of a situation in which men and women work together on the production of commercial crops—such as food, cotton, tobacco—and women somehow manage to produce food for the family as well.

Until changes really do take root in the village economy and alter the division of labor, one can only assume that it will be the women who perform a double task, unable to do justice to either. Moreover, given the poverty of Guinea-Bissau, it is not feasible for women to be paid wages for their work. Neither is this particularly desirable, as it could serve to entrench the present system of production and not alleviate their workload. In trying to increase production and build a surplus, cash crops need to be encouraged. Giving men the responsibility for this work keeps the division of labor unequal. If both men and women are involved in the production of cash crops, but women remain responsible for subsistence farming, the burden of women's labor simply increases.

Perhaps most importantly, women need political power commensurate with their productive contribution, while integrating men further into the agricultural work. At the same time women need to play a more positive role in the work of social transformation. Many of the leaders I spoke with showed a general and well-articulated consciousness about the need for change, but I felt that there remains a gap between theory and practice. I did not find a specific plan for future transformation of the village economy. While not anticipating on my return to Guinea-Bissau just one and a half years after independence the welcome sight of women and men sharing equally in all aspects of agricultural work, I did hope to find developing strategies that would help make these changes a reality for the future.*

This seemed to be lacking on a state level. Despite the third party congress in 1977 and the assessment of general goals for the future at the time, the years since my second visit apparently have not seen many changes on this score. Recent speeches such as those delivered by President Luiz Cabral—including the latest state of the nation message—tend to emphasize technical modernization and gloss somewhat lightly over the need for structural transformation.

There are no simple solutions to these needs. But as long as a country's agricultural work remains based in the present village economy as it has done in the past, there can be no solution to women's unpaid labor and no long-term solution to some fundamental causes of women's oppression.

The road ahead is not smooth. In the first place, the revolutionary process must be expanded to include the entire Guinean population, that is, a good 50 percent who were not in the PAIGC areas during the war, many of whom collaborated with the Portuguese or accepted Portuguese propaganda that characterized the guerrillas as terrorists and bandits. Maybe the horrors of yesterday's wars are today's memories, but, in terms of politi-

---

*With the reorganization at a government level that came in October 1978, the signs are that concrete planning will be stepped up. A new ministry for rural development was established, headed by Mario Cabral, a dynamic and talented young leader, who set up the Ministry of Education, one of the best organized and programmatically exciting of all ministries.

cal mobilization and national reconstruction, the task ahead is even more difficult.

Moreover, there are psychological factors to overcome in continuing revolutionary transformation, affecting even those committed to the process. The Portuguese colonialists represented a visible and common enemy who for decades had oppressed the people and, during the war, dropped bombs upon them daily. Mobilization was easier then. But once colonialism has been defeated and the wartime sense of urgency dissipated, it is more difficult to maintain the rate of change and the integrity of the revolutionary process. Underdevelopment is not as patently oppressive as colonialism, and people have a tendency to revert to what they know.

In addition, with independence coming as abruptly as it did, PAIGC had been forced to devote practically all of its time and resources to consolidating power and settling into the tasks of government. Thus, for the first time in its experience, and all of a sudden, the party had to begin functioning on a national scale. And although the population under its administration had nearly doubled, the number of trained cadres (relatively few of whom were women) remained about the same as during the armed struggle.

There were other, more subjective reasons why the women's struggle seemed to have lost some of its momentum. In as much as the struggle was part of the larger revolution, it confronted the same post-independence problems—the doubling of the female population to include those that had not been politicized during the war, in conjunction with a tendency on the part of some partisans to relax. The effect of this in terms of slowing down the progress of women's emancipation cannot be underestimated. For a period of time that cannot be calculated very precisely there will be regional disparities. And, until the varying levels of consciousness begin to approximate each other, PAIGC will have to establish a balance between mobilizing women for the first time, on the one hand, and making sure, on the other, that the gains achieved in the liberated zones are reinforced and not diluted.

Moreover, a superficial look at the post-colonial situation

might give rise to a question which related only to women's emancipation, and not at all to the overall revolution, and which would have its impact only after the women's struggle has moved into a more programmatic phase. The question is whether or not Guinean men as a whole will continue to support the idea of sexual equality, particularly now that the war is no longer there to serve as a force for unity.

The plain fact is that men have much to gain from national reconstruction, while women's liberation, now as never before, poses the "clear and present danger" that they will lose the last of their male privileges. Women's emancipation means that Guinean men, in the future, will have to work harder, both inside and outside the home, and to share political and decision-making power evenly. In this context, the war, for as long as it employed men as soldiers, also served to postpone really deep-going and radical changes in men's way of life, their traditional social roles, and their relationship to production.

Cadres tried to illustrate the need for an intensification of the struggle after independence when speaking at mass peasant meetings. "You know how a woman sweeps the front of her house," a political worker told one such meeting in an area that had previously been under Portuguese control. Then he picked a large leaf off the ground and bent over double as he swept the earth. "The woman will sweep and sweep but the broom can only remove the surface dust. The stones stay behind, embedded in the ground. It is necessary to use a bigger instrument to remove the stones. Now we must work harder to change the society further. We must not be satisfied with only sweeping away the surface dust."

This commitment is based in a new reality now that the war is over. And the current situation introduces both a new necessity (overcoming underdevelopment) and a new national target (building a nation-state) around which to organize the unity of men and women.

To put it another way, since PAIGC ideology generally holds that women's liberation is a necessary feature of a democratic society in each phase of development, the post-colonial situation has caused the party to alter the form of the struggle, but not the principle itself. The principle remains that the emancipation of women is ensured through their equal involvement in the process of social transformation.

It is a process that has but begun and is progressing *piconino, piconino*—"little by little." In the pages that follow I will try to bring to the reader, much as the Guineans brought to me, a sense of the achievements, the difficulties, the setbacks, the disappointments, above all the spirit—all part of a day's work in the process of starting anew.

Fighting Two Colonialisms

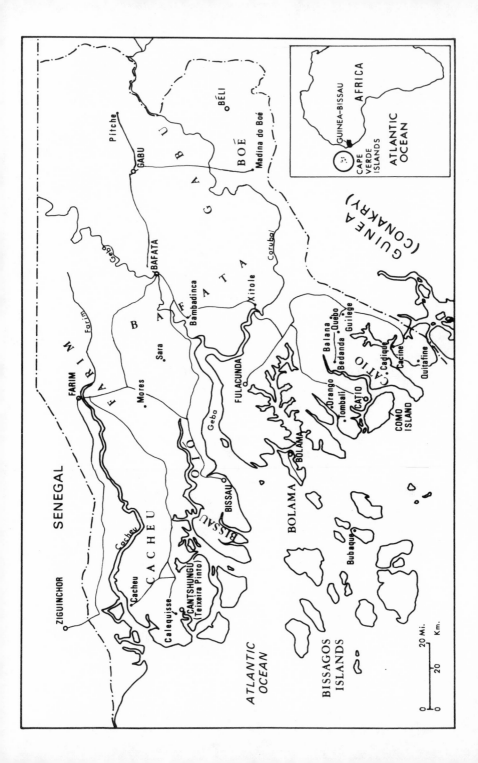

Part I
In the Liberated Zones

Chapter 1

"Nô Pintcha!"

My first experience of revolution, and revolutionaries. Everyday life in the liberated zones had to be adapted to the reality of living in a war zone. Out of this experience, new leaders—young and old—developed with a deep commitment to the struggle that the revolutionary liberation movement was waging and the new society that was envisioned. Out of it too emerged a special quality of friendship, comraderie, and support.

It was late in the afternoon when the Candjafara River finally came into view. We were hot, sticky, and covered with a not-so-fine layer of red dust. Our large Russian-built truck slowed down as it neared the water's edge and came to a halt. Behind us stretched the bumpy earth road we had traveled from Boké, through the alternately hilly and flat countryside of the Republic of Guinea (Conakry).

Ahead of us, way across the mile-wide river, lay the liberated territory of Guinea-Bissau. Through a bluish haze I could discern palm trees and forests, a mirror image of the scene on our side of the river. While we rested, a small dilapidated ferry could be seen making its slow way toward us from the opposite bank.

The banks themselves were thick, deep mud, now exposed as the river receded with the tides of the ocean bordering this low-lying coastal nation. This meant trouble for the driver of the truck who, expert though he was, could not maneuver his vehicle through the stubborn mud and onto the metal ramps of the ferry. Back and forth, back and forth he went, shouts from onlookers helping him on his way. In the end he had to admit defeat. But no sooner had we resigned ourselves to the long wait for the tide to return, than a black minibus/ambulance came along the road toward us, just ahead of a cloud of dust. Aboard were a number of PAIGC military men heading for the liberated zones. Because it was relatively light, this vehicle successfully negotiated the mud and made its way up the ramps.

There was room for two more passengers, and so I found myself one hour later aboard the ferry as it chugged its way back across the river, aiming for the road which picked up again on the other side and disappeared into a forest. The vibrating ferry was carrying me on the last lap of my journey to Guinea-Bissau. I stood silently next to my "guide," Teodora Gomes, as she supported herself against the rickety bar that served as a rail. We were dressed almost identically. Dark olive green army pants and short-sleeved cotton T-shirts of the same color. They could have come from the same place, although mine were bought at an army-surplus store in New York. On her feet were black leather Adidas-type running shoes; on mine were French rubber and canvas boots, also bought in New York, but which I discovered were identical to those worn by many guerrillas. Teodora's thick African hair was covered by a mottled emerald green and black turban, neatly twisted above her ebony face.

The similarities ended, however, with our uniforms. Looped onto Teodora's military belt, so that it rested against her right hip, was a large black leather holster holding her revolver. Slung over my shoulder was my camera inside its black leather case. The two instruments were symbolic of our very different relationships to the revolution we were about to enter. Teodora was a participant; I was an observer.

The ferryman guided his craft into place and lowered the metal ramps onto the mud. We got back into the ambulance, and the driver revved the engine. Without stopping, but with precarious sliding and skidding, he managed to reach the dry road—the same dry earth road that we had left behind in Guinea (Conakry). In fact, everything looked the same. Normal and very calm. Nothing immediately noticeable that would differentiate it from the ex-French colony we had just left behind that day in April 1974. As the ambulance bumped its way along the road, I noticed the same trees, the same bird calls, the same heat.

"Look," said Teodora, suddenly leaning forward from the back of the vehicle to tap my shoulder. "People of Guinea-Bissau!" Stepping out of the dense forest that lined the road was an elderly, wiry man, followed by a ten-year-old girl. They balanced large bundles of chopped wood on their heads, and the man rested slightly on a worn-looking axe, waving to us with his free hand as we passed. A scene from any West African country. Maybe. But I had to contain feelings of both romance and rising excitement; these were people of the revolution.

As we drove on, the difference between the independent nation of Guinea and the liberated territory of Guinea-Bissau became more apparent. It was a far bumpier ride, and much slower, as the driver carefully picked a zig-zag path between the large holes and cracks gouged out of the road. Opened only eight months earlier—after Guilege, a major Portuguese base some twenty miles inland, was routed by guerrilla forces—the road had not been repaired in years. For while the colonial base may have straddled the road, the surrounding area was in the hands of PAIGC, whose troops effectively denied the Portuguese further use of it. The trees of the forest had grown over, the branches meeting above and conveniently providing a cover for vehicles such as ours. This was the only road that could be used by vehicles in the whole south front, I was told, and it was safe for only about thirty miles. After that, and from one end of the country to the other, the sole method of transport would be on foot. And so dissolved any lingering impression I had that life in the two countries was the same.

We had not been traveling long when the ambulance veered off at a right angle, along a wide path cut through the bush and leading to Simbel, the first military base inside the borders of Guinea-Bissau. We made a one-day stopover here, a prelude to the trip I was about to begin. Reunited with our truck the following day, we prepared to depart Simbel in late afternoon, and leave behind the cluster of tents, hidden under trees, that represented "home" for many PAIGC soldiers. "For us camping is not a vacation, not something we do to relax," one of the military commanders commented to me with a laugh. "We have 'camped' for the past thirteen years."

I was given the front seat next to the driver, while everyone else—soldiers, a few young peasant women, Teodora and Espirito Santo Silva, the young Cape Verdian school teacher who would be our interpreter—piled into the open back of the truck, somehow finding seats amid the ammunitions, medical supplies, boxes of condensed milk and dried soup, not to mention a few live chickens. The condition of the road made it impossible to drive at even a moderate speed and so the truck kept at below fifteen miles per hour as the driver aimed for the firmer and flatter portions of the road. The din was terrific. The engine roared and the truck rattled. As we worked our way through the tunnel of trees, the overhead branches swished and scraped and cracked and every so often a springy thin branch would whip through the window of the cab and sting my arm.

Suddenly: *Para! para!* (Stop). There was an energetic banging on the roof from the people in the back and some shouts in

Creole, the most widely spoken language.* The driver brought the truck to a quick halt, grabbed his rifle from the ledge behind him, and jumped out. Some of the soldiers stood up in the back and took aim. I looked around in horror. Portuguese? But everyone else seemed unperturbed. A few shots were fired. At birds. They missed and we proceeded, having failed on this occasion to alleviate the food supply problem in the liberated zones.

As darkness fell, the lights of the truck were switched on to illuminate the jagged holes in the road ahead of us. The noise continued as before. Surely the bombers would spot our lights before we heard their engines, I thought nervously. *"Parapara-para!!"* This time the banging on the roof was urgent. *"Avion!"* In an instant, the engine was cut and the lights switched off. We all jumped out of the truck and walked a little way down the road. The drone of the circling plane could be heard for some time, but at a distance. It got no louder, and no bombs were dropped, before the drone receded into the silence of the night. In the weeks to come I would learn that the sound of the approaching jet bombers, however faint, could be heard above the most active noise of village or base life—over pounding, laughter, even blaring radios.

When we set off again, after waiting a while to make sure the bomber did not return, the driver fairly careered along the road until we were at the end of the drive. The contents of the truck were distributed among us and we set off for the half-hour walk to Donka, which served as base for Carmen Pereira, political commissar for the south front, and which also harbored a school and a hospital headed by a Cuban doctor. As I walked I could barely contain my anticipation. In the coming weeks I would experience a life I could not have imagined, however closely I followed the liberation struggle from America.

One of the first things that struck me was the special language that had evolved out of the struggle. I had entered a revolutionary world in which such words as "militant," "political commis-

---

*Creole, the *lingua franca*, is spoken by about 60 percent of the population on the mainland (nearly 100 percent on the Cape Verde Islands) and is a mixture of Portuguese and African languages which has evolved into a language in its own right.

sar," "*responsavel*," "mission," "cadre," were part of the everyday language, each with a meaning particularly adapted to the
work of PAIGC. At first, they sounded strange to my ear, but after
a few days' immersion in my new environment, I too began to
find them commonplace. I learned that cadre referred simply to a
member of a party in training for leadership or already taking a
leadership role; that *responsavel* meant a party militant who
was responsible for a particular task. And so in the days to come I
would meet education *responsavels*, health *responsavels*, and
come to understand that the term connotes the principle of
people being responsible for something, as opposed to being
leaders in the hierarchical sense. Political commissar, a literal
translation of *político comissário*, had no convenient English
equivalent but referred to a *responsavel* whose task was political
work and who had taken on a high level of leadership within the
party. Mission was any party assignment whatsoever, and could
include an attack on a Portuguese camp, attending a conference
abroad, or being responsible for a visitor to the liberated zones.
All members of the party were militants regardless of their
relation to the army and whether or not they carried arms. And
everybody was your comrade or, rather, *camarada*.

These terms both dispensed with, and reflected the lack of,
hierarchy within the liberation movement. There were no military ranks, no badges, no saluting. In fact, I found that the only
(but not always reliable) way of distinguishing party cadres with
higher responsibility was to check whether or not they were
wearing a wristwatch, and if it was a very sophisticated one, I
could safely presume they were in the military.

Then there were other words, such as *mato, Tuga, tabanca*,
and especially *nô pintcha*. *Mato* literally means forest, but had
come to mean liberated zones; *Tuga* means the Portuguese,
particularly the army, and was adapted into Creole from "Portugal"; *tabanca* means a village. But *nô pintcha* is a phrase con-
veying a variety of emotions and could crop up in any number of
different situations. Although literally meaning "let's go," and
as such interchangeable with *nô bai*, it had come to have a
very special significance in the Creole language: implicitly and
symbolically a call to continue the struggle, to fight to victory.

Nô pintcha! Forward! It was the PAIGC slogan, one to which even the most weary would respond.

Life in the liberated zones was frugal, arduous, and danger filled. Its joy lay first in the sense of solidarity people shared as they worked together for the same cause, and also in the victories, large or small, over the colonialists. Its pain was in the continual loss of compatriots and close friends in bombing raids or guerrilla action. In addition to the external threat, it was necessary to be constantly on the alert for subversion from within, whether in the form of counterrevolutionaries working as spies and saboteurs, or carelessness on the part of those not totally committed to the struggle. For even in the latter case, the consequences could be disastrous.

There is nothing romantic about armed struggle and I soon relinquished any such notions. The romance springs from the fantasies of the onlooker and is not intrinsic to the struggle itself. It arises from the hero-worshipping—unfortunately prevalent in the West—of guerrillas as bands of selfless young men, and perhaps women, accepting the grateful veneration of all their countrypeople, whom they have miraculously liberated by force of arms. These ideas place undue emphasis on the role of the gun. But the gun wins victories only when the people have first been mobilized behind it. In the war of liberation in Guinea-Bissau it was not only the soldiers who struggled. In fact, they were regarded not as heroic figures, but as people carrying out their work for the revolution much as anyone else. Every man, woman, and child participated, whether or not they bore arms. It was only through mass participation of the peasant population that total victory was possible. Everybody risked their lives daily, grieved at the deaths of family and friends, made innumerable sacrifices. There is nothing romantic about the continual hail of bombs, the scarcity of food and other necessities, the severe testing of one's emotional and mental resources, and the grinding physical exertion.

The reminders that life was being lived in a war zone were omnipresent. An ear was always tuned for the faintest sound of the bombers which, at any time of the day or night, might be circling above one or another area, dispensing their bombs. I was introduced to this state of reality soon after I entered the interior.

"Can you walk?" Teodora asked me as we sat finishing breakfast outside the hut we had slept in at Donka. She "walked" her index and middle finger across the small table for emphasis.

"Oh yes," I replied quickly. A little too quickly. "For two months I have walked for hours every day in preparation." Teodora was unimpressed. She looked at me hard, raising one eyebrow. "Ah, but can you *run?*" she responded, and her fingers picked up speed. This jolted me. I was not on an exciting jaunt. I had entered a real war zone.

A few days later there was no doubt about it. I was already accepting as routine the trips to the trenches whenever the bombers could be heard overhead. They would come so often— sometimes several times in a single day—that even I began to pick out the sound of the jets above the noises that were the regular backdrop to any village or base we might be in. The trenches, about two feet wide and about four and a half feet deep, were dug out of the orange earth, sometimes straight, sometimes L-shaped. The few earth steps at either end were usually ignored during raids, as people jumped right in. Much of the time I was sent to the trenches alone; sometimes a mother and baby would join me. But on one particular afternoon the sound of a plane grew so loud that we knew it was heading in our direction. Teodora grabbed my hand and we were all rushing for the trenches. People came flying out of huts. Children were hastily picked up by whoever was nearest. Women came running from their pounding. About twenty of us stood next to each other in a single trench, all our senses straining toward the sound of the engine which was getting louder and louder. Demonstrating as she spoke, Teodora told me: "Crouch down when you hear the bombs being released. *Comme ça!"*

Crack! Crack! The plane spat out two of its bombs, the harsh sound reverberating through the air. We waited, crouching, our heads down, arms pressed against the walls for balance. The explosions came, and then two more. Meanwhile, the militants discussed the bombing, estimating the distance and the direction, trying to work out what might have been hit. From the tone of their voices, they might have been discussing an everyday affair. Then it occurred to me they *were* discussing an everyday affair.

The consensus was that the bombs had been released on targets about a mile away. To my inexperienced ear it had sounded more like yards. We continued to crouch in the trench and heard two more bombs dropping. Finally the sound of the plane began to recede, and a militant came over to us from a second shelter. "You can get out now," he said. "It was a small plane and can only hold six bombs." Then he added, looking at me: "But stay near the trench. The *Tuga* don't warn us in advance when they are going to bomb us!"

The next day we learned that the militants had guessed correctly, and that the bombs had been dropped indiscriminately. Nothing was hit. Just a few weeks earlier, however, the Portuguese had been more successful. A twelve-year-old student of a school less than a mile from the base was killed by an exploding bomb as he went on an errand. On our way to visit the school, Teodora pointed out the spot where he had died—a charred hole ripped out of the forest floor.

Another night, while marching to our next destination, we had to contend with larger bombers that literally rained bombs down. This type of plane was invariably referred to by a word that sounded like "beekmun," and it took me a little while to realize the militants were not indicating some German-type jet, but using the Creole rendering of "big man." Still, when we heard them approaching, and if we were lucky to be near a village, we would join the peasants in the trenches they had constructed. If not, we ran for the nearest trees for cover. The shout of *"la luz"* meant bombers had been detected and was an instruction to turn off our flashlights immediately. (The flashlights were mainly for my benefit in the first place. After years of marching at night, my companions had learned to make their way without artificial aids.)

The way, the only way, to travel in the liberated zones was by foot, regardless of whether the destination was a mile, fifteen miles, or over one hundred miles away. The pace was brisk. Soldiers had to keep up a faster pace than others, their marching spurred by the pressures of a military mission, or the necessity of transporting from one camp to another vital arms and ammunition. This sense of extreme urgency did not apply to marches of PAIGC militants involved in political work or those transporting nonmilitary goods. Nonetheless, there were considerable distances to cover, and being out in the open, or in the forest but away from trenches, exposed them to bombing raids. Keeping up a fast pace meant survival. Although African peasants were used to walking long distances on foot, they had to learn how to march. As Nino Vieira, the top PAIGC commander and strategist of many of the war's victories (and now prime minister), put it: "Although the average African is a born walker, a soldier must learn what we call disciplined marching. This means reaching a level of nine hours daily, nonstop, for four days, at four miles an hour with arms and pack. He must also learn to go hungry at the same time."[1]

In order to reach the furthest point on the itinerary planned for me, our group marched for six to eight hours a night for the first five days, sleeping at schools or hospitals or political bases along the way. We always set off after five, when the oppressive heat of the day gave way to the relative cool of the evening. In the south, the land was blissfully flat—I was spared the mountains and hills of the north front—and I could generally keep up with the steady pace, although I presumed they had slowed it somewhat out of consideration for their city-dwelling visitor.

"At night, I walk ahead," Espirito instructed the first time we set out. The vision of his springy strides in front of me, and his off-white canvas rucksack hanging from his back seem forever embedded in my mind. For hour after hour after hour, night after night, we walked like this, sometimes talking, sometimes silent, sometimes joking, and occasionally angry, as on one night, when after only two hours' sleep, I was so tired that I could hardly place one exhausted foot in front of the other. Espirito was a cheerful and considerate companion and I found the marches far less taxing because of his presence.

We followed the narrow paths through the forests, where branches grew in twirls and twists on either side of us, and I marveled at how easily my companions found their way through the maze. Every now and then we would break out of the forest onto the open plains, bordered with stands of palm trees. At dusk the brown grass would glow golden under an incandescent red setting sun as it disappeared behind the differently shaped fronds of the various palm trees. Many times we had to dash across the rice fields, or *bolanhas* as they were referred to in Creole, stepping up and down over the sunbaked ridges. I was relieved that it was not the rainy season, when the heavy and constant tropical rains transform this dry, brown, and dark green land into a spectacle of luscious colors; when the mud is deep everywhere and the grasses grow to shoulder height; when the hard, cracked earth surface dissolves into marshes and mangrove swamps, and rivers overflow their banks. Throughout September it rains virtually nonstop. The forests, even in the dry season, are thick, but with the rains they become tightly knit webs of dense undergrowth and new leafy vines. Hiding from the bombers in that season could mean hours up to one's shoulders in water, under cover of the mangroves. One time, as I scrambled to the bottom of a dry river bed in order to make the crossing, I looked above to see militants effortlessly skimming across a long tree trunk which straddled the creek and served as a bridge. Stumbling over stones and clumps of dry earth, I congratulated myself on having avoided the rainy season. But I could not avoid the makeshift *pranças* that had been strung across the many narrow but gently flowing rivers. Every time we neared one of these bridges made from loose planks and logs, with no poles or rope for support, I found my heart sinking. I was thankful more than once for Teodora's sturdy presence as she held my hand in a firm grasp and guided me across, urging me to look ahead and not down. Despite my fears, I never actually managed to fall into the water below.

Accompanying Teodora, Espirito Santo, and me were ten members of FAL, the local armed forces, and at various times political *responsavels* from different regions or sectors we were visiting. The guerrillas, marching with their guns, bazookas, and ammunition as well as sacks of food and clothing, also carried my heavy bag of cameras, lenses, and tape recorder. The *responsavels* carried their rifles and whatever they needed with them. But whenever I picked up something of mine to carry, it was whisked away from me onto someone else's shoulder. They did this not only out of kindness, but also of necessity. PAIGC's experience had been that those unused to marching would find any item a tremendous burden after an hour or two and slow down the column.

Nonetheless, the kindness and hospitality shown me by the many different people I met became a mark of my visit. Hospitality in Africa generally evinces a particular generosity, but in the liberated zones it had an even deeper quality. It was directed not only toward me as a visitor, but also toward PAIGC militants, constantly on the go, when they arrived at a village or base. For me, hospitality on the part of militants was expressed in a great gentleness and concern for my well-being, the underside of which was appreciation of the fact that all visitors to their war-torn country braved conditions that were anything but ideal.

There were numerous and daily instances: an anonymous shoulder in the dark hoisting me through the deep mud of a riverbank toward a waiting canoe—although the additional weight must have sunk my slightly built helper up to his thighs; an exclamation by a militant when he caught sight of my boots, still muddy after I had washed them in a stream, and who proceeded to fill his canteen with water and meticulously wash away the residue; a gift of three fresh eggs from an elderly, wizened peasant woman who had carefully nursed them in the palms of her hands throughout a three-hour meeting; a gift from a nearby village of a gourd full of ripe mangoes and a chicken— despite the scarcity of meat—brought by a member of their village council who traveled specially to the school to present it; fresh oysters steamed just right by a *responsavel* who also saw to it that the eggs were soft boiled; the care taken so that I had the best seat, that I was not sitting in the sun, that I got plenty of rest—even when I felt it unnecessary.

But the most lavish display of generosity came from Teodora. At mealtimes she took delight in choosing the meatiest part of the chicken or stew and piling my plate high with food. I would inwardly groan as I battled to consume the mound of rice and supplements placed before me, a battle I lost more times than once. Teodora was not one to let this go by without comment. "You say you like our food, but you don't *eat!*"

Rice was the staple diet. Everything else was peripheral. If I did not eat the mound of rice she heaped in front of me, she inferred that I had not liked the food and therefore must still be hungry. My protestations that I was incapable of finishing the amount she expected fell on deaf ears. The food *was* good. The average meal prepared when guests were present included a large bowl of vegetable soup, made from packages sent as a gift from the German Democratic Republic. At lunch and supper the main dish consisted of as much rice as Teodora could maneuver onto my plate, topped with a tasty stew of chicken, fish, or wild meat. Breakfast too was substantial: a rice porridge or rice-flour bread, called *cus-cus*, and a large mug of coffee with condensed milk. I was never hungry, yet Teodora was never satisfied that I had eaten enough. On one such occasion she tried another tactic on her overfed visitor. "Food is not a luxury for us," she cajoled. "Without food we cannot march."

I felt uncomfortable, even guilty. In a few weeks I would return to the abundance of America, while the militants with me would have to continue living their spartan lives, including the necessity to march on empty stomachs, sometimes for days at a time, on those occasions when food was simply not available. Thoughts such as these would not have deterred Teodora; hardship was the reality of life. What did concern her was that her guest be made to feel as comfortable, as healthy, and as welcome as possible. Everyone who knew her was familiar with her generous spirit. She would express it in whatever way she could, and although in the liberated zones there was not much to give other than food, she still found ways.

But a special quality of friendship was reserved by the militants for each other. In a war zone it was never certain that a "good-by" was not the last one. People were constantly on the move so that friends did not see each other for months, even years at a time. A coming together was always full of spontaneity and joy, expressed in hearty and loving hugs, so that I often saw men in long embraces, breaking to slap each other's back. It was as common to see men, as it was women, holding hands with each other as they walked, or with arms around each other's shoulders or waists.

The life that dictated infrequent time together for friends

applied no less to lovers and husbands and wives. It was rare for a couple to share the same base, and where they did there were always regular partings due to missions, along with the chance of prolonged separation should party work call one or the other to a different area.

For PAIGC cadres and those working outside of their village, the concept of "home" was a very loose one. Generally, it meant a reed hut at a political or military base, and then moving every six or eight months to avoid detection by the Portuguese army. A picture cut out of a magazine, an embroidered cloth placed over a table constructed from stripped branches, or a larger cloth to cover a straw mattress—these were the only personal items a militant had. Since everything had to be brought in from the outside on someone's head or back, the accumulation of personal things became a luxury no one could afford. Because it was also necessary to give up the need for a home base, security was sought in feelings of solidarity among those sharing the revolution.

For three weeks in the south front and ten days in the east front, as well as a number of weeks in Conakry and Boké, I was a guest of this revolution. The women and men I met shared with me their difficult life without ever dwelling on its hardships. Instead, they conveyed to me feelings of excitement, of challenge and joy in the rewards gained from collectively working toward—"step by step" as they would say—a totally new, humane, and equal society.

Chapter 2

"What can we consider better than freedom?"

Against the backdrop of brutal colonialist oppression the African Party for the Independence of Guinea and Cape Verde (PAIGC) was founded in 1956. After efforts to bring about a peaceful transition to indigenous rule failed, the liberation movement turned to armed struggle. Their ideology—encompassing the need to build a new revolutionary society—was founded on the analysis of the conditions in Guinea-Bissau done by their founder and leader, Amilcar Cabral.

For the Guinean peasant, daily life under Portuguese colonialism was very harsh. The harshness permeated every aspect of life and work, never ending.

When the territory that is now the Republic of Guinea-Bissau first came under the Portuguese imperial sphere five hundred years ago, the Portuguese did not venture beyond scattered coastal trading posts. The trade they came for, and which they were the first to develop on a large scale, was the trade in slaves. And as long as they could ensure this without political control, they had no need to penetrate into the interior.

While the direct presence of the Portuguese (and other Europeans) was not felt inland, their avarice for the riches provided by the slave trade resounded far into the interior. They had little difficulty in finding Africans willing to enter into the selling of their fellow men and women, causing disruptions in the social structure of many peoples over a vast area.

By the beginning of the 1940s transportation of slaves across the Atlantic was outlawed for the seamen of most European and American nations. Anticipating the suspension of this lucrative trade, the imperial powers of Europe turned to the prospect of exploiting the continent's natural resources, which they imagined as bursting out of the earth. The "scramble for Africa" was on. At the Conference of Berlin in 1884-1885, Britain, France, Germany, Belgium, and Portugal sat down to agree on how Africa should be divided among them. Noticeably absent were the Africans themselves, whom the Europeans considered irrelevant to decisions about their future. Although Portugal came away from the conference with less than it had hoped for, it did have Angola, Mozambique, "Portuguese" Guinea, and the islands of Cape Verde, Sao Tomé, and Principé carved out in its name.

During the years that followed, the European powers set about entrenching themselves politically in their new possessions, while at the same time extracting wealth. Portugal, no exception, cracked down hard, realizing that without tight political control over its colonies it ran the risk of losing out to Britain and France, both of which coveted the entire area. But years of resistance by different ethnic groups forced Lisbon to fight mini-wars in all of its colonies. In "Portuguese" Guinea, the wars of peasant resistance were extensive. Only by the late 1920s—when the colonial era began in earnest—could the Portuguese seriously claim to have pacified this small West African nation.

Up until then, the peasant family had eked out a subsistence living, growing only what it needed in order to survive. The staple product was rice, cultivated during a four-month season when the heavy tropical rains poured down virtually nonstop, and the corrugated fields retained the water that nurtured the rice plants. In addition, some of the groups raised cattle, and all kept some livestock, such as goats, pigs, and chickens. Their daily meal of rice was supplemented by the thick nutritious sauce of palm oil and by fish, game, and wild vegetation. It was not an easy life, but hard work would guarantee enough to eat, since the climate, ever hot with an abundance of rain, seldom varied from year to year.

With "pacification" came the intensification of the erosion of the precarious relation between the individual peasant and the village economy that had begun with the slave trade. The Portuguese, having reluctantly ended their lucrative trade in slaves a few decades earlier, now sought other ways to exploit their colonies. In Angola and Mozambique the quest for wealth was relatively straightforward. Natural resources were extensive and the climate was attractive, leading the Portuguese to emigrate in large numbers. It was not long before they had settled in and established coffee and cotton plantations cultivated by forced labor. Guinea-Bissau was not blessed with such resources; the hot, humid climate and the small size of the territory made it unappealing to prospective settlers, which exempted the potential for large plantations. Other methods had to be utilized to make the colony profitable. First the Portuguese imposed the cultivation of peanuts on the peasants' own land, which provided the metropolis with an export commodity more profitable than rice. (By the end of the 1950s an estimated fifty thousand families were cultivating the crop.) At the same time, heavy taxes were imposed on all aspects of life in the colony.

The concentration on peanuts had a dire effect on the already fragile system of subsistence farming, as cultivation of this

cash crop prevented the peasant farmers from producing sufficient food for their daily needs. Poverty and malnutrition
increased as the years went by. The land too was being adversely
affected. Impatient for short-term profits, the colonialists forced
the farmers to disregard traditional crop rotation, whereby the
land was left fallow. Instead they would harvest, burn off, and
replant immediately, each year turning more land into waste.
The exploitation was continued by obliging the peasants to
trade peanuts at Portuguese stores at fixed, rock-bottom prices.
In this way the colonialists had access to a cheap supply of
peanuts, the export of which provided sixty percent of all foreign
trade revenue by the beginning of the guerrilla war. Rice was
procured for export in much the same way, but because it generated less satisfactory profits, most of the crop was used for
home consumption. In fact, exports and imports were under the
monopolistic control of one Portuguese company, the Companhia
União Fabril, hence the largest beneficiary of the profits.

In order to pay their taxes, the peasants depended on the
trading stores to transform their crops into money. The system
was a double-edged sword which the colonialists wielded very
effectively indeed, gaining as they did both income from the
produce—after selling it abroad—plus taxes that were paid from
the income generated by the trade in the first place. So to fill the
colonial coffers, they expanded taxation to touch every aspect of
peasant life: not only personal taxes on huts, every pound of rice
grown, every palm tree on a plot of land, palm wine, palm oil,
and livestock, but also on weddings and other celebrations,
festivities, dances, burials, and so forth. But the real hardship
was that the pittance received from the trading stores was seldom
sufficient to cover the taxes, in which case the peasants faced
forced labor, jail, beatings, confiscation of livestock and other
property, or a combination of these.

"My family were peasants," a Balanta peasant woman told me.
"They worked in the rice fields and grew rice. When they needed
something, they took rice to the Portuguese store some distance
from our village, and traded it. But they had no knowledge of the
actual value of the rice, and the Portuguese paid them what they
pleased. If you argued you would be beaten. With the little

money we received, we had to pay taxes for things like palm trees, pigs, domestic animals, land. My father was often whipped because he could not pay."

If was not possible for peasant family members to supplement their income by taking odd jobs in the rural areas; there were none to be had. Road building contributed the only major activity, but work was done by forced labor, by peasants who had not been able to pay taxes.

"When I was very young," the same Balanta woman said, "I was taken with many girls and boys to work on the construction of a road. We were paid nothing. The older girls had to collect water all day long and the younger girls carried sand. We slept in the forest. They didn't give us any food, so we had to carry our own rice as well. To make things worse, there was a famine at the time and not even the people in the villages had enough to eat. Those who tried to run away were severely beaten."

A much younger woman who had grown up in a Balanta village and was a party *responsavel* told me of a similar experience she had had as a child.

"After my father had paid the taxes, there was barely enough rice left for us to eat. The Portuguese administrators did what they pleased. They would take men, women, and children and force them to work for nothing, on such things as building roads. I remember once when ships had to be loaded with rice, they came to our village and rounded up a group of children, including me, to load the ship. We worked from early morning to late at night, every single day. When the day's work was over they would decide what they were going to pay us, maybe one escudo* today, a handful of sugar tomorrow. 'That's it for today,' they would say and order us home. We could do nothing about it. If we refused to work we would be beaten."

Such stories of life under colonialism were the shared experience of peasants throughout the liberated zones.

Of all the colonial powers in Africa, Portugal did the least to develop its colonies, and Guinea-Bissau was without doubt one of the most underdeveloped countries on the continent. Portugal

---

*The exchange rate for the escudo is roughly thirty escudos per one U.S. dollar.

extracted labor and wealth and put very little back, so that the people of Guinea-Bissau had even less in terms of social services in comparison with other colonies in Africa. There was no attempt to provide education or health services in the rural areas. Both were available in the towns for the few Portuguese settlers and the very few Africans who could afford to pay—the three percent of the population considered wealthy enough, educated enough, and Christian enough to be classified as second-class Portuguese citizens.

The total lack of education facilities for the population was reflected in an illiteracy rate of ninety-nine percent at the beginning of the war of liberation. The absence of health services could be seen in the wide variety of debilitating diseases that affected the population. Even the Portuguese official, Texeira da Mota, working in Guinea-Bissau, found the extent of ill-health excessive. Reporting in 1954, he said that the majority of the population was infected by hookworm; sleeping sickness affected two-fifths of the rural population, while malaria, bilharzia, and dysentery were chronic. Malnutrition was the cause of other widespread ailments. The infant mortality rate in the rural areas was six out of ten.[1]

All attempts to organize against these conditions were thoroughly crushed. With political repression so shamelessly practiced in Portugal itself after the establishment of the fascist regime in the 1930s, the administration met little opposition to the naked exploitation of their colonies.

Set against this reality were the claims of the fascist government that life in their so-called overseas territories was exceptionally good. They were not colonies, it insisted, but provinces, extensions of Portugal itself, and boasting all the benefits thereof. Even after the armed struggle had begun, the Portuguese foreign minister asserted that "we alone before anyone else brought to Africa the notion of human rights and racial equality. . . . Our African provinces are more developed, more progressive in every respect, than any recently independent territory in Africa south of the Sahara, without exception."[2]

As he spoke repression was reaching unprecedented levels in the so-called African provinces, in response to the decision by the liberation movements in Mozambique, Angola, and Guinea-Bissau to take history into their own hands and to fight for their freedom.

During the fifties, when independence movements proliferated throughout the colonies of Africa, France and Britain began negotiations to ensure that their economic interests remained intact under African rule. A host of neocolonial governments came to power, led by elites carefully nurtured by the old colonial administrations. Portugal, one of the poorest countries in Europe, did not have this option: a virtual economic satellite of the European powers itself, it could not have maintained its economic hold in Africa once it had relinquished political control.

In September 1956—after Lisbon turned deaf ears to calls for independence—a small group of compatriots, called together by Amilcar Cabral, met clandestinely in Bissau to form the African Party for the Independence of Guinea and Cape Verde (PAIGC). The goal was the eventual independence of both Guinea-Bissau and the Cape Verde Islands, some four hundred miles off the coast, linked to the mainland through culture, language, and history.*

On that rainy September day, they mapped out a course of action that would join them to the tide of independence

---

*For the purposes of this book, I have excluded discussion of the Cape Verde Islands, despite the close connection between the two territories. There was extensive underground organization on the islands for the duration of the war on the mainland. Conditions did not permit the onset of armed struggle on the islands, however. A future PAIGC goal is the unification of the two republics into a yet unspecified form of federated state. Lars Rudebeck, observer to the third party congress, notes:

> There are several reasons for [unity] beside the old historical ties [since the fifteenth century]. Guineans and Cape Verdeans struggled together against Portuguese colonialism. Their common liberation and future union was always an important point in the program of PAIGC. Many Cape Verdeans had important functions within the liberated areas of Guinea during the war. Without the military victory on the mainland, it would not have been possible to force the Portuguese out of the islands. But there are also important objective differences between the two countries with regard to economic and social structure. These make it essential that the future union be prepared carefully and thoroughly. The union is thus probably a long-term political project, although it was strongly reaffirmed as a political goal by the third congress. For the time being, however, the PAIGC remains the political party of two independent but closely cooperating countries.[3]

movements throughout Africa. But they had to work underground, for political parties, demonstrations, and gatherings were forbidden. PAIGC's initial tactics were peaceful. Demonstrations and workers' strikes, they felt, would indicate they were serious about independence, and force the colonialists to the negotiating table.

This approach was met with increased repression, brutality, and violence, culminating in the "Pidgiguiti massacre" of August 1959, in which the colonial army opened fire on workers demonstrating peacefully at Pidgiguiti docks in Bissau. Twenty minutes later, when the hail of rifle fire ceased, fifty dockworkers lay dead, more than one hundred wounded. The young party turned to the one remaining avenue: armed revolt. It would meet the violence of the Portuguese colonialists with counterviolence. Once this decision was made, the party set itself on a revolutionary path based on an analysis and ideology formulated in the most part by Amilcar Cabral, who proved to be an extraordinary leader and a brilliant theoretician.

Armed struggle not based on mass participation of the people would fail, according to Cabral's analysis. Since ninety-five percent of the people were peasants, the movement turned away from organizing the workers in the towns, concentrating instead on the rural areas. To protect the leadership, and in order to work more freely, PAIGC moved its headquarters to Conakry, not long after neighboring Guinea had gained its independence from France. Hundreds of young recruits left the towns of Guinea-Bissau to join PAIGC in Conakry, many escaping arrest by the security police. From these were chosen the mobilizers who would go into the countryside and begin an intensive campaign to win mass support for a war of liberation. But only when mass support turned into mass participation could the war itself begin. Three years were to pass before the first shots heralding the armed struggle were fired in January 1963 in the south. It took six more months before actions began in the north and an additional six months for it to spread to other key regions. Even by the end of the war there were areas that had never been won over to PAIGC's view of a new society.

PAIGC's successes throughout the war were possible only

because the liberation movement was a mass movement. This was not simply a result of charismatic and talented leadership, but evolved from ideology and practice, the provision of a solid foundation upon which the revolution could be built. A point often stressed by Cabral was the need for an indigenous theory. Basing his analysis, which was Marxist in essence, on the realities of the situation in Guinea-Bissau,* he once wrote:

> National liberation and social revolution are not exportable commodities; they are, and increasingly so every day, the outcome of local and national elaboration, more or less influenced by external factors (be they favorable or unfavorable) but essentially determined and formed by the historical reality of each people, and carried to success by the overcoming or correct solution of the internal contradictions between the various categories characterizing this reality.[6]

---

*Cabral always used the term "Marxist" sparingly, shying away from applying such labels to the Guinean revolution.

> Is Marxism a religion? I am a freedom fighter in my country. You must judge from what I do in practice. If you decide that it's Marxism, tell everyone that it is Marxism. If you decide it's not Marxism, tell them it's not Marxism. But the labels are your affair; we don't like those kind of labels. People here are very preoccupied with the questions: are you Marxist or not Marxist? Are you Marxist-Leninist? Just ask me, please, whether we are doing well in the field. Are we really liberating our people, the human beings in our country, from all forms of oppression? Ask me simply this, and draw your own conclusions.[4]

Minimal use of Marxist terminology is still favored today. Rudebeck points out:

> The long-term, overriding goal of the PAIGC has always been the classically socialist one of abolishing, once and for all, "the exploitation of man by man." In spite of the explicit long-term goal, clearly reaffirmed at the 1977 party congress, the word "socialism" appears very rarely in authoritative declarations of PAIGC ideology. It is found neither in the original party program nor in the various documents of the 1977 congress. The theoretical reason for this is that Amilcar Cabral was always careful to make a clear distinction between the concrete goals attainable for a society in the historical situation of Guinea-Bissau, and the type of theoretical thinking necessary to come to grips with the reality of such a society. According to Cabral's view, which is still the party's official view, the goal of a socialist society in Guinea-Bissau is distant, as Guinea-Bissau is still an economically and technologically underdeveloped agricultural country, marked by the mechanisms of colonial dependency. The social and political analysis applied to the situation of Guinea-Bissau can and should, however, be socialist in the sense of using Marxist points of departure and consequently viewing socialism as a natural and desirable goal for the development of society. In this perspective socialism is simply synonymous with human emancipation and liberation from exploitation.[5]

One of Cabral's first tasks was to make a thorough analysis of the social structure of Guinea-Bissau. This provided the basis for devising strategies for a successful revolution, and for appreciating the revolutionary potential of the different classes. Cabral separated the population first into two groups: the ninety-five percent living in the rural areas, and those who lived in the towns. Meanwhile, the population of under one million was divided into a large number of ethnic groups. There were eight major groups, with the Balanta comprising thirty percent of the population, followed in size by the Mandjak (fourteen percent), the Fula (eleven percent), Mandinga (ten percent), Pepel, Mancagne, Felupe, Bissagos, and another ten or so small groups related to the larger ones. The Fula, Mandinga and a few of the smaller groups are Muslim, together representing thirty percent of the population, while the rest practice their own African religions and are referred to by PAIGC as "animists."[7]*

In discussing the social structure, Cabral refers to the Balanta and the Fula peoples as representing opposite limits of a spectrum. The Fula were a highly stratified, hierarchical society, divided into three groups. At the top of the pyramid were the chiefs, nobles, and religious leaders; next came the artisans and itinerant traders. At the bottom were the peasants, the most exploited group, and described by Cabral as semifeudal because they had to work part of each year for their chiefs. The chiefs owned the land and the labor of the peasants.

The Balanta, on the other hand, were essentially egalitarian. Decisions were made by a council of elders, often in consultation with the people of the village. The land was owned by the village, with portions allocated to each family for cultivation according to their needs.

------

*The way the Muslim religion is practiced in West Africa differs from North Africa and the Middle East. As Cabral points out: "There are still a lot of remnants of animist traditions even among the Muslims of Guinea; the part of the population which follows Islam is not really Islamic but rather Islamized: they are animists who have adopted some Muslim practices, but are still thoroughly impregnated with animist conceptions."[8] The small number of Christians, about two percent of the population, who lived only in the towns, reflected the limited Portuguese penetration into the rural areas and the lack of missionaries compared with other colonies in Africa.

The Fula chiefs were closely tied to the colonialist regime, which nurtured that support with privileges and special treatment. The artisans and traders, being dependent on the chiefs for their livelihood, represented a second section of the pyramid which was resistant to any idea of national liberation. On the other hand, the Fula peasants, like all peasants of Guinea-Bissau, initially appeared to have everything to gain from it. However, the rigid authority the chief exercised over the laboring stratum minimized its early integration into the independence movement. The less stratified groups, the Balanta in particular, were the first to rally their support, partly due to their lack of hierarchy. But the difference also resulted in the degree of suffering under the colonial yoke.[9]

It took an intensive campaign on the part of PAIGC to convince the peasants, regardless of ethnic group, of the need to struggle for national liberation. Cabral was specific in his assertion that the peasants of his country were not a revolutionary force:

> [In Guinea] . . . the peasantry is not a revolutionary force, which may seem strange, particularly as we have based the whole of our armed struggle on the peasantry. A distinction must be drawn between a physical force and a revolutionary force; physically, the peasantry is a great force in Guinea: it is almost the whole of the population, it controls the nation's wealth, it is the peasantry which produces; but we know from experience what trouble we had convincing the peasantry to fight.[10]

Cabral underscores this point by contrasting the peasantry of his country with the revolutionary peasantry of China, noting that the Chinese masses, due to their long history of revolt, readily supported and participated in the revolution. But Guinean history was different, less marked by outside intervention (because the Portuguese had not penetrated the interior until more recently), less feudal, less divided along class lines, and lacking in instances of national revolt because it had not evolved into a nation-state as a result of its own internal dynamics. Thus, Cabral reasoned, mobilization in the rural areas was a precondition for armed struggle: "In certain parts of the country and among certain groups we found a very warm welcome, even right at the start. In other groups and in other areas, all this had to be won."[11]

In fact, the initiative for the liberation struggle did not begin in the countryside where it took solid hold later, but in the towns. The urban population totaled some one hundred thousand people. Three-fourths lived in Bissau, the capital, most of the others in Bafata, the second largest town, but one-fifth the size of Bissau. The rest were dotted in even smaller concentrations, earning the right to bolder lettering on maps of "Portuguese" Guinea, towns such as Cacheu, Catio, Gabu, Fulacunda, Teixeira Pinto, Farim. None of these towns, not even Bissau, could be considered vast urban centers in the way that the cities of Mozambique and Angola are. As the majority of the townspeople had close links with relatives in the rural areas, with constant movement back and forth, it would be more accurate to think of them as linked to the rural areas rather than as strictly urban people.

Cabral distinguished a number of categories among the urban dwellers. The small European population in the towns corresponded to the class divisions in Portugal and consisted mostly of high officials and shop owners. The only Europeans in the rural areas were those who ran isolated trading stores here and there. With few exceptions, the settlers were united in their opposition to the idea of national liberation.

There were three groups of urbanized Africans—the petty bourgeoisie, the wage earners, and the *declassé*. The petty bourgeoisie itself comprised three groups: the high and middle officials, and members of the liberal professions whom Cabral hesitantly placed among the petty bourgeoisie; the petty officials; and those workers employed in commerce on contract.

The difference between the paid workers of the petty bourgeoisie and the majority of workers who fell into the category of wage earners was the precious contract. With it, a worker had job security; without it, he or she was likely to be paid an unlivable wage while subject to firing at a moment's notice. Dockworkers, boatworkers, domestic workers (mostly men), shop and small factory workers (there were no large factories in the country), performed the bulk of the uncontracted work.

The *declassé* were also divided into subgroups. The first was described as lumpenproletarian, although, as Cabral comments, there was no real proletariat in Guinea in the first place. The second represented a large proportion of the urban group, and merited special attention from PAIGC. They had some education, spoke Portuguese, but were unable to find work in the towns. Many had grown up in the rural areas and still maintained close links with family there. In the towns, they lived with relatives from the petty bourgeoisie or worker families, following West African custom which requires that a close relative living in a town support his younger relatives. This group provided a lot of support for the national liberation movement.

The economic interests of the different classes in Guinea-Bissau were a major determinant of their support, or lack of it, for the national liberation struggle. The high and middle officials among the petty bourgeoisie were totally committed to and compromised by colonialism. Among the rest there were those who swayed between support and antagonism. But most importantly, there was what Cabral called the "revolutionary petty bourgeoisie," composed of people who were nationalist and from whom the idea of a national liberation struggle first emanated. The wage earners gave strong and immediate support to the struggle—it was the dockworkers, for instance, who were behind the strike which led to the Pidgiguiti massacre—with notable exceptions among those who had managed barely to establish themselves economically. Desperately wanting to defend the little they had acquired, these workers aligned themselves with the petty bourgeoisie.

The "lumpenproletariat" supported the Portuguese, often working as spies and informers. But it was the youth of the *declassé* which proved a major source of support for the struggle from the first, and it was from this group that most of the early mobilizers and cadres of the party emerged. Their militancy grew out of their ability to compare the standard of living of the Africans and that of the Portuguese settlers. Meanwhile, the peasant, who rarely had experience outside the village, and whose only contact with whites was at the trading post, continued to bear his lot in life uncritically. Social mobility, in other words, was a key element in the raising of consciousness—a fact emphasized by Cabral:

Many people say that it is the peasants who carry the burden of exploitation. This may be true, but so far as the struggle is concerned it must be realized that it is not the degree of suffering and hardship involved as such that matters: even extreme suffering in itself does not necessarily produce the *prise de conscience* [dawning of truth] required for the national liberation struggle. In Guinea the peasants are subjected to a kind of exploitation equivalent to slavery; but even if you try to explain to them that they are being exploited and robbed, it is difficult to convince them by means of an unexperienced explanation of a technico-economic kind that they are the most exploited people. Whereas it is easier to convince the workers and the people employed in the towns . . . that they are being subjected to massive exploitation and injustice because they can see.[12]

Nor could the question of land reform be a rallying point for the revolution. In countries where peasants had been robbed of their land, the call for return of the land to the people was enough to win quickly the support of the masses. As the Portuguese had not expropriated the land in Guinea-Bissau, it remained the communal property of the village. "Telling the people that 'the land belongs to those who work it' was not enough to mobilize them, because we have more than enough land, there is all the land we need. We had to find appropriate formulae for mobilizing our peasants instead of using terms that our people could not yet understand."[13]

Once this social analysis was made, it could and did provide a jumping off point for action, and, through action, the theory could again be reassessed in light of experience. A fluid and continuous process, it enabled PAIGC leaders to seek militants from among the *declassé,* to understand the need for a long and intensive period of mobilization among the peasants, to see that the leadership of the movement would initially come from the so-called revolutionary petty bourgeoisie. But it enabled them also to understand that the revolution would fail if the leadership remained there. Everybody working in the revolution would have to develop what Cabral saw as a working-class mentality in order to make up for the lack of a working class per se. Those from privileged positions and hence alienated from the masses of the people, specifically the "revolutionary petty bourgeoisie," would have to rediscover their roots, their history, their culture. In order not to betray the objective of the struggle for national liberation, "the revolutionary petty bourgeoisie must be capable of committing suicide as a class in order to be reborn as revolutionary workers, completely identified with the deepest aspirations of the people to which they belong."[14]

National liberation meant many things to PAIGC: regaining and revaluing the culture and history of the Guinean people; freeing of the productive forces from colonial and imperial domination; freeing the people from all forms of exploitation; building a new society and a new nation based on the full participation of the people, both men and women; liberation of women from their dominated and oppressed state within the society. The form of struggle was a vital factor in determining whether these goals could be attained, and the only form that would ensure independence on Guinean terms was armed struggle. The years of passive resistance, the demonstrations and strikes, had led only to increased repression on the part of the Portuguese colonialists. This violence, part of the society for decades, could finally be met only by counterviolence, according to PAIGC. Fully aware of the hardships it would cause the people, the party adopted this course out of necessity, and as a last resort.

Cabral explained this as follows:

In our present historical situation—elimination of imperialism . . . —there are only two possible paths for an independent nation: to return to imperialist domination (neocolonial, capitalism, state capitalism) or to take the way of socialism. This operation, on which depends the compensation for the efforts and sacrifices of the popular masses during the struggle, is considerably influenced by the form of struggle and the degree of revolutionary consciousness of those who lead it. The facts make it unnecessary for us to prove that the essential instrument of imperialist domination is violence. If we accept the principle that the liberation struggle is revolution and that it does not finish at the moment when the national flag is raised and the national anthem played, we will see that there is not, and cannot be national liberation without the use of liberating violence by the nationalist forces, to answer the criminal violence of the agents of imperialism. . . . The important thing is to determine which forms of violence have to be used by the national liberation forces in order not only to answer the violence of imperialism but also to ensure through the struggle the final victory of their cause, true national liberation. . . . The only effective way of definitely fulfilling the aspirations of the people, that is to say of attaining national liberation, is by armed struggle.[15]

There were benefits from this form of struggle other than the ousting of the Portuguese colonialists from Guinea-Bissau. "While the armed fight demands sacrifices, it also has advantages," Cabral told an informal meeting in New York in 1972:

For us now, it [armed fight] is a good thing in our opinion . . . because this armed fight helped us to accelerate the revolution of our people, to create a new situation that will facilitate our progress. . . . Through this armed fight, we realized other things are more important than the size of the liberated regions or the capacity of our fighters, such as the irreversible change in the attitudes of our men. We have more sacrifices to make and more difficulties to overcome, but our people are now accustomed to this, and know that for freedom we must pay a price. What can we consider better than freedom?[16]

The "irreversibility" that Cabral referred to in the changed attitudes of men and women was a phenomenon immediately apparent to visitors to the liberated zones. It was reflected in the support for PAIGC, the political consciousness of the peasants, and the unity that had been forged among the many different ethnic groups comprising the Guinea-Bissau nation. The armed struggle provided an impetus for unity—an essential element for true liberation—that could not as easily have been attained through other means. When people are facing death every day and when they need one another's support and strength to fight the enemy, differences based on ethnic group, religion, and sex begin to play a much more muted role in the life and culture of the people.

"Life is so different now," a Fula peasant woman told me when I visited her village. "Before it was not possible to think like this, but now I see more light and know that everybody is my brother and my sister. Today we do not think about color or ethnic group the way we did before. We know one thing now: everybody is from Guinea-Bissau."

The armed struggle proved to be just one phase of the revolution. The mobilization of the people that began even before the beginning of the guerrilla war was concerned even more with preparing the people for the building of a new society than with preparing them for war. And once areas were liberated, plans for social reconstruction were immediately put into effect.

The armed struggle also set in motion a two-way process, a kind of revolutionary osmosis, vital for the future of the new society. On the one hand, it brought the leadership closer to the peasants. On the other, because it encouraged and was dependent upon mass participation of the people, it also meant that peasants rose to the ranks of leaders. As Cabral explained in a lecture he gave in the United States:

> The leaders of the liberation movement . . . all have to live day by day with various peasant strata in the heart of rural populations. They come to know the people better. They discover at the grass roots the richness of the people's cultural values (whether philosophic or political, artistic, social or moral). They acquire a clearer understanding of the economic realities of their country and of the problems, sufferings and hopes of the masses of their people.
>
> Not without a certain astonishment, the leaders come to realize the richness of spirit, the capacity for reasoned discussion and clear exposition of ideas, the facility for understanding and assimilating concepts on the part of populations who yesterday were forgotten, or else despised as incompetent by the colonizer and even by some nationals.[17]

The "osmosis" in the other direction—peasants gradually acquiring the prerequisites of leadership—meant that a population ninety-nine percent illiterate began to understand the potential for a totally new life, and to begin to live it. Cabral continued:

> On the other side, the working masses and in particular the peasants, who are generally illiterate and have never moved beyond the boundaries of their village and their region, lose, in contact with other groups, the complexes which constrained them in their relations with different ethnic and social groupings. They realize their crucial role in the struggle. They break the bond of their village universe. They integrate themselves, progressively

in their country and in the world. They acquire an infinite amount of new knowledge that is useful to their immediate and future action within the framework of the struggle. They strengthen their political consciousness by assimilating the principles of national and social revolution postulated by the struggle. And so they become more able to play a decisive role in providing the principal force of the liberation movement.[18]

That PAIGC based its revolution on a clearly thought-out theory, which in turn was affected by the practice, can be seen in the preceding pages. The question remaining is how did PAIGC set about the day-to-day task of making revolution, of putting their theory into practice.

Chapter 3

"A great deal of patience"

For three years prior to the launching of the war of national liberation an intensive and critical campaign of political mobilization was undertaken to win the support of the peasants. During the eleven-and-a-half-year war, two-thirds of the countryside was liberated. A system of social services was established throughout the liberated zones together with elected local and regional councils and people's courts. A new society was fast emerging despite the hardships of living under conditions of war.

It was one of those crisp, clear Conakry nights that come only in the middle of the dry season. The whine of the Volkswagen engine cut through the stillness as Amilcar Cabral and his wife Ana Maria drove home from a reception at the Polish Embassy.

Although it was nearly eleven, Cabral was not returning home to bed. He would drop Ana Maria at home and head for the party office for a meeting with Aristides Pereira, another of the top PAIGC leaders. Like most of his nights in Conakry, this one promised to be a long one.

Cabral and his wife were alone in the car. The PAIGC leader shunned guards, despite the number of attempts on his life. If he had to live under protection and in constant fear of his life, he reasoned, he might as well not live. His motto was to trust people. There was a guard at his house always, and many times the party insisted that he not travel alone. But now he was in Conakry and he felt safe. He did not even bother to carry his gun.

He had reason to feel good that night, January 20, 1973. The war was going well, the People's Assembly was about to proclaim the Republic of Guinea-Bissau, and President Sekou Touré, President of Guinea (Conakry), had special guests: Samora Machel, president of FRELIMO, the Mozambican liberation movement and other FRELIMO leaders, including Joaquim Chissano. The solidarity between the two movements was strong, and their leaders welcomed the exchange of ideas about their respective revolutions. In fact, at that moment, Chissano was addressing PAIGC cadres and militants at the PAIGC Training Center.

Suddenly, bright headlights blinded the driver. Surprised to recognize a party Jeep, Cabral stopped his car and got out.

"What is the matter?" he asked, with no trace of suspicion in his voice.

Three men climbed out of the army vehicle and pointed their guns at the secretary-general.

"Follow us," said Kani Inocencio, a PAIGC member.

Cabral refused and called to the guard posted at his house. There was no guard. He had been the one to inform the conspirators of the evening's program and that Cabral would be alone.

"Get in," he was ordered, "or we'll have to force you."

"You can't get me that way," snapped Cabral. "Nobody can

ever tie me up. I never accepted the tying up of others. We are fighting precisely to break such chains."

Fear and dismay swept Kani's face. But it was too late. He hesitated a moment, then raised his gun and shot, practically point-blank.

Hit in the liver, Cabral collapsed, bleeding profusely. Kani left the scene, and Cabral tried to rise from the ground, where a pool of blood was spreading. The leader was still conscious. In a final effort, he addressed the other two men who were standing motionless:

"Why, comrades? If there are differences, we must discuss them. The party has taught us . . ."

"What? You're still talking?" shouted Kani, who had suddenly reappeared. He turned to the men: "Finish him off. Quickly."

There was a brief burst of gunfire and Cabral, hit in the head, fell back dead. The glasses he always wore lay next to him.

Terrorized and powerless, Ana Maria witnessed the whole scene from the car. She was then taken prisoner.

The swift response of Sekou Touré averted further disaster. By the next day the putschist assassins had been arrested and the seized PAIGC leaders, including Ana Maria Cabral and Aristides Pereira, freed. Pereira had been forced aboard a PAIGC boat en route to Bissau when his abductors were overtaken by a government naval patrol ship. The putschists were discontented party members in search of an accommodation with Lisbon and personal gain.[1]

The Portuguese who contacted these men anticipated that by killing Cabral they would cause the disintegration of the liberation movement. It did not. Nor did it set back the war; if anything it provided an impetus to push harder toward victory. Cabral had laid the foundations of the party well; it could continue without his leadership. However, his death robbed not only his country, but also Africa and the entire third world, of a truly remarkable thinker and revolutionary.

Amilcar Cabral's parents were Cape Verdeans who moved to Bafata in Guinea-Bissau before his birth in 1925. As his family was *assimilado*, Cabral was fortunate in getting a complete education. In the 1940s he studied in Lisbon, where he came in contact with other young students from the colonies. Their informal discussions soon brought them to a thoroughly anti-colonialist consciousness, but attempts to organize themselves were hampered by the Portuguese injunction against forming political groups. Undaunted, the students obtained government permission to establish a cultural club, ostensibly to look into the culture of their homelands—Mozambique, Angola, and Guinea-Bissau. It never served this purpose. Their political discussions and debates went on late into the night as they integrated what they were learning of left politics in Europe with their understanding of the oppression of their own countries. It was here that the ideas for founding the liberation movements—FRELIMO, MPLA, and PAIGC—were sown.

When Cabral returned to Bissau in the early fifties, he was employed by the administration as an agronomist and instructed to conduct an agricultural census of the whole country. The administration could not have done the future revolution a more valuable service. For two years, between 1952 and 1954, Cabral traveled from one end of his country to the other, from one village to the next. It gave him a unique opportunity to talk with the peasants and to find out about their lives. He listened closely, asked sympathetic questions, and absorbed enough information to form a comprehensive picture of the various forces at work in the society. He could now adapt the theoretical framework he had acquired in Europe to the realities of the situation in Guinea-Bissau. Meanwhile, the contacts enabled him to break down the barrier which had separated him, as an *assimilado*, from his people. But he was not only a listener, and was already organizing youth in Bissau.

It was not long before the Portuguese administration began to single out Cabral as a troublemaker. Fortunately, the governor at the time had some liberal instincts. Instead of arresting him outright, he called Cabral into his office and gave him the choice of stopping political agitation or leaving the country, making it clear that noncompliance would lead to jail.

Cabral left and went to Luanda, but his political work did not stop; it was simply transferred. Not long after settling in the Angolan capital, Cabral joined Agostinho Neto in founding

MPLA, of which Neto remained president until independence. Simultaneously, the Guinean patriot continued his work toward the liberation of his own country. In September 1956, he returned to Bissau for a brief visit, ostensibly to see his family, but actually to form a clandestine party, grouping the anticolonial forces in the country.

A month after the Pidgiguiti massacre in 1959, he returned a second time to Bissau. At a historic meeting in a house in a *bairro* (district) a small group of PAIGC leaders decided that "in light of the Pidgiguiti experience and the nature of Portuguese colonialism . . . the only way to liberate the country is through struggle by all means, including war."[2] They also decided to transfer the leadership of the party outside the country, to guarantee its security and provide the mobility to prepare for the war. After bidding farewell to his mother and friends, Cabral left as quietly as he had entered. Exiled in Conakry, he established the PAIGC headquarters where it was to remain until the end of the war.

The policies of PAIGC, and their successes in struggle, have much to do with the outstanding leadership qualities exhibited by Cabral. But his main talent lay precisely in his ability to develop these qualities in others, so that the weight of the revolution was distributed among numerous cadres. Believing in the capacity of those about him to do the work as competently as he, Cabral never saw himself as indispensable. "I am a simple African man, doing my duty in my own country in the context of our time," he once told an audience in London, adding: "We have no heroes in our country—the only heroes are the African people."[3] On another occasion, perhaps anticipating the eventuality of his death, he said: "In our country we do not believe in the capacity of one man to liberate the people. Liberation is the job of all the people."[4] The fact that the armed struggle was spurred on to new victories after his assassination is testimony both to the impact Cabral had on people and the party's understanding that people, not individuals, are the motors of history.

Cabral's wit, his intense honesty, his uncompromising sense of justice and humanity, have become almost legendary. He could be stern, teasing, or kind, depending on the situation. All who met him came away with the sense of his being a great yet simple man.

Homage to him both as a leader and as a person respected and loved by the people throughout Guinea-Bissau could be elicited easily by any visitor to the liberated areas after his death. Discussion of the revolution inevitably meant discussion of Cabral. Whenever people were gathered together and could indulge in the rare luxury of just sitting and talking, they would begin to tell endless stories and funny anecdotes, slapping their sides and laughing as they recalled him. Among the many unsolicited tributes that I heard, one stands out in particular. It came from a Balanta peasant woman. As she talked she would rub her fingers and palms together in a nervous, jerky way, and I could not help noticing the skin of her bony hands, dry and cracked and calloused, evidence of many years of pounding rice and hard labor in her village. She spoke with a simple eloquence, looking at me directly, her voice swelling with emotion:

"We were exploited by the Portuguese. They stole everything from the people of Guinea for centuries. They massacred our people. They stole all our products. They took our people as prisoners.

"Before our eyes were closed and we could not see the world. It is the comrade Cabral who opened our eyes and showed us a new world so that we could stop this Portuguese domination, so that we could stop all this exploitation. Cabral has cleared the road where we must walk. Cabral has cleared our minds to help us understand.

"And now we are able to see how important the work of Cabral is. We are in a new world. For this comrade Cabral gave his life. They killed Cabral but Cabral is not dead. His work continues.

"This war is very important. It is not for one day. If it was for one day, we could not learn our story. This war must go slowly for the people to learn how important they are.

"We will fight until we kill the last Portuguese soldier. We will fight until our country is free. And we know why we are fighting. We don't want to fight, but the Portuguese came to our country and started the war. We did not go to Portugal to fight a war. We have a reason to be free. We are fighting in our own country.

"The fight goes forward, never backward. *A luta continua*—the struggle continues."

While Cabral was obviously comfortable dealing with abstractions, he was eminently capable of practical work as well. The PAIGC leader himself conducted the political preparation of the mobilizers. Drawn largely from the urban youth of the *declassé*, hundreds of these young men came to Conakry, some fleeing arrest, all inspired by the goals of the liberation movement and wanting to commit themselves to its work. About one thousand militants passed through the training "school," no more than an old, dilapidated cement house, small and always overcrowded. Some of the graduates would later become leaders of PAIGC, but one thing they all had in common was that they were all men.

There were reasons why none of these first mobilizers were women. The most obvious one is that, given their relative freedom in the society, it was easier for the men to leave Bissau and join PAIGC in Conakry. Women had virtually no mobility, in keeping with tradition, and were less likely to break from the patterns set for them by their socialization. The fact that many of the first mobilizers were from the *declassé* gives another clue. Only young men left the rural areas to live with relatives in the towns. For while uncles would feel duty-bound to support their young nephews, they were unlikely to consider doing the same for nieces. It was beyond the call of custom, and such behavior by women would never have been condoned in the first place. The third reason is a very practical one, relating to how mobilization itself took shape. It was essential to win the trust of first one peasant, then another, and slowly widen the contacts until the whole village was won over. This trust would never have been given to a woman, particularly one making the first contact between the party and a given locality. In the mind of the peasant there could be no good explanation for a woman to "happen" to pass through his village, and he certainly would not have responded to her questions about his life, much less any call for the overturning of his oppressors. This initial and very delicate task thus could be handled only by men.

The training given at the political school for activists was thorough. Cabral described it in an interview in 1969:

> In 1960 we created a political school in Conakry, under very poor conditions. Militants from the towns—Party members—were the first to come to receive political instruction and to be trained in how to mobilize our people for the struggle. After comrades from the city came peasants and youths (some even bringing their entire families) who had been mobilized by Party members. Ten, twenty, twenty-five people would come for a period of one or two months. During that period they went through an intensive education program; we spoke to them, and night would come and we couldn't speak any more because we were completely hoarse. . . .
>
> We performed in that school as in a theater, imagining the mobilization of the people of a *tabanca*, but taking into account social characteristics, traditions, religion—all the customs of our peasant population. . . .
>
> We could never mobilize our people simply on the basis of the struggle against colonialism—that has no effect. To speak of the fight against imperialism is not convincing enough. Instead we use direct language that all can understand:
>
> "Why are you going to fight? What are you? What is your father? What has happened to your father up to now? What is the situation? Did you pay taxes? Did your father pay taxes? What have you seen from those taxes? How much do you get for your groundnuts [peanuts]? Have you thought about how much you will earn with your groundnuts? How much sweat has it cost your family? Which of you has been imprisoned? You are going to work on road-building: who gives you the tools? You bring the tools. Who provides your meals? You provide your meals. But who walks on the road? Who has a car? And your daughter who was raped—are you happy about that?"
>
> In our new mobilization we avoided all generalizations and pat phrases. We went into detail and made our people preparing for this kind of work repeat many times what they were going to say. This is an aspect which we considered of great importance, in our specific case, because we started from the concrete reality of our people. We tried to avoid having the peasants think that we were outsiders come to teach them how to do things; we put ourselves in the position of people who came to learn *with*

the peasants, and in the end the peasants were discovering for themselves why things had gone badly for them. They came to understand that a tremendous amount of exploitation exists and that it is they themselves who pay for everything, even for the profits of the people living in the city. Our experience showed us that it is necessary for each people to find its own formula for mobilization for the struggle; it also showed that to integrate the peasant masses into the struggle, one must have a great deal of patience.[5]

The period of mobilization continued for three years before the beginning of the armed struggle. This period was stressed as the most important element in laying the foundation for the future revolution. Without this foundation, the armed struggle, more particularly, the active part played in it by the peasants, would not have been so successful. To have been lacking in patience, to have expected a spontaneous response from the peasants, would have entailed a dangerous naïveté on the part of the mobilizers. The peasants knew only too well how tightly and brutally the colonial administration governed Guinea-Bissau. The laws were formulated and justice controlled by the colonialists. How could they hope to change this? "We're blacks," they would say. "We don't even know how to make a safety-match. The whites have guns, airplanes. How ever can we get rid of them?"[6] But the mobilizers were persuasive, and they were persuasive partly because they had patience—a very reassuring quality in the eyes of the peasants, of people whose very lives depended on the recognition of the practical. And so over the months of mobilization they began to develop a new and more confident image of themselves, ignited by the idea that they themselves might throw their oppressors out of the country.

Among the many mobilizers I met (some of whom are now leading members of the party and government) were Braima Camara and Cau Sambu. Braima was a political commissar in the army during the war, Cau a member of the Superior Council for the Fight and regional political commissar in the Balana-Quitafine region in the south.

Braima was scarcely a teenager when he was mobilized by Cabral, even before PAIGC was founded.* He came from a very poor family and grew up in one of the *bairro* slums of Bissau, spending his childhood out on the streets with his friends from the neighborhood. Braima's father had died when he was an infant and his mother, sickly and aging, never had any regular employment. Education was out of the question; he seldom had enough to eat and dressed in little more than rags.

When he was twelve he set out in search of employment and eventually found it on an experimental government plantation in Bissau which grew peanuts, as well as such fruit as oranges, mangoes, papayas, and palm kernels. He joined one hundred other adolescents whose work was to carry water to the workers in the fields for drinking and watering the crops. The pay was three escudos per day. A pittance, but to Braima, twenty-one escudos at the end of a seven-day week felt pretty good. A change from nothing. He worked hard and made a lot of friends among the boys.

No sooner had he begun to work than an African agronomist was hired—Amilcar Cabral. And no sooner had Cabral sized up the appalling conditions than the boys were out on their first strike. Their foreman, Bakar Cassama,** was Cabral's close friend and it was he who spoke with the young workers about protesting their bad wages. All one hundred stayed away from work and the following day presented their demands to their highly agitated boss. "We did not come to work yesterday," they told him, "because you pay us very little money. And for three months now, we have not been paid at all. We have no money to buy food. We are hungry. We refuse to work here any longer under these conditions. We would rather go and find work elsewhere."

The boys refused to budge from their position. Finally, with much reluctance and no small amount of anger, their employers agreed to increase their salaries to five escudos per day, and to

---

*I interviewed Braima Camara after independence when he was based in Quebo, a small town in the Catio region in the south. He was the political commissar of a division of FARP, the national army stationed in barracks evacuated by the Portuguese.

**Bakar Cassama is now a leading member of both PAIGC and the government.

pay one month's back pay at the higher rate. They were paid that afternoon, but only after they had been rounded up by the plantation's armed guards who tried to intimidate them into telling who had instigated the strike. "We have nothing to tell you," they insisted. "You can kill us if you want to. We are not afraid. But we have nothing to tell you. We did it ourselves."

The success of this strike led to another, equally successful, a few months later, but this time all the plantation workers, young and old, took part.

Cabral was watching these young workers all the while, testing them for their political potential. In particular he favored Braima, and took him along on occasion when he traveled into the rural areas to work on the census. Meanwhile, he organized a football club among the youth, and he and the boys worked hard to clear land for a field. After the agronomist had purchased T-shirts of one color—their "uniform"—they began inviting other teams to play against them. Cabral's endeavors were supported by his employers who thought this was a fine idea to keep the boys out of trouble. But, like the cultural club in Lisbon, the sports club was largely a cover for political discussion, in which Cabral would talk for hours about the conditions in Guinea-Bissau. Not long after the *Clube Africano* was formed, its initiator had to leave Bissau. But Bakar Cassama took over where Cabral left off and continued to raise the young workers' consciousness.

Braima avidly took in everything that was being said and vowed that he would fight for the liberation of his country. As the years went by he and a group of friends spoke to young people of their age about the need for a national liberation struggle, and, after the party moved its headquarters to Conakry, he distributed pamphlets that had been sent clandestinely into the country.

When Cabral was in Bissau for the last time, Braima went to his house to see him. Cabral showed interest in the political work his young recruit was carrying on, asking many questions. "Braima, I have to leave Bissau," Cabral said to him before they parted. "But I will continue our work in Conakry. If you want to come and join us, you will find me there."

Braima mulled over these words during the ensuing weeks

and months. It was becoming clear that he could not go on with his political activities without being arrested. Besides, he knew that the only way to win freedom was by armed struggle. And so, at the beginning of 1960, he and a small group of comrades left for Conakry. For the next three months he trained under Cabral as a mobilizer before going into the interior of his country. He was one of the many mobilizers who formed the core of the revolutionary cadres.

Not all those who went into the interior became cadres. Some encountered suspicion and fear in the village they were trying to mobilize—all it took was one antagonistic peasant—and were turned over to the Portuguese authorities. Their fate was always the same: interrogation, torture, and imprisonment or summary execution. Other mobilizers, meantime, successfully carried out their assignments, and then proceeded to use their weapons to tyrannize the villagers for personal profit.

"These militants considered that the areas they mobilized 'belonged' to them," explained Cau Sambu, "and they did not want to collaborate with the rest of us. They thought they ruled the area. They used their guns to give themselves power. This was possible due to the fact that there were so few cadres, and mobilizers had to act as both political and military *responsavels*. Without revolutionary consciousness, they began to get caught up in their own power. One of the main items dealt with at the first Party Congress at Cassacá in 1964 was to rid the party of these attitudes. The *responsavels* in question were relieved of their positions and dismissed from the party. The worst offenders were arrested and detained in military bases. It took longer to develop political consciousness and mobilize people in the areas that these militants had worked."

Cau Sambu,* one of the movement's most successful mobilizers, was born in Campara, a village in the Quinara region of the south. At the age of ten he went to Bissau and became a tailor's apprentice. By age seventeen he had his own corner of

---

*Cau Sambu's story emerged out of a number of interviews and discussions I had with him both during the war, in the Balana-Quitafine region of the south front where he was political commissar, and after independence when he was regional secretary-general of PAIGC for the Catio region.

the veranda of a house where he sewed for his clients. He remained in this work for many years and left for Conakry only after the Pidgiguiti massacre, to train as a mobilizer.

It did not take long for him to become one of the party's most trustworthy and talented cadres. Loved and respected by all the people he mobilized and worked with, he was often called "man of the people." He wore that label proudly—there was no false humility about Cau—but it in no way belied his record, which spoke for itself. And the record grew more impressive with each year that he worked, driven by his unbounded energy and dedication to the liberation struggle. Although he was a member of the Superior Council and had numerous opportunities to leave the liberated zones, he remained inside from the time he first went in as a mobilizer to near the end of the war.

Cau arrived in Xitole, his first assignment as a mobilizer, with the name of just one potential contact. He set about winning this man's support in the way that became his general pattern:

"I arrived at the man's house, as if by chance, and asked if I could stay there a little while, giving some excuse as to why I was in the area. With the initial contact I had to be very cautious. I could not begin to discuss the war immediately, or even mention anything political. No, I just sat there, talking about this or that. I told stories, joked, talked in a friendly way—for one day, two days, three days, maybe even a week. It depended on the responses I got. All the time I was trying to size up my host and only when I felt the atmosphere between us was right, did I begin to mobilize Alfredo or Mamadou or João. A wrong judgment could be fatal, so I had to be extremely careful."

Slowly Cau would bring the conversation around to politics, to living conditions, to the need for change. Once his contact showed interest in the idea of national liberation, he would begin to divulge more details about PAIGC and its plans, and then suggest that the peasant bring two people that he trusted from his village to speak with him. At this point, Cau would leave the village as a security measure—an informer might have picked up wind of what was happenng—and go to live in the forest, where he had meetings with his first contacts.

"When this first group of people came to speak to me in the

forest, I would say things like, 'Ah, I understand that in Bissau people are beginning to organize,' or, 'In Cubucare, I hear that there are people living in the bush who want to fight the *Tuga*.' I would say, 'Huh, if this is true, then tomorrow I will go and fight them. But I don't have a gun. So what! I'll just fight them with what I can find.' While I spoke I would watch the expressions on their faces. If they reacted sympathetically to my bravado, then I could push a little harder."

Once the initial group was mobilized, they would speak with a few more and in this way the numbers would grow until everybody in the village was mobilized. Then Cau would hold a meeting of the whole village in the forest, making sure that one or two people remained behind to keep watch for Portuguese soldiers. He would also make sure they all had an alibi in case the villagers were questioned about where they had been. All the women brought their baskets and gourds to make it appear they had been to the forest to look for fruit, while the men carried their axes, so that they could say they had been to chop wood.

In his speeches, Cau would talk about oppression by the Portuguese colonialists and the need to take the fight into their own hands; he would talk about plans for the armed struggle and the need to build in the process a society that benefited all. He would also urge the women to participate in the struggle, insisting that achievements of the liberation movement would come to nothing if it meant that only men joined the fight. Meanwhile, addressing the men directly, he would cajole them into understanding this radical departure from tradition, into encouraging their wives and daughters to work together with the men.

Cau, like the other mobilizers, had come to understand from his training with Cabral that women did not have the same rights as men. Because the party recognized the crucial productive role of women, mobilization was directed consciously at both men and women, with the insistence that all Guineans be treated as equals and that men learn to respect women.

The women themselves, however, initially were hesitant about attending meetings and taking responsibility, and Cau experienced the difficulty of setting this aspect of the revolution in motion. There were noticeable exceptions, though, and one of the first people he mobilized was a woman. She was the wife of his first contact in a village he went to soon after he began his work. Every day the woman took food to him in his hiding place in the forest, and to avoid raising suspicion, hid the food at the bottom of a basket. With the excuse that she was going to the rice fields or to get water, she would set off toward her supposed destination and, as soon as she was out of sight, switch direction.

"When she arrived," Cau related, "I talked to her about the party while I ate the food. We would talk like this every day. I showed her the documents I had and the PAIGC flag. She was very eager to help. Back in the village she began to talk with a few people she trusted most. At first she did not tell them about me, only talked in a general way about the oppression and the need to fight against it. When they responded sympathetically, then she began to tell them about me and the plans for beginning the war of liberation."

Once a particular village was won to the cause of national liberation, Cau would move on to the next. Sometimes he would have to proceed differently, by laboring with the peasants, as opposed to waiting around the forest. He would go with them to the rice fields, or to the forest to chop wood, talking all the time about general things, winning their trust. Then, as they worked, he would begin to talk more concretely.

Cau's charismatic qualities, his skill in a singularly African way of oratory, and his ability to explain things so that they related directly to the lives of the peasants made him very effective. He soon became known to the Portuguese authorities, who placed a huge price on his head. Once, the Portuguese administrators of a town near Cau's area of responsibility called together the people of the sector and took them in trucks to Bafata, on the pretext of holding a festivity. After a few perfunctory ceremonies, the police and army assembled the people together for the real purpose of the festivity, to instruct them on how to capture Cau and the other terrible *bandidos*.

"The terrorists are destroying the villages," they said. "They are your enemy. They live like monkeys in the forest, eating only fruit. But they are very greedy and they love lots of food.

"The worst of these bandits is Cau Sambu. Now if he comes to your village, you must kill a nice, big chicken and prepare it well.

"How does he eat?" the commander then asked the crowd.

"Ah, he always eats with his hands," one man shouted back, with encouragement from those around him. "But he holds his pistol in one hand, while he eats with the other. He never puts his pistol down."

"OK," the Portuguese commander rejoined, "you must put the chicken in one bowl, the sauce in another, and place it on his right side. Then place a bowl of water to his left side. When he wants to drink water while he is eating, he will have to put down his pistol. Then someone can say, 'Ah, what a beautiful pistol you have,' and pick it up and pretend to look at it. Then you've got him. Hit him over the head until he begins to bleed. When he loses consciousness, you can kill him by cutting his throat. Whoever brings us the head of Cau Sambu will get fifty thousand escudos and twenty cows."

The commander then appointed one man, Tunga Labadna, to be responsible for overseeing the capture of Cau. "OK," replied Tunga, adopting a subservient air, "we can surely do this." In fact, Tunga was the first man Cau had ever mobilized, and it was he who helped the mobilizer gain the support of many people in his area. He always welcomed Cau in his home and looked after him in the forest.

When they returned home, Cau called a large meeting, where the peasants reported to him in minute detail what had happened in Bafata. Punctuated by the appreciative guffaws of the audience, the whole scene was acted out for his benefit.

A similar incident occurred a while later. But this time Cau was sitting in the crowd, clean-shaven and dressed like the peasants he had accompanied, having reluctantly parted for the day with the black T-shirt he always wore. The meeting had been called to the town of Xitole, where the Portuguese army was about to establish a camp. Cau was sent by PAIGC to find out as much as possible about it. When the commander addressing the crowd singled Cau out as the most dangerous bandit, the people around turned to look at him aghast. But the mobilizer kept a deadpan face, instructing them in their own language, "Don't look at me. He doesn't recognize me. Nothing will happen." The commander, ten feet away, continued the meeting, oblivious.

As Cau listened to the tirade against "terrorists," he noticed a small car nearby; the driver was a Portuguese soldier with a very fine rifle. Even as he began to scheme a way to steal the rifle, the car stalled, and when an African guard called for people to come and help push it, Cau jumped up at once. But as he neared the vehicle, the African guard shouted at him, "We called the *young* boys only. Go away! *Go away!*"

At first Cau was puzzled, but looking more closely, he realized the African was gesticulating furiously, not out of anger but in an attempt to warn him of danger. And then he recognized him. The guard had been a regular customer when Cau was tailoring in Bissau.

Cau would laugh heartily as he recounted these stories. But he could switch in an instant to a serious tone.

"The time of mobilization was a difficult one. A great number of mobilizers were captured and killed by the *Tuga*. Others were arrested. Many peasants were killed or tortured because they would not give information about us and about PAIGC. Also there were times when we went without food. Sometimes we had to manage off the fruit we gathered in the forest, and these were hard to find during the rainy season."

The last thing PAIGC wanted to do was rush the process of mobilization. Only when they felt sure they had the solid support of those they had mobilized did they move to the next vital step—the military. Armed revolt was begun three years later when the peasants themselves began pushing for it. Tired of the discussions and talk, they wanted action.

"In Xitole region, where I was, it was the people who directed the war," Cau told me, his forehead puckering in a slight frown as he remembered back. "If it was not for the commitment of the people, nothing would have happened. The people kept asking me when they could begin to fight. I wrote a letter to comrade Cabral telling him that the people were eager and ready. A small group of us then were sent across the border to fetch guns. But the arms were not to be utilized in the *tabancas*. No, attacks had to be made as far from the *tabancas* as possible so that the peasants would not be implicated.

"Those early actions were very important. We knew if they were successful that we would have all the people on our side. We had for so long just been using words. Now we had to show the peasants that the Portuguese were vulnerable and not invincible. Many were still skeptical, so our first combat missions had to be carefully chosen. I remember how one group of village militia came running back into the village after their first ambush displaying Portuguese army rifles high above their heads: 'We've attacked the *Tuga*! The *Tuga* fled from us! We have won against the *Tuga*!' They were so excited. They had managed to achieve something they had once thought impossible.

"We had very few arms, at first. We felled trees and placed them across the road. When the Portuguese army truck came to a standstill we shot the soldiers and took their weapons. Or we dug a large hole in the road and then covered over the top to camouflage it. When a truck fell in we would attack and take the arms. In this way, in the beginning, we were able to amass more weapons and so increase the number of ambushes.

"In this way the war of liberation began. Without total support of the people, it would never have been won."*

Throughout the areas liberated by PAIGC, a program of social and national reconstruction was already under way, providing services where none had existed before. Schools, hospitals, clinics, people's stores were established in every region and every sector, and I visited those in the regions and sectors of the south and east that I traveled in. I met people who had been elected to serve on village councils, sector councils, and regional councils as well as members of the People's National Assembly, and judges who had been elected by people in the villages onto the people's courts.

---

*This account by Cau Sambu illustrated how the *foco* theory of revolutionary practice would not have suited the conditions of Guinea-Bissau. This theory, effectively applied by the Cubans, for instance, emphasizes the launching of armed struggle as a mobilizing technique in itself, and dispenses with a period of prior political mobilization, which PAIGC found so critical to the development and ultimate success of their war of liberation.

The school system in the liberated zones was built from scratch, dispensing with colonial influence and establishing a new syllabus to reflect the conditions of Guinea-Bissau and the revolution. The school system included village schools, boarding schools, semiboarding schools, and two secondary schools outside the country, one—the "Pilot School"—in Conakry, and the other in Ziguinchor, Senegal.

Before the beginning of the war there were twelve thousand students in the whole country, the majority concentrated in the towns. Toward the end of the war there were over fifteen thousand pupils in the liberated zones alone, despite the enormous difficulties that had to be overcome in establishing schools.

Hospitals and health posts, like the schools, were buried in the forest and consisted of huts constructed from branches, vines, and palm fronds. The most severe medical cases were carried on stretchers to the border and then by ambulance to the Solidarity Hospital in Boké, which had been built with the help of friendly countries. All other cases—wounds from battle, illnesses, and injuries—were treated at the small hospitals in the interior which, although they lacked electricity, had facilities for minor surgery. Emphasis was placed on preventive medicine, and health brigades visited villages on a regular basis. They brought with them, for the first time in the experience of many peasants, scientific knowledge and relief from the enormous health problems that persisted from colonial Guinea-Bissau. Equally important, they provided the people with concrete experience of the changes the revolution could bring.

But at first these services were widely greeted with suspicion. Women were particularly hesitant to undergo a medical examination and to take their illnesses to the health posts. Only persistent education, as well as concrete results on the part of PAIGC, began to win support for these services. One health *responsavel* who worked in the north of the country recalled these early problems. "I remember how we tried so hard to get the people in the village to go to the hospital or medical post when they were ill," she told me. "Huh! They would have nothing to do with these newfangled ideas about medical care. We had to talk and talk and talk in order to encourage them to use these services. And then what happened? We could not *stop* them from going to the medical posts. Every little headache, every sneeze. . . !"

People's stores were another aspect of social reconstruction, operating throughout the country. The surplus produced in the fields (and, despite the war, there was a surplus) was traded at these stores for basic necessities. Peasants no longer had to submit to unfair trading practices at Portuguese-owned stores. In exchange for their rice, palm oil, as well as beeswax, crocodile skins, and livestock, peasants had access to such basic necessities as salt, sugar, soap, cloth, matches, batteries, flashlights, blankets. No money was used in the transaction; instead, a slip of paper indicating the value of the goods would be given the trader, who could exchange it then, or at a later date, for needed items. The stores, sometimes resembling small market places where people would gather and talk, also provided a place for political education, particularly in relation to the economy.

The people elected their own five-member councils at the village, sector, and regional level, and at the end of 1972 elections extended to the People's National Assembly. Meanwhile, the village councils were at the core of the administrative and political structure of the liberated zones. Each of the five elected members of a village council was responsible for a specific task: the president for the overall leadership; the vice-president for security and defense at a local level; another for "social affairs," ensuring that the sick got to the hospital, that the children attended school; another organized the delivery of food to the party and army, and provided meals for visitors to the village; the fifth was responsible for keeping a register of births, marriages, and deaths, with the help of the local schoolteachers if he or she could not write.

PAIGC tried not to influence the election of the village councils, unless a candidate supported the colonialists or was being chosen because he had been a leader in the area before the war. At times the party found it had to explain to some peasants new concepts of authority, that it was not a possession to be inherited, or forever attached to a given individual. Just because someone had been in authority before liberation did not mean he must be elected onto their new councils. "In principle the peasants' choice is respected," explained a regional political commissar in 1966:

> If in our opinion, they have chosen badly, we leave the candidate in office. We wait for the peasants to realize their mistake themselves. Naturally, the party deserves the right to remove those who use their prerogatives in their own interests. We don't want a new chieftainship system. A new committee is elected at the peasants' request; and elections are also held periodically just to avoid what you might call hardening of the arteries.[7]

In the last years of the war, elections for people's courts were held throughout the territory. Three members were elected in each village, or set of villages, depending on their size. Prior to this the execution of justice in the liberated zones had been the responsibility of the political commissars. They were terribly overworked as a result.

"With the election of people's courts," Fidelis Cabral d'Almada, the commissioner of justice, told me, "we could solve the problem of shortage of cadres, and also give new value to the traditional customs. This is very important in the political field, because the people could realize that much has changed and that *they* have the power and responsibility to make justice."

The members of the court were responsible for all the "small quarrels" among the people. This included petty theft, land disputes, family rights (such as forced marriage and divorce), and other aspects arising out of daily life. Their principal function was one of reconciliation, and their judgments made in accordance with the traditional law of the area, provided these were not in conflict with the progressive principles of PAIGC. The courts could not sentence an offender to prison, but imposed fines or other punishment commensurate with the crime.

"We are very encouraged by the people's courts," d'Almada told me with obvious pride. "Since they have been in existence the rate of crime has decreased. And we are able to educate our people through the courts, by the practice of real justice."

The war continued for eleven and a half years. During this time PAIGC liberated two-thirds of the countryside. They exercised such effective control that in September 1973, a year after elections were held for a People's National Assembly, they proclaimed Guinea-Bissau a state, partially occupied by Portugal.

All attempts by the colonialists to counteract these successes failed. General Antonio Spinola had arrived in Bissau in 1968, exuding confidence and proclaiming he would reverse the insurrection in no time at all. He set in motion a program dubbed "Better Guinea" in an attempt to improve the level of social services and to lure the Guineans away from struggle. It was simply preposterous, he thought, a matter of a few escudos unspent, that a terrorist organization had managed to achieve so many victories against the Portuguese army.

At the end of his four-year term, PAIGC was entrenched more than ever. Support by the masses of the people had grown steadily each year, and so had the military actions. Spinola extended his term of office for another two years, extra time to reach his goal. Before this deadline, however, he was removed due to "bad health." In a word, he had failed. Totally. He began to assert that there could be no military solution to the Portuguese wars in Africa. In acknowledging that the solution would have to be a political one, Spinola was also acknowledging the strength of PAIGC.

Some eight months after his dismissal as governor of Guinea-Bissau, young officers in the Portuguese army staged a coup, overthrowing the forty-nine-year-old fascist dictatorship of Portugal, and placing Spinola at the head of the new government (temporarily, as it turned out). The coup was a direct result of Portugal's failure to win the guerrilla wars in Guinea-Bissau, Mozambique, and Angola: the wars had so drained the already fragile Portuguese economy and caused so much disillusionment among the Portuguese people, that the dictatorship finally cracked under the strain.

In September 1974, the independent Republic of Guinea-Bissau was formally recognized by Portugal and became the newest member of the United Nations. Meanwhile, the foundations for the new society and for the state had already been effectively laid inside the liberated zones.

All these programs were not conceived only as matters of

necessity, pure and simple. Each one both reflected and put into practice the principles of PAIGC and, as such, furthered the goals of the liberation movement—to do away with exploitation, to encourage mass participation, to help the people control their own lives and their own destinies.

The struggle to end all forms of exploitation, furthermore, did not refer solely to colonialism and neocolonialism, or to exploitation based on ethnic differences or religion. PAIGC spoke also about an end to the exploitation of women. And when it encouraged mass participation, the party understood that women had to participate in the revolution equally alongside the men.

This special emphasis on women, the revolution within the revolution, formed the basis for my decision to visit Guinea-Bissau. In this small tropical country I found that behind the words and the rhetoric a practical program for women's liberation, in the context of the total revolution, actually exists. In discussing the one, I mean to illuminate the other.

Top: Maria Sá, sector committee member: "This is how all women are suffering. . . ." *Bottom:* Kumba Kolubali, Fula village councillor: "A boy can be a girl and a girl can be a boy."

Top: Bwetna N'Dubi, regional councillor in the south and one of the first women mobilized.
Bottom: Fatima Buaro, who fled from the restriction of Muslim customs to join PAIGC.

Top: Stephanie Urdang talking with Mario Ribeira (left) in a Fula village. *Bottom:* Amilcar Cabral (right) visiting a PAIGC child-care center in Conakry, with a U.N. delegation (courtesy of the United Nations).

Chapter 4

"First it is the women who pound. . ."

PAIGC recognized that despite women's intensive role in production and the greater input their work represents in the village economy, their status is consistently lower than men's and their contribution to political affairs minimal. It is among the Muslim group—thirty percent of the population—that women are the most restricted. The differential position of women and men in the society is not lost on peasant women themselves. At the same time, they know there was no hope for change before the revolution.

It was midday and the sun beat down relentlessly as we marched single file across the flat, open plain of the east front during the last week of my journey. Kumba Kolubali walked in front of me, her body swinging effortlessly in rhythm with her long strides. On her head she balanced a white enamel basin (which remained in that one spot throughout the march as if glued in place). A transparent plastic bag, patterned with orange and blue flowers, rested in the basin. A picture of a running soccer player was printed large onto the material of her long blouse, covering the top of the cloth that wound, West African style, around her waist. On her upper arm, just below her shoulder, a thin leather thong had been tied so tight it dented her flesh. In contrast, two silver bracelets clinked on her wrist as she walked.

It was all I could do to put one resisting foot in front of the other and try to keep up with her pace. On my heels came Fina Crato, the young woman accompanying me on my trip to the east front; N'Bemba Camara, a nurse who worked in the area; my interpreter, Mario Ribeira, as well as four armed militants. Hard as I tried, the heat was taking its toll, and my pace began to slacken. After two and a half hours, the soldiers, concerned about my weariness, insisted that we take a break. We stopped at one of the sparse clumps of trees that every so often broke the monotony of the open plain. I sat down in the spot Kumba had chosen for me as the most comfortable, and leant back against a tree. I reached out for Mario's metal canteen and took a mouthful of water. I spat it out instantly. It seemed hot enough to brew tea.

"Are we halfway yet?" I asked gingerly.

The question was translated from English into Creole to Fula. Kumba contemplated a moment. Yes, she thought it was halfway. Mario, remembering the destinations that were "just over the hill" but which required ten to twelve more hours to be reached, cautioned me not to hope too much. I thought longingly of the marches in the south where I had begun my visit to the liberated zones. There, seven or eight hours' marching would easily be forgotten in the cool of the evenings and the shelter of the vine-draped forests. But I recalled too the times when Teodora told me, "We're nearly there," and how my pace would liven at the news, only to fall off again as I found myself marching for another couple of hours.

The stop was short—a necessity if we did not want our muscles to stiffen and cramp. *"Nô pintcha! Nô pintcha!"* urged my companions, and I got heavily to my feet and began again. Kumba seemed as fresh as when we had begun, although she had already walked the distance from her village in the early morning to meet and escort us. Despite the fact that she had given birth to ten children, her body was erect and strong. N'Bemba and Fina talked and laughed together as they walked and I marveled at their energy.

Through the trees and out into the open. The landscape was beginning to change as the soft hills that edged the plain grew closer. Larger clumps of trees alternated with the palms. We soon began to descend into a long ravine. Below us was a striking and unexpected view of a sprawling valley with a small village nestling in it. Kumba turned round and looked at me with a smile. "Senta Saré," she said. Her village. We followed her down a narrow path which led straight into a cluster of huts. I looked at my watch. Less than half an hour had passed since we resumed our march. It struck me that halfway marks were alien concepts to peasants who seldom wore watches and who, without opportunity for formal education, were not instructed in the elements of linear measurement. For Kumba, who marched for hours and for miles each week, she started when she started, and got there when she got there.

There were about six or seven huts in the village or, rather, the segment of the village. Ever since the area had been liberated, villages had been subdivided into three or four segments. This way it was easier to camouflage the living areas from the Portuguese pilots as they flew overhead seeking bombing targets. It meant too, if the village were hit, that fewer people would be affected. Even with the division of the villages, they were moved approximately once a year as an additional precautionary measure. This was no small task in a Fouta Fula village where huts were intricate constructions. The walls were made of thick mud bricks, covered with woven thatch. The beehive-shaped roofs were swept down within a few feet of the ground. Adults had to bend to enter the huts through the low doorways.

As soon as we arrived we were greeted by the few people who were in the village. Most of the adults were tending the fields or doing other chores, and they arrived back in groups later in the afternoon. Reed mats, brought out for us to sit on, were placed under a tree which afforded some shade. We were given cool water to drink. Children came and stood shyly to the side, looking on with curiosity. It was still very hot and even the chickens sat sleepily in clumps in the limited shade offered by the huts.

During my visit to Senta Saré and other Fula villages in the predominantly Fula area of the east front, I was able to observe women's work.

I woke up early in the morning to the swishing sound of brooms made from reeds or branches tied with vines. The women, bent over double, were sweeping the ground around the huts, removing leaves and small loose stones that had accumulated the day before. The sun was just rising and the men were still asleep. The fire was already lit and breakfast of boiled rice was being prepared. Soon the swishing sound gave way to the steady thud, thud of the pounding, as three or four women stood in front of large wooden mortars which had been carved from the trunks of large trees. It was a sound that would provide a background noise to village life for hours on end. Concentrated in the first two hours, but present at all hours of the day and early evening, the pounding took many forms: pounding to husk the rice; pounding to make rice flour; pounding peanuts to a smooth butter for peanut stew; pounding manioc; pounding wild berries and fruits.

It is strenuous work. On each stroke the long wooden pestle, which broadens out at both ends, is lifted high above the head with both hands and brought firmly down into the mortar. The full weight of the woman's body is behind the rhythmic swinging motion. Up, down. Up, down. Thump, thump. Thump, clap, thump. Sometimes only one hand would be used, and then, without breaking rhythm, the other hand would take over. Or the woman would let go and clap her hands as the pestle descended, to give her arms a rest.

Pounding was a task that could be done alone or communally. A group of women would sometimes stand over their individual mortars or, for more strenuous work, two women would share a single mortar, one woman's arms high in the air, while the other was hitting the grain. Then the speed of the thumping would double. From the age of about six, girls would begin to learn from their mothers, and it was not uncommon to see a slight eight- or nine-year-old pounding with the older women. Young girls, sometimes young boys, would even incorporate it into their play. I watched a girl toddler, who could barely walk, trying with her still uncoordinated movements to "pound" into a small rusted enamel bowl with a short stick. She kept falling over and then resorted to "pounding" while sitting, the bowl between her chubby knees. I knelt down to take a photograph but she burst into terrified tears as I came close. Her mother leaned down and in a single movement grabbed her by the arm and swung her onto her hip. The child stopped crying but looked at me crossly.

Water had to be fetched almost every day. I noticed three young women in their mid teens set off from Senta Saré carrying buckets and gourds. They returned three hours later—I timed it—balancing the containers heavy with water on their heads. I asked whether they had stopped on the way to the well. No, it had been a brisk walk there and back. This was the dry season and we were in one of the few areas of the country that had no rivers. During the rainy season, throughout the country, water was taken from the wells as it was purer. And in the wetter areas of the country some of the deeper wells continued to provide water during the dry season, while the rivers could be used if necessary. In the east, people were not so fortunate. The wells tended to dry up, and those that did not could be far away. Many miles might have to be traveled to get sufficient water for cooking and drinking.

Women worked with their babies tied to their backs—in the fields, at pounding, while cooking. They also looked after the younger children, too big to carry on their backs. By the time a girl was about six years old, she would begin helping to care for her baby brothers and sisters, carrying an infant on her back or balanced on a hip jutted out to support the baby's weight. There were many more responsibilities that a woman had to undertake each day. Besides caring for the children, there was washing to do at the well or river, food to be cooked, and, during the six months of the agricultural season, work in the fields from morning to late afternoon. Field work for women involved clearing the land, planting the seeds, transplanting the seedlings, tending to their growth at all stages, harvesting. In addition, they often had to return to the villages to prepare food to take to the fields for the men at midday, and take care of their children's meals and their own.

It is a full day's work, every day of the week, every week of the year. This is not a situation peculiar to Guinea-Bissau. It is a pattern repeated throughout Africa. Not only do women have the full responsibility for child care, cooking, and housework, they frequently bear the major responsibility for food production. As one writer put it, "Africa is the region of female farming *par excellence.*"[1] Women are responsible, on average, for well over half the work in agriculture. In Guinea-Bissau this varies from one ethnic group to another, but, nonetheless, the burden of agricultural production and a great deal of other work still falls more heavily on the shoulders of the women than the men. This has been a subject of concern for PAIGC. Addressing a meeting of Mandinga (Muslim) peasants, Cabral said:

"We can praise a person who works, but the work somebody did yesterday is not about to give him special privileges today. You have got to work every day. . . . When I come back here there has got to be rice and a lot of it. *The only people who work around here are the women, and that has got to stop.* They will help you and that's all."[2]

Hence, when we talk of women as providers of food, it is not simply a question of going down to the local market, buying foodstuffs ready for cooking, or often precooked, and coming back to do the final preparation. For the African peasant woman, it means involvement in the entire productive process, from clearing the land through harvesting, and then pounding until the rice is ready for cooking. Even at this point, it is not a case of filling a saucepan with water from the faucet; it may mean walking a few hours to collect water from the well. And then, there is no knob to turn so that a stove can provide instant heat; rather a fire must be built and tended, which in turn requires that wood be collected from the forest beforehand.

Despite the fundamental importance of the provision of food—the most basic human need—PAIGC confronted the fact that women in Guinea did not have equal decision-making power in village life. In terms of women's affairs, yes. In terms of influencing men's decisions in an advisory way, yes. But for the ultimate decisions that had to be made for the whole village, decidedly not. These were made by the chiefs or the councils of elders, depending on the social structure of the particular ethnic group, and such positions were always held by men. The less stratified the society, the more discussion there tended to be before final decisions were made. Nonetheless, regardless of ethnic group, women lacked political power or real authority in their society. This is spelled out clearly by PAIGC. *"In spite of the importance of women in the life of African peoples,"* states a PAIGC document, "it is only rarely that they take an active part in political affairs. In our country, women have almost always been kept out of political affairs, of decisions concerning the life which they nonetheless support, thanks to their anonymous daily work."[3]

Along with women's lack of substantial authority over village life, there went a general lack of status. Men's work, whatever it was, acquired higher status than women's work, a pattern repeated through much of Africa, where the division of labor based on sex is strictly adhered to. Women in Guinea-Bissau, like their African sisters, were held in considerably less esteem than men of the same age group. This did not mean that they saw themselves actually as inferior to men, but to a greater or lesser extent they were expected to play a role subservient to men.

The variety of different ethnic groups in Guinea-Bissau resulted in considerable variation of women's roles and the degree to which they were submerged by men. Cabral's discussion of the social structure of Guinea-Bissau notes specific differences in the roles of women among the Fula and the Balanta, the two groups he presented as being at opposite ends of the spectrum in terms of social stratification in the rural areas. "Among the Fula," he stated, "women have no rights; they take part in production, but they do not own what they produce. Besides, polygamy is a highly respected institution and women are to a certain extent considered the property of their husbands."[4] By contrast, the Balanta were generally monogamous, although polygyny was practiced to a limited extent. Women participated in production, but owned what they produced, giving them, according to Cabral, "a position which we consider privileged, as they are fairly free."[5] He went on to state that one way in which they were not free was in matters involving custody of children in a marriage. Children were regarded as belonging to the head of the family, that is, the man. "This is obviously explained by the actual economy of the group," Cabral said, "where a family's strength is ultimately represented by the number of hands there are to cultivate the earth."[6]

Cabral's analysis showed the close relationship between ownership of land, the level of stratification of the society, and the level of the oppression of women. The women in the highly hierarchical society of the Fula were the most oppressed in Guinea-Bissau. Being "Islamized" rather than "Islamic,"* these women were not as restricted as Muslim women in Muslim societies outside West Africa. They were not veiled or secluded like their counterparts in Algeria or the Middle East, and had more freedom of movement. Nonetheless, they were regarded by their men as inferior and expected to behave toward men in a submissive manner. There was little they could do without permission or approval of men and, in comparison to Balanta women, their behavior was heavily circumscribed.

Whenever I entered a Fula village I was struck by the distinct separation of the sexes. There was the praying area, carefully marked out with rocks or tree trunks, where the men sat at various times of the day. In another part of the village the women clustered around the fire—the "kitchen"—with infants and toddlers of both sexes. From the age of four or five, boys began to spend most of their time with the men, receiving their informal, traditional education much as the girls were receiving theirs from the women. What was transmitted to the children established the roles of both sexes for later life.

In one particular village we visited—it was a little bigger than the others—the Muslim men themselves brought out mats and stools for us to sit on, placing them alongside the praying area. The women brought us water to drink. After greeting us, the women—some young, others much older—stood to one side, and looked on somewhat shyly. Mario Ribeira said to me quietly, "I am going to conduct an experiment." Turning to the women, he said in a friendly way, *"Sinta, sinta"* (sit down), and pointed to a long bamboo bench standing alongside the praying area, and therefore in the men's area. The bench was empty. According to custom, an invitation to sit is difficult to refuse, as it could be interpreted as rudeness. There was slight embarrassment on the part of the older women, who looked down, but did not move. After a moment's hesitation, a young woman did take up the offer, walking over to the bench and sitting down with a confident air. After a polite interval the older women returned to their work at the fire. The younger woman remained seated for a while and then followed them. But she had been able to do what the older women could not—go against custom. The incident showed both how deeply seated the traditions are, and how the younger generation is accepting them less readily.

On another occasion we arrived in a village unexpectedly and although we were made to feel welcome, the women were noticeably disturbed about whether or not to give us food. Feeding guests meant killing chickens and they did not want to act without approval from the village council president who was away at the time. And yet how could they express their welcome without giving the visitors food? The dilemma was eventually resolved after much discussion between the women and the cadres in our group. Instead of the usual two, three chickens were killed for us as a way of compensating for an initial hesitancy which could have been interpreted as unfriendliness. It had not been an easy decision for the women to make.

Of the Fula villages I visited, I spent the longest time in Senta Saré, Kumba Kolubali's village, which was also the furthest away from the base where we were staying. The president of the village council appeared extremely put out by the fact that we had traveled all that way to his village and spent our time speaking to the women. He fussed about and ordered the women around, including Kumba, a strong and outspoken woman, a member of the village council herself. The fact that she had walked for miles alone to escort us to her village was noteworthy and something a Muslim woman would not have done easily before the war. The one night we spent in Senta Saré was a particularly beautiful one. The air was fresh and cool, the atmosphere relaxed. A blind traveling musician, having heard there were visitors in the village, came to entertain us. He played his flute and other Fula instruments well into the night, while a group of young women stood in a row near him and provided a high-pitched chorus as background. Kumba came over to me as I stood among the people gathered around the musician, and put her arm around my waist. We stood close together, listening to the music. But not for long. Showing irritation, the president called her aside and spoke to her sharply, in a tone that one might use to scold a child. Perhaps he thought she was bothering me. Perhaps he did it as an outlet for his unhappiness at my special effort to communicate with Kumba rather than the president. Whatever the reason, she did not challenge his authority. Looking upset and embarrassed, she joined a group of women at the fire. I left the musician and went to join them, placing my stool close to hers. She looked at me and smiled.

Compared to their Fula counterparts, Balanta women certainly had much more control over their own lives. They could travel unrestrictedly and participate in village decision-making, albeit in indirect rather than direct ways, since the council of elders made the final decisions and its members were always men. In relation to men, however, the situation was different. A Balanta woman recalled the relationship between her parents:

"Balanta women are not free. I can give you an example from my own mother and father. My mother had to always ask my father's permission for the smallest thing, although she did such necessary tasks as cooking rice, fishing, pounding, caring for children. But this was considered merely women's work—she could do nothing else."

In discussion with Francisca Pereira, one of the leaders of the party and government, I asked about the position of women in the Balanta society. "The Balanta woman is freer than the Fula woman, but she is free up to a point. She does not choose her husband, for instance, and her husband can marry more than one wife." She added that a Balanta woman, however, was able to leave her husband for months at a time and travel to another area. What is more, it was accepted that she had lovers if she wished—a custom known as *cundunka*. Another government member, when commenting on the practice, laughed and said, "Ah, but if the wife is away at the beginning of the rainy season when the work in the fields begins, then he will go and look for her and make her return to work. That is when he needs her the most." The only other limitation on her behavior in relation to *cundunka* was that any children resulting from such a relationship would belong to her husband and not the father.

Francisca stressed the heavy burden of work on Balanta women. While women of most ethnic groups played a greater role in agricultural production, as compared to their men, the Balanta woman's share was greatest of all. And this did give them considerable say over the distribution of rice. However, she added, when it was a question of selling the rice in order to pay taxes to the Portuguese, or for such necessities as clothes, it was the men who took over responsibility. This inequality extended to other areas, Francisca emphasized: "In the Balanta village the *homem grandes* [old men, respected because of their age] make all the decisions. The older women are not respected like the *homem grandes*. They cannot make decisions and women in general are considered in need of protection by the men."

Fina Crato, the young party militant who accompanied me on my ten-day trip to the east front, became very heated whenever she spoke about the role of women in peasant society.

"The greatest difference between men and women comes out when a woman gets married," she said. "Before you don't feel it as much, but when you get married, ah, then it's clear. Among some groups, for instance, the men have four or five wives and they choose these wives when the women are still babies maybe three or four years old.

"And the women have to work so hard. Take for example the time we spent in Lala. [Lala was a village across the border in Guinea (Conakry) in which we stopped on our way into the liberated zones.] You remember the little boy who ran crying after a group of men? The men were only going to look at the fields, not to work. The women were busy doing all the necessary work, cooking and so forth, and the men were only going to drink hard and look over the fields. And even then, do you think they would take the little boy with them? The mother had to leave her work to fetch the child away from them.

"The women work like slaves, you know, for the men. They work very, very hard. But the worst is among the Fula and the Mandinga. The men sit at home and do nothing. Nothing, nothing. The women do all the work. The Fula live in a very poor area of the country. Sometimes a woman has to walk five, six hours to get some manioc or something like that. And her man? He just sits at home and waits for her. When she returns he takes the best food for himself. Ah, the women have to be very servile."

N'Bemba Camara, head nurse of the hospital at the military base where Fina, Mario, and I stayed on our visit to the east front, accompanied us on all our trips to the villages. She herself had grown up in a Muslim village, and echoed Fina's words:

"Muslim women are very badly treated by the men. Especially once they are married because they must do everything in the home. They must work in the fields as well. A woman cooks her husband's food and does everything for him. When he eats, the wife must wait outside until he is finished. Then he calls to her, 'you can come now.' She takes him water to wash his hands and face. She stands nearby waiting for him to finish and only when he says 'OK, you can go now,' does she leave. Really, they are just like servants, just like slaves."

Peasant women did not accept their unequal role in the society without complaining or with blind subservience. Many women were highly conscious of the fact that they were considered inferior by the men. They would discuss it among themselves in the villages and express their bitterness to each other, often in a joking way. But, as one militant expressed to me, what could they do? They saw that their husbands were oppressed by the Portuguese colonialists, as indeed they themselves were, and felt there was no way they could begin to make demands for change. So they continued to grumble about their hardships, and do nothing about it. Fina explained: "Take for example the woman who wants to revolt against the situation. All she gets for her efforts is her husband's whip. There is no possibility of change within that system.

"If she is fed up with being his servant she cannot just return to her parents. Her husband has rights over her now. He has paid for her, with a cow or something like that, no? If she doesn't want to stay with him, she has absolutely no place to go. Her children belong to her husband, so if she left, she would have to leave them behind. This is especially true among Muslim groups. Of course, it exists among the other groups as well, but much less so. Among the other groups the domination of women is more subtle; it is not so obvious to the observer. But the Muslims are proud of these customs and will show them openly. So I tell you, what could a woman do to change this?

"When it comes down to it, though, among the Balanta it is no different. When the woman gives birth to a child and is breast-feeding it, they say, 'Now you are a woman. This is your destiny.' If I am a married man, however, and after a number of years I get tired of the wife I married when she was fourteen, I can say, 'Now you must go. I want a young wife.' And I'll simply take a wife of fourteen again."

Njai Sambo, a Nalu, one of the first women I interviewed, was in her early thirties and a member of the Gambona village council in the Catio region of the south. The interview took place at a political base in Catio. It was seldom that women traveled from their villages alone when they came to meet me, and Njai was no exception. Sometimes they would be accompanied by male members of the village council; other times they would come, as Njai had, with their husbands. This was Njai's second husband. Her first, a Muslim like herself, had died a few years after the wedding. At the time of the marriage, which had been arranged when she was still a child, Njai was only in her mid teens and her husband already an elderly man. She married her present husband shortly before the beginning of mobilization.

Njai was shy and nervous in my presence. Perched on the edge of a bamboo bench, her hands clasped together on her lap, she sat straight and still throughout the interview. She wore a bright red chiffon scarf tied across her forehead and around her head. Her face was serious, showing little expression other than nervousness. When she was not answering a question she looked into her lap.

"Muslim men are very strict," Njai told me. "Muslim women

do not understand anything, because their men do not allow their women to really live. They feel they are more important than women and therefore the women must respect and obey them. My second husband is not Muslim. I married him just before the beginning of mobilization and, although I was not really free then, I was much freer than in my previous marriage."

Her first husband, the elderly Muslim, already had three wives when she married him, Njai said, adding, "I think this custom of men marrying more than one wife is very bad. I am much happier being the only wife. I have experienced both and can compare."

When I asked if her first husband had treated all his wives equally, a smile momentarily brightened her angular, attractive face. "No," she replied. "But I was the favorite! The other wives were always jealous of me. We did not get along well at all."

Maria Sá, a Pepel and non-Muslim, came from Cassacá in the south front and had been a member of the sector committee for her area for many years of the war. She had begun to work for PAIGC at the beginning of mobilization.

Maria was of an older generation than Njai, probably in her fifties. She had greeted me in a friendly manner, but remained in the background when men were around. I interviewed her late in the day when time was limited because we had to return to the place where we were to spend the night. The regional political commissar and the president of the sector sat with us during the interview. The president had actively participated in PAIGC and the armed struggle from the beginning and was a mine of information about the early days and the first party congress at Cassacá. The men presumed I had more to learn from the president than from Maria and got agitated when they felt I was taking too much time talking to her.

The presence of the two impatient men did not help Maria to relax. She would stop speaking if either of the men intervened, showing deference to them. She seldom looked toward them when she spoke. Despite all this, she held her ground. In her low-key but firm voice she told me what she felt about the role of women. Every now and then a look of anger would flash across her gentle face as she emphasized a point about the way in which women were oppressed. Her manner might have changed, because of the presence of the men, but the substance of what she had to say apparently did not.

"We women really suffer," she began. "First it is the women who pound, it is the women who go to fish, it is the women who cook for the men. And then sometimes they say, 'Ah, your food is not well prepared.' With all the work we have to do, and they protest! It is these things, these kinds of discrimination that we have suffered and continue to suffer from. When there is a lot of work to do, we women go and help the men. When the men are tilling the land, we have to cook fast and take it to them. And we must be sure that we are not late with the food! It is our responsibility, also, to find food supplements such as fish.

"It is very hard, our life. In addition to all of this, if his clothes are dirty, it is we women who must wash them. Very nice and clean. Because if the man walks in the village or the street wearing dirty clothes and people see him like this, who does it reflect on? Why, the women! Not the men. We do not like this or want this. All these things are ways in which women suffer. As for the men, the only thing they do is till the land. Once the men have tilled the land and the rice begins to grow we are then responsible for everything after that. The women alone harvest the rice and we have to transport it without their help to the village.This, I tell you, is how all women are suffering."

When I was told in Guinea-Bissau that it was the women who responded first and most strongly to mobilization, I could appreciate it. "Go and join the fight," women would tell their husbands. "If you don't, I'll wear the pants and go." The next level was for the women themselves to become active participants in the struggle.

Women carry the heaviest burden of both agricultural and domestic work. *Top, left:* women pounding in Quebo, a small town in the south. *Right:* preparing for a peanut crop. *Bottom, left:* washing in the river. *Right:* men's work: repairing a thatched house in Bissau.

Top: Muslim girls in a Fula village. While girls tended to be covered up by wraparound skirts, blouses, and turbans, the younger boys often wore no clothes. *Bottom:* members of the Young Pioneers, a PAIGC youth organization, at a mass meeting in the liberated zones.

"Children are the flowers of the revolution and the principal reason for our fight." *Top:* an army militant with a child from a village in the south; *bottom, left:* a mother and child in a Fula village in the east. *Bottom, right:* a member of a village council of a Fula village in the east.

Chapter 5

"We are part of the same fight"

From the beginning, PAIGC integrated the need for women's liberation into their ideology and practice. There were many women among those first mobilized, supporting the work of the movement in many ways. An important step in the process of entrenching PAIGC's position that women participate equally in the struggle was the stipulation that at least two of the five-member elected councils—village, sector, and regional—be women. Progress was uneven from one area to another, with the difference in rate of involvement most marked between Muslim and animist women.

Every day Bwetna N'Dubi did the work that was expected of her.* She pounded rice with the other women in her Balanta village until the callouses on her hands were hard and embedded. She fished. She cleaned the hut she and her husband slept in and swept the ground outside. She worked in the fields. And although she had no children herself, despite her thirty years, she helped care for the children of the village, carrying infants on her back, scolding them, comforting them. Her husband had been imposed as "chief" of the village because the Portuguese could never understand how to relate to the whole council of elders, the very core of local authority. What is more, the Balanta society was too democratic to allow a truly efficient exploitation on the part of the fascist regime. So Bwetna's husband, reluctantly acting as a single go-between, was responsible for tasks such as rounding up workers for the Portuguese and making sure that the taxes were paid.

The years went slowly by, with hatred for the *Tuga* increasing with each and every provocation. But the daily pattern of Bwetna's work and life continued much as it had been for her mother and her grandmother. The years ahead must have seemed to her to be cast in the same mold as those that had already passed. Nothing would ever change.

However, it did.

One hot day, early in 1961, a young man, barely more than twenty, arrived unexpectedly in their village. He was quiet-spoken and polite. After being welcomed as a visitor for a few days, he left, and the villagers assumed he had traveled on to another area. But he had not. "Nino" Vieira was in fact a PAIGC mobilizer, and, after having contacted a few people in the village he could trust, he had gone to live in the forest. Bwetna was among the first four people he mobilized. Later she would recall with pride that it was Nino himself who first came to her village, for by the end of the war he was something of a national hero.**

---

*Bwetna N'Dubi told me about her life when I interviewed her in the Balana-Quitafine liberated region of the south front.

**Bernardo "Nino" Vieira was a dynamic young mobilizer who quickly rose to top leadership of PAIGC. As commander of the people's revolutionary armed forces (FARP) he was the strategist behind many of PAIGC's key military actions. He was the commissioner of defense from the declaration of a state in 1973 to mid-1978 when he became prime minister (*comissario principal*) after the tragic death of Francisco "Chico" Mendes in an automobile accident.

While he was working as a mobilizer, she took him food every day and listened with tremendous excitement to his words. The ideas filled her head and she could think of little else. That they themselves could change their lives! When he talked it seemed so obvious, so possible. Soon Bwetna was beginning the work of mobilizing other people in her village. Like many women, she joined PAIGC before her husband, and it was she who mobilized him, convincing him of the need to begin the struggle against the *Tuga*.

It did not take more than a few weeks for the whole village to rally behind the idea of fighting colonial oppression, making it safe for Nino to call meetings of all the villagers in the forest.

Within a few months the seemingly unchanging rhythm of village life had been totally disrupted. Guerrilla camps were established in the forest, filled with men and women who had come from the villages, some to train as guerrillas, others to carry out the different supporting tasks.

Bwetna's husband was one of the first to leave for the camp, spurred on by the fact that the Portuguese were on his trail. The Portuguese had asked him, as "chief," to inform on the movements of the "terrorists," and when they suspected his involvement, sought to arrest him. Bwetna remained in the village and, with other women, organized the cooking and transport of food to those who had set up base in the forest.

Those early days were hard going. It was one thing to support the idea of liberation, quite another to risk one's life for it. Because once they got wind of what was happening, the Portuguese retaliated by attacking villages indiscriminately, and massacring the peasants living there. Bwetna was challenged to work even harder. Organizing the cooking of the rice was relatively easy. The more difficult task was to recruit people to transport it. The journey took two days and meant crossing a major river. For security, it had to be made under cover of night. If no one volunteered she would sit down and think: "My husband is in the forest. He is fighting for our country. Why don't I sacrifice a little and take them the rice?" She would then set off with the rice herself, even if she had transported it the time before, and the time before that. The women in the village felt responsible for providing the guerrillas with enough food. They appreciated that life was difficult enough for them without the additional hardship of going hungry. But while they spared no effort, there were times that those in the forest went without food for two or three days at a time.

In addition to the staple diet of rice, the women would try to take the guerrillas fish and even meat, along with water for drinking and washing. And although these were time-consuming tasks, they never questioned the sacrifices they made. "We know well what the guerrillas are fighting for," Bwetna would say to herself. "My husband is in the forest. Our sons and daughters are in the forest. I too must make an extra effort to see that they get enough food. We are part of the same fight."

It was not long before the Portuguese soldiers began to harass the peasants of her village. They arrived one day, demanding to know where Nino was. Only four people, including Bwetna, knew his hiding place. They said nothing. Bwetna argued with the soldiers, finally convincing them that they had no idea of his whereabouts. But the *Tuga* were put off only for a short while. They returned to the village on a later occasion and went straight to Bwetna, their rifles in firing position.

"Where is your husband?" they asked her.

"I don't know," she replied.

"If you do not tell us then we'll all go together and look for the camp."

"But it is you yourselves who say that the people of the forest are terrorists and kill people," she replied. "They will kill me."

"No, they won't," they sneered. "They know you."

She held her ground, thinking all the while of the many women like her who had been shot for refusing to comply.

"Kill me if you want," she retorted. "I won't tell you anything."

Bwetna was lucky. The soldiers finally left the village without harming her. But other women she worked with, and whom she had in fact mobilized, defied the *Tuga* at the cost of their lives. Once, after the guerrillas had ambushed and annihilated a Portuguese column, angry soldiers from a nearby base came to the village seeking information—and revenge. Bwetna was away taking food to the camp, but two other women were cooking a large amount of rice when the troops arrived. And when they refused to divulge the location of the camp, the Portuguese riddled them with machine gun fire.

On another occasion, after Bwetna and the women from her village had made a number of consecutive trips to the base, she organized two volunteers from a neighboring village in order to share the responsibilities. The two women were crossing a bridge on their return from the camp when they were spotted by soldiers waiting nearby. No warning was given. The volunteers were shot off the bridge and killed.

While Bwetna's bravery would still be recalled with respect and pride many years later by those who knew her, she was not unusual among Guinean women. Many like her responded with excitement and dedication to the call for national liberation. They too risked their lives in their work. They gathered information on the movements of Portuguese troops and prepared food which they carried to the guerrilla bases; they marched for hours transporting supplies to the front, and went into the bases to train as guerrillas and to fight in the militia.

Freeing their country from Portuguese colonialism was sufficient reason to spur many women to support PAIGC. But it was not the only reason. Teodora Gomes and others told me that many women initially began to support PAIGC because they saw in it the potential for their own liberation. They were angered by their oppressed situation but at the same time impotent to bring about change. Suddenly they were presented with the opportunity to radically affect the unequal balance of power. National liberation became for these women almost incidental to the promise of equal social status, and the right to play a political role previously denied them.

Women are potentially a formidable revolutionary force. They are so totally oppressed that once they do begin to move for change the momentum begun in order to unload the burden of their own oppression may simply keep on going until the structures that support both their oppression and the oppression of the whole society under colonialism is toppled.

"It was the women who were the easiest to mobilize," said Francisca Pereira, in an interview. "They realized that this was a great opportunity for their liberation. They knew the attitudes of the party, and understood that for the first time in the history of our country, *they would be able to count on political institutions to safeguard their interests."*[1]

The development of these institutions was not accidental. The position that women must be liberated in the process of overall revolution had been a clear and integral part of the ideology of PAIGC from before mobilization. In all guerrilla wars women have been the supply line—be it Yugoslavia during the Second World War, Vietnam, Algeria, Angola, or Mozambique. It is the women, given their historical condition, who have provided the food.

However, there is a distinct difference between the involvement of women in the guerrilla wars in countries such as Algeria on the one hand, and in countries such as Vietnam, Mozambique, and Guinea-Bissau on the other. This difference lies in the political ideology of the movements. In the case of the latter group the liberation of women is emphasized in order for socialism to become a reality. In Algeria, women played a very active role in the revolution, although it was generally restricted to tasks that men could not do, such as smuggling bombs out of the Kasbah. But there was no ideology to back it up, no policy that saw the liberation of women as an end in itself. Once colonialism was defeated, women were encouraged to don their veils again and return to their traditional roles in the family and to produce more children. The fight for the emancipation of women was stillborn.

The involvement of women in the Guinean revolution was not an afterthought brought about through necessity. This can be seen, for example, in a PAIGC directive of the early 1960s, which states:

> Defend the rights of women, respect and make others respect them (whether as children, young girls or adults), but persuade the women of our country that their liberation must be their own achievement on the basis of their work, dedication to the Party, self-respect, personality and decisiveness toward everything that can act against their dignity.[2]

There are, of course, some pragmatic reasons why the involvement of women was encouraged in Guinea-Bissau. Every member of the society—man, woman, and child—was needed to fight against the tremendous force of the colonialists. But armed struggle was never viewed as the final stage of the revolution; it was seen as a springboard for the creation of a completely equal society. And so the concept of equality was integrated into the ideology of PAIGC at its inception, and then put into practice in numerous notable ways.

Party mobilizers launched the battle for women's emancipation necessarily on a most elementary level. They began by talking. The need for the liberation of women, the fact that they were doubly oppressed by the Portuguese and by men, and what should be done about it—these were the subjects of many meetings in the rural areas. An address by Cabral to a mass peasant meeting was recorded by a journalist in 1966:

> Comrades, we are going to place women in high-ranking posts, and we want them at every level from the village committees up to the party leadership. What for? To administer our schools and clinics, to take an equal share in production, and to go into combat against the Portuguese when necessary.
>
> . . . The women and girls will go into the villages as nurses or teachers, or they will work in production, or in the village militias. We want the women of our country to have guns in their hands.
>
> . . . Comrades, young girls are going to be coming into the villages from our bases. But don't anybody think that these girls are up for sale as brides. They will get married if they wish, but there will be no forced marriages. Anyone who does that is worse than the Portuguese. These young girls are going to work in the villages, go to school, be in the militia and the party will exercise complete control.
>
> . . . The women must hold their heads high and know that our party is also their party. Our party repeats to everyone of you that the road we have taken is like the Farim River: it never returns to its source but flows toward the sea. Likewise the PAIGC will reach its goal, which is the true independence of our people.[3]

Years before, Cabral had given lectures such as this while training mobilizers in Conakry. He had insisted that the mobilizers understand and accept the need for the liberation of women before going into the interior.

"When we first arrived in Conakry we did not understand this," admitted Cau Sambu with a laugh. "Both men and women, we just didn't understand it. But Cabral explained these new ideas to us carefully, at the same time being very emphatic about the need to accept these ideas. He was very strict with us."

When the mobilizers began to call the village meetings in the forest, few women attended. They saw this as the man's domain and stayed away. So the mobilizers would insist that at least a few women attend to represent the others in their village. These would return to the village and discuss what had been said at the meeting. The next time, a few more women would attend. Slowly the numbers grew until the whole village was meeting in the forest, except for those who were responsible for security and remained behind. "The women understood quickly what I was talking about," Cau told me, "because they knew from their own experience that they were dominated by men."

The party's practice, however, went even beyond all the words. In order to achieve the emancipation of women, PAIGC believed an ongoing struggle had to be waged by the women themselves. It was not seen as something that would be conveniently realized at the time of independence "because now everybody is free."

"The people began to understand how serious PAIGC was," said Cau Sambu, "when the party began organizing the work, and insisted that both men and women take on the same responsibilities. Through our practice, not only through our words, women understood more clearly why they had to fight for their rights as women."

One of the most important steps the party took initially was to stipulate that at least two women be elected to the five-member village councils. These councils were established soon after an area had been liberated to carry out local party work, to handle the daily organization of life in the village, and to provide support for the war. Council members were elected by the peasants and replaced the traditional council of elders or chiefs. However, given the traditions of the society, it seemed amazing to me that both men and women had agreed to this radical departure from past practices.

How PAIGC implemented this was one of the first questions I

asked Teodora. It had not been easy, she agreed, to convince the women or to persuade the men that women should be members of the councils. "We solved the problem by a very practical method," she said. Each member of the council had a different area of responsibility. The task assigned the women at first related to the work they traditionally performed: women were responsible for providing rice for the guerrillas. This went beyond cooking, which had initially been done by women in the villages, to collecting quotas of raw rice from all the families in their respective villages, and which then had to be transported to the camps and military bases. Women, responsible for the harvest, were also responsible for the stores of rice in the village. Hence, provision of rice for the army was an extension of the work they performed daily in the village and, as such, was an acceptable task for women to perform—in the eyes of both men and women.

"It was not a simple matter for a man to cook for the fighters," added Teodora. "But for a woman it was easy, so she took up the task with eagerness. She was basically doing the same work she had always done."

Nevertheless a qualitative change had taken place: the integration of women into a decision-making body, once a male preserve, brought with it recognition and increased status for women's work. For the first time, the "anonymous daily work of women," as PAIGC referred to it, was given a status more in keeping with its real value in the society.

Teodora stressed that the task of cooking for the guerrillas was especially important at the beginning of the war. In fact, it was "the *most* important task that had to be done." Initially, women left their homes to cook for the fighters, who were based in different regions, and this gave them more mobility than they had had before. They would also participate in the constant discussions that were going on about the war and about the work of PAIGC. And not only among themselves. Because they were carrying out such an essential task, they were able to have new and more equal interactions with men. Food production was *consciously* perceived as vital to the society. And as the war itself stepped up, the provision of food for the PAIGC army necessarily became better organized. Hence, the task expanded both in scope and in value even as women joined the councils to carry it out.

Once on the councils, the women could take part in all discussions and decision-making, giving them an opportunity to develop self-confidence and leadership abilities. Meanwhile, a new world was unfolding, not only for themselves, but for all the women in the village. PAIGC represented an authority outside of the traditional councils or chiefs, and because it had given its approval and explicit encouragement to the idea of women taking on an equal political role, men could begin to accept this idea as legitimate. For women there was finally a structure through which to begin to move toward liberation. As Francisca Pereira had expressed it, they could now "count on political institutions to safeguard their interests."

Before too long some councils had a woman president or vice president. By the end of the war, there were many councils with more than two women members. On one occasion I was introduced to a council with four women members.

The tasks of the councillors also underwent changes, corresponding to the progress of social reconstruction in the liberated zones. After a while, the provision of food became the responsibility of one member of the council, rather than two. Next, the task of "social affairs" was added, in an attempt to overcome the suspicion with which the peasants greeted the introduction of the party's new social services. And generally, though not exclusively, this new council task went to a woman.

Responsibility for ensuring that PAIGC's services were in fact understood and used by the people for whom they had been intended represented a qualitative difference in women's roles. Persuading a sick person to go to a hospital and reluctant parents to send their daughters—not only their sons—to school, required the exercise of authority, a function denied Guinean women throughout their history.

Just how important this work can be is apparent from the description of her work given by the woman responsible for social affairs in Cã village in the south front. Explaining her duties to a visitor, Tale Na Sum said:

"I am responsible for the schools and the health care in the village. The Portuguese never built any schools before. They have started doing it now, when they are about to lose the struggle. Therefore the parents are not used to sending their children to school. We have to persuade them. This was not always easy to begin with. But I explain to the parents that they have to send their children to school, because it is important for our country. I also see to it that the teachers get what they need, food and laundry and other such things. . . .

"It is important that the school is not too far away from the village, so the children will not have to walk too far. I discuss this with the teachers. I also discuss with the parents. I ask them to keep their children neatly dressed and clean, and to take care that they get the help they need to do their schoolwork.

"I work with health care too. If anybody gets sick, I talk to the president, so the sick person can be brought to the sanitary post. When the health brigade comes to our village, I am always present and watch that the people listen to the advice offered by the brigade. I also see to it that the members of the brigade are received as well as possible when they come to our village."[4]

PAIGC's requirement that at least two women be members of the local decision-making bodies applied to sector and regional councils when they were elected later in the war. Women also became members of the People's National Assembly though the percentage was still very small. In addition, one out of three elected members of the people's courts was usually a woman. However, Commissioner of Justice d'Almada denied that this was conscious policy. "Election of a court is too sensitive a matter to make stipulations such as these," he said to me. "People must elect judges whom they trust absolutely." Another *responsavel* hotly contended that this was not so. "I was sitting right next to [Amilcar] Cabral when the issue was being discussed at a meeting of cadres, and he stated categorically that at least one member must be a woman."

I could only presume that d'Almada, supervising as he did most of the elections personally, must have been reflecting current policy. In any event, my experience showed that women were members in many cases, and I met a number of women judges in both the south front and the Fula (Muslim) east.

Policy or not, either villagers *were* being encouraged to elect a woman to their courts, or by the time these courts were established toward the end of the war, the peasants were already so accustomed to having women on their committees that they readily elected a woman of their own accord.

Throughout the liberated zones women were emerging to become militant, active members of the society and the revolution. Bwetna N'Dubi was one such woman.

I first met Bwetna when I visited Cau Sambu's base in the south front. The base was about one-and-a-half-hour's march from Teodora's, where I was staying at the time. Teodora and I had spent the afternoon visiting a clinic and a people's store, and ended up at Cau's base where Bwetna was waiting with two other women from her village, both members of their village council. Bwetna herself was a member of their regional council. She was a tall, bony women, with a proud countenance and a firm step. Her uneven smile seemed to be lurking around her mouth even when she was serious and would illuminate her face in a flash whenever she found something pleasing or amusing, which was often. She knew little Creole and spoke in Balanta. I watched with appreciation as she talked, giving vent to a wide range of gestures and facial expressions. Her speech was punctuated by the sharp "*eh!*" that so many Guineans use for emphasizing a particular point, along with the "*n'tchia*"—the Creole term to describe the peculiarly Guinean practice of sucking one cheek in against the teeth, so that a high-pitched sound resulted. Used in different ways it connoted anything from anger and disgust to contemplation or approval. Of the three women, Bwetna was the most outspoken. There was no trace of diffidence or self-consciousness in her demeanor, and she appeared to be enjoying my presence as thoroughly as I was hers. I asked if I could interview her and she agreed to come to Teodora's base the following day.

Her arrival before seven o'clock in the morning meant she had risen before five to begin the two-hour march from her village to the base. She traveled alone. We sat for a number of hours under the mosquito-netting tent, which had been erected over the large table and two long benches serving as the eating area. While we talked, chickens ran about outside, squawking and busily scratching in the dry, brown earth of the small clearing. Occasionally someone would enter or leave one of the five huts that edged the open space. A slight, elderly woman sat on a small carved stool outside one of the huts, looking after two preschool children. Nearby a young woman washed clothes in a metal basin. She had dug a shallow hole out of the ground and placed her chubby, nine-month-old daughter in it. The child contentedly watched her mother while she worked. Meanwhile, other sounds of the base drifted through the mosquito netting. Pounding. Radios tuned to music from Senegal or Guinea (Conakry). The voices of people working, walking by, or relaxing in the shade, as well as the occasional but inevitable drone of the Portuguese bombers. Radios were turned off at once and silence reigned as we cocked our ears toward the sound to check if they were approaching in our direction.

Bwetna, who acted as liaison between the people in the villages in her region and the regional representative to the People's National Assembly, spoke passionately—about the need for the revolution, about the importance of the war in mobilizing people for a new life, about the need to liberate women, about Cabral.*

Her husband had been chosen by her uncles, as her father was no longer alive. Her mother had had no say in the decision. Neither had Bwetna. "I did not understand anything; they give, I take," she said, adding that because of the changes since the beginning of the war she could now leave her husband if she wanted. "But it is not necessary as now he understands something about the need for equality between women and men."

Bwetna first heard about the need to fight for women's rights at the time of mobilization. It had meant a lot to her, as she understood from her own experience that equality was both necessary and possible. "Today I work together with men, having more responsibility than many men. This is not only true for me. I understand that I have to fight together with other women against the domination of women by men. But we have to fight *twice*—

---

*Bwetna N'Dubi is the peasant woman whose moving tribute to Amilcar Cabral is quoted in Chapter 3.

once to convince women, and the second time to convince men that women have to have the same rights as men."

Many changes had occurred in her life since the beginning of mobilization, Bwetna said. She felt much more confident now and was able to speak at meetings, something she could not have conceived of before. "Sometimes I have to leave my home for up to three days on a party mission and my husband stays home and takes care of everything. Two days ago, for example, I was told that I should come and meet a visitor. Yesterday I was at the commando and I met you, today I am here with you. Tomorrow we have a meeting at the regional commando which I have to attend and maybe I will return home only the day after tomorrow. This is not the first time that I am doing this, nor is it only me that does it." (In fact, she stayed away from her village even longer. Three days later we met by chance in the huge crowd that had assembled to welcome the first five ambassadors to Guinea-Bissau as they presented their credentials to President Luiz Cabral at a military base inside the liberated zones.)

"Before, life was very difficult for women," she concluded. "The party has brought new ways and a new life for women. But we must continue to defend our rights ourselves."

Media Té, a Muslim who grew up in the north of the country, spoke of similar changes. When she married she moved to the south where her husband's family lived. He joined PAIGC soon after, at the time of mobilization, and was arrested by the Portuguese. She had not seen or heard from him since, and could only assume that he was dead. In the short time I spoke with her after a mass meeting, Media gave me the impression of being a dynamic and confident woman. "I was very excited when the mobilizers began talking about the need for women to be equal," she told me. "Yes, I welcomed this very much. Now both women and men are considered people and can do the same work. We must work together. My life is completely different now. I live alone, but I am free."

During our meetings, I invariably asked women what resistance their husbands or fathers had initially given to their joining the struggle, or becoming members of the village councils. Without exception they told me the men had been supportive. Such a stream of unthreatened men! This was contrary to what women cadres told me or to the experience of mobilizers who often found men very hostile to their wives becoming active in the movement. I wondered if the advances made in the last ten to twelve years had not blurred history a little. Bwetna responded to my question with a chuckle. "If we tell the truth today about what happened at the beginning of the struggle, we would have to admit that many of the men were *very* unhappy about it. Life was difficult for the men too, before, but now that so much has changed in our lives, they refuse to remember their reluctance of the past. In fact, they deny it!"

Some women would allude to *other* women's husbands. Njai Sambo, the village councillor in the south whom I interviewed at the beginning of my visit, touched on these early attitudes of men.

"In my case this was not a problem," she began. "My father accepted what the party said about women at the time of mobilization. So did my husband. But I have seen cases where husbands refused to allow their wives to join the guerrillas or work for them. They felt that if their wives went to the camps, other men would take their women. This was a big problem. Women were not free and they had to do what their husbands said."

By the time I visited Guinea-Bissau it seemed to me that men supported, even took for granted, that women be on the village councils. There was also a consciousness among many men of the need to fight discrimination against women. The mass peasant meetings I attended were always addressed by both men and women. The women who stood up to speak had crossed many personal barriers since the first days of mobilization, when women hesitated even to attend such meetings and would have been put down by the men for such effronteries as speaking out.

Nonetheless, ideological development was not even. In my interviews I found discrepancies among individuals, and among different communities. Women would talk to me about their work as providers of rice with immense pride, and I could see that they felt their contribution to the war was extremely important, even a revolutionary act. One peasant women, asserting that women's work was equal to fighting because the guerrillas could not continue without them, said: "The men fight with guns, the women provide the food." She correctly understood the vital importance of her work. However, she, like a great number of her sisters, saw this as an end in itself and not a transitional step toward breaking down the division of labor based on sex. Life had changed so radically for them that they felt they were already free.

The gaps in the levels of individual consciousness were not lost on PAIGC cadres. They would reply that it was not possible to leap instantly from a society in which there was a strict division of labor along sex lines, to one in which all work is performed equally by both sexes; this was a goal that had to be worked for over many years.

Disparate levels of consciousness on the village level became apparent to me after I had attended two mass meetings in different areas of the south. The first was held in Tombali, near a semiboarding school, where we stayed for a few days. We set off at about ten in the morning for the hour's walk to the meeting place. We followed a road originally built by forced labor, now grown over by vegetation and in need of repair, and then turned off onto a narrow forest path. Suddenly, without warning, we were amid a crowd of about four hundred colorfully dressed people who stood up and clapped their welcome as we entered. The atmosphere was electric. People greeted us and shook our hands as we made our way to the table and benches newly constructed for the "guests of honor." Teodora and the *responsavels* for justice, health, and education who were accompanying us were surrounded and greeted with backslaps and warm hugs. After a while the meeting was called to order and we sat down, filling up the bench. Everyone else sat on the ground in front of us, crushed close together, row after row. Women, men, children, and infants, with no noticeable segregation between the sexes.

There were a number of speeches. The three *responsavels* each talked about their areas of work. Then it was Teodora's turn and she spoke at length about the role of women and about the coup which had recently taken place in Portugal. Her voice rang out to the crowd, which listened attentively. The speeches were being simultaneously translated from Balanta to Creole, or Creole to Balanta by an energetic militant who jabbed his hands in the air for emphasis. The people from the audience got up to speak, about six altogether, including two women. One was Sabado Ie, a frail-looking elderly woman, who directed her words to me.

"We women gave the men food and the men fought against the Portuguese colonialists. This is our fight, a fight of both women and men, and the bombs cannot stop our struggle for liberation. I am old, but this is not important because now I know what I want. We will fight until our lives have ended. Every day children are being born and will take our place and continue the struggle. We women fight together with men to defend our country."

When the meeting came to an end, Teodora led the *vivas* (long live!) in her powerful voice. No meeting or gathering, however small, failed to end with *vivas*, a unified expression of the participants' support for PAIGC. *Viva Amilcar Cabral!* Teodora's voice rang out. *Viva Amilcar Cabral!* responded the gathering, as they thrust their right arms upward. *Viva PAIGC! Viva PAIGC!* Then followed a veritable stream of these tributes in growing crescendo, ending with a special *Viva as mulheres da America!* Long live the women of America!

There had been a certain amount of moving around during the meeting, as a few men and women walked about. The sexes mingled with apparent ease. And when the meeting was over, people dispersed slowly, and again both men and women came up to talk with Teodora and the *responsavels*. It was men and women together with no noticeable sense of inequality. As we walked away, after the meeting finally ended, Teodora turned to me and said that what I had witnessed was an important marker in the progress of the revolution. Ten years before this scene could not have taken place.

Several days later, I attended a much smaller meeting of about one hundred fifty people at a village school in the sector of Cubisseco. Because the single "classroom"—constructed from wooden poles and thatch—was not large enough to hold everybody, rough-cut planks from benches and tables had been brought out and people sat on them in rows in front of us. That is, the men sat in rows. Most of the women sat in a circle on the ground at the back, attending to children and talking among themselves. The spirit and involvement so evident at the Tombali meeting was absent here. Part of this was due to the fact that the meeting was called at short notice—hence the fewer people—and it was held at a much hotter time of the day in a clearing that offered little shade. The atmosphere was decidedly less festive. On the other hand, despite the segregation of women, two of the four peasants who gave short speeches were women, one being Media Té.

While the differences between the Tombali and Cubisseco peoples had been marked (I never received explanations precisely as to why), the gap between the Muslim peoples and the rest of the Guineans presented no great mystery. Unlike the confidence and eagerness to talk to me shown by the animist women—although they were often shy and few were as forceful and articulate as Bwetna—one Fula woman I spoke with seemed to typify the general reticence of most of her Muslim counterparts. She gave such tense, cryptic replies to my questions that after a little while I decided to bring the interview to an end. We were getting nowhere and she was so obviously uncomfortable. Her ordeal over, the woman positively beamed with relief. For the next half hour or so, she spiritedly launched into comments and stories, joking with me and all those around her.

When I talked to women such as Teodora and Carmen Pereira who could speak for the party with authority, they tended to minimize the differences that still existed after eleven years in the liberated areas. The impression I got from them was that the differential, in terms of oppression, between Muslim and animist women had narrowed to such a point that it was virtually nonexistent.

"In the beginning of the struggle it was a problem because the Muslim women wanted to stay at home," Carmen told me. "But now it is the Muslim woman who brings her children to the party and asks that they go to school. We no longer have difficulties in this regard. The party mobilized everyone, insisting that we not be divided by ethnic group or by religion. We all belong to Guinea-Bissau. The people understand this. Now there are nurses who are Muslims and other Muslim women working for the party. One of the regional *responsavels* for health in the south is a Muslim woman.

"In the villages, you will meet Muslim women on the village councils. She works and talks with confidence. The men will sit and listen to her, just as if it was a man speaking. Before it was not so, a situation worsened by colonialism. At that time when two men sat down in a village, a woman could not go near them. If she did there would be trouble. The woman had to stay at home, shut up in the house. Today these things have been changed by the party through struggle."

An interview with another journalist gives additional insights into the difficulties confronting Muslim women.

"Among the Muslin tribes the position of women was very backward. To greet her husband, for example, a woman would have to kneel and put her forehead on the floor. She went to work and the husband stayed home. She worked till sundown, came home, greeted her husband, prepared the meal, got some water for him to wash with, brought him food and knelt before giving it to him. The party has struggled against such negative traditions and done away with most of that. Now men work with the women in the fields.

"In the past a Muslim man never wanted a woman to go to a meeting. There were many meetings during the struggle and women were very interested to hear what was going on. The men would refuse to let them go for three or four times, but the women would keep insisting. Finally, the men were obliged to accept. Now, women are on the village committees and are sometimes elected president. Men now accept women leading meetings because it is a party directive and they see why it is correct."[5]

What Carmen was saying about the development of Muslim women toward emancipation was true to the extent that Muslim women have advanced considerably in relation to their point of departure. There were, too, many women whose progress matched that of their animist compatriots. However, I also saw the still marked differences between Muslim and non-Muslim women. Those Muslim women who were cadres of the party, and the women confronting the restrictive customs in their villages head on, had to fight harder than their animist sisters. Male supremacist attitudes were more firmly entrenched in the customs of Muslim society. This did not mean that all women were now at an equal stage in their struggle.

The work of women on the village councils also was different in the south as opposed to the east. As the east was unsuitable for growing rice, the Fula did not supply rice for the army in the way that the people of the south had done throughout the war. It appeared that the work of the women in the Fula areas was to attend to visitors when they came to the village and to see that they had a place to sleep and food to eat. The task of "social affairs" had not yet been instituted there, judging from the villages I visited.

The women council members in the east were referred to as "president-for-women" and "vice-president-for-women," which seemed to indicate that they would be accepted on the council as long as they were responsible for women's affairs, but not as equals with the men. This, and the fact that women were less active on the councils as compared to men, had much to do with the high level of stratification in Fula society in contrast with the Balanta. The more rigid the stratification, the more rigid the authority figure—an authority always vested in men in Fula society as opposed to the Balanta.

Some of the younger women in the party were more open than top leaders in discussing the differences between the two groups. When N'Bemba spoke out so strongly about the subservient and oppressed position of women in Muslim society, for instance, she was not only referring to the past, before the beginning of the war. Such oppression was still a part of life in Muslim villages in the liberated zones. However, the south was liberated considerably earlier than the east and this contributed substantially to these differences, they emphasized.

"Women in the south have more responsibility, it is true," said N'Bemba. "The constant contact with the army there leads to this. In the east, women do not supply food for the guerrillas. Progress is slower here, but it is still progress. You must understand that the south and the east are very different. The social structure is different and this must be taken into account."

Kumba Kolubali, Fula and Muslim, best summed up the changes that had come about for women, Muslim women in particular, since the first mobilizers infiltrated the rural areas. She talked to me about this the day I visited Senta Saré. In the late afternoon the women had gathered in one place, while the men sat a little way off, excluded from the gathering. Kumba spoke at length, despite a severe toothache which had caused one side of her mouth to swell up. She began even before I could pose a single question.

"When the first comrade came here to mobilize us, we were very afraid. We did not know him so we did not trust him. We thought he was dangerous and that he would take our things and not pay for them. But he talked about all the bad things that the Portuguese were doing, which we understood very well. He said that the party believes that everybody is equal and that we are all one people.

"Later the party organized a committee in the village to take care of matters that related to the party and to the village. It was elected by the people in our village, and we elected two women as well. Before it had not been possible to even imagine that things like this could happen. But now life is very different. Now I see more light and now I know that everybody is my brother and my sister. Now we don't talk about color or ethnic group the way we did before. We know that everybody is from Guinea-Bissau.

"We have forced the Portuguese out by the war, and we are able to live much better than before. We used to go to Beli or Madina Boé [the nearest small towns, but a long distance from the village] if we needed things. Today we have shops that we can go and buy from and we can afford the goods. We have so many things since the party began to help us, things that I have never seen before and could not have dreamed of. Schools and hospitals, which are free. Before, we had no clothes and went barefoot. But now everybody can get material and clothes and we are well dressed. I am very happy for the things the party has done for us. I can't tell you enough how happy I am for my people and how pleased I am that the party exists."

Kumba spoke animatedly and her words flowed without hesitation. After a few sentences she would pause and wait patiently while the translation went from Fula to Creole to English, stoically ignoring the pain that her decayed tooth was causing her. As she adjusted the large, bunched-up cloth against the swollen side of her face, I remembered the tooth extraction a medical officer had performed on an elderly peasant man during my visit a few days before to a nearby clinic. The knowledge that Kumba would be able to have the same attention at a free medical service helped me appreciate the changes she was describing.

"The difference between my life as a woman before and my life now is very, very big. How could I have ever thought that it would be possible for me to be the vice president of a village council one day. Before this was always man's work. When the elections were held, both women and men voted for me and for the other woman on the council. I know they accepted us as members of the council, otherwise they wouldn't have voted for us.

"Life is so much better for women now. You see, before you were brought up to be a boy or to be a girl. Now things are different. For the party says everybody is the same and we understand this. A boy can be a girl and a girl can be a boy. In other words, each can do what the other can do.

"Oh yes, life is very different now. For example, I sit here at this moment and men are nearby. They have listened to what I have said and they have accepted it. They have made no objections. Before it was not possible for me as a woman to sit here and talk to you, a visitor. It would have had to be a man who talked with you. It would not even have been possible for a woman to sit and listen.

"Before, men and women could not work together doing the same work. The men had this idea that the women must work for the men. Not anymore. Now the men and the women work together."

Chapter 6

"Sold for a pig or a cow"

While stressing the importance of revaluing the customs of the people, PAIGC simultaneously began discouraging the practice of customs that were oppressive. Forced marriage, lack of divorce rights for women, and polygyny were singled out as particularly detrimental to women. Many young women joined PAIGC in order to escape the restrictions of these customs. When elected people's courts were established, these women were responsible for handling such cases.

There was a rebellious streak in Fatima Buaro.* She did not want to accept the husband—a much older man—her parents had chosen for her and whom she, a Fula girl, was expected to marry without question. The marriage had been arranged when she was just a child, and although she had more than a decade to get used to the idea, Fatima never overcame her dislike of the man.

At fifteen, sixteen, seventeen, she had met young men nearer her age whom she preferred. There were two she liked in particular and one she would have considered marrying had there been a choice. But what could she do? She could flirt a little. Yes, this was allowed. But girls her age, almost young women now, knew their limits.

Fatima was nearing her next birthday. At eighteen she would have to get married. Already the final preparations were being made for the African-Muslim wedding: the long discussions between the two families; the final exchange of gifts; the plans for the ceremony. The young woman saw all this happening around her and did not like it. No, there would be no wedding, and she told her father so in no uncertain terms. But he was adamant. Fatima became desperate. She cried and pleaded. Her father remained unmoved. Didn't she know that he was the best judge of what was good for his daughter? After all, wasn't this man economically stable? That was very important. She would get over her unhappiness in time and see what a good choice he had made.

Anyway, he thought angrily, what could he do now, at this stage? It was too late to go back. Hadn't he arranged the marriage ten years ago, knowing then that it was a good match? And hadn't he, since then, accepted the customary gifts from the bridegroom's family? The goats, the chickens, the rice, the few escudos. (In the old days there would have been cattle. Not any more, though. The *Tuga* had seen to that.) And wasn't it hard enough to just keep going? How difficult it was to produce even enough rice to take to the trading store so he could pay his taxes. And his family still had to eat. He worked hard. And so did his

---

*Fatima Buaro told me this story of her life during the week I spent at Vendoleidi base in the east front.

one wife. For although Fatima's mother had died and he had married again, there had never been any question of a second wife. He could not afford one.

Then his son had gone off to fight the *Tuga*. His only son. He needed him to help with the work. Hadn't he sacrificed much so that his son could go to school? Was this to be his reward—his son killed in battle? How could these guerrillas hope to defeat the *Tuga*? The *Tuga* were far too strong. They had guns and money. They had power. How could the poor people living in the villages hope to fight them? And win? First, his only son had got carried away with this nonsense. And now his only grown-up daughter was trying to go against his wishes. She knew he would have to return all the bride-price if the marriage did not take place. Poor as he was, how could he possibly do that?

As the preparations for the marriage progressed, Fatima became resolute. She decided to carry out the plan that had been in the back of her mind for some time now. Taking with her only the clothes she wore, she left her father's village and the Gabu area.

Somehow, she didn't know how, she would make contact with PAIGC. She would join her brother. Skirting the edge of the forest, she walked on, hoping she would be lucky. Suddenly she realized she was not alone. *"Hey!"* Hearing a man's voice call after her, she turned to see a man the age of her father coming up quickly behind her. "Where are you going?" She did not answer. "Young women don't walk alone. You are not from this area. Where are you going?" Still she did not answer."Ahuh, I know. You are going to the Republic of Guinea to join the *bandidos*. Yes, I know. I am going to take you to the *regulo*."*

The *regulo*, seventy-three years old, looked her up and down. And then up and down again. He was pleased with what he saw. His wives were also old, and he had been wanting a new young wife for some time. He would marry Fatima, he decided.

Fatima knew there was no way out this time. She told him

---

*In the Fula hierarchy there were several levels of chiefs, at the top being the *regulos* who wielded considerable power. They owned large tracts of land worked by Fula peasants on a semifeudal basis, were generally very wealthy, and collaborated with the Portuguese in order to safeguard their interests.

where she came from, hoping without hope that her father would intervene. The *regulo* then contacted her father, a bride-price was agreed upon, and the young woman returned to her village to wait for the wedding.

There, her father was totally unresponsive to her predicament. He brushed her anguish aside. "It serves you right. If you hadn't run away this wouldn't have happened. Now you must live with it." Besides, what could he possibly do? Go against the *regulo's* wishes? Impossible.

If Fatima had cried before it was nothing compared with the tears she shed now. She wasn't just unhappy. She was terrified. She hated this man and had heard that he was cruel. He was as bad as the *Tuga*, forcing his people to pay him huge amounts in livestock and rice. As if they didn't have a hard enough time paying their taxes. Once they had paid their taxes, and then the *regulo*, they were literally starving. And this was the man she was being forced to marry and with whom she would have her children. She did nothing but cry. Through her tears, though, she knew that her father was in a difficult position. The *regulo* had such power that her father, like the other villagers, was afraid of him. Were her father to say anything on her behalf, the *regulo* would simply punish him, when his life was already hard enough. And if she refused to marry the *regulo*, he would make life even harder for her father and she would have to marry him anyhow. There was no way out.

The wedding festivities were very grand. It was the biggest feast that had been held in Gabu for many years. People came from all over and partook of the sumptuous spread of food the *regulo* provided. He had ordered many animals killed, not only as a tribute to the bride but also because the occasion presented an opportunity to display his wealth.

When the ceremony finally ended after a few days, Fatima went to live with the *regulo's* other wives. They were in a separate compound and never came in contact with visitors. It was almost like a harem. Although Muslims were only allowed four wives, he had twelve ... well, thirteen, including her. Maybe he hadn't married all of them. She didn't know. Or maybe when you were very rich and powerful and favored by the Portuguese the way he was, you made your own rules.

The other wives were very jealous of Fatima and ostracized her. She spent most of her time alone, and bored. There were many servants and, anyway, the *regulo* did not want her to work. Occasionally, she cooked special dishes for him. Often when he traveled to Bissau and other towns he took her along. This simply increased the jealousy of the other wives and also their hostility toward her.

Fatima became pregnant a few months after the wedding and gave birth to a healthy boy. How pleased the *regulo* was. This was indeed a perfect wife. Young. Beautiful. Fertile. And the first-born was a son. For Fatima it meant that life was less lonely, as her child kept her company and occupied her. But it did not mean she was less unhappy.

One day the *regulo* told her that her brother was threatening to come and take her away. He laughed: "He thinks he can do that, but it is impossible." The *Tuga* would stop him and smash that puny PAIGC militia force he was commanding. Those *bandidos* could attack the Portuguese *gazernas* [barracks] all they wanted. No matter. The *gazernas* were impregnable, he thought smugly, and had been established near the Fula villages precisely because the Fula supported the Portuguese. (At least the *regulos* did, and hence at this early stage of the war, so did many of the Fula peasants.) Meanwhile, the young guerrilla anguished over the forced marriage of Fatima and continued sending messages to the *regulo* announcing that he would come and free his sister. Forewarned, the *regulo* took precautionary measures. Whenever he heard that PAIGC was in the vicinity he would remove Fatima to another one of his villages in a different area. Her once high hopes began to fade. Because she had been anticipating freedom, she felt more trapped each time it failed to materialize. After the fifth transfer she was desperate. No, this is enough, she told herself. I have to do something about this situation myself. So for the second time she ran away, taking her son, now a year old, with her.

Walking through the forest she was suddenly surrounded by a group of armed young Africans. Immediately they trained their rifles on her, demanding to know why she was there. "I have come to join the party," she replied. They were suspicious, however. She was a Fula, from a Fula village, and at that time most of the Fula were supporting the *Tuga* against the guerrillas. They had no grounds to trust her. But when she told them who her brother was and that she wanted to find him, their faces brightened. Her brother had talked about her often. So they helped her with her child and led her along the paths that wound through the mazelike forest to a military camp, hidden under the trees. After a joyous reunion with her brother she was taken to Amilcar Cabral, who was visiting the camp at the time. But Cabral too was suspicious because she had been married to a *regulo.* "But it's not *my* fault," she pleaded. "I was taken by force. What would you expect me to have done?" Convinced, Cabral then spent a long time talking to her about PAIGC. He went into detail about their work, about their achievements, their goals, their difficulties. He took out a large packet of photographs and went through them with her. They were of women who were working in the party. He proudly and carefully explained to her the need for the involvement of women and that in the liberated zones women were treated as equals and expected to play as full a part in the struggle as men. Fatima, whose own experience had been so different, was exhilarated.

She had never heard anything like this before, and her heart pounded faster and faster as Cabral unfolded his vision of free men and women in an independent Guinea-Bissau. After they had talked a long while, Cabral asked her what she would like to do. Perhaps she'd like to train as a nurse, he suggested. Yes, she'd like that a lot, she replied.

First Fatima went to the south where she was attached to a health post and began to train as a nurse's aide. After a few weeks she went out of the country to train in Boké at the nursing school attached to Solidarity Hospital. For the first time in her life, at the age of twenty, she began to learn to read and write, at the regular grade school for nurses in training.

Having completed her nursing studies after a year, she went to work at Cameconde Hospital in the south front. When she got there she learned it was one of the first hospitals established after liberation began, and this under sparse conditions without any fully trained doctors. But Fatima would work under the supervision of a fully trained doctor and as one member of the hospital's staff of twelve nurses, midwives, and nurse's aides. There were beds for over fifteen patients and a busy out-patient clinic, but Fatima's work was not confined to the hospital alone. She joined the health brigade, consisting of four or five nurses, which made weekly visits to the villages to attend to the health needs of the population, visit pregnant women, and educate the people about preventive medicine.

She began to enjoy her work at Cameconde, adapting easily to the exacting life of the *mato*. She learned to distinguish the sound of oncoming bombers and help the patients in and out of the trenches when the raids came. With her son at the child-care center in Conakry she was able to settle into her work quickly. She felt she was contributing something very concrete to her people. She grew close to the comrades she worked with. It was a new kind of home for her, and she began to experience the independence she had dreamed of when she first left her father's village to seek a new life.

This was not to last long. Shortly after her arrival at the hospital her work there came to a dramatic end.

The morning began like many others at Cameconde. Fatima and the other health brigaders had arrived at a village to begin their work for the day. Suddenly they heard the whirring of helicopters and looked up to see them disappearing behind the trees into a clearing in the forest.* In a second everybody scattered. Women picked up their babies and ran for shelter, while the men and nurses made sure that everybody was leaving the village. Then they followed amid the squawking of chickens rushing round in circles, flapping their wings.

Fatima, being new to this area, did not know where to hide. She ran into the forest and, after choosing a likely spot, watched the Portuguese soldiers charge into the village and set the huts on fire. But as they retreated, setting alight the bushes behind

---

*By 1970 it was obvious to Spinola that his "Better Guinea" program was doing nothing to woo the people away from PAIGC. Beginning to get desperate as he saw his dreams of reconquering "Portuguese" Guinea fade into oblivion, he reinforced his program with military action by increasing the bombing raids and the helicopter commando raids on liberated villages—parallel with the U.S. army's "search and destroy" operations in Vietnam. Unable to sustain these raids, they were forced to abandon the tactic.

them, they ran straight into her. She had chosen as her hiding place the very path they were following to link up with the helicopters. A few minutes later, when the helicopters lifted into the air, squashed together with the soldiers was Fatima, a prisoner. All the soldiers were African, including their officer, who volunteered a comment: "When we take prisoners in the forest and do not kill them on the spot, then we won't allow them to be handed over to PIDE [the secret police]." Fatima breathed an inward sigh of relief. She had heard much about PIDE and its methods—the brutal tortures, the murders, how they would leave their victims to rot in jail.

On touching down in Bissau, the soldiers remained true to their word. They handed their young prisoner over to the Portuguese army; Fatima underwent intensive questioning at military headquarters. But five military interrogators, a new one every day, got five different stories from their captive. When they realized what was going on they gave up and returned her to the African soldiers. She heard afterward that the officer who had effected her capture had called together a group of black soldiers, handed them guns, grenades, and ammunition, and threatened to wipe out PIDE in the event the young woman was turned over to it. While it was unlikely they would have succeeded, relationships between the African and the Portuguese soldiers were tense enough. The Portuguese officers had wanted to avoid a confrontation and so they released her into the custody of their Guinean allies.

The African soldiers lived on the outskirts of Bissau, in housing the Portuguese had provided for them. It was isolated and difficult to reach without transport. They told her she could work as a nurse at the hospital. Work for the Portuguese? No, thanks, she said. Well, then she would have to work for them, looking after their houses.

She thought this over. Her one objective was to return to the liberated zones as soon as she could. If she worked for them on the outskirts of the town it would be well nigh impossible to make contact with the PAIGC underground in Bissau. She would seldom meet anyone but soldiers. No she could not risk that. "*Stabon*, OK, I'll work at the hospital," she finally answered.

The African soldiers were kind to her. They even told her in a friendly way that she could choose any one of them for a husband. When she refused politely they were surprised. They thought they were doing her a favor. She knew they were disappointed, but they left her alone.

The PAIGC underground was very active in Bissau. It did not take long for them to hear that Fatima was there. PAIGC comrades came to the hospital to make contact. She was thrilled and relieved, and then disturbed. They were so evasive. Did they want to help her? she wondered. Then she understood from their questions that they were testing her. It was quite possible that she might have found life so difficult in the liberated zones that she had preferred to desert and work in the relative comfort of the Bissau hospital. It wasn't long, however, before they were convinced of her sincerity. They planned her return in detail, and ten months later she was back with PAIGC.

Up until the end of the war Fatima worked as a nurse in the hospital at the Vendoleidi base in Boé Oriental, a Fula area in the east front. She worked alongside an older nurse, then over sixty, who came from Bissau to join PAIGC in the early years with his wife and thirteen children, and who had, in fact, founded Cameconde Hospital. Every day she attended to the patients at the hospital. Twice a week she and other nurses in the health brigade went into the Fula countryside to take health care to the peasants in the villages. Being from a Fula village herself she communicated easily with her peers. In the afternoon, after the children of the base had finished their lessons for the day, she would join twenty or thirty other militants and continue her education in the small reed classroom that stood between the small huts and pup tents that the soldiers slept in.

The liberated zones of Guinea-Bissau had nurtured a new Fatima Buaro. Her life was so completely different from what she had grown up to expect that, at times, she was incredulous. What meant the most to her was the equality she felt working among men and women joined in common cause. When Fatima first arrived in the liberated zones she had noticed immediately the large number of women working for the revolution. She came to learn that a woman could work like a man and have the same rights and the same respect. And that marriage could be an institution based on free choice.

Soon after Fatima settled in Boé, she met and fell in love with a political commissar who worked in a different area of the east front. They decided to get married. The commissar's mother was Mandjak and his father Fula. But he, just as she, no longer believed in religion. Nor did they believe any longer that there were differences between ethnic groups. Fatima thought back to the attitudes she had grown up with. The discrimination against people who were not Fula. The way Muslims thought themselves superior to animists because they did not pray in the same way. The use of the derogatory word "Kaffr" (heathen) to refer to animists. Now she sincerely believed that there was no difference between people. They were all together in the same struggle and, because of it, they had been revolutionized themselves.

And because of it, Fatima was able to marry because she chose to marry. The wedding was held in Conakry in June 1974—a simple ceremony led by the commissioner of justice and followed by a small celebration. The couple returned soon afterward to the east and to their separate places of work. Sometime in the future they believed they would be able to live together—when the war was over, and a new era begun.*

Fatima's story highlights three oppressive customs practiced widely in Guinea-Bissau: forced marriage, denial of women's right to divorce, and polygyny. While PAIGC was insistent on the need to revalue the traditions of the people—so disparaged and attacked by colonialism—they were equally insistent that all discriminatory practices, including those affecting women, be discouraged and in time discontinued.

In stressing the vital role of culture in the liberation of a

---

*Just before we were to leave the base where I had stayed for a week, I asked Fatima if I could take her photograph. We were in a hurry, but she disappeared into her hut in another part of the camp. I thought, as we waited some time, that she must have wanted to get "pretty" and would come back dressed up for the photograph. She returned wearing a simple skirt, and a PAIGC T-shirt imprinted with a picture of Cabral and the PAIGC motto *Unidade e Luta*—Unity in Struggle.

But there is a sad conclusion to this story. When I returned to independent Guinea-Bissau, I was told that she had died a few months earlier in Gabu Hospital, where she had been working since independence.

people, a recurrent theme in all of his writings, Cabral has noted contradictions in the Guinean experience:

> The liberation movement must . . . base its action upon thorough knowledge of the culture of the people and be able to appreciate at their true value the elements of this culture, as well as the different levels that it reaches in each social group. The movement must also be able to discern in the entire set of cultural values of the people the essential and the secondary, the positive and the negative, the progressive and the reactionary, the strengths and the weaknesses. All this is necessary as a function of the demands of the struggle and in order to be able to concentrate action on what is essential without forgetting what is secondary, to induce development of positive and progressive elements, and to combat with flexibility but with rigor the negative and reactionary elements; and finally, in order to utilize strengths efficiently and to eliminate weaknesses or to transform them into strengths.[1]

Among the negative values is the belief in and reliance on fetishes to protect an individual. This had dire repercussions when the person placed faith above the necessary precautions. While insisting that such anachronistic beliefs have a destructive effect on the people practicing them, PAIGC went about its program to combat such beliefs with patience and with respect. Commenting on this in an interview, Cabral said:

> [One] aspect which we consider very important is the religious beliefs of our people. We avoid all hostility towards these religions, towards the type of relationships our people still have with nature because of their economic underdevelopment. But we have resolutely opposed anything going against human dignity. We are proud of not having forbidden our people to use fetishes, amulets and things of this sort, which we call *mezinhas*. It would have been absurd, and completely wrong, to have forbidden these. We let our people find out for themselves, through the struggle, that their fetishes are of no use. Happily, we can say today that the majority have come to realize this.
>
> If in the beginning a combatant needed the assistance of a *mezinha*, now he might have one near but he understands—and tells the people—that the best *mezinha* is the trench. We can state that on this level the struggle has contributed to the rapid evolution of our people, and this is very important.[2]

Another patently negative aspect of the culture is gerontocracy. Elected village councils have replaced the councils of elders that exercised complete political control in village life. This change did not come easily, as the elders were hardly eager to relinquish control. As one political commissar told a visitor, "Young people are often elected [to village councils]. The old people haven't always been happy to see their places in the village leadership taken over by the young."[3] Nonetheless, village councils existed throughout the liberated zones by the end of the war, and were highly effective in their work. Plenty of political education, talk, and meetings had helped this process along.

Among the main targets of PAIGC's cultural campaign are forced marriage and prohibition of divorce for women, both entrenched in the customary laws of all the ethnic groups in Guinea-Bissau. The practices were interconnected, as the society's ability to enforce a marriage would dissolve if a woman were able to divorce out of it once the ceremony had taken place.

According to custom, a girl's father chose her husband. Her age at the time of the arrangement varied among the ethnic groups: she could be just a baby or young child (in the case of many Muslim groups) or any age up to the time of puberty. Older men were often preferred as they were more economically stable. It was not uncommon for a fourteen-year-old to be married off to a fifty-year-old man. A man might have decided that in ten years time he would need an additional wife, as his present wife or wives would then be old. The thought of a new young sexual partner at that stage, as well as another worker in his household, was attractive, and he would choose a young daughter from an appropriate family. Once a father considered the man acceptable, negotiations began for the bride-price, which was to be paid over the years until the girl was ready for marriage, or in a few large installments shortly before the marriage if negotiations had begun only at puberty. The bride-price included items such as cattle, pigs, chickens, rice, money, the amount depending on the wealth of the husband-to-be.

"It's just as if a woman is being sold to a man," Teodora commented. "It's like selling babies or young children." In a similar vein, Francisca Pereira said, "A woman is sold for a pig or a cow. She then goes to the man's house and has no active voice whatsoever."

If a marriage failed to take place for any reason, the girl's parents would be expected to return the bride-price or its equivalent value. Hence, for economic reasons, a girl could expect no support from her parents if, at the last minute, she tried to refuse the marriage. And for the same reason, they would side with the man were she later to run back home.

Mothers had little say in the marriage arrangement and could do nothing to prevent it, even if sympathetic to the daughter's predicament. The general expectation was that the daughter would adjust to the marriage in time, particularly once children were born, and cease to resist. Any unhappiness at first was considered perfectly normal.

"If a girl falls in love before she gets married," Teodora said, "things get very complicated. Her parents do not take her feelings into account and they blame the boy for interfering. In the village nobody thought that the daughter had any right or desire to think for herself."

A husband could send his wife home in disgrace, repudiate her, if he considered her to be unsatisfactory. A range of different behavior could serve as cause for this: laziness, disobedience, and, in the case of most groups, unfaithfulness. He could also repudiate her should she prove to be barren. What sometimes happened, though, was that a disgraced wife would be totally ignored by her husband but kept in his household as a worker, even as he took additional wives to replace her. Regardless of how unhappy the woman was, or how badly she was treated, she had little redress, other than possible community support to try and change the husband's ways. If a woman ran away persistently, he could demand the bride-price back, unless children had resulted from the union. Children had such economic value that they supplanted a refund of the bride-price as a means of compensating the man. (The bride-price paid in the first instance was a way of compensating the father for the loss of a worker.) Nevertheless, in actual practice, a woman's reproductive ability did not diminish her entrapment in an unhappy marriage, since a decision to leave her husband also meant almost certain loss of her children. If there were no children it would be difficult, if not impossible, to raise the equivalent of the bride-price in a country as poverty-stricken and underdeveloped as Guinea-Bissau. The woman would have no access to an independent income as the product of her labor would go toward the household as a whole. The only latitude a wife had in marriage anywhere in the society occurred among the Balanta, where lack of divorce rights for women was mitigated by the practice of *cundunka.**

PAIGC began its campaign against regressive customs with political education. Speaking to a group of Mandinga peasants in 1966, Cabral took up the question of forced marriage:

> Why should a little girl go to school if afterwards she must be married by force? I'm telling you that the Party is not going to tolerate any more of these transactions and business deals involving daughters. . . . Some of the girls came to us at the bases, as you well know, in order to avoid being married against their will. A woman should marry the man she has chosen and not one her parents have chosen for her.
>
> The women here have been doing what they could in production and they deserve our respect for that. Meanwhile, a good many of the men have been content to go on trafficking. They buy and they sell, they sell and they buy, and finally they buy themselves a woman in order to put her to work. Now all that has got to stop.[4]

Since it was essential to go beyond political education PAIGC recognized the need to provide alternative structures to support the new attitudes and concepts. Thus, from the beginning of the war, the party accepted into its ranks a large number of young women who had left their villages and fled to the guerrilla bases in order to avoid a forced marriage or to leave their husbands.

Anselmo, an education *responsavel,* interviewed in 1966, described how young women were seeking PAIGC's protection:

*An interesting exception to the practice that denies women the right to divorce is prevalent among the people of the Bissagos Islands. Isolated from the mainland, they did not come under direct PAIGC influence during the war. They are a matrilocal people—the husband goes to live in his wife's village. If a woman decided she no longer wanted him as a husband, she would place all his belongings outside their hut when he was away from the village. When he returned he would quickly sum up the situation, pick up his goods, and leave.

With the girls, the custom of involuntary marriages creates a special problem we have to handle with particular care, As a result of the political lectures, the girls are no longer willing to be married off to somebody they were promised to at birth. In this very camp, for example, we have several little nurses who are no longer willing to return to their native villages but insist on staying here at the base and working for the Party. This is especially true among those coming from Islamized background. They are considered nubile at twelve or thirteen, whereas animist girls are marriageable at eighteen or thereabouts. The Party upholds the principle of freedom of choice.[5]

Sometimes, however, the problem of the bride-price that had already been paid drew PAIGC into family quarrels. If the man's family demanded to be reimbursed, cadres would intervene by discussing this with the two families, emphasizing, as Francisca Pereira said, that "a woman is not an object that can be bought." They would encourage the man to forfeit repayment. And they were usually successful, although sometimes only after lengthy and persuasive discussion. A male *responsavel* commented, however, that there had been occasions when both families continued to insist a marriage be enforced for economic reasons, and PAIGC would pay back the bride-price itself.

Political education was the first step. The next was to back it up by law. At first it was the responsibility of the sector and regional political commissars to mediate between parents and children, or wife and husband. With the election of people's courts the responsibility for these judgments became part of their work. Although forced marriages were illegal (decreed by the two hundred articles of law issued to guide the actions of all militants), PAIGC or the courts would not intervene if the girl agreed to go along with her father's wishes. The system was established to support those who refused, by far the majority, while political education continued to encourage the others to make independent decisions.

In disputed cases, the three-member court listened to what all the interested parties had to say before they made a decision. In the case of forced marriage, they focused on the father to try to make him change his mind. If he did not, the court decided in favor of the daughter.

Forced marriage had virtually disappeared in the liberated zones by the end of the war. When I visited the Fula villages, I asked the young women who had married in the last three or four years whether they had chosen their own husbands. Without exception, all had. "Perhaps if it was not for the war," Justice Commissioner Fidelis d'Almada postulated, "it would not have happened so fast. With political preparation and long explanations about why marriages like this should not take place, they are disappearing rapidly."

Nonetheless, changes come slowly. While marriages against the wishes of women appeared to occur only seldom, if ever, in the liberated zones, by the end of the war arranged marriages, with the consent of both parties, were still practiced to some extent, even among party cadres. Canadian Chantel Sarrazin, writing about her experiences in post-independence Guinea-Bissau in 1975, recalls the situation of one of the FARP militants, Dalme M'Bunde, who acted as her guard and translator during her visit to the south of the country. For ten years he had been part of the struggle, fighting in the *mato*. "Now that the war was over, his family had found him a wife—a girl he vaguely remembered having played with at his home village many years ago. He was proud to make the announcement; as a married man he would get a separate hut and an extra monthly allowance from the army." Reflecting on this, Sarrazin observes, "Was this marriage not a sign of political retrogression? I no longer think the answer is so simple. The revolution cannot change all aspects of negative traditions overnight." She noted that Dalme and his wife were both happy with the marriage. This "was neither forced, nor polygamous; it was therefore consistent with PAIGC principles. Still, that the relationship was not initiated by the two young people themselves shows there is some distance to go in transforming Guinea society."[6] Sarrazin, however, is presuming that the young woman was in favor of the arrangement—having to go by Dalme's account alone. One immediately wonders what, if any, pressure may have been applied to his future wife.

I myself was surprised to learn (during my second visit in 1976) from a top party cadre and one of the most effective mobilizers whom I had first met in the liberated zones, that when his wife died shortly after independence, a man whom he had mobilized and who had dedicated himself to the struggle suggested that the militant marry his daughter. The couple spent some time with each other before the final decision, but they did not take long to commit themselves. She was a lot younger than he, but it seemed to me—superficially at least—after spending some time in the company of the couple, that both were pleased with the arrangement. In telling me the story, the cadre appeared quite moved by the gesture of his father-in-law in "offering" his daughter, as he seemed to view it as an expression of the man's deep respect for the militant. I could not help but wonder, however, how his new wife had viewed the arrangement in the beginning and even later.

Like forced marriages, divorces in the villages were brought before the people's courts, who would request a six-month period of reconciliation. If this failed to reunite the couple, divorce would be granted.

During the war, divorces for party cadres were heard by the military tribunal, which had usually married them in the first place. A plea for divorce had to be submitted in writing. This overcame the problem of convening the court when either the litigants or cadres assigned to the tribunal might be anywhere in the country and therefore unable to attend a proceeding in a given locality. The six-month period of reconciliation was applied in these cases as well.

Teodora stressed that the right to divorce and an end to forced marriages was essential to help women in their fight for liberation. But passing decrees would not immediately bring an end to these repressive practices; social factors still played a part in maintaining them. It was still difficult, she said, for a woman who wanted to divorce her husband but felt she could not because, "due to prevailing attitudes, she would bring shame on her family." The general view of the community still maintained in many instances that a woman who could not live well with her husband was a disgrace. If she left her husband, her family pressured her to return "because traditions expect her to be tied to her husband."

Nonetheless, divorces were not infrequent, particularly among younger women. Older women had adapted to their husband's village, had given birth to children, and developed friendships with the other women of the community which bonded them to the life they were living and gave it meaning. Unless they were enormously unhappy with their husband or felt ostracized by the community, they were unlikely to seek a divorce. Young women, on the other hand, more mobile and restless, were quick to snap up the opportunity to gain more control over their lives. The war meant that young people were on the move. As members of the army, or involved in other work for the revolution, they traveled from one end of the country to the other, or were permanently stationed in areas far away from their villages. Thus, whether they traveled themselves or came in contact with young men working in their home area, women had opportunities to meet and fall in love with men from beyond their own localities. This in turn led to requests that the people's courts dissolve arranged marriages.

"Who is granted custody of the children in a divorce?" I asked Jeronimo Correia, a regional *responsavel* for justice, and other comrades, as we sat around a table at the semiboarding school in Tombali. We were having a lively discussion, after traveling together for a few days.

"Oh, the father. Always," he answered immediately.

"The *father*?" I queried.

"Yes, of course. The father."

Yes, of course. The father. I turned the thought over in my head, completely nonplused. Coming from a society in which the mother automatically gets custody of the children, unless the father can prove that the mother is "unfit," I had blindly assumed this to be universal. My almost casual question launched a heated debate about the custody of children. The men vehemently supported the idea that it was the right of the father to have custody over his children.

"How can you prove you are the father, if you don't have custody over the child?" one *responsavel* said with emphasis. "What would happen if the mother married someone else? The child would have the name of her husband, not the father."

"When I married my wife," another *responsavel* told me poignantly, "she already had a child by another man. I love that child as if he was my own son, and he loves me as if I was his father. But if his father came and said, 'I want my child,' I would agree to his taking the child. It is his right."

The spirited discussion continued for over half an hour. But we went round in circles. It seemed clear to me that the automatic designation of custodian emanated from the economic structure of the village, and paralleled the situation whereby children could supersede the need to repay the bride-price if a wife deserted her husband. What interested me though was the way economic necessity had given rise to repressive social values, the core of which was emotional and which could be so hotly defended by men whose political perceptions were otherwise unclouded. Theirs was a very normal and human response, which gave me added insight into the problems of bringing about change.

Teodora, who had not been participating in the discussion, came to join us after a while. She first explained to me that the concept of custody in their society did not mean that the mother loses her children. It was accepted that the children travel back and forth between the parents regularly. A few months with one, a few months with the other. The mother would continue to care for the child until age five or six, at which time she or he would go to the father. There was no question of having to establish visiting rights or of the parents fighting over time to see their children. The problem did not arise in the context of Guinean society, she said.

Then Teodora added a view of her own, which she stressed was not the position of PAIGC, but one she felt was valid: "It would be a form of oppression to insist that women have custody. This would result in the mother being bound by the children, having to stay home and look after them. It would entrench her lack of freedom, reinforcing her traditional role within the household. In this sense having custody would defeat the purpose of divorce, rather than the reverse. Eventually this will not happen, when mother and father are equal in the family. But now in our villages this is a problem. And if the father gets custody, it does not mean that the mother loses the children. But it does mean that the mother has more freedom."

This question of custody was taken up later in a discussion I had with the commissioner of justice. Traditional custom is the decisive factor in determining who gets custody of the children, d'Almada explained. All decisions of the people's courts went in accordance with the customs of the people living in the area, unless these customs were contrary to the principles of PAIGC. "The party does not interfere with the ruling of the court," he said. "The court can give custody to either. If the father is considered incapable of adequately providing education for his children, the court may give custody to the mother. The party stipulates that everything must be decided in accordance with the customs of the people. If these customs go against the principles of the party, then PAIGC will intervene. But in this case, the party has no reason to intervene and the court itself has the power to decide. Hence the father usually gets the children."

When I spoke with d'Almada, he commented further on a social custom that is also a factor in granting custody to the father. Even though forced marriage was on a speedy decline in the liberated zones, it was still expected that a young man ask his prospective wife's father for permission to marry her. "Only the father's family has the authority to give consent to the marriage," he said. "This is still very important in peasant society. It comes from the custom of giving the bride-price, and must be respected." D'Almada foresaw problems because the mother cannot make such a decision, and if the mother were to have custody of the daughter there would be no one to grant the permission. Given PAIGC's attitude that marriages be entered into freely by the decision of the couple concerned and no one else, the goal is eventually to eliminate the obligation to request permission. In the meanwhile fathers are being given custody of young children who may well not turn to them for "permission" by the time they are ready to be married. Nonetheless, PAIGC has to take into account what the customs are at the present time, as the people in the village are not looking ahead in this way.

For party cadres, where traditional custom did not apply, the military tribunal decided custody when granting a divorce, a decision based solely on whom they felt to be most responsible.

D'Almada gave two examples. The first concerned a man whose wife left the country to live with another. Custody was granted to the father. In the other instance, both husband and wife were cadres of the party, but the court felt that the mother was more stable than the father, and therefore granted the mother custody. However, for party cadres, there was no concept of the children "belonging" to one parent rather than the other, he explained. As in the villages, there was a lot of flexibility in the time spent with each parent. But with no economic gain attached to having custody, unlike the case of peasant society, the tribunal could decide that the child would live six months with one parent and six months with the other.

What would happen, I asked, if both parents were considered equally stable. Who would get custody then? "Generally the father," d'Almada replied with a smile. "It is not a right, but it is a duty to educate your children. Women do not yet have the same privileges in the society. The man leaves her more frequently and therefore it should be his duty to take on that responsibility. We are fighting for total equality, but we cannot pretend that we have achieved our goal. It is a long road."

Forced marriage and lack of divorce were "negative aspects of the beliefs and traditions" of the people which, in the short space of twelve years, had been almost fully transformed in the liberated zones. The elimination of polygyny is a much slower process.

If Africa can be looked upon as the "region of female farming *par excellence*," it can also be looked to as the continent—south of the Sahara in particular—where polygyny is the most preeminent. While these two statements might appear to be unconnected, in fact they are decidedly related to each other. In order to appreciate why this form of marriage is so widespread in Africa, it is necessary to look toward the village economy that nurtures it. A United Nations Economic Commission for Africa report states it succinctly: "One of the strongest appeals of polygyny to men in Africa is precisely its economic aspect, for a man with several wives commands more land, can produce more food for his household and can achieve a high status due to the wealth which he can command."[7]

In a large part of Africa it has been estimated that between one-third and one-fourth of marriages are polygynous. It is not, as d'Almada emphasized to me, "simply the sexual pleasure of having two or three wives. No, it is an economic necessity as well. The wives provide most of the labor in the rice fields. Each wife is necessary because she helps in production."[8]

The laws of land tenure adhered to by many of Africa's peoples give a particular society rights to a prescribed territory, with the land divided among the various clans and families. If land is not scarce, a man will be allocated an additional plot of land for cultivation with every new marriage. Accordingly, each additional wife enables a family to expand its production.

This relationship between the number of wives, increased production and, hence, wealth and status, can be seen among the people of Guinea-Bissau. The extent of a man's wealth, hence status in the community, is dependent on the number of wives and progeny he can acquire. The extent to which he can increase his workers in this way has the added gain of allowing the husband more leisure time. It is altogether a highly advantageous system for the man, and not one he is likely to relinquish easily.

For the wives, however, it is altogether another question. For the first wife, polygyny can be beneficial. She is accorded higher status in relation to other wives by virtue of being first and oldest. Comments Boserup:

> In a family system where wives are supposed both to provide food for the family—or a large part of it, a wife will naturally welcome one or more co-wives to share with them the burden of daily work. . . . In many cases, the first wife takes the initiative in suggesting that a second wife, who can take over the most tiresome jobs of the household, should be procured. A woman marrying a man who already has a number of wives often joins the household more or less in the capacity of a servant for the first wife, unless it happens to be a love match.[9]

There are societies where terminology refers to later wives as the "wives" of the first wife. A more persistent first wife may herself look for a woman she feels to be hard-working and trustworthy and even begin negotiations for her, in order to ensure that her husband does not marry someone unwilling to pull her weight in the community.

Being a second or third wife, then, can mean entering a life of hardship. The desire for more wives on the part of the first wife is dictated solely on grounds of economic necessity; it is this context that renders comprehensible the statements of many older African women that polygyny is preferable.

Another contributing factor to the hardships experienced by younger wives (and sometimes the first wife) is the substantial gap in age between the husband and his later wives. The choice of younger women is the main way of circumventing the problem of nonavailability of women in a society more or less evenly divided by sex. Despite this, many men have to postpone marriage until there are girls available from younger generations. While it is no doubt pleasurable for an older man to have a nubile young woman as a new sexual partner, it is likely to provoke the reverse reaction in the woman herself, particularly (as is common) when the difference in age is thirty, forty, or even—as in the case of Fatima—fifty years.

Hence, the tensions that permeate social life in the polygynous household can often be severe. The age gap does not only apply to the men and women, but between the wives themselves. While the older women benefit from the work contribution of new wives, this arrangement can also generate jealousy. These tensions are manifested in different ways, leading women cadres in Guinea-Bissau to observe that it is the exception to encounter a polygynous marriage where wives live in harmony, particularly among younger women. "In many cases of polygyny," Francisca Pereira told me, "there is rivalry between the wives due to jealousy because the husband prefers one wife more than another. There is also, many times, rivalry between the children. And if one child is brighter than another, his mother might be accused of witchcraft. Sometimes a woman will just leave the family and try to look for a different way to support herself and care for the children. But this is difficult to do."

Aware of these sources of tension in the community, there is a general attempt not to aggravate them by spending more time with one wife than another. It is customary for the husband to divide his time equally between his wives, eating and living with each one in regular rotation. But it is a system that does not

always hold, particularly as the first and second wives grow ·
older, and the husband brings an attractive new wife into the
family. However, each wife has her own hut and does her own
cooking for her immediate family, and benefits from not having
to cook each night for her husband.

Polygyny, because it is so tied in with other oppressive customs, is opposed by PAIGC. Men with two or three wives cannot
provide adequately for the emotional needs of each of them, they
argue. The goal is for marriages based on love and mutual
respect, as well as free choice. However, because it is so basic to
the social and economic structure of the society, it is not something that can be erased in a few years. Much more immediate
success has been accorded PAIGC's efforts to terminate forced
marriage and the taboo on divorce for women. Hence, this means
that with the possibility of divorce, women who are unhappy in
such a marriage are now in a position to leave it. With this
freedom established, education will further reduce the practice
of polygyny. "Although the party is against polygyny," explained
d'Almada, "we understand that we cannot change the customs
of the people suddenly, or they will turn against us. It is a custom
that has existed from generation to generation. We have to move,
but we have to move slowly."

Despite the acknowledged time such changes take, polygyny
is noticeably on the decline. A limitation has been placed on the
custom by stipulating that a man cannot automatically replace a
wife he has lost through death or divorce, unless he has only one
wife in the first place. For party cadres polygyny is not permitted,
not even for practicing Muslims. "Polygyny is dying out," Francisca told me. "People don't want it any more. If they accept it,
they do so against their will."

Young women in the Fula villages told me that they would
insist that their husbands not marry more than one wife. They
did not anticipate that this would ever become an issue for them.
I picked up this same attitude from other women I spoke to.
Re-evaluation of the marriage institution, so that it ceases to be
an instrument of women's oppression, ranks high among the
changes that have taken place in the daily life of peasant women
throughout the liberated zones. "Before, life was very difficult

for women," said Bwetna. "The party has brought new ways and a new life for women. But we must continue to defend ourselves."

Although these views were echoed by many other peasant women, who told me their "eyes have been opened to a new world," by and large peasant women still do "women's work" and men continue to carry out "men's work."

Women's work. Visible everywhere. My clothes were whisked from me and washed in the river, then neatly pressed with irons heated over smouldering coals. In villages and at most bases, women prepared our food. The rhythmic thud, thud constantly in the background of village life was nearly always the result of women rather than men pounding rice. Superficially, the villages I visited were typical of all African villages. Women cooking around the fire, women pounding, women calling after children, women collecting water. Some distance away men sitting together, talking or silently watching the afternoons go by.

And yet, while the superficial impression is true as far as it goes, a really sharp look brings other perceptions into bold relief. One sees men helping women in their work in numerous ways. Taking goods to the people's stores on their heads. Helping with children. Collecting water. Washing clothes. Sharing more equally the work in the fields. Listen beyond the rhythmic pounding and one hears the voices of Bwetna, of Kumba, of numerous peasant women, speaking simply but expressing profoundly the changes that have taken place in their lives since the beginning of the struggle. *"Before women worked for men,"* we hear Kumba say. *"Not anymore. Now men and women work together."* Focus yet deeper and one sees women addressing large meetings, mixing comfortably with men, talking as equals, functioning on village councils, on people's courts, on sector committees, choosing their own husbands, resisting polygyny. Hold this focus, and more subtle details come to the foreground— hurdles, obstacles still to be surmounted. Those women still diffident, still hesitant. Those peasant women who, because of the immense changes in their lives, say proudly, "now we are free," who view providing rice for the guerrillas not only as a revolutionary act, but also as an end in itself. Those men in the villages accepting women cadres, women leaders, but also asserting authority and domination over Kumba.

We have been viewing a process that has only begun, and in the nature of such processes, progress is uneven. The question is how to keep the momentum going. The need for the reorganization of the economy can be seen with particular clarity when considering the negative customs that perpetuate the dependent and exploited position of women. To ensure that the gains already achieved are not allowed to slip back before fully entrenched, the system which is supported by such practices needs to be eradicated. That system, of course, is the organization of the village economy with its enormous dependence on the intensive labor of women. However, the conditions of the *mato* did not permit any real inroads to be made on the existing economic structures.

Chapter 7

"Our education has to be conditioned by our life and history"

Education is considered a fundamental necessity for the emerging new society. Persuading parents to send daughters to school proved to be an uphill battle. By the end of the war the ratio of girls to boys in school was one to three. From the beginning the new school curriculum and work emphasized equality and political education included a focus on the position of women and the need for change.

The sound of drums, an insistent rhythmic beat, filled the still, twilight air and galvanized the young dancers as they stamped and swirled in a wide circle in the clearing of the forest school. As the beat quickened, the strands of their grass skirts fused into a pale yellow haze. And when Mario, the director of their school, rushed into the circle to exhort them to still greater efforts by his own example, the dancers stamped even more vigorously. Then, one of the students left the circle for the center and danced with a machete held high above his head. Tied to each leg was a tin can and an anklet of large dried pods which clinked and clattered in time with his stamping.

The vitality of the dancers was infectious. We in the audience watched appreciatively, clapping and calling out approval. The students, between ten and fourteen years old, smiled with obvious enjoyment and laughed back. But Mario, his large cowboy-style hat gleaming in the dusky light, grinned broadest of all. He was proud of his young charges. The scene we were witnessing could not have occurred before the armed struggle. Boys and girls together. Pepel, Mandinga, Balanta, Fula, all expressing in dance their different national cultures. The performance had opened with a Balanta dance, continued with songs about the revolution and satirical skits about Spinola and Salazar, and ended with dances of other ethnic groups.

We had arrived at the school in Orango, Tombali region of the south front, late the previous evening at the end of a long march. Mario greeted us with friendly hospitality. Only a few of the students were at the school, as the rest had not yet returned from their villages where they spent weekends visiting their families and helping with production. Mario had vacated his small hut for Teodora and me, brought us water for a bath, and warm milk to drink. He looked so young I initially took him for a student. But at twenty, he was director of the semiboarding school, or *semi-internato* as it was called. However, it was not just his youth which had caused me to mistake him for a student. Like most of the young directors of boarding schools, Mario did not project a sense of authority or distance from his students; he was one of the group of eighty young people at his school. And it became evident, as I watched him and his three co-teachers both in class and out, that the entire staff treated their students quite naturally as comrades.

The vitality of spirit I found in the school could not have developed by chance. No unusually felicitous combination of staff, students, and curriculum could have produced such unbounded enthusiasm among all concerned. Rather, that special atmosphere flowed directly from the innovative approach to learning which PAIGC had consciously formulated at the beginning of the struggle. And because it was not accidental, neither was it exceptional: I found a similar quality to the atmosphere in all the *internatos** I visited. It was a mark of education throughout liberated Guinea-Bissau, and consisted in a shared joy in learning and self-discovery, and a commitment on the part of teachers and students alike to understand the society in evolution around them; it expressed how it felt to be a revolutionary, consciously involved in developing the new woman and the new man that Amilcar Cabral and PAIGC had projected as the ultimate goal of Guinean education.

A tough task confronted PAIGC when they first set out to establish new schools. They had to begin from scratch, as those facilities the Portuguese had provided were limited to a few primary schools and one secondary school catering to the children of the privileged few, the *assimilados* in the towns who could afford the high fees. To realize that the illiteracy rate was ninety-nine percent at the beginning of the war, and that few of the remaining one percent had more than the most elementary of reading and writing skills, is to appreciate the extent to which Guineans were deprived of basic education. But the threadbare system was enough for the Portuguese, who needed only a small number of Guineans to administer the colonial apparatus. The African graduates, meanwhile, were not only few, they were alienated. Their education, steeped in Portuguese history and Portuguese culture, was synonymous with de-Africanization. As *assimilados* they learned early to denigrate their own culture, to accept that they had no history, and to deny

---

Internato or *semi-internato* was never translated for me. As the term "boarding school" tends to conjure up the idea of an authoritarian institution, isolated from society, I have used *internato* as is.

any links with or feeling for African identity. They spoke Portuguese rather than Creole and prided themselves on their second-class Portuguese status and on the way they had "come up" in the world.

This miserable school education, however, was not the first education that the people of Guinea-Bissau had known. Even if there were no schools as we know them today, every child in an African village was educated. Girls and boys were educated by their mothers and fathers, and by the other adults and elders with whom they related on a daily basis. They were trained to take their place in the society, a place defined by centuries of tradition. History was passed from generation to generation in the stories that elders told the young people. Social values and customs were absorbed from experiencing life in the village and from participating in the religious ceremonies, most particularly in the initiation rites which symbolized the passage from childhood to adulthood.

But colonial penetration had distorted this traditional process, making one of PAIGC's main goals the need to relearn and re-value Guinean history and culture, to inculcate in the people an integrated national culture transcending the tenuous boundaries between the different ethnic groups.

In this context, the process of revolution and the process of education became interdependent. Just as education had been the key to mobilization for the war, so the continuing revolution reciprocally influenced the shape of education. And since school could not be something separate, exempt from the revolutionary dynamic, the PAIGC school became a microcosm of the transformation toward socialism that was going on in the society. In other words, what happened to the students passing through the school "system" was in step with what was happening to the population as a whole, although, in the latter case, the pace of development was generally slower.

As PAIGC viewed it, education was not a way of mechanically providing students with the necessary skills to pass exams, to find jobs in order to support themselves as adults, and to learn to adjust to the system under which they lived. It did not prepare them for a life as an elite. Guinean youth was being prepared for the life that the masses of people will lead in a new society. In the revaluation of their own culture and their own history, they learned too about the world as a whole and their place within it, from the perspective of fighting imperialism and struggling for justice.

The very process of education was itself helping to develop a new society. The students were being prepared for a future that did not yet exist, and in this way were themselves molding the future. Their education was an insurance that the revolutionary direction of the society into which they would pass would be carried forward. "Our type of education," said Cabral, "has to be conditioned in each phase of the struggle by the life and the history we experience at a given moment."[1]

Thus, education went beyond the confines of the classroom. No brick buildings, rooms with doors and windows, no walls. None of the basic equipment that we take for granted, such as desks, writing material, sports gear, scientific apparatus. Few books. Instead, there was maybe one "classroom" built from the vinelike branches of the forest, a frame holding up a roof of branches or palm fronds. Often the school was simply a clearing in the forest. The benches and desks were rough poles strapped together by thin vines which worked well in place of rope. One precious blackboard, worn with age, would be propped up in front next to the teacher's desk. Equally precious was the chalk. Every pencil, every book, every writing tablet had to be brought in from outside on the heads or backs of militants who marched for days and miles into the interior. They were carried together with medical supplies, ammunition, food, and other critical necessities of life in the *mato*. Nothing was wasted, every scrap of paper valued. For these meager supplies PAIGC relied on the generosity of friendly countries and organizations. Every six months the school would have to be rebuilt at another location as a precaution against the bombing; schools, like villages and hospitals, were considered legitimate military targets by Portuguese bombardiers. A hundred yards or so from the classroom were the deep trenches—as essential as the benches and the blackboard. The first lesson to be taught at any school was survival.

There were three types of schools in the liberated zones:

village, *semi-internatos*, and *internatos*. By the time of my visit over sixty village schools dotted the *mato*. One, maybe two teachers taught a class of fifty to sixty pupils from nearby villages or groups of villages, spanning the first three grades and aged between seven and sixteen. The school term was adjusted to the agricultural season so that the children could help their parents with production.

From the village schools the student could go on to the *internatos*. Students at the *semi-internatos*—one for each region—attended school five days a week, returning home on the weekends to work in the villages and to be with their parents. Their parents provided rice for the school. Everything else was provided by PAIGC. From the *semi-internato*, pupils could go on to one of the four *internatos* in the countryside. Of these, one each was in the north and south fronts and two were in the east. (In addition, two secondary schools were situated outside the country, in Conakry and Ziguinchor, Senegal.)

The *internato*, more than the other school in the liberated zones, epitomized what PAIGC was trying to achieve in education. PAIGC's emphasis on the need for cooperation and collectivity in work, as well as in day-to-day relationships, was incorporated into its organization. The teachers had authority over the content of lessons, but beyond that it was left to the students to administer the school. No one was employed to work there, and all the tasks, such as cooking, cleaning, fetching water from the well, were divided among the students and performed on a rotating basis. A committee elected at the beginning of the year was responsible for leadership and for any disciplinary problems that might occur. However, regular meetings of the assembly were held to develop a consensus on these and other matters.

The school committee was composed of three boys and three girls. Although the actual percentage at the schools varied between twenty-five and thirty-three percent, equality was maintained at the committee level to demonstrate that the goal was to equalize the number of boys and girls in the general student population.

At first parents hesitated for economic reasons to send even their boys to school. And Cabral had to harangue a meeting of peasants a year after the first schools were established:

> Parents may no longer refuse to send their children to school. The children are caught up in the chores. . . . But children need to go to school just as parents need the children's help. . . . I am an engineer. Perhaps there are people present who are smarter than I. But there are not engineers among them because there were no schools. The Party wants to give all the children of our people a fair chance. Our people's main enemy is Portuguese colonialism. But any adult preventing the education of our children is also our enemy.[2]

That was 1966. In 1971, with the problem still pressing, Cabral was forced to take up the subject again. Addressing a meeting of the Superior Council for the Fight, he pointed out that in many countries the peasants had initially resisted education:

> We must not be discouraged because there are people in our country who do not like education. We must regret this, but we must not be discouraged. In Portugal for instance . . . the people rose and burnt schools when schools were built in the villages . . . because the school took their children away from home, and this harmed the work, for the children were taking care of the house, the pigs, the sheep, the cattle, etc. This is normal, and we must not be discouraged by it. We have to be able to understand it as well as possible, and find an acceptable solution, without aggravating the conflict between the schools (and thus the Party) and the population.[3]

While economics lay at the heart of early peasant resistance in Guinea-Bissau, its effects were not equal for both boys and girls. Parents eventually found ways of sending their sons to school. But daughters, no. It was not so much a matter of seeing the education of girls as less important as it was an uncritical response to the prevailing economic order. Girls were needed in the village to assist their mothers, and women's work, time consuming and arduous as it was, was the linchpin of the village economy. Besides, what possible use could education be to girls, fathers reasoned, when they were to get married, and the younger the better.

Political education around this issue was intensive, particularly in the Muslim villages where the women's role had been most rigidly defined. "Our party placed great emphasis on the children because they are the future of the country," nineteen-year-old Jacinta da Sousa, director of an *internato* in the east, told me. "Political commissars go to the villages and explain why education is so important, particularly for the girls. They explain that we want to construct a new society, a society without sex discrimination."

Still, after parents had finally agreed to educate their daughters, another problem emerged: girls were starting their schooling at a much older age than boys, usually once the younger girls in the village became old enough to take on their work. I discovered this for myself when I interviewed Njai Sambo, who was responsible for "social affairs" on her village council. Yes, she assured me, all the children in her village attended school, boys and girls. Education for all the children was very important. She added: "I want all my children to go to school. If they go to school, then they will know what they are able to do and what they will want to do when they are adults. I put my younger sister through school. I didn't know what she could do, but now she is a nurse in the east front."

But when I asked her whether all her own children were presently in school, I learned that her twelve-year-old daughter was not. "She will be going next year," Njai hastened to add. And then she touched on the core of the matter: "But what can I do? I have a baby and I need my daughter to help me look after him. There is just too much work to do in the village."

There were other hitches. A parent might turn up at a school from one day to the next to retrieve his or her daughter for work in the village, because something unexpected had come up. As a result, the child's education would be erratic and she would fall behind. In an attempt to overcome this, some girls had been placed in *internatos* far away from the villages and given special attention so that they might catch up. Hence, although it was usual for the lowest grade to be the third, at these *internatos* there was a class of second-graders who were all girls.

The ratio of girls to boys at the three *semi-internatos* and the two *internatos* I visited varied. At the *internato* at Boé in the east, there were eighty-eight students, of which eleven were girls. The percentage was higher at the *internato* in Candjafara, which had a second-grade class for girls only. Of the *semi-internatos* I visited, one near Teodora's base in the Balana-Quitafine region had only two girls out of a total of fifty-one students. The other two I visited were better, with about twenty-five percent girls. So was the *internato* in the north, where two years earlier in 1972 there were forty-three boys and ten girls.

However, these figures may not be as disheartening as they appear. A number of girls—probably as many as those in schools in the interior—went to Boké to study nursing and continue their regular education alongside the nurses' training. (Although boys studied nursing as well, this alternate schooling was consciously viewed as a way of ensuring further education for young women.) An American journalist who visited Guinea-Bissau in 1973 recalled that he attended a combined graduation ceremony for a group of schools in the north and the percentage of girls among the graduates was about one-third.[4] Party statistics for 1971–1972 indicate that one-third of the students in the north were girls.[5] Party statistics for the country as a whole, from 1965 to 1972, give the breakdown over those years.[6]

	1965-66	1966-67	1967-68	1968-69	1969-70	1970-71	1971-72
Students	13,361	14,386	9,384	8,130	8,559	8,574	14,531
Male	9,821	10,865	6,737	5,907	6,232	6,419	10,898
Female	3,540	3,521	2,647	2,223	2,327	2,155	3,633
% Female	26	24	28	27	27	25	25

The percentage of girls in school remained fairly level despite PAIGC consciousness of the problem and its attempts to change the attitudes supporting it. But by 1974 direct improvement could be seen, with the percentage of girls in school reaching thirty-three percent.

The best performance in terms of enrolling girls was that of the Pilot School in Conakry. Girls made up one-third of the one hundred twenty students who attended this secondary school in 1974. And this despite the fact that the school was outside the country—so far away from the villages as to discourage parents of prospective students from sending even their sons. Meanwhile, the relatively large overall percentage was even greater in the two lower grades. Here a good number of students were children of cadres or war orphans and therefore the number of girls was not affected by the attitudes of their tradition-bound parents. The classes were divided equally between girls and boys. The sixth and highest grade, however, had fourteen boys and only three girls, possibly due again to girls having chosen or having been encouraged to take up nursing. While day to day peasant resistance to educating girls was not so much of a factor at the Pilot School, it was still true that the majority came from the interior. The process of selection must have been weighted in favor of girls in order to set a national example and put into practice its political principles.

Teodora insisted that the number of girls attending school had increased over the years, despite the fact that official statistics appeared to say otherwise. Without exception, the village councillors I interviewed responded to my question about attendance from their village with the answer that all girls and boys went to school. I was puzzled by this contradiction. It seems, on looking beyond the statistics a little, that there is a less obvious dimension to the above table which helps clarify the relative number of girls who had some schooling. If instead of looking only at the flat yearly statistics of the percentage of girls versus boys in school at one particular time, one looks at the percentage of girls that attended school over a period of time in the school-going population as a whole, the gap between the sexes narrows considerably. Two facts pertain: girls went to school later than boys; boys and girls seldom continued their schooling beyond the age of sixteen (as they could more valuably direct their energies toward other aspects of the revolution once they reached that age). Hence, there was a greater turnover of girls in school. To be sure, quantitatively, schooling for girls was inferior in general, because they spent less time in school. However, the actual number of girls who passed through school compared with the number of boys who passed through school is not as unequal as the above table would suggest. Further, once girls left school, and presuming they did not return to their villages to marry and become reabsorbed into the traditional peasant life and economy, they would be able to join adult education classes and continue their studies, be it in Boké at the nursing school, working at a base, or at a hospital in the liberated zones. Thus their lesser education had a chance of being remedied.

As to the education of Guinean children generally, one fact stands out of the table of figures: the enrollment decreased rather dramatically in the third year (1967-1968), and then in 1972 leapt equally dramatically back to the previous level, before increasing steadily until the end of the war. Why? Some of the reasons are obvious. The initial enthusiasm of many parents waned with the inconvenience of having their children away from the village for a good part of the day, or a good part of the week and year in the case of *semi-* and full *internatos*. But most interestingly, this decline was actually the result of a conscious move on the part of PAIGC. When Cabral discussed the reduction of school services in his address to the Superior Council for the Fight (quoted earlier), he insisted on the need for realism. "It is more important for us to have a few schools and many young people without schools, than to have many schools that we cannot support, with fourth-grade teachers who have only finished second grade themselves, and similar things." PAIGC had been overoptimistic at first, established schools "everywhere" without a clear line on the matter, and then had to retrench. In addition, there was a need for teachers with a high level of political consciousness. "This is more important than increasing the number of schools," Cabral explained. "If the few teachers we have in the few schools we have perform their education and political functions properly, our struggle will advance much more than if we have 300, 500 schools, where the teachers are a bunch of cheating liars, without any connection with the political work of our Party."[7]

Consequently, enrollment rebounded only when PAIGC was in a position to provide more schools and teachers. In the meanwhile, political education regarding the need for sending children to school had more of an impact even as the peasants, encouraged by the military victories won by their guerrilla army, had come to see the bombing less as a danger to their children and more as an ineffectual response by the Portuguese to a losing situation.

There is one other factor that contributed to the acceleration of the enrollment of both sexes. Soldiers in the army played an important role in agricultural production, pulling their weight in the village at critical times in the growing and harvesting seasons. In so doing they helped alleviate the heavy burden of production supported by the peasants, enabled those who remained in the villages to accept their youth going to school, and affected attitudes to traditions such as forced marriage. By providing an alternate source of labor, the soldiers were able to undermine rigid adherence to repressive traditions.

No matter how many schools were in operation at any one time, PAIGC ideology was put into practice through the subjects taught. Standard subjects such as history, geography, mathematics, and language were part of the curriculum. But political education and agricultural production also had their place in the academic routine.

The teaching of history and geography was made political in the sense that students were able for the first time to learn about their country and the world from the perspective of their own lives and culture—and not from the Portuguese point of view. Rather than rely on unsatisfactory books from other countries or adaptations of them, teachers used no books at first and developed their own lessons. Mathematical problems, for example, related to their environment. How much rice would be needed to feed a village? How quickly do mosquitoes multiply in a swamp? How many swamps near the village? In this way, too, the danger of malaria would become part of the lesson with the children encouraged to talk to the people in the villages about the need to remove the swamps.

Readers in Portuguese, the first books to be written for each grade,* were produced collectively by village schoolteachers, based on their experiences. Colorfully and often humorously illustrated by PAIGC artists, they depicted life in Guinea-Bissau: the war, the village, the national reconstruction programs. The books were straightforward and simply written, with limited

---

*Portuguese is the language medium for all schools. Creole is not yet a written language and, besides, if Creole were to become the sole national language it would isolate Guinea-Bissau from the rest of the world. Since independence, plans are being developed to have Creole written and taught alongside Portuguese.

political content. That PAIGC refrained from using this opportunity to indoctrinate its youth was reflective of the confidence
the party had both in the people and its own ideology.

The political was dealt with more specifically in weekly
political education classes. These classes were considered vital
to the process of education, and featured lively discussion
and debate. Courses emphasized developing an understanding
of PAIGC, its program and its work, and an international perspective, including African history (independence and trade
union struggles in particular), the history of revolutions in
other parts of the world, colonialism, and the role of culture in
national development.

Another aspect of political education promoted in the schools
was that of learning through doing. Learning from books solely
within the confines of a classroom was considered inadequate to
equip the student for life in the new society. For example,
students grew their own food and cultivated land adjacent
to the schools, as an object lesson in self-sufficiency which,
by extension, demonstrated the importance of agricultural production to their society. At the same time, through sharing
the work of administering the schools, they learned principles
of collectivity and that the blind authority and bureaucracy of
the colonial system had no place in the organization of their
future state.

A question of relating future goals to a current reality was
particularly evident in the approach to the issue of exploitation
of women. Because many discussions focused around the need
to eradicate all forms of exploitation, students came more easily
to understand the nature of the oppression of women and to
broach different ways in which to work toward a society based
on true equality.

Jacinta da Sousa, the Boé *internato* director, explained how
these issues are taken up in the political education classes. "We
direct the discussion around the rights of women at the boys in
particular," she said, "so they can begin to understand that what
they learn at home in regard to women is not true. You know, the
boys come to school with the opinion that 'I am a man, she is
a woman, and therefore I am superior.' We try very hard to

eradicate these ideas from the boys' heads. We talk about women in the militia and now in our army also. We give examples of women such as Carmen [Pereira] and Titina [Silá] to show the girls that women can have the same responsibility as men and can become leaders in our country."

These discussions were reinforced by daily experience in the schools where equal participation by all students was consciously encouraged. No part of the curriculum was set aside for one sex or the other. Every aspect of school life—all classes, including sewing and gymnasitcs, all work in maintenance and adminis-tration of the school—was shared equally. And in an attempt specifically to counteract the sexual division of labor found in the villages, agricultural work was done by both boys and girls.

The contrast between school life and much of village life was marked. In the schools I saw boys fetching water from the well and carrying buckets on their heads, just like the girls. I saw boys cooking and both girls and boys taking part in the early morning gymnastics and quasimilitary training. (In fact the gymnastics teacher at the Pilot School was a young woman.) I saw boys looking after the young children of women working at schools, children of a nurse on one occasion, the administrator of a *semi-internato* on another. I saw girls and boys rebuilding two large huts that had burnt down at the *internato* in Candjafara, both carrying the long, heavy wooden poles used in such con-struction and defying the long tradition that marked building huts as "men's work." This was the school at which Espirito Santo taught. He was very proud of the way his students shared work, regardless of the traditional sex-based work roles. "At my school everything is equal," he would declare.

It was something of a challenge for the students to appeciate sympathetically the contradiction between the future-oriented nature of daily experience in school and the reality of village life. Village life could not be changed because one wished it, any more than it could be changed by force. Such a result could only come about "step by step" through the peasants' own strivings. Meanwhile, the school readers appeared to reflect a point of view intermediate between the past derogation of women and their future equality. In the process, women's work was reevaluated and women themselves accorded higher status, in keeping with the conscious effort of PAIGC to emphasize everywhere that the economy was based primarily on their labors. And so we read in the second-grade reader, under the section entitled "Mother's Work":

"In our section of the village who is it that always goes from one side to the other, working without stop? It is our mother. She is the first to awaken and to go at once to the kitchen to prepare some rice with milk. Then the whole family eats. The men leave for the fields and the children for school. Our mother goes to clean the house and to make lunch. Such a delicious meal mother makes.

"Moreover, after working in the house, mother still goes to till the fields. Now many mothers are members of the party. They work in the house, in the fields, and struggle as well. Our mothers know that it is necessary to work harder in order to help build a better life for their children. We must respect the work of our mothers."

What is most significant about this passage is that children were being encouraged actively to comprehend the value of the work their mothers did, probably for the first time. "The anonymous daily work of women," as PAIGC called it, would no longer be permitted to remain so in the minds of the new generation. Consciousness was the first step toward change.

In another section, entitled "The Day of Women" and commemorating the March 8th International Women's Day, respect was expressed again for women along with suggestions that alternative roles were possible. "The women clean the house, plow, cook, and do the laundry, even for our soldiers. But the women also perform other work. Many of them are soldiers, nurses, teachers, and others are officials in the party. Isn't it true the women of our land work hard? . . . Also, do not forget to help the women in their work. And now let us applaud all the courageous women." To underscore that different roles were possible, the drawing accompanying this story was of a woman in army uniform, carrying a rifle on her back and a baby in her arms. Another way the reader hinted at new roles was through the use of the word "companion." Women were portrayed as companions of, i.e., equals to men. This was an important element in the new relationships between men and women which the text posed as possible in a transformed society.

What these texts portrayed, then, was the reality of the daily life of peasant women. To suggest that the division of labor no longer existed or to depict a society that was already equal would not make sense to the children leaving their peasant village to attend school. The readers reflect where the society *is*, not where one would ideally like it to be. Nonetheless, elements of contradiction are evident in the discussion of international women's day—the contradiction of celebrating a still unequal role. As such the spirit of "women's day" seems to have been confused with that of "mothers' day." The passage reads: "The 8th of March is women's day. In all the countries, the children give presents to mothers; brothers to sisters; grooms to brides; boyfriends to girlfriends. The woman is honored on that day as the companion of man, as the mother of all men. It is a great celebration, and in some countries women do not work the whole day, because men do the work for them. Women are very happy with such proof of affection and gain courage to proceed with the great tasks they perform every day. Also in our land in the new life we will build after the Portuguese colonialists leave, we will celebrate the women's day with great happiness."

In contrast with the schools in the *mato*, discussion around the emancipation of women was apparently downplayed at the Pilot School, possibly because it was more removed from the contradictions of the interior. Lilica Boal, the director of the school, told me, "This problem is not discussed in the Pilot School because it is a problem of the past. The boys treat the girls completely as equals. Now the young people have received a completely different education. They belong to the new generation and they accept this equality."

This may be overhopeful; certainly it has not always been the case. Fina Crato, who studied there for four years after being evacuated from Como Island at the height of the 1964 siege by the Portuguese army, recalled both the discussion of the oppressed role of women and the equality she experienced in the school.

"Here for the first time in my life I discovered that boys and girls can be equal. We lived it in our lives each day. We did everything together—studying, playing, working. All the pupils shared in the work of the school equally, which included cooking, cleaning, laundry. And besides our regular lessons we did sports and learned to sew together. For a while Carmen Pereira was our sewing teacher for both boys and girls."

It was the practical situation which had made the deepest impact on Fina, enabling her to understand both the need for and the potential of emancipation. From Lilica Boal's statement, however, it seems that practice was emphasized while theoretical discussion on women's liberation was not. (Lilica became director after Fina was a student.) Although I could accept that the problem of sexism was minimal in the day-to-day life of the school, I did feel—looking about me at the society I was in—that this ideal situation existed in a very small section. The students, the party's future cadres, needed to understand the realities of the world outside their protected enclave, and to combine that understanding with a broad political perspective. It seemed to me that these needs meant that there was still an important place for continual political education around the issue of women's oppression.

In the interior education *responsavels* grappled head-on with the myriad contradictions of peasant society. "We have to utilize all methods of education that will be of use for the development of our society," said Teodora, voicing a basic principle of PAIGC and pointing out that education in the schools, along with lectures in the villages by cadres, had gone a long way toward overcoming the anachronistic aspects of their culture. In fact, polygyny, forced marriage, and denial of divorce rights for women were no longer considered acceptable options among youth with even a few years' education.

One striking example of how school education can influence such change is evident in the effect it has had on the practice of circumcision, and most particularly female circumcision or clitoridectomy. The practice of clitoridectomy is not confined to Africa, although outside the continent it is prevalent mainly among Muslims. This is not the case in Africa, where it can be found in at least twenty-eight countries.

One study defines clitoridectomy as follows:

> The terms "female circumcision" or "excision" cover a variety of practices involving the mutilation of the female genitals. Basically, three different operations may be distinguished: clitoridectomy, the removal of whole or part of the clitoris; labiadectomy, the excision of all or part of the labia minora, occasionally including the labia majora; and infibulation, in which the labia are sewn together, or a girl's legs are tied together for several days in order that the amputated edge of the labia may join through healing. . . . The risk of haemorrhage and infection is always present, as the indigenous instruments of iron, stone, wood or glass, are never sterile.[8]

The most commonly practiced of the three operations is clitoridectomy. Such mutilation of the genitalia—apart from the pain and possible infection—has a horrific effect on women. While anthropologists tend to view male and female circumcision as equatable aspects of initiation rites in a given society, this is not so. As the study cited above indicates: "Whatever the parallels might be in the ritual and surgical operations, the physiological effect of male and female circumcision is fundamentally different. For boys, the operation has little lasting effect; but for girls, the removal of their clitoris may drastically damage the capacity for sexual enjoyment."[9] For boys it can be argued that there is a valid hygienic reason for the practice. For girls it is a conscious or unconscious method of maintaining the subordination of their gender.

The time in the life cycle of women at which the operation is performed varies among the different ethnic groups of Africa, and might differ within a region. In Nigeria, for instance, it can be done at birth, at puberty, as part of the bridal preparations, prior to childbirth, and after several years of marriage. However, the time that is the most prevalent throughout the continent is during the initiation ceremonies of girls into womanhood. It is tragically ironic, therefore, to find young girls eagerly looking forward to the event as the mark of the transition from girlhood to adulthood. Only then is she considered mature and marriageable: a woman.

Not all societies appear to understand the correlation between the clitoris and sexual pleasure, although it is impossible to know at this stage why the practice was initially instituted. The passing of time clouds and modifies the ostensible reasons: that it makes the girl strong, ensures her fertility, prevents a difficult childbirth or the future sickness of the baby are among the rationales. These reasons have undergone changes, in some instances, corresponding to changes in the society itself. For example, among the Yoruba of Nigeria, when infant mortality was higher than it is at present, the operation was considered necessary to safeguard the life of the baby, for it was believed that if the head of a baby touched its mother's clitoris during birth it would die. This belief has since died out, and been replaced by one which directly addresses the connection between the clitoris and sexual pleasure, namely that the operation will prevent young girls from becoming prostitutes and bringing disgrace on themselves and their families.[10]* But the most usual explanation for the practice was tied to tradition, a continuation of a practice "always performed."

This latter reason was prevalent in Guinea-Bissau, where clitoridectomy is to be found only among the Muslim groups, representing thirty percent of the population. As far as I could ascertain, total excision is not performed; rather, the tip of the clitoris is removed. Male circumcision is not confined to Muslim peoples, but is practiced by all ethnic groups, and, being integral to the initiation rites into manhood is, like female circumcision, performed at puberty. The girls undergo the procedure just prior to puberty, and, like their sisters elsewhere in Africa, view it as a symbol of passing from a girl to a woman.

Given the sensitive nature of the subject, I was not able to gain conclusive insights into the reasons behind the practice in the short time I was in the country, and the problem was further compounded by language barriers. The older women I spoke to in the Muslim community seemed very much in favor of clitoridectomy. My questions as to why it was practiced invariably produced the answer "it has always been done," or "she cannot

---

*The practice of clitoridectomy is not confined to third world countries. There were numerous cases of the operation being performed as a "cure" for masturbation and nymphomania in nineteenth-century England.

be a woman if it isn't done." I asked N'Bemba, who was trusted by the women in the Fula villages we visited, to try and elicit a more concrete rationale. She was given the same answer. And I came to see that the direct connection between circumcision and womanhood provided one of the clues to the unquestioning continuation of the practice. From early childhood, girls learned that in order to become a woman they must go through the initiation rites. Each year they saw the rites carried out for older girls in the village and eagerly anticipated their turn. They understood that only then could they be considered a woman. The initiation rites, therefore, played an important role in the conscious process of growing up.

The effectiveness of this connection makes PAIGC's efforts to change the practice difficult. Yet, as with all such customs, they do not deny the interrelationship between the custom and the social structure of the society; instead they emphasize it. Were they to ban the practice the result probably would be its continuation in secret, causing more harm to women, at the same time generating hostility and mistrust toward the party. Neither have they followed the path chosen by leaders in other newly independent African nations, however: the blind return to traditional customs, however detrimental, which had been outlawed or disdained by the oppressive colonial regimes. As an expression of victory over the colonialists, for example, clitoridectomy was reinstituted and encouraged in Kenya. And in Sierra Leone young women proudly adhere to the practice in an effort to distinguish themselves from westernized urban women.

As we saw in the previous chapter, PAIGC draws a bold line between those customs that enhance the culture of the people and those that provide only negative influence. Yet unlike the customs discussed in that chapter—polygyny, forced marriage, and denial of divorce rights for women—clitoridectomy was not singled out as a target for PAIGC's opposition and was not made illegal in the liberated zones. This, according to party leaders, was because women themselves did not consider the procedure oppressive. Realizing that a call for an end to the practice would not have won much support, PAIGC decided other tactics needed to be used.

They designed an information campaign directed at the younger generation: girls were told circumcision was unnecessary while boys were warned of infections resulting from traditional methods. And both sexes were told that the procedure was no precondition of true adulthood. However, the older generation basically was left alone. Teodora, expressing PAIGC's characteristic patience in such matters, explained: "It is not possible to stop overnight a custom that has arisen out of centuries of tradition. In particular it is very difficult to prevent any practice that relates to sexuality and which emanates from very old and deep-rooted ideas. Hence, the party has not taken any concrete measures, directed at the older people, to try and stop this practice. But those who have been educated—the youth—understand that it is not necessary."

It had been PAIGC's experience that when young students went to study in the *internatos,* in the secondary schools in Conakry and Senegal or abroad, they found themselves in a social environment completely different from that in which they grew up. Here they saw that clitoridectomy was not practiced by others, and that it was even considered harmful. After these impressions had sunk in, they quickly reached the conclusion that it is irrelevent to attaining womanhood, and, on returning to their villages, insisted that their younger sisters not be circumcised. The teachers in the village schools and *semi-internatos* also took up the issue, but because of the counterpressure that parents could apply directly on their daughters, they were not as successful as their counterparts in the *internatos* and secondary schools.

Teodora pinpointed another aspect that PAIGC took into account: "Someone who has grown up knowing that at a certain age, he or she *must* go and be circumcised, might suffer psychological problems if they do *not* have it done." An individual would have to live with these doubts for the rest of his or her life unless the process of political education was done so sensitively that it gained the full support of the individual child. "Teachers do not say that those who have been circumcised are better or worse than those who have not," Teodora added. "Rather they stress that there are other ways of living and the practice itself is unnecessary and not beneficial.

If parents still insisted, then PAIGC encouraged them to send their children to a clinic or hospital to have the operation done more hygienically. But it appeared, at least in the case of girls, that in the villages the ritual was considered as important as the actual operation. Girls were, once more, the last to be released from tradition. So while the party had some success in steering boys to clinics, girls by and large were circumcised in the ways demanded by tradition.

PAIGC's experiences in the circumcision campaign were not without their lighter moments. I listened on one occasion as a group of cadres jokingly but sympathetically recalled the predicament of a young teacher. A group of fathers had come to his school to retrieve their sons for an initiation ceremony and took them back to the village. The teacher followed in hot pursuit, arriving just as the ceremony was about to take place, and rushed in to demand that they stop. Only he had forgotten something: according to tradition, if an uncircumcised man witnesses these sacred rites, he too must undergo the procedure. As the teacher was uncircumcised he found himself running again—this time in the other direction.

The effectiveness of PAIGC's school education program in the ten years of its existence can be measured by reference to the new generation of Guineans that grew up in it.

At one of the *internatos* I visited, I talked with the two "political commissars"—a boy and a girl—of the elected student committee. The boy explained the workings of his school with a clarity and political insight which quite belied his youth. While he spoke, the girl, also fourteen, sat quietly next to him, looking down, her hands resting in her lap, interjecting no comments into his authoritative presentation. Adama Sambu seemed a perfect image of her mother and grandmother. But when I asked her questions after her comrade had finished, referring particularly to the role of women, her seemingly subservient demeanor disappeared without a trace. Showing an equal political grasp of the revolution, she confidently described her perceptions:

"In our school the girls live and work on a completely equal basis with our male comrades. So here it [sexism] is not a problem.

Nonetheless, we talk frequently about the role of women in our country and the problems confronting women because of their inferior status. On March 8th, the day of women, for instance, we hold special meetings, and a teacher, who is a member of the party, visits each class to talk about the rights of women, the work we must do in our country in order to free women, and the necessity for women to have equal rights with men.

"Outside the school, I see immediately the difference between the role of women there and the special situation of equality in our school. There, a woman does *all* the work around the home. She works continuously and very hard. Men do not help with this work at all, although they could very easily. Men are, of course, engaged in other work, work which women may not do although they are perfectly capable. This is because they are treated unequally in the society and are expected to serve the men.

"In order to develop our country, in order to make the women of our country advance toward complete equality, women and men must have the same rights. We women must do the same work as the men, which they believe we cannot do, and men too must free women from the enormous amount of work they have to do in the home. In this way our country will advance so that men and women will have the same responsibilities and the same rights."

Top: Fina Crato (center) with Jacinta da Souza, school director (second from left), and Conceiçao Goia, teacher (right) at east front *internato*. *Bottom, left:* Carmen Pereira, PAIGC leader. *Right:* Mariama Camara interviewed at her house in Cacine. To the right is her co-wife.

Top, left: Ana Maria Gomes, PAIGC *responsavel. Right:* Juliana Gomes, hospital director, examining malaria victim in the liberated zones. *Bottom:* Ule Bioja (left), health *responsavel,* with nurses at Cameconde Hospital. Nurses often worked with babies on their backs.

Top, left: Cau Sambu, one of the first and most effective mobilizers. *Right:* Satu Djassi, a leader of the Organization of Women, addressing a peasant meeting. *Bottom:* Teodora Gomes, regional political commissar, at work at her base in the south front of the liberated zones.

Chapter 8

"At the same time fighting for personal independence"

As the war progressed, increasing numbers of women were found entering such diverse areas of work as different facets of political mobilization, health, education, and information, and women worked their way up through different levels of leadership. Markedly lacking, however, were women soldiers. I found PAIGC's reasons for this were more connected to social and economic factors than to attitudes that discriminated against women.

It was the last week in January 1973. From north, south, and east, from every region and sector, *responsavels*, party militants, soldiers, representatives from villages, young people and old, emerged from villages, bases, schools, camps, and hospitals and set out on foot for the border with neighboring Guinea. They were on their way to pay their last respects to their leader and hero, Amilcar Cabral, whose funeral was to be held in Conakry. They marched in sorrow and anger, but also with determination. For however deeply they mourned his death, they knew that their struggle was not embodied solely in Cabral; his assassination would not mark the end of the revolution, but a strengthening of their will to press on more resolutely to victory.

The journey meant days of marching, especially from the north front. For seven or eight days, nonstop, the people marched, following the paths that wound through the forest, sprinting across the open *bolanhas* under cover of darkness. At the edge of the rivers they waited in mangroves for a peasant to take them across in a dugout canoe. Although the peasants were notified ahead of the travelers' arrivals, invariably there was a wait, as precise timing under such conditions was impossible. The crossing time varied: a few of the rivers were miles across, while others were much narrower. No journey could be made without such crossings, however, as rivers carved their way in all directions through the Guinean landscape. Six or eight people balanced on their haunches on the floor of the dugouts as the expert paddlers negotiated across to safety.

The Portuguese colonialists, meanwhile, realizing that many militants would be traveling to mourn the murder of their prime target, intensified their attacks, hoping to hit less illustrious ones. One such was Titina Silá, one of the most loved leaders of the revolution. Crossing the broad Farim River on February 1, as part of an advance guard to make preparations for the funeral, she and her comrades fell into a Portuguese ambush. This was not the first—more likely the seventh or eighth—but this time her presence of mind and bravery could not help her as before. When the comrades were in the middle of the river, the Portuguese army boat appeared and shot at their rubber dinghy, hitting Titina. A Cuban doctor in the dinghy tried to grab her, but he missed, and she fell into the water. The others managed to get away, but Titina, unable to swim, did not, and the revolution lost its political commissar for the whole north front.

Ernestina ("Titina") Silá was born in Cadique Betna, Tombali region, in April 1943. By the time mobilization began she had moved with her mother to Cacine; it was there, in 1961, that she was first contacted by two mobilizers, Nino Vieira and Umaro Djallo. From the first time they approached her, she threw all her energies into the struggle. Her initial task was to distribute clandestine literature, which she hid in a can in her backyard. Later she acted as a liaison between the mobilizers living in the forest and the peasants. Ever active, she went between forest and village, working nonstop, talking incessantly about the struggle. It was not long before she had convinced all the people she knew, all those she contacted, both young and old, to support the PAIGC and fight for the liberation of their country.

But her mother, meanwhile, looked with distrust on the young mobilizers who visited Titina. What were they encouraging her young daughter to do? She worried herself sick and tried to persuade Titina to stop. Titina would not listen. Already she was dedicated and accepted without question the need for national liberation. So her mother decided to send her to Bissau to live with an aunt and continue her studies. The entreaties of Nino and Umaro proved unavailing. But Titina had also made up her mind. Though she loved her mother, she had to follow her conscience. She ran away and took refuge in the base at Galā, in the sector of Cubucare. There she trained as a guerrilla, and was soon taking part in combat missions.

The following year Cabral began a program for the mobilization of girls and young women and chose Titina to study in the USSR, under the auspices of the Soviet youth organization. Affected by the extreme cold, she returned in 1964 before she had completed her course, but her revolutionary fervor was not dampened, and she continued her political work among the people as a *responsavel*. When Titina attended the first party congress in Cassacá in 1964, she was lauded for her work in the south front. She had shown such exceptional leadership qualities that Cabral took a special interest in her, treating her like a daughter. A year later she returned to the Soviet Union, this time to Kiev, as co-leader with Carmen Pereira of a group of women—between fourteen and thirty years old—who had won scholarships to study nursing.

Back in Guinea, she went to the north front, where she set up a militia training camp, as assistant to the front commander. Later she was assigned to one of the most responsible positions in the liberated zones—political commissar for the whole north front. Since the north was the most strongly contested of the three war fronts it was the most challenging, and Titina seldom left, except to represent PAIGC at a conference, accompany Cabral or another leader on a foreign visit, or attend a meeting of the seventy-five-member Superior Council for the Fight, of which she was a member. Her militancy extended to the liberation of women, a question she made a central issue in all facets of her work.

In the meanwhile, Tia (aunt), as her mother Eva was affectionately called, had herself joined the struggle; the words of her daughter had not fallen on totally deaf ears. Throughout the war she helped in whatever way she could. Later, because of a heart condition, she left the liberated zones and went to Boké, where she continued to work for PAIGC.

Titina married a PAIGC militant and had two children, the eldest of whom died in the *mato* when a few years old. Distraught at the thought that the same fate might befall Eva, her youngest, she placed her in the care of Tia in Boké, where she would be beyond the reach of the war. The decision meant she seldom saw her daughter, so as she journeyed toward the border for Cabral's funeral, the pain of her mission was slightly alleviated by the rare opportunity to visit.

Francisca Pereira, who had been a close friend and comrade, recalled Titina with emotion, her voice breaking as she talked. "Titina symbolized the kind of woman that PAIGC is trying to produce. Strong enough to withstand even the kind of test that the north front presented, she was always able to find a solution to the most difficult problem. She had natural leadership qualities and the people responded to her because she was neither selfishly demanding nor authoritarian. Everybody loved her. Everybody. That is why we were all crying when we heard that she had been killed. She was always willing to sacrifice herself for the struggle and that is how she died. She was someone formed by the revolution and who had attained the ideal of what the Guinea-Bissau woman should be."

Many women in Guinea-Bissau have been formed by the revolution, including Francisca herself. She had been a political commissar in the north before acting as the PAIGC representative to the Pan African Women's Organization in Algeria, where she was when the war ended. There was also Carmen Pereira,* one of the top leaders of the party and the political commissar for the south front, and Teodora Gomes, regional political commissar in the south. These women had joined PAIGC as young adults: Francisca and Teodora were sixteen or seventeen, Carmen slightly older. They were joined by women like Ule Bioja, Ana Maria Gomes, and Fina Crato, only ten or eleven when they joined the struggle. They came straight out of their villages, with no formal schooling, and grew up in the revolution, later holding positions of responsibility and leadership. Ana Maria was a political commissar for a sector of the north, Ule Bioja a regional health *responsavel* in the south, and Fina Crato a film maker working in the Department of Information.

On an absolute scale, the number of women cadres was abysmally small. However, in light of the fact that no women had previously worked on an equal footing with Guinean men, the number was not unimpressive. And PAIGC was constantly looking to improve its performance in this regard. Responding to a question about the role of women at an informal meeting in New York shortly before his death, Cabral said,

> Yes, we have made great achievements, but not enough. We are very far from what we want to do, but this is not a problem that can be solved by Cabral signing a decree. It is all part of the process of transformation, of change in the material conditions of the

---

*Francisca and Carmen Pereira are not relatives. Names such as Pereira, Cabral, and Gomes are very common in Guinea-Bissau. Many Guineans, particularly those from the towns, have Portuguese surnames. This is mainly due to an early custom whereby Africans were given the names of their Portuguese masters. It does not necessarily indicate mulatto background, although this was a factor in the towns.

existence of our people, but also in the minds of the women, because sometimes the greatest difficulty is not only in the men but in the women too. We have a big problem with our nurses, because we trained about 300 [women] nurses—but [some of them] married, they [had] children and for them it's finished.[1]

"Women cadres work harder than men cadres," another PAIGC leader said to me with a troubled air. "They have to do the work they are responsible for, like the men. But they also have to work with women, to encourage them to join the struggle and to make them understand that they can have equal rights. The shortage of women cadres is a big problem."

The lack of women cadres was starkly brought home to me at a ceremony at a military base in the south in May 1974, when the first five ambassadors to the country presented their credentials to President Luiz Cabral. I felt totally surrounded by men— soldiers, *responsavels*, members of the government. The only women present among the thirty to thirty-five male cadres were Carmen Pereira, Teodora Gomes, and Lucette Andrade, the director of the Department of Information.

While the event provided confirmation of the length of time it takes to involve women on an equal basis with men, reminders were everywhere of the seriousness and commitment with which PAIGC confronted this problem. Women were being encouraged to take on a more active and positive role in the revolution and had responded by demanding that they be allowed to take their rightful place in the political life of the country.

At the time of my visit a few women had risen to high-ranking posts. Two of the seventy-five members of the Superior Council for the Fight were women—Carmen Pereira and Francisca Pereira; a third had been Titina Silá. One of the twenty-five members of the Executive Council was a woman: Carmen. Two of the fifteen-member State Council were women: Carmen and Chica Vaz. Carmen was also elected vice president of the recently constituted National Assembly. But none of the newly appointed commissioners were women.

I asked Teodora why there were not more women on these bodies. "It would be tokenism if there were *more* members," she replied without hesitation. "We have to face the reality of our society, and in light of the reality this number is not small and it is certainly not tokenism. If we wanted to, we could put more women on this council or that, but it would be pretending that we have come further than we have. It is a slow process, this emancipation of women. And members of the Superior Council for the Fight, for example, have to work hard and have to attend meetings regularly. This means a lot of traveling. We do not have enough women cadres who can spare the time. We need them to work inside the country. We need them to help develop new cadres."

Carmen, Teodora, and Francisca represented a vanguard for the younger generation which was growing up in the revolution and taking on positions of responsibility at an ever-increasing rate. "The older women have shown us the way," Fina said to me. "We have great respect for what they have done." They had, through their work, been able to demonstrate that women could enter fields of work traditionally reserved for men and also the new areas which might automatically have become "men's work" had women been content to follow uncritically patterns of history in Guinea and elsewhere in Africa.

The crucial role played by women in the fight was apparent even to the strategists of the colonial army. The very presence of Carmen Pereira in the liberated zone provoked the Portuguese to design a special strategy for her elimination. They spent six weeks bombing the area around Donka, her base, and when she moved to another area, they shifted their bombing targets. During those six weeks in the late 1960s, she seemed to spend more time in trenches than anywhere else, unless it was *en marche* to yet another adjacent area in the hope of throwing the bombers off her trail. But she never fled her region or took refuge in Conakry. Such was the courage of this militant. And it paid off in the end, when the bombing halted as suddenly as it began, and she returned to her work, undefeated.

To look at Carmen and watch her among comrades, it was hard to believe she was such a dangerous militant. But as time passed I came to observe a few of the different sides of Carmen: the leader, sitting in front of her hut, quietly and patiently explaining a course of action to three young militants; the speechmaker, addressing a crowd of one thousand people in fiery tones; the comrade, joking and teasing with the cadres over whom she ostensibly had authority, the teasing as much at her own expense as at theirs. Her hair was braided into a number of points that stopped just short of her shoulders, but which invariably stuck out below one of those patterned woolen hats that had become the mark of PAIGC militants.* In fact, she had become so identified with the head covering that when I wanted to take her photograph she laughed, touching her bare head, and, with a look of mock embarrassment, joked: "Oh, but I am not wearing my *cap!* How can I possibly be photographed?" The photograph did not show her hat, but it did capture the hint of a smile and gentle expression which often played about her face.

What impressed the visitor too about Carmen was the ease with which she worked in the liberated zone and accepted the rigorous life it offered. Perhaps because she was a woman, she had won the special respect of the peasants for the way she traveled constantly around the region, investigating problem areas, exhorting people to further efforts for the revolution, organizing the myriad aspects of the social reconstruction program; and no less for the way she was in and out of the trenches with them, risking the bombs without ever flinching or changing expression. Donka had been her home for eight years, a "home" that moved at least twice a year to lessen the chance of detection by the Portuguese army. Her reed-matting hut contained only a few personal items. And in a small clearing next to the hut was what she laughingly called her "office." Its furnishings consisted of a table of rough-cut poles and four canvas chairs, all of which were built so low that the heads of those sitting round seemed to peer just above the table top.

There were years when she hardly left the liberated zones at all, others when she went on numerous missions abroad, accompanying Cabral or attending conferences, and always returning as quickly as possible to continue her work as political

---

*Many militants, following the example of Amilcar Cabral, had adopted the habit of wearing the blue, green, or brown woolen caps from a number of ethnic groups in Guinea-Bissau and Senegal, who traditionally wore them regardless of heat or rain.

commissar of the south front and member of the movement's most important decision-making bodies. Nonetheless, these episodic sojourns in the big cities—with such comforts as running water, hot showers, sanitation, abundance and variety of food, the possibility of shedding guerrilla uniforms and donning attractive West African or European dress, the pleasure of traveling by car—must have been unsettling. Yet Carmen slipped so easily back into the spare life of the *mato* that one would have thought she had been born to it, or at least had grown up in a peasant village. But her mulatto complexion and fluency in Portuguese and French hinted at her background: Carmen had grown up in Bissau, the daughter of one of the few indigenous Guinean lawyers. As her family had acquired a fair amount of status in the small town, a status her father took seriously, she and her three sisters were sent to school up to the fourth grade. Then their schooling stopped. Carmen's father did not want them to attend the secondary school in Bissau where students were equipped only to join the civil service. Such an occupation did not befit his daughters, he thought, preferring instead that they spend the next few years engaged in such ladylike activities as embroidery and sewing, and waiting for suitable husbands. He got his wish. Carmen married a man who appeared to be satisfactory and, in the following few years, gave birth to two sons and a daughter.

While she was pregnant with her third child, the "suitable" son-in-law joined PAIGC. It was 1961.

"One day I noticed my husband and two of his friends up to something unusual," Carmen recalled. "They had papers and these they hid in the house. But I thought I had a right to know what my husband was doing, so I found the hiding place and looked at the papers. They were documents about the PAIGC, a photo of Cabral, and a drawing of the flag."[2]

She was reproached by her husband for going into his belongings. But Carmen was not one to play the submissive wife. She retorted that he should have told her about the party in the first place and not left her out.

The next few months saw a lull in Portuguese repression. Then the secret police, responding to an escalation of the guerrilla war and a corresponding increase of underground activity in Bissau, conducted massive raids and dawn swoops throughout the area. Although hundreds of people were arrested, Carmen's husband left the country just in time, and she followed his example in short order. Gathering her three children, the youngest just a few months old, she set off for Senegal. The move was the beginning of her total commitment to the liberation struggle. "Although my life was not unpleasant, I could see the sufferings of my compatriots around me," Carmen said.[3] "I saw what the Portuguese did in my country: wealth for a few, with extreme poverty for the great majority. I saw them putting my Guinean brothers and sisters in prison for the smallest protest, and I realized that this life was not a good one."[4] She could not accept this with complacency. "Eventually I was drawn into the revolution. I had felt myself gravitating toward revolt, but the question for me had been how to contribute to the fight like a man."[5]

Any doubts she might have carried with her as she traveled toward Senegal soon dissolved. "On the way we passed by a concentration camp in Tite and saw prisoners being treated very badly by the Portuguese. Some had been so badly tortured they were bloody and lying on the ground, unable to get up. This confirmed my decision to go and join the Party."[6]

In Senegal she met Amilcar Cabral, who encouraged her to work full time for the party. She went to Ziguinchor, a town near the country's northern border, where the party had established a rather tenuous base. The president of Senegal initially looked upon the movement with a great deal of ambivalence, making life awkward for PAIGC militants in his country and arresting some of them, as well as preventing even medical supplies from crossing the border. Carmen, twenty-one at the time, threw all her energy into her work in Ziguinchor. She ran the small party house, always overcrowded with people moving to and fro across the border. "The movement was so poor then, and we all offered whatever help we could. I prepared meals for them, took in sewing, and treated our wounded brought in from the Guinea war zones across the frontier. We had no money for hospital bills in those days."[7] At the same time she looked after her own children who lived with her in the house.

In 1963 Carmen was offered a scholarship to the Soviet Union to study nursing for ten months. Leaving her children in the care of people at the house, she departed for Moscow and her first chance to further her education and acquire a skill that would be of more substantial use to the armed struggle. Two years later she went again to the Soviet Union with Titina Silá. On her return, the party posted her to the interior, where she was to remain—except for her brief diplomatic visits abroad—until the war ended in 1974. The first few months of the transition were not easy. Growing up in the relative comfort of Bissau had not equipped her for the rigorous life of the forest. "I had my own problems in the beginning," Carmen remembered. "I couldn't march for more than a few hours and I didn't know the village people. I needed about three months to orientate myself, to adjust to the life here."[8]

For the first year she worked as a health *responsavel* in the south, where she opened the first hospital in the liberated zones. In 1967 she was appointed political commissar for the south front, one of the most taxing positions in the revolution. "At that time many people thought a woman couldn't carry out a responsibility like that. My work required a lot of travelling, and walking was the only way. Many ambushes were set up by the colonialists. I was responsible for the political mobilization of all people—men and women—in that region."[9] With her children in PAIGC boarding schools, she could devote all her time to her work. Within the first few months of her new task, she had covered the whole of the front on foot. "My only companions were men because we had so few women [cadres] at that time," she said, adding that the men treated her with respect. "I think their attitude under these circumstances would always have depended upon my own behavior. I gave and took respect."[10]

Her work in the revolution contributed to a profound personal development. "Before I joined the struggle I was very timid and didn't speak much. I couldn't be among people too long because I was shy. And I was very afraid when seeing people with guns. Now I don't hesitate to talk and have learned to use a gun myself." Noting that this change was due to the great influence Amilcar Cabral had had on her life, his books, lectures, and conversations, she concluded: "I have learned that the first thing one must have is political determination. To win the people's respect and confidence it is necessary to be disciplined and serious about one's responsibilities. It is especially important to follow every directive and line of the Party. With the people's respect and confidence one can work without too many difficulties."[11]

Although she was trained to handle weapons, Carmen, unlike other cadres, men and women, chose not to carry them herself. Never far from her was a member of the army, rifle slung over his back, and when she was on a march, a group of armed militants would always escort her.

Not so Teodora Gomes. She seemed proud to be armed; her revolver and holster were always strapped to her waist. "I was the best shot in my class," she once proclaimed with a self-satisfied grin. Teodora's manner then, as always, was totally in keeping with her forceful verve for life that allowed nothing in half measure. Her generosity, her anger, her laughter, her defense of those women in a less fortunate situation than herself, her demand that she be taken seriously by those around her, all this she projected strongly. Many were the times I saw her burst into infuriated shouts at someone who was behaving in a less than correct manner. I remember on one occasion, when a male cadre criticized me for being withdrawn, she flew to my defense and attacked him for his inhospitable comments—only after she told me that I needed to rest. From my hut I heard her bellowing at him; he hardly ventured a response. The next day, though, she looked on like a proud older sister, all smiles, when the militant and I hugged each other good-by, the rift healed. On another occasion, a militant, seeing me for the first time, asked her in sexist tones, "And *who* is *that*?" "*That*," she immediately responded, bringing herself up to her ample full stature, "is my friend!" He made no further comment. In fact, most men spoke to her and of her with respect and affection: "Ah, Teodora, she has such a big heart." Or, referring to her hard work and sound political sense, they would say: "Ah, Teodora—it is easy to see that her work is political." Other men, though, who were more easily threatened by strong women, were more cautious in their comments.

During the three weeks I was with her, Teodora learned more

English than I did Creole (although I heard it constantly all around me). She was always asking the English for this word or that, wrestling with the difference in pronunciation between such fundamental verbs as "work" and "walk," puzzling over the similarity in sound of "two" and "shoe." Her eagerness to learn as much English as possible in the short time available was one indication of the gusto with which she approached all challenges. In this case, her smattering of English represented the beginning of her tenth language. She was fluent in most of the other nine—four European, Creole, and four indigenous African languages.

Unlike Carmen, who grew up in the rather rarefied atmosphere of the Bissau elite, divorced from the rural areas and the culture of the people, Teodora grew up in small towns that dotted the south, towns scarcely larger than the villages which surrounded them, where her father, an *assimilado*, ran his small business concerns. The ethnic make-up of her family traversed five animist groups. Unlike many *assimilados*, Teodora's father was not mulatto and her mother's parents were peasants.

Teodora had observed the life of the women around her and resolved somehow to escape from the mold.

"I knew that women were dominated," she told me. "But the way to free ourselves from that domination? This I did not know and couldn't conceive. I saw how women lived in misery, struggling to survive. They had to contend with a lot of problems from their husbands. But what could we do at the time? What the men wanted was for the women to stay at home. They had control over all the money. If they chose to give some to their wives, they gave it. If not, they didn't. We could do nothing, because we were oppressed."

While Teodora was taking all this in, her parents were telling her a woman's main goal in life should be to get married. But the thought of marriage was not a happy one: "To me it meant that I would enter a life of hardship, but one that could not be avoided. There was no alternative." Except through education: "In this way I could defend myself. I realized that the more ignorant a woman was, the more she was dominated. The domination of women is the result of economic domination."

Her quest for education began at an early age. While it was taken for granted that the boys in her family went to school, the presumption did not extend to girls. So she began to pester her father. "Why do you want to learn to write?" he would chastise her. "You just want to write love letters." But he finally succumbed to his daughter's persistence, and when she was eight employed a tutor to come to his home and teach Teodora and her younger sister, Juliana. Six years later, they had only passed through second grade; the teacher was incompetent. When Teodora complained each year, her father ignored her. She'd got what she wanted, what more did she expect? Eventually he gave in and sent her to a missionary school, where she completed two more grades in as many years. No sooner had she got this far than her teacher was arrested for cooperating with PAIGC, and her schooling came to an abrupt end. But the year was 1962, and events were occurring which began to take precedence in her life.

First, her father was mobilized by PAIGC, the culmination of a process that had begun years before. When he returned from Lisbon without having completed his studies in construction engineering, and with only a small sum as seed money, he developed a number of moneymaking enterprises: building houses on speculation and then selling them at a large profit; buying large tracts of land and growing rice for export; buying boats to transport the rice; growing sugar cane and exporting that. At the height of his success, he had purchased his own pier to handle his boats and employed a large number of workers. But several features of the colonial situation combined to undermine his endeavors. The first—widespread poverty—fed right into an African custom which required wealthier members of a family to support less fortunate relatives. "And did we have a big family!" Teodora laughed.

Then, despite his diminishing wealth, her father felt committed to provide benefits which Lisbon never saw fit to extend to workers in its "overseas provinces," and few other employers even contemplated. The Portuguese did not and there were few Guineans in his position. "My father was a generous man," Teodora reminisced. "He helped his workers pay their taxes. He supplied them with food, medical services, and he established a school for his workers' children."

Finally, there were the heavy Portuguese taxes: all facets of his business and property were taxed by the administration. There were the arbitrary expenses too—such as the 5,000 escudos (about $175) he had to pay to replace his lost identity card—so that by the time he was mobilized at the beginning of the war he was virtually bankrupt.

Her father never said a word to his daughters about the war or his membership in PAIGC, but it did not take long for the curious sixteen-year-old to see that something out of the ordinary was happening.

"I remember the night I first noticed that something unusual was going on. I was at home and a large group of people gathered outside. In the morning they were gone. I asked who they were, but no one would talk about it and this only increased my interest. More and more incidents occurred which puzzled me; I went inside a few days later to listen to the news as always, and the radio was gone. Then a number of Portuguese soldiers arrived in our town, looking for guerrillas in the forest, and demanded to know where they were. Nobody told them anything. The people I saw that first night returned to our house soon afterward and my father gave them food and clothing. I asked where the food was going, and again nobody would tell me, but by then I knew it was for the guerrillas.

"Knowing that my father would refuse to answer my questions, I began to plague one of his workers. Eventually he agreed to talk about it and take me to visit a camp. I was very excited. Portuguese propaganda had been maintaining that the guerrillas were just like monkeys, covered with hair! I was curious to see them!"

One night, when her father was asleep, they went to the guerrilla camp. The insurgents welcomed her as a friend, and talked about the struggle and the mobilization for two hours. She listened avidly, taking in all that was said, and stared about her, wide-eyed. "Yes, they were a bit hairy because they had beards, but that was all!"

It was a turning point in her life. A few months later, in 1963, the war began in earnest. (The comrade who had taken her to the camp joined the guerrilla army and was later killed in combat.) But Teodora was still answerable to her father and could not actually get involved until a brutal incident jolted the entire household. The Portuguese soldiers rounded up ten well-known people in her town, all supporters of PAIGC, and shot them to death in full view of the townspeople. This attempt to terrorize the population, and nip the insurrection in the bud, had precisely the opposite effect. "That day my whole family decided to join the guerrillas and we went to live in the forest," Teodora said.

Later that same year, she was chosen to study youth organization in the Soviet Union. When she returned twelve months later, she worked in the PAIGC hospital in Boké where there was a dire shortage of nurses. Then it was back to the Soviet Union a year later, this time for four years, to study child psychology. When Teodora came home for good, she was assigned to work as a regional political commissar in the Balana-Quitafine region of the south, and, like Carmen, rarely left her post until the end of the war.

But her sense of self and what she would do in the future had been irrevocably changed. At the time Teodora joined PAIGC she thought her life was heading inevitably toward marriage. In the crucible of the revolution, however, she became a person in her own right. When she spoke of women joining PAIGC because they had found a way they could fight for their own liberation, she was talking as much for herself as for a peasant woman. "We did not know how to fight together to change our lives as women. This we have now learned through PAIGC." In fact, Teodora had never married.

The supportive climate offered by the party was perhaps the determining factor in the recruitment of Francisca Pereira, a self-reliant fighter since childhood. She made the defense of women a principal component of all her work for the revolution. Always on guard against male supremacist attitudes, she presented a prickly exterior to male comrades whose sensitivity to the issue left much to be desired. And this was hardly mitigated by her expressed conviction that those Guinean women who had taken up the issue for their liberation were in fact more politically advanced than many of their male counterparts.

When Francisca defended women, she was likely to show anger, her forehead creasing into a slight frown and her face shining as she talked. But the anger was cool, and so contained that she became extremely articulate. It was a demeanor with which not a few male cadres became familiar; from the time she joined PAIGC Francisca fought her way to equality with the comrades working with her. As one of the top leaders in the party, she directed those energies on behalf of younger women who, sometimes tentatively, were beginning to take their place in the revolution. A case came to her attention of a young woman who had been studying in a socialist country in Europe when she became pregnant as a result of a relationship with a male student. The first response from PAIGC headquarters had been to recall her, despite the fact that it would have meant the end of her studies and possibly the loss of a cadre. Francisca took up the issue immediately, criticizing this attitude and the double standard implicit in it. "If she comes home, then he comes home!" she protested, in order to underscore the inherent unfairness. She won. The young woman remained to complete her studies.

Francisca's staunch belief in the need for all women to be independent from men can be traced back to the view of the world she acquired as a child. "I watched my mother. I watched her struggle through great difficulties just because she was a woman. I decided from a very early age that I would always be responsible for myself, and not have to rely on a man for anything." So she set about ensuring that she would be economically independent and, from the age of thirteen, was already making a bit of money for herself by sewing. Later, she was able to integrate these perceptions into her political views. "Nothing is better than if women can become economically independent. We can talk about discrimination against women and about domination by men because the woman does not have economic independence, because she depends on her husband."[12]

It was not only economic self-sufficiency she resolved to maintain in her personal life. She was by nature independent, and not about to let others control her life, even when according to custom she should have been obedient. Consequently, numerous acts of defiance dotted her formative years: by age sixteen she had left her uncle's house and the secondary school in Bissau because she did not like her aunt; she walked out of another uncle's home in Conakry when he refused to allow her to marry the man of her choice; she packed her bags and left her husband when the marriage did not work out.

Although her family was *assimilado*, she grew up in Bolama in relative poverty. Her father had died a few years after her birth and the small family income vanished with him. The situation began to ease only when her mother remarried some years later. In the interim, the money problems represented a barrier to the child's schooling, a stumbling block all the more frustrating because the family, unlike most others, held that both girls and boys should be educated. Fortunately for her, an uncle agreed to pay for her education and she began her schooling in a small town to which they had moved after her father's death. She remembers the next years as happy ones. She worked hard and was liked by the teachers. All this changed abruptly, however, when her family returned to Bolama as she was about to enter third grade. Her mother took her to the Portuguese school to enroll her, only to discover that they would not admit the child without a birth certificate. Francisca's was nowhere to be found. "My mother didn't know anything about my father's affairs, where he kept his papers, where he kept his money. Typical of Africa, where the woman is the last person to know anything about her husband." All efforts to find the precious document were in vain. In the end she was enrolled at a missionary school, but only after she had agreed to become a Catholic. She did not like this at all. "My mother was a Christian, which is why I am called Francisca. But I didn't believe. I now had to take communion and go to church every single day! I hated it." But what she hated even more was the racism at the school. Incidents happened regularly which caused her great distress. For instance, she remembered that "One day a white pupil began fighting with an African pupil. The priest came and separated them and then gave the African child such a vicious beating. It wasn't even his fault. He ran home crying. Of course his parents could do nothing as there was no justice in cases like this. It was this kind of discrimination that created a lot of antagonism against both religion and whites."

When Francisca had completed fourth grade, she went to Bissau to continue her studies at the secondary school. As was the custom, relatives provided her with board and lodging in return for domestic work, virtually the only way that children from outside Bissau could attend secondary school. But often they were treated like servants, as Francisca herself was to discover: "My aunt treated me so badly that I ran away and returned to my mother. My schooling stopped there. Mine was not an unusual case."

Not long afterward, a different uncle, who had recently married in Conakry, invited her to live in his household. Francisca's acceptance of the offer proved to be a critical decision in her life. Arriving in Conakry in 1957, one year before independence, she witnessed a period of political ferment as Sekou Touré, the president-to-be, maneuvered to thwart France's desire for a neo-colony. The energetic debates of the time struck a responsive chord in the young visitor. Supporting the independence stand, Francisca began gravitating toward politics herself—and to the house where PAIGC had established its headquarters and school in 1959. There, Amilcar Cabral was quick to spot her talent. He saw in her the makings of a strong leader and, with few women in the party at that stage, personally encouraged her to take an active role.

In the meanwhile her life in Conakry had been unhappy. Her aunt resented her presence and treated her unkindly. The climax came when she wanted to marry: "My uncle opposed it, so I just said 'ciao' and left them." Her happiness in her married circumstances was short-lived, however; when her husband began to maltreat her she took her infant daughter and left him too.

Francisca was as decisive in getting into situations as she was in getting out of them. When the chance of working for the liberation of her country presented itself, she jumped at it. By the age of seventeen, she was living in the PAIGC house and working full time for the party. She was also growing into an extremely attractive young woman. Carrying herself with an ease and confidence which belied her teenage years, she had a ready, winning smile which spread wide across her face and showed a large gap between her teeth. Her face glowed whenever she expressed feelings of particular friendship. But being the only woman living in the PAIGC house at the time proved problematic. In fact, it was a battle which she fought without ever compromising, to make the young militants around her treat her with respect and not as a young woman there for their pleasure. "In the beginning they treated me as inferior," Francisca recalled. "Even those with whom I had equal responsibility would keep thinking that whatever a woman does cannot be as good as they do. 'Huh! she's just a woman,' they would think. It is a continual fight even now. However, things have changed enormously since those early days. But this does not mean that the problem has disappeared. Men need to be polished! I am still having to fight with my comrades about these attitudes. Toward me, yes, but more so in their treatment of younger women. Cabral helped women a lot over these issues. Now our women have become even more aware than the men, and women are carrying on their own struggle for liberation."

In 1965 Francisca joined the group of young women led by Titina Silá and Carmen Pereira and went to study nursing in the Soviet Union for one year. During the course she and Titina became very close friends, sharing similar attitudes toward life and a special aversion to the Moscow winter. When they returned, they were both assigned work in the north front as health *responsavels*. Much later Francisca represented PAIGC at the Pan African Women's Congress and was based in Algeria until the end of the war, returning regularly with Carmen and Titina, to carry out her responsibilities as one of the three women members of the Superior Council for the Fight. Her quick rise to leadership in the party, rather than setting her apart, served to intensify the common cause she felt with women comrades. Francisca regarded leadership not as an end in itself, but as a facet of the general independence that all women must fight for: "It is not enough to fight for political independence, if we are not at the same time fighting for personal independence."

Carmen, Teodora, and Francisca are examples of the transformation taking place in Guinea-Bissau. They are not tokens; each has fought her own way to a position of equality with men. While their *assimilado* background had given them a relatively privileged position, as compared with peasant women, they still had to overcome severe disavantages vis-à-vis men in terms of education. And while they were not as bound by the kind of culture which so severely circumscribed their peasant sisters, they still had to reverse tradition in order to exercise authority.

But the revolution was a great equalizer in many other respects, not the least being the way in which it gave peasant women some upward mobility even as women from *assimilado* backgrounds were finding their roots again. Women participated in all facets of work for the revolution, including education, information, and, of course, politics. They played a particularly strong role in health. Although PAIGC began the war with no more than three male nurses, by its end there were over ten qualified Guinean doctors (one woman) and an equal number of medical assistants, some of whom were women. (These were supplemented by doctors from friendly countries, Cuba in particular.) Of the five hundred nurses who were working by the end of the war, more than half were women. And while not all of these had gone through the full nurses' training course, all did have sufficient preparation to work effectively in the health service, whether at a health post, on a health brigade, or in a hospital.

One of the medical assistants was Teodora's sister, Juliana Gomes, head of Guerra Mendes Hospital in Tombali, in the south's Catio region. My itinerary in the south included a visit to the hospital, where I stayed overnight. Juliana was two years younger than Teodora and very different in temperament, her expansive patience a contrast to Teodora's energetic and dynamic nature. The personalities seemed to match their choice of work.

Juliana was born in Fulacunda, a small town in the south where her father was working at the time. Her overriding passion as a child and young teenager had been that someday she would work in the health field, nursing being the highest position she could imagine. It took a revolution, however, for such a dream to enter the realm of the possible in Guinea-Bissau. After Juliana had joined the liberation movement she was given a scholarship to study in the Soviet Union. She left Guinea equipped with a fourth-grade education and returned four years later, trained as a medical assistant, possessing more skills than the nurses who had inhabited her early dreams.

In fact, she had many of the skills of a doctor, the difference lying primarily in her less extensive diagnostic and surgical training. This more limited training was due in part to starting with a fourth-grade education, in part to expediency on the part of the party: cadres could not go away for training for indefinite periods when people with a certain modicum of skill were required on the scene of the revolution. Besides, the party knew the gap in her expertise would not be of immediate consequence, since most of the cases she would encounter would likely be diseases endemic to the country, arising from social conditions and not requiring surgery. Most importantly, her training gave her sufficient expertise to run a hospital such as Guerra Mendes, and provided a highly trained cadre to the revolution.

When she returned from her studies in 1969, Juliana first worked at Solidarity Hospital in Boké for one year and then went into the interior, to a hospital in Cubucare. She had not been there long when the Portuguese selected the area as a prime bombing target and it became essential to have a fully trained doctor on hand. So Juliana exchanged posts with the head of Guerra Mendes. "I never believed as a child that my dreams could possibly come true," she told me. "Maybe when the war is over, I'll be able to continue my studies and become a full doctor."

Guerra Mendes Hospital was a typical *mato* hospital. Camouflaged in the forest, the "wards" were built from thatch and palm fronds. There were about four beds to each hut, covered in pale green sheets. In the late afternoon, a four-year-old girl with a high fever was brought to the hospital by her parents. They had walked a number of miles to get there and now stood next to Juliana as she examined their daughter and quickly diagnosed malaria—a chronic complaint. After giving the child an injection of quinine, Juliana handed the parents a box of phials of more quinine, explaining that they should take these to a health post near their village so that the child could be treated each day without having to walk for miles.

A few days later I spent two nights at Cameconde Hospital in the region of Cubisseco. The main purpose for this visit was to meet Ule Bioja, the regional health *responsavel*. Although based at the hospital, she was regularly away in the villages. The work of a health *responsavel* was essentially political and educational. It involved educating the population about hygiene and preventive medicine and encouraging them to use health services which at first they had viewed with suspicion. The political significance of all this was simply a variation of PAIGC's mobilizing theme— that national independence demanded people let go of destructive customs, including the dependence on traditional medicine. For the *responsavel* it meant traveling constantly between villages, from one sector to another, often for days at a time, covering the whole region to coordinate the work of the health brigades and check on the problems of each area.

One morning at Cameconde we sat on a makeshift bench outside one of the carefully constructed huts that served as a ward, and Ule talked about her life. She was reserved and quiet spoken, but also relaxed. As she spoke, I recognized that quality of self-possession I had grown accustomed to finding in the women cadres I met.

A Balanta, Ule was eleven when mobilizers first came to the village on Como Island where she was born. She was not aware of anything unusual. "In the beginning only a few adults were mobilized. The children were only told what was going on once the whole village was supporting PAIGC. I suspected nothing."

She was thirteen when the Portuguese launched their massive— and ultimately unsuccessful—attack against the islanders. "Many people went into the forest, under the protection of PAIGC, and helped to fight off the *Tuga*," Ule recalled. As the siege wore on, she joined the work in support of the guerrillas. "I helped the women cook for the guerrillas. At the same time we did some gymnastics training, not full military training. There was a serious lack of guns and ammunition and these tended to be used by the men. I was young, but I remember at least one woman who had a gun and fought with the men."

During this period, Ule lived in the forest. Then she was evacuated from the island with a group of young people and taken to the mainland. But she never had a chance to settle down. The party soon sent her to Ghana for three months to begin training as a nurse. A few months later, at the age of fifteen, she joined Carmen and Titina's group to study nursing in the Soviet Union. The course there had been specially designed to accommodate people who had had no formal schooling. In fact, Ule began to learn to read and write only when she returned to Guinea-Bissau; the hospital where she first worked, like all PAIGC hospitals, was attached to a school for the workers. She had completed fourth grade by the time I met her.

While Ule was growing up she was conscious of how women were oppressed. "My mother was a classic example. She could not sit with the men or speak with other men in front of my father. All she could do was pound rice, cook, wash all my father's and her children's clothes. She had to attend to all his needs. She had no choice. But I have seen a great change in her. She responded very strongly to what the mobilizers were saying about the need for women to be equal. Now she attends meetings and does things independently. It was she who encouraged me to join the party and to study. She is very supportive of my work.

"Before mobilization I thought my life would be just like my mother's and my grandmother's. I could not visualize anything else. I was very hopeful when I heard what the party was saying about the need for women to take part equally in the struggle. I understand now clearly that women must be equal with men, but we have to fight for that equality. The conditions for women have been very bad, so it's going to take a long time. PAIGC stresses that women must be as free as men and I believe that in the future this will happen. There is such a difference between living under Portuguese colonialism and with the party's view of society. Now women can have the same responsibility as men. Now men must hear the women's voice."

Ule had two children. At the time of my visit, the older one was one and a half years old, the younger seventeen days. Since her husband was away, studying in the German Democratic Republic, I asked her how she managed to look after her new baby and work at the same time. She responded by telling me that PAIGC suggests pregnant women work only up to their seventh month, and take off a few months after the birth to care for their child. Those who wished to work longer before the birth or begin again sooner could do so. As for herself, she said, "I did not stop working until the day my child was born. Even in the last month I was attending meetings away from the hospital. I am back at work already."

And did having a child make it more difficult to travel long distances now? "When I have to do that, I carry my child with me," she responded with a shrug of her shoulders. She did not consider this a "problem" that needed solving. Her older child was with her husband's parents and, although they lived in the same region, it was still some distance away. "I have to cross two broad rivers to get there," Ule continued. "If I have work to do in the area, I can go and visit him, but this does not happen too often. I cannot let my child interfere with my work. The struggle must come first now. He is being well looked after, so I don't have to worry."

Encouraging women to train as nurses was not only a health expedient; for young peasant women it represented a basis for acceptance as equals. For some women nursing became a stepping stone to greater responsibility and leadership in the movement.

Ana Maria Gomes was another example of a woman who took this route out of obscurity and ignorance. Like all the women in her poor Mandjak village, she received a traditional education which prepared her for an adulthood of arduous work in production and in the home. By the age of six she had already learned the time-consuming and backbreaking task of pounding rice. She helped to look after the younger children, wash clothes in the river, collect water from the well; she learned to work the land, and was soon balancing large bundles on her head as she walked the long distances from one place to another.

Still, she was a sickly child, prone to regular bouts of fever, cold shivers, and attacks of vomiting. The nearest health station in her area of the south was a six-hour march away, and the Portuguese fees for treatment were beyond what her parents could pay. So for Ana Maria and the people of her village, the health post was as good as nonexistent. There was no question of her attending school either. It was too expensive and far away for even the boys of her village.

A predictable life pattern was established from a young age: soon after puberty she would have to marry a man chosen by her father, then move to her husband's village and, if she survived childbirth, bear many of his children, some of which, with the high mortality rate, could be expected to die young. Such was her mother's life and Ana Maria could imagine no other.

Ana Maria was ten years old when she noticed that unaccountable things were happening in her village. For instance, there was her mother, cooking mounds of rice and palm oil—far too much for their family, large though it was. When she asked, her mother would brush her aside: "Oh, it's nothing. It's nothing. Don't worry about it." She was even more puzzled by the strangers visiting their village, once unusual now almost a regular practice. Eventually, even though the adults tended to stop in midsentence when the children joined them, Ana Maria began to pick up a word here, another there. She learned that men were living in the forest, that they were talking about something called the "party," and that they were planning to make life better for the peasants.

The people of her village responded quickly to what the mobilizers were saying, at last seeing a way out of their oppressed existence. By the beginning of the war in 1963 many had joined PAIGC, some to fight in the guerrilla war, others to take on whatever tasks were needed to support it, such as transporting ammunition and other goods, acting as guides, cooking for the fighters. "We organized it," she told me, "so that different people took turns with the cooking and washing. This way everybody did a little extra and no one had the full burden."

At first Ana Maria did not understand much about what was being said regarding the need for women to participate equally with men. However, she did see how women were speaking out more and more at these meetings, standing up and expressing what was on their minds. Later, sitting with the women around the fire, she would listen to their talk about all the changes that were taking place. The excitement was infectious. In terms of her own life, she understood that she would be able to choose her own husband and saw how young women had joined PAIGC in the camps in order to escape forced marriages or to divorce men they had not wanted to marry in the first place.

Ana Maria was far from docile, even as a child. Bright and talkative, she was full of questions and eager to try the new things that brought excitement into her life. She was one of the first chosen to join a PAIGC camp established in 1964 specifically for girls.

"The camp was created so that girls could begin to participate in the struggle," she explained. "When boys wanted to join—and there were many—they just did it. One day they would be off, just like that. They were boys, it was easy. But for the girls? Oh, no. This was out of the question. Many parents were more comfortable about allowing their daughters to participate in the revolution if they knew they were being well cared for. But not all the parents. Some thought their daughters would be taken by force and so they quickly arranged a marriage for them, even if they were very young. Others thought: 'If the party takes my children, who will help me at home?' There were those who were afraid of the bombing and so would not let them go."

In cases where there was reluctance, PAIGC militants would talk patiently with the parents and encourage them to send their daughters, Ana Maria said, adding, "If a mother had only one daughter, though, they would not try to mobilize her, unless her mother wanted her to go."

When Ana Maria arrived at the camp, scarcely more than skin and bones, she had her first medical examination ever and discovered that she was a chronic malaria sufferer. After treatment she began to blossom into a healthy and very attractive teenager. With the other girls, about sixty of them, she started learning to read and write and to do semimilitary training. All the while, they had to be on constant alert for Portuguese bombers which were trying to rout the camp. No sooner had they established themselves in one area, when they had to move again to the next. Eventually, it became too dangerous to remain, and PAIGC decided to escort the girls out of the country for further training. It was a difficult journey from the north to the south and across the border to Guinea (Conakry). Only one-third of the country had been liberated at the time and they had to march through hostile territory, hiding both from the *Tuga* and the other so-called liberation movement, FLING.* On occasion they went without food for days. Never before had Ana Maria marched like this. But although she was exhausted, her still spindly legs hardly managing to carry her, she made it. It was her first of many lessons of endurance.

Subsequently, she joined twenty other young women, including Ule, who went to Ghana to begin training as nurses. The program was so badly organized by the Ghanaians, however, that after a few months they all returned to Conakry. She then went to the Soviet Union for the year's nursing training course.

When she returned to Guinea-Bissau she was stationed as a health *responsavel* in Mores sector. It was the first time she had been to the north, which, as the most contested area, was most steadily bombarded. Although Ana Maria was just sixteen then and her responsibilities extremely taxing, she worked as hard as any adult, displaying courage and determination. These qualities distinguished her as a promising leader and in 1970 she was chosen to participate in a seminar for cadres held by Amilcar Cabral in Conakry. There he told her that she was to be given a greater responsibility, that of political commissar for the sector of Sara, also in the north.

"Oh no," she replied, maybe only half in jest, "the work is too hard for me. I will collapse under the strain!"

"Oh, if you fall down," replied Cabral with mock nonchalance, "we'll just pick you up again so that you can go on."

Round this time she married a young military commander, and a year later became pregnant. From the beginning it was clear that it was going to be a difficult birth. The doctors felt she could not get special care in the *mato*, and so, with her child heavy inside her, she marched over the hilly terrain to the border with Senegal, and gave birth in Dakar.

---

*FLING, the Front for the Liberation of Guinea, was an organization based in Senegal whose aims were independence in the form of neocolonialism. They were never a serious threat to PAIGC, but at the beginning exerted their energies toward harrassing PAIGC rather than the Portuguese.

"I knew it was going to be difficult, but I did not anticipate that it would be as bad as it was," she recalled. "It was awful! I was ill for a month afterward." She also knew that had her life continued as she once imagined it she would have been one more young peasant woman who died in childbirth.

Eager to return to Guinea-Bissau, however, she left Dakar earlier than was wise, still weak, and carrying the added weight of her one-month-old daughter, tied to her back. Crossing the Farim River—the same river that claimed Titina—the guerrilla party heard the sound of a Portuguese patrol boat approaching. The women with children were told to get out of the *pirog* first and to start marching fast. Ana Maria stumbled along with the few other women, none of whom knew the way, and almost got lost.

Back in Sara she returned to her work immediately, her baby on her back. An important aspect of this work was the political education of women. "We can see what the party has done for our women," she said to me, "because now there are women *responsavels* in both the party and the government. This was never seen before. Women are everywhere in the life of our country.

"The women are very glad that their lives are changing. Now we understand that when the party talks about independence, there is another independence—not only national independence, but personal independence. This has opened a new road for us. A road to equality. We know it will take a long time, but we are working steadily so that things can change little by little. The women are very grateful for what the party has done for them. Thanks to it, we women know there is a way to free ourselves. I feel this particularly. I never, never knew anything about life beyond my village. My life has changed."

By the end of the war, with six years' experience behind her, Ana Maria had become a forceful, articulate, and vibrant woman. She was twenty-two years old, an impressive young leader in the party, and a long way from malaria and bare survival in a peasant village.

Although not in such numbers as in nursing, women could be found in all fields in the liberated zones in 1974. They were being trained as agronomists, working as teachers, and working with the party in such areas as information. About half of the schools I visited had women teachers on the staff, and two of those—one boarding school and the Pilot School—had women directors. As the comparative lack of education for girls was overcome, this would in turn lead to more women teachers in the future. In 1974 over one-third of the students going outside of Guinea-Bissau for further study—to socialist Europe, Cuba, and Africa—were women.

One of these students was Fina Crato, who began to work in the Department of Information upon her return from Cuba and Senegal.

I first met Fina in Conakry, when she came to my hotel with a young militant from PAIGC headquarters. She was to be my companion on my second trip to the interior, this time to the east. Fina was small and fairly thin, her youth accentuated by her short red cotton dress. Her thick hair was hidden under a floral scarf, loosely tied around her head, and looking as if it might fall off any minute. On her feet was a pair of the molded plastic sandals that many of the militants wore, a gift in bulk from one of the socialist countries, probably Cuba. What struck me most was her shyness. She sat next to me, not uttering a word, looking nervously down into her hands. She hardly ever raised her head and never once allowed her eyes to look directly at my face. She answered a stifled "yes" or "no" to my questions, and after she left I wondered how we were going to get along together. I was pleased to have the opportunity to travel with someone young, so that I could get a sense of that generation, but alas, it looked as if our communication would be limited.

When I arrived at the headquarters the following afternoon, ready for our drive down to Boké, I was startled to find a totally different Fina. Dressed in guerrilla uniform, she was with a group of young people, telling jokes and roaring with laughter. She waved in a friendly, self-confident way, smiling directly at me. The Fina of the day before had totally vanished, never to return for all the time I was with her, not even in the presence of top party leaders. Anxious about our initial lack of interpreter, she rushed over to Aristides Pereira, secretary-general of PAIGC and Cabral's successor, who was walking toward his office. "I'm in a fix!" she exclaimed, her jocular tone masking her anxiety.

"How can I travel with the journalist if I can't speak English?" "What, Fina," he replied with a twinkle in his eye, "you mean to say you can't use a *dictionary?*" She jumped at any chance to retell the story with gusto, laughing heartily each time. In fact, my more vivid memories of Guinea-Bissau include Fina, her hearty, chuckling laughter, and the fact that during the two weeks I spent with her, in Boké and in the east front, she seldom seemed to stop talking, the words coming out fast and staccato, like a machine gun. Always ready with an opinion, a comment, a joke, she was pleasure to be with, and through her I began to understand what it meant to grow up in the revolution, a generation behind Francisca, Teodora, and Carmen.

Fina's political awakening had been sudden. She was born in Catchanga in the south, where her father worked long hours in a Portuguese store, at abysmal wages. The family had a hard time making ends meet. They moved first to Catio, where Fina's father died: "We now lost the family income, which had not been very big in the first place. My mother worked to try and support the children by doing housework and washing clothes." And then they moved once or twice more before they decided to settle in Catum. Fina was eleven.

One morning she was sitting outside the house in the sun when she heard a drone in the distance getting louder and louder. She ran inside to her mother, shouting excitedly, "Mama! Mama! Planes are coming." "Oh, stop your nonsense," her mother shouted back, not breaking from her work, "You're always making up things." But a few minutes later, the planes could be seen approaching in the distance and the noise was unmistakable. All the villagers ran out of their houses into the open, filled with curiosity at this unexpected event. They had never seen planes so close before and stared up at the sky, smiling at each other and exclaiming, some even waving at the metal birds. Then the planes proceeded to disgorge their bombs on the upturned faces. One after another. They bombed nonstop for a few days.

It was the beginning of daily raids that were to last over a period of four or five months. Many people were killed at first, but the casualties diminished as the villagers began to adjust their lives around the raids. By five o'clock in the morning they were up, preparing food. By seven o'clock they were ready to leave the village, which was out in the open and highly visibly, to hide in the mangrove swamps, where they would remain the whole day, in water up their waists. The Portuguese then began to bomb before seven, this time using napalm.

Ten years later, Fina was able to recall the resourcefulness of the people with a chuckle. "The villagers were very inventive. They would take the empty napalm cannisters and make spoons and combs and such things!"

But her mother had had enough, and she decided to move to Como Island, an area already liberated by PAIGC, in 1964.* As luck would have it, the Portuguese began their historic siege just a few days after the Crato family had unpacked their small bundles. Fina was at a New Year's Eve party at one of the PAIGC bases when they heard a shot ring out. Some of the militants went to investigate and saw Portuguese soldiers landing at the port. They quickly relayed the news and the people were escorted back to the village. A few days later, the villagers all moved to the center of the island, as the Portuguese were landing their helicopters on the rice fields which ran around the edge of the island. For seventy-five days and nights the attack continued nonstop—from the air, from boats, and on the ground. Fina remembered, "When the bombs were dropped, my mother would lie on top of me to protect me, or she would hide me in the hollow of a *pilom* tree."

When PAIGC wanted to evacuate children, women, and old people, the women refused to go along, saying they would rather die than forsake their island. They played a key role in the

---

*The battle on Como Island was a decisive point in the escalation of the war and the refining of PAIGC'S military techniques. Cabral spoke of the battle as follows:

Being the first part of our national territory to be liberated by our forces, Como's reconquest became for the Portuguese at the beginning of 1964, a matter of basic and even vital necessity to their military and political strategy. . . .
   The battle of Como was a test for the Portuguese, but even more for ourselves. Indeed, it has helped us to make a better judgement of our own forces. We have learned about the capacity of our fighters and our people when confronted with the most difficult situations; about the political consciousness and fierce determination of the civilian population (men, women and children) in the liberated zones—now definitely liberated— not to fall again under Portuguese rule.[13]

counteroffensive. Some took up arms, others kept the provisions moving from the mainland to the island, including ammunition and food for the guerrillas. All continued production as best they could so that the population could be fed.

Fina worked alongside her mother during this period. "We worked hard during the attack, cooking and carrying ammunition for the fighters. We had to find ways to cook so that there would be no smoke. And when we pounded, we buried the *pilla* in a large hole to deaden the noise. But still the Portuguese managed to locate some of the villages and bomb them. There was one large Nalu village which they bombed heavily, killing the whole population. But we finally won and drove the Portuguese off the island for good."

Since Fina's birth, her mother resolved that her daughter would have a better chance in life than she had had. From her meager income she had scraped enough money together to send her to school. And so, despite all their moving, Fina had managed to complete a few grades before the war began and Como Island became a combat zone. Later, when PAIGC gave many of the young people on the island the opportunity to leave it for training, Fina was among those chosen to go. For the next three years she studied at the Pilot School. After that she went with three male comrades to study film making in Cuba for four years. Then it was on to Senegal. After spending a year in further training with the Senegalese Film Institute, Fina returned to Guinea-Bissau. She was waiting for a camera in order to begin filming in the liberated zones when the war ended.

Had Fina been able to get her hands on a camera prior to the ceasefire, her footage would have shown relatively few women carrying arms.

Women in all fields of work? No, not quite. Few women fought in combat. And I seldom saw women armed.

A consistent reply to my questions was that arming women was "not necessary." This view was in line with comments made by Cabral to a mass meeting early in the war. Although the speech might have been tempered in order to lessen the reaction of the peasants, Cabral said: "[We want our women] to administer our schools and clinics, to take an equal share in production and to go into combat against the Portuguese *when necessary.* . . . [They] will work in the villages . . . in the village militia. We want the women of our country to have guns in their hands."[14]

When necessary. If the goal of PAIGC is an equal society in every respect, I asked, how could something be considered necessary for men but not for women? The regular response was that Guinea-Bissau is a small country with a small population. They could rely on a proportionately smaller army than Mozambique, for instance, where vast territory had to be defended. Therefore Guinea-Bissau was in a situation unique for a guerrilla war, having more than enough men to fill the ranks of the national army, FARP. While this was less true for the local armed forces (FAL) or the village militia, it was FARP that engaged in the major combat. "In our country," Teodora said to me, "we do not have women who fight in combat, although there are women members of the army in the field of telecommunications and as nurses. We have enough men and therefore we do not need women."

This had another aspect as well. Luisa and her husband, Battista, both of whom were in the diplomatic field, saw the central issue as the necessity to increase the population. When Cabral had been asked this question, Luisa said, he would stress that they have an extremely small population: "We cannot put women in our army and risk their death, because we want to increase the population when the war ends. We cannot work without people. To develop our country we need as large a population as possible."

This is not an insignificant point. The devastation wrought by decades of colonialism and eleven years of guerrilla war, meant that the population had decreased drastically. PAIGC saw as legitimate the need to halt this trend, to make special efforts to preserve the female population so as to guarantee a rising birth rate.

Further, I was told by one of the leaders of PAIGC that many younger peasant women hesitated to join the army due to the deep-set custom of having children at a very early age— beginning at sixteen or seventeen, sometimes younger. In fact, this was more than custom; it was an economic imperative

dictated by the seemingly unalterable social factors—the requirement for child labor of the village economy, a high infant mortality rate, and low life expectancy generally. "It is a problem
and we need to overcome it," the cadre said. "But still at present
it is a factor which cannot be ignored."

Teodora also mentioned the problem of tradition. "You see, in
order to put women into the front line in combat, we have to fight
very hard against our traditions which maintain that women are
not suitable for this work. The people who feel this way are very
much against having women fighting in the army. Our priority is
to expel the Portuguese from our country and we cannot slow
down the war, change these traditions, and then continue. It
would set us back and we can't afford to lose time. If we did not
have sufficient men, we would have had to set this as a priority."

The reasoning behind this argument did not surprise me, for I
had heard it before in discussions of the party's practice as
regards clitoridectomy and placing women on the village councils. In general, it was consistent with PAIGC's overall strategy,
in not moving too fast in sensitive areas or in ways that would
alienate the people. All of these arguments, however, did not
impinge on the central one: that had there been too few men,
women would have been encouraged to join up.

At the time of mobilization, when volunteers were first being
recruited for the guerrilla force, many women came forward
to fight. Then it *was* necessary and women were actively encouraged. A regional FAL *responsavel* reminisced about how
recruiters would often go to a village with a group of armed
women. "Then *all* the men would join up so as not to be shown
up by the women!"

Titina Silá, for instance, was always armed either with a rifle
or a revolver, and worked as assistant commander of the military
training camp she helped to set up early in the war. When Cabral
introduced her to a peasant meeting attended by Chaliand, he
said proudly, "Comrade Titina Silá, who is in overall charge of
our public health program in the North. She saw combat in the
South, gun in hand."[15]

However, when FARP, a well-organized national army, as
opposed to a guerrilla militia, was formed in 1967, women were

no longer encouraged to take part in combat, although those who insisted were not prevented. Meanwhile, the army did require such support personnel as radio operators and nurses, and women joined in large numbers to work in these capacities. Others continued to be members of the village militias and, to a lesser extent, FAL. The village militia had a purely defensive role, and were not active in combat because the Portuguese attacked villages from the air, not the ground.

Fatmata Silibi, a twenty-one-year-old Fula woman, had been in combat at the age of sixteen. She told me when I met her at Senta Saré that she had been the only woman member of a unit of thirty youths, between the ages of fifteen and seventeen. During the period of training, both she and her instructor had felt she was equal to her comrades. But this was not the case in actual combat. She recalled one particular mission that had been very strenuous from the beginning and on which her group was later ambushed. Fortunately, they managed to escape. "I think we wounded some *Tuga* soldiers, but we didn't wait to find out!" Then on the retreat to the base, she experienced such difficulty in keeping up with the speed of the march, that her comrades had to help her carry her equipment. This she ascribed to being a woman: "I am just not as strong as a man." And she never went into combat again.

This personal account seemed to corroborate what I was told on various occasions, that PAIGC experience had led them to conclude that women could not fare as well in combat as the men. I wondered while listening to Fatmata, however, how much her performance could have been affected by attitudes, rather than her inherent capability. Did the men project onto her any feelings that she would not be able to keep up because she was a woman? If there had been a number of women with her, would she have derived support from them to keep up, which she may not have received from the men? There was probably an additional psychological element, having to do with the fact that she is Fula and as such had been brought up to denigrate herself as a woman. This could have contributed to the fact that she gave in easily, in a self-fulfilling prophesy.

I unfortunately did not have the opportunity to interview

women who had fought in combat in the south, the area that had the highest number of guerrillas, or interview women members of FAL. Fina commented a number of times: "Ah, but in the *south* there are many, many women who fought in combat alongside the men." She did not feel that they were less capable than their male comrades.

Moreover, it was a generally accepted fact, based on the history of guerrilla war elsewhere, that while men may have had a better capacity for short expenditures of brute force, women are better able to handle tasks requiring physical endurance, certainly over the long haul. Women fighters in Mozambique or Vietnam, for instance, always stressed that women fared equally with men.* Why then, should the Guinean experience have been all that different? As far as I was able to ascertain, the young women I spoke to did not harbor hidden frustrations or resentment because they were not playing a combat role in the army. I asked Fatmata if she regretted not going into combat again. "No," she replied, "I had a baby. I had to look after it. That is the way things go. I had a choice. I am doing other work for the struggle now. All work is important."

Even though few women went into combat, all cadres, whether male or female, attended the political and military training school at Madina Boé in the east front for two months, before taking up their first assignment inside the country. "All women who are participating in the struggle know how to shoot and handle weapons," said Teodora. This was imperative for self defense. Their work took them to all parts of their respective

---

*For instance, Pauline Mateos, a seventeen-year-old commander of the women's detachment in Mozambique told Barbara Cornwall:

> We undergo the same program as the men because we will be doing men's work. We stay in the same camps often and we regard them as our brothers. We suffer hunger and thirst and heat as they do, and we learn to handle all kinds of arms. When we first begin our training we think that we will die of hunger and fatigue. With the men we are marched past water holes and rivers and not permitted by our trainer to drink although we might be near collapse with thirst. This is done to toughen us for the times when we might want to drink water from sources suspected of being poisoned by the enemy.
> Finally, when we are strong enough to have overcome all of these trials, we find that we can suffer as much and march as long as any of the men, even with our packs and rifles. Sometimes we overpass men who have collapsed.[16]

fronts and the danger of ambushes and attacks was ever present.

Yet by the end of the war, PAIGC had apparently reversed its policy in principle. Combat roles for women became a national goal, and women were being given the same military training as men in a special camp in Madina Boé. Because the war ended shortly after, these women never entered combat, but the fact that the party changed its practice reflected an ongoing debate within the leadership. This concerned expedience more than principle; Cabral always recognized the symbolic importance of arming women, the trade-off was between advancement of the women's struggle and the arguments presented above.

A hint of the debate's evolution was provided by Information Director Lucette Andrade during an informal speech she made at the World Youth Festival in 1973: "We have great respect for the women of Vietnam. We have not yet been able to achieve the level that they have. We do not have a commander of a battalion who is a woman."[17]

Comparisons with the wars in Vietnam and Mozambique were also evoked whenever the subject of women in the military came up during my travels in the liberated zones of Guinea-Bissau. "We do not yet have the situation that exists in Mozambique," Fina said to me, referring to the large number of women that fought in FRELIMO's army, "but we are trying to change this."

Nevertheless, had all things been equal, it is not clear whether the Vietnamese and Mozambican liberation movements would have supported an ideology which maintains that women should be soldiers as readily as men. In fact, a closer look at these two countries seems to give weight to PAIGC's argument about necessity. Mozambique, for example, has a land mass twenty times that of Guinea-Bissau but only eight times as many people. And although Mozambican women were armed far more extensively than women in Guinea-Bissau, and a women's detachment was created by FRELIMO in order to increase the mobilization of women, the fact remains that relative to men, they did not play as decisive a role.

Josina Machel, one of the leading women in FRELIMO until her unfortunate death at the age of twenty-five, said, in discussing the role of the women's detachment:

As in the case of military units composed of men, one of the principal functions of the Women's Detachment is naturally, participation in combat. In Mozambique, the military activities of women are generally concentrated, together with the militia, in the defense of the liberated zones. In this way, the men are partly freed from the task of defense and can concentrate on the offensive in the advance zones. Nevertheless there are women who prefer to participate in more active combat and fight side by side with men in ambushes, mining operations etc. They proved to be as capable and courageous as their male comrades.[18]

In North Vietnam, too, although women played a major role in the war, they were not, on the whole, sent to the front. An American journalist who visited North Vietnam shortly after the end of the war observed:

Few women are members of the regular Viet Nam People's Army (VPA)—the mobile, full-time soldiers who usually travel far from home. It was not general policy to send women to the front. But few North Vietnamese would suggest that women are incapable of becoming full-time members of the VPA. I asked a Vietnamese friend if the VPA discriminated against women and if women had a lower status than men in society because they rarely went to the front. Her answer was proud:

"Every country must limit its full-time army because the army cannot be economically self-sufficient. Some people must stay home to take care of production and the children. Besides, the militia is very important. We could not win the war without village defense. The entire country recognized the contribution of women in fulfilling the 'Three Responsibilities'—production, defense, and the family—not just defense. In any case, we do whatever the revolution requires without calculating personal gain.[19]

In the final analysis, then, the contribution of women in the Mozambican and to a lesser extent the Vietnam wars was supportive, secondary to that of men, and reflective of the historical division of labor.

In Guinea-Bissau, no special heroism was attached to being an armed soldier; in fact, any tendency to value this role above any other was consciously discouraged. The guerrilla was considered the liberator of the country no more than any other worker for the revolution. "We are armed militants, not militarists," Cabral would insist. No sense of the *macho* was attached to the image of the guerrilla. In fact, none of the movements in the Portuguese colonies tolerated the development of such *macho* qualities and one sees photographs of Cabral, and of other leaders, holding a child or baby more often than brandishing a gun.

This gentleness in the way they projected themselves, reflected party ideology: revolution meant total transformation of the society so that any person engaged in any aspect of social transformation was considered a revolutionary. Cabral told a group of peasants:

> This work cannot be done by one person alone. It must be done by everybody, and most especially by those who understand the meaning of their action. The people must work. . . . The armed struggle is very important, but the most important thing of all is the understanding of our people's situation. Our people support the armed struggle. We must assure them that those who bear arms are the sons of the people and that arms are no better than the tools of labor. Between one man carrying a gun and another carrying a tool, the more important of the two is the man with the tool. We've taken up arms to defeat the Portuguese, but the whole point of driving out the Portuguese is to defend the man with the tool.*[20]

Women whom I interviewed were united in their opinion that armed struggle was not the highest form of revolutionary activity. They would say in essence what Fina said: "But we do not see some work as being more important than other. The important thing is to work for the revolution. And there are many different and equally essential ways of doing that."

Pointing to the temporary nature of the war, they would also assert that national reconstruction will continue long into the future, as will the fight to change attitudes. As such, there was no direct connection between military activism and the fight

---

*Cabral fluctuated in his use of the word "man." In other addresses, he specifically said, "When I say 'man,' I mean both man and woman." Other occasions he would say "man and woman" or "brothers and sisters" without qualification. This speech was recorded in 1966, before the question of sexist language had been raised as an issue in the United States.

for their own liberation in particular. Women would win their emancipation in the long run, the very long run, and maybe the fact that they did not fight in combat would have no measurable effect on the outcome.

But this "maybe" lingers in my mind. Despite the understanding I took away from Guinea-Bissau, the lack of armed women soldiers seems to present an objective problem. I saw guns *everywhere*—in villages, in the bases, at meetings, propped up against trees while people were eating or relaxing. Wherever there were people, there were guns, men carrying guns.

Guns and power are often equated, and I wondered what psychological effect this could have on the girls and boys growing up in Guinea-Bissau. "We are fighting to change attitudes," they told me over and over again; liberation has value only when minds are liberated in the process. But would minds not change a little faster if women too, like men, had been carrying guns?

Top, left: students from a Bissau secondary school and a rural *internato* work on production. *Right:* a father takes care of infant during a meeting. *Bottom, left:* a school in a liberated zone: girls were often older than the boys. *Right:* a man pounding is still uncommon.

Top: a Cacine town meeting after independence is divided by sex—men on one side, women on the other, the men benefiting from the only shade. *Bottom:* a member of a Fula village court (center) with other peasant women.

Top: rest stop during a long march. *Bottom, left:* a radio operator, member of the national army. *Right:* Titina Silá, political commissar for the north front, with her child. Later killed in ambush while crossing the Farim River, she is now a national hero.

Chapter 9

"The woman of today is a new woman from the woman of yesterday"

A slow but perceptible change in sexist attitudes could be traced between the period of mobilization and the end of the war. Those women who joined PAIGC at the beginning of the war were denigrated at that time by many of the men they worked with, most particularly when in positions of authority. Toward the war's end the younger women who had grown up under PAIGC were experiencing greater equality. Other problems were beginning to be confronted, such as the need for child care and sharing domestic work with the men.

Heading back across the dry, open plain to Vendoleidi base in the east front in early June we did not march in an ordered column. Neither did we keep an ear on constant alert for the drone of approaching bombers. We were spread out rather haphazardly, chatting easily among ourselves. We knew the planes were not going to come. The coup in Portugal had taken place a few weeks earlier and a ceasefire was in effect.

As we neared the base, returning from my first outing to a nearby Fula village, Mario pointed to the two hills that rose up from the edge of the plain and the clump of trees at the foot of the nearest hill. "Look," he said. "Those trees are a perfect camouflage for the base. The Portuguese pilots have to fly high to avoid the hills. And so, *bom*, they can't pick out the camp from among the trees."

So effective was the camouflage that the camp had never been moved during the war, other *responsavels* told me as we walked. Looking for myself, I could appreciate what they were saying. Long before we could discern human life among the trees, the noises of the camp reached us across the stillness of the plain: the crowing of cocks, barking of dogs, the thump, thud of women pounding, music and voices from the radios.

Vendoleidi was a large base, housing over one hundred fifty soldiers, who slept in small huts or pup tents crowded under the trees. The space also harbored a hospital, a school, and the political commissars of the region. The small, typically constructed school was shared between the children of the base in the morning, and the adults—nurses, soldiers, *responsavels*—in the afternoon. At any time of the day I would see groups of two or three women or men sitting under a tree or on a protruding rock and, laboriously pouring over one of the PAIGC readers, teaching each other to read.

As we entered the base along the narrow path that cut through the clearing, I stopped to watch two young militants in green guerrilla uniforms, cleaning their automatic rifles. As they rubbed each one meticulously with oil, I wondered if it would be for the last time. I thought back to a recent afternoon in Conakry, when the head of Solidarity Hospital drove me to my hotel from PAIGC headquarters in his Volkswagen. He told me then that the hospital in Boké, which I had visited not too long before, had been partly destroyed in the first torrential rains of the season. The filler between the prefabricated walls of the wards had been devoured over time by termites and part of the building had washed away. And now, the director told me, some of his comrades were arguing for the hospital not to be rebuilt. Independence was so near, they had said, that the whole hospital would be transferred to the interior any day. "This is incorrect thinking," he said to me, shaking his head. "We must not allow ourselves to give in to the idea that independence is just around the corner. We cannot trust the Portuguese. Who knows, we might still have to pick up arms again. No, we must continue the struggle until we are absolutely sure. The hospital must be rebuilt in Boké.

Coming as it did in the midst of a fluid diplomatic situation in Lisbon, the ceasefire caught us all off balance. People were divided over how to proceed. Some of the leaders, evincing extremes of optimism, sported broad grins and teased: "You'll see, you will leave from Bissau!"

Others, like the hospital director and the militants at the Vendoleidi base, carried on as if the war were still in progress. But as the days went by, a new atmosphere began to pervade the *mato*. Discipline was relaxed unmistakably and replaced by a tentative but growing elation on the part of the guerrillas.

In the end, I did not leave from Bissau. But it took only four months for the new Portuguese government to grudgingly recognize the de facto independence of Guinea-Bissau. As for the Solidarity Hospital, it never did get rebuilt in Boké, and those rifles I had watched being oiled were never again used in combat.

During those last, more relaxed days of my visit—and as it turned out, of the war—I had time to reflect on my experiences of the past weeks, and on the perceptions I had gained of the women in Guinea-Bissau. I thought particularly about the "new woman" that was emerging and the differences I perceived between the generation of Teodora and Francisca and that of Fina and Ana Maria.

Young women usually had more easy-going and naturally equal interactions with men of the same age. The older generation of women had had to struggle against the conditioning of a lifetime, both their own and men's, in order to break ground which their younger sisters could follow. In the process, they gave vent to an anger and resentment that before had burned below the surface.

I witnessed a number of encounters involving women cadres and their male comrades who had not totally rid themselves of chauvinist ideas. The women's response was often angry, but it always included a firm declaration of their rights and a demand for equal respect.

One such incident happened on my first night inside the liberated zones, a night which I spent with Teodora at the military base in Candjafara. It was after supper and we were sitting round a table with Joaquim Baro, a member of the PAIGC executive, who was also a commander of the south front. Baro's English was good and, mellowed by strong, sweet Cuban coffee and the gentle, flickering light of a kerosene lamp, we began to talk about general matters. Then, on learning the purpose of my visit, his face lit up and he exclaimed, "Ah, the women have achieved so much. It is such an important aspect of our struggle." So enthusiastic was he that I began to ask him questions about the role of women. He answered without referring to Teodora, except to translate the interchange. Teodora listened for a few minutes. Then, while Baro was in midsentence, she drew herself up, her elbows planted firmly on the table, and spoke to him sharply in Creole. He turned to me with a sheepish but good-humored grin and translated: "Teodora says she is better qualified to answer your questions than I am." From then onward, until late into the night, he was interpreter only.

Male supremacist ideas were manifested in myriad ways, both overt and subtle, but the most common expressions of sexism saw men refusing to take women's work or leadership seriously, presuming that women could be treated as sexual partners only, feeling that men are more capable than women in carrying out political tasks. And when I first broached the subject with Teodora, asking whether she found this a problem, I had hardly got all the words out of my mouth before she burst forth emphatically: "*Sim, sim, sim!*" (Yes, yes, yes.)

"It is a very important question you have asked," she went on, "because this is one of the aspects of our society that has been present, still is present, and will continue to be present for a long time. In our society, men have very particular ideas about women. At the beginning of the struggle when women and men first began working together, the men brought these conceptions with them from their previous experience. They found it difficult to conceive of a woman as a comrade, a companion, or to treat her with the respect due to her, as someone who is equal in the struggle and working for the same goal. It was common to find comrades having relationships with more than one woman, and saying blithely that he loved them all!"

Amilcar Cabral gave these attitudes special attention when he spoke with young men individually or at meetings. "Women are not like shirts," he would tell them, "so that you put on one today, another tomorrow. If I find any of you treating women in this way, you'll marry the woman!"

Teodora chuckled at the memory and quipped: "There were *lots* of marriages in the early days of the struggle!" Then, returning to Cabral, she recalled how he insisted from the first that woman is an equal companion of man and that the basis for choosing a spouse must be mutual respect and a desire to live together. Actions that were not in keeping with this, he had made clear, were in violation of the principles of PAIGC, and he never let up in his insistence that the young men act accordingly.

"The belief that all women are good for is to do the domestic work and to be a sexual partner and bear children still manifests itself in our society," Teodora acknowledged. "We continue to battle with these ideas and I can say that there has been a very perceptible change over the years. Nonetheless, we cannot deny that in reality and despite our efforts, they still exist. But it is not just the men. As Cabral used to point out, women themselves must have a clear understanding of how these attitudes affect them. No one can fight for their rights except women themselves."

Both women and men have to learn to take responsibility for their actions, she said. This was often easier for them to do if they had had some education and exposure to the party's position on harmful social customs. Only recently, for example, did it become possible for a woman to choose her own boyfriend and decide if she wants to marry him or not. By taking responsibility for their actions, they were becoming stronger women and hence respected in their own right.

"We feel sure that if our people are able to have mutually respectful and trusting relationships, it will be advantageous to their own children who will grow up in a new kind of environment. These children will learn early and consciously about the respect that men must have toward women and women toward men. This is our great task in the revolution."

Although Teodora began her work inside the country and Francisca in Conakry, their experiences had been similar in regard to the attitudes of the men they worked alongside. Both of them joined PAIGC as young adults, around the age of seventeen, and won respect after proving themselves over the years. "Now, though," Francisca told me, "these difficulties seldom occur between comrades working together. For women like Carmen, Teodora, and myself, these problems do not arise. Women in our position in the party have their opinions and decisions taken seriously and with respect." Nevertheless, she lamented that older men with more than residual sexist attitudes were continuing to mistreat younger women, those just beginning to work with the party. In many of these cases the men were not according them the respect they deserved and the young cadres were hampered in carrying out their work.

"The party gives her a particular mission and often she can do the work better than a man," Francisca explained, "but when she gives an order, he feels that he doesn't have to obey it, simply because he is a man. This problem exists in the family as well. The husband will go ahead and act without consulting his wife, even if his actions affect her. And then there is a huge uproar if she acts without consulting him—perhaps by taking contraceptives or having an abortion. This is the sort of thing we are fighting against."

It was not only the women who spoke of the continuing need to change such attitudes. At an informal meeting in New York in 1972, Amilcar Cabral, responding in English to a question about the role of women, referred both to the achievements and to the difficulties. "But we have big problems to solve and we have a great problem with some of the leaders of the party. We have, even myself, to combat ourselves on this problem, because we have to be able to cut this cultural element, with its great roots, until the day we put down this bad thing—the exploitation of women. But we have made great progress in this field in these ten years."[1]

Progress has indeed been made, but for many men it appeared that notions of equality had not penetrated into the homes. This reality was underscored for me during a conversation I had with a male cadre. He commented that some party cadres, even leaders, accept that their wives should work in responsible positions in the party. They accepted in principle that the liberation of women is very important. "But in *my* home? Never!"

Meanwhile, women turned to each other for support, the older cadres feeling a special responsibility to look out for the young women. I saw this in Teodora on a number of occasions. One evening, she, Espirito Santo, and Starr, another regional political commissar who shared her base, got into a heated debate. One of the men had brought up the case of two teenagers from Bissau, who were in love with each other and had decided to join PAIGC in the liberated areas. The young man had gone first, and a few months later the woman followed. They were assigned work in different areas, but before they could be reunited, the young woman fell in love with a *responsavel,* who was older than her boyfriend from Bissau and higher up in the party. Compounding the problem, she had not written to tell her boyfriend and he still harbored the thought that she was waiting for him. The argument about who was in the right went on for a long time, Teodora's voice getting louder and more emphatic with each point she made. Espirito Santo became so involved that it was barely possible to get a translation, as he would dive back into the argument himself, leaving me dangling on the end of incompleted sentences. Both Espirito and Starr were denouncing the young woman with vehemence, contending that she was interested only in glamor, while Teodora stood stoutly in her defense. She was wrong not to write, Teodora acknowledged, but how could they presume that her feelings for the second man were not genuine. In any case, the role of the men was not to condemn but to try and understand the woman's position and educate her. Given the society in which she grew up, she might well have acted "fickle." But they had to remember that men, simply by virtue of the fact that they were men, had both education and privileges that were denied women and that pressures existed for women to live vicariously through men. While Teodora maintained that men were failing as revolutionaries if they did not understand the context of this behavior, Espirito and Starr did not agree, and the argument continued for a long time. However, not only did Teodora show solidarity with the woman, she also used the debate as an opportunity for political education, directed particularly, I suspect, toward Espirito, who had recently joined the party.

Throughout my trip I found myself in the company of both men and women cadres and the main impression I gained, particularly from the younger cadres, was that the men and women felt equally at ease with each other. I never felt that men were just giving the appearance of combating sexism or that they were self-conscious about women being in positions of higher authority.

For example, during my stay at the *internato* at Boé in the east front, a mixed group of adults sat around the table after supper. There were four young women—Fina, the director, a teacher, and the school nurse—as well as about five men, all teachers. Everyone participated in the discussion, the women taking as active a part as the men. In fact, they soon were outdoing the men; when the talk turned to the role of women in Fula society Fina and one other woman passionately aired their feelings on the subject. While this was going on, Mario turned to me, a look of wonderment on his face, and observed: "It was absolutely impossible to see men and women sitting around a table talking like this at the beginning of the struggle, or even six years ago. [He had been out of his country for the past six years, and had returned shortly before my visit.] Maybe the women would have eaten together with the men. But afterward they would have excused themselves and left. This difference is truly remarkable."

The following morning I interviewed Jacinta da Sousa, the school's nineteen-year-old director, while an open-air class was in progress nearby. At one point Jacinta stopped talking, her attention caught by something the teacher was doing. Walking over, she called the teacher aside and, after they had talked briefly, the lesson continued in an apparently different vein. It seemed the teacher, who was male and a few years older than she, had been able amicably and without defensiveness to accept Jacinta's comment that he had been using an outdated lesson.

It was through the young women, those who were nineteen or in their early twenties, that I was able to glimpse the future women of Guinea-Bissau. Most had grown up in the revolution and had been educated by PAIGC. Some, like Fina, had attended the Pilot School and then gone abroad for further study. Others, like Ana Maria and Ule, had trained as nurses abroad and learned to read and write only on their return to the *mato*. And then there were women like Jacinta, who had grown up in Bissau and chosen to leave the city to join PAIGC in the liberated zones, where they quickly assimilated the ideology of the movement.

In the case of Jacinta, a child when the war began, she had heard so much about the liberation movement before she left Bissau that the transition was not difficult. Her parents supported the PAIGC, so eight-year-old Jacinta supported it too. Every day they tuned in the radio for news and talked about the bad conditions under colonialism and what was happening to change all that. Jacinta shared the excitement about PAIGC victories and by the time she was thirteen had resolved to share them.

The daughter of a privileged Bissau family, she attended a school in Bissau catering only to girls and geared toward providing "good wives" for the elite. Although it was part of Spinola's "Better Guinea" program, it was also one of the only ways that girls could be educated past elementary school. The best thing about it was that she received some training as a teacher. Meanwhile, Jacinta and Conceiçao Goia, a classmate just a year younger, had become inseparable friends. Together they dreamed and schemed of ways to get to the liberated zones—in secret. "We couldn't talk about it to anybody else," Jacinta told me, "because of the informers. Everyone in Bissau was afraid of informers. You didn't even talk about such things with your best friends."

When Jacinta was seventeen and Conceiçao sixteen they put their plans into action. First they made contact very discreetly with the PAIGC underground and convinced them that they were serious about leaving. Their route was planned and a young militant assigned to travel with them to Cô, where they would contact another underground member who would escort them into the liberated zones. They were told that another young woman from Bissau would be traveling with them.

The next obstacle was to obtain permits to leave Bissau. Presenting themselves to the Portuguese authorities with their hearts pounding, they lied about their names, ages, and destination, saying they were going to visit relatives in Teixeira Pinto. After additional formalities they left the building, clutching the precious document and grinning at each other in victory. But before they could leave their contact was arrested, so they decided to go alone to find the man who was to escort them. When they got to Cô, along the route to Teixeira Pinto, they were greeted with sour suspicion by the inhabitants, most of whom had found it safer to support the Portuguese. People came up to the young strangers and began to question them: Why did their permit say Teixeira Pinto and they were staying over in Cô? Oh, they replied, affecting nonchalance, we have come this way first to visit relatives. But Jacinta panicked. She split from the others and made a hasty retreat back to Bissau, only to hear later that the others had made it across into PAIGC territory. Then she got angry with herself, immediately began work on another plan, and in May 1973, a few months after her friends, she was escorted by a PAIGC militant into the liberated zones.

Jacinta was quickly put to good use, first as a teacher at a school in the north and after she had proved her capabilities as director of the *internato* at Boé. There she was reunited with Conceiçao, who had been assigned to the school as a teacher. Their friendship was still strong, and had expanded to include the nurse at the school, Babtida Nambuna. The three women spent much of their spare time together. Relaxed, at ease, supportive, they talked easily with one another and treated each other as equals.

Jacinta got much satisfaction from teaching in her new surroundings. She was able to work in an education system she could get excited about and, at the same time, feel she was making a contribution to the building of a new society. PAIGC's emphasis on equality between the sexes particularly impressed her, she told me.

While she was growing up she was conscious of women's inequality and she saw how her father treated her mother. "My father had three other women, though it was my mother he was married to. Had she not been his favorite, it might have been a problem between them. My mother never said anything about this, but it made me angry as a child. I could see she found it very hard to accept. But what could she do? It is our custom. I will never accept this custom."

Jacinta also spoke of change. "We have been colonized twice, but it is not the woman's fault. But although we are aware of it now, it is not something that can be resolved quickly. It must be part of building a new society and this takes time. What I find so remarkable is that only a few years ago it was impossible to conceive of what has already transpired."

While Jacinta's commitment to PAIGC was obvious, she showed signs of someone new to the movement—a slight hesitancy in explaining theoretical points and a tendency to resort to the pat phrase. N'Bemba Camara, the head nurse at Vendoleidi hospital, was the complete opposite. At the age of nine, when Jacinta was first hearing about PAIGC, N'Bemba had already joined.* Her

---

*During the war of liberation PAIGC resembled a mass movement, the criteria for membership being a) support for the party's principles and b) anticolonialism vested in unwavering support of the armed struggle to oust the Portuguese. No system of membership cards or files of registered members was developed. So children working for the struggle alongside adults saw themselves and could be considered members of the party.

Assessing the nature of the party after being present at the third party congress in 1977, Lars Rudebeck noted that "the backbone of the organization, i.e., all members with special responsibilities and tasks from the local committees up, were, however, often referred to as 'the party within the party.'" This open political movement, with its core of committed and trained cadres, provided the administrative and judicial structure of the new society emerging in the liberated areas. It was, in other words, both a party and a state at the same time. This changed, as he points out, at independence, with the need to separate the two. After debating whether the new party should be an open mass organization or a vanguard party of the most dedicated and politically conscious, the 1977 congress decided on the latter.[2]

whole way of thinking, her basic approach to life, reflected the ideology of PAIGC—but in a completely unself-conscious way. She was what the revolution is all about.

I first met N'Bemba at Vendoleidi base. Her people, the Beafada, are one of the smallest ethnic groups in Guinea-Bissau, and she had grown up in a Muslim village in the south where her father was chief. When PAIGC mobilizers first arrived, N'Bemba's father was quick to join and soon had the whole village supporting the liberation struggle. But he had to walk a tightrope to carry it off. At night he would allow the mobilizers into the village and during the day the Portuguese would come to ask him to tell them what was going on. Although he pretended ignorance, the Portuguese were suspicious. One day troops took his wife to Fulacunda, a nearby town, and threatened to kill her unless he talked. Although he knew they were serious, N'Bemba's father refused to give them information, and eventually the Portuguese released her.

Unlike many peasant parents, N'Bemba's father talked to his daughter from the first and at length about PAIGC and what they were going to do. In fact, he encouraged all his children to begin working for the party. So did his wife. "She was just as tired of the oppression by the *Tuga*," the young nurse told me. With this kind of encouragement N'Bemba developed a consciousness of women's condition and how it was changing. When she was thirteen, a time when she could expect her family to marry her off to some older man, she found she could continue to assert her wish to become an independent person. "What PAIGC was saying about women made great sense to me. I had seen how women in the villages were oppressed, how they had to do all the work in the village all day. This angered me. Then I saw how women members of the party were taking on equal responsibilities with the men."

N'Bemba was quiet spoken and seemed to consider seriously all that was happening around her. She did not make quips or tease and she gave the impression of being mature beyond her years. Completely unflustered, she never hesitated and carried out her work with responsibility and thoroughness. She showed her respect for the people she worked with in the villages, and was respected in return. All this is not to say that N'Bemba did not laugh or joke. She did so often, and her oval face and even features would light up instantly.

In talking about the changes that had come about since the beginning of the war, N'Bemba contrasted the young women who had joined PAIGC and gone to live in the *mato* as she had done with those who remained in the villages; the difference in outlook and in lifestyle was enormous. "But there have been vast changes in the villages as well," she added. "Life for women in the villages is very hard, but they are much freer now. I see how women have taken on more responsibility and are accepting the new way of life."

In the generation growing up behind her she saw the changes most clearly: "I feel that the woman of tomorrow will not be like the woman of today. And the woman of today is a new woman from the woman of yesterday. The situation has changed not only for us, but for the men as well. But the struggle for emancipation will be a long one. There is still potential for much more change. We are building a new society and therefore more things are possible."

I detected a noticeable difference in the way that Fina and her generation approached men, compared to Teodora's attitude. The younger women all stressed how men treated them as equal comrades in working relationships; they did not see these as a battle. The key to the difference probably lies in the fact that Fina's generation reached adulthood some eight or ten years after the beginning of the armed struggle, eight or ten years of pressure on men to change their attitudes. Fina studied in Cuba with three young men who had been classmates at the Pilot School and had shared the same political education. "At no point did I feel that I was not being taken seriously or being considered inferior," she told me. I asked the women at the Boé *internato* whether they felt that men treated women as sex objects, despite the fact that in work they were treated as equals.

"Sometimes it is a problem," Jacinta answered, "because some men feel that they have to make advances to women, because if they do not, they are not men. It is true that men have these ideas. For example, a comrade came here a little while ago.

He had never been here before and did not know the women. After a few hours he began making propositions. Not directly—you know how men are. However, if a woman likes a man, if she has no commitment to another, she can accept if she wishes. Why not? We don't think that by accepting, it is a commitment for life. For if a man has a desire, a woman has a desire as well. That is natural and it is the same for both.''

I was informed that contraceptives, mainly pills, were available at the hospitals in the interior and in Boké and Conakry. An older male nurse at the Vendoleidi base, the one who had joined PAIGC at the beginning of the war, tried to tell me that pills were available only for married women. But Fina and N'Bemba denied this vigorously. "We *know!*" they laughed, leaving the old nurse completely nonplused, fumbling to readjust his attitudes about sexual relationships.

The women also said it was possible to get an abortion, although it is not encouraged officially and was seen as a last resort. Emphasis was placed on the development of attitudes which would make young people feel responsible for their actions and decide in advance whether or not they wanted children. If they did not, then they could take preventive measures. "We are trying to educate our young women about birth control," Teodora said, "in order to avoid the situation that has been so common where a very young woman would get pregnant against her wishes and hardly know how it happened. Sometimes girls who are studying become pregnant. And suddenly we have lost a cadre. We want to prevent unwanted pregnancies from happening. We try to discourage our young women from feeling ashamed or shy about discussing these problems. We encourage them to take measures in order to ensure a healthy sex life. And we are being successful."

Nonetheless, there were still many problems in this area. While I was in the south I was told that a sixteen-year-old pupil at one of the *internatos* had become pregnant and that the father was a teacher at the school. This had upset Espirito Santo very much, as he felt the teachers, as party cadres, should be particularly correct in their relationships with pupils. And, worse, he assumed the girl would now have to stop or suspend her studies. Nevertheless, if Francisca continues to have her way, this will cease to be automatic and cadres will not be lost. As she insisted in the case involving two students: "After all, nobody expects the young man to stop studying as well. That is completely unfair."

Peasant women married by age eighteen at the latest, and in the case of Muslim women such as the Fula, years earlier. But many of the younger cadres I met were not married, although they were in their early twenties. For most, the desire for children would be the deciding factor about whether or not to get married. Teodora talked about this one afternoon as we rested on a mat outside our hut at the *semi-internato* we were visiting. She was twenty-nine, she told me, and loved children. Sometimes when she saw friends of hers with their own children she felt sad because she had none. But the struggle had to come first, and consumed her life totally. Once the war was over? Well, then things would change. But as long as the war continued, she had no choice.

N'Bemba saw the situation differently. Her two-year-old son lived with her at the base, superenergetic and brazen. He was loved by all and could always find a playmate in one of the older children or one or more of the militants. N'Bemba told me frankly that she was not married, a situation I thought was not something taken lightly. "I did not love the father," she said, "so why should I marry him?" When I asked if anyone had shown antagonism toward her she shrugged and looked at me in her direct way. "No," she said, "even my parents have accepted the situation. A war is going on. They have got used to living a new life in so many ways."

N'Bemba told me that there were many women who had left the villages and who were deciding not to marry if they got pregnant. If they wanted a child there would be no problem in caring for it, and should they wish to marry later, children from a previous relationship did not present an obstacle. A child was not the sole responsibility of the mother, she said, adding that PAIGC would also look after it and provide medical care and education. "There is no problem. My child is the child of the revolution."

The problem of child care in Guinea-Bissau has its own particular nature, which makes the whole question more complex. It needs to be considered in the light of the African situation, of the fact that caring for children during a war creates unusual problems, and of the fact that new patterns are emerging and being tested as the society changes.

Throughout Africa the extended family, not the nuclear family, provides the context of the child's care and upbringing. Children do not relate only to their mother and father in their day-to-day activities, but also to their mother's co-wives, aunts, uncles, cousins. This means that, although the mother is mainly responsible for caring for her children, she can rely on other women for assistance if she needs to leave the village to work in the fields, to collect water from the well, or in case of illness or any circumstance that makes the care of her children impossible. The helping hands of other women are taken for granted as the care of children is viewed as a collective responsibility among the women. Additionally, when the child is still small the mother will tie her or him onto her back before starting work or leaving the village. Even once the boys have begun to learn "men's work," with their fathers and older brothers, the mothers feed all the children and look after their welfare—again much of this collectively.

For peasant women the provision of child care by the state has not arisen as an issue, given the organization of social and economic life at a village level. As reorganization of the village economy begins to take place and collective villages are established, this is likely to change. The benefit of having child-care facilities in the village which would help free up the enormous amount of time women invest in reproduction might then be appreciated. But the advantages of conceptualizing such a need at this early stage were not seen as a necessary part of the political education process. A prior step is the need for education and for the development of women cadres. The lack of child-care facilities was not a hindrance here, as there were other women in the village who would step into the breach when necessary. Hence the communal tradition of child care to some extent facilitated the release of women for work in the revolution. I asked N'Bemba, for example, what happened to her son when she had to leave the base for short visits to nearby villages (a major part of her work) or when she spent entire days with me visiting the Fula villages, and on one occasion sleeping over.

"For the first six months," she replied, "while I was breast-feeding him, he was with me all the time. And it did not interfere with my work. But afterward, no problem. There is always someone at the base to look after him. I have never seen a child being a problem to a woman. Whatever her work, there is always someone to look after her child."

That Teodora viewed this differently resulted from the fact that she was involved in intensive political work, demanding constant travel and undivided attention. But for nurses or teachers it was easier. Ule, for instance, accustomed to carrying her seventeen-day-old baby with her when she had to visit areas away from the hospital, did not anticipate that the infant would ever be a hinderance. While she was taking me on a "tour" of her hospital we passed an elderly man, a patient, sitting upright on his bed, very still, and holding Ule's baby in front of his chest. He had a gentle smile on his face and had been sitting like that for some time. As we got near, the baby began to yell with hunger. Ule took her from him, and breastfed her as we continued the tour. When the child was satisfied, Ule handed her back to the patient and we proceeded. There was barely a change of pace. All in a morning's work. I saw variations of this behavior whenever I met women with young babies.

Moreover, it seemed to me that children in Guinea-Bissau seldom cried, and it was very rare to see a child give way to a tantrum. They had free run of the base, the school, or other living area, and whoever was nearby would keep a watchful eye for trucks driving in and out or bombers overhead. When I interviewed N'Bemba in her hut after nine o'clock one night, her son sat on the bed they both shared and played with a small car. Sometimes he would run the car up one of my arms, across my back, and down the other. He entertained himself like this for over an hour and a half. Later, when I was transcribing the tape of my interview with his mother, I could hear his little voice in the background, occasionally asking N'Bemba a question, but most of the time going "brrr, . . . brrr, . . . brrr," as he drove his car around the bed.

During my travels in the liberated zones, it was common to see women working with babies tied to their backs—at hospitals, schools, bases. At the schools the women could count on help from the students, so the children seemed to spend more of the day with students than with their mother. I watched a young male student patiently wheel a two-year-old around a clearing on a bicycle, back and forth, back and forth. But it was always the girl students who looked after the very young babies, even though these students were fewer.

Nonetheless, the men I met were in general very gentle with children. I noticed it everywhere. One of the militants who accompanied us on a march was rather *macho* in the way he related to women, always ready for a flirtation. But as soon as we arrived at our destination, he immediately sought out the children and played with them for long stretches of time. At one school we visited, the two-year-old son of the administrator was not feeling well and was crying constantly, and yet this militant was the only person, other than his mother, that the child allowed near him.

I asked Teodora whether the men had always related to children that way or if it was a by-product of the revolution. She said that men had always shown attention to children, but on a limited scale. Men that were not really interested remained so, but more and more men were feeling freer to express their affection for children and helping with child care in ways that had not been customary in the villages in the past.

The women cadres, meanwhile, insisted that their husbands share equally all tasks associated with domestic life. Fina explained: "The child would not only be mine. It would be the father's as well. We must share all the domestic work and child care. I just don't accept that it is only women's work. Both husband and wife are working and both must have the same rights. However, I am proud. I would not ask a man to do things like change diapers. If he is prepared to do it, fine. But I would not demand it. Everything else, yes, I would demand. There are many things around the house to do—cleaning, cooking, washing, taking care of the children. This work must be shared."

"It is an absolute necessity," said Francisca with similar emphasis, "that men help equally with child care and housework. But to reach this goal we have to educate the men and there are still many women who do not understand this. In many cases, if a man helps with the housework or with the children, changing diapers, for instance, or cleaning the house, his friends laugh at him. This has got to stop."

However, women's insistence that men must take on half the responsibility for child care spoke more to the ideal situation than to the real one. Because families were fragmented as a result of the war, the husband working in one region, the wife in another, it was invariably the mother who had the young children with her. Sometimes, as in the case of Ule or Titina, a grandmother would take on a lot of the child care, but it was always a woman.

This is the point N'Bemba overlooked when she commented that there is always someone to look after a child: that "someone" was usually a woman not working actively outside of the home. It was still the women, not the men, who carried babies on their backs, and it was the women, either sisters or mothers or friends, who were responsible for the children. Men helped. A good sign for the future, but the reality was that children in Guinea-Bissau received adequate care largely because many women had a unidimensional conception of their social role.

PAIGC cadres told me that many women still opted for full-time child care once they had a baby, giving up their work in the revolution. Cabral regarded the conflict with particular concern. Raising the issue at the 1971 meeting of the Superior Council, he referred to the phenomenon of nurses leaving their work as soon as their first child was born: "This cannot be. Either we find a way of obliging our nurses to continue working after having children, or otherwise we will have to stop recruiting female nurses for our struggle." This problem was not peculiar to Guinea-Bissau, he admitted, but that did not mean that PAIGC must not seek ways to solve it. "We have to be capable of understanding this reality, but also capable of struggling in order to improve it. And the best way of improving the work of our women is to demand of them that they hold themselves in due consideration."[3]

In other words, that they be liberated. If its success in other areas is a guide, PAIGC ultimately will succeed in raising women's consciousness to a point where nonagricultural work and child care are no longer mutually exclusive. Such an eventuality, however, brings with it two related problems. First, contradicting the views of Ule and N'Bemba, one of the leaders said PAIGC's experience had been that women cadres returning to work after childbirth were often hampered by the presence of a child and did not perform as efficiently as before. Teodora said this depended a lot on the type of work they were engaged in and the number of children they had. A school administrator would be able to manage with little real difficulty, particularly with the help of students, and if there was only one child. But women like herself, a political commissar, would never be able to work with children alongside them, as their work demanded all their attention and constant travel, from region to region, and in and out of the country.

And then again, Teodora, noted, the masses of Guineans tended to have large families. "How can it be possible," she asked, "to even consider a woman free if she has seven or eight children dependent solely upon her? How can she be free if she is unable to send her children to kindergarten, and to school?"

Thus as more women participate in the revolution and cease to see their work centered around home and children, there is the problem that existing child-care resources are certain to be strained, even if men are doing more than just helping.

Everyone concerned agreed about the need to provide child-care centers throughout the country. During the war it was impossible to establish these in the liberated zones. With the Portuguese bombing constantly, people had to be ready to rush for the trenches at any moment of the day or night, so in a center with many young children virtually one adult per child would have been necessary to make sure they all made it to the trenches in time. Besides, it was too dangerous to keep large groups of children together in one place. *Infantarios* were established during the war in Mozambique because they could be adequately hidden from the Portuguese in the large liberated territories. However, as Guinea-Bissau is so small, every acre was vulnerable to bombing and the risk too high. As a result, the one child-care center PAIGC had was located in Conakry. It housed sixty children, all of whom had one or both parents fighting or constantly on the move (Fatima's son by the *regulo* lived at this center). But the war was over, and party leaders were only too aware that a much larger beginning had to be made to make an impact on the population in general and the role of women in particular.

As we have seen, changing the role of women was expressed by the Guineans as having to engage in a battle on two fronts. I asked Guinean women what exactly they meant by "two colonialisms," the phrase I heard so often throughout the liberated zones. In reply, they emphasized that the men were no more the enemy of women than the Portuguese people were the enemy of the Guinean people;* the real contradiction was the system under which they all labored. This system gave rise to so-called male colonialism and has to be eradicated; it is a system of values stemming from a subsistence economy and further distorted by the influence of colonialism. The women see it as a question of changing both attitudes and the economy, not of fighting men.

Teodora talked at length when I asked her how she perceived the need for the liberation of women and what it means to her.

"In our country women are considered the instruments of production," she began. "For instance, in marriage and particularly

---

*That the Portuguese people did not represent the enemy in the eyes of the people of Guinea-Bissau was demonstrated for me shortly after the coup was announced. Up until May 1974 a great deal of skepticism existed among the people in the liberated areas about the nature of the coup and whether Portugal's new leaders were serious about independence for their African colonies. On May Day, however, demonstrators poured out in their thousands into the streets of Lisbon, waving PAIGC, MPLA, and FRELIMO flags and carrying banners proclaiming support for the liberation movements and demanding an immediate end to the war. As this news came over the radio the comrades with me were very moved. It was seen as the first real sign that the coup could bring an end to the war. One militant said to me later, his voice filled with emotion, "Cabral always used to say that we are not fighting the Portuguese people, but the Portuguese system. Now I really understand what he meant."

in polygynous marriage, she is considered the property of men, just like cattle." What is seen as important, Teodora continued, is the number of children a woman can produce for her husband and the size of the harvest she can reap from the fields. This is her role in life, a role devoid of any rights or any freedom, and it is from this that a woman must be liberated.

"By a liberated woman I mean a woman who has a clear consciousness about her responsibility in the society and who is economically independent. By a liberated woman I mean one who is able to do all the jobs in the society without being discriminated against, a woman who can go to school to learn, who can become a leader.

"The liberation of women is one aspect of our revolution. It is one element of our struggle. Because without equality of all people, without equal opportunity to go to school, to get medical care, without equality in work, it is not possible for a woman to be free. Without a revolution in the system of education, so that both girls and boys are educated to have the same responsibilities, there will be no liberated women in our society."

Teodora spoke of the need for women to be free to make their own decisions about their lives, not only to combat such practices as forced marriage but also to bring change in the relationship between men and women in family life, where men had too much control over decision-making in the lives and actions of women. She stressed, however, that personal freedom could not be individual: "The old men—and young men as well—must understand that freedom cannot be individual. You cannot be free if your neighbors are not free.

"While women are fighting for their freedom at present, a new system is evolving which is preparing the young people of the next generation. And this new system is trying to change their idea of liberty, their idea of freedom, and their idea of sexual equality between the members of the family and within the society in general.

"The struggle for the liberation of women has to be done in different ways. First of all, women must fight together with men against colonialism and all systems of exploitation. Secondly, and this is one of the most fundamental points, every woman must convince herself that she can be free and that she has to be free. And that she is able to do all things that men do in social and political life. And thirdly, women must fight in order to convince men that she has naturally the same rights as he has. But she must understand that the fundamental problem is not the contradiction between women and men, but it is the system in which we are all living.

"If we build a society without exploitation of one human being by another, then of course women will have to be free in that society. Our struggle for national liberation is one way of assuring the liberation of women because, by doing the same work as men, or by doing work that ensures the liberation of our country, women convince themselves that they are able to do the same work as men. In the process women will learn that they are able to do many things that they could not have conceived of before. They will learn that in our party there are women in the highest level of leadership and that women are working in all different sectors of our lives. It is important because it convinces women that they have potential and it also shows men what that potential is.

"You cannot isolate the liberation of women in circumstances such as ours because there is one goal for our society—which is to transform it step by step."

As Teodora finished speaking I thought of Ana Maria Gomes, not a relation but a sister in revolution. Had liberation of women in Guinea-Bissau remained a distant goal, unconnected to a process of change, Ana Maria probably would have died in childbirth. Or had she somehow survived that first difficult delivery, she would be illiterate still and surrounded by four or five children, rather than the two she deliberately chose to have, still pounding rice in a village together with her husbands' co-wives, worn out by the incessant toil and weakened by malaria.

National independence resulting in a change in the color of the dominating minority would not have improved the life of Ana Maria and her sisters. A neocolonial elite would continue to exploit the peasant masses, especially the women, in order to build skyscrapers in Bissau and keep the country open to Portuguese and other Western capitalist profits. Instead, independence brings with it both hope for the future and questions about women's emancipation. The armed struggle represented several things at one and the same time: a force for rapid change, a unifying focus for contradictory social tendencies, and a limitation on the initiatives of a progressive movement. In peacetime, however, unencumbered by the restrictions of the guerrilla war, PAIGC confronts problems of rising expectations, especially from women, even as they search for ways to maintain the pace of forward motion in the absence of the galvanizing effect of armed struggle.

Part II
After Independence

Chapter 10
"We are not fighting for a piece of the pie. . ."

After independence in 1974 the awesome tasks of developing the nation brought the need to confront numerous issues. Among the measures taken to assist the continuing struggle for equality between the sexes during the first year of independence were the establishment of the Organization of Women, the passing of laws to protect the rights of women, and the continued political mobilization of women, particularly those who had lived in the Portuguese-controlled areas.

I swung my camera bag over my shoulder and behind me so that my back could take its weight, and with my free hand grasped the door frame of the old ex-Portuguese troop-carrying plane which now bore the gold, green, and red flag of the new African republic. Below me a rickety metal ladder extended four feet to the rough tarmac of Bissau Airport. Weighted down by cameras, tape recorder, lenses, tapes, film, notebooks, I descended rung by rung until my feet were on terra firma, on the soil of independent Guinea-Bissau. I exulted inwardly as I followed the other passengers across the runway toward the small, shabby building which served as the air terminal. African and East European diplomats, two Danish film makers, PAIGC militants, an old peasant woman, and a North African agronomist had all shared the bumpy flight from Dakar to Bissau that Saturday morning in April 1976. As we walked, the heat pressed down from above and rose up from the dark, tarred surface to envelop us. I knew I was back.

But this time I was in Bissau, once the very core of colonialism in "Portuguese Guinea." A small town, with barely eighty thousand inhabitants, it had been for many years the generally unwilling host to thousands of Portuguese army members: soldiers, officers, generals, and the numerous and various functionaries in the Portuguese administration, who grumbled at the boredom of it all and sweated from the humidity and oppressive tropical heat. They filled the small sidewalk cafés, sitting on the rusty chairs and balancing their imported drinks on wobbly metal tables with faded white or pink enamel paint. Rocking back in their chairs, they would eye the women who passed by, discuss their attributes among each other, shout out comments, and occasionally call them over for a drink. And when they tired of entertaining the young *assimilado* women who eagerly responded to their interest and their money, the soldiers could turn their attention to the prostitutes. There was a shortage of neither.

Another feature of colonial life was the small stores. Set back a little under the two- or three-story buildings with their neat balconies and shutters, they were fairly bursting with luxury goods imported from Europe to add variety to the lives of the military men, as well as the roughly two thousand white settlers and the *assimilado* elite. Occasionally, no doubt, the soldiers would consider the idiocy of being there in the first place, and certainly an active group among them was plotting to ensure that it would not be for too much longer.* In the evenings the military men would stroll along the pleasant, though short, boulevard that ran parallel to the broad Jeba River and past Pidgiguiti dock. After dark, when the moon filtered through the rows of tall palm trees along the waterfront, the scene was positively romantic, especially since the African dockworkers, in their torn shirts and faded pants, had long since gone to their homes.

Home for the Portuguese was in the town proper, scarcely a half-hour's walk from one side to the other, and an ordered concentration of neat streets. Then the city, "their city," gave way to miles of ugly African slum, without running water or electricity, where families had to survive for a month on what one officer casually fished out of his pocket to pay for one night's consumption of alcohol.

When the Portuguese army grudgingly left Guinea-Bissau at independence, this life vanished entirely. The rows of houses on the tree-lined streets were evacuated by the military families and panicked settlers and reoccupied by PAIGC militants and officials of the new government. In the shops the remaining luxury items were gathering dust, looking oddly incongruous alongside the new stock—including brightly colored cloth or T-shirts with the imprint of Cabral's portrait—that could be afforded more easily by people who were not elite or settlers. But many shops, stripped bare, stood dark behind padlocked metal gates, a stark reminder of the large numbers of Portuguese who preferred to desert the new nation rather than give up their exclusive priveleges.

And now, a little way from the center of Bissau, near a wide street lined with small, tidy houses, I sat drinking Guinean beer on the newly completed patio of the Hotel 24 de Setembro, which had been converted from army officers' quarters. Next to

---

*It was in Guinea-Bissau that officers in the Portuguese army first began to plot to topple the Portuguese fascist regime, eventually culminating in the April 1974 coup led by the Armed Forces Movement.

me sat Teodora Gomes. Instead of her green uniform and revolver, she wore a patterned African cloth wound around her waist, topped by a green blouse. Her hair, cropped fairly short and combed flat, was no longer covered by the familiar turban.

But it was the same Teodora. Vital, spontaneous, generous. She worked in the Department of Veterans, in charge of the program for disabled veterans of the war, and her office, like most of the offices, was in a small and run-down building. But it was a brick office and not a reed hut. And seeing her sitting behind her desk the following day, I flashed back to a scene which had become so familiar during my travels in the liberated zones of the south: Teodora, in the middle of an open clearing at her base, sitting on a chair in front of a makeshift table and typing on a portable Adler typewriter, while, in the background, automatic rifles hung by their straps from the low branches of the trees.

Yes, it was a far cry from life in the *mato*. And yet no large, modern concrete and glass buildings "graced" Bissau as they do Luanda and Maputo. Only the simplest of structures, and these had gone to seed, evidencing Portugal's historical ambivalence toward this colony and the sense of hopelessness the colonial military felt at ever being able to contain the insurgents. And now, with the drastic economic situation in which the new government found itself, it would be quite a while before the impact of renovation and construction would be felt here.

During the war the freeing of Bissau had come, for many militants, to symbolize total liberation. Two-thirds of the national territory had been safely under the control of PAIGC. But not Bissau, nor for that matter any of the towns such as Bafata, Gabu, Farim, Catio, Bambadinca. The symbolic importance of Bissau existed regardless of the relationship to the city. Militants such as Carmen Pereira, who had been born and raised there and who subsequently made the adjustment to the spartan and dangerous, though rewarding, life in the *mato*, never knew when or if they would see their city again. Others had only visited Bissau. Teodora, for instance, joined PAIGC after having paid only a brief visit there. Still others—such as Fina Crato and Ana Maria Gomes—had never seen Bissau in their entire lives. But they all knew that the day they set foot in the capital would be the day on which they would experience the true and complete liberation of their country.

After September 1974 this fantasy became reality. Militants who had lived in the *mato* for over a decade began to come to Bissau, either to visit or to work. Fina, now working in the Commission of Information as a film maker and film editor, first arrived in Bissau in December 1975. "I had always heard so much about Bissau that I was very curious to see it. When I got here the first thing that struck me was the way that the colonialists had destroyed the people of Bissau. They had been terribly corrupted by the Portuguese. Everywhere people were drinking, drinking, drinking. They were only concerned with enjoying their life, taking no responsibility—just drinking and fooling around. This is one instance where there is no discrimination between men and women! Both drink too much! We have a lot of work to do here."

Apart from the spiritual devastation, colonialism had left other legacies. I was spared nothing when I was taken through the *bairros* of the city by the deputy mayor who along with the mayor had been an active cadre of PAIGC in the *mato* for many years. Rather than avoid the worst eyesores, he seemed eager to show me the vestiges of colonialism so that I could appreciate the problems that lay ahead. We drove over "roads" that were gouged deep with ruts and barely passable. In a month or so, when the rainy season began, they would disintegrate into muddy rivers. And then there were the slum dwellings. An occasional small tiled-roof house that seemed reasonably livable stood out among badly weathered mud huts and brick hovels patched together with flattened metal oil drums or crates which had originally contained Portuguese war material. We also passed small oblong houses, each of which was divided by three sets of stable doors, with narrow cement verandas running around the four sides. Each door was the entrance to a family's home—behind which parents, children, grandparents, and other close relatives crowded into two small rooms—while the few windows were too small to provide adequate ventilation. As with all the houses in the *bairros*, here there was no running water, no sanitation, no electricity. The "kitchen" was not in the house, but behind it, in an open place where fires could be made for cooking. The corrugated iron roofs kept out the rain but absorbed the sun and heat, so that by afternoon, the temperature inside must have seemed akin to that of a furnace. Roofs that were patched together with cardboard or wood or bits of metal or anything that could be salvaged were not as hot. But they were no effective barrier to the heavy rains either. More effective were the thatch roofs which, nonetheless, needed replacement or patching each year. During the rainy season empty oil drums were used to collect the rain and reduce the number of trips people made to the communal water pump. At any time of the day a large group of women and children could be seen standing around the pumps waiting to collect water for cooking, drinking, and washing.

The squalor of the various slums was uniformly grim, although, in one of the *bairros* we drove through, it unexpectedly gave way to rows of neat houses connected to electricity and running water and topped by corrugated iron roofs which, although impractical, were considered a status symbol. Built during the Spinola administration for African supporters of the Portuguese regime, the houses were, the deputy mayor told me, the product of forced labor by political prisoners who had worked from early morning to dusk without stop and without shade from the blinding sun. Lunch had invariably consisted of a handful of cold rice which the prisoners grabbed in one motion as they marched single file, and at quick time, past a huge metal container. Many horror stories could be readily recalled. One stands out: a sick baby, tied to the back of its mother as she worked, succumbed to heat stroke. Forced with the other prisoners to continue without stop to the end of the day, she could only then remove the stiff body of her dead infant from her back.

The imprint and cruelty of the colonial administration that had pervaded the fabric of life for all but the privileged in Bissau gradually gave way to the realization that, yes, the war *had* ended in victory. The euphoria of being back in the capital soon began to fade, superseded by the stern realities of the enormity of the task ahead. Independence was not the end of an era. It was a new beginning. A new nation had to be forged from the rubble of colonialism, a period of history that had so gravely wounded all facets of the social, political, and economic life of the people of Guinea-Bissau. And so, with strengthened resolve, PAIGC militants began once more the immediate task at hand: political mobilization. Among the critical items on the vast agenda for the rebuilding of the nation, through the efforts and participation of the people themselves, was the question of emancipating women.

In order to facilitate this, the Organization of Women was established three months after independence, its leadership invested in a ten-member Commission of Women. Each of the members, with the exception of Carmen Pereira who was co-ordinator, was responsible for a different region of the country. Because of its size, Bissau, had two representatives while the other seven regions of the country had one each.

All ten women had been active militants in the armed struggle. They included Teodora, Francisca, Carmen, Ana Maria, and Lilica Boal, as well as women whom I had not met on my first visit, or had met only briefly. Some were from peasant backgrounds, others not. The youngest was twenty-one-year-old Satu Djassi, who lived in Catio and worked as a nurse in addition to being the commission's representative for her region. Another member was Lucette Andrade Cabral, then wife of President Luiz Cabral and a leader in her own right, who had headed the Department of Information and who never accepted the designation or role of full-time "president's wife." Carmen, meanwhile, headed the PAIGC Secretariat as well as taking on other major responsibilities (such as National Assembly vice president). Although she was coordinator of the Commission of Women, she carefully pointed out that she was not its president. The leadership was collective.

This was not the first time that PAIGC had formed a women's organization. In 1961, before the beginning of the armed struggle and shortly after the beginning of mobilization, the Democratic Union of Women (UDEMU) was founded in Conakry. "In those early days," Franciscâ told me, "there were few women working for the party. The women who were involved in the organization in Conakry were mostly daughters of exiles who were living there. Many had never been in Guinea-Bissau themselves and their commitment was weak.''

By 1965, UDEMU had been disbanded. ''As the struggle began to intensify and develop,'' Francisca explained, ''these women [the daughters of exiles] did not want to participate fully in the struggle. They felt outsiders. Hence, the UDEMU began to slowly die. In 1966 PAIGC decided that the organization had ceased to be effective and that the women should actively join the struggle in the interior and work toward the liberation of women inside the country.''

The early experience of the women's organization showed that despite well-intentioned and revolutionary goals, success is not automatic if the practice does not live up to the theory. UDEMU failed to fulfill its role because it lagged behind the pace of the overall struggle, due to the influence of a petty-bourgeois elite group who did not want to foresake their positions and go into the *mato*. They had preferred to support the revolution from the safety and relative comfort of Conakry. Thus, it is to PAIGC's credit that they allowed the organization to die rather than pretend that their goals were being implemented through it. They could have hidden behind rhetoric, but chose not to.

Eight years later, when the country was fully independent, the creation of a new women's organization became one of the immediate tasks of the new government. However, its goals and practice now rest on a firm foundation of years of experience gained during the armed struggle.

The members of the Commission of Women traveled regularly to the areas they represented and, continuing the political education program, talked about the necessity to continue the struggle for women's rights, why women should take part in all activities, why they should help in national reconstruction. There were committees of five members of the women's organization on a *bairro* or sector and regional level; a political organizer, who was the president of the committee for each region, worked closely with the appropriate commissioner based in Bissau. At the time of my visit, these committees were newly established and their effectiveness varied from region to region depending on the objective conditions and the capabilities of the local president and those working with her. Teodora was the commission's representative for the Gabu region, and working with her as political organizer was N'Bemba Camara whom I first met at Vendoleidi in the liberated east front. The town of Gabu had been in a Portuguese stronghold and the population was one of the most resistant to the new government. Other areas which were in ex-liberated zones proved easier to organize. The region of Bafata, however, also one of the ex-Portuguese areas, responded well after the war. A contributing factor was the leadership of Satu Camara, who was president of the local women's organization. She had grown up in a Beafada village, began working for PAIGC when she was thirteen, did military training, and then trained as a nurse. She had spent most of the war years as a health *responsavel* in the north front, with particular responsibility for educating mothers about health care for their children. Since independence she had worked in Bafata Hospital. Satu was one of the many women cadres I met on my second visit who had been active throughout the armed struggle, and who evinced strength of purpose and political sense, combined with commitment to their work and to the continuing revolution. Indeed, it seemed to me that most of these women were even more serious about their political work than were their male counterparts. I attributed this to the extra burden—fighting a second "colonialism"—which gave them added direction as political beings. And I began to understand more concretely why Francisca could contend that once they were mobilized women develop politically even faster than men.

However, the paucity of women cadres* adversely affected the work of the women's organization. There were simply not

---

*By 1977 the number of women in top leadership positions was still abysmally low. There was no lack of strong and extremely competent women, even if they were less educated and less technically qualified. A breakdown of women in some of the leadership positions is as follows: *State*: Peoples National Assembly: 19 women among 150 delegates, including Carmen Pereira as vice president; State Council: 2 women of 14 members, namely, Ana Maria Cabral and Francisca Pereira; regional presidents (governors): 1 woman of 8, namely, Francisca Pereira. *Party*: Permanent Commission of PAIGC: 8 members, no women; Executive Committee of the Struggle: 1 woman of 26 members, namely, Carmen Pereira; Superior Council of the Struggle: 2 women of 90 members, namely, Francisca Pereira and Carmen Pereira. The figures are not enhanced by the fact that there is an overlap in the women, reducing the absolute total.

enough cadres who could give the organization their full-time attention. For instance, the very fact that the members of the Commission of Women had been chosen from among the most experienced and committed PAIGC militants also meant that they held other responsible positions in the party and/or government. Work with the commission took up their "spare" time. It was something of a vicious circle: cadres' inability to devote more time to the Organization of Women in turn affected the rate at which new women cadres were trained.

The staggering array of responsibilities handed Francisca Pereira illustrates this problem quite graphically. Francisca was appointed president (governor) of the geographically isolated region of Bolama when the country was redivided into eight regions after independence. Before that, and during much of the colonial period, the area had been sorely neglected and its people subjected to greater suffering than most. As a result, the new government felt a special need to integrate the region into the country as a whole and had chosen it as the focal point for a number of development projects.

Thus, by the time I visited Bolama the projects had just been launched, and Francisca was presiding over a center of growing activity. In addition, the town of Bolama itself was the new site of the Pilot School—which had moved there directly from Conakry—as well as a nursing school and a training center for primary school teachers. But on top of her political responsibility for all this, she had her duties as representative for Bolama region on the Commission of Women as well as her role as active fighter for women's rights.

Bolama was the place of Francisca's birth and had once been the capital of Guinea-Bissau. But it was rather inaccessible, situated on a coastal island far to the south of the country, so the Portuguese transferred the capital to Bissau rather than invest in building roads and bridges. In its heyday Bolama had been a haven for settlers, who attended lavish parties at the sprawling Governor's Palace or at the hotel, a large, magnificently designed building up the street from the palace. The rooftop of the *palácio* served as an open-air ballroom, and on hot tropical nights it would fill with elegantly dressed Portuguese men and women who lived the life of the aristocracy—simply transplanted to African soil—and spent their time bemoaning the "laziness" of the natives. Meanwhile, below in the kitchen and hallways of the palace itself, these same "natives" were serving, attending, cleaning, and scrubbing so that the building shone and sparkled.

After the settlers deserted the capital, it rapidly went to seed. Rooms of the palace were closed up, the hotel had trouble surviving. Then came the mobilization. Bolama was one of the first areas to respond, and so did the Portuguese, who bombed the town, isolating it even further, and arrested hundreds of people. The supporters of PAIGC fled to the *mato* and Bolama became a ghost town. "I am crying for Bolama," begins a Guinean song that came out of the war.

When Francisca returned to Bolama after independence, she found the town of her youth falling apart. The palace had served as a barracks for the Portuguese army; ignoring the worn paint and the cracked walls, she moved in with her husband and two young daughters.

When I visited her there I saw that Francisca had blossomed into an even more self-possessed woman than I remembered. Dressed in elegant cotton dresses or long West African robes, her hair cut in a short Afro, I observed the ease and tact with which she interacted with her co-workers and with the people of Bolama. She was pregnant with her fourth child at the time, and her daughter from her first marriage, now fifteen, was with her on a brief vacation from studies in Moscow.

Francisca's days were full. She had just returned from a trip with Luiz Cabral to Scandinavia and Yugoslavia and would soon resume a routine which also took her away from Bolama and which saw her attending conferences in Bissau or traveling through her region. "Whenever I return to Bolama," she lamented to me, "even if I have been away only a short time, I spend the return journey worrying myself sick about all the problems that will greet me as soon as the plane lands. If I can spend an hour a day with my two daughters and my husband, I consider myself fortunate." Her husband directed the teacher training college in Bolama. He appeared to have taken on a responsibility for his children which was far from common in Guinean households.

When his youngest child began to yell in the courtyard while we were eating supper one evening, it was he who jumped up spontaneously and rushed out to see what the matter was. Francisca remained in her seat without reacting at all. The pattern of behavior that I would have anticipated in other households when such incidents arose would have been for the husband to respond by telling the *wife* to go and see what the matter was.

My visit coincided with the last of many trials of collaborators with the Portuguese that had been held throughout the country during the previous six months. As president of the region, Francisca was a member of the tribunal and participated actively in the proceedings. After one of the accused had been handed a two-year sentence for stealing cattle and selling it to the Portuguese, she delivered an impassioned speech, directed as much at the general audience as at the culprit. It was an exercise in political education, and Francisca carefully explained how difficult conditions had been for the guerrillas and the people living in the forests. But they had done it for the freedom of their country and for people such as him. And while they had been starving in the *mato*, the accused was selling cattle to the Portuguese army so that they could remain fit and continue perpetrating their atrocities on the people of Guinea-Bissau, his people.

While Francisca's daily calendar was crowded with appointments, somehow she found time to be an active host—which meant showing me Bolama, driving out to a state cooperative run by FARP soldiers, and taking me on tours of the schools and child-care center in the town of Bolama. Besides the meetings that had been planned, there were also the spontaneous ones, when people arrived at the *palácio* with their problems. Francisca was available for everybody. She had regular meetings with cadres working as area *responsavels* for health, education, people's stores, agriculture, justice, and so forth. There were also weekly meetings with members of the regional council and regular meetings relating to the establishment of the regional structure of the Organization of Women.

But Francisca was not the only woman cadre bogged down with work. One morning I spent a few hours with Carmen

Pereira in her office. It had not been easy to set up time for our meeting as she was continually traveling to the interior of the country as well as outside. I finally managed to catch a few days with her before I left Guinea-Bissau and after her return from a visit to other African countries. Carmen, in addition to coordinating the Commission of Women, was responsible for the organization of the party at a national level and worked with the eight regional party secretaries. She also had recently been reelected vice president of the National Assembly.

Despite the lack of cadres and the lack of finances, Carmen told me, the Organization of Women was beginning to tackle the various problems affecting women. Illiteracy was one of these, and Lilica Boal, who now coordinated all the PAIGC boarding schools out of the Friendship Institute in Bissau, had been delegated to supervise a nationwide literacy campaign that would place special emphasis on women. "It is possible to travel to different regions," Carmen commented, "and not find one woman who knows how to read and write. The situation is scarcely better in the towns." Another problem was unemployment, and special programs were being organized to begin to overcome this. One example involved a sewing center where women could either work full time or take material home and do it there.

But it was not only the lack of jobs that concerned the new government. There was widespread lack of understanding among women about the value of work outside the home. "In the cities and towns there are some women who worked before independence," Carmen said. "But we know that these women worked during the colonial period because of the poverty they were experiencing. It was necessary for a young woman to work in order to help support her family. Every member of the family that could bring in a salary worked. Now we want these women to understand that the goal of working is not only for a salary. There are more important and far-reaching reasons. They must contribute to the reconstruction of our country. They must understand that they are every bit as important as the men, and that they have to make an extra effort to gain more experience and knowledge."

In order for them to do this, the provision of child-care centers across the whole country had become one of the priority tasks. And a major program, involving the establishment of a few pilot centers, was due to begin in a few months with help from the Soviet Union.* These were already long overdue and would come as a welcome addition to the child-care center in Bolama, which served much the same purpose as it had in Conakry during the war—housing children of cadres and youngsters who had lost their parents in the armed struggle.

Meanwhile, true to form, PAIGC had not taken long to size up the situation of women in the towns and to use the people's structures to further tasks of mass mobilization. Once again, they respected the institutions already in existence and instead of supplanting them began to develop them so they could better serve the women of Guinea-Bissau.

The government's growing relationship with traditional women's societies was a case in point. A feature of life throughout the countries of West Africa, these societies were to be found in even the smallest of towns (but not the villages) in Guinea-Bissau. Known in Creole as *manjuandades*, the societies were ethnically integrated, a facet of organization which distinguished them right away from typical village structures. Members of a particular *manjuandade*, having all joined at about the same time, were also about the same age and remained in the same group throughout their lives. This informal grouping, I was told, represented a relatively recent departure from tradition, whereby women usually joined a society some time in their teens and then moved through a succession of other groups which corresponded to different age brackets.

The societies function essentially as support groups. Members will make financial contributions to one of their group who is experiencing hard times economically, and they also organize wedding and birth celebrations, among other festivities.

"These are not political groups," Carmen told me when I spoke with her, "but they are well organized and the women

---

*By mid-1978 these had not yet been established, the funding still a problem. Plans for their development were continuing. An additional center, organized on the lines of the one at Bolama, had been established.

provide strong support for each other. They are traditional organizations which have existed for a long, long time and we found them still to be an important aspect of town life when we arrived in Bissau."

One afternoon I accompanied Isabel Bushkardin, one of the two representatives of the Commission of Women in Bissau, to a schoolroom in a *bairro*, where a meeting had been set up with members of *manjuandades* from the area. About thirty women of all ages, representing six different societies, sat in rows at the desks which had been hurriedly vacated a few minutes earlier by the students. (The grave shortage of places to meet meant that whatever was available had to be shared.)

Among them were representatives of the oldest *manjuandade* in Bissau, the members of which were as old as eighty. There was friendly competition among all the groups. The younger women said that times were changing and that they think of themselves more as "clubs" rather than traditional societies. They wanted to learn new dances and "modern" ways, while the older women continued to pride themselves on being reposi- tories of the traditions of their culture. The women spoke out easily and seemed to treat the meeting as something of a festive occasion. They were dressed in their best clothes, with bright- colored turbans piled high on their heads.

Each of the groups selected one spokeswoman who explained their basic structures, which appeared to differ little among them. The societies had up to eighty members who elected a "queen" and an "assistant queen." In all other respects the groups were highly egalitarian. For example, at all festivities, the women wore dresses made of identical cloth, chosen before- hand, so that one woman did not look better off than another. Each group also elected a man, only one, to handle affairs with the administration or government when necessary. While an obvious anomaly, this appeared to reflect the reality that women encountered in such matters, given their low political status within the community. However, I was unable to confirm this with the women themselves. "That is the custom," was the fullest reply I could elicit. The male representative was usually the husband of one of the members or a man respected in the community. In this way, I was told, he would not generate jealousy or competition among the women.

Each *manjuandade* had its own name. *Pe di mesa*—legs of table—was the name of one, but the women shook their heads when I asked if they knew its significance. It had been chosen because the grandmother of one of the founders had belonged to a *manjuandade* of that name. Another was called *Confortavel*, comfortable. "We are called this, " their spokeswoman explained, "because we do not want too much. On the other hand, we do not want too little either. We just want to be comfortable."

The Organization of Women wanted to benefit from the existence of such societies, Carmen Pereira told me. "They will form the basis for organizing women in the towns. We have begun working with them in order to organize them politically and mobilize them for the continuing work of national reconstruction. They are giving strong support to the Organization of Women and are beginning to participate in our work."

While PAIGC was politicizing the women's societies slowly, it had lost no time at all in enacting a number of new laws concerning women. Three of the first six laws passed by the National Assembly covered provisions for divorce, abolition of the concept of "illegitimate" children, and the legalization of common law marriages.

The fact that they moved so quickly is not insignificant, given the amount of work and shortage of cadres trained in judicial affairs. The entire legal system needed to be reorganized. One of PAIGC's first tasks had been to review the cases of every person jailed by the Portuguese to see who were the political prisoners and who were the common criminals. Generally, the task had been to evaluate the colonial laws to ascertain which were acceptable, which could be lived with until new ones could be passed, and which had to be discarded. It readily became apparent that there were no laws protecting the rights of women.

Under Portuguese law and the influence of Catholicism, divorce was prohibited in colonial times, as it had been for women under customary law. Now, however, divorce is a fairly straightforward procedure for the whole population, as it was in the liberated zones, with a recommended period of attempted reconciliation. The law states that if a marriage does not "fulfill the social task that is expected of it, then it can be dissolved." In order to ensure that a man's wife and children were not abandoned, the law established that a certain percentage of his income would go for the upkeep of his children. In addition, the wife kept the house they lived in, with the husband paying the rent. This latter arrangement only ceased if the woman lived with or married another man.

The second law, which relates to women indirectly, calls for all children to be regarded as "legitimate," whether they are born in or out of marriage. This means that a man can no longer disclaim responsibility for children he has fathered, whether or not the relationship with the mother is ongoing or legally registered. Under Portuguese law all such children would not have been recognized as the man's and their support left to the woman and her family. "A child does not choose his parents," one woman militant commented to me. "Men *must* be responsible. A child cannot be made guilty for the circumstances in which he or she was created."

The legislation legalizing common law, or "informal" marriages as they were referred to, is the most far-reaching. These marriages had been widely practiced in the towns of Guinea-Bissau for as far back as people could remember. The couple established a domestic arrangement and the community treated them as married and the children as "legitimate." However, colonial law did not. This led to complications for both parties. For instance, women who had lived with their men for many years sometimes discovered, at the man's death, that all his assets—a result of both their work—were inherited by a woman the man had formally married years before and with whom he had lost contact. And the children of the common law relationship were denied rights of inheritance.

Another problem highlighting the need for such a law grew out of the war and involved militants who had lived with

278   Fighting Two Colonialisms

peasant women in the *mato*. After independence many of these young men went to work in Bissau or other towns and some decided to marry young women they met there. Meanwhile, their previous common law marriages were thrust into the realm of past history, much as the war itself.

In order to try to protect women caught in this situation, the new law invests common law marriages with the same status as those legally established through a marriage ceremony. It allows for a simple registration of the common law marriage, if it has been in existence for three years or more. Registration can be done together, or separately by either spouse, with or without the consent of the other, and makes the union a legal marriage that can be dissolved only by divorce. A man can no longer simply "forget" his former spouse. By going through a divorce procedure if he wants to leave her, and having to bear a continued responsibility for financial support, he acknowledges the commitment he made to her. At the time of its enactment, the law was widely publicized through newspapers, over the radio, at political meetings, and by reports the deputies to the People's National Assembly took back to their constituencies.

"Thorough propaganda was made about this law; it was discussed everywhere," Commissioner of Justice Fidelis d'Almada told me. "If a man wants to marry another woman in Bissau, then his common law wife can come here and we will explain the law to her. 'OK, how many years were you living with him?' we'll ask. If she replied more than three years, we'll say, 'OK, you must ask for the recognition of your marriage and we will prevent this second marriage.' Of course, you cannot force a man and woman to live together, but now he will have to go through with a divorce and take responsibility for his children and ex-wife."

In fact, all three laws were seen as a mechanism for developing greater respect for women. PAIGC anticipated that when a man is faced with the prospect of taking equal responsibility for all the children he brings into the world, or when he knows his wife can walk out on him, or that he cannot simply deny a common law wife in favor of a more attractive situation, he is likely in the future to weigh his actions vis-à-vis women much more carefully.

The most striking examples of PAIGC's attempt to bring about a change of attitudes as quickly as possible, as well as provide protection for women, involved a "regulation" concerning battered wives. Because laws take time from formulation to enactment, and the National Assembly meets just once a year, a regulation ratified only by the party was promulgated to put violent husbands on notice. A wife beaten up by her husband can report the case to the Commission of Justice and if she can show marks on her body the man will be jailed immediately for a minimum of twenty-four hours. In addition, he has to pay a fine which goes in part to his wife. Wife-beating was basically a regional phenomenon and confined to the towns. The practice had ceased entirely in the former liberated zones and occurred only rarely in the rural areas, but it continued in Bissau on such a scale that the government was forced to move decisively and without delay.

"We have to show men who beat up their wives that we are serious about changing these attitudes," d'Almada emphasized. "Men must learn to respect women, and if they do not, we have to take actions to combat this. The situation was scandalous. Every single day wives would be beaten so badly that some even died. Men who were oppressed by the colonialists, and unable to retaliate against their oppressor, took their frustrations out on their wives, and even their children. It was an urgent situation."

Meanwhile, the women's organization faced obstacles of time, finances, human resources, and political underdevelopment standing in the way of its attempts to achieve concrete goals. On speaking with young people in Bissau, I had the sense that there was some impatience about the organization's lack of speed in setting up programs.

Frustration was articulated to me by Maria Santos,* a young woman who had studied in Portugal and returned to Guinea-

---

*This is the only instance where I have substituted a fictitious name. It was the specific request of the woman in question.

Bissau after independence to take up a responsible position on one of the commissions. She felt generally that at the time of my visit too much emphasis was being placed on political education—such as mass meetings and rallies on International Women's Day, which she nonetheless threw her energies into to help organize—and not enough on the development of services for women. Despite her criticisms, however, she was a strong supporter of the women's organization and an outspoken campaigner for women's rights at her place of work.

Maria, a lively young woman under thirty, projected a nervous energy which did not detract from her appealing personality. When I arrived at her office with a tape recorder, she became very agitated and said with a laugh she was shy about being interviewed. I told her I was not conducting an examination and she laughed again before confessing she had been so afraid of going blank that she had prepared something in writing the night before. Should she read it? Maria asked, fingering the pages laid before her on a desk. When I agreed, she began to read immediately, stopping every now and then, her face slightly flushed, to add a spontaneous comment. Eventually, though, she had relaxed completely and she just kept going in her energetic and passionate way, hardly giving herself time to catch her breath as she jumped from one thing to another.

"The fundamental problem," she said, "is to change the values of the society which characterize women as inferior. But it is very difficult to change the conditions of life for women when they continue to live according to these old conditions." She was critical of the government for being too slow in preparing for and providing essential social services. "It is not enough to just do political work. We must also provide services to free women, such as day-care centers, improved working conditions, and so forth, that take the problems of women into account. I think the state is not attacking these problems quickly enough or seriously enough."

As evidence of how hard it is to change attitudes, she referred to her own circumstances. Both she and her husband worked in government jobs; they had two young children and paid someone to come in and take care of them during the day. But they could not afford to pay someone to babysit at night. It was expected, then, that Maria stay home to look after the children, whereas her husband, without once thinking it might be unfair, was free to go and visit friends, take in a movie, or go out for a beer. If she needed to go out at night and it was in connection with her work, that was fine too. Her husband willingly stayed home with the children. But only if it was "official." He would never consider staying home so she could visit friends or go to the cinema. Maria laughed, but the laugh did not mask some bitterness: "I resent this very much. But at least I know I am economically independent and can leave my husband if I choose. Not that I want to, as it is a very good marriage otherwise."

Compared to the other women, particularly those women in Bissau—by far the majority—who were not educated, she felt she was fortunate. They grew up ignorant of the liberating potential of education and with just one thought in mind: they had to marry and their husbands would support them. But what alternative was there really? The society did not provide jobs enough for the men. And in the rare cases where a young woman held a job, tradition demanded that she stop working as soon as she married. Thus, the marriage institution, since it required the woman to be in the home and only the home, served to reinforce her dependency, a dependency which multiplied each time another child was born. Husbands, on the other hand, knowing their wives could never leave them, often took advantage of the situation to act as they pleased. And if the woman didn't like it, she just had to bottle it up inside her and say nothing.

Maria insisted that education and employment opportunities were fundamental. These would enable women to be economically independent, and then emotionally independent. This in turn would bring respect from men.

"Also," Maria continued, "if a woman is economically independent, then she does not need to get married. Why shoud she *have* to get married. The traditional attitude, which is still strong, is that a woman is only a complete woman if she has a husband and a house and some children. Single women are looked down upon. This is wrong. And then if a single woman gets ill, people say, 'Oh, she needs a man to look after her so she won't get ill.'

"But every day we are trying to educate both women and men, and so these attitudes are changing. Now women are more easily able to live alone and have normal sexual relationships, which both men and women need."

She stopped and thought a minute so that her next point would be clear. "But some confusion has come with this freedom in regard to sexual relationships. These young women in Bissau confuse sexual liberation with the emancipation of women. Young women just sleep with anyone they wish and think this is fine. They do not understand the value of relationships with men. And they say, 'Oh, the Organization of Women says we must be free. We are free because we are sexually liberated.' They think this is freedom. It is not."

She shook her head. "We do not want women to behave like men, like animals. No, it is for women and men to change their attitudes. We are not becoming emancipated in order to act like men, to behave according to their values; we are being emancipated to create a new and responsible man and woman, to create a new society. When both men and women understand this, then we will have passed the halfway mark to true liberation."

While Maria was talking in Portuguese and I was waiting for the translation, I thought back to a conversation I had a few days earlier with a young militant of the youth organization. He had said essentially the same thing about some of the young women in Bissau, the women who came from privileged, elite families. "All they are interested in," he told me, "is getting married. And to go out with members of the government. They sit in groups at the cafés and all they talk about is who they have gone out with, whether he is good-looking, whether he has a car." I asked if party militants took it upon themselves to try and educate these women instead of going out with them to have a good time. Yes, he replied, this did happen on occasion. "But that can become a problem in itself. Maybe he will give her some books to read about revolution. Then she will carry these books under her arm wherever she goes to show that she is 'revolutionary' and that this man has given her some gifts!"

I remembered, too, how a party militant who now holds a highly responsible position in the government, had teased Ana Maria Gomes one afternoon when we were all together. "Ah, Ana Maria, you are so ugly, ug-*ly!*" he joked at this very beautiful woman. "I remember when you came into the camp, all legs and ugly. You are very lucky, very fortunate that Lucio married you when you were still in the *mato*. Because if he had not, you would not have had a chance. No, not a chance! Why, when I first came to Bissau, I was driving a battered old Jeep. But still the girls came running, and look at how awful-looking I am! And *now* I have a *Volvo!*"

And yet, even though these two militants had spoken from principle, and their criticisms of the young women had merit, they had addressed only one side of the equation. What of the men, even party members, who were involved in this continuing transaction? The women would not be persisting in their behavior if it were not met with a positive response from a lot of men. And it was these same men, the men who were encouraging the women to be sexually "liberated," who complained all over town, "there are no girls in Bissau that are good enough to marry any longer." A familiar hypocrisy. The age-old double standard survived, unadulterated, in the Guinean capital.

I brought my attention back to Maria. "It is totally wrong," she was continuing, "for virginity to be equated with a 'good woman.' The problem is to explain to *both* men and women that virginity is not important, but neither is sexual freedom of this kind the answer. What must be valued is the new and meaningful relationships that can develop between the new woman and the new man in our revolutionary society."

Maria stopped again, this time to think of a way to sum up. Her face serious, she searched for a metaphor to convey the essence of her meaning.

"We are not fighting for a piece of the pie," she said. "The men control the pie and we don't want men to give us a piece of *their* pie. For if we accept something that is given to us, even if it is half, we will never have the same power as those who gave it. They will still control it. What we want to do is to destroy this pie so that men and women, *together*, can build a new pie where women will be totally equal with men."

Chapter 11

"For our country to develop, it must benefit from both men and women"

Priority for development has been given to the rural areas because of the importance of agriculture to the economy and because it was the people in the rural areas that suffered most during the war. PAIGC cadres from the liberated zones can be found in leadership positions within the state, focusing now on the continuing struggle. The system of education is based on that established during the war, with a reemphasis on agricultural production as part of the school curriculm, as well as on the liberation of women.

The six-seater airplane flew low. Below us huts, rivers, forest, palm trees, marshes, villages, spread out like a tapestry map come alive. Tones of browns and greens, rich textures of earth, foliage, human life.

A similar scene must have greeted Portuguese pilots as they reconnoitered for targets, instantly transforming the tranquil landscape into a nightmare as their bombs scorched the green vegetation, gouged holes out of the fertile earth, and reduced the huts to smoldering cinders. Two years before I had listened keenly for the sound of those bombers. Now it was I who was surveying the scene from above. I could almost feel the tranquility of the countryside rising up to engulf me. But something was different below, something insubstantial which the Portuguese pilots could not have experienced no matter how many missions they flew. And that was the difference between tranquility and peace. For without freedom, it is not possible for the latter to exist.

I was jerked out of my reveries as the plane bumped down at Catio "airport"—a dirt clearing in the midst of rice fields, palm trees, and huts. The veneer of calm created by the altitude dissolved in an instant. Children, their thin brown legs moving fast, came running from the huts to greet the plane, their small bodies exuding the excitement they felt at this arrival from above. And so began my return journey to the rural areas of Guinea-Bissau and an attempt to find out what freedom means.

Traveling through the region of Catio for ten days—on the first of a number of visits I made to the countryside—I saw for the first time how different rural life could be outside a war zone. Now planes could be treated as a novelty, and the children, instead of diving for the nearest trenches, ran to greet them.

It was a Land-Rover that provided the means of transport for the rest of my journey, this time out in the open roads and not confined to some circuitous route under the cover of dense foliage. The vehicle passed quickly over ground that had once taken days to cover by foot, the shrinking of distance suddenly making sense of the fact that Guinea-Bissau is a very small country. The villages, meanwhile, were built in the open, next to trees, not camouflaged beneath them, and the vigorous pounding

by the women was not curtailed by the fear that it would alert the
enemy. The women had also begun again the cultivation of
vegetable gardens, marked out behind the huts, which they had
had to abandon during the war. The villages themselves had
many new huts, the thatch still golden and the branches freshly
cut. There was more livestock and even cattle; the people could
now begin to breed their animals for the communal benefit and
not for taxation or for destruction by bombing and fire. The many
people's stores that were already built in the villages were solid
cement structures—simple, functional, and easily accessible to
the people living in the area.

I made the journey from the town of Catio, and from one
village to the next, squeezed between two PAIGC cadres in the
front seat of our Land-Rover. Pressed up against the right-hand
window was the youngest member of the Commission of Women,
Satu Djassi. Her one-year-old daughter Branca sat on her lap
throughout the trip, occasionally sleeping but mostly giving
vent to her active self, obviously resentful at being cooped up for
hours in a car. Satu worked as a nurse at a hospital just outside
the town, living in converted army barracks, which now served
as the site for an *internato*. Her husband, a top commander in the
army, was stationed in Bissau.

Sitting on my left, exercising his new driving skills as he
directed the vehicle around deep corrugations and through
wide puddles, was Cau Sambu. Every now and then he would
turn to me, particularly after negotiating a tricky maneuver
through slippery mud, and give me a few staccato nudges
and grin his wide grin. His pipe, as always, was clenched
between his teeth, and he carefully rationed out his supply
of Dutch tobacco to avoid having to smoke the pungent-smelling
local leaf. Slightly broader now, Cau was the same energetic
man, working as party secretary for the region of Catio. He
lived in a small house in the town of Catio with the young
woman he had recently married. His first wife had been killed
in a tragic accident a few weeks after independence, when a
land mine, a legacy of Portuguese colonialism, exploded under
their passing car. The war had managed to reach out its tentacles
beyond independence, claiming a few more lives before finally

subsiding. Cau, sitting in the back seat, had sustained only minor injuries.

One of the first villages on my itinerary was Cassacá, which being the venue of the first party congress was something of an historic site and had become absorbed into the folklore and oral history of the revolution. The full support given PAIGC by the people of Cassacá had been met with reprisals from the Portuguese army, which destroyed the village totally soon after the congress. Some of the inhabitants took refuge in neighboring Guinea, but the rest transferred their village to the *mato* and continued to work for liberation. When the war ended, the people returned to the original site of their village, by then completely overgrown and unrecognizable, and together they cleared the land, rebuilt their houses, and began to work the fields. Later I would spend a day in the newly constructed village which was still to be surrounded by fresh tree stumps sticking out of the ground.

A meeting of the people of the surrounding villages was due to start in Cassacá at nine o'clock the morning of our visit. But at ten-thirty we were still making our way toward the village. We were not the only ones late. As we got nearer we passed groups of people heading in the same direction, the women balancing on their heads stools carved from tree trunks, shiny and smooth with years of use. The villagers had prepared for our arrival. In a clearing to the side of the road was a table and a few chairs for the visitors and speakers. A number of makeshift benches provided some seating, others were brought by the audience. Already a few had taken their places, but it was at least another hour before we began. By then about one hundred and fifty people had arrived, some forty of them women. When the party *responsavel* for the area made the introductions he apologized for the generally small audience. It had rained heavily the day before, one of the first days of the rainy season, and the opportunity to begin to prepare the land for planting could not be allowed to pass by. As a result, individuals were chosen from each household to attend the meeting. This may have explained in part the smaller proportion of women, since it was they, more than the men, who were needed to work in the fields; but it was doubtless not the sole reason.

Cau spoke first, and I found his energy had not diminished with independence. He kept his audience transfixed as he graphically illustrated, through mime and metaphor, the need for the revolution to continue and for the people themselves to carry on the struggle. He spoke for over an hour and a half, describing the conditions of the country, reporting on decisions made at the recent meeting of the National Assembly, and emphasizing both the need for vigilance against counterrevolutionaries and to protect what had been gained during the armed struggle. Repeating once again his extended metaphor of "sweeping away the stones," Cau spiced his speech richly with other examples from the daily lives of the people. If a fisherman has a canoe full of fish, he hypothesized, and one fish goes bad, then it is necessary to throw away the fish immediately or it will turn the whole lot. Or take the man stung by a bee. Why was he stung? He was wearing a sweet-smelling perfume, that's why. It was his fault he got stung as the bee was only acting according to its nature. Those who are responsible for the security of the villages are like the bees, Cau opined,

While he spoke, he radiated energy and vigor. He would thrust his arms into the air and then point his fingers to the ground. He bent over double, he jumped from one side to the other, his voice now raised and shouting, now soft. And sometimes he would stop in midsentence, then beam his brilliant smile and launch right back into his story. As always, by the end of his "performance," he was breathless and dripping with perspiration. But he kept the undivided and appreciative attention of his audience from beginning to end. Even after he stopped they continued to exclaim, "*aiyee, Cau!*"

They were still reacting to him when Satu got up to speak. Satu did not look a day older than her twenty-three years, and her slight build emphasized her youth, particularly when she stood next to Cau. She wore a scarf tied neatly around her head, a blouse, and a long cloth wound African-style around her waist. Her slightly protruding teeth seemed to accentuate her serious expression. How could she hope to capture the audience's attention after Cau's virtuoso display, I found myself thinking reluctantly. But I need not have worried. Her initial nervousness soon vanished, and in her quiet way Satu proved herself as capable a speaker as Cau.

She began, in her soft, melodious voice, to speak about the family. It is important for men and women to live together in harmony, she said, and for men and women to work together. Production was the priority task for all Guineans and they should be prepared to do without consumer goods for a good while.

"We went through the war with nothing," Satu told her audience. "We do not need as our example a woman with lots of dresses and flashy things, but who does not work. All women of the party should continue to wear the clothes that we had in the war time. Our priority now is to help our men rebuild the villages. If you desire only expensive cloth—so, you can fill your suitcase full of pretty cloth. And then what? Where will you go with it? Into an ugly house. But if you build a nice-looking house, people will pass and see the work you have done and will learn from your example. When our villages are rebuilt and when we have the basic necessities of life and the standard of living has improved for everyone, then it will be time enough to think of acquiring beautiful things. Life is not expensive here and we have plenty of time."

While Satu was exhorting women to help build their houses, I recalled that in peasant society this work is usually done by men, and it began to dawn on me that she was beginning to touch on aspects of women's liberation in the Guinean context. "If both husband and wife build their houses," she was saying, "then they will have to have equal rights in that house. He cannot say, 'This house is mine, not yours.' And from now on, he cannot do what many men do. He cannot send you away because both of you have shared in building the house. The house belongs to the wife as much as the husband. One does not have more rights than the other. Your husband cannot send you away."

Smiles spread across the faces of the women and their applause was loud. "Maybe some of the men think they are stronger than women and that they can still send their wives away," Satu continued. "But no man is stronger than the state, and the people's courts can intervene. Men must respect us and treat us as equals."

She then pointed out that there are two sides to the problem. "If a woman thinks, 'no, I am inferior,' then there is little we can do to change the situation. This is not right. We women are *not* inferior. We can do what the men do. Some women work much harder than men. Women must be able to travel around the country if they wish, and we must be able to do what work we choose. There is no work that is just for men or just for women. Women must help to rebuild the country.

"Historically, the women of Guinea-Bissau and of Cape Verde participated in the struggle. Through this participation we learned that we are not inferior. Women, I am asking you to hold on to what you gained during the war and to continue the struggle for equality. Do not allow the rebuilding of our country to go ahead and to leave you behind.

"Maybe, because I am not from Cassacá, you are thinking, 'Ah, but Satu has no business to talk to us like this.' This is not so. All the women of Guinea-Bissau are one."

Satu had captured the attention of the women. Their eyes were fixed on her and the expressions of their faces would change from serious concentration to smiles and then dissolve into laughter. Satu was enjoying herself and she laughed with the women.

"The colonialists were against us. They oppressed us. Both men and women. Then, on top of that, we were oppressed by our men. This is why I say that we women had two colonialisms on our hands: we had the *Tuga* in our country and our husbands in our house.

"The problem of the colonialism in our own home is a more difficult one. We are part of the same family. Our husband lives in our house and he is the father of our children. But it is the woman who cares for the children. The father does not even buy his children a shirt. He has other things to think about, he says. But then the children grow up. Oh yes, suddenly the father is interested. 'This is *my* daughter,' he says with pride. From that time on he begins to pay much attention to her. 'Oh, my daughter, come here to your father,' he will say whenever he sees her. But we know about the marriages our daughter is expected to make. The father is doing this because her marriage will profit him. If the mother or daughter is unhappy about the husband he has chosen, what can they do? Nothing. Why can't the mother also make decisions about her daughter?"

Satu began to direct her words to the men.

"This cannot be, comrades. We must all decide together what the daughter is going to do. You must ask your wife's opinion. You must consider your daughter's wishes. When you decide to give your daughter to someone without her consent, it is as bad as living in the time of the *Tuga*. This practice must stop once and for all. If you talk about freedom, then it must exist in your own home, not just outside. As *Comarada* Amilcar Cabral said, we must leave these bad traditions behind us. Your daughter and your wife know that you are the head of the house and they respect you. You must respect them the same way and not practice your colonial ideas on your family."

Satu addressed the question of a family environment that would be conducive to nurturing respect for all members, saying that men must respect their wives, must not beat or shout at them. She added that they shared responsibility to educate their wives, but that it was important to go slowly. "You cannot expect your wife to grow by beating her. Talk to her. Talk to her with respect and she will change. You cannot change her by force. Your wife is your comrade. She must be equal in your house. The future of your children depends on the quality of life within the family."

When Satu was nearing the end of her speech, the meeting was well into its third hour. Everything she and the other speakers said had to be translated from Creole to Susu, one of the local languages spoken by a number of ethnic groups, and this drew things out considerably. And yet the people were still with her, even though the sun was at its peak and the shade of the leafy mango and towering *pilom* trees hardly lessened the heat.

"*Comaradas*, men and women," she went on, "it is my responsibility, as representative of the Commission of Women for this region, to talk to you about these things and to help the women understand why they are being oppressed so that they can begin to change their lives. Women, we must tell the men to let us be free. Free to rebuild our country, our village, our house, with our own hands.

"Unfortunately, however, there are some women who are confused about the meaning of the liberation of women. These women think freedom means doing what they want without responsibility. Maybe after I leave tomorrow some women will begin to do as they please, not taking others into consideration. They will say: 'Ah, but Satu says I must be free. The party says I can do what I like.' I am not talking about this so-called freedom. I am talking about respect between men and women. I am talking about building a new life together.

"We all know that times are hard now. It is often difficult to find a husband because so many men died in the war. But this does not mean that, because there is a shortage of men, men can do simply what they like and treat their wives as they wish. Not at all. We would rather live without men than accept this kind of oppression from men any longer."

Throughout the meeting a soldier, his rifle propped up against a large tree behind him, sat patiently with his six-month-old baby on his lap. A white cloth was neatly spread out over his knees and under the child, while she moved around, put her hands to her father's face, pressed his nose, grabbed his ear. The father was all gentleness. Sitting next to him was his three-year-old daughter, who played with her sister or quietly watched what was going on. The man's wife was president of the sector committee of the women's organization, and she was sitting with the speakers up front. The scene accentuated the changing times.

When Satu came to the end of her speech, the women's applause filled the muggy quiet of the afternoon. Their faces were bright with smiles as they nodded at each other and exclaimed their approval. The clapping of the men was polite. Elsewhere in the region, and on several occasions, I saw other signs of a less than supportive response from men. On one occasion, Satu's interpreter was a local resident, active in PAIGC. He had a rather aggressive and lively personality which added flavor to the translations. But when he translated Satu's words, he would add his own version of what she was saying, softening her points, even twisting them, to try and lessen their impact. His efforts did not pay off, however. Most of the women understood both languages and laughed at him when he made his own interpretations. At one point, when the women responded with particular delight and chuckles to something Satu had said, he got angry and shouted: "What are you applauding for? You have no business to applaud!" But they ignored him, and treated it as a joke.

At this same meeting, Cau himself expressed some impatience with the women. The meeting had been a particularly long one and the election for the first village council—the main reason for his visit to the town—had still to be organized. After Satu finished speaking, she asked whether any women wanted to respond to what she had said. She was greeted by silence. A few women looked at each other, some were given encouraging nudges by their friends, but no one came forward. We waited. There was a feeling of mounting tension as the women remained reticent. I thought back to meetings in the liberated zones where women had been ready and eager to speak, and many more than one. The interpreter began to get agitated and press for the business to continue. Cau matched his impatience and said with some irritation, *"Nô pintcha! Nô pintcha!"* meaning in this case, come on, come on, let's get on with the proceedings. But Satu was not about to be stampeded. She turned to Cau, her face shining with anger. "This is not right," she said sharply. "We must not hurry the women. They are not used to speaking. It is important to encourage them and to go slowly." Cau said nothing more.

At last an older woman stood up to speak. She had caught my attention a number of times because of her demeanor. She had been especially engrossed listening to Satu, and her face glowed when the representative made a point which particularly appealed to her. Then, when the speech was over, she had been one of the first to applaud. During all of this, she would light up a small pipe from time to time and puff away at it. Her own speech was short, although she did not appear particularly shy.

"I had not intended to speak, but after hearing Satu I felt it is very important that a woman speak. I know that all the women here agree with me when I say that she spoke the truth to us today. At home we women discuss these problems. I heard very well what *Comarada* Satu said. We want to ask her please to continue to help us to rebuild our country."

Later, when I asked if I could interview her at her home, she agreed. Mariama Camara was the first woman I interviewed who had not lived in the liberated zones during the war and hence had not benefited from PAIGC's mobilization of women. Her home was right in the town of Cacine, where the meeting had taken place. Throughout the war, Cacine had been a Portuguese *aldeamento*, that is, a fortified village or strategic hamlet, an enclave carved out of a vast liberated zone.* Although the true population barely exceeded eight hundred inhabitants, its strategic importance had earned it the title of "town" and a particular designation on the Portuguese-drawn maps. However, to the visitor, Cacine differed from a village not in terms of its size—there were villages with larger populations—but because it boasted permanent structures: a cement administrative building, a sizable brick house, and two brick shops. The construction materials of the other houses ranged from mud, to a combination of mud and brick, to all cement. The center of the town was not more than half a mile long, spread out between two parallel roads. The main road, a wide earth track, ran the length of the center, passed through a dense avenue of mango trees, heavy with the bright orange fruit, and then went down to the Cacine River and onto a dilapidated pier.

Halfway between the pier and the entrance to the town stood Mariama Camara's small house, built by her husband years before the war. Its age was revealed by the numerous cracks which traced their way across the cement walls. Typically, it had an iron roof and no electricity or running water. When Satu and I arrived there late in the afternoon, we were greeted by members of her family, who immediately brought out carved stools for us. Mariama then perched herself on the edge on the concrete veranda that ran around her house, letting her legs dangle over the edge. A few feet away sat Fatmata, her co-wife, balanced on a small stool.

---

*Cacine's vital importance during the war derived from its position on the Cacine River. The Portuguese built one of their largest marine bases there, strengthened with a considerable garrison. The town itself was fortified by uprooting some sixteen hundred people from the surrounding areas and concentrating them into a "strategic hamlet," providing a human hedge between the base and the vast liberated territory.

"The Portuguese colonialists oppressed us," Mariama began, without prompting. "They smashed us—both the men and the women. But for women it was particularly bad. The men were oppressed by the Portuguese and then they turned around and oppressed us. So we were oppressed twice.

"Now at meetings women want to stand up and speak their minds freely. Many women want to express their own independent personalities, but they are afraid of the men. And the men think we do not speak because we do not understand what is going on. This is not so. We understood only too well the situation. We are not stupid. We are not inferior. The men think this is why we do not stand up and speak. But we do not speak out because they have oppressed us.

"In order for our country to advance, these attitudes must end. For the country to develop, it must benefit from both men and women. Otherwise we will all suffer by losing the contribution that women can make. If this changes, we will advance more quickly than we are doing now. But it is not easy. Even though our country has been liberated, it does not mean that these attitudes, this mentality, can change suddenly. Oh no. It will take a long time to free both women and men from these attitudes."

Mariama's words were always accompanied by graphic facial expressions and other body gestures. She would jab her fists into the air, shake her head, sigh, put her hands on her hips and thrust her chin forward or exclaim a high-pitched "hé!" at the end of sentences. Although she spoke in Susu, her mannerisms were so expressive that I had a sense of what she was feeling, even before the translations were relayed to me.

"Many women could have spoken at the meeting," she continued. "They understood what Satu said, but we have been so oppressed, it's terrible. This isn't the first time I spoke at a meeting, but often I do not. But after Satu spoke I felt I had to say something to express our support for what she had said to us women."

Mariama had moved to Cacine when she got married, about twenty-five years ago. Or was it twenty-two? No, maybe as much as twenty-seven. She could not be exact as she did not know her age. In any case, she had been there long enough to give birth to and rear three children, one boy and two girls. Long enough to see them marry and be delighted by her numerous grandchildren. She had remained in Cacine all this time and had never traveled. After the war began there was no chance of leaving anyway. The town was one of those circles on a colonial map that had lines surrounding it. The lines showed the large liberated areas, the circles the fortified camps of the Portuguese. To have left would have meant the suspicion, or rather the presumption, by the *Tuga* that you were collaborating with the terrorists. When you returned you would be arrested, yet if you stayed away, your family would be the target of reprisals. If she had known more about PAIGC at the beginning of the war, she said, then maybe she would have left Cacine to live in the *mato*. But they (her family) did not, so they missed the chance. Later it was too dangerous. "Hé"—she shook her head—you just tried to live through those days as best you could. What else could you do?

Once Mariama had a close escape. Her brother had come to visit her while ill with a fever, so she took her basket and set out for the forest on the edge of the town to gather medicinal herbs. So engrossed was she in looking for the right plants that she did not hear the soldiers arrive. And when she looked up, she gasped at finding five rifles pointed at her.

"You're a *bandido!*" they accused her.

"No, I'm from Cacine," she protested. "I'm looking for medicines for my brother."

"Bah! You liar! What can you find among these dry bushes?"

They grabbed her by the arm, forced her into the back of the truck, and squashed an empty oil drum over her head so that no one would see her as they drove through the town. She could barely breathe. "We're going to kill you," they yelled at her. "When we get to the camp we will shoot you."

When they had reached their destination, Mariama was taken down from the truck and tied up. But a young African soldier walking past stopped and looked at her.

"What are you doing?" he asked the other soldiers, puzzled. "Why have you arrested the mother of Fatima?"

"Oh no, she is a *bandido*. We found her in the forest. We are going to kill her."

"Don't be ridiculous. She lives in Cacine. I have been to her house."

The soldiers reluctantly let her go.

Her husband had not been so fortunate, however. It was soon after the beginning of the war that the soldiers came to get him. One morning he got up and went about depressed and pre-occupied. Both Mariama and Fatmata noticed and asked him what was wrong. "Nothing," he said, and they watched him go out and sit under the kola nut tree. That tree just to the side of the house. But he did not eat the breakfast they brought him. Then the *Tuga* drove up in an army car and took him away. Just like that. They never saw him again.

Mariama stared past me out to the kola nut tree and began to cry silently. She took the corner of her skirt and dried her eyes before continuing.

They had no idea why he was arrested. All the *Tuga* would say was that he had been working for PAIGC. Mariama said this was not true. Of course, he supported the movement, but that was all. She remembered hearing him talk to a young man once, telling him to go and join PAIGC. "I am too old," he said. "I have my two wives to take care of. But you are young. It is best that you go and join the struggle."

At independence, when the prisoners were released, his wives waited eagerly for his return. But he never came.

"He never returned to us," Mariama said. Tears ran down her cheeks again. "Only then did we hear that they had killed him soon after his arrest."

Mariama and Fatmata looked toward each other consolingly. The relationship between them was relaxed and supportive. They were like two close sisters. (Satu commented later on how unusual this was in polygynous marriages. The young women in particular were always quarreling.)

After their husband had been arrested, the two women lived together in the house they had all built, and brought up their children. Life became very hard. Now they had to do all the work because there were no men to help them. Only men could clear the land for growing rice and dig up the trenches for planting, so they grew peanuts instead. But this did not provide sufficiently, and when they had some money, which wasn't often, they would buy rice. Other times they exchanged peanuts for rice at the Portuguese store. They were constantly short of food.

"*Aiye*," Mariama exclaimed, "but the difficulties, the troubles we have seen in this village! I can't begin to tell you. I'd prefer to forget it all, it was so bad." Then, as she added another "*hé*" to underscore her anger, her hands sprang to her hips as she jutted her chin and right shoulder forward in a defiant manner.

"The *Tuga* did bad things to us, really bad things. But those who committed the worst acts were the sons who turned against us. Yes, the very sons and grandsons of Cacine hurt us the most. They were armed and paid by the *Tuga* and told to fight against PAIGC in our town. But they took the war out of the hands of the *Tuga* and waged it against their own people. Because we all lived in the same town they knew everything, everything about us, and they used this knowledge to commit atrocities against us. They would accuse people of working with PAIGC, even when they were not, and have them arrested. They would kill people for no reason. Once these boys fired a bazooka at our house. Luckily it missed and went over the roof. They threatened to kill us and called us *bandidos* and said we were collaborating with PAIGC. In the end they left our family alone. *Hé*, it was hard. And they were the sons of our town!"

Then Mariama's face broke into a vivid smile. "But now our country is independent. This makes us so happy. Life is much better. Before I was just like a stick. I have put on weight and we are all healthier. Oh, you should have seen us the day we heard we were free! The excitement in this town! You can't imagine it. And the festivities! I have never seen anything like it. It was wonderful."

And now? What of the future, I asked.

"Everything in life comes to an end," she replied. "The war has ended and now there is only one thing to do. Just one thing to do. We must all join our hands together and with our power to work, we will build up our country. The past and the suffering is behind us. This is what we must do now."

When she had finished talking, Mariama fished around in the folds of her skirt, took out her small pipe, filled it carefully with the coarse, sharp-smelling local tobacco, and lit it. She puffed at it pensively, all the while clenching the pipe between her teeth, and every now and then opening her lips just enough to blow out smoke in gentle bursts. We sat in silence, thinking over what she had told us. Finally, Mariama called her grandson over and spoke to him in Susu, pointing at their orange tree. Quickly he climbed the tree, and began shaking its branches until all the ripe fruit fell to the ground. His grandmother then got up, carefully picked up each orange, placed them one by one in a cloth normally used as a turban, and handed it to me as a gift. I was very touched.

But the most enduring impression I took away with me from Cacine had to do with the level of political consciousness, which matched that of many women mobilized by PAIGC at the beginning of the war. My first reaction was to consider this extraordinary in light of the fact that these women had been suppressed throughout the war by a Portuguese garrison, and therefore denied any real involvement in PAIGC's political education process.

On the other hand, their experience of oppression had been acutely personal, more drawn out than that of Guineans in the liberated zones, and marked by brutality due to the continued Portuguese presence in the town. It was not difficult for them to understand what PAIGC was talking about when they spoke of the need for change. As a result, after the war had ended, PAIGC's continuing politicization campaign was readily received, since what they were saying about women related so closely to the facts of their own lives.

In fact, this ability of PAIGC to articulate the people's experience in language they could understand was an important reason why so many women had been quick to throw their support behind the party fifteen years earlier, and why, after independence, most of the peasants living in the region of Catio, male and female, responded favorably to the new phase of mobilization. Nevertheless, PAIGC's success in postwar reconstruction depended on other factors also, and these explained the fact that development was anything but uniform across the country. Peasants who had lived in the heart of Portuguese-controlled areas—as opposed to towns like Cacine which had been colonial pockets within vast liberated territories—regarded the new regime with suspicion and put up some resistance to the political mobilization. For too long they had been recipients of the colonial pacification programs. To win either the allegiance or political neutrality of these people, the colonial administrators had waged an unrelenting campaign of psychological subversion. They left in place and manipulated to their own advantage repressive local customs, spread propaganda depicting the guerrillas as terrorists bent on destroying the traditional way of life, and offered consumer staples at prices set artificially low, to be competitive with the people's stores.

Such tactics would not have worked in the garrison towns, the military enclaves surrounded by liberated territory, and the colonialists knew it. Some children of Cacine, for example, may have hired themselves out to the Portuguese army, but many more, including Titina Silá, had joined the guerrillas in the nearby *mato*. Consequently, those they left behind had intimate and ongoing connections with the liberation movement, connections which proved impermeable to all attempts at subversion. Moreover, the Portuguese occupation force had its hands full in keeping the guerrillas at bay, and no time to administer a network of alternative social structures based on bribery of the local population. They had difficulty enough assuring their own supply lines.

After the war, the amount of resistance emanating from former Portuguese areas thus varied from place to place, and a lot depended on the abilities of the PAIGC *responsavels* and the amount of time and energy they were prepared to put into their work. And with the shortage of cadres more severe than at any time in PAIGC's history, the problem was compounded considerably, as for example, in the Calequisse area, which I visited on a later occasion.

As we drove from Bissau toward Cantshungu (formerly Teixeira Pinto), the central town of the region, I looked out of the window of the car onto an already familiar scene. Few cars passed us in either direction. But we were still sharing the road with the local population, who were walking the long distances from their village to one or another destination. Meanwhile, others waited patiently, often next to a pile of luggage, under large mango trees which cast their shade over the road. They would rise as a car approached, hoping for a ride. I watched the women as they walked, their backs perfectly straight, with the ease and rhythm of people used to walking long distances. Heavy bundles or baskets balanced on their heads, and not a few had the additional weight on their backs of a baby, tied with a long piece of cotton cloth. Their clothes were not more than a piece of cloth wound around the waist, and invariably grayed from countless washings, which could no longer remove the stain of earth or retrieve the color. I tried to look beyond the silhouettes along the side of the road and to conjure up the reality of their daily lives. The distances they walked, the clothes they wore, the conditions of the houses and the huts we passed, all pointed to the harshness of the life these women shared. But I was not able to fully appreciate this until I had spent a day and night in the Calequisse village.

I stayed in the compound of the president of the village council, which, like the other compounds comprising the large sprawling village, included a main house of mud bricks and thatched roof and a number of smaller huts surrounded by neat thatch fences, compressed and tied by thin branches. From early morning to late into the evening the women never stopped working: sweeping the ground to clear the leaves, pounding for hours, preparing palm kernels for palm oil by boiling them and then pounding and sifting, roasting large mounds of cashew nuts which they had spent hours collecting, and then, after removing them from the heat, sitting in front of the mound to shuck the tough bitter shells. The daily routine also involved tending the fire and cooking, caring for the children, fetching water from the well where they also washed the clothes—a good hour's walk from the village—and cleaning and tidying their houses. Moreover, the rainy season was approaching and they had aleady begun to work in the fields and to prepare food to take to their men who were breaking up the ground. In the evening each woman placed her husband's food—a good portion of chicken, meat, or fish and rice—in his hut, where he ate alone or was joined by male relatives. On the night we were there, my interpreter and I were invited to eat with the village councillor and his brother. While the women did not appear to act in a particularly subservient way toward the men (this was not a Muslim village) they did stay at a distance, so that the separation of the sexes was immediately obvious. The men were our hosts and the women were supposed to have nothing to do with our presence. They never came to talk to us and seemed puzzled that I would want to speak with them.

The following morning, when I spent some time with the women, they were shy and seemed unused to visitors. They asked if I had come to take photographs for postcards—the only reason for them that would explain the presence of myself and my camera. The concept of the liberation of women was totally alien to all the villagers. So, apparently, was the concept of liberation itself. Our host reminisced about the "good times" of the Portuguese rule. "They just left us alone," he told me, "and we could live our lives every day without interference." PAIGC forced them to pay taxes and tried to control their lives. However, there was something suspect in the man's criticism of PAIGC, his use of the words "us" and "we" and in the defensive way he spoke. I inferred that in some way his relationship with the Portuguese had been beneficial to him and his family. Now he had no such privileges and therefore no real incentive to accept PAIGC's egalitarian program. As a result, political mobilization in the area had been a slow process, and I found nothing here to match the spirit of the Catio region and its support for the new government. (I was told later in Bissau that this situation had been aggravated by the ineffectiveness of the politcal commissar for the sector, and that he was replaced shortly after my visit.)

Meanwhile, the process of council elections was under way here and in other former Portuguese-controlled villages, and also in villages which had seen a large part of their populations flee from the war and then return after independence. The delay of one and a half years had been deliberate. It gave PAIGC time to encourage mass participation in the process, and also served to prevent the automatic elections of those who had held positions of authority under colonial rule—the chiefs, the collaborators with the Portuguese, the wealthier men. What PAIGC had learned from earlier mobilization was being applied again: that a prior period of political education is essential before institution of any large-scale reform. The first elections in the liberated zones had taken place only after the mobilization had moved into the phase of armed struggle, and in the wake of victory, when the peasants could see that what the mobilizers predicted was beginning to materialize. They were indeed able to liberate their land, govern themselves representatively, and extend this democracy to include women.

But the situation was very different ten years later in areas which had no experience of revolutionary life. A mass peasant meeting at which the new councils of five villages were presented demonstrated for me that this second phase of the revolution was going to move slowly in relation to the pace of events in the old liberated zones. Without exception, any woman elected was made responsible for relatively low-status activities, like keeping the treasury and cultural affairs. Provision of rice for the guer-rillas could no longer be used as a politicizing tactic, and, while the stipulation of at least two women per council had been adhered to, none of the councils exceeded the minimum, as they often did in the PAIGC-influenced villages. However, cadres regarded these developments as a good beginning. An element of national uniformity was now in place, and the presence of women on the new councils meant that they had opportunities to assert themselves politically where once there had been none. In Cacine, for instance, Mariama Camara was elected to her council and I doubted that her contribution and participation would be token.

Elsewhere, the political mobilization of the people was being conducted at still higher levels. The eight regions of the country and the sectors into which they were subdivided each had their elected councils, all with a minimum of two women. Discussions with the regional presidents I met reinforced for me the leader-ship's contention that Bissau would not become the focus of national life. These governors knew their regions from one end to the other, were familiar with local problems in every way, and generally impressed visitors in terms of their own commitment and the high caliber of many of the *responsavels* who worked with them. The government leaders, for their part, regularly traveled through the countryside and the smaller towns, addressing meetings and speaking to the people. They had not insulated themselves in the capital.

Nevertheless, regional disparities were such that PAIGC leaders told me they were expecting some setbacks in an upcoming vote to replace the National Assembly that had been elected in the liberated zones four years earlier. (The first national elections were duly held in December 1976, at the same time as those for regional councils. Basil Davidson, who was in Bissau at the time, reported that the party did not simply compile a list of candidates and ask the people to vote for them. Desiring elections in which voters should actively participate in the whole process of selection and choice of candidates, as well as discussion of problems, they spent some months reviewing possible candidates with an electoral commission for each region, until the people were satisfied with those chosen. Since "a large fraction of the electorate was voting for the first time in their lives, and without the slightest experience even of the superficial forms of electoral democracy," there were some disappointments. "In the two main regions of the north where hereditary chiefs in Portuguese pay (mainly Fula) had always opposed the movement of national liberation . . . the PAIGC list could manage to secure only 50.4 per cent of the votes (Bafata) and 56 per cent (Gabu)." The picture had been very different in most of the other areas, with PAIGC gaining over ninety percent of the votes. Even the city of Bissau responded with eighty-four percent, "a striking tribute to the effective work of party militants there."[1])

So while all was not rosy in the early days of independence, Guinea-Bissau militants tended to view with patience their compatriots who maintained backward views on women's liberation, and PAIGC's policies of social reconstruction. It was not, they felt, that such people were actively, or even essentially, opposed to the party or its policies. The problem was one involving underdevelopment. They saw this as a direct result of the ideological damage suffered by the population who lived with colonial propaganda for so many years.

An anecdote related to me by Francisca Pereira captured

the disparities between the people's consciousness and demonstrated the difference in political development between those
who had remained active participants in the struggle and those
who had not. An elderly Muslim chief who had joined PAIGC
right at the beginning of mobilization risked much in his work
for the party and the revolution. For his efforts he was arrested
by the Portuguese before the beginning of the war and spent
the duration of the armed struggle isolated behind the bars
and walls of his tiny prison cell. At independence, however,
when all political prisoners were released, the chief returned in
triumph to Bolama, his hometown. Still a respected and loyal
member of the party, he was elected onto the regional council.
But all regional councils function under the leadership of a
regional president, with whom the members work closely. The
president in this case was Francisca, not only a woman, but
virtually young enough to be the chief's granddaughter. For the
twelve years this elderly Muslim headman had languished in
the prisons of the *Tuga*, he had remained a supporter of PAIGC.
But he had not experienced daily life in the liberated zones,
where old attitudes and practices had been drastically altered in
the context of armed struggle and national reconstruction. In
short, the chief was not prepared to deal with women on equal
terms and was finding it extremely difficult to adjust to the new
world into which he had been released. Francisca spoke about
him with understanding, saying she appreciated what he must
have been going through. However, while she was trying to
handle the situation tactfully, she would not compromise her
leadership. "He must learn to let go of his backward ideas about
women," she told me. "Not since the beginning of the armed
struggle have I been confronted with this kind of problem. If
he had not been isolated during the war, his attitudes would
have changed gradually as did those of the other militants, old
and young."

In sum, if we take a bird's-eye view of the society that is
emerging since independence, our attention necessarily focuses
on an apparently motley array of inharmonious situations. In
Bissau, our eye is caught by a group of young women flirting, a
seemingly major preoccupation in their lives, with members of

the government; in Catio region we find a nurse trained in the liberated zones, newly wed and not working outside the home, while the hospital in the same town is short of nurses. But then our eye fixes on a meeting of peasants, mainly women, in Mansoa, not far from Bissau. The women's clothes strike a blaze of rich colors against the green trees and brown earth as they listen to a speech by Ana Maria Gomes. The interpreter, however, a party *responsavel* in the sector, is stung by her words and takes it upon himself to defend "men's rights" and to remind the women how much they must respect men. Ana Maria then jumps up and launches into a lively defense of women's liberation and a deft put-down of his male chauvinism. Throughout, the women clap energetically in support of her words. An overview also has to include Mariama Camara listening with rapt attention to the speech of a young woman, younger than her youngest daughters, drinking in the words and trying to translate them into action in her everyday life. And yet, at the same time we cannot help noticing that the physical separation between the men and women is as if a rope had been dividing them.

These apparent contradictions are not antagonistic, however. They permit eventual reconciliation even as they now give life and movement to a new society that is breaking out—painfully here, spontaneously there. And most important, they do not detract from the dominant trend that emerges from the bird's-eye view, the view of Guinean society taken as a whole. And this is that women in the towns and the villages are taking up the idea of their own liberation; that women cadres, government representatives such as Teodora, Satu, Francisca, Ana Maria, and Fina are working as hard as anyone to ensure that this movement remains an integral part of the continuing revolution, and that the state, which sees women's emancipation as indispensable to the fight against underdevelopment, is planning programs and services directed especially toward women.

But political education and exhortations are not enough. Laws are not enough. The work of the Organization of Women, its establishment of services for women, even these are not enough. Critically important, yes. But not enough. True women's emancipation will not come in Guinea-Bissau if the revolution does not get past the superstructure. A vital next step is the need to change the organization of agricultural production, a step that, as we have seen, PAIGC still relegates to the future. Fundamental changes in the social life of the peasants cannot happen without it. For instance, how can repressive customs such as polygyny cease unless men—and women—experience the reality that innovations such as cooperatives, technological improvements, retraining of both women and men, will in the long run produce more at the least physical cost? Marrying that extra wife will not, under these circumstances, have any impact on the amount of work a family puts out to feed itself or to increase the wealth of a particular individual. Only when time spent in agricultural work is more equitably divided between women and men can a community afford, on a lasting basis, to release all its daughters from the heavy workload imposed upon them from an early age and allow them to benefit from a full schooling.

While the pace of rural transformation remained slow in the first years succeeding independence, the work remained strenuous. As I drove through the rural areas, I saw peasants everywhere working a long day in the fields. My visit coincided with the coming of the rains and the planting of rice, peanuts, manioc and other produce—but mainly rice. And the Guineans accompanying me would point to all the land under cultivation for the first time. PAIGC was emphasizing the need to work, for both ideological and pragmatic reasons, and the people seemed to be responding with great optimism about prospects for the future.

N'Fansu Thiam, an elderly peasant and PAIGC militant who lived in Cassacá for many years and who walks with a limp as a result of his participation in one of the first guerrilla actions against the Portuguese, said to me:

"This is our land, our country now. Only work can take us forward. Our country has such potential, such possibilities for the future. Our land is very good for agriculture, our soil is very rich. Already we are seeing the results, and we are benefiting from them, not the Portuguese. Fruit that was grown here before the war—bananas, apples, oranges—were all taken from us by the Tuga. Rice too. Then the war destroyed everything. Now that the war is over, we must work hard so that we can have all this again. It will all return. I am old. Many of us in this village are old. But our hearts are young. We can all work to rebuild the society. But we must do it together. Step by step. Yes, it's like that."

Thus, the emphasis was not only on the need for hard work, but on the need to work together. Bwetna N'Dubi expressed it best when I met her again in Catio. She now lives in a village twenty kilometers away from the town and is a member of the party's regional council.

"Rebuilding Guinea-Bissau is like work in the rice fields. Some of the rivers are salty, so everybody must build a wall around his portion of the rice field to keep the salt water out. If just one person does not build his wall, or builds it badly, it will let the water in to all the fields and destroy everyone's rice."

"The children are the flowers of our revolution and the principal reason for our fight" goes the oft-quoted saying of Cabral. Thus it is only in the coming generations that the ambitions of the present-day revolutionaries can be realized. In this context, the PAIGC educational system becomes a crucial element in any assessment of what the future holds for the people generally, and women particularly. For as much as new laws and economic development strengthen the process of revolutionary social change, education helps people to understand the need for that change, thus empowering them to become in their own name, the major protagonists of the revolution.

Of all the programs of social reconstruction under way, probably the most alive and innovative was education. In fact, although there were new and more difficult obstacles along the path, the party has actually redoubled the commitment it made to all its children some fifteen years earlier.

The Kwame Nkrumah Secondary School—new name, old facility—stands adjacent to the Commission of Education and in front of the small Titina Silá Square, where a plaque has been mounted as a memorial for one of ten national heroes of the country. The building is large by Bissau standards, and rises two stories. I was struck by the lively atmosphere in which students mingled easily with the teachers, many of whom were hardly older than the pupils. Along the corridors were taped wall newspapers, written and illustrated by the students. One commemorated the first years of Mozambique's independence, while another denounced apartheid and the Soweto massacres and expressed solidarity with the people of South Africa. Still others depicted the role of women in the Guinean armed struggle or explained aspects of preventive medicine. Although the school buildings were old, rambling, and in poor repair, the freshness of the atmosphere bespoke the excitement permeating all other aspects of education in independent Guinea-Bissau. Because here too the government was challenging the old colonial structures and continuing the process by which the society would be transformed into one based on freedom.

During the colonial period, this had been the only secondary school in the country, and catered exclusively to the sons and daughters of the *assimilados* and the small settler community. With wives of army officers for teachers, the students were trained to perpetuate the civil service while they wrestled with the dates and events of Portuguese fascist history. As a result, they learned nothing of their own. And they absorbed values entrenching their feelings of superiority over and alienation from the masses of their countrymen and women. They were told, and generally believed, that PAIGC was not a liberation movement trying to free their people, but a band of terrorists— *bandidos*—who, in their efforts to bring dreaded communism to Guinea-Bissau would cause great suffering for the people in general and for the *assimilados* in particular.

When the new government took over its first inclination was to replace such schools with those developed in the liberated zones, but a shortage of teachers, for one thing, made this not feasible. So for the first year of independence a dual system of education was in operation: the system inherited from the Portuguese administration, of which the Kwame Nkrumah School was part, existed side by side with the PAIGC *internatos*, now numbering ten.

The adoption of the old Portuguese system in the towns was a pragmatic decision, not an ideological one. PAIGC first set about making certain changes that could not wait, and then designed a program to transform the system year by year, over six years, when it would fully reflect their ideology and effectively complement the *internato* network in the rural areas.

At the time of my visit, they were confronted with many difficulties. There was a great shortage of teachers and, except for the eighty Portuguese nationals on contract from Lisbon, few of the teachers had any formal training. In fact, the primary schools in Bissau, which were staffed mostly by instructors who were themselves pupils in the secondary schools, would not have teachers with formal training until the return of large numbers of student-teachers who had been sent outside the country for study. These would be supplemented by graduates from the school for primary school teachers in Bolama, still small, which had been taken over from the Portuguese and completely restructured. Meanwhile the texts that had been used by the colonialists had to be discarded. The teachers at the Kwame Nkrumah School, for instance, were writing their own lessons and discussing them collectively, so that they might form the basis for the new textbooks still to be written. Often I walked into the teachers' room to find one or another pounding away on an old manual typewriter, preparing stencils for mimeographing his or her lessons. Regularly, however, the school would run out of paper and they would then have to dictate the text to the class before they could begin the lesson.

One of the English teachers, Lucette Tavares, a Guinean and a young PAIGC militant, was my interpreter for part of my visit to Bissau. During the many hours that I spent with her, we talked at length about the school and the problems educators were facing. Most of her students, thoroughly imbued with the colonial mentality, were uncritical and resistant to a political way of thinking, she said. Rather than aggravate this by the use of overtly political English texts, she selected works of African writers and of progressive writers from other continents and used the subject matter as a basis for discussion, which she insisted be done in English.

"What I do is take a sentence from the text and begin a discussion around that," Lucette told me. "For instance, one African story referred to the woman standing outside the door. 'Why did the woman stand outside the door, away from the company of men?' I asked my class, and we got into a discussion of the oppression of women. On another occasion we were discussing the well. I showed a picture of women collecting water from a well.'Why are only women collecting water from the well?' I asked, and again we began to talk about the role of women in our society."

Sometimes these discussions can get very heated, she told me, but the most heated one was when they were reading a text about native Americans. "A boy in the class made the comment: 'But they are lazy.' I said, 'OK, class, close your books. We'll stop right there.' I then took up the point he had made and for over an hour we had an intense debate about these attitudes. I began by pointing out that this was exactly what the Portuguese said about us. By the end of the discussion all the pupils agreed and the boy tried to make out that this was not what he had meant!"

At the end of the term, however, during the criticism–self-criticism session in which pupils evaluate their teachers, she had been criticized for being "too political," although she herself felt her pace had been slow and deliberate. "Some of my students told me that they had come to class to learn English, not for political education!" Lucette recalled with a laugh. Nonetheless, not all the students had been resistant to the ideas of PAIGC—although most, for lack of contact, had little knowledge of the party—and the overall level of political consciousness continued to rise with each succeeding year. This process, Lucette added, had been given a boost by another factor. As time went by, the composition of the school had changed substantially, with students from nonelite backgrounds entering for the first time. And, as none of these could ever have hoped to go to secondary school in colonial times, they brought progovernment ideas into the classroom which affected the changing attitudes of the other students in a positive way.

The ten *internatos* were a different story. In keeping with the dual principle of giving developmental priority to the towns and not alienating the students from peasant culture, none of the *internatos*—except the Pilot School and kindergarten in Bolama—were situated in the towns. The exception was made for the express purpose of rebuilding Bolama after its destruction. Given its isolation and size, the environment was not all that different from the rural areas and certainly anything but "urban." One of the few useful inheritances from the colonialists was the proliferation of brick army barracks throughout the countryside, which PAIGC put to good use as school buildings. With a coat of paint and the planting of flowers, they had been made to look quite attractive. One aspect had not changed, however: the one-to-three ratio of girls to boys in these schools had not improved since the war. The problems that had confronted PAIGC in this area during the war had not diminished after independence.

Of the several *internatos* that I visited throughout the country, one stands out most particularly. The *internato* at Mores is in the heart of the old liberated zones. I traveled there by bus one Sunday with a large group of students from the Kwame Nkrumah School who were to spend the day helping with production. This was not a token effort. For hours the students and teachers of both schools worked side by side in hand-plowing the land and planting corn. But even if I had not known already which students were from which school, it would have been easy to spot. Those from the *internato* expertly wielded their implements, while the "city" students, because production had only recently been added to their curriculum and because of growing up in an urban area, were awkward still.

As I watched the young people, both boys and girls, waging their sweaty battle to unlock the abundance of the earth, it occurred to me that no young person was destined anymore to a strictly anonymous life devoted exclusively to productive toil. Some were even going to be future leaders of Guinea-Bissau, leaders who had actual experience of the backbone activity of the country and, therefore, *responsavels* who had come from the people and whose consciousness had been formed in the revolutionary educational system.

Take Helder Proença for example. At nineteen he was the *responsavel* for education for the Bolama region and a veteran of PAIGC. A few years earlier, during the war, he had left off his own schooling in order to teach at a village school in the liberated zones, and now combined his duties as *responsavel* with further study at the Pilot School.

I got to know him on my visit to Bolama and was able to

observe him one evening interacting with his young comrades at the school, where we had gathered for a rally in solidarity with the student uprising in South Africa, to be followed by a poetry reading intended especially for the visitors. The room was filled with students of all ages who had much to say and many questions to ask. Although they were to rise at six o'clock the following morning, it was midnight before the front desks were removed to make room for the small school band which would provide background music for Helder's poetry.

During the rally my eyes kept returning to Helder. Possessed of one of the most pleasant and easy smiles I have seen, he projected almost constantly a quiet enthusiasm about his work and the revolution. And although his personality was not forceful (if anything, he was a little shy) his presence was always felt. Even his *vivas*, which he shouted in unison with the other students at the end of the meeting, had a naturalness to them which seemed the integrated expression of the unforced way in which he held his beliefs.

Helder was also a very fine poet. As I listened to him read in his sonorous voice I remembered how so many people in Guinea-Bissau had insisted to me that in order for women to be liberated, men's attitudes—perhaps more than women's—must be changed; and that for a sign of real change we have to look to the next generations, not only in young women but in young men. And Helder's poetry did conjure up rich images of the revolution, of solidarity with oppressed people, of *Comarada* Amilcar Cabral. But when he announced his last poem would be a love poem, I had an involuntary reaction of disappointment and braced myself to hear something saccharine and naïvely romantic. Then he read his poem about love. It was addressed to a young woman he had met in the *mato*. The verses spoke of how they had fought together for the revolution, which had formed their love, a new kind of love, based on mutual respect and real equality. They had found new smiles, he read. And these new smiles would be multiplied on the faces of their children and on those of all the children that would be born into the coming generations.

Notes

Introduction

1. Amilcar Cabral, *Our People Are Our Mountains*, text of a speech given in London, 1971 (London: Committee for the Freedom of Mozambique, Angola, and Guiné, 1972).
2. See Ester Boserup, *Women's Role in Economic Development* (New York: St. Martin's Press, 1970), pp. 53ff, 119ff, and United Nations, Report of the Secretary-General, *Development and International Economic Co-operation: Effective Mobilization of Women in Development*, A/33/238, October 26, 1978.
3. Memorandum of 1965, quoted in Basil Davidson, *Liberation of Guiné* (London: Penguin, 1969), p. 122.
4. Ibid., p. 137.
5. Basil Davidson, "No Fist Is Big Enough to Hide the Sky," *The Socialist Register* (London: Merlin Press, 1973).
6. See Denis Goulet, *Looking at Guinea-Bissau: A New Nation's Development Strategy* (Washington, D.C.: Overseas Development Council, 1978), p. 20.
7. Quoted in Lars Rudebeck, *Guinea-Bissau: A Study of Political Mobilization* (Uppsala: Scandinavian Institute of African Studies, 1974), p. 177.
8. Lars Rudebeck, *Guinea-Bissau: Difficulties and Possibilities of Socialist Orientation* (Uppsala: AKUT, 1978), p. 23.
9. Peter Aaby, *The State of Guinea-Bissau: African Socialism or Socialism in Africa?* (Uppsala: Scandinavian Institute of African Studies, 1978), p. 26.

10. Rudebeck, Guinea-Bissau: Difficulties and Possibilities, p. 24.
11. Ibid., p. 25.
12. Goulet, Looking at Guinea-Bissau, p. 40.
13. Ibid., p. 40.
14. See Aaby, The State of Guinea-Bissau, p. 32.

Chapter 1. "Nô Pintcha!"

1. Barbara Cornwall, The Bush Rebels (New York: Holt, Rinehart and Winston, 1972), p. 166.

Chapter 2. "What can we consider better than freedom?"

1. Texeira da Mota's observations are quoted in Amilcar Cabral, Report to the United Nations, 1961, cited in Basil Davidson, Liberation of Guiné: Aspects of an African Revolution (Baltimore: Penguin, 1969), p. 27.
2. Basil Davidson, Joe Slovo, and Anthony R. Wilkinson, Southern Africa: The New Politics of Revolution (London: Penguin, 1977), p. 25. Davidson's extensive writings on Guinea-Bissau have been invaluable to me in the preparation of this chapter.
3. Lars Rudebeck, "Development and Class Struggle in Guinea-Bissau," Monthly Review 30, no. 8 (January, 1979): 18–19.
4. Amilcar Cabral, Our People Are Our Mountains, text of a speech given in London, 1971 (London: Committee for Freedom in Mozambique, Angola, and Guiné, 1972), p. 21.
5. Rudebeck, "Development and Class Struggle," pp. 15–16.
6. Amilcar Cabral, "The Weapon of Theory," in Revolution in Guinea (New York: Monthly Review Press, 1969), p. 92.
7. Amilcar Cabral, "Brief Analysis of the Social Structure of Guinea," in ibid., pp. 56ff.
8. Ibid., p. 61.
9. See, for example, Peter Aaby, The State of Guinea-Bissau: African Socialism or Socialism in Africa? (Uppsala: Scandinavian Institute of African Studies, 1978), p. 11.
10. Cabral, "Brief Analysis," p. 61.
11. Ibid.
12. Ibid., p. 63.
13. Cabral, "Towards Final Victory," in Revolution in Guinea, p. 159.
14. Ibid., p. 110.
15. Ibid., pp. 104–8.
16. Amilcar Cabral, "National Liberation and Culture," in Return to the Source: Selected Speeches, ed. Africa Information Service (New York and London: Monthly Review Press, 1973), p. 79. Cabral was speaking English to a group of black Americans. While he spoke many languages, English was not his most fluent.
17. As quoted in Davidson et al., Southern Africa, p. 51.
18. Ibid., p. 52.

Chapter 3. "A great deal of patience"

1. *Afrique-Asie* 24 (February 19-March 4, 1973), translated in *Southern Africa* 6, no. 4 (April 1973). Shortly after the assassination journalist Aquino de Bragança went to Conakry. This section is based on his report, parts of which have been used verbatim.
2. Confidential party record, quoted in Basil Davidson, *Liberation of Guiné: Aspects of an African Revolution* (Baltimore: Penguin, 1969), p. 32.
3. Amilcar Cabral, *Our People Are Our Mountains*, text of a speech given in London, 1971 (London: Committee for Freedom in Mozambique, Angola, and Guiné, 1972), p. 3.
4. Speech delivered by Amilcar Cabral at Lincoln University in Pennsylvania, 1972, mimeo.
5. Amilcar Cabral, "Towards Final Victory," in *Revolution in Guinea* (New York: Monthly Review Press, 1969), pp. 158–60.
6. Davidson, *Liberation of Guiné*, p. 54.
7. Gérard Chaliand, *Armed Struggle in Africa: With the Guerrillas in "Portuguese" Guinea* (New York and London: Monthly Review Press, 1971), p. 47.

Chapter 4. "First it is the women who pound . . ."

1. Ester Boserup, *Women's Role in Economic Development* (New York: St. Martin's Press, 1970), p. 16. On the role of women in rural societies Ester Boserup concluded:

   > The joint result of women's high rate of participation in agricultural work and their generally long working hours was that women, in nearly all the cases recorded, were found to do more than half of the agricultural work; in some cases they were found to do around 70 per cent and in one case nearly 80 per cent of the total. Thus, the available quantitative information about work input by sex seems to indicate that even today village production in Africa south of the Sahara continues to be predominantly female farming. (Ibid., p. 22)

2. Gérard Chaliand, *Armed Struggle in Africa: With the Guerrillas in "Portuguese" Guinea* (New York and London: Monthly Review Press, 1971), p. 67.
3. PAIGC, "Report on the Politico-Socio-Economic Role of Women in Guinea and the Cape Verde Islands," published in English in *Women in the Struggle for Liberation* (New York: World Student Christian Federation, 1973), p. 52. Emphasis mine.
4. Amilcar Cabral, "Brief Analysis of the Social Structure in Guinea," in *Revolution in Guinea* (New York and London: Monthly Review Press, 1969), p. 57.
5. Ibid.
6. Ibid.

Chapter 5. "We are part of the same fight"

1. "There was not room for sex discrimination during the struggle," Interview with Francisca Pereira, *Ceres* 8, no. 2 (March-April 1975): 40. Emphasis mine.

2. Ibid., pp. 40–41.
3. Gérard Chaliand, *Armed Struggle in Africa: With the Guerrillas in "Portu-guese" Guinea* (New York and London: Monthly Review Press, 1971), p. 93.
4. Lars Rudebeck, *Guinea-Bissau: A Study of Political Mobilization* (Uppsala: Scandinavian Institute of African Studies, 1974), pp. 130, 186–87.
5. Chantal Sarrazin and Ole Gjerstad, *Sowing the First Harvest: National Reconstruction in Guinea-Bissau* (Oakland: LSM Information Center, 1978), p. 63.

Chapter 6. "A woman is sold for a pig or a cow"

1. Amilcar Cabral, "National Liberation and Culture," in *Return to the Source: Selected Speeches,* ed. Africa Information Service (New York and London: Monthly Review Press, 1973), p. 52.
2. Ibid., p. 160.
3. Gérard Chaliand, *Armed Struggle in Africa: With the Guerrillas in "Por-tuguese" Guinea* (New York and London: Monthly Review Press, 1971), p. 45.
4. Ibid., p. 67.
5. Ibid., 63–64.
6. Chantal Sarrazin and Ole Gjerstad, *Sowing the First Harvest: National Reconstruction in Guinea-Bissau* (Oakland: LSM Information Center, 1978), pp. 43–44.
7. Quoted in Ester Boserup, *Women's Role in Economic Development* (New York: St. Martin's Press, 1970), p. 38.
8. Boserup states it thus:

   In regions . . . where women do all or most of the work of growing food crops, the task of felling the trees in preparation of new plots is usually done by older boys and very young men. . . . An elderly cultivator with several wives is likely to have a number of such boys who can be used for this purpose. By combined efforts of young sons and young wives he may gradually expand his cultiva-tion and become more and more prosperous, while a man with a single wife has less help in cultivation and is likely to have little or no help for felling. Hence there is a direct relationship between the size of the area cultivated by a family and the number of wives in a family.

9. Boserup, *Women's Role,* p. 43.

Chapter 7. "Our education has to be conditioned by our life and history"

1. Quoted in Lars Rudebeck, *Guinea-Bissau: A Study of Political Mobilization* (Uppsala: Scandinavian Institute of African Studies, 1974), p. 220.
2. Gérard Chaliand, *Armed Struggle in Africa: With the Guerrillas in "Por-tuguese" Guinea* (New York and London: Monthly Review Press, 1971), p. 93.

OBSESSIVE–COMPULSIVE DISORDER AND ITS SPECTRUM

A LIFE-SPAN APPROACH

EDITED BY
ERIC A. STORCH
AND
DEAN McKAY

American Psychological Association • *Washington, DC*

Copyright © 2014 by the American Psychological Association. All rights reserved. Except as permitted under the United States Copyright Act of 1976, no part of this publication may be reproduced or distributed in any form or by any means, including, but not limited to, the process of scanning and digitization, or stored in a database or retrieval system, without the prior written permission of the publisher.

Published by
American Psychological Association
750 First Street, NE
Washington, DC 20002
www.apa.org

To order
APA Order Department
P.O. Box 92984
Washington, DC 20090-2984
Tel: (800) 374-2721; Direct: (202) 336-5510
Fax: (202) 336-5502; TDD/TTY: (202) 336-6123
Online: www.apa.org/pubs/books
E-mail: order@apa.org

In the U.K., Europe, Africa, and the Middle East, copies may be ordered from
American Psychological Association
3 Henrietta Street
Covent Garden, London
WC2E 8LU England

Typeset in Goudy by Circle Graphics, Inc., Columbia, MD

Printer: Maple Press, York, PA
Cover Designer: Naylor Design, Washington, DC

The opinions and statements published are the responsibility of the authors, and such opinions and statements do not necessarily represent the policies of the American Psychological Association.

Library of Congress Cataloging-in-Publication Data

Obsessive-compulsive disorder and its spectrum : a life-span approach / edited by Eric A. Storch, Dean McKay.
    pages cm
  ISBN 978-1-4338-1563-8 — ISBN 1-4338-1563-X 1. Compulsive behavior. 2. Obsessive-compulsive disorder. 3. Evidence-based psychiatry. I. Storch, Eric A., editor of compilation. II. McKay, Dean, 1966- editor of compilation.
  RC533.O2645 2014
  616.85'84—dc23
                                    2013025897

British Library Cataloguing-in-Publication Data

A CIP record is available from the British Library.

Printed in the United States of America
First Edition

http://dx.doi.org/10.1037/14323-000

I dedicate this book, with all my love, to Jill, Maya, and Noah.
—*Eric A. Storch*

For Dawn and Rebecca, thank you for your constant support and love.
—*Dean McKay*

129946

CONTENTS

CONTRIBUTORS

Jonathan S. Abramowitz, PhD, Department of Psychology, University of North Carolina—Chapel Hill

Nicole M. Alberts, MA, Department of Psychology, University of Regina, Regina, Canada

Margaret S. Andover, PhD, Department of Psychology, Fordham University, Bronx, NY

Gordon J. G. Asmundson, PhD, Department of Psychology, University of Regina, Regina, Canada

Catherine Ayers, PhD, ABPP, Research Service, VA San Diego Healthcare System, Psychology Service, VA San Diego Healthcare System, Department of Psychiatry, University of California, San Diego

Heather A. Berlin, PhD, MPH, Department of Psychiatry, Icahn School of Medicine at Mount Sinai, New York, NY

Shannon M. Blakey, BA, Department of Psychology, University of North Carolina—Chapel Hill

Aaron J. Blashill, PhD, Department of Psychiatry, Massachusetts General Hospital and Harvard Medical School, Boston, MA

Christiana Bratiotis, PhD, LCSW, Grace Abbott School of Social Work, University of Nebraska at Omaha

Obsessive–Compulsive Disorder and Its Spectrum

monitoring for side effects, and combining treatments. Chapter 15 (Grant, Odlaug, & Schreiber) reviews pharmacological approaches for adults with OCSDs, especially monotherapies; augmentation strategies; and evidence supporting pharmacological approaches for OCD, body dysmorphic disorder, trichotillomania, and skin picking.

Part IV concludes the volume with a discussion of the biological bases of OCSDs from genetics and neuroscience research. Chapter 16 (Taylor) reviews the heritable features of OCD and indicates, in considerable detail, the extent to which genetics contributes to a variety of OCD features. The chapter also suggests future directions for the field of study. Finally, Chapter 17 (Lapidus, Stern, Berlin, & Goodman) examines the cognitive neuroscience of OCD with regard to behavioral inhibition, error monitoring, motor suppression, cognitive inflexibility, reward processing, and emotional processing. The chapter's focus on brain imaging and neurophysiology studies of disgust and neural fear circuits is particularly interesting, as is its review of neuropsychological factors for OCSDs, including trichotillomania, body dysmorphic disorder, and hoarding.

Researchers, clinicians, and students will appreciate the detailed information in this volume. It provides a strong basis for understanding the clinical features and underlying mechanisms for expression of OCSDs. Not surprisingly, many commonalities are evident in the types of evidence-based behavioral, cognitive, pharmacological, and family interventions across these disorders. There are also commonalities in the delivery methods for these interventions. This is a strength and also a concern for clinicians and researchers who struggle to achieve maximum benefit from interventions without prolonging their duration and cost. Accordingly, readers will appreciate the treatment findings and implementation strategies, at least so far as our understanding of these disorders permits.

opportunity to expand our behavioral and cognitive processing treatment repertoire, as well as to search for biological interventions that improve outcomes, accessibility, and ease of application for clinicians and patients.

With 17 chapters (in four parts) written by top specialists in their fields, this volume provides a solid grounding in conceptual models for understanding OCSDs. Part I describes assessment and psychological treatments. Chapter 1 (Worden & Tolin) covers OCD in adults. Chapters 2 through 4 (Gryczkowski & Whiteside; Walther, Josyula, Freeman, & Garcia; Lewin) consider the unique treatment needs of children and adolescents with OCD, and Chapter 5 (Ayers & Najmi) considers the needs of older adults with OCSDs. Together with Chapter 1 on OCD in adults, these detailed reviews examine the cognitive, behavioral (including avoidance), and emotional symptoms and features across the developmental span, as well as assessment strategies and evidence-based behavioral and cognitive treatments. These chapters enable clinicians to consider special features of adult and child cases of OCD, including pediatric acute-onset neuropsychiatric syndrome, and help translate implementation of assessment and therapy methods, including family-based cognitive behavior therapy for children.

Chapter 6 (Muroff, Levis, & Bratiotis) closely examines hoarding disorder, an especially timely topic in view of the inclusion of this new diagnosis in the fifth edition of the *Diagnostic and Statistical Manual of Mental Disorders*. Chapter 7 (Hartmann, Blashill, Greenberg, & Wilhelm) focuses on body dysmorphic disorder, a particularly challenging problem with a significant risk of suicidality and a need to address low motivation for treatment. Using examples, the authors detail cognitive and behavioral methods for this disorder in adolescents and adults. Chapter 8 (Snorrason & Woods) addresses body-focused repetitive behavioral disorders such as trichotillomania, skin picking, and tic disorders, especially in children and young adults. Chapter 9 (Himle & Hayes) covers Tourette's syndrome. Finally, Chapter 10 (Hadjistavropoulos, Alberts, & Asmundson) examines hypochondriasis among youth, adults, and older adults.

Part II details co-occurring problems that may present together with OCSDs. Chapter 11 (Abramowitz & Blakey) addresses depression in OCSDs. Chapter 12 (Andover & Morris) examines similarities and distinctions between suicidal and nonsuicidal self-injury on the one hand and OCSDs on the other. Concluding Part II is Chapter 13 (Francis, Kim, & Jacob), which examines the possible link between autistic conditions and OCSDs. This chapter covers theoretical considerations, research findings, and treatment strategies and outcomes.

Part III focuses on pharmacological treatment. It begins with Chapter 14 (Stewart & Stachon), a review of medications for children and adolescents with OCSDs, including the challenges of determining dosage,

FOREWORD

GAIL STEKETEE

It is my pleasure to introduce you to this fine volume. As Drs. Eric Storch and Dean McKay rightly note in their introduction, although we have gained considerable knowledge about obsessive–compulsive spectrum disorders (OCSDs) and evidence-based treatments for these disorders, new research emerges at a regular rate, and much remains to be learned. Particularly interesting for the field as a whole are genetic studies and basic neuroscience and biological investigations that help us better understand brain dysfunction in OCSDs.

Although exposure and response prevention remains the gold standard behavioral treatment, cognitive therapies have added another tool set for resolving symptoms in OCSDs. Nonetheless, well-trained and accessible clinicians specializing in the treatment of these disorders are hard to find, perhaps especially for children with these conditions. Various medications, mainly the serotonin reuptake inhibitors, have been well studied and have positive outcomes for OCD patients, but recovery is often incomplete. Patients with other OCSDs may benefit from a variety of medications. The editors of this volume point to areas of study that are not yet well tapped, such as behavioral inhibition and reward processing. Certainly there is much

INTRODUCTION: DEFINING THE SCOPE AND BOUNDARIES OF THE OBSESSIVE–COMPULSIVE SPECTRUM

DEAN McKAY AND ERIC A. STORCH

Clients' obsessive, intrusive, and unwanted thoughts and images pose a unique challenge for clinicians. These experiences are difficult to assess objectively given the private nature of the problem. Obsessions are also difficult to treat because clinicians cannot verify the experiences or the success of any treatments beyond the self-report of the client. In the case of obsessive–compulsive disorder (OCD), there are typically overt behavioral signs that imply the presence of obsessions, and these indirect expressions of the underlying mental event serve as our best estimate of the effectiveness of treatments. An added challenge in clinical practice is that many diagnosed conditions have components that resemble obsessions and behaviors that are similar to compulsions. This book focuses on how best to conceptualize and treat the problems of obsessions, compulsions, and the conditions that have signs and symptoms that resemble obsessions and compulsions.

http://dx.doi.org/10.1037/14323-001
Obsessive–Compulsive Disorder and Its Spectrum: A Life-Span Approach, Eric A. Storch and Dean McKay (Editors)
Copyright © 2014 by the American Psychological Association. All rights reserved.

3

In 1965, Kringlen declared that any treatment for obsessional problems was actively harmful and that the best course of action was to avoid intervention. The next year, Meyer (1966) published the first paper detailing the application of what is now known as *exposure with response prevention* (ERP) as a psychosocial intervention for OCD. At present, ERP is the leading intervention for the disorder, and numerous meta-analyses have documented large effect sizes supporting its efficacy in adults (see, e.g., Olatunji, Cisler, & Deacon, 2010; Olatunji, Davis, Powers, & Smits, 2013) and children (Watson & Rees, 2008). In addition to the findings of efficacious outcome for ERP, pharmacologic approaches have emerged that alleviate substantially the symptoms of OCD. Selective serotonin reuptake inhibitor (SSRI) medications have provided significant relief to sufferers of the conditions, and meta-analyses have also supported the efficacy of this approach (Eddy, Dutra, Bradley, & Westen, 2004; Kobak, Greist, Jefferson, Katzelnick, & Henk, 1998). Between the application of ERP and SSRIs, comprehensive empirically supported treatment now exists for this severe and disabling condition.

Although there are now well-established and efficacious treatments for OCD, limitations in outcome remain, and controversies persist, in how best to treat the disorder. For example, although ERP is considered highly efficacious, it is also an approach that is not widely embraced by practitioners for reasons that have little to do with outcome and much more to do with clinician discomfort with applying a procedure that might lead to distress before providing relief (Richard & Gloster, 2007). Indeed, as an alternative, one major treatment manual describes cognitive therapy for OCD, with a note on the back cover that states successful treatment may be conducted without the use of exposure (Wilhelm & Steketee, 2006).

Controversies also exist on the pharmacotherapy side. Among these is the degree to which SSRIs are adequate interventions as stand-alone therapeutics and whether these approaches will persist should a specific and robust genetic model of OCD emerge. On this front, the controversy is especially robust given that some have suggested there are hopeful signs that a unique genetic profile is close to being identified (Stewart et al., 2013). Such a development may be promising if it leads to better treatment, given that OCD has been described as a serious and debilitating disorder and that despite the efficacy of available therapies, many sufferers remain partially symptomatic after treatment. The recent genetic findings notwithstanding, there remains deep skepticism in the research community regarding the heritability of the disorder via specific gene expression (Taylor, 2013) despite the apparent strong support for its familial transmission (Taylor & Jang, 2011). These are rich and productive debates in the scientific literature on the disorder and will likely serve to promote additional advances in treatment and phenomenological understanding.

EMERGENCE OF THE OBSESSIVE–COMPULSIVE SPECTRUM

Since the development of these major therapeutic methods, other disorders have been conceptualized as obsessive–compulsive in nature. These disorders, referred to as *obsessive–compulsive spectrum disorders* (OCSDs) or *obsessive–compulsive (OC)-related disorders* (as they are categorized in the *Diagnostic and Statistical Manual of Mental Disorders*, Fifth Edition [DSM–5]; American Psychiatric Association, 2013) are characterized by a basic deficiency in behavioral inhibition (Hollander, Braun, & Simeon, 2008). The concept of a spectrum of obsessive–compulsive disorders has been developing for many years. At present, although behavioral inhibition is a unifying feature of all OCSDs, the conceptualization has not led in a clear way to unifying therapeutic approaches. As documented in this volume, there are variants in the basic implementation of ERP for OCD, and the basic conceptualization of treatment for putative OCSDs is diverse.

Critics of the OCSD category have taken the most exception to the neuroscientific basis of this proposed class of conditions, especially the contention that shared clinical features between disorders justify the development of this class of disorders (Abramowitz, Storch, McKay, Taylor, & Asmundson, 2010; McKay, Abramowitz, & Taylor, 2008; Storch, Abramowitz, & Goodman, 2008). The supporters of the conceptualization of the OCSD counter that reward processing—as regulated through not only serotonergic pathways but also dopaminergic pathways—is dysregulated in the proposed group of OCSDs and that future research will support this hypothesis across these seemingly disparate conditions (Stein & Lochner, 2008). As of this writing, the critiques and supporting literature seem largely confined to psychology and psychiatry, respectively.

The OCSD category was originally defined so broadly that it encompassed any disorder featuring a behavioral inhibition disruption. For this reason, virtually all the disorders in the *DSM* could be said to fall under the OCSD category (i.e., Hollander & Rosen, 2000), including disorders that are more compulsive in nature (i.e., hypochondriasis, body dysmorphic disorder) and disorders that are more impulsive in nature (i.e., trichotillomania, compulsive gambling). Over time, the definition of OCSD has become narrower, including only those disorders with purported compulsive behavior, whether the core features in the diagnosis were impulsive or not. Therefore, trichotillomania was considered a potential OC–related disorder (not spectrum anymore) because individuals with this condition often have preferred regions where hair is pulled and do so in a stylized and ritualistic manner (Hollander, Braun, & Simeon, 2008).

Currently, the DSM–5 category of OCSDs encompasses OCD, as well as hoarding disorder (formerly a symptom within OCD), body dysmorphic disorder, excoriation, Tourette's syndrome, hypochondriasis, and trichotillo-mania. For the purposes of this book, we retain the label of OCSDs because the conditions that are potential candidate disorders have been the subjects of considerable debate and the final set that forms the OCSD category for the *DSM–5* may be subject to revision.

It was expected that developing a broader class of disorders related to OCD would facilitate the development of treatment for this new class of con-ditions. At the very least, having the view that these disorders are obsessive or compulsive in quality provides a starting point for treatment development, particularly in light of the challenge in treating some of these disorders. For example, although there are empirically supported treatments for trichotil-lomania, most clinicians agree that this disorder is quite challenging (see Chapter 8). Rather than reliance on conceptualization based solely on the defining characteristics of the disorder, using an obsessive–compulsive frame-work allows for operationalization of mechanisms of the disorder and mecha-nisms of intervention that can be tested and compared against the efficacy of analogous methods for other OC–related disorders.

CLINICAL APPLICATIONS, CLINICAL LORE, AND THE FUTURE OF THE OCSD

Despite the controversy about conceptualization of OCD and the puta-tive OCSDs, robust treatments are available. These treatments are derived from the fields of both psychology and psychiatry and are discussed in this book. Yet there are vast gaps in our ability to treat all sufferers who arrive in our offices. Take, for example, OCD in cases characterized primarily by scrupulosity, which clinicians see with relative regularity (Abramowitz, 2008). Conducting ERP in this instance raises specific ethical and logistical concerns that are not well described in the literature and that have been the subject of relatively limited investigation. There are many variants of the disorder that nonetheless would unambiguously meet criteria for OCD (see, e.g., Abramowitz, McKay, & Taylor, 2008a, 2008b).

Fortunately, we have come a long way from the clinical lore proposed back in the mid-1960s—namely, that treatment for OCD was futile. However, a significant percentage of the clinical community has not embraced the idea of empirically supported approaches to OCD or has not fully grasped the complexity of the disorder. For example, OCD and related disorders remain poorly understood in the general treatment community, with incorrect diag-noses frequently determined for sufferers (i.e., Rasmussen & Eisen, 1992). Clinicians remain greatly reluctant to engage in ERP for individuals diag-nosed with the disorder, as noted earlier.

AIMS OF THIS BOOK

The formal adoption of a category of diagnoses that are collectively OC–related is a new development. Direct service providers will be well served to understand how to conceptualize conditions that are considered part of this group, which aspects of these conditions closely resemble OCD, and which aspects make these conditions distinct. The methods of treating these conditions are also important to highlight, including methods that are similar to and distinct from OCD treatments. Because this book also covers the conceptualization and treatment of OCD, it is expected to be an important resource. Clinicians and researchers will have information about the similar and distinct aspects of OCD and OCSDs in one text.

Given these limitations and caveats to developing comprehensive treatment programs for individuals with OCSDs, clinicians will require additional skills in identifying disorders that have a basic behavioral inhibition regulation deficit. Better documentation of the types of interventions that best relieve these conditions is also warranted. It is our hope that this volume will be a useful guide for clinicians in proceeding to effectively treat those with OCD and OCSDs. We also hope that this volume will serve as a reminder to clinicians that, despite the apparent widespread availability of interventions for OCD and OCSDs, we should remain humble in our approach to conceptualizing cases with any of these disorders. In light of this, we would like to leave readers of this introduction with a quote from Nobel Laureate and quantum physicist Neils Bohr, who said, "If quantum mechanics hasn't profoundly shocked you, you haven't understood it yet." In the same way, to fully appreciate OCD and OCSDs is to admit that the complexity of the conditions is startling.

REFERENCES

Abramowitz, J. S. (2008). Scrupulosity. In J. S. Abramowitz, D. McKay, & S. Taylor (Eds.), *Clinical handbook of obsessive-compulsive disorder and related problems* (pp. 156–172). Baltimore, MD: Johns Hopkins Press.

Abramowitz, J. S., McKay, D., & Taylor, S. (2008a). *Clinical handbook of obsessive–compulsive disorder and related problems*. Baltimore, MD: Johns Hopkins Press.

Abramowitz, J. S., McKay, D., & Taylor, S. (2008b). *Obsessive–compulsive disorder: Subtype and spectrum conditions*. Amsterdam, the Netherlands: Elsevier.

Abramowitz, J. S., Storch, E. A., McKay, D., Taylor, S., & Asmundson, G. J. G. (2010). The obsessive–compulsive spectrum: A critical review. In D. McKay, J. S. Abramowitz, S. Taylor, & G. J. G. Asmundson (Eds.), *Current controversies in the anxiety disorders: Implications for DSM–V and beyond* (pp. 329–352). New York, NY: Springer.

American Psychiatric Association. (2013). *Diagnostic and statistical manual of mental disorders* (5th ed.). Arlington, VA: Author.

Eddy, K. T., Dutra, L., Bradley, R., & Westen, D. (2004). A multidimensional meta-analysis of psychotherapy and pharmacotherapy for obsessive-compulsive disorder. *Clinical Psychology Review, 24,* 1011–1030. doi:10.1016/j.cpr.2004.08.004

Hollander, E., Braun, A., & Simeon, D. (2008). Should OCD leave the anxiety disorders in *DSM–V?* The case for obsessive compulsive–related disorders. *Depression and Anxiety, 25,* 317–329. doi:10.1002/da.20500

Hollander, E., & Rosen, J. (2000). Obsessive–compulsive spectrum disorders: A review. In M. Maj, N. Sartorius, A. Okasha, & J. Zohar (Eds.), *Obsessive–compulsive disorder* (pp. 203–252). Chichester, England: Wiley. doi:10.1002/0470846496.ch5

Kobak, K. A., Greist, J. H., Jefferson, J. W., Katzelnick, D. J., & Henk, H. J. (1998). Behavioral versus pharmacological treatments of obsessive-compulsive disorder: A meta-analysis. *Psychopharmacology, 136,* 205–216. doi:10.1007/s002130050558

Kringlen, E. (1965). Obsessional neurotics: Long-term outcome. *The British Journal of Psychiatry, 111,* 709–722. doi:10.1192/bjp.111.477.709

McKay, D., Abramowitz, J. S., & Taylor, S. (2008). Discussion: The obsessive–compulsive spectrum. In J. S. Abramowitz, D. McKay, & S. Taylor (Eds.), *Obsessive–compulsive disorder: Subtype and spectrum conditions* (pp. 287–300). Amsterdam, the Netherlands: Elsevier.

Meyer, V. (1966). Modification of expectations in cases with obsessional rituals. *Behaviour Research and Therapy, 4,* 273–280.

Olatunji, B. O., Cisler, J. M., & Deacon, B. J. (2010). Efficacy of cognitive-behavioral therapy for anxiety disorders: A review of meta-analytic findings. *Psychiatric Clinics of North America, 33,* 557–577. doi:10.1016/j.psc.2010.04.002

Olatunji, B. O., Davis, M. L., Powers, M. B., & Smits, J. A. J. (2013). Cognitive-behavioral therapy for obsessive–compulsive disorder: A meta-analysis of treatment outcome and moderators. *Journal of Psychiatric Research, 47,* 33–41.

Rasmussen, S. A., & Eisen, J. L. (1992). The epidemiology and differential diagnosis of obsessive compulsive disorder. *The Journal of Clinical Psychiatry, 53* (Suppl. 4), 4–10.

Richard, D. C. S., & Gloster, A. T. (2007). Exposure therapy has a public relations problem: A dearth of litigation amid a wealth of concern. In D. C. S. Richard & D. L. Lauterbach (Eds.), *Handbook of exposure therapies* (pp. 409–425). Amsterdam, the Netherlands: Academic Press. doi:10.1016/B978-012587421-2/50019-3

Stein, D. J., & Lochner, C. (2008). The empirical basis of the obsessive-compulsive spectrum. In J. S. Abramowitz, D. McKay, & S. Taylor (Eds.), *Clinical handbook of obsessive-compulsive disorder and related problems* (pp. 177–187). Baltimore, MD: Johns Hopkins Press.

Stewart, S. E., Yu, D., Scharf, J. M., Neale, B. M., Fagerness, J. A., Mathews, C. A., Arnold, P. D., Evans, P. D., . . . Pauls, D. L. (2013). Genome-wide association study of obsessive-compulsive disorder. *Molecular Psychiatry, 18,* 788–798.

Storch, E. A., Abramowitz, J., & Goodman, W. K. (2008). Where does obsessive–compulsive disorder belong among the anxiety disorders in DSM–V? *Depression and Anxiety, 25*, 336–347. doi:10.1002/da.20488

Taylor, S. (2013). Molecular genetics of obsessive–compulsive disorder: A comprehensive meta-analysis of genetic association studies. *Molecular Psychiatry, 18*, 799–805.

Taylor, S., & Jang, K. L. (2011). Biopsychosocial etiology of obsessions and compulsions: An integrated behavioral-genetic and cognitive-behavioral analysis. *Journal of Abnormal Psychology, 120*, 174–186. doi:10.1037/a0021403

Watson, H. J., & Rees, C. S. (2008). Meta-analysis of randomized, controlled treatment trials for pediatric obsessive–compulsive disorder. *Journal of Child Psychology and Psychiatry, 49*, 489–498. doi:10.1111/j.1469-7610.2007.01875.x

Wilhelm, S., & Steketee, G. S. (2006). *Cognitive therapy for obsessive–compulsive disorder: A guide for professionals*. Oakland, CA: New Harbinger.

I

ASSESSMENT AND PSYCHOLOGICAL TREATMENT

1

OBSESSIVE–COMPULSIVE DISORDER IN ADULTS

BLAISE WORDEN AND DAVID F. TOLIN

Epidemiological studies typically suggest a lifetime prevalence of obsessive–compulsive disorder (OCD) in approximately 2% to 3% of adults (Ruscio, Stein, Chiu, & Kessler, 2010; Weissman, Bland, Canino, & Greenwald, 1994). OCD tends to follow a chronic course (Leckman et al., 2010), being unlikely to remit without treatment (Houghton, Saxon, Bradburn, Ricketts, & Hardy, 2010). Adults with OCD report high rates of impairment in work, role (Mancebo et al., 2008), and social functioning (Huppert, Simpson, Nissenson, Liebowitz, & Foa, 2009).

Although the fifth edition of the *Diagnostic and Statistical Manual of Mental Disorders* (*DSM–5*; American Psychiatric Association, 2013) allows the diagnosis to be made in the presence of either obsessions or compulsions, the vast majority of individuals with OCD present with both (Foa et al., 1995). Obsessions and compulsions tend to cluster into commonly occurring dimensions, with the most common dimensions reflecting (a) fears of

http://dx.doi.org/10.1037/14323-002
Obsessive–Compulsive Disorder and Its Spectrum: A Life-Span Approach, Eric A. Storch and Dean McKay (Editors)
Copyright © 2014 by the American Psychological Association. All rights reserved.

contamination paired with washing or cleaning behaviors; (b) "not just right" feelings paired with symmetry or arranging behaviors; and (c) fears of religious blasphemy, aggression, or unwanted sexual thoughts, which can be paired with a variety of compulsions.

The chapter begins with a discussion of cognitive aspects of OCD, describing commonly occurring types of obsessions and other cognitive processes that maintain OCD, such as maladaptive belief systems. We then review behavioral aspects that maintain OCD, such as ritualizing and avoidance. The chapter then covers differential diagnosis of OCD along with empirically supported psychotherapeutic treatments, including cognitive therapy and exposure with response prevention. (Psychopharmacologic treatments for adult patients are discussed in Chapter 15 of this volume). We conclude with a brief review of other treatment modalities, such as group therapy and self-help formats, and suggestions for future directions in OCD psychotherapy research.

COGNITIVE FEATURES OF ADULT OCD

Obsessions

OCD is typically characterized by the presence of obsessions, defined as recurrent intrusive thoughts, urges, or images that cause marked anxiety or distress (American Psychiatric Association, 2013). In this section, we describe some of the more common obsessions.

Contamination Fears

Individuals with contamination fears may excessively fear germs and related illness or may fear a feeling of "dirtiness," which can be sensory (e.g., difficulty tolerating a feeling of grease on one's fingers) or emotional, the latter of which is likely more similar to difficulty tolerating a feeling of things being "not just right."

Harming Fears

Individuals with harming fears have pronounced concerns about harming oneself or others. Examples include the patient who fears that she will stab her child, one who fears he may become a pedophile and molest children, or one who worries that she may have just hit a pedestrian with her vehicle.

Symmetry Obsessions

Patients with symmetry obsessions often endorse a feeling of discomfort if items are "not just right." These patients often remain preoccupied with the position, order, or arrangement of items if they are unable to ritualize.

Somatic Obsessions

Somatic obsessions involve discomfort with perceived abnormalities in one's appearance or bodily functioning. Individuals with somatic obsessions may obsess that they have a physical problem or that they will develop one (e.g., a patient who obsesses that she will develop an allergy to certain foods and therefore avoids many foods and often checks herself for signs of an allergic reaction). Differential diagnosis of OCD versus disorders such as body dysmorphic disorder or hypochondriasis can often be difficult.

Scrupulosity or Unwanted Imagery

Scrupulosity obsessions reflect an exaggerated concern that one's thoughts or actions, even objectively minor ones, are sinful or blasphemous or will lead to damnation or other punishment from God. Similarly, many OCD patients describe unwanted or "forbidden" thoughts, such as those of a sexual nature (e.g., a patient who identifies as heterosexual but who fears that his ego-dystonic sexual thoughts about men may reflect latent homosexuality) or intrusive violent images (e.g., mental images of violent accidents or assaults to loved ones).

Maladaptive Beliefs

In addition to the intrusive obsessions, individuals with OCD commonly endorse certain maladaptive beliefs, thoughts, and appraisals (Steketee et al., 2003). Beliefs thought to be related to OCD include the following.

Inflated Sense of Responsibility

Responsibility beliefs have been hypothesized to be central to OCD (Salkovskis et al., 2000). Some individuals with OCD endorse the belief that they are uniquely responsible for preventing harm to self or others or that failing to prevent harm is as bad as causing harm. For example, an individual with inflated responsibility beliefs may believe that he is responsible for making sure a public walkway is entirely free of debris that someone might trip over and might also believe that failing to do so would be as bad as actually causing someone to trip.

Thought–Action Fusion

Thought–action fusion (TAF) occurs when patients believe that having thoughts about an action are morally synonymous with completing that action (moral TAF; Storch & Merlo, 2006) or that thoughts about an event will increase the likelihood of that event occurring (likelihood TAF; Rachman, 2004; Shafran, Thordarson, & Rachman, 1996). For example, an individual may feel that thinking about harming her newborn infant is morally equivalent to actually harming her child, or she may feel that the more she has obsessions about harming the child, the more likely she is to become aggressive and actually do so.

Control of Thoughts

Many individuals with OCD believe that control of inappropriate thoughts is possible and necessary and therefore engage in strong efforts to control their thoughts, using techniques such as distraction, thought stopping, or self-punishment (Tolin et al., 2007). These efforts typically backfire because individuals with OCD who attempt to suppress thoughts often experience a paradoxical increase in those thoughts (Purdon, Rowa, & Antony, 2005; Tolin, Abramowitz, Przeworski, & Foa, 2002).

Intolerance of Uncertainty

Intolerance of uncertainty (IU) is characterized by discomfort with ambiguous situations or limited information. For example, an individual high in IU may be upset by not knowing with certainty whether she locked the front door of her house. IU often manifests behaviorally as excessive reassurance seeking or data gathering.

Perfectionism

Perfectionism may be conceptualized as an exaggerated concern with making mistakes (Flett & Hewitt, 2002). Individuals high in perfectionism often believe that there is a perfect way to do a given task, and anything less than a perfect performance is unacceptable. For example, an individual high in perfectionism may feel that her carpet should be clean at all times in case visitors arrive; any speck of dirt is unacceptable and is considered a failure to keep the carpet clean.

Overestimation of Threat

Individuals with OCD often perceive themselves as more likely to suffer feared outcomes than do other individuals (Moritz & Jelinek, 2009). Patients tend to overestimate both the probability and severity of feared events. For example, an individual with contamination fears might estimate that the likelihood of getting ill from touching toilets is 90% (erroneously high), and might also predict that getting ill would yield catastrophic results, such as death (erroneously severe).

BEHAVIORAL FEATURES OF ADULT OCD

Compulsions

Compulsions are repetitive behaviors that a person feels driven to perform in response to an obsession or according to rules that must be rigidly applied and are aimed at preventing or reducing distress or preventing some dreaded event or situation (American Psychiatric Association, 2013). Compulsive behaviors are thought to reduce anxiety associated with maladaptive appraisals of obsessive thoughts (Tolin, 2010) and are negatively reinforced via reduction in anxiety. In some cases, particularly compulsive checking behaviors, compulsions may actually cause some increase in subjective fear, yet patients continue to feel compelled to perform the behaviors. Herrnstein's (1969) learning model proposes that these individuals may be substituting a milder form of distress to avoid more severe anxiety or prevent a more severe outcome. Therefore, although the compulsion creates some degree of anxiety, the patient may believe that noncompletion of the compulsion would lead to even greater distress.

Compulsions maintain anxiety by blocking the natural habituation that would occur with prolonged exposure to cues. Compulsions also maintain fear by preventing the individual from forming realistic appraisals of the likelihood and severity of feared outcomes. For example, if an individual with contamination fears engages in excessive washing behaviors, he or she is unlikely to learn that contact with "germy" surfaces is unlikely to cause illness. We now discuss some of the most common adult compulsions.

Checking

Patients with checking compulsions may have low memory confidence, as well as high levels of IU or perfectionism, threat overestimation, or responsibility beliefs. As a result, they may doubt whether they completed routine activities (or completed them perfectly), such as locking a door or turning off appliances or faucets. They therefore recheck several times to obtain reassurance that the activity was indeed completed.

Excessive Washing or Cleaning

Cleaning or washing compulsions involve excessive cleaning of one's self or objects—for example, excessive showering or hand washing or excessive scrubbing of surfaces in the home.

Repeating

Repeating compulsions typically appear as recompletion of routine activities, such as opening or closing a door or drawer, rereading or rewriting, or repeating a phrase. These compulsions are often accompanied by desire for a "just right" feeling, with the action repeated until the feeling is obtained.

Mental Rituals

Mental rituals can be some of the most difficult compulsions to assess and treat because of their covert nature. The presumption in distinguishing a mental compulsion from an obsession is that the mental compulsion is done voluntarily, with intent to reduce anxiety or minimize risk, whereas the obsession is intrusive or involuntary and causes feelings of anxiety or distress (Leckman et al., 2010). Examples of mental compulsions include silent repetition of phrases, words, or prayers or having to think positive thoughts to neutralize an obsession.

Ordering or Arranging

Ordering or arranging compulsions involve arranging or categorizing according to rigid rules. For example, a patient may spend several hours per day arranging books on a shelf alphabetically or ensuring that all of the items in her medicine cabinet are equally spaced and symmetrically arranged.

Compulsions by Proxy

Many individuals with OCD incorporate others into their rituals. For example, an individual with fears of contamination may request that all others in the household wash in a routinized way before preparing food. Another might insist that a family member assist him with arranging compulsions by ensuring that used objects are always put back in a specified position and location. Excessive requests for reassurance are another, more subtle form of compulsions by proxy, which often take the form of persistent questioning of others. Some OCD sufferers will repeatedly ask friends or family members "is [feared situation] OK to enter? Will I be safe?" or questions such as "Did I wash enough?" or "Are you sure I didn't harm anyone?"

Passive Avoidance

In addition to overt compulsions, many patients with OCD demonstrate a high level of passive avoidance. Some individuals may have adopted such a lifestyle of avoidance that they might appear to have few to no compulsive behaviors because most triggers for these behaviors are avoided. For example, an individual with fears of harming others may restrict socializing, or another who excessively checks her written work for errors may seek out low-pressure jobs that involve little to no written work. Therefore, it is important to assess for situations or activities in which the client has reduced engagement over time.

ASSESSING ADULT OCD

Differential Diagnosis

The terms *obsession* and *compulsion* can be used quite loosely by both the public and clinicians, and we have received many referrals for clients with "compulsive" gambling, eating, or sexual behavior, or "obsessions" about previous traumatic experiences. The obsessive thoughts in OCD must be distinguished from the typically more ego-syntonic thoughts characteristic of intense worries in generalized anxiety disorder, ruminations about loss and worthlessness in depression, intrusive trauma memories in posttraumatic stress disorder, and many other mental phenomena.

In addition, obsessions and compulsions can be more difficult to identify when they are not the more commonly known dimensions (e.g., contamination or washing, checking, arranging) and take more idiosyncratic forms. Patients sometimes complete behavior patterns that outwardly appear unrelated to the outcomes they are used to forestall, such as a patient who walks in a ritualized pattern of steps to prevent her loved ones from dying. In addition, patients do not always have insight into the outcomes that they fear will occur when rituals are not completed, which can make drawing connections between compulsions and obsessions difficult.

Measures of OCD Severity

A description of all of the measures of OCD topography and severity that have been developed is beyond the scope of this chapter. In this section, we describe some of the most widely used and well-validated measures. For additional information on the psychometric properties of these measures, see Grabill et al. (2008).

Interviews

The gold standard of OCD measures is the Yale–Brown Obsessive-Compulsive Scale (Y-BOCS; Goodman, Price, Rasmussen, & Mazure, 1989), a semistructured interview consisting of a checklist of 40 obsessions and 29 compulsions and severity rating scales. The Y-BOCS demonstrates excellent interrater reliability, sound internal consistency, and strong test–retest reliability (Goodman, Price, Rasmussen, Mazure, Fleischmann, et al., 1989;

Woody, Steketee, & Chambless, 1995). The Y-BOCS is also available in a self-report version (Steketee, Frost, & Bogart, 1996) and a dimensional version (Dimensional Yale–Brown Obsessive-Compulsive Scale; Rosario-Campos et al., 2006) in which related dimensions of obsessions and compulsions are assessed together, with severity ratings calculated for each factor.

Self-Report Measures

The Obsessive–Compulsive Inventory—Revised (OCI–R; Foa et al., 2002) is an 18-item questionnaire based on the earlier 84-item OCI (Foa, Kozak, Salkovskis, Coles, & Amir, 1998). The OCI–R has six subscales: Washing, Checking, Obsessing, Hoarding, Neutralizing, and Ordering. A cutoff of 15 on the OCI–R showed good sensitivity (84%) and specificity (78%) in its ability to distinguish individuals with OCD from nonclinical participants (Foa et al., 2002).

Measures of OCD-Related Cognitions

The Obsessional Beliefs Questionnaire—44 (OBQ–44; Obsessive Compulsive Cognitions Working Group, 2003) is a 44-item self-report measure that examines the strength of three factor-analytically derived OCD-related beliefs. The OBQ–44 consists of three empirically derived factors: Responsibility/Threat Estimation, Perfectionism/Certainty, and Importance/Control of Thoughts.

EVIDENCE-BASED PSYCHOLOGICAL TREATMENT FOR OCD

Cognitive Behavior Therapy

Cognitive behavior therapy (CBT) continues to be the recommended first line of psychological treatment for OCD (Chambless & Ollendick, 2001; Koran, Hanna, Hollander, Nestadt, & Simpson, 2007; National Institute for Health and Clinical Excellence, 2005). Research indicates that 77% to 86% of individuals receiving CBT for OCD show significant improvement (Mancebo, Eisen, Sibrava, Dyck, & Rasmussen, 2011). Effect sizes (Cohen's d) for CBT for OCD tend to range from around 1.0 to 1.24 (Jónsson, Hougaard, & Bennedsen, 2011; Rosa-Alcanzar, Sanchez-Meca, Gomez-Conesa, & Marin-Martinez, 2008). Benchmarking studies suggest that results from randomized controlled trials translate well to routine clinical practice (Houghton et al., 2010). CBT also appears to be efficacious for individuals who have shown nonresponse to several trials of serotonin reuptake inhibitor medications (Anand, Sudhir, Math, Thennarasu, & Reddy, 2011; Tolin et al., 2007).

Exposure and Response Prevention

Exposure and response prevention (ERP) consists of prolonged, repeated exposure to fear-eliciting stimuli or situations, combined with instructions for strict abstinence from compulsive behavior. The purpose of these exercises is to allow the client to experience a reduction of her fear response, to recognize that these situations are not dangerous (or that the level of risk is acceptably low), and to learn that anxiety will subside naturally if she does not make efforts to avoid it.

An initial step in completing ERP with a client is to identify situations or activities that elicit obsessions and avoidant or compulsive behavior. Many patients with OCD present with multiple symptom dimensions (Foa et al., 1995); therefore, the clinician and patient must negotiate where to begin treatment. We suggest that the primary consideration should be to choose exposure exercises that are feasible and have a high probability of success (reduced fear). Early treatment successes can help to maintain a high level of patient motivation, whereas discouraging experiences early in treatment may lead to noncompliance or dropout.

Once an inventory of obsessional triggers has been completed, patients can begin to create an exposure hierarchy. Patients can rate their triggers—for example, ranking them in order or using a subjective units of distress (SUDS) scale (0–100, where 0 indicates a complete absence of anxiety and 100 equals the most discomfort the patient has ever felt). A hierarchy is then developed by ordering the exposures from least to most difficult. Exposures can be expected to elicit mild to moderate anxiety, but if the therapist finds that the patient is unable to complete an exposure, it may be modified slightly to reduce the level of anxiety produced. For example, an individual with contamination fears initially may be asked to hold his hand over the feared object rather than directly touch it; once the patient becomes more comfortable with this exposure, he can be asked to directly touch the object. In arranging an exposure hierarchy, having one to two exposures per 10-point increment is typically sufficient to allow for a gradual increase in difficulty.

The patient should be instructed in how to properly complete the exposures. We recommend that during initial exposures, the clinician should demonstrate full contact with the feared stimuli. The therapist should emphasize the importance of response prevention during and after exposures are completed. Across treatment, the clinician can gradually transfer responsibility to the patient to demonstrate thorough contact with feared cues. For exposures to be maximally effective, the patient will need to persist with them until she learns that anxiety will reduce naturally. Rituals will often be permitted in response to cues that have not yet been addressed in the hierarchy; once a hierarchy item has been practiced in session, patients can be instructed to avoid responding to any cues or situations with a lower SUDS rating than the exposures that have been completed in sessions.

During completion of the exposures, the therapist can solicit thoughts, emotional reactions, and ratings of anxiety or discomfort level. Patients are instructed to focus directly on aspects of the feared situation that increase anxiety and obsessive thoughts, and they may need to be reminded to do so during an exposure because many will engage in subtle avoidance or distraction. Patients can be warned that habituation to exposures can take an extended period of time and that prolonged exposure is more effective than spaced exposure. If anxiety does not decrease over an extended period, the patient may be continuing to complete some sort of subtle avoidance. It is important for the clinician to help the patient monitor for avoidance and to redirect the patient's attention to the obsessional cues.

Once the patient demonstrates sufficient habituation to the exposure stimulus in session, the patient is then instructed to repeat the exposure as homework. Patients will typically be requested to complete the exposure daily, keeping their own record of anxiety and discomfort ratings and frequency and duration of exposure completion. Patients are often encouraged to vary the task somewhat and to complete the exposure task in several contexts to maximize generalization. Clinicians may want to warn patients that anxiety or distress levels may be somewhat higher outside of the treatment session because the safety cues of the therapy environment are no longer present.

Occasionally it will be difficult or impossible to arrange for exposures to feared stimuli; in these cases, imaginal exposure may be substituted. For example, if a patient is worried that he will make insulting and obscene comments to his boss, he can be asked to imagine doing so and can imagine the feared outcomes of this act. The therapist may ask the patient to write out the narrative of this feared outcome in detail and then encourage him to read the narrative repeatedly. Another option is to make a loop-tape recording of the narrative. The patient can listen to this tape repeatedly to facilitate habituation.

Consistent with the theme of gradually transferring responsibility for exposure completion to the patient, around the midpoint in treatment we begin to increase the patient's role in deciding which exposures to do and when. Often, a late-treatment exposure session begins with the therapist asking, "What kind of exposure do you think would be helpful for you to do today?"

Cognitive Therapy

Formal cognitive therapy (CT) may also provide relief from OCD symptoms. Cognitive treatment protocols (e.g., Steketee & Wilhelm, 2006) tend to be based on Beck's (1976) model, which holds that negative emotions arise as a result of maladaptive or erroneous beliefs, thoughts, or appraisals. Like CT for other forms of psychopathology, CT for OCD focuses on teaching patients to identify and correct their dysfunctional beliefs about feared situations (Whittal & O'Neill, 2003; Wilhelm, 2003). In most cases, this has taken a form such as that used by Beck, Emery, and Greenberg (1985) in which Socratic questioning, behavioral experiments, and other cognitive strategies are used to challenge the validity of distorted thoughts. However, CT for OCD involves an additional component in which patients are instructed on how attempts to control intrusive obsessions often backfire, resulting in an increase in obsessional thought frequency (Salkovskis, 1985; Wegner, Schneider, Carter, & White, 1987). Patients are therefore instructed to relinquish efforts to control the content of their obsessions.

Identifying and Challenging Maladaptive Cognitions

To reduce efforts at control of obsessions and to challenge magical thinking, the content of obsessions is often normalized early on in treatment. Patients are informed that obsessions are simply thoughts, the content of which is not out of the range of normal human experience. Patients are therefore instructed in how their maladaptive appraisals, or the meaning that they attribute to cognitions, can maintain distress. Clinicians can explain the cognitive philosophy that events do not necessarily lead to distress but that negative interpretations of those events do and that obsessions are an event patients are interpreting negatively. The patient might then begin to self-monitor both obsessions and the appraisals that he or she is making about the obsessions. Appraisals are likely to reflect patients' belief in the importance of controlling their thoughts, or their overestimation of threat, intolerance of uncertainty, overestimation of responsibility, perfectionism, or concerns about their ability to tolerate anxiety or distress (Purdon, 2007). To normalize intrusive thoughts, the clinician can review with the patient the findings of studies showing that many individuals without OCD often experience distressing intrusive thoughts (e.g., Fullana et al., 2009; Rachman & de Silva, 1978).

Patients can then be instructed to practice identifying their appraisals of obsessions and, after they are skilled at identifying appraisals, can begin to practice challenging these interpretations. A downward arrow method can be used to identify feared appraisals. This method involves asking patients for their feared outcomes and then asking questions such as, "So if that [feared outcome] happened, what would that mean to you? To you, what would be bad about that particular outcome?" Once identified, appraisals can be challenged using cognitive methods such as identifying common cognitive distortions, for example, discounting positives, personalizing, "should" statements, or emotional reasoning (Leahy, 1996).

Effective techniques for challenging cognitions in OCD are similar to those used in CT for depression and other forms of anxiety (Leahy, 1996). Although the range of cognitive challenging techniques is broad, techniques often used for treating OCD include the continuum technique, direct calculations of the probability of feared outcomes, making "responsibility pie charts," and weighing advantages and disadvantages of thought styles.

The continuum technique can be used when patients overestimate responsibility or are feeling excessive guilt about their obsessions. This technique is designed to directly challenge all-or-nothing thinking. For example, if a participant is feeling that she is a "horrible person" for having thoughts that she may harm her child, she can be asked to make a continuum from "the worst person ever" to "the best person ever," describing behavioral anchors for how she is arriving at these judgments. The patient will likely acknowledge that having obsessions, although distressing, is not comparable to someone who actually harms her children.

Direct calculations of probability can be used to challenge overestimations of threat. For example, a patient who has obsessions that he may kill someone by mistakenly hitting them with his car can be asked to estimate how many times he has driven in the past and how many of these times he has hurt someone with his vehicle. He can be asked to list the conditions that would need to be present for him to actually murder someone with his car, such as (a) he would need to be driving, (b) he would need to lose control of himself or his vehicle, (c) a pedestrian would need to be nearby, (d) the pedestrian would need to be hit, and (e) the pedestrian would need to be injured so severely that the injury was fatal. He can then be asked to calculate probabilities for each of these individual events occurring. Then these probabilities can be multiplied to obtain a total probability or likelihood of the worst outcome occurring. Often, the total probability is a fraction of a percent chance of the feared outcome occurring. This exercise can highlight probability overestimations and emotional reasoning distortions for the patient, reinforcing that although feared outcomes often feel likely, these feelings do not necessarily reflect the evidence for the likelihood of these consequences occurring and their severity.

Responsibility pie charts can be used to directly challenge an excessive sense of responsibility. For example, a participant who worries that if she makes an error in a report, the company will fail and she will be fired can be asked to make a pie chart outlining who would be responsible for this feared outcome. Patients with an inflated sense of responsibility often begin this exercise believing that if their feared outcome occurred, it would be 100% due to their behaviors. Socratic questioning can be used to assist the patient in examining who or what other factors could also have played a role in such a feared outcome occurring (e.g., the employer, coworkers who also worked on the report). The clinician may need to offer examples to get the patient started on this exercise.

Weighing advantages and disadvantages can be used to have patients examine the utility of their beliefs. Even participants who are reluctant to directly challenge the content of their appraisals will often recognize that there are many more disadvantages than advantages to using their negative appraisals as an operating framework.

Finally, behavioral experiments may be used in which the patient is encouraged to use the scientific method to directly test assumptions. For example, a patient who fears that she will become gravely ill if she touches contaminated items can be asked to generate alternative hypotheses for this outcome (e.g., she does not become sick at all, she becomes only mildly sick). The patient can then design an experiment or series of experiments to test which of these possible hypotheses is correct. For example, the patient may be asked to touch a range of "dirty" items, keeping a log of how often she becomes ill in the days afterward. Although it clearly involves behavioral components, many therapists conceptualize the behavioral experiment as a cognitive technique and emphasize the importance of using the experiments to disconfirm fearful expectations.

Matching Patients to ERP or CT

Our preference, based on the data, is to use ERP whenever possible. However, incorporating CT may be important when ERP has not produced optimal results or when patients refuse ERP. Approximately 20% to 30% of OCD patients refuse to begin ERP (Franklin & Foa, 1998), many because of apprehension about the difficulty and intensity of the treatment and because of environmental barriers (e.g., difficulty locating a CBT provider, scheduling conflict; Mancebo et al., 2011). However, once patients enter treatment, they appear to be equally likely to stay in exposure based-treatments as non-exposure treatments: At least two meta-analyses (Hoffman & Smits, 2008; Kobak, Greist, Jefferson, Katzelnick, & Henk, 1998) found no significant differences in dropout rate between exposure-based therapies and alternative psychotherapies or pharmacotherapies. There appear to be no consistent pretreatment predictors of individuals who are likely to drop out of ERP due to negative aspects of the treatment (Aderka et al., 2011). Individuals who drop out of CBT for OCD later in treatment tend not to do so for negative reasons but rather may leave treatment after experiencing a substantial improvement in symptoms (Aderka et al., 2011). One potential strategy for facilitating treatment enrollment in reluctant patients is to begin with CT, first introducing behavioral experiments and then integrating prolonged exposures and response prevention. Alternatively, some patients may benefit from medications, which, although rarely effective as a stand-alone treatment for OCD, may alleviate OCD symptoms enough that the prospect of ERP is no longer overwhelming. Once engaged, giving patients a detailed rationale and an appropriate explanation of the treatment, or appropriate "socialization to treatment" (Haaland et al., 2011), is associated with higher rates of compliance.

There are few variables to aid clinicians in matching patients to ERP. Many therapists will elect to emphasize ERP for patients with more overt compulsions. Some studies have suggested that individuals who have primary obsessions (i.e., those who appear to have obsessions without compulsions) are less likely to respond to ERP-based treatment (Starcevic & Brakoulias, 2008). However, recent research has suggested that these individuals may not be "pure obsessionals" but instead may have rituals that may be more difficult to identify and observe, such as mental neutralizing or reassurance seeking (Williams et al., 2011). Therefore, these individuals may be more difficult to treat with ERP due to the difficulty of identifying mental compulsions and preventing these cognitive responses. Some studies have suggested that certain comorbid conditions, such as major depression, panic disorder, generalized anxiety disorder (Hansen, Vogel, Stiles, & Gotestam, 2007), post-traumatic stress disorder (Gershuny, Baer, Jenike, Minichiello, & Wilhelm, 2002) and obsessive–compulsive personality disorder (Pinto, Liebowitz, Foa, & Simpson, 2011), are associated with a poorer response to ERP for OCD. However, many studies suggest that some concurrent anxiety and affective disorders, including depression, have been associated with minimal to no diminution of treatment benefit with ERP (e.g., Orloff, Battle, Baer, & Ivanjack, 1994; Steketee, Eisen, Dyck, Warshaw, & Rasmussen, 1999).

Currently, no patient variables are known to reliably predict response to CT. CT is clearly a viable alternative for patients who may not be willing to participate in ERP. It appears that concurrent depression and anxiety are not contraindications to successful CT (Anholt et al., 2011; Steketee et al., 2011), but the total number of comorbid Axis I disorders does appear to be associated with less benefit (Steketee et al., 2011).

Treatment Structure of CBT for OCD

Individual CBT for OCD tends to follow a format similar to CBT for other anxiety and mood disorders. Individual treatment sessions typically commence with a review of homework completion and agenda setting. Sessions focus on psychoeducation in early sessions and then move to practice and application of skills (i.e., cognitive challenging or exposure). Individual sessions typically end with a discussion of homework to be completed. A course of treatment may end with one to two sessions focusing on relapse prevention; in these sessions, patients can be given psychoeducation about how relapse risk is higher during times of stress. Patients may be asked to identify potential upcoming stressors and to create a plan to avoid relapse at those times, such as reimplementation of an exposure hierarchy and a cognitive challenging record. The clinician may also discuss the heightened potential for relapse when the patient has negative, catastrophic cognitions about lapses.

Many authors recommend that CBT for OCD be delivered in an intensive format. When daily or near daily treatment is not possible, treatment may begin with sessions twice per week and taper down to once per week (Steketee, 1999). Studies directly comparing intensive with weekly sessions have suggested that the two are comparable in effectiveness (Oldfield, Salkovskis, & Taylor, 2011; Storch et al., 2008); however, treatment benefit may result earlier from intensive treatment because the treatment is completed more quickly. After a full course of treatment (approximately 20–24 therapy hours), many therapists will elect to taper off treatment. If possible, booster sessions as needed may be offered.

Often, inclusion of family members in treatment is helpful. This is especially indicated when the family members are accommodating the patient's ritualizing. We educate family members about the negatively reinforcing effect of avoidance and encourage them to reduce accommodations (with the patient's consent). Family members can also be recruited to assist the patient in the completion of exposure homework. Friends or relatives may be effective at reminding patients to complete homework assignments, modeling exposures, and providing support. The role of the assistant in helping with homework should be negotiated with the patient because although many patients find the support helpful, some may find the involvement of family members intrusive.

Other Treatment Modalities

Group Therapy

Direct comparisons of individual and group CBT for OCD have largely found that individual therapy tends to have somewhat better outcomes. In two studies, approximately 41% to 45% of those who completed group CBT for OCD were classified as "recovered" based on measures of clinically significant change, compared with 62% to 63% of those who completed an individual modality (Anderson & Rees, 2007; Cabedo et al., 2010). Open trials of group CBT for OCD show reductions of approximately 7 to 8 points on the Y-BOCS, or a 37% to 44% reduction, with a pre–post effect size of approximately 0.81 to 1.13 (Fenger, Mortensen, Rasmussen, & Lau, 2007; Jónsson, Hougaard, & Bennedsen, 2009; Kearns, Tone, Rush, & Lucey, 2010). This magnitude of change is somewhat lower than that of individual therapy for OCD, showing a change of about 10 to 15 points (Houghton, Saxon, Bradburn, Ricketts, & Hardy, 2010). However, these open trials of group therapy often offered fewer sessions than trials of individual therapy, typically around 12 sessions (e.g., Haaland et al., 2010; Raffin, Fachel, Ferrao, de Souza, & Cordioli, 2009). Some studies that have examined a longer course of treatment (e.g., 20–24 sessions; Fals-Stewart, Marks, & Schafer, 1993; Jaurrieta et al., 2008) found that group therapy led to outcomes similar to those found with individual therapy.

Self-Help and Guided Self-Help

Some studies have investigated therapist-guided self-help modalities, such as bibliotherapy and computer-guided interventions. The small literature base does suggest that bibliotherapy or self-help interventions are less effective than individual therapy. Small-scale open trials of self-help or computer-based CBT for OCD have shown mild to moderate decreases on the Y-BOCS of about 6 points, or clinically significant change in approximately one third of participants (e.g., Fritzler, Hecker, & Losee, 1997). Consistent with this, one of the programs that has been most investigated, BTSteps (also known as "OC Fighter"; Greist et al., 1998), has been shown to result in decreases on the Y-BOCS of 5 to 8 points, with an effect size of 0.08 to 1.3 in one study (Kenwright, Marks, Graham, Franses, & Mataix-Cols, 2005).

Although these self-help treatments tend to show less benefit than individual treatment, they may be useful in situations in which individual treatment is not readily accessible or is financially unfeasible. In addition, self-help modalities may be a good first step in stepped care models (Moritz, Wittekind, Hauschildt, & Timpano, 2011). Preliminary research on the use of these interventions in stepped care models (e.g., Tolin, Diefenbach, & Gilliam, 2011; Tolin, Diefenbach, Maltby, & Hannan, 2005) suggests that therapist-guided bibliotherapy may be a cost-effective initial step.

Summary and Future Directions

In conclusion, OCD is a common, often debilitating disorder that tends to cluster into distinctive patterns of obsessional content and compulsive behaviors. Although ERP and CT are highly effective psychotherapies for OCD, there remains room for improvement. It is recommended that future research investigate methods of enhancing CBT and improving outcomes, possibly with the use of concurrent medications such as D-cycloserine. Investigation into neurobiological processes, particularly those surrounding attentional biases in OCD, may elucidate some potential treatment targets. Additional research on subtyping of OCD and differential responses to treatment by subtype may be useful because some treatments may be more efficacious with some subtypes than others. Finally, additional investigation of predictors of response to CT versus ERP may aid clinicians in matching patients with the best available treatment.

REFERENCES

Abramowitz, J. S., Whiteside, S., Lynam, D., & Kalsy, S. (2003). Is thought-action fusion specific to obsessive–compulsive disorder? A mediating role of negative affect. *Behaviour Research and Therapy, 41,* 1069–1079. doi:10.1016/S0005-7967(02)00243-7

Aderka, I. M., Anholt, G. E., van Balkom, A. J. L. M., Smit, J. H., Hermesh, H., Hofmann, S. G., & van Oppen, P. (2011). Differences between early and late drop-outs from treatment for obsessive–compulsive disorders. *Journal of Anxiety Disorders, 25,* 918–923. doi:10.1016/j.janxdis.2011.05.004

American Psychiatric Association. (2013). *Diagnostic and statistical manual of mental disorders* (5th ed.). Washington, DC: Author.

Anand, N., Sudhir, P. M., Math, S. B., Thennarasu, K., & Reddy, Y. C. J. (2011). Cognitive behavior therapy in medication non-responders with obsessive–compulsive disorder: A prospective 1-year follow-up study. *Journal of Anxiety Disorders, 25,* 939–945. doi:10.1016/j.janxdis.2011.05.007

Anderson, R. A., & Rees, C. S. (2007). Group versus individual cognitive-behavioural treatment for obsessive–compulsive disorder: A controlled trial. *Behaviour Research and Therapy, 45,* 123–137. doi:10.1016/j.brat.2006.01.016

Anholt, G. E., Aderka, I. M., van Balkom, A. J. L. M., Smit, J. H., Hermesh, H., de Haan, E., & van Oppen, P. (2011). The impact of depression on the treatment of obsessive–compulsive disorder: Results from a 5-year follow-up. *Journal of Affective Disorders, 135,* 201–207. doi:10.1016/j.jad.2011.07.018

Beck, A. T. (1976). *Cognitive therapy of the emotional disorders.* New York, NY: International Universities Press.

Beck, A. T., Emery, G., & Greenberg, R. L. (1985). *Anxiety disorders and phobias: A cognitive perspective.* New York, NY: Basic Books.

Cabedo, E., Belloch, A., Carrio, C., Larsson, C., Fernandez-Alvarez, H., & Garcia, F. (2010). Group versus individual cognitive treatment for obsessive–compulsive disorder: Changes in severity at post-treatment and one-year follow-up. *Behavioural and Cognitive Psychotherapy, 38,* 227–232. doi:10.1017/S135246580999066X

Chambless, D. L., & Ollendick, T. H. (2001). Empirically supported psychological interventions: Controversies and evidence. *Annual Review of Psychology, 52,* 685–716. doi:10.1146/annurev.psych.52.1.685

Fals-Stewart, W., Marks, A. P., & Schafer, J. (1993). A comparison of behavioral group therapy and individual behavior therapy in treating obsessive–compulsive disorder. *Journal of Nervous and Mental Disease, 181,* 189–193. doi:10.1097/00005053-199303000-00007

Fenger, M. M., Mortensen, E. L., Rasmussen, J., & Lau, M. (2007). Group therapy with OCD: Development and outcome of diagnosis specific treatment of patients with OCD in groups. *Nordic Psychology, 59,* 332–346. doi:10.1027/1901-2276.59.4.332

Flett, G. L., & Hewitt, P. L. (Eds.). (2002). *Perfectionism: Theory, research, and treatment.* Washington, DC: American Psychological Association. doi:10.1037/10458-000

Foa, E. B., Huppert, J. D., Leiberg, S., Langner, R., Kichic, R., & Hajcak, G. (2002). The Obsessive–Compulsive Inventory: Development and validation of a short version. *Psychological Assessment, 14,* 485–496. doi:10.1037/1040-3590.14.4.485

Foa, E. B., Kozak, M. J., Goodman, W. K., Hollander, E., Jenike, M. A., & Rasmussen, S. A. (1995). DSM–IV field trial: Obsessive–compulsive disorder. *The American Journal of Psychiatry, 152,* 90–96.

Foa, E. B., Kozak, M. J., Salkovskis, P. M., Coles, M. E., & Amir, N. (1998). The validation of a new obsessive compulsive disorder scale: The obsessive compulsive inventory. *Psychological Assessment, 10,* 206–214. doi:10.1037/1040-3590.10.3.206

Franklin, M. E., & Foa, E. B. (1998). Cognitive-behavioral treatments for obsessive–compulsive disorder. In J. M. Gorman (Ed.), *A guide to treatments that work* (pp. 339–357). New York, NY: Oxford University Press.

Fritzler, B. K., Hecker, J. E., & Losee, M. C. (1997). Self-directed treatment with minimal therapist contact: Preliminary findings for obsessive–compulsive disorder. *Behaviour Research and Therapy, 35,* 627–631. doi:10.1016/S0005-7967(97)00024-7

Fullana, M. A., Mataix-Cols, D., Caspi, A., Harrington, H., Grisham, J. R., Moffitt, T. E., & Poulton, R. (2009). Obsessions and compulsions in the community: Prevalence, interference, help-seeking, developmental stability, and co-occurring psychiatric conditions. *The American Journal of Psychiatry, 166,* 329–336. doi:10.1176/appi.ajp.2008.08071006

Gershuny, B. S., Baer, L., Jenike, M. A., Minichiello, W. E., & Wilhelm, S. (2002). Comorbid posttraumatic stress disorder: Impact on treatment outcome for obsessive–compulsive disorder. *The American Journal of Psychiatry, 159,* 852–854. doi:10.1176/appi.ajp.159.5.852

Goodman, W. K., Price, L. H., Rasmussen, S. A., & Mazure, C. (1989). The Yale-Brown Obsessive Compulsive Scale: I. Development, use, and reliability. *Archives of General Psychiatry, 46,* 1006–1011. doi:10.1001/archpsyc.1989.01810110048007

Goodman, W. K., Price, L. H., Rasmussen, S. A., Mazure, C., Delgado, P., Heninger, G. R., & Charney, D. S. (1989). The Yale–Brown Obsessive Compulsive Scale. II. Validity. *Archives of General Psychiatry, 46*, 1012–1016. doi:10.1001/archpsyc.1989.01810110054008

Grabill, K., Merlo, L., Duke, D., Harford, K., Keeley, M. L., Geffken, G. R., & Storch, E. A. (2008). Assessment of obsessive–compulsive disorder: A review. *Journal of Anxiety Disorders, 22*, 1–17.

Greist, J. H., Marks, I. M., Baer, L., Parkin, R., Manzo, P., & Mantle, J. (1998). Self-treatment for OCD using a manual and a computerized telephone interview: A US–UK Study. *M.D. Computing, 15*, 149–157.

Haaland, A. T., Vogel, P. A., Launes, G., Haaland, V. O., Hansen, B., Solem, S., & Himle, J. A. (2011). The role of early maladaptive schemas in predicting exposure and response prevention outcome for obsessive–compulsive disorder. *Behaviour Research and Therapy, 49*, 781–788. doi:10.1016/j.brat.2011.08.007

Hansen, B., Vogel, P. A., Stiles, T. C., & Gotestam, K. G. (2007). Influence of co-morbid generalized anxiety disorder, panic disorder and personality disorders on the outcome of cognitive behavioural treatment of obsessive–compulsive disorder. *Cognitive Behaviour Therapy, 36*, 145–155. doi:10.1080/16506070701259374

Herrnstein, R. J. (1969). Method and theory in the study of avoidance. *Psychological Review, 76*, 49–69. doi:10.1037/h0026786

Hofmann, S. G., & Smits, J. A. J. (2008). Cognitive-behavioral therapy for adult anxiety disorders: A meta-analysis of randomized placebo-controlled trials. *Journal of Clinical Psychiatry, 69*, 621–632. doi:10.4088/JCP.v69n0415

Houghton, S., Saxon, D., Bradburn, M., Ricketts, T., & Hardy, G. (2010). The effectiveness of routinely delivered cognitive behavioural therapy for obsessive–compulsive disorder: A benchmarking study. *British Journal of Clinical Psychology, 49*, 473–489. doi:10.1348/014466509X475414

Huppert, J. D., Simpson, H. B., Nissenson, K. J., Liebowitz, M. R., & Foa, E. B. (2009). Quality of life and functional impairment in obsessive–compulsive disorder: A comparison of patients with and without comorbidity, patients in remission, and healthy controls. *Depression and Anxiety, 26*, 39–45. doi:10.1002/da.20506

Jaurrieta, N., Jimenez-Murcia, S., Alonso, P., Granero, R., Segalas, C., Labad, J., & Menchon, J. M. (2008). Individual versus group cognitive behavioral treatment for obsessive–compulsive disorder: Follow up. *Psychiatry and Clinical Neurosciences, 62*, 697–704. doi:10.1111/j.1440-1819.2008.01873.x

Jónsson, H. H., Hougaard, E., & Bennedsen, B. E. (2011). Randomized comparative study of group versus individual cognitive behavioural therapy for obsessive compulsive disorder. *Acta Psychiatrica Scandinavica, 123*, 387–397. doi:10.1111/j.1600-0447.2010.01613.x

Kearns, C., Tone, Y., Rush, G., & Lucey, J. V. (2010). Effectiveness of group-based cognitive-behavioural therapy in patients with obsessive–compulsive disorder. *The Psychiatrist, 34*, 6–9. doi:10.1192/pb.bp.106.011510

Kenwright, M., Marks, I., Graham, C., Franses, A., & Mataix-Cols, D. (2005). Brief scheduled phone support from a clinician to enhance computer-aided self-help for obsessive–compulsive disorder: Randomized controlled trial. *Journal of Clinical Psychology, 61*, 1499–1508. doi:10.1002/jclp.20204

Kobak, K. A., Greist, J. H., Jefferson, J. W., Katzelnick, D. J., & Henk, H. J. (1998). Behavioral versus pharmacological treatments of obsessive compulsive disorder: A meta-analysis. *Psychopharmacology, 136*, 205–216. doi:10.1007/s00213 0050558

Koran, L. M., Hanna, G. L., Hollander, E., Nestadt, G., & Simpson, H. B. (2007). Practice guideline for the treatment of patients with obsessive–compulsive disorder. *The American Journal of Psychiatry, 164*, 5–53.

Leahy, R. L. (1996). *Cognitive therapy*. Northvale, NJ: Aronson.

Leckman, J. F., Denys, D., Simpson, H. B., Mataix-Cols, D., Hollander, E., Saxena, S., . . . Stein, D. J. (2010). Obsessive–compulsive disorder: A review of the diagnostic criteria and possible subtypes and dimensional specifiers for *DSM–V. Depression and Anxiety, 27*, 507–527. doi:10.1002/da.20669

Mancebo, M. C., Eisen, J. L., Sibrava, N. J., Dyck, I. R., & Rasmussen, S. A. (2011). Patient utilization of cognitive-behavioral therapy for OCD. *Behavior Therapy, 42*, 399–412. doi:10.1016/j.beth.2010.10.002

Mancebo, M. C., Greenberg, B., Grant, J. E., Pinto, A., Eisen, J. L., Dyck, I., & Rasmussen, S. A. (2008). Correlates of occupational disability in a clinical sample of obsessive–compulsive disorder. *Comprehensive Psychiatry, 49*, 43–50. doi:10.1016/j.comppsych.2007.05.016

Moritz, S., & Jelinek, L. (2009). Inversion of the "unrealistic optimism" bias contributes to overestimation of threat in obsessive–compulsive disorder. *Behavioural and Cognitive Psychotherapy, 37*, 179–193. doi:10.1017/S1352465808005043

Moritz, S., Wittekind, C. E., Hauschildt, M., & Timpano, K. R. (2011). Do it yourself? Self-help and online therapy for people with obsessive–compulsive disorder. *Current Opinion in Psychiatry, 24*, 541–548.

National Institute for Health and Clinical Excellence. (2005). *Obsessive compulsive disorder: Core interventions in the treatment of obsessive–compulsive disorder and body dysmorphic disorder* (Clinical Guideline 21). Retrieved from http://www.nice.org.uk/CG031

Obsessive Compulsive Cognitions Working Group. (2003). Psychometric validation of the Obsessive Beliefs Questionnaire and the Interpretation of Intrusions Inventory: Part I. *Behaviour Research and Therapy, 41*, 863–878. doi:10.1016/S0005-7967(02)00099-2

Oldfield, V. B., Salkovskis, P. M., & Taylor, T. (2011). Time-intensive cognitive behaviour therapy for obsessive–compulsive disorder: A case series and matched comparison group. *British Journal of Clinical Psychology, 50,* 7–18. doi:10.1348/014466510X490073

Orloff, L. M., Battle, M. A., Baer, L., & Ivanjack, L. (1994). Long-term follow-up of 85 patients with obsessive–compulsive disorder. *The American Journal of Psychiatry, 151,* 441–442.

Pinto, A., Liebowitz, M. R., Foa, E. B., & Simpson, H. B. (2011). Obsessive compulsive personality disorder as a predictor of exposure and ritual prevention outcome for obsessive compulsive disorder. *Behaviour Research and Therapy, 49,* 453–458. doi:10.1016/j.brat.2011.04.004

Purdon, C. (2007). Cognitive therapy for obsessive–compulsive disorders. In M. A. Antony, C. Purdon, & L. J. Summerfeldt (Eds.), *Psychological treatment of obsessive-compulsive disorder: Fundamentals and beyond* (pp. 111–145). Washington, DC: American Psychological Association. doi:10.1037/11543-005

Purdon, C., Rowa, K., & Antony, M. M. (2005). Thought suppression and its effects on thought frequency, appraisal and mood state in individuals with obsessive–compulsive disorder. *Behaviour Research and Therapy, 43,* 93–108. doi:10.1016/j.brat.2003.11.007

Rachman, S. (2004). OCD in and out of the clinic. *Journal of Behavior Therapy and Experimental Psychiatry, 35,* 207–208. doi:10.1016/j.jbtep.2004.04.010

Rachman, S., & de Silva, P. (1978). Abnormal and normal obsessions. *Behaviour Research and Therapy, 16,* 233–248. doi:10.1016/0005-7967(78)90022-0

Raffin, A. L., Fachel, J. M. G., Ferrao, Y. A., de Souza, F. P., & Cordioli, A. V. (2009). Predictors of response to group cognitive-behavioral therapy in the treatment of obsessive–compulsive disorder. *European Psychiatry, 24,* 297–306. doi:10.1016/j.eurpsy.2008.12.001

Rosa-Alcazar, A. I., Sanchez-Meca, J., Gomez-Conesa, A., & Marin-Martinez, F. (2008). Psychological treatment of obsessive-compulsive disorder: A meta-analysis. *Clinical Psychology Review, 28,* 1310–1325. doi:10.1016/j.cpr.2008.07.001

Rosario-Campos, M. C., Miguel, E. C., Quatrano, S., Chacon, P., Ferrao, Y., & Findley, D. (2006). The Dimensional Yale–Brown Obsessive–Compulsive Scale (DY-BOCS): An instrument for assessing obsessive–compulsive symptom dimensions. *Molecular Psychiatry, 11,* 495–504. doi:10.1038/sj.mp.4001798

Ruscio, A. M., Stein, D. J., Chiu, W. T., & Kessler, R. C. (2010). Epidemiology of obsessive–compulsive disorder in the National Comorbidity Survey Replication. *Molecular Psychiatry, 15,* 53–63. doi:10.1038/mp.2008.94

Salkovskis, P. M. (1985). Obsessional–compulsive problems: A cognitive-behavioural analysis. *Behaviour Research and Therapy, 23,* 571–583. doi:10.1016/0005-7967(85)90105-6

Salkovskis, P. M., Wroe, A. L., Gledhill, A., Morrison, N., Forrester, E., & Richards, C. (2000). Responsibility attitudes and interpretations are characteristic of obsessive compulsive disorder. *Behaviour Research and Therapy, 38,* 347–372. doi:10.1016/S0005-7967(99)00071-6

Shafran, R., Thordarson, D. S., & Rachman, S. (1996). Thought-action fusion in obsessive compulsive disorder. *Journal of Anxiety Disorders, 10,* 379–391. doi:10.1016/0887-6185(96)00018-7

Starcevic, V., & Brakoulias, V. (2008). Symptom subtypes of obsessive–compulsive disorder: Are they relevant for treatment? *Australian and New Zealand Journal of Psychiatry, 42,* 651–661. doi:10.1080/00048670802203442

Steketee, G. (1999). *Therapist protocol: Overcoming obsessive–compulsive disorder: A behavioral and cognitive protocol for the treatment of OCD.* Oakland, CA: New Harbinger.

Steketee, G., Eisen, J., Dyck, I., Warshaw, M., & Rasmussen, S. (1999). Predictors of course in obsessive–compulsive disorder. *Psychiatry Research, 89,* 229–238. doi: 10.1016/S0165-1781(99)00104-3

Steketee, G., Frost, R., & Bogart, K. (1996). The Yale-Brown Obsessive Compulsive Scale: Interview versus self-report. *Behaviour Research and Therapy, 34,* 675–684. doi:10.1016/0005-7967(96)00036-8

Steketee, G., Siev, J., Fama, J. M., Keshaviah, A., Chosak, A., & Wilhelm, S. (2011). Predictors of treatment outcome in modular cognitive therapy for obsessive–compulsive disorder. *Depression and Anxiety, 28,* 333–341. doi:10.1002/da.20785

Steketee, G., & Wilhelm, S. (2006). *Cognitive therapy for obsessive–compulsive disorder: A guide for professionals.* Oakland, CA: New Harbinger.

Storch, E. A., & Merlo, L. J. (2006). Obsessive–compulsive disorder: Strategies for using CBT and pharmacotherapy. *The Journal of Family Practice, 55,* 329–333.

Storch, E. A., Merlo, L. J., Lehmkuhl, H., Geffken, G. R., Jacob, M., Ricketts, E., . . . & Goodman, W. K. (2008). Cognitive-behavioral therapy for obsessive–compulsive disorder: A non-randomized comparison of intensive and weekly approaches. *Journal of Anxiety Disorders, 22,* 1146–1158. doi:10.1016/j.janxdis.2007.12.001

Tolin, D. F. (2010). Compulsions. In I. B. Weiner & W. E. Craighead (Eds.), *The Corsini encyclopedia of psychology* (pp. 371–372). New York, NY: Wiley. doi:10.1002/9780470479216.corpsy0210

Tolin, D. F., Abramowitz, J. S., Przeworski, A., & Foa, E. B. (2002). Thought suppression in obsessive–compulsive disorder. *Behaviour Research and Therapy, 40,* 1255–1274. doi:10.1016/S0005-7967(01)00095-X

Tolin, D. E., Diefenbach, G. J., & Gilliam, C. M. (2011). Stepped care versus standard cognitive-behavioral therapy for obsessive–compulsive disorder: A preliminary study of efficacy and costs. *Depression and Anxiety, 28,* 314–323. doi: 10.1002/da.20804

Tolin, D. F., Diefenbach, G. J., Maltby, N., & Hannan, S. (2005). Stepped care for obsessive–compulsive disorder: A pilot study. *Cognitive and Behavioral Practice, 12,* 403–414. doi:10.1016/S1077-7229(05)80068-9

Tolin, D. F., Hamlin, C., & Foa, E. B. (2002). Directed forgetting in obsessive–compulsive disorder: Replication and extension. *Behaviour Research and Therapy, 40,* 793–803. doi:10.1016/S0005-7967(01)00062-6

Tolin, D. F., Hannan, S., Maltby, N., Diefenbach, G. J., Worhunsky, P., & Brady, R. E. (2007). A randomized controlled trial of self-directed versus therapist-directed cognitive-behavioral therapy for obsessive–compulsive disorder patients with prior medication trials. *Behavior Therapy, 38,* 179–191. doi:10.1016/j.beth.2006.07.001

Wegner, D. M., Schneider, D. J., Carter, S. R., & White, T. L. (1987). Paradoxical effects of thought suppression. *Journal of Personality and Social Psychology, 53,* 5–13. doi:10.1037/0022-3514.53.1.5

Weissman, M. M., Bland, R. C., Canino, G. J., & Greenwald, S. (1994). The cross national epidemiology of obsessive compulsive disorder: The Cross National Collaborative Group. *Journal of Clinical Psychiatry, 55,* 5–10.

Whittal, M. L., & O'Neill, M. L. (2003). Cognitive and behavioral methods for obsessive–compulsive disorder. *Brief Treatment and Crisis Intervention, 3,* 201–216. doi:10.1093/brief-treatment/mhg015

Wilhelm, S. (2003). Cognitive treatment of obsessions. *Brief Treatment and Crisis Intervention, 3,* 187–199. doi:10.1093/brief-treatment/mhg014

Williams, M. T., Farris, S. G., Turkheimer, E., Pinto, A., Ozanick, K., Franklin, M. E., . . . Foa, E. B. (2011). Myth of the pure obsessional type in obsessive–compulsive disorder. *Depression and Anxiety, 28,* 495–500. doi:10.1002/da.20820

Woody, S. R., Steketee, G., & Chambless, D. L. (1995). Reliability and validity of the Yale–Brown Obsessive–Compulsive Scale. *Behaviour Research and Therapy, 33,* 597–605. doi:10.1016/0005-7967(94)00076-V

2

PEDIATRIC OBSESSIVE–COMPULSIVE DISORDER

MICHELLE R. GRYCZKOWSKI AND STEPHEN P. H. WHITESIDE

The nature and treatment of obsessive–compulsive disorder (OCD) in children and adolescents ages 7 to 17 (henceforth collectively termed *children*) is largely consistent with that of adults. Diagnostically, the only difference is that children need not recognize that their obsessions or compulsions are irrational. This distinction is supported by recent findings indicating that nearly half of children with OCD demonstrate poor insight into their symptoms (Storch et al., 2008). Children are also more likely than adults to hide their symptoms and have poorer distress tolerance and tend to involve other family members in their rituals (March & Mulle, 1998), rendering treatment more complex. Indeed, pediatric OCD presents unique challenges to the treating clinician and may require therapeutic skills beyond those required to treat adult OCD. Important considerations when assessing and treating pediatric OCD include the developmental level of the child, familial factors that may be maintaining symptoms or providing barriers to treatment, and

http://dx.doi.org/10.1037/14323-003
Obsessive–Compulsive Disorder and Its Spectrum: A Life-Span Approach, Eric A. Storch and Dean McKay (Editors)
Copyright © 2014 by the American Psychological Association. All rights reserved.

comorbid externalizing disorders. The purposes of this chapter are to provide a thorough discussion of the nature of pediatric OCD and to offer detailed guidance on its treatment.

NATURE OF PEDIATRIC OBSESSIVE–COMPULSIVE DISORDER

Epidemiology

Pediatric OCD is relatively common, with lifetime prevalence reaching 2% to 3% by late adolescence (Rapoport et al., 2000). The prevalence is greater in boys during childhood due to the earlier age of onset in males; however, by adolescence, the sex distribution is equal (Flament et al., 1988; Zohar, 1999). Symptoms typically present initially in childhood or adolescence (Rasmussen & Eisen, 1990), although some individuals develop symptoms in adulthood (Delorme et al., 2005; Taylor, 2011). The idea that childhood-onset and adult-onset OCD represent two distinct subtypes has been proposed by a number of researchers (e.g., Geller et al., 2001; Geller, Biederman, Jones, Park, et al., 1998; Taylor, 2011).

Course

Without treatment, OCD is a chronic condition (Micali et al., 2010), although the intensity of symptoms waxes and wanes (Stewart et al., 2004). Complete remission rates are highly variable across studies, with meta-analytic findings indicating mean persistence rates of 41% for clinically significant symptoms and 60% for subclinical symptoms (Stewart et al., 2004). A subset of pediatric OCD cases are characterized by an abrupt, dramatic onset or exacerbation of OCD symptoms that tend to be episodic. When combined with two or more neuropsychiatric symptoms (i.e., anxiety; emotional lability/depression; irritability, aggression, or severely oppositional behaviors; deterioration in academic performance; sensory or motor abnormalities; or somatic symptoms such as urinary incontinence or frequency and sleep disturbance), a diagnosis of pediatric acute-onset neuropsychiatric syndrome (PANS) may be most appropriate (Swedo, Leckman, & Rose, 2012). This recently proposed diagnosis encompasses a wider variety of etiologies than the original term pediatric autoimmune neuropsychiatric disorders associated with streptococcal infections (PANDAS; Larson, Storch, & Murphy, 2007; Swedo et al., 1998), which is a now a proposed subtype of PANS. The current standard of care is to treat PANDAS with a selective serotonin reuptake inhibitor (SSRI) or behavioral treatment (Larson et al., 2007); however, there is some preliminary evidence for the effectiveness of antibiotic prophylaxis, plasma exchange, and intravenous immunoglobin (IVIG) in treating this subset of children (Larson et al., 2007; Perlmutter et al., 1999; Snider & Swedo, 2003; Swedo et al., 2012). There is also some evidence that children with PANDAS may be at greater risk for adverse reactions to SSRIs (Murphy, Storch, & Strawser, 2006). Finally, preliminary findings suggest that cognitive behavior therapy (CBT) is effective in treating PANDAS-related OCD in some children (Storch et al., 2006). More rigorous, controlled trials with larger sample sizes are needed to determine the most effective treatment for PANS/PANDAS-related OCD.

Clinical Description

Although the course of OCD is relatively stable, the types of obsessions and rituals change over time. Rettew, Swedo, Leondard, Lenane, and Rapoport (1992) assessed symptom constellations in 79 children with OCD over a span of 2 to 7 years; no patient's combination of symptoms remained the same from baseline to follow-up. Moreover, only 15% displayed symptoms from only one category at any given time, indicating that the presence of multiple, concurrent obsessions and/or compulsions is the norm. The most common symptom typology involves themes of cleanliness and contamination (Geller, Biederman, Jones, Shapiro, et al., 1998). Other common categories include fear of harm, symmetry and exactness, repetition, checking, touching, and aggression (Geller, Biederman, Jones, Shapiro, et al., 1998; Rettew et al., 1992). Relative to adults, children have greater preoccupation with harm, are more likely to display hoarding symptoms, and have fewer intrusive sexual thoughts (Geller et al., 2001; Moore, Mariaskin, March, & Franklin, 2007). Girls tend to have more "phobic" symptoms, whereas boys tend to have more "just right" feelings (Swedo et al., 1989). Finally, symptom presentation is similar across a variety of cultures (Thomsen, 1991).

Comorbidity

The majority of children with OCD also meet criteria for one or more additional psychiatric disorders (Franklin et al., 2011). The most common comorbid disorders include other anxiety disorders, tic disorders, depression, attention-deficit/hyperactivity disorder (ADHD), and disruptive behavior disorders (DBDs; Franklin et al., 2011; Geller et al., 2003; Pediatric OCD Treatment Study Team, 2004; Swedo et al., 1989). Noncompliance, inattention and hyperactivity, and depression (particularly if severe) are likely to interfere with behavioral treatments if not treated concurrently (Storch et al., 2008); thus, assessing for comorbid mood and externalizing behaviors is particularly important. In some cases, these conditions may require clinical attention before implementing behavioral treatments for OCD. Comorbid anxiety disorders, however, do not appear to have a negative impact on OCD treatment (Storch et al., 2010).

Differential Diagnosis

Many symptoms of OCD may appear similar to those expressed in other disorders commonly diagnosed in childhood; therefore, differential diagnosis is critical. For example, stereotypies exhibited by individuals with a pervasive developmental disorder, such as repetitive vocalizations or rocking, may appear similar to OCD compulsions at a surface level but are self-soothing rather than distressing. Tics—repetitive body movements or vocalizations— also differ from repetitive behaviors seen in OCD because tics lack the goal-directedness of OCD-related rituals and are not tied to specific fears (Walitza et al., 2011). Notably, oppositional behaviors are typical of pediatric OCD and tend to fluctuate along with the OCD symptoms (Lebowitz, Vitulano, Mataix-Cols, & Leckman, 2011). Episodes of rage are also common in children with OCD (Storch et al., 2012). Thus, an understanding of the nature and functions of coercive, disruptive, and aggressive behaviors as they relate to OCD is important for accurately distinguishing between those behaviors that typify pediatric OCD from those that warrant a separate, comorbid diagnosis.

Impairment

Symptoms of OCD are likely to have a significant impact on children's academic and social functioning (Piacentini, Bergman, Keller, & McCracken, 2003). Children who perform more frequent, bizarre, or disruptive rituals may be at greater risk for teasing or peer rejection. In addition, children with greater insight may withdraw from social activities out of shame or embarrassment. Regarding academics, Piacentini and colleagues (2003) found concentrating on schoolwork and homework completion to be the most commonly reported impairments associated with children's OCD symptoms. Indeed, rituals that involve repeating, rechecking, rewriting, rereading, and seeking reassurance often come into play when engaging in schoolwork. Declines in grades are common when symptoms increase and may lead to treatment seeking by parents.

Pediatric OCD also causes significant family disruption. In fact, many families who present to treatment describe feeling as though OCD has taken over their household because the child's OCD may put demands or restrictions on the behavior of others. For example, the child may demand that others perform an action in a particular way (e.g., repeat a word or phrase, stand in a specific spot) or forbid them to perform an action (e.g., move, touch certain objects) to follow OCD's rules (Lebowitz, Vitulano, & Omer, 2011). Note that the function of these behaviors is to reduce anxiety or distress due to OCD-related urges as opposed to efforts to get one's way or elicit stimulation as in oppositional defiant disorder or ADHD. Targets of coercive behavior are typically mothers, but these behaviors are also directed toward fathers and siblings in approximately half of cases (Lebowitz, Vitulano, Mataix-Cols, et al., 2011). The means through which children attempt to control others' behavior to follow OCD's rules include threats of harm to self or others, physical or verbal aggression, and emotional blackmail (e.g., "You don't love me"). Such extreme behaviors are likely to lead to accommodation of the child's OCD symptoms by family members in an effort to avoid outbursts and aggression, which in turn may lead to increased functional impairment (Lebowitz, Vitulano, & Omer, 2011; Storch et al., 2012),

Family Accommodation

Family accommodation (FA) of pediatric OCD has been a topic of focus in recent research. FA characterizes the vast majority of families in which there is a child with OCD (Merlo, Lehmkuhl, Geffken, & Storch, 2009; Peris et al., 2008; Storch, Geffken, Merlo, Marni, et al., 2007). In fact, virtually all parents provide some mode of accommodation, with more than three fourths of parents engaging in daily accommodation (Flessner et al., 2011; Storch, Geffken, Merlo, Marni, et al., 2007). The most frequent types of accommodation reported were providing reassurance (63.5%), assisting in avoidance (33.3%), and participating in rituals (32.3%; Flessner et al., 2011). This accommodation not only reinforces the avoidance behaviors, thus contributing to the maintenance of OCD, but may also lead to the generalization of these coercive behaviors to situations unrelated to OCD due to the learning history of successfully escaping demands and responsibilities as a result of these behaviors. Families high in accommodation tend to have children with more severe symptoms (Merlo et al., 2009) and associated functional impairment (Storch et al., 2010; Storch, Geffken, Merlo, Marni, et al., 2007), and greater reductions in FA lead to improved treatment response (Merlo et al., 2009). Thus, family involvement in treatment and targeted interventions aimed at reducing FA are highly recommended.

Assessment

A diagnostic assessment of pediatric OCD should include information about the specific types of obsessions and compulsions or rituals, the duration of time spent obsessing or ritualizing per day, the level of distress associated with the obsessions and performance of rituals, and the resulting functional impairment. Information regarding school attendance, grades, social activities and relationships, and family dysfunction related to the OCD symptoms is important for determining symptom severity. When assessing OCD in children, one must take developmental level into account. Children develop through stages during which they may demand that things be done in a particular manner and have tantrums when these demands are not met. Children in these stages are likely to adhere rigidly to routines or collect random objects such as rocks or rubber bands and become upset if they are thrown away. Although these behaviors may be appropriate and even adaptive for younger children, they are developmentally inappropriate for older children. It is important to consider whether the behavior is normative for that child's age and intellectual level and whether it is causing significant distress and impairment (Geller & March, 2012).

Assessment of OCD symptoms in children should include multiple informants because parent–child agreement is often poor (Canavera, Wilkins, Pincus, & Ehrenreich-May, 2009), as is children's insight into their symptoms and the impact of their symptoms on their own or their families' lives (Storch et al., 2008). In addition, children are likely to attempt to hide their symptoms. As such, it is often helpful for the clinician to normalize "bad" or "strange" thoughts through examples from previous patients (without compromising confidentiality) or even from his or her own life. Parents also play an important role in the assessment by providing information that the child may be unable or embarrassed to report and by providing examples of their own intrusive thoughts. This may encourage children to open up about obsessive content, mental rituals, or physical rituals done in private. Examples regarding aggressive or sexual thoughts may be particularly helpful because many children believe that they are the only ones with such thoughts and may have been told that such thoughts are inappropriate.

Demonstrations of physical or verbal rituals by the patient or parents can help the therapist and parents identify ritual performance for baseline assessment, symptom monitoring, and treatment design. Identifying the specific fears tied to the rituals that lead to the perceived need to perform them can be vital for successful treatment, particularly in adolescents who are more cognitively advanced and thus more likely to have developed specific expectations and feared scenarios. If specific fears are present and are not adequately targeted through exposure exercises, habituation may not occur.

The gold standard measure for assessing OCD severity in children is the Children's Yale–Brown Obsessive Compulsive Scale (CY-BOCS; Scahill et al., 1997), a clinician-administered semistructured interview that provides information about the specific obsessions and compulsions experienced in the past and present, the categories to which these belong (e.g., contamination, checking, aggression, scrupulosity), the severity of the symptoms (i.e., how much time they take, how much distress they cause, attempts at and success with resisting urges to ritualize or diverting attention from intrusive thoughts), and the functional impairment due to the symptoms. The CY-BOCS can be used for diagnosis, development of an individualized treatment plan, and assessment of treatment progress. To supplement the CY-BOCS, the Anxiety Disorders Interview Schedule (Silverman & Albano, 1996) can provide a more complete overview of anxiety disorders and common comorbid conditions. Two psychometrically sound self-report measures that are commonly used to assess OCD symptom severity and functional impairment, respectively, include the Obsessive Compulsive Inventory—Child Version (Foa et al., 2010) and the Child OCD Impact Scale—Revised (Piacentini, Peris, Bergman, Chang, & Jaffer, 2007). The Family Accommodation Scale (Calvocoressi et al., 1999) is a clinician-rated questionnaire that assesses the extent to which family members accommodate the child's OCD symptoms. This measure provides specific information regarding the types of family accommodation that may be contributing to symptom maintenance and must be addressed during treatment.

TREATMENT

According to the current practice parameters of the American Academy of Child and Adolescent Psychiatry (American Academy of Child and Adolescent Psychiatry Committee on Quality Issues, 2012), CBT is the recommended first–line treatment for pediatric OCD when symptoms are mild or moderate in severity. Augmenting CBT with medication (i.e., serotonin reuptake inhibitors [SRIs]) is indicated in more severe cases of OCD, when individuals fail to respond to an adequate trial (i.e., several months) of CBT, or when comorbid psychopathology, family factors, or poor insight or motivation are barriers to behavioral treatment. Medication may also be required when CBT is not available; however, combined treatment is preferred over medication alone when CBT is available, even in the absence of a highly skilled CBT clinician. Food and Drug Administration–approved medications for pediatric OCD include clomipramine, fluoxetine, sertraline, and fluvoxamine. A more comprehensive discussion of pharmacologic treatments, associated efficacy, and side effects for children and adolescents with OCD is provided in Chapter 14.

CBT

The efficacy of CBT is supported by numerous studies, including six randomized controlled trials demonstrating the efficacy of CBT in individual, family, and family group-based formats (for a review, see Franklin, Freeman, & March, 2010). Effects from CBT appear durable (Barrett, Farrell, Dadds, & Boulter, 2005; Franklin et al., 1998). For example, Shalev et al. (2009) evidenced sustained treatment gains beyond 24 months, and O'Leary, Barrett, and Fjermestad (2009) found that 79% of patients in family-based CBT and 95% of patients in family-based group CBT had no diagnosis at 7-year follow-up. Treatment gains have been found to persist even after withdrawal of medication treatment (March, Mulle, & Herbel, 1994).

CBT for children with OCD mirrors the treatment for adults, with some age-based modifications and the addition of parental involvement. Treatment takes place across 12 to 20 sessions with key components, including (a) psychoeducation, (b) cognitive coping, (c) building a fear ladder, (d) exposure and response prevention (ERP), (e) parent involvement, and (f) relapse prevention. Emphasis is placed throughout treatment on the importance of between-session homework exercises.

Psychoeducation

Proper psychoeducation is imperative because parents and patients alike need to understand the treatment rationale to consent to a treatment that will produce distress in the short term. One approach to education involves presenting OCD as a neurobehavioral disorder that is not caused by poor parenting and is not a manifestation of a behavioral problem. For example, March and Mulle (1998) described obsessions as "brain hiccups" that occur due to faulty wiring and likened them to a problem with the volume control on the brain. Rituals can be described as behaviors that OCD tells the child that he or she must do to feel better. March and Mulle also suggested that OCD be externalized as an enemy to be fought off by the child, therapist, and parents, who are all allies. Preteens may enjoy giving OCD a nasty nickname, such as "Germy."

Another point of education that is important to convey to parents is that because the child does not initially have control of the OCD behaviors, he or she should not be punished for engaging in rituals. Despite how illogical or silly the thoughts or behaviors may seem, OCD "tells lies" to the child, and not listening to these lies, in the child's mind, could have devastating consequences (e.g., death of others, going to hell). Indeed, OCD has a powerful voice and can be quite convincing, even for adults with the disorder. However, with the necessary knowledge and tools and a good support system, children can gradually learn to gain control of their symptoms.

It can also be helpful to explain the persistence of OCD symptoms from a cognitive–behavioral perspective that emphasizes the role of beliefs, avoidance, and negative reinforcement (i.e., the anxiety cycle). Given the unusual nature of many OCD symptoms, it can help to initially present the anxiety cycle through a common concrete experience, such as a fear of dogs. Using an illustration, the therapist begins by explaining that some people are afraid of dogs because they believe that dogs are likely to bite people. When they see a dog and become fearful, they naturally run away or avoid the animal. This reaction is quite successful for reducing anxiety in the moment. However, because they still believe that dogs are likely to bite people, they remain scared of dogs and stuck in this cycle of fear and avoidance. The therapist emphasizes that (a) it is the thoughts (not the dog) that lead to anxiety, (b) avoiding dogs prevents people from learning through their own experience that dogs are relatively safe, and (c) because avoidance is so effective at reducing unpleasant anxiety, people rely on this strategy more and more frequently. The majority of families, even fairly young children, can readily understand the self-perpetuating nature of the anxiety cycle as it applies to a fear of dogs.

The therapist can then describe how the cycle is broken through exposure. Here it should be explained to the child and parents that exposure will be a gradual process, beginning with, for example, looking at pictures of dogs, then being near a small dog in a cage, then petting a small dog, then petting a larger dog. The importance of continuing to pet the dog until the child feels safe to prove that the child can feel better without running away should be underscored. It is often helpful to have the child explain the model in his or her own words to demonstrate understanding. At this point, the therapist can work with the family to map the child's OCD triggers, maladaptive beliefs, and rituals onto the cycle and explain the persistence and exacerbation of symptoms in terms of a natural learning process involving negative reinforcement. This model for understanding OCD is particularly valuable because it provides a clear rationale for treatment with ERP.

Cognitive Coping

Although the cornerstone of CBT is ERP, cognitive strategies can assist in preparing a child to engage in ERP and help him or her to learn from these experiences. Identifying and modifying cognitive distortions such as over-estimation of likelihood and risk are primary objectives of therapy. Asking the child how often he or she or others have been in the same situation and have *not* experienced the ultimate negative event, and asking how horrible the feared outcome would be compared with other possible negative events, can help facilitate more accurate, logical estimations. Undue emphasis on the power, or danger, of thoughts is another cognitive distortion common to OCD that may be manifested as thought–action fusion (the belief that having a thought is the same as carrying out the thought), the belief that one's thoughts are abnormal, or the belief that one should be able to control or stop one's thoughts. To address beliefs about the abnormality of intrusive thoughts, it can be helpful to review research demonstrating that the contents of the thoughts reported by individuals with OCD do not differ from those without OCD (Rachman & de Silva, 1978). Rather, those with OCD attend more and assign power to the thoughts, leading to anxiety. Powerlessness of thoughts to control actions or events can be demonstrated by repeating a thought while doing the opposite (e.g., repeat "I can't walk" while walking around the room).

It is important to remember that cognitive restructuring exercises frequently are not sufficient for lasting symptom improvement but rather help to set the stage for ERP. Children who are open to beginning exposure should not be delayed by unnecessary emphasis on cognitive coping. Not only is the amount of focus on cognitive coping dependent on the child's willingness to engage in exposure, it is also affected by the child's developmental and intellectual level. Although there is little research on the effectiveness of CBT for children with mental retardation or developmental disorders, there is preliminary evidence to suggest that modified treatment protocols with a greater emphasis on behavioral approaches (e.g., shaping, overcorrection, differential reinforcement) can be effective (Storch et al., 2010). It is also important to ensure that cognitive coping itself does not become a ritual or relied on during exposure to reduce anxiety: Some individuals may repeatedly remind themselves of their cognitive distortions as a way of reducing anxiety by providing reassurance rather than allowing habituation to occur.

Building a Fear Ladder

An understanding of the child's anxious beliefs and the situations that trigger them leads to the creation of the "fear ladder." The fear ladder is the list of activities that the child will complete to test whether his or her feared consequences are likely to occur and, for those that do, determine if they are manageable. Generation of items for fear ladders can begin with identifying stimuli (objects, situations, thoughts, people) that provoke anxiety, lead to rituals, or are avoided. These stimuli are then phrased to reflect a concrete activity that the child will complete to induce anxiety (while refraining from rituals). The therapist then arranges the items in descending order based on the child's ratings of the degree of anxiety associated with each activity. To be most successful, the creation of the fear ladder should be a collaboration among the therapist, child, and parent. Assessment tools such as the CY-BOCS, information provided during the clinical interview about OCD's "rules," and identified cognitive distortions should be used to guide this process. Because children often have a much more difficult time identifying fears than adults, the therapist will likely need to take an active role in creating effective exposure scenarios.

Careful consideration of the items placed on the ladder is of utmost importance because it serves as a targeted, individualized treatment plan. If the patient's specific fears are not adequately identified, the devised exposure exercises may not target the true fears and thus be ineffective. Active involvement in choosing exposure exercises increases compliance with treatment, and therefore it is critical that the child be offered the opportunity to have some control over the items on the hierarchy. A well-built fear ladder will include an activity that is easy enough to do tomorrow, an activity that represents the patient's greatest OCD fear and is more challenging than the situations typically encountered in everyday life, and enough items to move gradually from the former to the latter. The therapist may need to explain to the child that placing items on the hierarchy does not lock him or her into having to conduct an exposure to that item before he or she feels ready to do so and that typically the items on the top of the ladder are not nearly as scary by the time they are reached as they are at the present time. For younger children, mapping OCD symptoms into three categories (child wins, child and OCD both win some of the time, OCD wins), as described by March and Mulle (1998), may increase engagement in the therapeutic process.

ERP

As with treatment for OCD in adults, ERP is the core component of treatment for pediatric OCD. Once the child gains an adequate understanding of the role of rituals in the maintenance of OCD through psychoeducation, he or she should be encouraged to resist ritualizing as much as possible. However, the child should not be expected to be successful in doing so at this time. Throughout therapy, the child will systematically face feared situations (exposure) while simultaneously refraining from performing any rituals that serve to reduce the anxiety associated with that specific situation (response prevention). Because ERP exercises are experiments in which the child tests his or her OCD beliefs, they must be set up in a manner to support or disconfirm these beliefs. The process begins with the child selecting (typically with therapist assistance) an item that he or she is prepared to complete. The therapist then helps the child specify what OCD predicts will happen as a result of doing an activity that breaks OCD's rules without a neutralizing ritual. For example, a child may fear that he will get sick and that he will feel dirty if he does not wash after touching a doorknob. Including a prediction about persistent distress applies to most patients but is particularly important with children who may not have a clearly defined feared consequence or "just-right" symptoms.

After the exposure is set up, it is typically advisable to have the therapist complete the exposure with, or before, the child. The goal of an exposure is to clearly and completely test OCD's predictions. For example, a contamination exposure should include touching the item and rubbing it over one's body rather than touching it with a fingertip. At the beginning and every couple of minutes throughout the exercise, the therapist asks the child to rate his or her anxiety. Most children are able to use a 1-to-10 scale to rate their anxiety, but there is considerable variability in how they use these ratings. Some children remain at a 9 or 10 until suddenly dropping to a 0, and others predictably decrease by 1 point (or a tenth of a point) at a time. Although it is preferable for the child to use the ratings as accurately as possible, the process is unavoidably subjective, and it is more important for the child to learn that he or she can manage facing his or her fears rather than using precise ratings.

It is important to continue an exposure exercise until the child's anxiety decreases. The degree of decrease will depend on the child's use of the rating scale and the difficulty of the exposure. The exposure should continue until the child's anxiety has reduced by at least 50%, with the goal of being reduced to zero. At the very least, the exposure should continue until the child's anxiety begins to decrease so that he or she can see that anxiety is manageable and will eventually go down. The clinician should incorporate her or his judgment so that the child does not report a low number to escape the exposure. If an exposure cannot be carried out to completion, the focus should be on the fact that the child was able to manage his or her anxiety throughout the exposure, even if it has not yet come down as much as expected. It is also important to ensure that the child's anxiety does not decrease because a ritual was completed, which precludes the testing of OCD's prediction. Often it is possible to "recontaminate" if the child performs a ritual. For example, if the child removes contamination from his hands, he can touch the object again. A similar process can be applied to noncontamination rituals. For example, if a blinking ritual is performed while thinking about a "bad" thought, the child can return to the original thought that led to the ritual or a milder thought if that specific thought is too anxiety provoking for the child to handle at that time. Recontamination in effect reduces the reinforcing power of the ritual by being immediately followed by an increase in anxiety.

During the exposures, it is important for the therapist to provide frequent positive feedback and encouragement. Some exposures may take as long as 60 minutes, although many can be completed within 30 minutes or less. The goal of exposure is for anxiety to reduce due to habituation over time even though the child is focusing on the feared object or thoughts. As such, distractions should be avoided. Conversation between the therapist and child should focus on encouragement, monitoring anxiety, and cognitive restructuring when needed. It is certainly appropriate to engage in small talk or to use humor during exposures if doing so does not distract the child, and the therapist should make an effort to periodically refocus the child on the anxiety-provoking stimulus.

Following the exposure task, the therapist should promote cognitive change by helping the child reflect on his or her experience. Specifically, the child and therapist should determine if the feared outcome occurred. If it did, the child should be encouraged to decide if it was manageable. Specific focus should be placed on what happened to the child's anxiety level—if it did not decrease substantially, emphasis should be placed on the fact that the anxiety did not spiral out of control and the child was able to manage it. Because it is typically easier to acquire than to reduce a fear, each exposure exercise will need to be repeated, and the therapist should emphasize that it will likely be easier the next time. Throughout most of treatment, each exposure should be conducted first in the therapy session for instructional purposes and then repeated between sessions as homework. With repetition, the child will realize that his or her fears rarely come true, are manageable when they do, and that anxiety comes down on its own over time. Once a child is able to refrain from ritualizing during planned exposure to a specific stimulus, he or she should practice response prevention when faced with that stimulus naturally. For some, urges to ritualize seem to occur at random, and intentionally evoking the urge to ritualize can be difficult. In such situations, designating periods of time during which the child refrains from rituals may be necessary.

Several factors make exposures with children challenging. To begin with, some children, especially younger ones, may be reluctant to participate in exposures if they have limited insight into the severity of their symptoms or difficulty understanding the trade-off between immediate discomfort and future improvement. In such cases, a carefully designed fear ladder that begins with small manageable steps can be augmented with parental praise and a reward system contingent on their efforts rather than success. For example, to engage a 6-year-old girl who was reluctant to participate in exposures, a reinforcement plan was designed such that she earned one marble for completing her daily exposure and two bonus marbles for each additional exposure that day. She could then cash in her marbles for small daily rewards or save them for larger rewards. The child was involved in delineating a number of rewards of different value that she was motivated to work toward, and her parents assisted in adding additional rewards, such as five marbles equals 20 minutes of playing dolls with mother. As a result of the plan, the child was excited about doing exposures to earn rewards, and the potential for reward gave her extra incentive to challenge herself beyond the expected once-daily exposure. For more severe oppositional behavior that interferes with ERP, more advanced behavioral management may be necessary before or in conjunction with ERP.

Another challenge involves parents' and therapists' reservations about tolerating children's distress. These concerns can lead to underuse of exposure or avoidance of the most challenging exposures, increasing the risk that children will remain symptomatic or relapse in the future. It is important to remember that the success of numerous clinical trials that included ERP attests to the ability of children to tolerate and benefit from challenging exposures. Abramowitz, Deacon, and Whiteside (2010) provided detailed guidance for implementing exposure treatment, including strategies for working with children.

Parental Involvement

Treatment of OCD requires difficult work by the child and, often, the parents as well. In general, the younger the child, the more parental involvement is needed. For children with multiple caregivers, it is best for all parties to receive psychoeducation and training on exposure for consistency. For all children and adolescents, but particularly for younger children, it can be helpful to include the parents in all treatment sessions to train them to become "exposure coaches." Parents initially observe the therapist leading the child through an exposure, then work with the therapist, and eventually lead exposure under the therapist's supervision. Such experiential learning helps prepare the parent to lead successful exposures at home. For adolescents who prefer more independence and are able to complete exposures on their own, parent involvement can be limited to psychoeducation and providing regular updates on their child's symptoms, provided treatment is progressing. Increased parental involvement may be indicated if the adolescent is having difficulty completing homework or if symptoms are not improving.

Training in exposure coaching encompasses a number of principles that may need to be addressed directly to facilitate generalization. To a large extent, the role of the parents is one of a cheerleader or coach who provides support, encouragement, and positive reinforcement for the child's efforts to fight OCD. Some parents may need additional assistance to refrain from expressing frustration or criticism. More frequently, parents may need additional support regarding their own distress about witnessing their child's anxiety. It is a natural reaction for parents to want to rescue their child from painful experiences; however, it is important for children to remain in the exposure situation until their anxiety reduces independently. Although learning to coach exposure involves praising efforts to defy OCD and not responding to anxious behaviors, some parents may benefit from an emphasis on how to apply these principles of differential attention outside of planned exposures. It can also be instructive to help parents identify how they are participating in rituals or facilitating avoidance (i.e., accommodating OCD). Reducing family accommodation can be included in the response prevention plan. Because it would be distressing for family members to suddenly stop providing reassurance, it is preferable to gradually decrease participation in rituals in a prearranged fashion.

Relapse Prevention

Once the child has mastered the majority of the items on the fear ladder, therapy sessions can be spread out from weekly to every 2 or 3 weeks while planning for termination. The termination session should review what the child and parents have learned, what has been most helpful in overcoming OCD, and the plan for maintenance of gains. It is important to explain to the family that OCD symptoms may never completely go away and that the goal is to be able to manage the symptoms that are present without functional impairment. Even if the child is symptom free at the time of termination, the family should be prepared for the likelihood that symptoms may recur in the future. Following the termination session, it is recommended that a booster session be scheduled to reassess symptom management. Families should be encouraged to view symptom exacerbation as expected rather than as a failure. When such lapses occur, the family should set up exposure exercises to target the fear that led to the ritual until symptoms remit.

Intensive Treatment Options

Although CBT is the recommended treatment of choice for pediatric OCD, it is difficult to access outside of academic medical centers (Franklin et al., 2010; Lewin, Storch, Adkins, Murphy, & Geffken, 2005). One potential option for families who do not have access to weekly exposure-based therapy in their area or who are not benefitting from this level of treatment is to attend an intensive outpatient treatment program (Lewin, Storch, Merlo, et al., 2005). These programs typically vary in length from about 1 to 3 weeks and appear to be equally effective as weekly therapy (Storch, Geffken, Merlo, Mann, et al., 2007). For children who do not respond to outpatient or intensive treatment or appropriate medication management, participation in an inpatient or residential program may be indicated. Another option that is likely to become increasingly available as technological advances in psychological treatment continue is Internet-based therapy (Storch et al., 2011).

CONCLUSION

Tremendous advances in the identification and treatment of pediatric OCD have been made over the past few decades. OCD is no longer the hidden epidemic it once was, and successful treatments are available. Overall, treatment of children with OCD is similar to that of adults with a clear focus on ERP. Special attention should be paid to the family environment, such as the challenges of accommodation and the opportunities to train parents as exposure coaches. Despite the availability of effective treatments, not all children benefit from treatment, and the limited access to therapists in the community who are well trained in and use ERP presents a barrier to receiving appropriate treatment. The dissemination of research findings and treatment manuals, the proper training of practitioners in ERP, and the harnessing of technological advances in psychological treatments are of utmost importance for increasing availability of treatment to children with OCD. To improve response rates, future research should continue to identify and address factors that influence treatment outcome. Increased efforts toward prevention and early identification are also warranted. Finally, the relative importance of CBT with ERP, medications, and combination therapy needs to be better understood, as does the best approach for treating PANS.

REFERENCES

Abramowitz, J. S., Deacon, B. J., & Whiteside, S. P. H. (2010). *Exposure therapy for anxiety: Principles and practice*. New York, NY: Guilford Press.

American Academy of Child and Adolescent Psychiatry Committee on Quality Issues. (2012). Practice parameter for the assessment and treatment of children and adolescents with obsessive–compulsive disorder. *Journal of the American Academy of Child & Adolescent Psychiatry, 51*, 98–113. doi:10.1016/j.jaac.2011.09.019

Barrett, P., Farrell, L., Dadds, M., & Boulter, N. (2005). Cognitive-behavioral family treatment of childhood obsessive–compulsive disorder: Long-term follow-up and predictors of outcome. *Journal of the American Academy of Child & Adolescent Psychiatry, 44*, 1005–1014. doi:10.1097/01.chi.0000172555.26349.94

Calvocoressi, L., Mazure, C. M., Kasl, S. V., Skolnick, J., Fisk, D., Vegso, S. J., . . . Price, L. H. (1999). Family accommodation of obsessive–compulsive symptoms: Instrument development and assessment of family behavior. *Journal of Nervous and Mental Disease, 187*, 636–642. doi:10.1097/00005053-199910000-00008

Canavera, K. E., Wilkins, K. C., Pincus, D. B., & Ehrenreich–May, J. T. (2009). Parent-child agreement in the assessment of obsessive–compulsive disorder. *Journal of Clinical Child and Adolescent Psychology, 38*, 909–915. doi:10.1080/15374410903258975

Delorme, R., Golmard, J. L., Chabane, N., Millet, B., Krebs, M. O., Mouren-Simeoni, M. C., & Leboyer, M. (2005). Admixture analysis of age of onset in obsessive–compulsive disorder. *Psychological Medicine, 35*, 237–243. doi:10.1017/S0033291704003253

Flament, M. F., Whitaker, A., Rapoport, J. L., Davies, M., Berg, C. Z., Kalikow, K., . . . Shaffer, D. (1988). Obsessive compulsive disorder in adolescence: An epidemiological study. *Journal of the American Academy of Child & Adolescent Psychiatry, 27*, 764–771. doi:10.1097/00004583-198811000-00018

Flessner, C. A., Freeman, J. B., Sapyta, J., Garcia, A., Franklin, M. E., March, J. S., & Foa, E. (2011). Predictors of parental accommodation in pediatric obsessive–compulsive disorder: Findings from the Pediatric Obsessive–Compulsive Disorder Treatment Study (POTS) trial. *Journal of the American Academy of Child & Adolescent Psychiatry, 50*, 716–725. doi:10.1016/j.jaac.2011.03.019

Foa, E. B., Coles, M., Hupper, J. D., Pasupuleti, R. V., Franklin, M. E., & March, J. (2010). Development and validation of a child version of the Obsessive Compulsive Inventory. *Behavior Therapy, 41*, 121–132. doi:10.1016/j.beth.2009.02.001

Franklin, M. E., Freeman, J., & March, J. S. (2010). Treating pediatric obsessive–compulsive disorder using exposure-based cognitive-behavioral therapy. In J. R. Weisz & A. E. Kazdin (Eds.), *Evidence-based psychotherapies for children and adolescents* (pp. 80–92). New York, NY: Guilford Press.

Franklin, M. E., Kozak, M. J., Cashman, L., Coles, M. E., Rheingold, A. A., & Foa, E. B. (1998). Cognitive-behavioral treatment of pediatric obsessive–compulsive disorder: An open clinical trial. *Journal of the American Academy of Child & Adolescent Psychiatry, 37*, 412–419. doi:10.1097/00004583-199804000-00019

Franklin, M. E., Sapyta, J., Freeman, J. B., Muniya, K., Compton, S., Almirall, D., ... March, J. S. (2011). Cognitive behavior therapy augmentation of pharmacotherapy in pediatric obsessive–compulsive disorder: The Pediatric OCD Treatment Study II (POTS II) randomized controlled trial. *JAMA, 306*, 1224–1232. doi:10.1001/jama.2011.1344

Geller, D., Biederman, J., Jones, J., Park, K., Schwartz, S., Shapiro, S., & Coffey, B. (1998). Is juvenile obsessive–compulsive disorder a developmental subtype of the disorder? A review of the pediatric literature. *Journal of the American Academy of Child & Adolescent Psychiatry, 37*, 420–427. doi:10.1097/00004583-199804000-00020

Geller, D. A., Biederman, J., Faraone, S., Agranat, A., Cradock, K., Hagermoser, L, ... Coffey, B. J. (2001). Developmental aspects of obsessive–compulsive disorder: Findings in children, adolescents, and adults. *Journal of Nervous and Mental Disease, 189*, 471–477. doi:10.1097/00005053-200107000-00009

Geller, D. A., Biederman, J., Jones, J., Shapiro, S., Schwartz, S., & Park, K. S. (1998). Obsessive–compulsive disorder in children and adolescents: A review. *Harvard Review of Psychiatry, 5*, 260–273. doi:10.3109/10673229809000309

Geller, D. A., Biederman, J., Stewart, S. E., Mullin, B., Farrell, C., ... Carpenter, D. (2003). Impact of comorbidity on treatment response to paroxetine in pediatric obsessive–compulsive disorder: Is the use of exclusion criteria empirically supported in randomized clinical trials? *Journal of Child and Adolescent Psychopharmacology, 13*(Suppl. 1), S19–29. doi:10.1089/104454603322126313

Larson, M. J., Storch, E. A., & Murphy, T. K. (2007). Is it PANDAS? How to confirm the sore throat/OCD connection. *Current Psychiatry, 4*, 33–34, 39–48.

Lebowitz, E. R., Vitulano, L. A., Mataix-Cols, D., & Leckman, J. F. (2011). When OCD takes over . . . the family! Coercive and disruptive behaviours in paediatric obsessive–compulsive disorder. *Journal of Child Psychology and Psychiatry, 52,* 1249–1250. doi:10.1111/j.1469-7610.2011.02480.x

Lebowitz, E. R., Vitulano, L. A., & Omer, H. (2011). Coercive and disruptive behaviors in pediatric obsessive–compulsive disorder: A qualitative analysis. *Psychiatry, 74,* 362–371.

Lewin, A. B., Storch, E. A., Adkins, J., Murphy, T. K., & Geffken, G. R. (2005). Current direction in pediatric obsessive–compulsive disorder. *Pediatric Annals, 34,* 128–134.

Lewin, A. B., Storch, E. A., Merlo, L. J., Adkins, J. W., Murphy, T., & Geffken, G. A. (2005). Intensive cognitive behavioral therapy for pediatric obsessive–compulsive disorder: A treatment protocol for mental health providers. *Psychological Services, 2,* 91–104. doi:10.1037/1541-1559.2.2.91

March, J. S., & Mulle, K. (1998). *OCD in children and adolescents: A cognitive-behavioral treatment manual.* New York, NY: Guilford Press.

March, J. S., Mulle, K., & Herbel, B. (1994). Behavioral psychotherapy for children and adolescents with obsessive–compulsive disorder: An open trial of a new protocol–driven treatment package. *Journal of the American Academy of Child & Adolescent Psychiatry, 33,* 333–341. doi:10.1097/00004583-199403000-00006

Merlo, L. J., Lehmkuhl, H., Geffken, G. R., & Storch, E. A. (2009). Decreased family accommodation associated with improved therapy outcome in pediatric obsessive–compulsive disorder. *Journal of Consulting and Clinical Psychology, 77,* 355–360. doi:10.1037/a0012652

Micali, N., Heyman, I., Perez, M., Hilton, K., Nakatani, E., Turner, C., & Mataix-Cols, D. (2010). Long-term outcomes of obsessive–compulsive disorder: Follow–up of 142 children and adolescents. *British Journal of Psychiatry, 197,* 128–134.

Moore, P. S., Mariaskin, A., March, J., & Franklin, M. E. (2007). Obsessive–compulsive disorder in children and adolescents: Diagnosis, comorbidity, and developmental factors. In E. A. Storch, G. R. Geffken, & T. K. Murphy (Eds.), *Handbook of adolescent obsessive–compulsive disorder* (pp. 17–45). Mahwah, NJ: Erlbaum.

Murphy, T. K., Storch, E. A., & Strawser, M. S. (2006). Selective serotonin reuptake inhibitor-induced behavioral activation in the PANDAS subtype. *Primary Psychiatry, 13,* 87–89.

O'Leary, E. M., Barrett, P., & Fjermestad, K. W. (2009). Cognitive-behavioral family treatment for childhood obsessive–compulsive disorder: A 7-year follow-up study. *Journal of Anxiety Disorders, 23,* 973–978. doi:10.1016/j.janxdis.2009.06.009

Pediatric OCD Treatment Study Team. (2004). Cognitive-behavior therapy, sertraline, and their combination for children and adolescents with obsessive–compulsive disorder: The pediatric OCD treatment study randomized controlled trial. *JAMA, 292,* 1969–1976. doi:10.1001/jama.292.16.1969

Perlmutter, S. J., Leitman, S. F., Garvey, M. A., Hamburger, S., Feldman, E., & Swedo, S. E. (1999). Therapeutic plasma exchange and intravenous immuno-globulin for obsessive–compulsive disorder and tic disorders in childhood. *The Lancet, 354,* 1153–1158. doi:10.1016/S0140-6736(98)12297-3

Peris, T. S., Bergman, L., Langley, A., Chang, S., McCracken, J. T., & Piacentini, J. (2008). Correlates of accommodation of pediatric obsessive–compulsive disorder: Parent, child, and family characteristics. *Journal of the American Academy of Child & Adolescent Psychiatry, 47,* 1173–1181. doi:10.1097/CHI.0b013e3181825a91

Piacentini, J., Bergman, R. L., Keller, M., & McCracken, J. (2003). Functional impairment in children and adolescents with obsessive–compulsive disorder. *Journal of Child and Adolescent Psychopharmacology, 13*(Suppl. 1), S61–S69. doi:10.1089/104454603322126359

Piacentini, J., Peris, T. S., Bergman, R. L., Chang, S., & Jaffer, M. (2007). Functional impairment in childhood OCD: Development and psychometrics properties of the Child Obsessive–Compulsive Impact Scale—Revised. *Journal of Clinical Child and Adolescent Psychology, 36,* 645–653. doi:10.1080/15374410701662790

Rachman, S., & de Silva, P. (1978). Abnormal and normal obsessions. *Behaviour Research and Therapy, 16,* 233–248. doi:10.1016/0005-7967(78)90022-0

Rapoport, J. L., Inoff-Germain, G., Weissman, M. M., Greenwald, S., Narrow, W. E., Jensen, P. S., . . . Canino, G. (2000). Childhood obsessive–compulsive disorder in the NIMH MECA Study: Parent versus child identification of cases. *Journal of Anxiety Disorders, 14,* 535–548. doi:10.1016/S0887-6185(00)00048-7

Rasmussen, S. A., & Eisen, J. L. (1990). Epidemiology of obsessive compulsive disorder. *The Journal of Clinical Psychiatry, 51,* 10–14.

Rettew, D. C., Swedo, S. E., Leondard, H. L., Lenane, M. C., & Rapoport, J. L. (1992). Obsessions and compulsions across time in 79 children and adolescents with obsessive–compulsive disorder. *Journal of the American Academy of Child & Adolescent Psychiatry, 31,* 1050–1056. doi:10.1097/00004583-199211000-00009

Scahill, L., Riddle, M. A., McSwiggin-Hardin, M., Ort, S. I., King, R. A., Goodman, W., . . . Leckman, J. F. (1997). Children's Yale–Brown Obsessive Compulsive Scale: Reliability and validity. *Journal of the American Academy of Child & Adolescent Psychiatry, 36,* 844–852. doi:10.1097/00004583-199706000-00023

Shalev, I., Sulkowski, M. L., Geffken, G. R., Rickets, E. J., Murphy, T. K., & Storch, E. A. (2009). Long-term durability of cognitive behavioral therapy gains for pediatric obsessive–compulsive disorder. *Journal of the American Academy of Child & Adolescent Psychiatry, 48,* 766–767.

Silverman, W. K., & Albano, A. M. (1996). *Anxiety Disorders Interview Schedule for DSM–IV Child and Parent Versions.* San Antonio, TX: Psychological Corporation.

Snider, L. A., & Swedo, S. E. (2003). Childhood-onset obsessive–compulsive disorder and tic disorders: Case report and literature review. *Journal of Child and Adolescent Psychopharmacology, 13*(Suppl. 1), S81–S88. doi:10.1089/104454603322126377

Stewart, S. E., Geller, D. A., Jenike, M., Pauls, D., Shaw, D., Mullin, B., & Faraone, S. V. (2004). Long-term outcome of pediatric obsessive–compulsive disorder: A meta-analysis and qualitative review of the literature. *Acta Psychiatrica Scandinavica, 110,* 4–13. doi:10.1111/j.1600-0447.2004.00302.x

Storch, E. A., Bjorgvinsson, T., Riemann, B., Lewin, A. B., Morales, M. J., & Murphy, T. K. (2010). Factors associated with poor response in cognitive-behavioral therapy for pediatric obsessive–compulsive disorder. *Bulletin of the Menninger Clinic, 74,* 167–185. doi:10.1521/bumc.2010.74.2.167

Storch, E. A., Caporino, N. E., Morgan, J. R., Lewin, A. B., Rojas, A., Brauer, L., . . . Murphy, T. K. (2011). Preliminary investigation of web-camera delivered cognitive-behavioral therapy for youth with obsessive–compulsive disorder. *Psychiatry Research, 189,* 407–412. doi:10.1016/j.psychres.2011.05.047

Storch, E. A., Geffken, G. R., Merlo, L. J., Mann, G., Duke, D., Munson, M., . . . Goodman, W. K. (2007). Family-based cognitive-behavioral therapy for pediatric obsessive–compulsive disorder: Comparison of intensive and weekly approaches. *Journal of the American Academy of Child & Adolescent Psychiatry, 46,* 469–478. doi:10.1097/chi.0b013e31803062e7

Storch, E. A., Geffken, G. R., Merlo, L. J., Marni, L. J., Murphy, T. K., Goodman, W. K., . . . Graybill, K. (2007). Family accommodation in pediatric obsessive–compulsive disorder. *Journal of Clinical Child and Adolescent Psychology, 36,* 207–216. doi:10.1080/15374410701277929

Storch, E. A., Jones, A. M., Lack, C. W., Ale, C. M., Sulkowski, M. L., . . . Murphy, T. K. (2012). Rage attacks in pediatric obsessive–compulsive disorder: Phenomenology and clinical correlates. *Journal of the American Academy of Child & Adolescent Psychiatry, 51,* 582–592. doi:10.1016/j.jaac.2012.02.016

Storch, E. A., Milsom, V. A., Merlo, L. J., Larson, M., Geffken, G. R., Jacob, M. L., . . . Goodman, W. K. (2008). Insight in pediatric obsessive–compulsive disorder: Associations with clinical presentation. *Psychiatry Research, 160,* 212–220. doi:10.1016/j.psychres.2007.07.005

Storch, E. A., Murphy, T. K., Geffken, G. R., Mann, G., Adkins, J., Merlo, L. J., . . . Goodman, W. K. (2006). Cognitive-behavioral therapy for PANDAS-related obsessive–compulsive disorder: Findings from a preliminary waitlist controlled open trial. *Journal of the American Academy of Child & Adolescent Psychiatry, 45,* 1171–1178. doi:10.1097/01.chi.0000231973.43966.a0

Swedo, S. E., Leckman, J. F., & Rose, N. R. (2012). From research subgroup to clinical syndrome: Modifying the PANDAS criteria to describe PANS (pediatric acute-onset neuropsychiatric syndrome). *Pediatrics & Therapeutics, 2,* 1–8.

Swedo, S. E., Leonard, H. L., Garvey, M., Mittleman, B., Allen, A. J., Perlmutter, S., . . . Dubbert, B. K. (1998). Pediatric autoimmune neuropsychiatric disorders associated with streptococcal infections: Clinical description of the first 50 cases. *The American Journal of Psychiatry, 155,* 264–271.

Swedo, S. E., Rapoport, J. L., Leonard, H., Lenane, M., & Cheslow, D. (1989). Obsessive–compulsive disorder in children and adolescents: Clinical phenomenology of 70 consecutive cases. *Archives of General Psychiatry, 46,* 335–341.

Taylor, S. (2011). Early versus late onset obsessive–compulsive disorder: Evidence for distinct subtypes. *Clinical Psychology Review, 31,* 1083–1100. doi:10.1016/j.cpr.2011.06.007

Thomsen, P. H. (1991). Obsessive–compulsive symptoms in children and adolescents: A phenomenological analysis of 61 Danish cases. *Psychopathology, 24,* 12–18.

Walitza, S., Melfse, S., Jana, T., Zellmann, H., Wewetzer, C., & Warnke, A. (2011). Obsessive–compulsive disorder in children and adolescents. *Deutsches Ärzteblatt International, 108,* 173–179.

Zohar, A. H. (1999). The epidemiology of obsessive–compulsive disorder in children and adolescents. *Child and Adolescent Psychiatric Clinics of North America, 8,* 445–460.

3

OBSESSIVE–COMPULSIVE DISORDER IN YOUNG CHILDREN

MICHAEL R. WALTHER, KRISHNAPRIYA JOSYULA,
JENNIFER B. FREEMAN, AND ABBE M. GARCIA

This chapter focuses on young children (ages 5–8 years) with obsessive–compulsive disorder (OCD). First, we describe the clinical characteristics of young children with OCD. Next, we review the assessment of young children with OCD, including ways in which assessment can be modified for this young population. Finally, we discuss the treatment of young children with OCD, including an overview of a family-based cognitive–behavioral approach.

CLINICAL CHARACTERISTICS

Clinical Description

OCD is a neurobiological disorder with a lifetime prevalence of 1% to 2% in children and adolescents (Zohar, 1999). Point prevalence estimates of

http://dx.doi.org/10.1037/14323-004
Obsessive–Compulsive Disorder and Its Spectrum: A Life-Span Approach, Eric A. Storch and Dean McKay (Editors)
Copyright © 2014 by the American Psychological Association. All rights reserved.

OCD are between 0.5% and 1% of the pediatric population (Flament et al., 1988). These figures may underestimate the true prevalence of the condition in children younger than 8 years because children of this age may lack the ability to articulate their symptoms and distress to others. OCD has been diagnosed in children as young as 3 years (Nakatani et al., 2011). Data related to gender distribution in those with early-onset OCD are mixed; some data suggest that early-onset OCD is more common in males (3:2; Geller et al., 1998), whereas other data (Garcia et al., 2009) suggest that the gender ratio is closer to 1:1 (as it is in adolescence).

OCD in young children impairs academic, social, and family functioning and may also disrupt normal developmental milestones (Palermo et al., 2011; Piacentini, Bergman, Keller, & McCracken, 2003). Given that young children are just beginning formal schooling and forming peer relationships, OCD symptoms can seriously hinder the formation of a strong academic foundation as well as peer functioning. OCD is also related to increased morbidity over time. A meta-analysis showed that an earlier age of OCD onset predicts persistence of OCD symptoms (Stewart et al., 2004). The concept of "kindling" (Post et al., 1996), which suggests that the presence of a psychiatric disorder can cause neuronal changes that result in heightened sensitivity to stress, is another reason treatment for early-childhood-onset OCD should start early.

As many as 80% of children with OCD have an additional Axis 1 disorder, and 50% of children have multiple comorbid conditions (Piacentini & Graae, 1997). In young children with OCD, comorbid diagnoses such as attention-deficit/hyperactivity disorder (ADHD), other anxiety disorders, tic disorders, and learning disabilities are common (Garcia et al., 2009). Freeman et al. (2008) conducted a study involving 38 children ages 5 to 8 years with OCD and reported that 21.0% of them had a tic disorder ($n = 8$), 18.4% ($n = 7$) had ADHD, 57.9% ($n = 22$) had a comorbid internalizing disorder, and 34.2% ($n = 13$) had a comorbid externalizing disorder. Garcia et al. (2009), with a sample of 58 children with OCD ages 4 to 8 years, reported the following comorbidity rates: 20.7% ($n = 12$) with tic disorder, 22.4% ($n = 13$) with ADHD, and 20.7% ($n = 12$) with generalized anxiety disorder. Family studies have shown increased rates of comorbidity between OCD and tic disorders (Pauls & Leckman, 1986), and this finding was especially strong for children with OCD onset before age 9 (Pauls, Alsobrook, Goodman, Rasmussen, & Leckman, 1995).

Symptom Expression

Young children with OCD have a modestly different pattern of symptom expression than older children and adults with OCD (Nakatani et al., 2011). In young children, compulsions without obsessions are common, as are sensory-related compulsions, such as tapping or touching until it feels "just right" (Nakatani et al., 2011). Compulsions in young children often involve another family member (e.g., reassurance seeking, verbal checking; Flessner et al., 2011). These differences in symptom expression between young children and adolescents/adults may be largely due to developmental factors. Limitations in cognitive ability may be one reason obsessions are endorsed less frequently in young children. Young children may not be able to differentiate their obsessions from more normative thoughts or identify the connection between their obsessions and subsequent compulsions and express that connection to others. Young children also have greater dependence on their family for guidance and direction, which may be why many of their rituals involve other family members.

ETIOLOGY

Pediatric OCD imaging studies have shown similar results as adult imaging studies, with the frontal cortico-striatal-thalamic circuit displaying structural abnormalities in cingulated cortex, basal ganglia, and thalami (Rosenberg & Keshavan, 1998). In early-childhood-onset OCD only, the severity of OCD symptoms correlated positively with cerebral blood flow in the left orbitofrontal region (Busatto et al., 2001), indicating that brain mechanisms may differ depending on age of OCD onset.

Beginning in the late 1990s, researchers have found that in some young children, OCD symptoms develop or are worsened by group A beta-hemolytic streptococcal infection (GABHS). This OCD subtype is called *pediatric autoimmune neuropsychiatric disorders associated with streptococcal infection* (PANDAS; Swedo et al., 1998) and is associated with an abrupt onset or worsening of OCD or tic symptoms. The OCD symptoms in PANDAS are thought to be a result of swelling from an autoimmune reaction between caudate tissue and antineuronal antibodies formed against GABHS. More recently, a shift toward a less specific etiology has been proposed by acknowledging the possibility that OCD symptoms may abruptly develop despite the absence of streptococcal infection. This newly proposed subgroup has been termed *pediatric acute-onset neuropsychiatric syndrome* (PANS; Swedo, Leckman, & Rose, 2012).

Twin and family studies have shown that OCD has a genetic basis (Nestadt et al., 2000; Pauls et al., 1995). The concordance rate for "obsessive symptoms or features" has been shown to be higher in monozygotic twins (87%) than dizygotic twins (47%; Carey & Gottesman, 1981). Family studies have demonstrated a greater genetic loading in childhood onset OCD, such that first-degree relatives of pediatric OCD probands have a greater risk of OCD (24%–26%) than first-degree relatives of probands without OCD

(12%; Nestadt et al., 2000). Although the genetic underpinnings of OCD remain poorly understood, emerging data have highlighted the role of the glutamate transporter and receptor genes (MacMaster & Rosenberg, 2009).

ASSESSMENT

When a family presents for treatment, it is important to conduct a thorough assessment of the child's overall clinical picture. Ideally, this assessment captures (a) information about the child's OCD symptoms, (b) information about potential comorbid symptoms, and (c) general information about the family. This section focuses mostly on the first two points.

It is often useful to incorporate a semistructured interview, such as the Anxiety Disorders Interview Schedule (ADIS; Silverman & Albano, 1996). This type of interview may be helpful for several reasons. First, the ADIS can be a useful tool in differential diagnosis. Second, even if making a diagnosis of OCD is relatively straightforward, conducting a semistructured interview before treatment can yield important information about comorbidities that may in turn inform decisions made about treatment planning.

An initial interview with the family may be conducted with or without the child present. However, it is generally advisable to have the child present because the initial visit gives the child a chance to get acquainted with the setting. In addition, even children in this young age range may have important information about their symptoms that parents are not able to provide.

As discussed later in this chapter, the treatment of OCD is individually tailored. Therefore, it is important that an assessment include OCD-specific measures. The gold standard interview for assessing OCD severity in children is the Children's Yale–Brown Obsessive Compulsive Inventory (CY-BOCS; Scahill et al., 1997). The CY-BOCS is a clinician-administered interview, and its psychometric properties for use with 5- to 8-year-olds are strong (Freeman, Flessner, & Garcia, 2011). It contains a general checklist of common present and past obsessions and compulsions as well as Likert-rated items (rated from 0 to 4) on two subscales (Obsessions and Compulsions) that are summed for subscale and total scores. What follows is a general guide for administering the CY-BOCS in young children.

1. Administer the CY-BOCS in "Reverse" Order by Starting With Compulsions and Finishing With Obsessions

The CY-BOCS is structured such that the clinician begins by completing the obsessions checklist, which can be problematic when working with young children. In the case of a young child, the clinician will likely have to rely on parent report more than when working with an older child. As such, parents tend to have more information about what they can observe (i.e., compulsions) than what they cannot (i.e., obsessions). Moreover, as discussed previously, it is not uncommon for OCD in younger children to have "not just right" symptoms. In these cases, obsessions are often inferred from compulsions. For example, for a child who ritualizes by touching or tapping a certain number of times, an obsession with "numbers" may be inferred. By starting the interview with compulsions, it also frames information in such a way that the clinician can probe for obsessional content (e.g., "Earlier you told me that you wash your hands a certain number of times. What do you think about right before you do that?"). One helpful question along these lines can be, "What happens if you are unable to perform the compulsion?" Information about feared consequences directly informs obsessional content and also gives important information about treatment planning, such as exposure targets.

2. Ask Questions in a Developmentally Informed Manner

Even though the CY-BOCS differs in language from its adult counterpart (the Y-BOCS), it is important that the clinician choose language that the child can understand. Words such as *secretions*, *bodily waste*, *contaminants*, *obscenities*, and *impulses* may be too complex. In addition, clinicians may feel uneasy about probing for OCD content that is sexual in nature despite the fact that such symptoms are often present in young children. A calm and up-front manner in discussing such potential symptoms is both professional and thorough.

3. After Completing Both Checklists, Attempt to Derive Functional Relationships Between Related Obsessions and Compulsions

OCD is not a disorder of separate and unrelated symptoms. Rather, obsessions and compulsions are functionally related; obsessions give rise to anxiety or discomfort, and compulsions are aimed at reducing such distress. Thus, even though the CY-BOCS has the clinician collect information separately about obsessions and compulsions, it is critical that the clinician synthesize information in a way that allows them to understand the child's OCD.

It may be useful to jot notes next to a particular obsession or compulsion about what the symptom relates to (e.g., hand-washing compulsions are related to obsessions about a certain number and not contamination). At times it may even be helpful to use a whiteboard or large piece of paper and organize the child's symptoms, with obsessions in one column and compulsions in another. Then the clinician can "match" each obsession to a particular ritual and vice versa. This is particularly helpful in obtaining a broad overall perspective of the patient's major OCD themes.

4. Complete the CY-BOCS Severity Items

This portion of the CY-BOCS involves making ratings from 0 (*none*) to 4 (*extreme*) across 10 items, five of which relate to obsessions and five of which relate to compulsions. Although a detailed procedural outline is beyond the scope of this chapter, the following information may be helpful in completing these items with young children:

a. Time occupied by the obsession or compulsion: Ask how long each obsession or compulsion typically lasts and try to get a sense of what the average day has recently looked like (e.g., how many times the child washes his or her hands in an average day).

b. Interference: Ask the child and family what they enjoy doing. Ask them if they feel like OCD interferes with those types of activities.

c. Distress: Attempt to find a balance between how frequently the symptom occurs versus how much the child and family are bothered by it. Being "bothered" can mean many things to a child. Ask the child and parents about reactions such as crying, getting frustrated, feeling physical symptoms of anxiety (e.g., racing heart, sweating).

COMORBID SYMPTOMS AND OTHER CONSIDERATIONS

A semistructured interview and CY-BOCS administration will give the clinician a thorough account of the child's psychological picture. At this point, a decision as to whether and how to proceed with treatment may need to be made. In the case of comorbidity, it should not be assumed that OCD treatment will begin first. Following are some general guidelines.

Decide whether a comorbid condition (or other concern, such as family stress) will interfere with treatment. If another psychiatric condition is more interfering, it may be sensible to address that problem before treating OCD. Similarly, other psychiatric conditions, even if not more severe, may make it difficult to conduct exposure treatment. For example, with comorbid depression, a child may lack motivation to persevere through difficult exposure tasks. Clinical judgment in proceeding with such cases is needed.

An additional consideration that often presents during evaluations for OCD involves the consideration of PANDAS and PANS. In PANDAS, OCD-like symptoms begin soon after streptococcal infection, whereas PANS refers to abrupt onset or worsening of OCD symptoms and is etiologically unspecified. The diagnoses of PANDAS and PANS are controversial, with researchers and clinicians falling on either side of the coin regarding the disorders' validity. Although a detailed description of these disorders and their set of diagnostic procedures is beyond the scope of this chapter (for an in-depth review of PANDAS, see Kurlan & Kaplan, 2004), the clinician should consider several things when conducting an evaluation of a child with symptoms of OCD.

- *Inquire about the presence of recurrent streptococcal infection and relation in time to OCD symptoms.* An inquiry into the onset of the child's OCD symptoms may reveal that they began soon after a streptococcal infection. It is important to recognize the difference between a long-standing history of OCD, in which OCD symptoms appear to increase in severity when the child is sick, versus a rapid onset of OCD symptoms following infection. Acute onset of symptoms that occurred at the same time as infection may warrant further investigation into the potential role of PANDAS in the case.
- *When indicated, refer to a physician for management of the acute infection.* In cases in which a diagnosis of PANDAS is being considered, a referral to a physician is recommended. The clinician and physician may work together to determine whether such a diagnosis is appropriate.
- *Discuss the implications of a possible PANDAS diagnosis with the family.* Families of children who may have PANDAS will often ask how PANDAS affects treatment and prognosis. Families who have followed up with a physician and have received a PANDAS diagnosis should be encouraged to follow the physician's recommendations, which often involve prophylactic antibiotic treatment.
- *Psychotherapy with cases of PANDAS remains the same.* Although OCD symptoms that emerge because of PANDAS may have a different cause than the "typical" case of OCD, cognitive behavior therapy (CBT) with exposure and response prevention (ERP) remains the treatment of choice for reducing OCD symptoms (Storch et al., 2006). Even if PANDAS-related symptoms reemerge after treatment, families who have undergone CBT will be armed with tools to manage the symptoms.

TREATMENT

This section discusses the treatment of young children with OCD. For a more in-depth explanation of using family-based CBT for early-onset OCD, the reader is referred to Freeman and Garcia (2008).

History of Treatment for Early-Onset OCD

In recent years, treatment for early-onset OCD has been adapted in an age-downward trajectory from CBT used to treat adult OCD. Protocols for OCD found effective in adults (Foa & Kozak, 1996; Foa et al., 2005; Simpson et al., 2008) were tested in children with single case studies, open clinical trials, and then randomized controlled trials. Although OCD treatment for both children and adults involves ERP, treatments for these populations may differ in terms of specific therapeutic tools and the relative emphasis placed on each of those tools. The role of these tools in treating early-onset OCD is explored in greater detail later in this chapter. In the past few years, research has examined the efficacy of family-based CBT treatment for young children (younger than 9 years) with OCD. Freeman and colleagues (2008) randomized 38 children to receive either family-based CBT or relaxation therapy (RT). In the completer sample, 69% of children receiving family-based CBT achieved symptom remission compared with 30% in the RT group. Currently, a more rigorous, randomized controlled trial involving 124 children ages 5 to 8 years is underway.

Overview of Family-Based CBT for Young Children With OCD

The family-based CBT approach for young children with OCD used by Freeman and Garcia (2008) consists of 12 sessions over 14 weeks. The first two sessions include the parents only, are 90 minutes in duration, and are designed to educate parents on the nature and treatment of OCD, provide a rationale for CBT, and obtain information about the family (e.g., parenting style, parental accommodation). The remaining 10 sessions involve parent(s) and the child and are 60 minutes in duration. After the 14 weeks of treatment, follow-up or booster sessions can be added as necessary. CBT for young children with OCD involves five treatment components: Psychoeducation, Parent Tools, Externalizing OCD, ERP, Family Process Components, and Relapse Prevention. See Table 3.1 for a summary of how these components are covered across sessions. These components are described in the following subsections.

Psychoeducation

In this phase of treatment, the nature of OCD is discussed with the family, and a rationale for CBT is provided. It is helpful during psychoeducation to use visual imagery, metaphors, and examples so that concepts are clear. For parents, psychoeducation occurs during the first two parent-only sessions, and for the child, it occurs during the third session. Parents often blame

TABLE 3.1

An Overview of Family-Based Cognitive Behavior Therapy
for Young Children With Obsessive–Compulsive Disorder (OCD)

Visit	Session goals
1 (Parents only)	Psychoeducation: Assess impact of OCD on family functioning, explain treatment rationale, and provide overview of treatment
2 (Parents only)	Psychoeducation: Misperceptions of OCD, OCD symptom hierarchy
	Parenting tools: Overview of treatment tools, introduce reward plan
3 (Parents and child)	Psychoeducation: treatment rationale
	Child tools: Feelings thermometer, self-monitoring, hierarchy building
	Parenting tools: Introduce Praise and Encouragement
4 (Parents and child)	Child tools: Introduce "bossing back OCD" and ERP
	Parenting tools: Introduce Removal of Attention
5 (Parents and child)	Child tools: ERP parenting tools: Introduce Modeling
6 (Parents and child)	Child tools: ERP parenting tools: Introduce Scaffolding
7 (Parents and child)	Child tools: ERP parenting tools: Continue Scaffolding
8 (Parents and child)	Child tools: ERP parenting tools: Managing OCD in public
9 (Parents and child)	Child tools: ERP parenting tools: Apply tools to other areas
10 (Parents and child)	Child tools: ERP parenting tools: Review and practice tools
11 (Parents and child)	Child tools: ERP parenting tools: Relapse prevention
12 (Parents and child)	• Review child's OCD symptoms
	• Review course of treatment and maintenance plan

Note. ERP = exposure and response prevention.

themselves or their child for not being able to control OCD symptoms. It is crucial to inform the family that OCD is a neurobiological disorder with many causes that are out of their control. Many children come to treatment believing that OCD is a part of themselves or a part of their identity. It is important to teach the child to view OCD as separate from themselves (see the externalizing techniques described below).

The therapist should also describe to parents in careful detail what they can expect in therapy. Parents should be told that treatment will not only be occurring in the therapist's office but that the parents are the "treatment coaches" at home and play an integral role in therapy. The inherent challenges of ERP should also be explained. ERP involves gradual exposure to feared stimuli without performing any of the anxiety-reducing compulsions. Often, it is difficult for parents to observe their children being anxious or in a state of distress, thereby making participation in exposure a challenge. The therapist should remind parents that although ERP is challenging for everyone involved, it is extremely effective in reducing OCD's control and helping the child stand up for himself or herself. Furthermore, it is critical that the rationale behind ERP is explained, which should involve a discussion of what obsessions and compulsions are and how compulsions serve to reduce the anxiety or distress associated with obsessions. In addition, the therapist should explain that although this strategy "works" in the short term, ritualizing only serves to maintain anxiety over time. The therapist may explain this concept to parents in the following way:

> We know that obsessions increase anxiety, and compulsions serve to decrease anxiety. In other words, what your child is doing makes sense: When she experiences anxiety, which is uncomfortable to anyone, she does what comes naturally (ritualizes) to feel better. The problem with this pattern is that your child never really learns that the fears that OCD tells her about are unfounded. We know that anxiety is a temporary emotion. When your child feels anxious, her anxiety would go away on its own, without engaging in the compulsion. That's what we are going to do here in treatment: break that pattern of obsession, compulsion, obsession, compulsion, and so forth, and allow anxiety to come down on its own. This will be done in a gradual manner. Over time, your child will experience fewer and fewer compulsions, and her anxiety associated with obsessions will decrease.

Thus, in ERP, the child will be asked to face anxiety-provoking situations while refraining from ritualizing. During these exposures, anxiety will abate on its own, and through repeated exposure, situations will produce less and less anxiety over time. Thus, the rationale behind exposure therapy is to break the counterproductive cycle and instead implement a strategy that reduces anxiety in the long term. Although the majority of psychoeducation occurs during the first three sessions, the therapist should frequently reflect back on key concepts with the family as treatment progresses.

Parent Tools

Parents play a vital role in therapy. Therefore, it is important for the therapist to teach them the skills necessary to be successful treatment coaches. The three main skills that are taught to parents are differential attention, modeling, and scaffolding. *Differential attention* involves attending to the child's behaviors that are consistent with therapy goals and not attending to the child's behavior that are inconsistent with therapy goals. For example, if the child balks at completing ERP exercises, the parent should not inadvertently reinforce this type of behavior by engaging the child in an argument or pleading with the child to engage in the exposure. In contrast, when the child tries hard to engage in therapy homework exercises, the parent should reinforce the child's behavior. Reinforcing treatment-consistent behavior can be done several ways, such as providing praise and use of contingency management.

Unlike older kids and adults who may have intrinsic motivation for treatment, young children may benefit from rewards. A reward system is often helpful in encouraging children to participate in exposures and complete homework assignments. Before implementing a reward system, the therapist should discuss the family's history (or lack thereof) with reward systems as well as their values and beliefs behind such practices. It is also helpful to discuss the rationale behind using a reward system, with the therapist making sure to differentiate between "bribery" and the use of reward systems. Parents often have useful information about what they have found helpful about using such systems.

Next, before implementing the reward system, it is helpful to emphasize several important aspects of structuring reward systems to maximize the likelihood that they are effective. A reward system needs to be feasible, simple, and implemented consistently. Small rewards or redeemable objects (e.g., stickers, tokens) should be delivered as immediately as possible following the target behavior. It is often helpful to have the reward system be visible to the child. Sticker charts and jars where tokens can be placed are recommended.

After a discussion of these topics, a basic structure of the reward system can be set up. It may be necessary to tweak aspects of the system to ensure that it is properly motivating. Furthermore, the reward system will likely need to be changed as the family progresses through treatment. Target behaviors, for example, should change as the child gains more ground against OCD, and the frequency of rewards may decrease.

Modeling is another skill taught to parents. Modeling involves demonstrating behaviors that are consistent with the therapy goals in the hope that the child is motivated to follow suit. Parents may be asked to "boss back" some of their own anxieties. Exercises like this serve as good examples of modeling, but these types of exercises also highlight the team atmosphere that a family-based treatment aims to achieve. Because the child is the focus of treatment, modeling may be difficult to discuss. Thus, it is recommended that this discussion take place after good rapport has been developed.

> As you know, your child has been working really hard on facing his fears by doing exposures. Although your child is learning a lot about himself and OCD through this process, kids also learn a lot about the world through a process we call *modeling*. Modeling refers to learning by watching. Kids are very perceptive about those close to them, and I'm sure you'd agree that your child has learned a lot by observing you. Kids learn about fears this way. You told me that you have a really hard time using public restrooms. What does your child learn when he observes you having trouble with this? Is that message consistent with what your child has been learning in here? We find it to be very powerful when children can observe others in the family interacting with their fears in a different way. How can you move in that direction this week?

The final skill that parents are taught is *scaffolding*. Scaffolding involves encouragement from the parents during exposure exercises, especially as they increase in difficulty. Therapists may choose to teach parents scaffolding in a didactic way or by example. Examples of scaffolding include validating the child's feelings during exposure and brainstorming with the child ways to tackle the exposure. Scaffolding in these types of situations typically involves the following: (a) the parent asking the child to identify the situation as an OCD situation, (b) the parent asking the child about what is difficult about the situation (e.g., "What is OCD making you worry about?"), (c) asking the child if she can think of a way to boss back OCD, and (d) encouraging the child to follow through with bossing back OCD.

Externalizing OCD

Externalizing OCD refers to how OCD is discussed as being separate from the child, as opposed to being "part of" the child (March & Mulle, 1998). The inherent message in externalizing is: The child is not his OCD. To shape externalizing into the culture of treatment, children are asked to complete two homework assignments early in treatment: (a) name their OCD and (b) draw a picture of their OCD. The therapist and family are encouraged to refer to the child's OCD by name (e.g., "The Bully") throughout treatment.

ERP

ERP is the heart of family-based CBT for young children with OCD and involves gradual exposure to feared stimuli without engaging in fear-reducing compulsions. The rationale behind ERP is that the child will habituate to the feared stimuli without ritualizing, and anxiety will decrease over time. The phrase "bossing back OCD" is helpful during ERP to help the child externalize OCD and stay motivated during the exposure. Bossing back OCD refers broadly to having the child resist ritualizing. It does not involve getting into a battle with OCD regarding obsessional content.

Therapists typically use a "fear thermometer" of some kind so that the child can report his anxiety level during the exposure. The fear thermometer may be a drawing of an actual thermometer or scale of some sort. With young children, the range of the fear thermometer is typically small (e.g., 0–10, 0–5). To design appropriate exposures, the therapist works with the parent and child to create a fear hierarchy, which is a systematic ranking of hypothetical exposures that are specific to each child's OCD. It is important to note that ERP ideally involves having the child engage in an exposure while simultaneously refraining from ritualizing. Thus, it is important for the therapist to communicate, during the course of hierarchy building, that rankings should be provided with the assumption that one cannot ritualize during or after the exposure.

ERP proceeds with tackling the easiest items first and slowly progressing up the hierarchy. An exposure item that is practiced in session is then assigned as homework, to be completed daily outside of session. When an exposure no longer elicits significant anxiety levels, the next item on the hierarchy is addressed. It is important that exposures selected early in treatment be able to be completed, when possible, in the office, where the therapist is able to demonstrate key aspects to the child and family (e.g., addressing parental accommodation, appropriate titration of the difficulty of the exposure). If exposures cannot be completed in the office because of the nature of the child's symptoms, the therapist may wish to consider conducting exposures in his or her presence outside of the office, such as in the community or in the home.

Cognitive Techniques

Cognitive techniques, such as thought challenging, may be used in conjunction with the family-based treatment. However, we recommend several guidelines for their use. First, given that the goal of ERP is to allow habituation to occur naturally (e.g., without ritualizing, without parental accommodations), cognitive techniques should not be used during an exposure because doing so may serve to lessen anxiety. For example, if thoughts about contamination-based feared consequences are challenged during an exposure, the anxiety associated with the exposure may be substantially lessened. Thus, cognitive techniques, during an exposure, may function similarly to rituals and accommodation. Therefore, cognitive techniques should be used outside of the exposure context.

Typically, then, cognitive techniques, such as thought challenging, are used after the exposure has been completed—when the child's anxiety has reached near-zero levels. This allows the therapist to avoid some of the pitfalls described earlier, while allowing cognitive techniques to provide additional therapeutic benefit. After an exposure is complete, it is helpful for the therapist to "process" the exposure with the child and family. Often, processing the exposure will involve a discussion of cognitive testing. Typically, this would be framed in an externalizing manner, for example,

> What did OCD tell you would happen if you did that exposure without doing your rituals? Now that we've done the exposure, how true do you think that was? What do you think of that? What does that tell us about what OCD says?

Cognitive techniques may occasionally be used in the context of an exposure task to appropriately "titrate" an exposure to the desired level of difficulty. Early on in the course of conducting exposures, tasks should be in the easy-to-moderate range. However, it is important to note that the ratings given during hierarchy building are predictions. A child may initially rate an exposure task as being a "4" out of "10" during hierarchy building, and then report a higher number during the actual exposure. In these cases, the therapist may wish to ease the child's anxiety down to a more manageable level, especially if the therapist feels that the child will balk at the exposure and jeopardize a positive course of treatment. Cognitive techniques, such as questioning the likelihood of the feared outcome, may be helpful in this regard.

Family Process Components

During treatment, various family process components arise that the therapist needs to address. The component that we focus on in this chapter is parental accommodation.

Parental accommodation refers to actions that parents take to reduce their child's momentary anxiety or distress. It is critical that parental accommodation is addressed in treatment because any action to reduce anxiety or distress in the moment is contrary to therapy goals. Often, parents accommodate their child's OCD symptoms because it is difficult for them to see their child anxious. Parents may also accommodate to avoid the child from displaying angry or hostile behavior. The therapist should help the parents decrease accommodation that interferes with treatment goals and come up with more adaptive problem-solving techniques to manage their child's behavior or handle their own anxiety.

One of the most common examples of parental accommodation involves responses that parents give to their child's reassurance seeking. Children may often ask their parents questions that relate to feared consequences (e.g., "Will I get sick if I touch that?"). Accommodating responses to these types of questions often involve reassuring the child that the feared consequence will not take place (e.g., "Oh, I don't think you'll get sick") or providing direct ways to ensure that the child does not risk coming into contact with the feared consequence (e.g., wiping an object with a decontaminating cloth).

Even if a parent is not exhibiting overt signs of accommodation, it is important to inquire about other, more subtle, forms of accommodation. Many parents will report changing the child's schedule to minimize the likelihood that the child will encounter anxiety-provoking events. Parents may also report that they will attempt to soothe their child when their child is anxious or distressed (e.g., patting them on the back, giving them a kiss). The therapist should be sensitive in discussing these issues with parents because soothing a child during times of distress is a natural reaction and normative in most situations. However, it must be explained how such actions are inconsistent with ERP because they artificially reduce anxiety and prevent habituation from occurring naturally.

Just as ERP is conducted in a gradual manner, so are steps to remove accommodation. The therapist should discuss with the family a plan to gradually reduce the level of accommodation that is occurring. In that discussion, the therapist should explain that a temporary increase in anxiety may result when accommodation is lessened. Over time, however, the child's anxiety is expected to decline.

Relapse Prevention

In the family-based treatment of pediatric OCD, there are two main ways that maintenance is taken into account. First, treatment tools themselves should be used in a manner that maximizes generalization. Second, ample time should be provided toward the end of treatment to discuss a maintenance plan moving forward.

There are several ways to maximize generalization. First, it is important for an exposure hierarchy to contain as many elements that are relevant to the child's OCD as possible. For example, if a child has OCD symptoms related to contamination, symmetry, and checking, ERP should address all of those areas. Second, it is important that ERP be conducted in as many environments as is feasible. It is often helpful for the therapist or parents (or both) to talk to their child's teacher about how OCD may be interfering in the classroom. If exposure work can be done in the classroom setting as well as the home and therapy settings, it will help ensure that child is gaining ground on OCD in the major areas of his or her life. Third, it is important, when possible, to emphasize that bossing back OCD involves not only structured ERP but also the ability to boss back OCD spontaneously as well. Although successful completion of target exposures is an important part of the therapeutic process, it needs to be emphasized that bossing back OCD in all areas of life is the ultimate goal.

To increase the likelihood that treatment gains will be maintained, the family-based treatment of pediatric OCD involves explicit discussion of maintenance over the last few sessions. During these sessions, it is important to review the major tools that were learned in treatment. By the end of treatment, families should be comfortable with the idea of using these tools for novel situations in the future. In that vein, it may be helpful to discuss a hypothetical new OCD symptom that may arise in the future and have the family come up with ways in which they would use what they learned in treatment to address it.

By the end of treatment, it is critical that the family understand ERP from not only a procedural perspective (e.g., how to set up an exposure, how to build a hierarchy, the steps used in scaffolding) but a conceptual one as well. In other words, we want families to understand the *why* as well as the *how*. Understanding the concepts behind ERP (e.g., habituation, how avoidance and escape serve to maintain OCD) increases the likelihood that the family will be able to apply the tools learned in treatment in an effective manner.

Finally, when discussing maintenance, it is important to discuss realistic goals and expectations for the future. Some families may hold the idea that "success" necessitates the absence of symptoms. Other families may need to be reminded that the treatment of OCD is an ongoing process. The therapist should communicate to families that the goal of treatment was not to permanently erase OCD symptoms. In fact, obsessions are not an uncommon experience in the general population (Fullana et al., 2009). Rather, it should be emphasized that the goal of treatment was to put the family in a position in which they have the tools in place to manage OCD. How frequently and intensively one needs to use such tools in the future depends on the situation, and some guidelines around this should be discussed. For example, transient OCD symptoms (e.g., occasional urges to ritualize, when parents observe a quick compulsion every now and then) do not require the same attention as a more enduring return of symptoms.

BARRIERS AND PITFALLS

Working with young children can present unique challenges to the therapist and family. This section highlights and discusses some of those challenges.

Cognitive Developmental Factors

Although there is much variability from child to child, younger children will generally display more cognitive limitations than older children. These limitations can affect how therapy is conducted. Several are discussed here.

1. Young Children May Possess Limitations in What Is Understood in Therapy

It is important that the therapist and family use language that the child is able to understand and that concepts be explained in a simple manner. For example, a young child may have difficulty following the logic of how ritualizing is negatively reinforced by a reduction in anxiety. We find it helpful to use real-world analogies that depict OCD in a way that the child can understand. One analogy that can be helpful in explaining the rationale behind ERP is the "lunch bully."

> OCD can be a lot like the lunch bully. Do you know what the lunch bully does? The lunch bully is the kid at school who comes up and tells you to give him your lunch. Let's pretend that the lunch bully comes up to you today, and you give him your lunch. What is the bully is going to do tomorrow? And the next day? Now, instead of giving the bully your lunch, what do you think will happen if you don't give in? Let's pretend you do this for several days. What do you think the bully will eventually do?

Any analogy or example can be used, of course, and it is recommended that examples be used that are relevant to the family being seen in treatment. For instance, sports examples may resonate with some children but not others. Using relevant examples allows the child to better understand abstract concepts that are discussed in treatment.

2. Young Children May Have Difficulty "Catching" Their Rituals

The family-based treatment of pediatric OCD discussed in this chapter takes many steps to increase parental involvement, given the likelihood that younger children may have more difficulty implementing treatment by themselves. "Catching" rituals is one such area that younger children can struggle with, especially for those who engage in quick, subtle rituals.

It may be useful to assign homework for "catching" rituals. If an exposure that is being addressed in treatment relates to a reliable ritual, the child can attempt to catch that ritual as it occurs in real time outside of the exposure context. This type of assignment can be readily incorporated into an existing reward program in which the child earns a sticker for each time she is able to catch a ritual by herself.

Furthermore, it is important that the therapist discuss ways in which parents or other caregivers can assist the child in catching his rituals. In-the-moment feedback can be helpful in this regard. However, one also needs to be careful that the collaborative spirit of treatment is not compromised. For example, a child may become frustrated or upset if those around her are constantly pointing out rituals. Thus, is it is often useful to address one type of ritual at a time, with a discussion around how often to prompt the child about their rituals. For instance, if a ritual corresponds to a particular situation in which the child has experience dealing with in vivo exposures, the therapist can discuss with the parents how to implement scaffolding techniques (refer to the Parent Tools section of this chapter for a discussion of scaffolding).

3. Younger Children May Lack Motivation to Beat OCD

At times, younger children may lack the intrinsic motivation to beat OCD. For example, they may be less likely to have encountered some of the negative consequences that older children and adults have encountered in life. First, we find it useful to inquire about consequences of OCD early in treatment. Young children, with the help of family members, are often able to provide several good reasons why they want to beat OCD. Many young children, for example, state that their rituals take up a lot of time or that they get into arguments with their parents about OCD. These reasons can be revisited throughout treatment as needed.

The potential lack of intrinsic motivation in young children highlights the importance of external motivators. For this reason, as already discussed, the family-based treatment of pediatric OCD emphasizes parental attention and a reward system. In those contexts, immediately delivered reinforcers can be properly motivating for a child to engage in the day-to-day tasks involved in treatment, such as completing in vivo exposure tasks and resisting rituals.

SUMMARY AND DIRECTIONS FOR FUTURE RESEARCH

Treatment research on pediatric OCD, especially as it relates to the young age range of 5- to 8-year-olds, is in its infancy. Nonetheless, preliminary data are promising and suggest that a family-based cognitive–behavioral approach may be efficacious.

The family-based cognitive–behavioral approach for pediatric OCD involves several modifications to "traditional" CBT. These modifications include increasing the role of parental involvement, teaching parents additional behavior management tools, placing a heavier emphasis on external motivation (i.e., the use of reward systems and tangible reinforcers), and making changes to the language and delivery of the treatment (e.g., focusing on externalizing OCD, using developmentally appropriate language and examples).

Future research should focus on dissemination efforts. Although family-based CBT appears to be effective in clinical trials, it is unclear how readily available such treatment is in the community. Furthermore, dissemination efforts may be able to identify potential pitfalls in dissemination (e.g., difficulties in training therapists how to conduct the treatment, systematic issues in clinics, parental resistance to certain treatment techniques). Finally, given the complex nature of therapy with this age range, an investigation of moderators and mediators of treatment may help guide how therapy is conducted or modified in the future. For example, identifying such variables may provide valuable information about who is not responding to therapy and why family-based CBT is not working. Such efforts may guide clinicians in how to modify treatment for such cases (e.g., a heavier emphasis on parent training techniques for those cases with more significant comorbid externalizing symptoms).

REFERENCES

Busatto, G. F., Buchpiguel, C. A., Zamignani, D. R., Garrido, G. J., Glabus, M. F., Rosario-Campos, C., . . . Miguel, E. C. (2001). Regional cerebral blood flow abnormalities in early-onset obsessive–compulsive disorder: An exploratory SPECT study. *Journal of the American Academy of Child & Adolescent Psychiatry,* 40, 347–354. doi:10.1097/00004583-200103000-00015

Carey, G., & Gottesman, I. I. (1981). Twin and family studies of anxiety, phobic, and obsessive disorders. In D. F. Klein & J. Rabkin (Eds.), *Anxiety: New research and changing concepts* (pp. 117–136). New York, NY: Raven Press.

Flament, M. F., Whitaker, A., Rapoport, J. L., Davies, M., Berg, C. Z., Kalikow, K., . . . Shaffer, D. (1988). Obsessive compulsive disorder in adolescence: An epidemiological study. *Journal of the American Academy of Child & Adolescent Psychiatry, 27,* 764–771. doi:10.1097/00004583-198811000-00018

Flessner, C. A., Freeman, J. B., Sapyta, J., Garcia, A., Franklin, M. E., March, J. S., & Foa, E. B. (2011). Predictors of parental accommodation in pediatric obsessive–compulsive disorder: Findings from the pediatric obsessive–compulsive disorder treatment study (POTS) trial. *Journal of the American Academy of Child & Adolescent Psychiatry, 50,* 716–725. doi:10.1016/j.jaac.2011.03.019

Foa, E. B., & Kozak, M. J. (1996). Psychological treatments for obsessive–compulsive disorder. In M. R. Mavissakalian & R. F. Prien (Eds.), *Long-term treatments of anxiety disorders* (pp. 285–309). Washington, DC: American Psychiatric Press.

Foa, E. B., Liebowitz, M. R., Kozak, M. J., Davies, S. O., Campeas, R. B., Franklin, M., . . . Tu, X. (2005). Randomized, placebo-controlled trial of exposure and ritual prevention, clomipramine, and their combination in the treatment of obsessive–compulsive disorder. *The American Journal of Psychiatry, 162,* 151–161. doi:10.1176/appi.ajp.162.1.151

Freeman, J., Flessner, C. A., & Garcia, A. M. (2011). The Children's Yale–Brown Obsessive Compulsive Scale: Reliability and validity for use among 5 to 8 year olds with obsessive–compulsive disorder. *Journal of Abnormal Child Psychology, 39,* 877–883. doi:10.1007/s10802-011-9494-6

Freeman, J. B., & Garcia, A. M. (2008). *Family-based cognitive-behavioral treatment for young children with OCD—Therapist guide and parent workbook.* New York, NY: Oxford University Press.

Freeman, J. B., Garcia, A. M., Coyne, L., Ale, C., Przeworski, A., Himle, M., . . . Leonard, H. L. (2008). Early childhood OCD: Preliminary findings from a family-based cognitive-behavioral approach. *Journal of the American Academy of Child & Adolescent Psychiatry, 47,* 593–602. doi:10.1097/CHI.0b013e31816765f9

Fullana, M. A., Mataix-Cols, D., Caspi, A., Harrington, H., Grisham, J. R., Moffitt, T. E., & Poulton, R. (2009). Obsessions and compulsions in the community: Prevalence, interference, help-seeking, developmental stability, and co-occurring psychiatric conditions. *The American Journal of Psychiatry, 166,* 329–336. doi:10.1176/appi.ajp.2008.08071006

Garcia, A. M., Freeman, J. B., Himle, M. B., Berman, N. C., Ogata, A. K., Ng, J., . . . H. Leonard. (2009). Phenomenology of early childhood onset obsessive compulsive disorder. *Journal of Psychopathology and Behavioral Assessment, 31,* 104–111. doi:10.1007/s10862-008-9094-0

Geller, D., Biederman, J., Jones, J., Park, K., Schwartz, S., Shapiro, S., & Coffey, B. (1998). Is juvenile obsessive–compulsive disorder a developmental subtype of the disorder? A review of the pediatric literature. *Journal of the American*

Academy of Child & Adolescent Psychiatry, 37, 420–427. doi:10.1097/00004583-199804000-00020

Kurlan, R., & Kaplan, E. L. (2004). The pediatric autoimmune neuropsychiatric disorders associated with streptococcal infection (PANDAS) etiology for tics and obsessive–compulsive symptoms: Hypothesis or entity? Practical considerations for the clinician. *Pediatrics, 113*, 883–886. doi:10.1542/peds.113.4.883

MacMaster, F. P., & Rosenberg, D. R. (2009). Neuroimaging studies of pediatric obsessive–compulsive disorder: Special emphasis on genetics and biomarkers. In M. S. Ritsner (Ed.), *The handbook of neuropsychiatric biomarkers, endophenotypes, and genes: Vol. 2. Neuroanatomical and neuroimaging endophenotypes and biomarkers* (pp. 201–213). New York, NY: Springer Science + Business Media.

March, J. S., & Mulle, K. (1998). *OCD in children and adolescents: A cognitive-behavioral treatment manual.* New York, NY: Guilford Press.

Nakatani, E., Krebs, G., Micali, N., Turner, C., Heyman, I., & Mataix-Cols, D. (2011). Children with very early onset obsessive–compulsive disorder: Clinical features and treatment outcome. *Journal of Child Psychology and Psychiatry, 52*, 1261–1268. doi:10.1111/j.1469-7610.2011.02434.x

Nestadt, G., Samuels, J., Riddle, M., Bienvenu, O. J., Liang, K. Y., LaBuda, M., . . . Hoehn-Saric, R. (2000). A family study of obsessive–compulsive disorder. *Archives of General Psychiatry, 57*, 358–363. doi:10.1001/archpsyc.57.4.358

Palermo, S. D., Bloch, M. H., Craiglow, B., Landeros-Weisenberger, A., Dombrowski, P. A., Panza, K., . . . Leckman, J. F. (2011). Predictors of early adulthood quality of life in children with obsessive–compulsive disorder. *Social Psychiatry and Psychiatric Epidemiology, 46*, 291–297. doi:10.1007/s00127-010-0194-2

Pauls, D. L., Alsobrook, J. P., Goodman, W. K., Rasmussen, S. A., & Leckman, J. F. (1995). A family study of obsessive–compulsive disorder. *The American Journal of Psychiatry, 152*, 76–84.

Pauls, D. L., & Leckman, J. F. (1986). The inheritance of Gilles de la Tourette's syndrome and associated behaviors. *The New England Journal of Medicine, 315*, 993–997. doi:10.1056/NEJM198610163151604

Piacentini, J., Bergman, R. L., Keller, M., & McCracken, J. (2003). Functional impairment in children and adolescents with obsessive–compulsive disorder. *Journal of Child and Adolescent Psychopharmacology, 13*, S61–S69. doi:10.1089/104454603322126359

Piacentini, J., & Graae, F. (1997). Childhood obsessive–compulsive disorder. In E. Hollander & D. J. Stein (Eds.), *Obsessive–compulsive disorders: Etiology, diagnosis, and treatment* (p. 23–46). New York, NY: Marcel Dekker.

Post, R. M., Weiss, S. R. B., Leverich, G. S., George, M. S., Frye, M. A., & Ketter, T. A. (1996). Developmental psychobiology of cyclic affective illness: Implications for early therapeutic intervention. *Development and Psychopathology, 8*, 273–305. doi:10.1017/S0954579400007082

Rosenberg, D. R., & Keshavan, M. S. (1998). Toward a neurodevelopmental model of obsessive–compulsive disorder. *Biological Psychiatry, 43*, 623–640. doi:10.1016/S0006-3223(97)00443-5

Scahill, L., Riddle, M. A., McSwiggin-Hardin, M., Ort, S. I., King, R. A., Goodman, W. K., ... (1997). Children's Yale–Brown Obsessive Compulsive Scale: Reliability and validity. *Journal of the American Academy of Child & Adolescent Psychiatry, 36*, 844–852. doi:10.1097/00004583-199706000-00023

Silverman, W. K., & Albano, A. M. (1996). *Anxiety Disorders Interview Schedule for DSM–IV—Child and Parent Versions.* San Antonio, TX: Psychological Corporation.

Simpson, H. B., Foa, E. B., Liebowitz, M. R., Ledley, D. R., Huppert, J. D., Cahill, S., . . . Petkova, E. (2008). A randomized, controlled trial of cognitive-behavioral therapy for augmenting pharmacotherapy in obsessive–compulsive disorder. *The American Journal of Psychiatry, 165*, 621–630. doi:10.1176/appi.ajp.2007.07091440

Stewart, S. E., Geller, D. A., Jenike, M., Pauls, D., Shaw, D., Mullin, B., & Faraone, S. V. (2004). Long term outcome of pediatric obsessive–compulsive disorder: A meta-analysis and qualitative review of the literature. *Acta Psychiatrica Scandinavica, 110*, 4–13. doi:10.1111/j.1600-0447.2004.00302.x

Storch, E. A., Murphy, T. K., Geffken, G. R., Mann, G., Adkins, J., Merlo, L. J., . . . Goodman, W. K. (2006). Cognitive-behavioral therapy for PANDAS-related obsessive–compulsive disorder: Findings from a preliminary waitlist controlled trial. *Journal of the American Academy of Child & Adolescent Psychiatry, 45*, 1171–1178. doi:10.1097/01.chi.0000231973.43966.a0

Swedo, S. E., Leckman, J. F., & Rose, N. R. (2012). From research subgroup to clinical syndrome: Modifying the PANDAS criteria to describe PANS (pediatric acute-onset neuropsychiatric syndrome). *Pediatrics and Therapeutics, 2.* Retrieved from http://intramural.nimh.nih.gov/pdn/PANDAS-to-PANS2012.pdf

Swedo, S. E., Leonard, H. L., Garvey, M., Mittleman, B., Allen, A. J., Perlmutter, S., . . . Dubbert, B. K. (1998). Pediatric autoimmune neuropsychiatric disorders associated with streptococcal infections: Clinical description of the first 50 cases. *The American Journal of Psychiatry, 155*, 264–271.

Zohar, A. H. (1999). The epidemiology of obsessive–compulsive disorder in children and adolescents. *Child and Adolescent Psychiatric Clinics of North America, 8*, 445–460.

4

TRACTABLE IMPEDIMENTS TO COGNITIVE BEHAVIOR THERAPY FOR PEDIATRIC OBSESSIVE–COMPULSIVE DISORDER

ADAM B. LEWIN

Pediatric obsessive–compulsive disorder (OCD) is a chronic and impairing condition that affects 1% to 2% of youth (Zohar, 1999). The vast preponderance of OCD cases across the lifespan have their onset in childhood (Douglass, Moffitt, Dar, McGee, & Silva, 1995) and run a protracted course without adequate treatment (Stewart et al., 2004). Unfortunately, functional impairment secondary to OCD has a marked impact on development, often disrupting lifelong psychosocial functioning and contributing to continued impairment in adult interpersonal, educational, and occupational attainment (Piacentini, Bergman, Keller, & McCracken, 2003), cementing OCD as one of the leading causes of disability (World Health Organization, 2005). Fortunately, there are two treatment modalities with demonstrated efficacy among pediatric OCD patients: namely, cognitive behavior therapy (CBT) with exposure and response prevention (ERP) and serotonin reuptake inhibitors (SRIs) pharmacotherapy (American Academy of Child and

http://dx.doi.org/10.1037/14323-005
Obsessive–Compulsive Disorder and Its Spectrum: A Life-Span Approach, Eric A. Storch and Dean McKay (Editors)
Copyright © 2014 by the American Psychological Association. All rights reserved.

Adolescent Psychiatry, 2012). Despite these advances in treatment, OCD remains a chronic and impairing affliction for youth and their families, and there is room for improvement in obtaining treatment response. In the first large-scale randomized controlled trial of pediatric OCD to include CBT, remission rates were 21% for sertraline (an SRI), 39% for CBT, and 54% for combined CBT + sertraline (Pediatric OCD Treatment Study, 2004). Sequelae of untreated OCD disorder contribute to academic, familial, and social dysfunction (Piacentini, Bergman, Keller, & McCracken, 2003). Further refinement of interventional approaches remains central to minimizing suffering and impairment while increasing the likelihood that youth with OCD can maintain relatively unafflicted lives. Unfortunately, lack of access to providers with expertise in treating childhood OCD, especially ERP, is an additional hindrance. Consequently, it is critical to understand factors that mitigate treatment response to obtain maximal clinical gains with the available resources.

Among youth with OCD, a number of factors have been associated with attenuated treatment response (Storch, Bjorgvinsson, et al., 2010). These include intangible factors such as OCD severity, symptom presentation and typology, neurocognitive impairment, and comorbidity profile. Notably, in addition, there are a number of more *tractable factors* (e.g., family functioning, insight, motivation, expectancy) that have an impact on treatment outcomes. The former have been more extensively discussed in the extant adult and child OCD literature, but attention to the latter group of barriers to treatment, which represent areas for potential intervention, is increasing. Understanding the impact of inherent, intangible factors such as psychiatric comorbidity, disease severity, and cognitive impairment may provide information on probability and rate of response to a particular intervention. However, it is difficult, if not impossible, to mitigate these factors. An appropriate analogy may be that this is the hand that is dealt: Understanding the impact may help guide appropriate intervention, but it is difficult to directly target these barriers. In contrast, the more malleable, tractable factors better represent targets for ancillary intervention. To continue the metaphor, these tractable factors could be akin to how skillfully the cards are played—they are putatively more vulnerable to intervention.

Both intangible and more tractable factors relate to medication and CBT response. Understanding predictors of medication response is a key area for research, especially in improving targeted, individualized intervention. Nevertheless, although the aforementioned factors may represent endophenotypes associated with medication response, determination of medication response is likely secondary to anatomical, neurochemical, and genetic variants. In other words, family functioning or expectations may correlate with SRI response, but it is unlikely that these factors affect medication response directly. As a consequence, the focus of this review is on factors that can be addressed within the context of CBT. Specifically, this chapter reviews existing research on treatment expectancy, accommodation, family functioning, and patient insight in the context of CBT for OCD. Although each can be an impediment to maximal CBT outcome, these factors can be addressed within the context of therapy. The focus of this chapter is on pediatric OCD, but relevant research from adult studies is also discussed.

TREATMENT EXPECTANCY

Patients' expectations have long been thought to color their perception of and participation in treatment, with links between higher expectations of treatment efficacy and improved medical, surgical, and mental health outcomes (Greenberg, Constantino, & Bruce, 2006). Given that CBT with ERP techniques are predicated on active engagement and participation, the extent to which treatment expectations shape future participation and treatment experience is logically a candidate for influencing clinical outcome for youth undergoing CBT. Not surprisingly, higher expectation for favorable CBT response has been linked with increased magnitude of treatment response and completion among youth with OCD (Lewin et al., 2011). Additionally, children with greater pretreatment expectancies of successful treatment were less likely to report significant OCD-related impairment following treatment. Notably, the research found higher expectations for treatment success to be associated with better ERP homework compliance. These associations were identified as early as the third treatment session and were generally consistent throughout the remainder of treatment. Similar associations between patient adherence with ERP and outcomes have been observed in adult OCD studies (Simpson et al., 2011). Interestingly, youth treatment expectancy was a better predictor of outcome, improvement, and homework compliance than parental treatment expectancy (Lewin et al., 2011). Given that children (vs. parents) are the targets of the intervention and that they are ultimately responsible for doing the bulk of the work in therapy, it is not surprising that their beliefs about treatment are most closely related to outcomes. Although parental participation is central to successful treatment of childhood OCD, if a child does not believe the exposure will be helpful, he or she may be less likely to engage. Notably, children and parents are good judges of successful outcome (Lewin, Peris, De Nadai, McCracken, & Piacentini, 2012). This is particularly important for the treatment of OCD in which exposure exercises are considered the active ingredient for progress (Piacentini, March, & Franklin, 2006).

Psychoeducation

Taken together, these findings underscore the value of harnessing engagement in and early buy-in of treatment. Treatment expectations should be assessed and concerns sufficiently processed before treatment. Expectancy can be enhanced via the provision of positive information about treatment (Di Blasi et al., 2001), suggesting that a significant portion of the initial psychotherapy sessions for pediatric intensive OCD treatment should focus on psychoeducation and "selling" the treatment procedure to ensure that the child and family understand and buy into the procedures (Piacentini, Langley, & Roblek, 2007b). With minor modifications to an ERP protocol, measures to assess and bolster patients' confidence in the intervention can be implemented. Procedures may include additional, developmentally appropriate psychoeducation regarding ERP outcomes and child OCD (Lewin, 2011). For an adolescent, this may include citing treatment data on robust response and remission rates. For a younger child, pictorial or anecdotal representations of treatment successes should be presented early and often. Regardless of age, choosing early exposure exercises at which the children will likely experience habituation to anxiety is central. Additionally, monitoring early adherence, especially with ERP homework, is key to maximizing outcomes (Lewin & Piacentini, 2010).

Family Factors: Accommodation and Family Dysfunction

Family accommodation refers to the incorporation of family members (or other caregivers) into rituals. In some cases, family members participate in elaborate rituals with the individual with OCD. More commonly, accommodation manifests via provision of reassurance, accepting or minimizing a confession, acquiescing to a child's demands, or allowing for escape or avoidance. For example, a parent may (a) repeatedly provide calming statements in response to a child's obsessive fears, "It's OK, God is not angry with you for saying 'devil' "; (b) prepare only beige foods in airtight packages, delivered on a "sterile" plate at a table separate from any other family member; (c) participate in elaborate bathing and bedtime routines, repeating them if the child becomes distressed; or (d) go to the wholesale market to buy industrial quantities of soap or toilet paper weekly. Essentially, accommodation becomes entwined in the obsessive–compulsive cycle and presents a significant hindrance to exposure-based therapy. Although reliable estimates are lacking, prevalence of OCD-related accommodation is high (Calvocoressi et al., 1995), with estimates of 60% for adults (Shafran, Ralph, & Tallis, 1995) and 70% for youth (Allsopp & Verduyn, 1990; Storch, Geffken, Merlo, Jacob, et al., 2007), occurring at least daily in 56% of child cases (Peris, Bergman, et al. 2008). Accommodation often begins innocuously and with the parents' best intentions, functioning to soothe a child's distress. However, family efforts to reduce anxiety prevent development of appropriate tolerance of distress and proliferate into excessive and sometimes bizarre routines that maintain a child's OCD and cause significant family burden. In fact, family accommodation efforts may temporarily mask OCD-related impairment to the outside eye, or even to family members themselves as they lose awareness of how disabled and dependent on accommodation a child has become. Disruption of accommodation is initially highly distressing to the child and can be objectionable to parents, despite the resulting impairment, given the perceived role in elevating the child's anxiety (albeit for the short term) in the context of eliminating accommodation.

Not surprisingly, elevated family accommodation is associated with worse response to both behavioral and pharmacological treatments (Lebowitz, Panza, Su, & Bloch, 2012) for adults (Calvocoressi et al., 1999; Ferrão et al., 2006) and youth (Garcia et al., 2010; Merlo, Lehmkuhl, Geffken, & Storch, 2009; Piacentini et al., 2011; Storch, Geffken, Merlo, Jacob, et al., 2007). Moreover, family accommodation has been associated with elevated OCD symptom severity (Amir, Freshman, & Foa, 2000; Calvocoressi et al., 1995, 1999; Ferrão et al., 2006; Lebowitz et al., 2012; Peris, Bergman, et al., 2008; Storch, Geffken, Merlo, Mann, et al., 2007), functional impairment (Piacentini, Bergman, Keller, & McCracken, 2003; Storch, Merlo, et al., 2008, Storch, Larson, et al., 2010), mood and anxiety disorder comorbidity (Amir et al., 2000; Storch et al., 2012), and family dysfunction (Peris, Bergman, et al., 2008, 2012; Storch, Geffken, Merlo, Jacob, et al., 2007). These findings have led experts to strongly encourage extensive family involvement in behavioral treatments for OCD, especially for youth (Barrett, Healy-Farrell, & March, 2004; Flessner et al., 2011; Lewin, 2005, 2011; Peris et al., 2010; Piacentini et al., 2007b; Steketee & Van Noppen, 2003; Storch, Geffken, Merlo, Mann, et al., 2007).

In applying ERP to children with OCD, family involvement in ritualization can be added to a fear hierarchy (Lewin et al., 2005; March & Mulle, 1998; Piacentini, Langley, & Roblek, 2007a) as targets for removal with successive practice. For example, a step of the fear hierarchy may be for a parent to ignore reassurance seeking about a particular symptom. Subsequent steps may involve ignoring additional requests for reassurance for other fears, followed by discontinuing purchasing of certain cleaners, and so on (as congruent for with the child's spectra of OCD). Notably, discontinuing accommodation may result in an increase in rage or externalizing symptoms (Storch, Jones, Lewin, Mutch, & Murphy, 2011), requiring specific intervention to address these problems (Lebowitz, Omer, & Leckman, 2011; Storch, Lewin, Geffken, Morgan, & Murphy, 2010). Additionally, characteristics of the caregiver (e.g., distress, OCD) may compromise their ability to disengage in their children's rituals (Futh, Simonds, & Micali, 2012; Geffken et al., 2006). If caregiver characteristics impede their ability to systematically decrease their involvement in rituals, individual therapy for the parent may be indicated.

Even beyond accommodation, family functioning is relevant to the impact and treatment of OCD. Family dysfunction (e.g., hostility, rejection, blame, coercion, discord) is commonplace among patients with OCD (Hibbs et al., 1991; Peris, Benazon, Langley, Roblek, & Piacentini, 2008; Peris, Bergman, et al., 2008) and can maintain and exacerbate the clinical presentation of OCD (Waters & Barrett, 2000). Distress is a mainstay among families of youth with OCD (Peris et al., 2012) with 20% of parents disclosing overtly hostile reactions to their child's OCD symptoms (Allsopp & Verduyn, 1990). Although some data suggest that comorbidity (e.g., attention-deficit/hyperactivity disorder) may account for problematic family dynamics among youth with OCD (Sukhodolsky et al., 2005), family pathology burdens youth with and without externalizing comorbidity.

Similar to family accommodation, family dysfunction is associated with diminished treatment outcomes (Amir et al., 2000), with notable changes to family functioning following ERP for adults (Diefenbach, Abramowitz, Norberg, & Tolin, 2007) and youth (Peris & Piacentini, 2013; Peris et al., 2012; Przeworski et al., 2012). Strikingly, Peris et al. (2012) reported that 10% of youth with marked family dysfunction (e.g., high blame and conflict) responded to CBT, whereas 93% of youth without these pathological family characteristics responded. These findings are not surprising given the impact of family dynamics on key treatment-related activities such as ERP (Lewin et al., 2005) as well as the overall burden that OCD places on the family system (Piacentini et al., 2003). Accordingly, to maximize the propensity for favorable outcome, family dysfunction should be targeted in the context of OCD treatment (Peris & Piacentini, 2013; Steketee & Van Noppen, 2003).

Despite a growing amount of data supporting higher effect sizes for ERP approaches that emphasize substantial parental participation, sampling increasing the extent of family participation may not mitigate the impact of family pathology on the treatment of OCD. Cases of severe family pathology may necessitate additional interventions before or in conjunction with evidence-based CBT. For family problems believed to be child-driven (e.g., marked oppositionality, anger, combativeness) parent-training based approaches may be sufficient for certain families. Notably, in other cases, family therapy targeting dynamics that may impede delivery of CBT to the child may be indicated. Pilot data suggest support for an intervention targeting family pathology incorporated within the CBT for OCD framework (Peris & Piacentini, 2013). Whereas the family can be a pivotal asset to overcoming

OCD-related impairment, coercive, toxic family environments can provide among the most significant barriers. Thoughtful, ongoing assessment of family dynamics is integral for any child with OCD.

INSIGHT

Insight is considered to play a pivotal role in the outcome of CBT with ERP. *Insight*, in the context of OCD, refers to recognition of the senselessness of one's obsessions and compulsions (Kozak & Foa, 1994). Insight into the irrationality of OCD symptoms is a diagnostic requirement for OCD in the fifth edition of the *Diagnostic and Statistical Manual of Mental Disorders* (*DSM*; American Psychiatric Association, 2013) for adults but not youth. However, experts have noted that it is not uncommon for patients to lack insight into the bizarre or excessive nature of their thoughts and behaviors (Carmin, Wiegartz, & Wu, 2008). Indeed, in the field trial of the fourth edition of the *DSM*, nearly 25% of patients meeting criteria for OCD also presented with poor insight (Foa et al., 1995). Preliminary estimates have identified 15% to 36% of adults (Alonso et al., 2008; Türksoy, Tukel, Ozdemir, & Karali, 2002) and 45% of youth (Storch, Milsom, et al., 2008) as presenting with poor insight. Poor insight occurs on a continuum. On the milder side, patients may report transient doubt into the illogicality of their symptoms. Toward the extremely low end of insight are schizotypal features (Alonso et al., 2008; Bellino, Patria, Ziero, & Bogetto, 2005; Matsunaga et al., 2002; Poyurovsky et al., 2008) or even psychotic-like presentations that may mimic OCD (Insel & Akiskal, 1986; Raveendranathan et al., 2012; Rodowski, Cagande, & Riddle, 2008). Even experts in OCD struggle to differentiate OCD symptoms from frank delusions and other phenomenology of schizophrenia (including catatonia) in these extreme cases. The degree to which a person with OCD possesses insight into the irrationality of his or her obsessions and compulsions has been linked to both the severity of OCD presentation and response to intervention (Bellino et al., 2005; Catapano et al., 2010; Lewin, Bergman, et al., 2010; Storch, Milsom, et al., 2008; Vogel, Hansen, Stiles, & Gotestam, 2006). Overall, regardless of age, individuals who fail to recognize the irrationality of their obsessions and compulsions are less able to challenge them and consequently have a worse prognosis (O'Dwyer & Marks, 2000).

Among adults with OCD, poor insight has been associated with increased OCD symptom severity (Bellino et al., 2005; Catapano, Sperandeo, Perris, Lanzaro, & Maj, 2001; Jakubovski et al., 2011; Ravi Kishore, Samar, Janardhan Reddy, Chandrasekhar, & Thennarasu, 2004) and psychiatric comorbidity (Bellino et al., 2005; Ravi Kishore et al., 2004), longer duration of illness and earlier onset of symptoms (Ravi Kishore et al., 2004), as well as a more chronic course and increased family history of OCD (Bellino et al., 2005). Decreased willingness to resist obsessive and compulsive symptoms (Alonso et al., 2008; Turksoy et al., 2002) was also reported among adults with poor insight. Among adults with OCD, poor insight has been connected to diminished response to both CBT (Foa, Abramowitz, Franklin, & Kozak, 1999) and pharmacotherapy (Ravi Kishore et al., 2004; Shetti et al., 2005).

Similarly, findings in youth suggest an inverse relationship between insight and OCD severity (Storch, Milsom, et al., 2008). In addition, studies have identified a link between lower insight and higher family accommodation (Storch, Milsom, et al., 2008) and increased impairment (Storch, Larson, et al., 2010). Although one study reported decreased insight among younger children (Lewin, Bergman, et al., 2010), the majority of findings suggest poor insight occurs across the lifespan (Phillips et al., 2012). Findings in both youth and adults (Alonso et al., 2008) have linked poor insight with depressive symptoms. Depressive pathology (e.g., hopelessness, anhedonia, limited motivation, diminished locus of control), combined with data suggesting that youth with poor insight experience decreased perception of control over their environments, bode poorly for ERP (Lewin, Caporino, Murphy, Geffken, & Storch, 2010; Storch, Merlo, et al., 2008, 2010a)—an intervention that requires active participation in anxiety-provoking (and often aversive) exercises. In fact, youth with low insight enrolled in the multimodal Pediatric Obsessive–Compulsive Treatment Study (2004) demonstrated a lower response across treatment conditions (CBT, sertraline, and CBT + sertraline; Garcia et al., 2010).

Unfortunately, most studies thus far have assessed insight at a single time point, preventing a strong understanding for how insight may change with intervention or development. Notably, in a sample of 132 adults, Alonso et al. (2008) reported that insight regarding OCD symptoms "constitutes a dynamic phenomenon" (p. 305) that improves with a pharmacotherapy intervention (with fluoxetine, fluvoxamine, or clomipramine). Given that depressive symptoms were prominent among individuals with OCD and poor insight in this sample, it is possible that that the change in insight reflected amelioration of mood symptoms.

Drawing from the schizophrenia literature, training focused on increasing insight can be incorporated into CBT, resulting in improved outcomes and treatment adherence (Rathod, Kingdon, Smith, & Turkington, 2005). Although changes in insight with CBT are yet to be systematically investigated in OCD, findings thus far offer guidance for adapting behavioral treatment. Youth with poor insight into the senselessness of their OCD symptoms may be less able to engage in cognitive therapy: for example, challenging irrational thoughts (O'Dwyer & Marks, 2000; Storch, Milsom, et al., 2008) or incorporating new information that is inconsistent with current schemata (Foa, Abramowitz, Franklin, & Kozak, 1999; Tolin, Abramowitz, Kozak, & Foa, 2001). Thus, emphasis on behavioral aspects of CBT (i.e., ERP) instead of cognitive treatments appears indicated.

CONCLUSION

Despite promising treatments for pediatric OCD, a sizable number of youth fail to respond. Combined with limited access to trained CBT providers, relatively poor dissemination of evidence-based psychotherapy, and direct and indirect patient costs, refinements are necessary. Fortunately, research has identified a number of relatively consistent factors to be associated with treatment outcome. As medical technology accelerates, there is every reason to believe that experts will identify biomarkers associated with OCD risk and perhaps responses to specific treatments. Fortunately, the tractable impediments to OCD treatment discussed in this chapter are not constrained by the state of biomedical imagining, genetics, and other factors. On the contrary, thoughtful assessment and often subtle modifications to CBT protocols offer the potential for cost-effective, personalized enhancements to evidence-based treatment.

REFERENCES

Allsopp, M., & Verduyn, C. (1990). Adolescents with obsessive–compulsive disorder: A case note review of consecutive patients referred to a provincial regional adolescent psychiatry unit. *Journal of Adolescence, 13,* 157–169. doi:10.1016/0140-1971(90)90005-R

Alonso, P., Menchon, J. M., Segalas, C., Jaurrieta, N., Jimenez-Murcia, S., Cardoner, N., . . . Vallejo, J. (2008). Clinical implications of insight assessment in obsessive–compulsive disorder. *Comprehensive Psychiatry, 49,* 305–312. doi:10.1016/j.comppsych.2007.09.005

American Academy of Child and Adolescent Psychiatry. (2012). Practice parameter for the assessment and treatment of children and adolescents with obsessive–compulsive disorder. *Journal of the American Academy of Child & Adolescent Psychiatry, 51,* 98–113. doi:10.1016/j.jaac.2011.09.019

American Psychiatric Association. (2013). *Diagnostic and statistical manual of mental disorders* (5th ed.). Washington, DC: Author.

Amir, N., Freshman, M., & Foa, E. B. (2000). Family distress and involvement in relatives of obsessive–compulsive disorder patients. *Journal of Anxiety Disorders, 14,* 209–217. doi:10.1016/S0887-6185(99)00032-8

Barrett, P., Healy-Farrell, L., & March, J. S. (2004). Cognitive-behavioral family treatment of childhood obsessive–compulsive disorder: A controlled trial. *Journal of the American Academy of Child & Adolescent Psychiatry, 43*, 46–62. doi:10.1097/00004583-200401000-00014

Bellino, S., Patria, L., Ziero, S., & Bogetto, F. (2005). Clinical picture of obsessive–compulsive disorder with poor insight: A regression model. *Psychiatry Research, 136*, 223–231. doi:10.1016/j.psychres.2004.04.015

Calvocoressi, L., Lewis, B., Harris, M., Trufan, S. J., Goodman, W. K., McDougle, C. J., & Price, L. H. (1995). Family accommodation in obsessive–compulsive disorder. *The American Journal of Psychiatry, 152*, 441–443.

Calvocoressi, L., Mazure, C. M., Kasl, S. V., Skolnick, J., Fisk, D., Vegso, S. J., . . . Price, L. H. (1999). Family accommodation of obsessive–compulsive symptoms: Instrument development and assessment of family behavior. *Journal of Nervous and Mental Disease, 187*, 636–642. doi:10.1097/00005053-199910000-00008

Carmin, C., Wiegartz, P. S., & Wu, K. (2008). Obsessive-compulsive disorder with poor insight. In J. S. Abramowitz, D. McKay, & S. Taylor (Eds.), *Clinical handbook of obsessive–compulsive disorder and related problems* (pp. 109–125). Baltimore, MD: Johns Hopkins University Press.

Catapano, F., Perris, F., Fabrazzo, M., Cioffi, V., Giacco, D., De Santis, V., & Maj, M. (2010). Obsessive–compulsive disorder with poor insight: A three-year prospective study. *Progress in Neuro-Psychopharmacology & Biological Psychiatry, 34*, 323–330. doi:10.1016/j.pnpbp.2009.12.007

Catapano, F., Sperandeo, R., Perris, F., Lanzaro, M., & Maj, M. (2001). Insight and resistance in patients with obsessive–compulsive disorder. *Psychopathology, 34*, 62–68. doi:10.1159/000049282

Di Blasi, Z., Harkness, E., Ernst, E., Georgiou, A., & Kleijnen, J. (2001). Influence of context effects on health outcomes: A systematic review. *The Lancet, 357*, 757–762. doi:10.1016/S0140-6736(00)04169-6

Diefenbach, G. J., Abramowitz, J. S., Norberg, M. M., & Tolin, D. F. (2007). Changes in quality of life following cognitive-behavioral therapy for obsessive–compulsive disorder. *Behaviour Research and Therapy, 45*, 3060–3068. doi:10.1016/j.brat.2007.04.014

Douglass, H. M., Moffitt, T. E., Dar, R., McGee, R., & Silva, P. (1995). Obsessive–compulsive disorder in a birth cohort of 18-year-olds: Prevalence and predictors. *Journal of the American Academy of Child and Adolescent Psychiatry, 34*, 1424–1431.

Ferrão, Y. A., Shavitt, R. G., Bedin, N. R., de Mathis, M. E., Carlos, L. A., Fontenelle, L. F., . . . Miguel, E. C. (2006). Clinical features associated to refractory obsessive–compulsive disorder. *Journal of Affective Disorders, 94*, 199–209. doi:10.1016/j.jad.2006.04.019

Flessner, C. A., Freeman, J. B., Sapyta, J., Garcia, A., Franklin, M. E., March, J. S., & Foa, E. (2011). Predictors of parental accommodation in pediatric obsessive–compulsive disorder: Findings from the Pediatric Obsessive–Compulsive Disorder

Treatment Study (POTS) trial. *Journal of the American Academy of Child & Adolescent Psychiatry, 50,* 716–725. doi:10.1016/j.jaac.2011.03.019

Foa, E. B., Abramowitz, J. S., Franklin, M. E., & Kozak, M. J. (1999). Feared consequences, fixity of belief, and treatment outcome in patients with obsessive–compulsive disorder. *Behavior Therapy, 30,* 717–724. doi:10.1016/S0005-7894(99)80035-5

Foa, E. B., Kozak, M. J., Goodman, W. K., Hollander, E., Jenike, M. A., & Rasmussen, S. A. (1995). DSM–IV field trial: Obsessive–compulsive disorder. *The American Journal of Psychiatry, 152,* 90–96.

Futh, A., Simonds, L. M., & Micali, N. (2012). Obsessive–compulsive disorder in children and adolescents: Parental understanding, accommodation, coping and distress. *Journal of Anxiety Disorders, 26,* 624–632. doi:10.1016/j.janxdis.2012.02.012

Garcia, A. M., Sapyta, J. J., Moore, P. S., Freeman, J. B., Franklin, M. E., March, J. S., & Foa, E. B. (2010). Predictors and moderators of treatment outcome in the Pediatric Obsessive–Compulsive Treatment Study (POTS I). *Journal of the American Academy of Child & Adolescent Psychiatry, 49,* 1024–1033, quiz 1086. doi:10.1016/j.jaac.2010.06.013

Geffken, G. R., Storch, E. A., Duke, D. C., Monaco, L., Lewin, A. B., & Goodman, W. K. (2006). Hope and coping in family members of patients with obsessive–compulsive disorder. *Journal of Anxiety Disorders, 20,* 614–629. doi:10.1016/j.janxdis.2005.07.001

Greenberg, R. P., Constantino, M. J., & Bruce, N. (2006). Are patient expectations still relevant for psychotherapy process and outcome? *Clinical Psychology Review, 26,* 657–678. doi:10.1016/j.cpr.2005.03.002

Hibbs, E. D., Hamburger, S. D., Lenane, M., Rapoport, J. L., Kruesi, M. J., Keysor, C. S., & Goldstein, M. J. (1991). Determinants of expressed emotion in families of disturbed and normal children. *Journal of Child Psychology and Psychiatry, 32,* 757–770. doi:10.1111/j.1469-7610.1991.tb01900.x

Insel, T. R., & Akiskal, H. S. (1986). Obsessive–compulsive disorder with psychotic features: A phenomenologic analysis. *The American Journal of Psychiatry, 143,* 1527–1533.

Jakubovski, E., Pittenger, C., Torres, A. R., Fontenelle, L. F., do Rosario, M. C., Ferrao, Y. A., . . . Bloch, M. H. (2011). Dimensional correlates of poor insight in obsessive–compulsive disorder. *Progress in Neuro-Psychopharmacology & Biological Psychiatry, 35,* 1677–1681. doi:10.1016/j.pnpbp.2011.05.012

Kozak, M. J., & Foa, E. B. (1994). Obsessions, overvalued ideas, and delusions in obsessive–compulsive disorder. *Behaviour Research and Therapy, 32,* 343–353. doi:10.1016/0005-7967(94)90132-5

Lebowitz, E. R., Omer, H., & Leckman, J. F. (2011). Coercive and disruptive behaviors in pediatric obsessive–compulsive disorder. *Depression and Anxiety, 28,* 899–905. doi:10.1002/da.20858

Lebowitz, E. R., Panza, K. E., Su, J., & Bloch, M. H. (2012). Family accommodation in obsessive–compulsive disorder. *Expert Review in Neurotherapeutics, 12,* 229–238. doi:10.1586/ern.11.200

Lewin, A. B. (2011). Parent Training for Childhood Anxiety. In D. McKay & E. A. Storch (Eds.), *Handbook of child and adolescent anxiety disorders* (pp. 405–417). New York, NY: Springer. doi:10.1007/978-1-4419-7784-7_27

Lewin, A. B., Bergman, R. L., Peris, T. S., Chang, S., McCracken, J. T., & Piacentini, J. (2010). Correlates of insight among youth with obsessive–compulsive disorder. *Journal of Child Psychology and Psychiatry, 51*, 603–611. doi:10.1111/j.1469-7610.2009.02181.x

Lewin, A. B., Caporino, N., Murphy, T. K., Geffken, G. R., & Storch, E. A. (2010b). Understudied clinical dimensions in pediatric obsessive–compulsive disorder. *Child Psychiatry and Human Development, 41*, 675–691. doi:10.1007/s10578-010-0196-z

Lewin, A. B., Peris, T. S., De Nadai, A. S., McCracken, J. T., & Piacentini, J. (2012). Agreement between therapists, parents, patients, and independent evaluators on clinical improvement in pediatric obsessive–compulsive disorder. *Journal of Consulting and Clinical Psychology, 80*, 1103–1107. doi:10.1037/a0029991

Lewin, A. B., Peris, T. S., Lindsey Bergman, R., McCracken, J. T., & Piacentini, J. (2011). The role of treatment expectancy in youth receiving exposure-based CBT for obsessive compulsive disorder. *Behaviour Research and Therapy, 49*, 536–543. doi:10.1016/j.brat.2011.06.001

Lewin, A. B., & Piacentini, J. (2010). Evidence-based assessment of child obsessive compulsive disorder: Recommendations for clinical practice and treatment research. *Child & Youth Care Forum, 39*, 73–89. doi:10.1007/s10566-009-9092-8

Lewin, A. B., Storch, E. A., Merlo, L. J., Adkins, J. W., Murphy, T. K., & Geffken, G. R. (2005). Intensive cognitive behavioral therapy for pediatric obsessive compulsive disorder: A treatment protocol for mental health providers. *Psychological Services, 2*, 91–104. doi:10.1037/1541-1559.2.2.91

March, J. S., & Mulle, K. (1998). *OCD in children and adolescents: A cognitive-behavioral treatment manual.* New York, NY: Guilford Press.

Matsunaga, H., Kiriike, N., Matsui, T., Oya, K., Iwasaki, Y., Koshimune, K., . . . Stein, D. J. (2002). Obsessive–compulsive disorder with poor insight. *Comprehensive Psychiatry, 43*, 150–157. doi:10.1053/comp.2002.30798

Merlo, L. J., Lehmkuhl, H. D., Geffken, G. R., & Storch, E. A. (2009). Decreased family accommodation associated with improved therapy outcome in pediatric obsessive–compulsive disorder. *Journal of Consulting and Clinical Psychology, 77*, 355–360. doi:10.1037/a0012652

O'Dwyer, A. M., & Marks, I. (2000). Obsessive–compulsive disorder and delusions revisited. *The British Journal of Psychiatry, 176*, 281–284. doi:10.1192/bjp.176.3.281

Pediatric OCD Treatment Study. (2004). Cognitive-behavior therapy, sertraline, and their combination for children and adolescents with obsessive–compulsive disorder: The Pediatric OCD Treatment Study (POTS) randomized controlled trial. *JAMA, 292*, 1969–1976. doi:10.1001/jama.292.16.1969

Peris, T. S., Benazon, N., Langley, A., Roblek, T., & Piacentini, J. (2008). Parental attitudes, beliefs, and responses to childhood obsessive compulsive disorder: The Parental Attitudes and Behaviors Scale. *Child & Family Behavior Therapy, 30*, 199–214. doi:10.1080/07317100802275447

Peris, T. S., Bergman, R. L., Asarnow, J. R., Langley, A., McCracken, J. T., & Piacentini, J. (2010). Clinical and cognitive correlates of depressive symptoms among youth with obsessive compulsive disorder. *Journal of Clinical Child & Adolescent Psychology, 39*, 616–626. doi:10.1080/15374416.2010.501285

Peris, T. S., Bergman, R. L., Langley, A., Chang, S., McCracken, J. T., & Piacentini, J. (2008). Correlates of accommodation of pediatric obsessive–compulsive disorder: Parent, child, and family characteristics. *Journal of the American Academy of Child & Adolescent Psychiatry, 47*, 1173. doi:10.1097/CHI.0b013e3181825a91

Peris, T. S., & Piacentini, J. (2013). Optimizing treatment for complex cases of childhood obsessive compulsive disorder: A preliminary trial. *Journal of Clinical Child and Adolescent Psychology, 42*, 1–8.

Peris, T. S., Sugar, C. A., Bergman, R. L., Chang, S., Langley, A., & Piacentini, J. (2012). Family factors predict treatment outcome for pediatric obsessive–compulsive disorder. *Journal of Consulting and Clinical Psychology, 80*, 255–263. doi:10.1037/a0027084

Phillips, K. A., Pinto, A., Hart, A. S., Coles, M. E., Eisen, J. L., Menard, W., & Rasmussen, S. A. (2012). A comparison of insight in body dysmorphic disorder and obsessive–compulsive disorder. *Journal of Psychiatric Research, 46*, 1293–1299. doi:10.1016/j.jpsychires.2012.05.016

Piacentini, J., Bergman, R. L., Chang, S., Langley, A., Peris, T., Wood, J. J., & McCracken, J. (2011). Controlled comparison of family cognitive behavioral therapy and psychoeducation/relaxation training for child obsessive–compulsive disorder. *Journal of the American Academy of Child & Adolescent Psychiatry, 50*, 1149–1161. doi:10.1016/j.jaac.2011.08.003

Piacentini, J., Bergman, R. L., Keller, M., & McCracken, J. (2003). Functional impairment in children and adolescents with obsessive–compulsive disorder. *Journal of Child and Adolescent Psychopharmacology, 13*(Suppl. 1), S61–S69. doi:10.1089/104454603322126359

Piacentini, J., Langley, A., & Roblek, T. (2007a). *It's only a false alarm*. New York, NY: Oxford University Press.

Piacentini, J., Langley, A., & Roblek, T. (2007b). *Overcoming childhood OCD: A therapist's guide*. New York NY: Oxford University Press.

Piacentini, J. C., March, J. S., & Franklin, M. E. (2006). Cognitive-behavioral therapy for youth with obsessive–compulsive disorder. In P. C. Kendall (Ed.), *Child and adolescent therapy: Cognitive-behavioral procedures* (Vol. 3, pp. 297–321). New York, NY: Guilford Press.

Poyurovsky, M., Faragian, S., Pashinian, A., Heidrach, L., Fuchs, C., Weizman, R., & Koran, L. (2008). Clinical characteristics of schizotypal-related obsessive–compulsive disorder. *Psychiatry Research, 159*, 254–258. doi:10.1016/j.psychres.2007.02.019

Przeworski, A., Zoellner, L. A., Franklin, M. E., Garcia, A., Freeman, J., March, J. S., & Foa, E. B. (2012). Maternal and child expressed emotion as predictors of treatment response in pediatric obsessive–compulsive disorder. *Child Psychiatry and Human Development, 43*, 337–353. doi:10.1007/s10578-011-0268-8

Rathod, S., Kingdon, D., Smith, P., & Turkington, D. (2005). Insight into schizophrenia: The effects of cognitive behavioural therapy on the components of insight and association with sociodemographics—data on a previously published randomised controlled trial. *Schizophrenia Research, 74*, 211–219. doi:10.1016/j.schres.2004.07.003

Raveendranathan, D., Shiva, L., Sharma, E., Venkatasubramanian, G., Rao, M. G., Varambally, S., & Gangadhar, B. N. (2012). Obsessive compulsive disorder masquerading as psychosis. *Indian Journal of Psychological Medicine, 34*, 179–180. doi:10.4103/0253-7176.101800

Ravi Kishore, V., Samar, R., Janardhan Reddy, Y. C., Chandrasekhar, C. R., & Thennarasu, K. (2004). Clinical characteristics and treatment response in poor and good insight obsessive–compulsive disorder. *European Psychiatry, 19*, 202–208. doi:10.1016/j.eurpsy.2003.12.005

Rodowski, M. F., Cagande, C. C., & Riddle, M. A. (2008). Childhood obsessive–compulsive disorder presenting as schizophrenia spectrum disorders. *Journal of Child and Adolescent Psychopharmacology, 18*, 395–401. doi:10.1089/cap.2007.0027

Shafran, R., Ralph, J., & Tallis, F. (1995). Obsessive–compulsive symptoms and the family. *Bulletin of the Menninger Clinic, 59*, 472–479.

Shetti, C. N., Reddy, Y. C., Kandavel, T., Kashyap, K., Singisetti, S., Hiremath, A. S., . . . Raghunandanan, S. (2005). Clinical predictors of drug nonresponse in obsessive–compulsive disorder. *Journal of Clinical Psychiatry, 66*, 1517–1523. doi:10.4088/JCP.v66n1204

Simpson, H. B., Maher, M. J., Wang, Y., Bao, Y., Foa, E. B., & Franklin, M. (2011). Patient adherence predicts outcome from cognitive behavioral therapy in obsessive–compulsive disorder. *Journal of Consulting and Clinical Psychology, 79*, 247–252. doi:10.1037/a0022659

Steketee, G., & Van Noppen, B. (2003). Family approaches to treatment for obsessive compulsive disorder. *Revista Brasileira de Psiquiatria, 25*, 43–50. doi:10.1590/S1516-44462003000100009

Stewart, S. E., Geller, D. A., Jenike, M., Pauls, D., Shaw, D., Mullin, B., et al. (2004). Long-term outcome of pediatric obsessive–compulsive disorder: A meta-analysis and qualitative review of the literature. *Acta Psychiatrica Scandinavica, 110*, 4–13.

Storch, E. A., Bjorgvinsson, T., Riemann, B., Lewin, A. B., Morales, M. J., & Murphy, T. K. (2010). Factors associated with poor response in cognitive-behavioral therapy for pediatric obsessive–compulsive disorder. *Bulletin of the Menninger Clinic, 74*, 167–185. doi:10.1521/bumc.2010.74.2.167

Storch, E. A., Geffken, G. R., Merlo, L. J., Jacob, M. L., Murphy, T. K., Goodman, W. K., . . . Grabill, K. (2007). Family accommodation in pediatric obsessive–compulsive disorder. *Journal of Clinical Child & Adolescent Psychology, 36*, 207–216. doi:10.1080/15374410701277929

Storch, E. A., Geffken, G. R., Merlo, L. J., Mann, G., Duke, D., Munson, M., . . . Goodman, W. K. (2007). Family-based cognitive-behavioral therapy for pediatric obsessive–compulsive disorder: Comparison of intensive and weekly approaches. *Journal of the American Academy of Child and Adolescent Psychiatry, 46*, 469–478. doi:10.1097/chi.0b013e31803062e7

Storch, E. A., Jones, A., Lewin, A. B., Mutch, P. J., & Murphy, T. K. (2011). Clinical phenomenology of episodic rage in pediatric obsessive–compulsive disorder. *Minerva Psichiatrica, 52*, 89–95.

Storch, E. A., Larson, M. J., Muroff, J., Caporino, N., Geller, D., Reid, J. M., . . . Murphy, T. K. (2010). Predictors of functional impairment in pediatric obsessive–compulsive disorder. *Journal of Anxiety Disorders, 24*, 275–283. doi:10.1016/j.janxdis.2009.12.004

Storch, E. A., Lewin, A. B., Geffken, G. R., Morgan, J. R., & Murphy, T. K. (2010). The role of comorbid disruptive behavior in the clinical expression of pediatric obsessive–compulsive disorder. *Behaviour Research and Therapy, 48*, 1204–1210. doi:10.1016/j.brat.2010.09.004

Storch, E. A., Lewin, A. B., Larson, M. J., Geffken, G. R., Murphy, T. K., & Geller, D. A. (2012). Depression in youth with obsessive–compulsive disorder: Clinical phenomenology and correlates. *Psychiatry Research, 196*, 83–89. doi:10.1016/j.psychres.2011.10.013

Storch, E. A., Merlo, L. J., Larson, M. J., Marien, W. E., Geffken, G. R., Jacob, M. L., . . . Murphy, T. K. (2008a). Clinical features associated with treatment-resistant pediatric obsessive–compulsive disorder. *Comprehensive Psychiatry, 49*, 35–42. doi:10.1016/j.comppsych.2007.06.009

Storch, E. A., Milsom, V. A., Merlo, L. J., Larson, M., Geffken, G. R., Jacob, M. L., . . . Goodman, W. K. (2008b). Insight in pediatric obsessive–compulsive disorder: Associations with clinical presentation. *Psychiatry Research, 160*, 212–220. doi:10.1016/j.psychres.2007.07.005

Sukhodolsky, D. G., do Rosario-Campos, M. C., Scahill, L., Katsovich, L., Pauls, D. L., Peterson, B. S., . . . Leckman, J. F. (2005). Adaptive, emotional, and family functioning of children with obsessive–compulsive disorder and comorbid attention deficit hyperactivity disorder. *The American Journal of Psychiatry, 162*, 1125–1132. doi:10.1176/appi.ajp.162.6.1125

Tolin, D. F., Abramowitz, J. S., Kozak, M. J., & Foa, E. B. (2001). Fixity of belief, perceptual aberration, and magical ideation in obsessive–compulsive disorder. *Journal of Anxiety Disorders, 15*, 501–510.

Türksoy, N., Tukel, R., Ozdemir, O., & Karali, A. (2002). Comparison of clinical characteristics in good and poor insight obsessive–compulsive disorder. *Journal of Anxiety Disorders, 16*, 413–423. doi:10.1016/S0887-6185(02)00135-4

Vogel, P. A., Hansen, B., Stiles, T. C., & Gotestam, K. G. (2006). Treatment motivation, treatment expectancy, and helping alliance as predictors of outcome in cognitive behavioral treatment of OCD. *Journal of Behavior Therapy and Experimental Psychiatry, 37*, 247–255. doi:10.1016/j.jbtep.2005.12.001

Waters, T. L., & Barrett, P. M. (2000). The role of the family in childhood obsessive–compulsive disorder. *Clinical Child and Family Psychology Review, 3*, 173–184. doi:10.1023/A:1009551325629

World Health Organization. (1999). *The newly defined burden of mental problems* (Fact Sheet No. 217). Geneva, Switzerland: Author.

Zohar, A. H. (1999). The epidemiology of obsessive–compulsive disorder in children and adolescents. *Child and Adolescent Psychiatric Clinics of North America, 8*, 445–460.

5

TREATMENT OF OBSESSIVE–COMPULSIVE SPECTRUM DISORDERS IN LATE LIFE

CATHERINE AYERS AND SADIA NAJMI

Research on late life obsessive–compulsive (OC) spectrum disorders is modest. The little we do know about the characterization and treatment of these disorders in geriatric populations comes from the limited body of work in obsessive–compulsive disorder (OCD) and hoarding. This chapter provides an overview of the clinical characteristics, assessment considerations, and treatment of late life OCD and hoarding. The geriatric treatment accommodations and implications presented will likely generalize to other OC spectrum disorders.

OCD IN OLDER ADULTHOOD

Until the past few decades, OCD in late life was considered to be an uncommon occurrence. Although late-onset OCD is indeed rare (Rasmussen & Eisen, 1992), given the chronicity of the disorder, it tends to persist into

http://dx.doi.org/10.1037/14323-006
Obsessive–Compulsive Disorder and Its Spectrum: A Life-Span Approach, Eric A. Storch and Dean McKay (Editors)
Copyright © 2014 by the American Psychological Association. All rights reserved.

late life for a large proportion of OCD sufferers. Studies have found that OCD occurs in as many as 1.5% of adults over age 65 years (Blazer, George, & Hughes, 1991; Flint, 1994; Kolada, Bland, & Newman, 1994). Certain subtypes of OCD, such as contamination concerns, that are common in young adults are also common in elderly patients (e.g., Calamari, Faber, Hitsman, & Poppe, 1994; Kohn, Westlake, Rasmussen, Marsland, & Norman, 1997). However, other subtypes, such as fear of forgetting, especially names (Grant et al., 2007; Jenike, 1991), and fear of having sinned (Fallon et al., 1990; Kohn et al., 1997), appear to be more frequent among older adults with OCD, whereas concerns related to symmetry, counting, and need to know appear to occur less frequently in this age group (Kohn et al., 1997).

Late-Onset OCD

There is an important distinction between late- and early-onset OCD. Late-onset OCD appears to be fairly uncommon, although when it does occur, it is more frequent in elderly women (Nestadt, Bienvenu, Cai, Samuels, & Eaton, 1998). Case studies mostly indicate that late-onset OCD is associated with cerebral lesions (Weiss & Jenike, 2000), although there have been more recent reports of late onset with no cerebral abnormality (Bhattacharyya & Khanna, 2004). The reports indicating brain abnormalities implicate intracerebral lesions in the frontal, temporal, and cingulate cortices and basal ganglia—in particular, the caudate nuclei. Philpot and Banerjee (1998) argued that the cerebral lesions likely trigger a sudden onset of OCD symptoms but that elderly patients are unlikely to be completely asymptomatic before the onset. For instance, as Cottraux and Gerard (1998) suggested, dysregulation in serotonergic pathways involving the basal ganglia and orbital frontal cortex likely represents an underlying vulnerability to OCD in these patients.

Teachman (2007) suggested that another vulnerability to late-onset OCD is subjective concerns about a decline in cognitive functioning. In an investigation of concerns among elderly adults, more than 60% reported that they perceived their memory had declined with age, although this perception was not supported by objective changes in memory functioning (Jorm et al., 1994, 1997). Moreover, Sinoff and Werner (2003) found that perceived decline in cognitive functioning in the elderly, not surprisingly, predicted anxiety and negative affect. Calamari, Janeck, and Deer (2002) have suggested that this might lead to greater monitoring of thoughts, thereby increasing the salience of normal, unwanted intrusive thoughts, which in turn leads to effortful, albeit counterproductive, attempts to suppress the intrusive thoughts. Substantiating this suggestion, Teachman found, in a cross-sectional study with older adults, that the fear of declining cognitive functioning partially mediated the relationship between obsessive beliefs (i.e., beliefs about the importance of thoughts and about the need to control thoughts) and their OCD symptoms.

Assessment of Geriatric OCD

The fundamental principles underlying assessment of OCD are no different for elderly patients than they are for younger ones. As with any patient, the therapist needs to examine the context of the target behaviors to determine the presence of clinically significant obsessions and compulsions. That said, there are certain common associations with aging, and a consideration of these can assist therapists in assessing symptoms in elderly patients. Carmin, Pollard, and Ownby (1999) presented a detailed account of how clinical assessment may be honed for older adults. Their principal recommendation is that therapists work closely with the elderly patient's physician to gain a comprehensive depiction of the patient's diagnosis. In particular, therapists must pay close attention to conditions common in elderly people that result in symptoms similar to obsessions and compulsions. These include medical problems such as cerebrovascular events that tend to occur more frequently in the elderly and may produce OCD symptoms in otherwise healthy patients (Simpson & Baldwin, 1995).

Another diagnostic challenge that necessitates close collaboration with the elderly patient's physician is the presence of physical disability, which can often become a source of fear for the patient. As a result, the therapist must determine whether the fear is based in reality. For example, auditory or visual impairment are common in late life; a patient's repetitive request to have questions repeated to him could be the result of hearing loss, an attempt at compulsive reassurance seeking, or both. Similarly, repetitive checking behaviors might be a realistic response to a loss of visual acuity rather than a manifestation of OCD, just as cautious behaviors that accompany the use of medical aids may or may not be indicative of OCD. Carmin, Pollard, and Ownby (1999) illustrated this issue with the example of two patients, one who developed complex rituals for placing and aligning her inhalers and medication containers, and another who checked repeatedly to ensure his walking aid was in a position that felt "just right." The former was simply a manifestation of her existing OCD symptoms, whereas the latter was an adaptive precaution to prevent falling. In both cases, the onus is on the therapist to obtain the information necessary to assess the extent of danger in the situation and then to determine whether the cautious behavior is motivated by a realistic assessment of the threat. Once again, collaboration with the elderly patient's physician can assist with making that determination.

The extent to which physical impairment may interfere with the patient's ability to comprehend instructions may also have consequences for diagnosis. Carmin, Pollard, and Ownby (1999) described a patient undergoing chemotherapy who was advised by her oncologist to minimize exposure to sources of infection. There was a clear disconnect between what the physician had intended for her to do (e.g., to stay away from family members who were ill) and how she interpreted the advice (e.g., to carefully and repeatedly clean her hospital room with disinfectants). The nursing staff found her behavior excessive and requested assessment from an OCD therapist, who determined that what appeared to be ritualistic cleaning was simply the result of misinterpreting the physician's advice. In an example such as this one, a trial of response prevention helped determine that the patient had not been ritualizing.

Regardless of the age of the patient, the therapist must consider cultural norms when assessing the presence of obsessions. When working with elderly patients, for example, social taboos regarding sex or blasphemy may well interfere with an accurate assessment of obsessions. One way to encourage an open discussion during assessment is for the therapist to normalize the occurrence of unwanted, intrusive thoughts and to highlight that they differ from obsessions only in frequency and intensity of distress, not necessarily in content. Another strategy is to allow patients to be somewhat vague about the content of the obsession during the assessment phase, although with the expectation that more specific details will be required during the in vivo or imaginal exposure phase of treatment. Yet another possibility is to ask patients to write out the content of their obsessions rather than reporting them verbally.

A final challenge is the dearth of assessment materials that have been validated for evaluating OCD in elderly people (Carmin, Pollard, & Gillock, 1999; Hersen & van Hasselt, 1992). For instance, the Yale–Brown Obsessive Compulsive Scale (Goodman, Price, Rasmussen, & Mazure, 1989; Goodman, Price, Rasmussen, Mazure, Delgado, et al., 1989) is a clinician-rated measure used extensively in research and clinical practice, both to assess OCD symptom severity and to monitor improvements during treatment; however, its psychometric properties have not been evaluated with elderly OCD patients. Indeed, to our knowledge, the Brief Symptom Inventory (Derogatis & Spencer, 1982), a self-report questionnaire of OCD symptoms, is the only measure that has published norms for the elderly sample (Francis, Rajan, & Turner, 1990; Hale, Cochran, & Hedgepeth, 1984), and even these may not be generalizable to clinical patients with OCD because the samples were drawn from the community.

Treatment Literature on OCD

The efficacy of pharmacological treatments for OCD in late life has been assessed primarily using case studies (Austin, Zealberg, & Lydiard, 1991; Bajulaiye & Addonizio, 1992; Shader, Kennedy, & Greenblatt, 1987; Sheikh & Saltzman, 1995; Stoudemire & Moran, 1993). On the basis of the limited evidence available for pharmacological treatments for OCD in late life, serotonergic drugs appear to be somewhat effective in this group. Jenike (1991) suggested the use of the serotonergic drug fluoxetine and warned against the use of some serotonergic drugs used with young adults, such as clomipramine, because the side effects (e.g., constipation, memory problems) may be particularly pronounced in older adults. Carmin, Pollard, and Ownby (1999) also warned more generally about the possibilities of complication with pharmacological treatment in this age group because of the potential for age-related changes in response to the pharmacokinetic and pharmacodynamic properties of drugs. Moreover, given the higher likelihood of medical comorbidities, they cautioned against a greater potential for interaction with other medications (Markovitz, 1993; Stoudemire & Moran, 1993). Until these concerns are addressed in systematic research on the effectiveness of pharmacological interventions for OCD in older adults, nonpharmacological interventions appear to be the treatment of choice for late life OCD.

Regardless of age of onset of OCD, cognitive behavior therapy (CBT) in the form of exposure and response prevention (ERP) is the recommended first line of treatment for this disorder (March, Frances, Carpenter, & Kahn, 1997). Although a normal decline in cognitive functioning has the potential to affect the patient's ability to process a treatment that is facilitated verbally, and a normal decline in physical functioning has the potential to affect the patient's ability to engage actively in behavior therapy, there does exist some sparse evidence to suggest that CBT is effective with older adults with anxiety disorders (King & Barrowclough, 1991).

To our knowledge, no controlled studies have examined this question specifically for ERP with older adults. Instead, most of these are case studies (Bajulaiye & Addonizio, 1992; Calamari et al., 1994; Hirsh et al., 2006; Junginger & Ditto, 1984; Price & Salsman, 2010; Rowan, Holburn, Walker, & Siddique, 1984) or single-case designs (S. M. Turner, Hersen, Bellack, & Wells, 1979). In their study, Carmin, Pollard, and Ownby (1998) compared the effectiveness of intensive, inpatient ERP in a small group of older adult OCD patients with their younger counterparts, matched for sex and severity of OCD and depression. They found no meaningful difference in treatment outcome for the two groups, despite the fact that the older patients had been symptomatic for much longer than their younger counterparts. However, these findings need to be replicated in randomized controlled trials to test more systematically the effectiveness of existing treatments for older adults.

Course of Treatment for Geriatric OCD

In their research, Carmin and colleagues have focused primarily on suggestions for modifying CBT to better suit older adults (e.g., Carmin, Pollard,

& Ownby, 1999). A summary of their recommendations is presented here. It is important to highlight that the fundamental principles of ERP for older adults are the same as for young adults. Much in the way that ERP for a young patient must necessarily consider the physical, psychological, and social makeup of the specific individual, it must do the same for an older patient. That said, there are certain physical, psychological, and social issues that tend to occur more frequently in older adults, and it behooves the therapist to attend to these challenges when treating late life OCD. Common issues to consider in this age group are medical comorbidity, perceived or actual physical and cognitive limitations, cultural beliefs, and the influence of caretakers and family members (Carmin, Pollard, & Ownby, 1999).

As one would with patients of any age, the therapist must consider older adults' cultural context to understand therapy-interfering behaviors. For example, older adults are a product of a time when psychiatric problems where more stigmatizing than they are today. The notion that psychiatric problems, unlike nonpsychiatric medical problems, signify a weakness of character exists to some extent today but was considerably more prevalent some decades ago. It follows that for some older patients, the shame associated with acknowledgment and disclosure of these problems may be severe enough to deter them from seeking treatment. Indeed, only 10% of older adults with OCD seek treatment (Grenier, Préville, Boyer, O'Connor, & the Scientific Committee of the ESA Study, 2009). Carmin, Pollard, and Ownby (1999) suggested that instead of insisting on presenting the cognitive–behavioral conceptualization of patients' condition, the therapist may encourage their buy-in for ERP by framing their condition in terms of the medical model and then drawing analogies with behavioral interventions that are used routinely for common medical conditions such as diabetes or hypertension.

According to Carmin, Pollard, and Ownby (1999), treating OCD in older adults with physical or cognitive difficulties requires patience and flexibility. More specifically, therapists must be prepared for interruptions in therapy to accommodate complications in the older patient's health and to work harder to reduce the potential for negative consequences of these interruptions for treatment. For patients who are unable to attend a session due to an exacerbation of comorbid symptoms (e.g., being bedridden or hospitalized), home visits and therapy sessions over the phone are examples of how the therapist may need to increase effort to prevent disruption of treatment. Throughout treatment, the therapist must involve family members and other caregivers to promote ERP-consistent behaviors in the patient, but at times when therapist contact is disrupted due to comorbid physical illness, extra effort on the part of the therapist to address the role of these significant others becomes crucial.

Within ERP sessions, the therapist must consider the impact of limitations to physical health and stamina on the patient's ability to engage in extended exposure exercises. Carmin, Pollard, and Ownby (1999) presented an example of a patient with emphysema who had supplemental oxygen needs and was hence unable to participate in exposures that required much physical activity. As with any other patient, the treatment plan comprised exposure exercises, but for this patient they were graded to contain the anxiety response, which necessarily slows progress in treatment, which in turn can be disheartening for the patient. Carmin, Pollard, and Ownby (1999) recommended discussing this situation with the patient openly and closely monitoring the intensity of the exposure exercises to maintain a level that is neither discouraging nor physically overwhelming.

As mentioned earlier, the perception of decline of cognitive functioning in the elderly is not always supported by objective changes in cognitive functioning (Jorm et al., 1997). That said, there are changes in cognitive functions (e.g., memory functioning) that may in fact occur in old age (Lindesay, Briggs, & Murphy, 1989), and these have the potential to interfere with ERP unless the therapist makes adjustments to take them into account. For example, if a patient is unable to remember the guidelines for response prevention, treatment effectiveness may indeed be jeopardized (Carmin, Pollard, & Ownby, 1999). Therapists can preempt this by providing written guidelines for response prevention and written reminders of where the patient is in his or her exposure hierarchy. Moreover, the therapist can enlist the help of caregivers to place the written guidelines and reminders where the patient is likely to see them. Finally, as with any patient, family and caregivers can be good resources for reminding patients to do the ERP homework.

As with assessment, visual or auditory impairment can interfere with treatment, in particular, by undermining the effectiveness of exposures. For instance, for a patient with contamination concerns, an exposure exercise high on the patient's exposure hierarchy might entail coming into contact with a dirty toilet; however, if the patient is unable to see clearly the amount of dirt on the toilet, he will likely not activate the fear structure to the intended extent. Thus, at the outset of treatment, the therapist must have an open discussion with the patient about the potential impact of sensory deficits on his treatment so that the patient might correct the impairment if possible. If it is not possible, the therapist must adapt exposure exercises to maximize processing of the fear, given the constraints of the patient's sensory functioning. For example, for a patient with visual impairment, Carmin, Pollard, and Ownby (1999) suggested the use of audiotaped scripts for imaginal exposure instead of written scripts, or vice versa for a patient with auditory impairment. Critical to all these accommodations is an assessment of the extent of sensory impairment, and the onus is on the therapist to coordinate care with the patient's physician to determine this before engaging in ERP.

Including families in treatment of OCD is valuable regardless of the age of the patient. For one thing, it is helpful in correcting misinformation families may have about the diagnosis and treatment of OCD, which is often depicted inaccurately or sensationalized in the media. For young and old patients alike, reactions from family can range from high expressed emotion (in particular, high criticism and overinvolvement; Shanmugiah, Varghese, & Khanna, 2002) to an overprotective accommodation of the patient's rituals, both of which are detrimental to treatment outcome. There are, however, some family issues that are specific to older adults, for instance, the adjustment for the patient's adult children as they take on the parental role with their aging parents. In such cases, the therapist must be mindful of issues of confidentiality. The logic of including private caregivers or nursing home staff in the treatment of OCD is the same as for including family, and similar issues of confidentiality must be taken into consideration.

Finally life stressors may exacerbate OCD symptoms in any age group. To address this, general stress management and problem-solving skills are part of most ERP protocols, often during the discussion on relapse prevention. This is no different for treatment of late-life OCD. That said, there are some stressful life events that tend to occur more often in the lives of the elderly, and it is important for the therapist, early in treatment, to be vigilant for the impact of these stressors on OCD symptoms. Examples include the experience of a fall or a fear of falling, the onset of a medical problem, the death of a spouse, or the move to a nursing home. According to Wisocki's (1994) research, older adults commonly experience fears of losing mobility and of becoming dependent or a burden on others. As with treatment of OCD in any age group, anxiety from other sources may interfere with ERP and hence must be considered to prevent an exacerbation of OCD symptoms.

Summary of Geriatric OCD

Assessment and treatment of OCD in late life are fundamentally no different from assessment and treatment of younger adults. However, certain challenges tend to occur more frequently in older adults and must be taken into account. For instance, the presence of medical comorbidities and the presence or perception of physical and cognitive impairments associated with aging can pose a diagnostic challenge that necessitates consultation with the treating physician. Additionally, most of the measures used to assess OCD have not been validated in older adults, calling into question their utility with this age group. The sparse research on treatment outcome in this age group presents preliminary data to suggest that ERP is the treatment of choice for older patients, as it is for young adults with OCD. However, as outlined by Carmin, Pollard, and Ownby (1999), during treatment, adjustments are often needed to address the physical, psychological, and social challenges that occur commonly in late life.

HOARDING IN OLDER ADULTHOOD

Evidence suggests that hoarding disorder in older adulthood is a debilitating, chronic, and progressive condition that has significant health implications (e.g., Ayers, Saxena, Golshan, & Wetherell, 2010; Kim, Steketee, & Frost, 2001). Clinically significant hoarding is defined by difficulty discarding or parting with possessions (regardless of value) due to strong urges to keep items (Frost & Gross, 1993). These urges to save items result in a large volume of clutter that impairs the use of living spaces. In some cases, individuals excessively acquire more items than they need. Clinically significant hoarding is not uncommon in nongeriatric populations, with estimates at approximately 5.3% (Samuels et al., 2008). Prevalence in community geriatric populations may be as much as 3 times greater than in younger adults. In older adult medical samples, the prevalence rates may be higher. Marx and Cohen-Mansfield (2003) found that 25% of elderly day-care participants and 15% of nursing home residents report clinically significant symptoms of hoarding. Given age-related physical and cognitive changes, hoarding is particularly dangerous in late life due to increased risk of falls, fire hazard, nutritional deprivation, social isolation, and health and medication mismanagement (e.g., Ayers et al., 2010; Dong, Simon, Mosqueda, & Evans, 2012; Kim et al., 2001).

Onset and Course of Geriatric Hoarding

There is consistent and compelling evidence that hoarding symptoms initially appear in childhood or adolescence (Ayers et al., 2010; Grisham et al., 2006; Tolin, Meunier, Frost, & Steketee, 2010). The clinical course of hoarding is likely progressive, with severe levels of hoarding starting in the mid-20s and mid-30s (Ayers et al., 2010; Grisham et al., 2006). Hoarding symptoms are more severe in older than in younger adults (Reid et al., 2011). In a retrospective analysis, older adults reported increasing hoarding severity with each decade of life, with no reports of late-onset hoarding (Ayers et al., 2010). However, there are reports of late-onset hoarding symptoms, particularly in dementia or schizophrenia samples (e.g., Hwang, Tsai, Yang, Liu, & Lirng, 1998; Poyurovsky, Bergman, & Weizman, 2006; Rabinowitz, et al., 2005). An important note is that available investigations in elderly dementia or schizophrenia samples did not use established hoarding assessments. Thus, it is unclear whether observed hoarding behaviors were due to true urges to save and distress from discarding.

Assessment of Geriatric Hoarding

Older adults are unlikely to have received previous assessment or treatment for hoarding (Ayers et al., 2010). The initial assessment session may mark the first time they have revealed information about their symptoms to a professional. The patient may fear that the clinician will report them to authorizes or respond negatively as family or friends have done over the years. Thus, patients present as hesitant, distrustful, or embarrassed at the initial interview.

A clinical assessment of late-life hoarding should consist of a clinical interview, home visit, family or caregiver reports, neurocognitive screening, and self-report instruments. The clinical interview is roughly the same as one would conduct with a midlife hoarding patient with a few exceptions. Typical domains assessed are hoarding symptom severity, acquisition behaviors, impairment domains, available resources, and safety (Steketee & Frost, 2007). A geriatric assessment should also focus on health status, sanitation problems, cognitive dysfunction, and falls given specific reports of problems in these areas (e.g., Dong et al., 2012; Steketee et al., 2012). It is also necessary to explore the reasons for saving, which in geriatric groups are typically related to use or need, avoiding waste, and sentimental value (Steketee et al., 2012). Available caregivers, friends, and family can provide useful historical information. It should be noted that family members tend to view the hoarding problem as more significant than the identified patient (Steketee et al., 2012). Other agencies such as Adult Protective Services may be involved, and thus it is important to query about all the key players in the case because many public safety and ethical dilemmas may arise in geriatric cases (Koenig, Chapin, & Spano, 2010).

Additional assessment should be given in the form of self-report and clinician-administered measures to pinpoint hoarding severity. Although none of the following hoarding symptom measures have been specifically normed for use with older adults, they still provide useful information. The Hoarding Rating Scale (Tolin, Frost, & Steketee, 2010), a five-item questionnaire, is a quick and relatively easy screening tool for hoarding symptoms. The Savings Inventory—Revised (Frost, Steketee, & Grisham, 2004) is a comprehensive, 23-item self-report measure that contains specific subtests on clutter, acquisition, and ability to discard. The UCLA Hoarding Severity Scale (Saxena, Brody, Maidment, & Baxter, 2007) is a 10-item, clinician-administered scale that assesses the urges to save, difficulty discarding, excessive acquisition, indecisiveness, procrastination, and impairment from hoarding. This scale assists in drawing out specific information about hoarding and associated symptoms. Finally, the Clutter Image Rating Scale (Frost, Steketee, Tolin, & Renaud, 2008) consists of a three photographs of a kitchen, living room, and bedroom with varying levels of clutter in which the patient indicates which photo best represents his or her specific rooms.

A risk assessment is necessary, particularly when working with older adults. Health hazards and safety issues may be compounded by age-associated physical limitations and medical comorbidity (e.g., Steketee et al., 2012). Areas to address include but are not limited to fire hazards, infestations, structural problems with the home, and mold problems. Activities of daily living and functional impairment should be assessed as they are affected by clutter as well as age. Measures such as the Activities of Daily Living—Hoarding (Grisham et al., 2006) and the Functional Disability Index (Jette et al., 2002) may serve as useful guides for exploration of abilities.

Non-hoarding-specific neuropsychiatric testing provides important information to complete the clinical picture. Psychiatric comorbidities—namely, anxiety and depressive symptoms and disorders—are prominent in geriatric hoarding patients (Ayers et al., 2010; Reid et al., 2011). Therefore, a comprehensive diagnostic interview (e.g., MINI-International Neuropsychiatric Interview; Sheehan et al., 1998) should be administered to determine contributory and primary psychiatric diagnoses. Other geriatric-normed mood and anxiety symptom self-reports may be indicated.

Neurocognitive testing may be required given reports of the association between hoarding and neuropsychological deficits. Studies have shown deficits in multiple aspects of neurocognition in midlife samples, including the acquisition and retention of new information, attention, response inhibition, decision making, categorization, and organization of information (Bechara, Damasio, Damasio, & Anderson, 1994; Grisham, Brown, Savage, Steketee, & Barlow, 2007; Grisham, Norberg, Williams, Certoma, & Kadib, 2010; Hartl, Duffany, Allen, Steketee, & Frost, 2005; Mackin, Arean, Delucchi, & Mathews, 2011; Tolin, Villavicencio, Umbach, & Kurtz, 2011). Mackin et al. (2011) found that older adults with comorbid depression and hoarding have deficits in categorization pinpointing potential underlying executive dysfunction. Furthermore, when comparing geriatric hoarding participants with healthy control subjects, multiple aspects of executive dysfunction were found, yet there were no significant differences in attention, working memory, visuospatial skills, delayed memory, category fluency, or processing speed (Ayers et al., 2013). Geriatric hoarding patients demonstrated deficits in multiple areas of executive functioning, such as categorizing, utilizing feedback, abstract thinking, set shifting, and generating hypotheses. Neuropsychiatric status has direct implications for the treatment plan.

Treatment Literature on Geriatric Hoarding

Although there are no available medication investigations in geriatric groups, a combined approach of medication and behavioral treatment is recommended (Saxena, 2011). One study found no differences between OCD patients with and without hoarding symptoms in response to paroxetine for midlife samples (Saxena et al., 2007). There are also promising preliminary results from 13 hoarding patients in which 61% were categorized as treatment responders to venlafaxine at posttreatment (Saxena, 2011).

CBT specifically developed for the treatment of hoarding has provided positive results in midlife samples (Steketee, Frost, Tolin, Rassmussen, & Brown, 2010; Tolin, Steketee, & Frost, 2007). This treatment consists of motivational interviewing; problem solving, decision making, and organizational skill building; cognitive restructuring techniques to address maladaptive beliefs; and exposure to discarding and acquiring. Results are promising, with 50% of treatment completers rated as "much improved" or "very much improved" at posttreatment and symptom severity ratings reductions of 28% on the Savings Inventory—Revised and 31% on the Clutter Image Rating Scale in an open trial (Tolin et al., 2007). A randomized controlled trial using this approach showed promising results, with a 27% decrease in patient-reported hoarding severity (Steketee et al., 2010).

Unfortunately, there are no randomized controlled trials of late-life hoarding. Studies investigating behavioral treatments are largely limited to case reports (e.g., Franks, Lund, Poulton, & Caserta, 2004; K. Turner, Steketee, & Nauth, 2010), with the exception of one open CBT trial (Ayers, Wetherell, Golshan, & Saxena, 2011). An investigation using the aforementioned CBT approach found less support for use in a geriatric sample, with only 25% of completers considered responders posttreatment (Ayers et al., 2011). Symptom severity reductions were not strong (21% Savings Inventory—Revised; 15% UCLA Hoarding Severity Scale). Another investigation of 11 elderly community mental health center patients evidenced only six treatment completers and modest improvement in at home functioning using a similar CBT approach (K. Turner et al., 2010). Although not systematically researched, harm reduction approaches are popular agency interventions and have been outlined in case reports (e.g., Tompkins, 2011). There are no known reports of remission without intervention in geriatric samples. Taken together, older adults with hoarding may require an enhanced or alternative treatment.

Course of Treatment for Geriatric Hoarding

The following section outlines a geriatric-focused course of treatment for hoarding patients. Generally, the initial phase treatment is similar to that of younger adults with a few important distinctions. Accommodations may be necessary for cognitive impairment, physical illness, limited mobility, and health hazards (e.g., Ayers et al., 2011; K. Turner et al., 2010). For all patients with hoarding, psychoeducation is a critical component to the initial session due to lack of information about hoarding. Brief motivational interviewing to foster internal motivation may be necessary early in treatment.

Deficits in executive functioning may have an impact on the typical course of CBT for geriatric hoarding given requisite abilities required for the generalization and implementation of CBT skills. We know that these deficits exist in both midlife and late-life hoarders (e.g., Grisham et al., 2007; Mackin et al., 2011); however, there have been no direct comparisons of functioning between groups. Nevertheless, the clinician may have to remediate cognitive weaknesses due to potential worsening of deficits or age related cognitive decline exacerbated by hoarding symptoms. Starting with cognitive remediation will allow participants to better utilize exposure techniques and increase homework compliance (Ayers, Bratiotis, Saxena, & Wetherell, 2012). The pretreatment assessment will directly inform the therapist what components of cognitive rehabilitation may be necessary. However, given that older adult patients with hoarding likely possess deficits or relative weaknesses in executive functioning, those domains should be the primary target area for remediation. Specific areas of focus include problem solving, planning, organization, goal setting, and cognitive flexibility.

After the incorporation of the cognitive rehabilitation, exposure to discarding and acquiring becomes the focus of treatment. If the older person is actively acquiring large numbers of possessions, the incoming items should be the initial target of treatment. As in younger populations, this would start with limit setting on incoming clutter and exposures to not acquiring. After patients have mastered acquiring exposures, discarding exposures become the focus of treatment. The basic premise of exposure therapy for discarding and acquiring is akin to the treatment of anxiety disorders. Through repeated exposure, a patient will habituate to the fear-provoking trigger (discarding or not acquiring) and learn to tolerate her distress (Craske et al., 2008). Ample time must be devoted to the rationale of exposure to discarding and acquiring. Often patients may be confused with family intervention "clean outs" and structured exposure sessions. As in other exposure therapies, the session begins with the rationale of exposure, reviewing the hierarchy, the exposure itself, and reporting subjective distress ratings and throughout. Although it is helpful for patients to see changes in their distress ratings over time as well as differences between actual and expected distress, it is most important that the patient sticks with and tolerates his distress. In young and midlife hoarding patients, exposure sessions are conducted in conjunction with cognitive therapy techniques to challenge beliefs about possessions (Steketee & Frost, 2007). However, in older adults, these cognitive therapy techniques have limited utility (Ayers et al., 2010, 2012). Geriatric exposure accommodations include repetition of exposure rationale, large visual signs or reminders of exposure rules, concrete exposure assignment, and working on hierarchy items that will make the most impact on health and safety.

Treatment barriers include poor homework compliance, low motivation, and lack of insight. Homework compliance is important given the negative impact on treatment outcomes in older adults with hoarding (Ayers et al., 2010). Reasons for homework incompliance include poor motivation, poor insight, or skill deficits. Although most older adult patients are able to master in-session exposure exercises, many struggle to maintain their practice at home. Skill deficits should be addressed through cognitive remediation. Poorly motivated or those with lack of insight often require additional psychoeducation, motivational intervention, and a multidisciplinary approach (Koenig et al., 2010). The multidisciplinary team may include family members, mental health experts, adult protective services. Fire, police, and code enforcement personnel may be necessary when there are significant health, public safety, and ethical challenges.

Delivering care to dementia patients with hoarding may be challenging (Baker, LeBlanc, Raetz, & Hilton, 2011; Hogstel, 1993). In dementia cases, treatment should be behaviorally based with environmental reinforcements (e.g., removal of stimuli, sorting practice). If the patient is living at home, ideally the caregiver will be involved in setting up a behavioral plan with a clinician. However, many of these patients are institutionalized, and thus, the treatment is designed and delivered by the facility multidisciplinary staff.

Summary of Geriatric Hoarding

The assessment and treatment of hoarding in late life are complicated by age-related physical, neurocognitive, and social challenges. The initial step in working with geriatric hoarding patients is a thorough assessment using clinical interviews, caregiver reports, team member or agency collaboration, clinician administered, and self-report assessments. Treatment must be tailored to specific medical comorbidities, treatment setting, cognitive functioning, and health status. A combination of medication, cognitive rehabilitation, and exposure therapy appears to be a promising treatment for geriatric hoarding.

REFERENCES

Austin, L. S., Zealberg, J. J., & Lydiard, R. B. (1991). Three cases of pharmacotherapy of obsessive–compulsive disorder in the elderly. *Journal of Nervous and Mental Disease, 179*, 634–635. doi:10.1097/00005053-199110000-00009

Ayers, C. R., Bratiotis, C., Saxena, S., & Wetherell, J. W. (2012). Therapist and patient perspectives on cognitive-behavioral therapy for geriatric compulsive hoarding: A collective case study. *Aging & Mental Health, 16*, 915–921. doi:10. 1080/13607863.2012.678480

Ayers, C. R., Saxena, S., Golshan, S., & Wetherell, J. L. (2010). Age at onset and clinical features of late life compulsive hoarding. *International Journal of Geriatric Psychiatry, 25*, 142–149. doi:10.1002/gps.2310

Ayers, C. R., Wetherell, J. L., Golshan, S., & Saxena, S. (2011). Cognitive-behavorial therapy for geriatric compulsive hoarding. *Behaviour Research and Therapy, 49*, 689–694. doi:10.1016/j.brat.2011.07.002

Ayers, C. R., Wetherell, J. W., Schiehser, D., Almklov, E., Golshan, S., & Saxena, S. (2013). Executive functioning in older adults with hoarding disorder. *International Journal of Geriatric Psychiatry*. Advance online publication. doi:10.1002/gps.3940

Bajulaiye, R., & Addonizio, G. (1992). Obsessive–compulsive disorder arising in a 75-year-old woman. *International Journal of Geriatric Psychiatry, 7*, 139–142. doi:10.1002/gps.930070212

Baker, J. C., LeBlanc, L. A., Raetz, P. B., & Hilton, L. C. (2011). Assessment and treatment of hoarding in an individual with dementia. *Behavior Therapy, 42*, 135–142. doi:10.1016/j.beth.2010.02.006

Bechara, A., Damasio, A. R., Damasio, H., & Anderson, S. W. (1994). Insensitivity to future consequences following damage to human prefrontal cortex. *Cognition, 50*, 7–15. doi:10.1016/0010-0277(94)90018-3

Bhattacharyya, S., & Khanna, S. (2004). Late onset OCD. *Australian and New Zealand Journal of Psychiatry, 38*, 477–478. doi:10.1111/j.1440-1614.2004.01397.x

Blazer, D., George, L. K., & Hughes, D. (1991). The epidemiology of anxiety disorders: An age comparison. In C. Salzman & B. D. Liebowitz (Eds.), *Anxiety in the elderly: Treatment and research* (pp. 17–30). New York, NY: Springer.

Calamari, J. E., Faber, S. D., Hitsman, B. L., & Poppe, C. J. (1994). Treatment of obsessive compulsive disorder in the elderly: A review and case example. *Journal of Behavior Therapy and Experimental Psychiatry, 25*, 95–104. doi:10.1016/0005-7916(94)90001-9

Calamari, J. E., Janeck, A. S., & Deer, T. M. (2002). Cognitive processes and obsessive compulsive disorder in older adults. In R. O. Frost & G. Steketee (Eds.), *Cognitive approaches to obsessions and compulsions: Theory, assessment, and treatment* (pp. 315–335). New York, NY: Pergamon. doi:10.1016/B978-008043410-0/50021-0

Carmin, C. N., Pollard, C. A., & Gillock, K. L. (1999). Assessment of anxiety disorders in the elderly. In P. Lichtenberg (Ed.), *Handbook of assessment in clinical gerontology* (pp. 59–90). New York, NY: Wiley.

Carmin, C. N., Pollard, C. A., & Ownby, R. L. (1998). Obsessive–compulsive disorder: Cognitive behavioral treatment of older versus younger adults. *Clinical Gerontologist, 19*, 77–81.

Carmin, C. N., Pollard, C. A., & Ownby, R. L. (1999). Cognitive behavioral treatment of older adults with obsessive–compulsive disorder. *Cognitive and Behavioral Practice, 6*, 110–119. doi:10.1016/S1077-7229(99)80019-4

Cottraux, J., & Gerard, D. (1998). Neuroimaging and neuroanatomical issues in obsessive–compulsive disorder. In R. P. Swinson, M. M. Antony, S. Rachman, & M. A. Richter (Eds.), *Obsessive–compulsive disorder: Theory, research, and treatment* (pp. 154–180). New York, NY: Guilford Press.

Craske, M. G., Kircanski, K., Zelikowsky, M., Mystkowski, J., Chowdhury, N., & Baker, A. (2008). Optimizing inhibitory learning during exposure therapy. *Behaviour Research and Therapy, 46*, 5–27. doi:10.1016/j.brat.2007.10.003

Derogatis, L. R., & Spencer, P. M. (1982). *Administration and procedures: BSI manual I.* Townson, MD: Clinical Psychometric Research.

Dong, X., Simon, M. A., Mosqueda, L., & Evans, D. A. (2012). The prevalence of elder self-neglect in a community-dwelling population: Hoarding, hygiene, and environmental hazards. *Journal of Aging and Health, 24*, 507–524. doi: 10.1177/0898264311425597

Fallon, B. A., Liebowitz, M. R., Hollander, E., Schneier, F. R., Campeas, R. B., Fairbanks, J., . . . Sandberg, D. (1990). The pharmacotherapy of moral or religious scrupulosity. *The Journal of Clinical Psychiatry, 51*, 517–521.

Flint, A. J. (1994). Epidemiology and comorbidity of anxiety disorders in the elderly. *The American Journal of Psychiatry, 151*, 640–649.

Francis, V. M., Rajan, P., & Turner, N. (1990). British community norms for the Brief Symptom Inventory. *British Journal of Clinical Psychology, 29*, 115–116. doi:10.1111/j.2044-8260.1990.tb00857.x

Franks, M., Lund, D. A., Poulton, D., & Caserta, M. S. (2004). Understanding hoarding behavior among older adults: A case study approach. *Journal of Gerontological Social Work, 42*(3–4), 77–107. doi:10.1300/J083v42n03_06

Frost, R. O., & Gross, R. C. (1993). The hoarding of possessions. *Behaviour Research and Therapy, 31*, 367–381. doi:10.1016/0005-7967(93)90094-B

Frost, R. O., Steketee, G., & Grisham, J. (2004). Measurement of compulsive hoarding: Saving inventory-revised. *Behaviour Research and Therapy, 42*, 1163–1182. doi:10.1016/j.brat.2003.07.006

Frost, R. O., Steketee, G., Tolin, D. F., & Renaud, S. (2008). Development and validation of the clutter image rating. *Journal of Psychopathology and Behavioral Assessment, 30*, 193–203. doi:10.1007/s10862-007-9068-7

Goodman, W. K., Price, L. H., Rasmussen, S. A., & Mazure, C. (1989). The Yale–Brown Obsessive Compulsive Scale. II. Validity. *Archives of General Psychiatry, 46*, 1012–1016. doi:10.1001/archpsyc.1989.01810110054008

Goodman, W. K., Price, L. H., Rasmussen, S. A., Mazure, C., Delgado, P., Heninger, G. R., & Charney, D. S. (1989). The Yale–Brown Obsessive Compulsive Scale: II. Validity. *Archives of General Psychiatry, 46*, 1012–1016.

Grant, J. E., Mancebo, M. C., Pinto, A., Williams, K. A., Eisen, J. L., & Rasmussen, S. A. (2007). Late-onset obsessive compulsive disorder: Clinical characteristics and psychiatric comorbidity. *Psychiatry Research, 152*, 21–27. doi:10.1016/j.psychres.2006.09.015

Grenier, S., Préville, M., Boyer, R., O'Connor, K., and the Scientific Committee of the ESA Study. (2009). Prevalence and correlates of obsessive–compulsive disorder among older adults living in the community. *Journal of Anxiety Disorders*, *23*, 858–865.

Grisham, J. R., Brown, T. A., Savage, C. R., Steketee, G., & Barlow, D. H. (2007). Neuropsychological impairment associated with compulsive hoarding. *Behaviour Research and Therapy*, *45*, 1471–1483. doi:10.1016/j.brat.2006.12.008

Grisham, J. R., Frost, R. O., Steketee, G., Kim, H., & Hood, S. (2006). Age of onset in compulsive hoarding. *Journal of Anxiety Disorders*, *20*, 675–686. doi:10.1016/j.janxdis.2005.07.004

Grisham, J. R., Norberg, M. M., Williams, A. D., Certoma, S. P., & Kadib, R. (2010). Categorization and cognitive deficits in compulsive hoarding. *Behaviour Research and Therapy*, *48*, 866–872. doi:10.1016/j.brat.2010.05.011

Hale, W. D., Cochran, C. D., & Hedgepeth, B. E. (1984). Norms for the elderly on the Brief Symptom Inventory. *Journal of Consulting and Clinical Psychology*, *52*, 321–322. doi:10.1037/0022-006X.52.2.321

Hartl, T. L., Duffany, S. R., Allen, G. J., Steketee, G., & Frost, R. O. (2005). Relationships among compulsive hoarding, trauma, and attention-deficit/hyperactivity disorder. *Behaviour Research and Therapy*, *43*, 269–276. doi:10.1016/j.brat.2004.02.002

Hersen, M., & van Hasselt, V. B. (1992). Behavioral assessment and treatment of anxiety in the elderly. *Clinical Psychology Review*, *12*, 619–640. doi:10.1016/0272-7358(92)90135-U

Hirsh, A., O'Brien, K., Geffken, G. R., Adkins, J., Goodman, W. K., & Storch, E. A. (2006). Cognitive-behavioral treatment for obsessive–compulsive disorder in an elderly male with concurrent medical constraints. *The American Journal of Geriatric Psychiatry*, *14*, 380–381. doi:10.1097/01.JGP.0000196636.88245.16

Hogstel, M. O. (1993). Understanding hoarding behaviors in the elderly. *The American Journal of Nursing*, *93*, 42–45.

Hwang, J. P., Tsai, S., Yang, C., Liu, K., & Lirng, J. (1998). Hoarding behavior in dementia: A preliminary report. *The American Journal of Geriatric Psychiatry*, *6*, 285–289.

Jenike, M. A. (1991). Geriatric obsessive compulsive disorder. *Journal of Geriatric Psychiatry and Neurology*, *4*, 34–39. doi:10.1177/089198879100400107

Jette, A. M., Haley, S. M., Coster, W. J., Kooyoomjian, J. T., Levenson, S., Heeren, T., & Ashba, J. (2002). Late life function and disability instrument: I. development and evaluation of the disability component. *The Journals of Gerontology: Series A, Biological Sciences and Medical Sciences*, *57*, M209–M216. doi:10.1093/gerona/57.4.M209

Jorm, A. F., Christensen, H., Henderson, A. S., Korten, A. E., MacKinnon, A. J., & Scott, A. (1994). Complaints of cognitive decline in the elderly: A comparison of reports by subjects and informants in a community survey. *Psychological Medicine*, *24*, 365–374. doi:10.1017/S0033291700027343

Jorm, A. F., Christensen, H., Korten, A. E., Henderson, P. A., Jacomb, P. A., & MacKinnon, A. (1997). Do cognitive complaints either predict future cognitive decline or reflect past cognitive decline? A longitudinal study of an elderly community sample. *Psychological Medicine, 27,* 91–98. doi:10.1017/S0033291796003923

Junginger, J., & Ditto, B. (1984). Multitreatment of obsessive–compulsive checking in a geriatric patient. *Behavior Modification, 8,* 379–390. doi:10.1177/01454455840083005

Kim, H. J., Steketee, G., & Frost, R. O. (2001). Hoarding by elderly people. *Health & Social Work, 26,* 176–184. doi:10.1093/hsw/26.3.176

King, P., & Barrowclough, C. (1991). A clinical pilot study of cognitive-behavioural therapy for anxiety disorders in the elderly. *Behavioural Psychotherapy, 19,* 337–345. doi:10.1017/S0141347300014038

Koenig, T. L., Chapin, R., & Spano, R. (2010). Using multidisciplinary teams to address ethical dilemmas with older adults who hoard. *Journal of Gerontological Social Work, 53,* 137–147. doi:10.1080/01634370903340353

Kohn, R., Westlake, R. J., Rasmussen, S. A., Marsland, R. T., & Norman, W. H. (1997). Clinical features of obsessive–compulsive disorder in elderly patients. *The American Journal of Geriatric Psychiatry, 5,* 211–215. doi:10.1097/00019442-199700530-00004

Kolada, J. L., Bland, R. C., & Newman, S. C. (1994). Epidemiology of psychiatric disorders in Edmonton: Obsessive–compulsive disorder. *Acta Psychiatrica Scandinavica, 376,* 24–35. doi:10.1111/j.1600-0447.1994.tb05788.x

Lindesay, J., Briggs, K., & Murphy, E. (1989). The Guys/Age Concern Survey: Prevalence rates of cognitive impairment, depression, and anxiety in an urban elderly community. *The British Journal of Psychiatry, 155,* 317–329.

Mackin, R. S., Arean, P. A., Delucchi, K. L., & Mathews, C. A. (2011). Cognitive functioning in individuals with severe compulsive hoarding behaviors and late life depression. *International Journal of Geriatric Psychiatry, 26,* 314–321. doi:10.1002/gps.2531

March, J., Frances, A., Carpenter, D., & Kahn, D. (1997). The Expert Consensus Guideline Series: Treatment of obsessive–compulsive disorder. *Journal of Clinical Psychiatry, 58*(Suppl. 4), 1–72.

Markovitz, P. J. (1993). Treatment of anxiety in the elderly. *Journal of Clinical Psychiatry, 54,* 64–68.

Marx, M. S., & Cohen-Mansfield, J. (2003). Hoarding behavior in the elderly: A comparison between community-dwelling persons and nursing home residents. *International Psychogeriatrics, 15,* 289–306. doi:10.1017/S1041610203009542

Nestadt, G., Bienvenu, O. J., Cai, G., Samuels, J., & Eaton, W. W. (1998). Incidence of obsessive–compulsive disorder in adults. *The Journal of Nervous and Mental Disease, 186,* 401–406.

Philpot, M. P., & Banerjee, S. (1998). Obsessive–compulsive disorder in the elderly. *Behavioural Neurology, 11,* 117–121.

Price, M. C., & Salsman, N. L. (2010). Exposure and response prevention for the treatment of late-onset obsessive–compulsive disorder in an 82-year-old man. *Clinical Case Studies, 9*, 426–441. doi:10.1177/1534650110387294

Poyurovsky, M., Bergman, J., & Weizman, R. (2006). Obsessive–compulsive disorder in elderly schizophrenia patients. *Journal of Psychiatric Research, 40*, 189–191. doi:10.1016/j.jpsychires.2005.03.009

Rabinowitz, J., Davidson, M., De Deyn, P., Katz, I., Brodaty, H., & Cohen-Mansfield, J. (2005). Factor analysis of the Cohen-Mansfield Agitation Inventory in three large samples of nursing home patients with dementia and behavioral disturbance. *The American Journal of Geriatric Psychiatry, 13*, 991–998. doi:10.1176/appi.ajgp.13.11.991

Rasmussen, S. A., & Eisen, J. L. (1992). The epidemiology and differential diagnosis of obsessive compulsive disorder. *Journal of Clinical Psychiatry, 53*, 4–10.

Reid, J. M., Arnold, E., Rosen, S., Mason, G., Larson, M. J., Murphy, T. K., & Storch, E. A. (2011). Hoarding behaviors among nonclinical elderly adults: Correlations with hoarding cognitions, obsessive–compulsive symptoms, and measures of general psychopathology. *Journal of Anxiety Disorders, 25*, 1116–1122. doi:10.1016/j.janxdis.2011.08.002

Rowan, V. C., Holburn, S. W., Walker, J. R., & Siddique, A. (1984). A rapid multi-component treatment for an obsessive–compulsive disorder. *Journal of Behavior Therapy and Experimental Psychiatry, 15*, 347–352. doi:10.1016/0005-7916(84)90100-9

Samuels, J. F., Bienvenu, O. J., III, Grados, M. A., Cullen, B. A. M., Riddle, M. A., Liang, K., . . . Nestadt, G. (2008). *Behaviour Research and Therapy, 46*, 836–844. doi:10.1016/j.brat.2008.04.004

Saxena, S. (2011). Pharmacotherapy of compulsive hoarding. *Journal of Clinical Psychology, 67*, 477–484. doi:10.1002/jclp.20792

Saxena, S., Brody, A. L., Maidment, K. M., & Baxter, L. R. (2007). Paroxetine treatment of compulsive hoarding. *Journal of Psychiatric Research, 41*, 481–487. doi:10.1016/j.jpsychires.2006.05.001

Shader, R. I., Kennedy, J. S., & Greenblatt, D. J. (1987). Treatment of anxiety in the elderly. In H. Y. Meltzer (Ed.), *Psychopharmacology: The third generation of progress* (pp. 1141–1147). New York: Raven Press.

Shanmugiah, A., Varghese, M., & Khanna, S. (2002). Expressed emotions in obsessive compulsive disorder. *Indian Journal of Psychiatry, 44*, 14–18.

Sheehan, D. V., Lecrubier, Y., Sheehan, K. H., Amorim, P., Janavs, J., Weiller, E., . . . Dunbar, G. C. (1998). The Mini-International Neuropsychiatric Interview (M.I.N.I.): The development and validation of a structured diagnostic psychiatric interview for *DSM–IV* and *ICD–10*. *Journal of Clinical Psychiatry, 59*, 22–33.

Sheikh, J. I., & Saltzman, C. (1995). Anxiety in the elderly. *Psychiatric Clinics of North America, 18*, 871–883.

Simpson, S., & Baldwin, B. (1995). Neuropsychiatry and SPECT of an acute obsessive compulsive syndrome patient. *The British Journal of Psychiatry, 166*, 390–392. doi:10.1192/bjp.166.3.390

Sinoff, G., & Werner, P. (2003). Anxiety disorder and accompanying subjective memory loss in the elderly as a predictor of future cognitive decline. *International Journal of Geriatric Psychiatry, 18*, 951–959. doi:10.1002/gps.1004

Steketee, G., & Frost, R. O. (2007). *Compulsive hoarding and acquiring: Therapist guide*. New York, NY: Oxford University Press.

Steketee, G., Frost, R. O., Tolin, D. F., Rasmussen, J., & Brown, T. A. (2010). Waitlist-controlled trial of cognitive behavior therapy for hoarding disorder. *Depression and Anxiety, 27*, 476–484. doi:10.1002/da.20673

Steketee, G., Schmalisch, C. S., Dierberger, A., DeNobel, D., & Frost, R. O. (2012). Symptoms and history of hoarding in older adults. *Journal of Obsessive–Compulsive and Related Disorders, 1*, 1–7. doi:10.1016/j.jocrd.2011.10.001

Stoudemire, A., & Moran, M. G. (1993). Psychopharmacologic treatment of anxiety in the medically ill elderly patient: Special considerations. *Journal of Clinical Psychiatry, 54*, 27–33.

Teachman, B. A. (2007). Linking obsessional beliefs to OCD symptoms in older and younger adults. *Behaviour Research and Therapy, 45*, 1671–1681. doi:10.1016/j.brat.2006.08.016

Tolin, D. F., Frost, R. O., & Steketee, G. (2007). An open trial of cognitive-behavioral therapy for compulsive hoarding. *Behaviour Research and Therapy, 45*, 1461–1470. doi:10.1016/j.brat.2007.01.001

Tolin, D. F., Frost, R. O., & Steketee, G. (2010). A brief interview for assessing compulsive hoarding: The Hoarding Rating Scale—Interview. *Psychiatry Research, 178*, 147–152. doi:10.1016/j.psychres.2009.05.001

Tolin, D. F., Meunier, S. A., Frost, R. O., & Steketee, G. (2010). Course of compulsive hoarding and its relationship to life events. *Depression and Anxiety, 27*, 829–838. doi:10.1002/da.20684

Tolin, D. F., Villavicencio, A., Umbach, A., & Kurtz, M. M. (2011). Neuropsychological functioning in hoarding disorder. *Psychiatry Research, 189*, 413–418. doi:10.1016/j.psychres.2011.06.022

Tompkins, M. A. (2011). Working with families of people who hoard: A harm reduction approach. *Journal of Clinical Psychology, 67*, 497–506. doi:10.1002/jclp.20797

Turner, K., Steketee, G., & Nauth, L. (2010). Treating elders with compulsive hoarding: A pilot program. *Cognitive and Behavioral Practice, 17*, 449–457. doi:10.1016/j.cbpra.2010.04.001

Turner, S. M., Hersen, M., Bellack, A. S., & Wells, K. C. (1979). Behavioral treatment of obsessive compulsive neurosis. *Behaviour Research and Therapy, 17*, 95–105. doi:10.1016/0005-7967(79)90017-2

Weiss, A. P., & Jenike, M. A. (2000). Late-onset obsessive–compulsive disorder: A case series. *The Journal of Neuropsychiatry and Clinical Neurosciences, 12*, 265–268. doi:10.1176/appi.neuropsych.12.2.265

Wisocki, P. A. (1994). The experience of worry among the elderly. In G. C. L. Davey & F. Tallis (Eds.), *Worrying: Perspectives on theory, assessment and treatment* (pp. 247–261). New York, NY: Wiley.

6

HOARDING DISORDER

JORDANA MUROFF, MAXWELL E. LEVIS, AND CHRISTIANA BRATIOTIS

Hoarding is a serious psychiatric condition that, in its most severe form, can be life-threatening to individuals and a significant burden to community members (Frost, Steketee, & Williams, 2000). Hoarding is associated with severe difficulty discarding everyday possessions and a powerful urge to save objects as well as acquire new ones. These behaviors lead to large amounts of clutter that prevent the use of space for intended purposes, high levels of stress, and impaired daily living (Frost & Hartl, 1996; Saxena, 2008). People who hoard often lack insight about these behaviors (Frost, Tolin, & Maltby, 2010). The *Diagnostic and Statistical Manual of Mental Disorders* (fifth edition; *DSM–5*) Obsessive–Compulsive (OC) Spectrum Working Group proposed criteria for hoarding disorder that include specifiers for excessive acquisition and level of insight (American Psychiatric Association, 2011), which were adopted in the *DSM–5* (American Psychiatric Association, 2013).

http://dx.doi.org/10.1037/14323-007
Obsessive–Compulsive Disorder and Its Spectrum: A Life-Span Approach, Eric A. Storch and Dean McKay (Editors)
Copyright © 2014 by the American Psychological Association. All rights reserved.

Additionally, these symptoms must not be attributable to any other medical or mental health condition (e.g., schizophrenia).

In several recent studies, hoarding has an estimated prevalence of 2% to 5%; 2.3% among twins in the United Kingdom as measured by the Hoarding Rating Scale—Self Report (Iervolino et al., 2009), 4.6% in Germany as measured by a modified Saving Inventory Revised (Mueller, Mitchell, Crosby, Glaesmer, & Zwaan, 2009), and 5.3% within the United States measured via psychiatric observations and multiple assessments (Samuels et al., 2008). (See the discussion of assessments later in the chapter.) Hoarding is 3 times more common among populations older than 55 years, twice as common among men, and 4 times more common among people with an annual household income under $20,000 (Samuels et al., 2008). Although treatment is not typically sought until middle age, the average age of hoarding symptom onset is 12 to 13 years (Grisham, Frost, Steketee, Kim, & Hood, 2006; Samuels et al., 2002; Seedat & Stein, 2002). Retrospective data show that 80% of people with hoarding report the onset of symptoms by age 18 (Grisham et al., 2006).

Hoarding can lead to significant physical health problems and work impairment. On average, a person with hoarding disorder misses 7 workdays per month, a number consistent with serious mental illnesses such as schizophrenia and bipolar disorder (Tolin, Frost, Steketee, Gray, & Fitch, 2008). Hoarding also affects housing stability; 8% to 12% of self-identified hoarders reported a threat of eviction or eviction as a result of amassed clutter (Tolin, Frost, Steketee, & Fitch, 2008). The broader costs of health inspections, home clean-outs, and multiple agency intervention are also markedly high, with 79% of hoarding cases involving multiple agencies (Frost & Hunt, 2000). The investment of time and resources by multiple community agencies to resolve hoarding cases that come to public attention has led to the formation of more than 85 community hoarding task forces in the United States and Canada (Bratiotis, 2013). In addition to economic and social burdens, hoarding is frequently associated with pronounced family stress and hostility, frustration, anger, and feelings of social rejection (Frost & Gross, 1993).

Commonly thought of as a subtype of obsessive–compulsive disorder (OCD), hoarding is a related but separate condition. Although hoarding symptoms are detected in 25% to 30% of OCD clinic patients (Frost, Krause, & Steketee, 1996; Frost, Steketee, Williams, & Warren, 2000; Samuels et al., 2002), among those who hoard, 18% have comorbid OCD (Frost, Steketee, & Tolin, 2011). Hoarding has higher comorbidity rates with major depression at 50.7%, generalized anxiety disorders at 24.4%, social anxiety at 23.5%, and attention-deficit/hyperactivity disorder—inattentive type at 27.8% and hyperactive type at 13.7% (Frost, Steketee, & Tolin, 2011). Furthermore, unlike OCD, hoarding is linked with impulse control disorders (Frost et al., 1998; Frost, Meagher, & Riskind, 2001; Frost, Steketee, & Williams, 2002;

Samuels et al., 2002) and decreased personal insight (Meunier, Tolin, Frost, Steketee, & Brady, 2006; Tolin, Frost, & Steketee, 2010). Furthermore, hoarding, in contrast to OCD, is associated with more significant levels of social disruption and distress.

Additionally, treating hoarding with behavior therapy and medication, which have been successful for OCD, has had limited benefit. Exposure and response prevention (ERP), serotonin reuptake inhibitors (SRIs), and combined ERP and SRI treatments have not led to significant improvement in hoarding symptoms (Abramowitz, Foa, & Franklin, 2003; Pertusa et al., 2010). Accordingly, a specialized cognitive behavior therapy (CBT) protocol for hoarding (see Steketee & Frost, 2007a, 2007b; discussed later in the chapter) has been developed, and the *DSM–5*, released in May 2013 (American Psychiatric Association, 2013), includes hoarding disorder as distinct from OCD (Mataix-Cols et al., 2010).

The purposes of this chapter are to review and summarize specific assessment and CBT treatment strategies for hoarding, to present studies examining the effectiveness of these techniques, and to discuss important treatment considerations for clinical practice and research.

SPECIALIZED CBT FOR HOARDING

This section provides a basic summary of the cognitive–behavioral tools and techniques depicted in the *Therapist Guide for Compulsive Hoarding* and accompanying *Client Workbook* (Steketee & Frost, 2007a, 2007b), with some practical guidelines for implementation.

Treatment Structure

The manualized CBT treatment protocol for hoarding is designed as a series of 26 weekly individual sessions spread over a half-year period. Each month, three 1-hour weekly sessions occur in the therapist's office, and one 2-hour visit occurs in the home. The first two sessions focus on assessing hoarding symptoms, related impairment, and general mental health and are typically 90 minutes each. All sessions have a common structure, beginning with an initial 5-minute check-in that assesses recent events, affect, and accomplishments. The therapist and patient collaborate to set an agenda for each session, prioritizing pressing issues, and to assign and review homework. Patients summarize their new learning and write down their particular homework assignments. Homework consists of between-session practice of specific treatment techniques (e.g., sorting, Thought Records) that the patient commits to working on and self-monitoring. Therapists and patients collaboratively decide on appropriate homework, often practicing a cognitive or behavioral strategy introduced during that session. Sessions close with a summary of topics and skills, intervention strategies, as well as an opportunity for feedback.

Assessment

The assessment and treatment of hoarding have been greatly enhanced by the development and publication of several measures over the past decade that specifically assess hoarding symptoms and severity, hoarding-related impairment, and evaluate CBT treatment effectiveness. Several are patient self-report measures, and others can also be rated by a therapist or observer.

- The Saving Inventory—Revised (SI–R; Frost, Steketee, & Grisham, 2004) is a patient-rated 23-item measure scored on a 0-to-4 scale and organized in three subscales measuring difficulty discarding, clutter, and acquisition.
- The Hoarding Rating Scale's (HRS; Tolin et al., 2010) five questions assess clutter, acquisition, difficulty discarding, distress, and impairment using a 0-to-8 severity rating scale that can be used by the patient, therapist, or both.
- The Clutter Image Rating scale (CIR; Frost, Steketee, Tolin, & Renaud, 2008) includes nine sequenced photos of three rooms (i.e., kitchen, living room, bedroom) used to assess the relative severity of clutter and can be rated by the patient, therapist, or other associates (e.g., those in fire and public safety, in-home coaches, family).
- The Saving Cognitions Inventory (SCI; Steketee, Frost, & Kyrios, 2003) is a 24-item patient-rated measure consisting of four subscales (i.e., emotional attachment, memory, control, and responsibility) that assesses beliefs experienced while trying to discard objects.
- The recently revised Activities of Daily Living for Hoarding (ADL-H) includes 15 items that assess the effect of clutter on the ability to do specific daily activities (Frost & Hristova, 2011).

Across these measures, higher scores signify more hoarding symptoms, severity, or impairment. The psychometric properties of these scales demonstrate excellent reliability and validity.

In addition to scales measuring symptoms, several instruments are helpful in assessing the environment for this home-based problem.

- The Home Environment Index (HEI; Rasmussen, Steketee, Frost, & Tolin, 2013) measures the extent of cleanliness/squalid conditions in the home.

- The HOMES Multidisciplinary Hoarding Risk Assessment (HOMES; Bratiotis, 2009; Bratiotis, Schmalisch, & Steketee, 2011) assesses the nature and level of risk associated with a hoarded environment. It assesses the effect of hoarding and clutter on health, obstacles, mental health, endangerment, and structure, and includes evaluation of household composition, imminent risk, capacity, postassessment plan sections.

The first few sessions of treatment are typically centered on completing the Hoarding Interview assessment to gain a comprehensive understanding of (a) the patient's hoarding-related beliefs and behaviors, (b) severity and associated impairment, (c) past and current life circumstances related to the hoarding problem (e.g., home of origin, current living situation), and (d) his or her own reasons for engaging in treatment. The detailed information from the interview and supplemental assessments is then incorporated into the patient's cognitive-behavioral theoretical model for understanding hoarding, which provides the basis of the treatment plan.

Building the CBT Hoarding Model

The cognitive–behavioral conceptual model of hoarding identifies specific elements associated with saving, acquiring, and clutter. These include personal and family vulnerabilities, difficulties with information processing, thoughts, beliefs and attachment to possessions, emotional responses, and reinforcement patterns. The therapist and patient collaborate to build the model, and typically start by writing the behaviors (e.g., difficulty discarding) at the bottom of the paper and then elaborating on the specified elements above, using arrows to exhibit their connections (see Steketee & Frost, 2007a). Model building supports patients in gaining some distance from their hoarding and investigating their thoughts and behaviors with the therapist, who asks open-ended questions. Patients may complete specific parts of the model for homework, to be reviewed with the therapist during the following session. Once a "working model" is developed, it becomes the basis for the goals and treatment plan.

It is essential that the therapist and patient work together to unpack potential factors and vulnerabilities that led to the development and manifestation of hoarding. Together, they consider specific vulnerabilities that may predispose someone to hoarding problems. These may include biological and familial factors such as genes, inherited traits, brain activity, and the interaction between genetic markers and the environment, including family-based learning (e.g., family-based rules, poor modeling of organizational and decision-making skills). Additionally, coexisting mental health problems are important to identify because they may cause or interact with the hoarding symptoms and greatly affect how the symptoms manifest. Severe hoarding may also lead to or exacerbate other mental health conditions (e.g., depression, personality features). Physical illness and limitations may lead to worsened clutter, which result in unclean conditions that aggravate the patient's physical health (e.g., allergies).

The therapist and patient work together to identify problems with cognitive processing and executive functioning commonly associated with hoarding, such as a lack of confidence in one's memory and difficulties making everyday decisions (e.g., "Which sweater should I wear?"), categorizing and organizing objects (e.g., "The shampoo bottle belongs in the bathroom"), focusing and sustaining attention on one targeted activity, and problem solving. Specific beliefs about objects may mediate the effects of these vulnerabilities and cognitive processes. Objects may be tied to one's identity or history or represent a period in one's life (e.g., "I was a literature major and am a writer—I can't get rid of these books"). Other beliefs focus on the emotional attachment and comfort provided by an object and concerns around enduring the anguish of letting it go. Humanlike qualities are sometimes attributed to items (e.g., "That stuffed bear has been with me for 40 years through very hard times. How can I abandon him and give him away?"). Beliefs may also be about the intrinsic value (e.g., beauty, unique) or a sense of responsibility for objects (e.g., a specific item needs to go to someone who will use it well— "I need to find it a good home"). Although these beliefs often impede patients' efforts to manage their clutter, they also reveal strengths (e.g., strong sense of accountability and social responsibility, creativity).

In addition to identifying the type of thoughts, the therapist and patient pinpoint the positive (e.g., joy, satisfaction) and negative emotions (e.g., grief, frustration) that reinforce the hoarding beliefs and behaviors. For example, when an individual decides not to discard an object under consideration or acquires a new object to avoid distress and negative emotions, his or her avoidance is negatively reinforced by the associated relief, increasing the likelihood of more avoidance in the face of distress. Additionally, the pleasures of acquiring a new object and handling one's own possessions are positively reinforcing. Negative beliefs about oneself are also reinforced by the continued hoarding behavior and cluttered home environment.

Establishing Personal Goals and Values

Through the processes of assessment and developing the patient's hoarding model, specific areas emerge for clinical focus. It is essential that patients identify their personal values and goals for treatment, regardless of whether they initiate treatment by their own volition or because it has been imposed (e.g., a spouse/partner threatening to leave unless the patient gets help, landlord threatening eviction). Therapists may ask patients to reflect on what they care most about and what they want to do most during the remaining years of their life (e.g., entertain guests in their living room). Such goals and values may be referred to throughout the course of treatment to elucidate ambivalence and ease indecisiveness. For example, when engaged in a sorting task, a patient might ask herself whether discarding a specific item fits with her goal to be able to cook using the stove.

Home Visits

Home visits and home-based assessments are integral to this specialized form of CBT; it is preferable that the first home visit is scheduled within the first four sessions (after assessment and model building). Home visits are critical to assessing the extent of the clutter and kinds of items saved, to connect with patients' families as appropriate, and to establish a baseline from which to monitor changes. Therapists need to communicate the importance of home visits while simultaneously addressing patients concerns, feelings of shame, and possible resistance. The visit may be framed as an opportunity for the therapist to learn about patients' thoughts and feelings about their possessions while in their presence, collaborate to identify specific areas to focus the therapeutic work, and remind the patient that the role of the therapist is not to handle or remove possessions. Taking photographs of all rooms of the home is highly recommended. This establishes a baseline level of clutter, and the photos can be used to assess and illustrate progress in treatment over time. The major goals of subsequent home sessions are to monitor daily activities, assess progress in reducing clutter, and chart intervention goals. When a therapist first visits the patient's home, it is essential to build a relationship of trust, establish a nonjudgmental stance, and not react negatively to the degree of clutter present or the condition of the home.

Additionally, while at the house, therapist and patient collaboratively select where to start the process of sorting, organizing, and getting rid of clutter. It is recommended to begin with more manageable spaces and those that offer maximum benefit for patients (e.g., bathroom). The therapist and patient collect a sample of clutter to illustrate the mix of possessions in the home; patients are encouraged to bring a similar collection of clutter to office sessions for in vivo sorting and discarding. If a patient is living with family members, these individuals should be included as much as possible. Family members may be encouraged to support and advocate for their loved one but not to accommodate the patient's hoarding impulses. If there are friends, roommates, family members, or professional assistants who seem capable and ready to aid the therapeutic process, it is recommended to include them in the treatment as coaches for in-home sorting and discarding work (i.e., exposure-based homework). It is important to note that the professional visiting the patient's home needs to be prepared for potential personal discomfort and to assess for danger. A plan for handling difficult situations should be set ahead of the home visits. At each of the monthly home visits, the therapist completes (at minimum) the HRS and CIR forms and takes photographs of the rooms of the home.

Motivational Interviewing

Treatment for hoarding symptoms is often impeded by patients' lack of insight into the nature of their condition and their fluctuating motivation to pursue changes. It is important to determine patients' level of insight and motivation (e.g., do they have insight but are reluctant?). Initial motivation may be undermined by skills deficits or challenges in learning skills. Miller and Rollnick's (2002) motivational interviewing (MI) approach may be an important adjunctive treatment used before engaging in CBT. MI may need to be "front loaded," with several sessions at the beginning of treatment dedicated to determining a patient's interest in addressing his hoarding. Motivational enhancement strategies may also be integrated throughout CBT treatment (e.g., in response to cancelations, lateness, homework noncompliance, avoidance when making decisions about objects).

Motivational techniques center on supporting patients to (a) identify and acknowledge that the hoarding behavior is problematic, (b) express concern about their condition, (c) work to address the hoarding, and (d) be positive about being able to make changes. Ambivalence is to be recognized, examined, enhanced, and resolved. It is essential that the therapist emphasize the patients' personal choice, acknowledge that ambivalence is normal, communicate respect, and use reflective listening statements to demonstrate interest in and understanding of patients' perspectives. Additionally, the therapist highlights patients' recognition that their present situation does not fit their goals and encourages them to develop their own arguments for change (i.e., developing discrepancy). It is essential that the therapist not "push back" or argue when patients show resistance but rather see that they are coping as best they can and "roll with it" by inviting them to present other solutions. Additionally, the therapist needs to believe in patients' capacity to solve their problems and help them realize their ability (i.e., self-efficacy) through supportive, respectful statements acknowledging their struggles and accomplishments.

Techniques that apply these principles and facilitate goal attainment involve the following: (a) asking open-ended questions (e.g., what? why? how?) that encourage patient engagement; (b) repeating patients' feelings, thoughts, and directly commenting on ambivalence; and (c) emphasizing personal choice and agency. Other common motivational strategies include asking patients to examine the pros and cons of their hoarding behavior and asking evocative questions that guide patients to talk about the consequences of their hoarding. Therapists may use extreme contrasts (e.g., "If you continue hoarding, what is the worst that can happen?") or ask the patient to look forward or back (e.g., "Looking ahead 5 years, what would you like your life to look like?") to identify concerns and emphasize benefits. It is important that therapists avoid provoking arguments, asking too many questions, or appearing to blame anyone for a patient's condition.

Cognitive Therapy

After working with patients to establish initial motivation, therapists apply cognitive techniques to identify and modify thoughts to reduce avoidance and clutter and manage strong negative emotions. CBT for hoarding combines cognitive methods with behavioral exposure. Helping patients to observe, identify, and change patterns of inaccurate and unhelpful thinking is an important component of hoarding treatment. Engaging in cognitive methods while doing behavioral exposures (e.g., sorting) contextualizes the thinking and beliefs. A number of cognitive strategies can be used. For example, during a sorting session, perhaps a patient picks up an item (e.g., book), and the therapist assists her to express her automatic thought (i.e., stream of thoughts: "I can't get rid of this. I need this"), along with a justification ("My sister gave it to me as a gift. I should keep it. I haven't read it yet. I will miss out on important information if I don't keep it").

Using the Problematic Thinking Style List, patients note their particular problematic thinking patterns. Examples from the list include the following:

- All or Nothing Thinking, shaped by absolutist and perfectionist thinking;
- Overgeneralization, categorized by using a single situation to generalize about all other situations (e.g., "If I get rid of this book, I will never have the opportunity to read it");
- Jumping to Conclusions, classified by assuming negative results without supporting evidence;
- Catastrophizing, defined by exaggerating the significance of actions (e.g., "If I throw away these holiday cards from my aunt, she's likely to experience a heart attack");
- Discounting the Positive, a thinking model that discounts achievement (e.g., "Even though I cleared most of the spare bedroom, that doesn't matter, the rest of the house is still packed full.");

- Emotional Reasoning, defined by the tendency to rely on emotions in place of logic (e.g., "It makes me sad to throw away these old magazines, so I think I'll just keep them");
- Moral Reasoning, characterized by the use of should statements stemming from perfectionism and guilt; Labeling; defined by negatively labeling oneself or others (e.g., "It's useless, I'm so stupid, I'm never going to figure out how to file these papers"); and
- Under- and Overestimating, characterized by underestimating personal capacities and overestimating difficulty.

This list can be initially applied during office-based sessions and then incorporated into homework assignments. After identifying their unhelpful thinking styles, patients work to develop alternative thoughts (e.g., "My sister doesn't expect me to keep this forever. The book likely has interesting information but if I require it in the future, I could get the book or look up the information then"). Thought Records are helpful tools for managing challenging decisions by illustrating the association between the activating event, thoughts, emotions, and behaviors as well as structuring the identification of thinking errors and development of alternative thoughts.

Sorting and making decisions about items may activate the patient's core beliefs and schema. The Downward Arrow is a cognitive strategy used to uncover core beliefs. If a patient seems at least somewhat distressed about discarding an item, she should first rate her level of distress (0 = *no distress* to 10 = *the most distress ever*). The therapist would ask the patient to believe that she ought to keep it because it's a gift from her sister or she will miss out on important information if she discards it without first reading it. The therapist then asks the patient a sequence of questions, such as: "What would that mean (about you)?" ("If I throw out her gift, I will seem life an ungrateful sister.") "What would be the worst part about that?" ("She'll be mad at me.") "What would happen then?" ("She won't want to talk to me, and I'll be alone.") These questions examine the underlying meaning of these thoughts and uncover the core belief (e.g., "I am unlovable"). Other examples of negative core beliefs are "I am worthless or helpless," "Others are not trustworthy," and "The world is unsafe." Of course, core beliefs can be positive ("I am safe in the world," "I am capable") as well.

Other helpful cognitive techniques may be applied during sorting exposures. Questions about Possessions encourage patients to ask themselves about the consequences of keeping or the reasons for not keeping items (e.g., "How many do I have? How many would be enough? Is keeping this item helping or detracting from decluttering goals?"). When using the Advantages and Disadvantages Worksheet, patients list the benefits and costs of keeping and discarding items. The task can be used either in regard to a single item or a category of items.

Socratic questioning is a strategy that guides patients' exploration of beliefs, helps them test evidence that supports or disconfirms beliefs, and consider alternative interpretations and outcomes. Taking Another Perspective is an exercise in which a patient is asked to consider his situation from the perspective of a close other (e.g., "Would your sister agree with your perspective? Is this a thought you would want your child to adopt?"). In Taking the Opposite Perspective, the patient chooses an item and then explains why it should be discarded while the therapist argues for keeping it. Valuing Time is an approach that focuses on time usage, how much time is spent engaging in hoarding behaviors, and how time could otherwise be used. When using the Need Versus Want form, patients rate how much they need a specific item and how much they want that item. The patient is then prompted to reflect on the item's actual value and how that coincides or differs with their goals and values. It is advantageous for the therapist to draw from the variety of cognitive methods to use in session during sorting tasks or as homework assignments. When assigning cognitive strategies as homework, it is important that the therapist and patient first have used the strategy in session together to help ensure the patient's comfort and confidence when practicing at home.

Skills Training

Many individuals with hoarding symptoms have difficulty with organization and problem solving. These problems may stem from challenges with attention and categorizing objects. CBT for hoarding addresses these issues by introducing problem-solving methods and basic organizational skills. Although these skills can be integrated into CBT treatment and may need to be reinforced throughout, the protocol advises spending two consecutive sessions working through them early on in treatment.

Problem-solving skills are best learned by applying them to a specific problem area. It is essential that the problem be framed as solvable. The steps include first defining the problem and identifying the issues contributing to the problem, brainstorming potential courses of action, selecting a solution, and devising small achievable and measurable outcomes, applying these steps (often outside of session as part of homework), and reviewing the final outcome. This process can be done in a creative way that engages the patient and promotes feelings of agency.

Problems with attention and distraction are frequently associated with hoarding and can limit the successes of interventions. Timing how long it takes to sort a range of materials is a simple method for assessing attention span. If distractibility is a problem, a timer may be used to gauge how long a patient works without distraction; using the timer, therapist and patient can work to increase the patient's attention span. Structured time management also protects against distraction and aids the patient's daily functioning. Toward this end, using a calendar to schedule activities, assignments, and appointments helps establish and track one's routine. The Task List is a form that requests patients to detail specific task descriptions, the importance of accomplishing a task, date it was added to list, and the date of completion. This exercise is particularly well-suited as homework. Other strategies for minimizing distraction include deconstructing larger tasks into smaller, easier component parts, writing down distractions to deal with them at another time and not during the time reserved for task completion, and novel ways of removing distracting stimuli. Therapists can reinforce the use of calendars, task lists, and other tools by asking about patients' use of them and integrating them into session (e.g., reminding patients to record the homework assignment in their calendar).

One of the first steps in organizing is the patient's decision to save or remove possessions. Objects that patients decide to remove from their home may be categorized as trash, recyclables, donations, items to sell, and undecided. It is crucial that the therapist and patient set an action plan for removing discarded items. The plan should set routines around trash and recycle pickup, identify local charities for donations, and identify places to sell select unwanted items. Saved items should be categorized by type of possession (e.g., toiletries, clothing, office supplies), making note of the location where that possession will be stored (e.g., toiletries will be stored on the shelf in bathroom). The Personal Organization Plan is helpful in this process, encouraging patients to identify the types of possessions that they have and where they should be kept. Before starting sorting initiatives, it is important to ensure that there is available and appropriate storage furniture (filing cabinets and shelving), cartons and containers, and organizational supplies (tape and labels). Creating interim staging areas for sorting, temporary storage, and final storage is also helpful. A decision tree is a useful way of guiding the patient through these preparatory steps for organizing possessions.

Managing paper documents is of particular concern and requires a separate process of organization. Papers may be organized according to how long the materials should be kept, and separate categories created for various kinds of paper. For example, everyday receipts and deposit and withdrawal slips (1 month); paycheck receipts and monthly bank and investment information (1 year); tax return information and yearly bank or investment summaries (6 years); major receipts, tax returns, real estate records, and will and trust information (indefinitely); and insurance policy information, marriage licenses, birth and death certificates (kept in safe deposit box). Guided questions that address timing, duration, frequency, short-term goals, and long-term goals are a helpful tool for planning the filing process. The Filing Paper Form (Steketee & Frost, 2007b) reviews common filing categories and is useful for constructing a unique filing plan.

Mail is a distinct kind of paper category and one that is difficult for many patients. Mail can be managed by making categories for the type of mail to be discarded and how it should be discarded, and for the type of mail to be saved and where it should be kept. Magazines and newspapers can be similarly categorized, allowing a certain time limit for materials to be kept and reviewed before disposing of them. Strategies for maintaining these systems prioritize punctuality, orderliness, and consistency, addressing issues such as regular trash removal, routine house cleaning, and scheduled mail sorting.

Exposure

Hoarding functions as a way to avoid the stress of making incorrect decisions, dealing with pain or loss, forgetting important information, or discomfort of having guests in one's home. Exposure techniques may help patients break with past avoidance behaviors, confront their fears, and achieve productive change. Habituation is a physiological process of desensitizing to fears. Graphing one's exposure and habituation process can be helpful. Exposure is associated with an increase in discomfort that diminishes over time and enhances one's control over his or her anxiety.

An exposure hierarchy (i.e., a list of progressively more challenging exposure tasks) is a strategy to facilitate this process. Patients begin sorting materials and areas on the list that are associated with less discomfort and gradually work toward achieving more challenging goals. General parameters include identifying the specific target area, selecting the type of items to be dealt with and their final destination (where they should go), and preparing for storage of items. Materials are ranked from easiest to hardest, and patients select the kind of possession with which to start. Patients apply the organizational and filing systems described and use cognitive skills when faced with a challenging decision. When sorting, a temporary category called "undecided" may be used, but possessions in this pile must be limited and attended to before the end of the sorting session. Once the area is clear, the patient can use the space and determine strategies for maintaining the clutter-free zone. These skills should be taught and practiced in the office and at home. Therapists socialize their patients to bring objects (e.g., mail) to the office to sort for maximum exposure opportunities. Cognitive therapy techniques are incorporated into the exposure exercises in the office and at home. It can be expected that progress and motivation for exposure-based work ebb and flow throughout treatment.

Home clean-outs are considered "extended exposures" and may be helpful under specific circumstances. When timed and prepared appropriately, clean-outs may lead to significant improvement. It is recommended that large-scale clean-outs be incorporated into the treatment plan when a patient is sophisticated in his or her cognitive reasoning and exposure skills (typically after Session 18).

Imagery-based exposures (in contrast to in vivo exposures) are useful in situations in which sorting and discarding is not initially possible because of issues of fear, paranoia, or beliefs in unrealistic outcomes. In a structured exercise, patients are told to imagine themselves within a given situation (e.g., sorting papers) and recount their sensory and emotional experiences as well as their thoughts. The therapist guides the patient to focus on parts of the imagery that evoke the most discomfort and anticipated negative outcomes and asks them to rate their feelings every 5 to 10 minutes until ratings have significantly declined. This method is used with patients who are particularly afraid of a catastrophe destroying their home and possessions. These patients are asked to imagine themselves in the context of such a catastrophe with time to save only certain items. This task prepares them to be able to let go of certain items while maintaining others. Imagined exposures are also useful in dealing with patients who are reluctant to discard newspapers and magazines. These patients are asked to imagine all of the worlds' newspapers and the wealth of information and opportunity associated with them. Then they are asked to imagine all the newspapers that they have not read and the information missed. Imagined exposure may also be applied to prepare an individual for in vivo exposure.

Therapists collaborate with patients to develop behavioral experiments to test specific hoarding-related hypotheses and beliefs. Patients articulate a hypothesis about what will happen in a specific sorting, discarding, or non-acquisition situation (e.g., "If I get rid of these books, I won't be able to handle it. I will think about them all the time and be really upset") and then rate how confident they are about this hypothesis and the consequences (e.g., their degree of discomfort). After completing the task, patients rate their actual discomfort and assess the degree to which their initial prediction was accurate. It is essential that therapists use their clinical judgment about what is an appropriate behavioral experiment, selecting opportunities in which it is probable that a prediction will not come true and that patients will be able to recognize the errors in their thinking. The Behavioral Experiment Form (Steketee & Frost, 2007b) is a helpful tool for structuring the activity. Because viewing a possession may enhance its perceived value, the Needing Object in Sight experiment involves patients physically distancing themselves from an object for a specified period of time (e.g., a week) by temporarily giving it to a friend, the therapist, or another person; subsequently, they decide whether to get the item back or discard it unseen. With the Influence on Your Life experiment, patients select an object for the therapist to hold for a specified period and then rate how not having the object influenced their life during that period (i.e., how the patient coped with not having the object). With time and separation from the object, patients' need for the object may lessen and the experience may lead to a shift in how other objects are valued. Similar experiments can be used over the course of therapy to evaluate and help shift a patient's thinking process.

Nonacquisition

Not all who suffer with hoarding also struggle with excessive acquisition; however, strong urges to acquire and difficulty with compulsive buying and acquiring free things are common. The degree to which acquisition is a problem and the patient's motivation to address it will influence when and how it is addressed in treatment. In cases in which acquisition is more severe, it may be helpful to focus on it earlier in treatment to reduce the volume of items entering the home. The Acquiring Form (Steketee & Frost, 2007b) is a helpful tool for patients to record the items that they typically acquire, where they are acquired (e.g., yard sale), and a discomfort rating associated with the thought of not acquiring the specific item. A functional analysis of the acquisition may be applied to explore and evaluate the triggers for acquiring and the thoughts, behaviors, and emotions involved in the acquisition process. The items and how they are acquired (e.g., yard sales, online) are critical to understanding the strong reinforcement patterns surrounding this behavior as well as developing an appropriate exposure hierarchy and exercises (e.g., nonacquisition trip to a favorite store). As noted in the earlier discussion of the CBT model for hoarding, the positive emotions associated with acquiring an object (e.g., pleasure, excitement) are strong positive reinforcers for further acquisition. An acquiring visualization exercise in which patients imagine experiencing a strong urge to acquire may help them verbalize their thoughts and beliefs. Cognitive strategies can be helpful in modifying beliefs associated with acquiring, resisting urges, and coping with exposure exercises. Furthermore, acquiring may be a coping behavior to boost a low mood; thus, it is essential that patients find other pleasurable activities as replacement for buying.

Once the goal to reduce acquiring is established, the therapist and patient collaborate to create a set of detailed rules to achieve it. For example, before acquiring any item, the patient agrees to identify the specific immediate use of the item, have cash available to pay for it, and have a designated clear space for storage. Another rule may state that for every one item that enters the home, at least one similar item must be removed (e.g., when a new magazine arrives, at least one other magazine must be removed). It is also helpful to use the cognitive strategy of advantages and disadvantages of acquiring, taking into account the short-term pleasure and the long-term negative consequences.

Although initially it may be helpful to avoid contexts that trigger acquiring, the exposure principles mentioned earlier are applicable for managing urges and acquisition over the long term. Together, the therapist and patient construct an exposure hierarchy that lists progressively more challenging situations (in which urges are more difficult to resist) and the accompanying discomfort ratings. During nonacquisition exposure trips, patients first pass by stores or areas where they have acquired in the past, but without stopping to shop. Next, they spend time in a store (or related location) without touching the merchandise. Finally, they handle specific items but leave the store without purchasing them (and without plans to return or buy them).

Additionally, identifying and planning other pleasurable activities as alternatives to those associated with acquisition are crucial. Because acquiring is often a coping behavior, alternative coping strategies for stress, low mood, or other affective responses are also critical. Problem-solving skills may be applied to generate a list of pleasurable and coping activities; behavioral experiments may be used to test out the level of enjoyment that the patient predicted versus that experienced.

Furthermore, cognitive strategies help with identifying thoughts and beliefs specific to acquisition. The List of Problematic Thinking Styles may help identify thought patterns that contribute to giving in to urges to acquire. For example, the thought "I should get 20 of these [notebooks] because they are an awesome deal—I'll never find it for this price anywhere" includes All or Nothing thinking. The Downward Arrow may reveal deep core beliefs about perfectionism, self-worth, and other concerns. Socratic questioning techniques are helpful for examining the evidence for beliefs about acquiring, such as the double standard, devil's advocate, evaluating the logic, generalizing to other conditions, or taking another perspective. Another important use of Socratic questions is to help patients recognize that they may be overestimating the beauty, usefulness, or uniqueness of an item and undercalculating the time required to fix or use it. The therapist may ask, for example, how long it would take for the patient to use 20 thick notebooks and also ask them to consider the amount of space required to store them. It is essential that the patient and therapist discuss these ideas in collaboration. The Want Versus Need worksheet helps the patient consider the various aspects of need (e.g., Is it required for life, safety?), the distinction from convenience, and where these factors falls on the spectrum of want (e.g., Is it their most favorite item?). Patients may consider additional questions to use when experiencing an urge to acquire, such as those on the list Questions for Acquiring (e.g., Do I own something similar? Do I have a specific space to put this? Will not getting this help me solve my hoarding problem?). Patients identify the questions that are most useful and relevant to them; some write these questions on a card, store it in their wallet or purse, and ask themselves the questions before purchasing anything.

Maintenance and Relapse Prevention

The two final sessions of the specialized CBT treatment protocol are typically scheduled 2 weeks apart, and booster sessions may be added. A goal of these sessions is to guide the patient to review the progress that he or she has made during the treatment. Patients' sense of self-efficacy will be boosted by recounting the specific techniques that they applied to reach their current accomplishments. It is also essential to orient the patient toward the future to maintain and increase gains but also because progress for hoarding tends to be slow, incremental, and unsteady. To encourage continued practice after treatment and between booster sessions, therapists may help patients schedule self-sessions in which they work independently to apply the strategies. More formal plans may be necessary for continued sorting and discarding and for maintaining gains. Resources and reminders such as audio recordings of specific techniques, treatment notes, published client workbook (Steketee & Frost, 2007b), a self-help book (Tolin et al., 2007a) or self-help groups may help structure and reinforce these techniques. At the end of treatment, it is also important to review the CBT model for hoarding to assess its accuracy and whether changes are needed. The therapist and patient review the initial treatment goals and actual achievements, as well as a comprehensive list of treatment strategies. Therapists normalize, anticipate, and plan for lapses before their occurrence. Discussion of anticipated and possible unexpected stressors are opportunities to consider reactions to and thoughts about these situations and identify specific CBT skills (e.g., identify thinking styles, behavioral experiments) and coping techniques that would be relevant. Progress is also a prompt for the therapist and patient to plan for how patients can spend additional "free time," that is, time that was previously consumed by hoarding symptoms (e.g., pleasant activity scheduling), or to utilize the cleared space (e.g., placing flowers on a cleared table). We recommend that the therapist and patient again complete the assessments (e.g., HRS, SI–R, CIR) noted earlier to evaluate change over the course of treatment. While reviewing these scores, it is essential to note the particular successes and areas for future improvement to help guide the patient toward self-efficacy, responsibility, and continued progress.

REVIEW OF EMPIRICAL STUDIES ON CBT FOR HOARDING

The CBT protocol developed by Steketee and Frost (2007b) and described in this chapter has been tested in an open trial and a wait-list control trial; it has been modified for delivery through various modalities (group CBT, webcam CBT, Internet-based support group, biblio-based support group), demonstrating promising results. These studies have been conducted with predominantly White, middle-aged, unmarried, well-educated women with hoarding behaviors as their primary psychiatric problem. In an initial open trial, 10 patients reported reductions of 30% on the CIR, 28% on the SI–R, and 50% of patients were therapist-rated as "much" or "very much" improved on the Clinical Global impression—Improvement (CGI; Tolin, Frost, & Steketee, 2007b). In the first randomized controlled trial of CBT for hoarding (Steketee, Frost, Tolin, Rasmussen, & Brown, 2010), after 12 weeks, CBT patients showed decreases of 15% on the SI–R and 27% on the HRS, whereas the waitlist group showed little reduction. After 26 sessions, CBT patients ($n = 37$) demonstrated significant reductions on the SI–R (27%) and HRS (39%) with large effect sizes (converted Cohen's $d = 1.81$ and 2.30, respectively). On the CGI, therapists rated 71% of patients as "much" or "very much" improved; 81% of patients rated themselves similarly. To extend access and increase home-based practice, Muroff, Steketee, and Frost (2009a) launched a pilot study exploring the effectiveness of CBT for hoarding delivered via webcam that showed promising effects for three of four patients, as well as shorter treatment duration. Additionally, two pilot studies tested individual CBT for hoarding specifically with older adults. Six patients completed 35 individual, primarily home-based CBT sessions and reported a 28.2% reduction on the CIR (Turner, Steketee, & Nauth, 2010). Another study of 12 patients found 20% reductions on the SI–R and little improvement on the CGI (Ayers, Wehterell, Golsshan, & Saxena, 2011).

Seeking to create a more time- and cost-effective alternative to individual therapy, Muroff, Steketee, Rasmussen, and colleagues (2009) developed and tested a 16- to 20-week group CBT (GCBT) manual for hoarding that included home visits (five to eight people per group, $n = 27$). They showed a 14.3% decrease on the SI–R (Cohen's $d = 1.57$). One group ($n = 8$) used a more formal manualized protocol and showed a 22% reduction on the SI–R. Gilliam et al. (2011) also tested GCBT for hoarding without home-based sessions, reporting a decrease of 27% on the SI–R (Cohen's $d = 1.31$); 73% rated themselves as "much improved" or "very much improved." Muroff and colleagues (2012), examined the efficacy of GCBT compared with self-help bibliotherapy for hoarding (BIB) using Buried in Treasures (Tolin, Frost, & Steketee, 2007a; $N = 38$) and measured the effects of additional home visits with nonclinician coaches. Participants in both GCBT conditions reported significant reductions on the SIR (23%–30%) and HRS–SR (25%–27%) and large effect sizes (Cohen's ds = 2.0–3.4), whereas BIB participants showed minimal reductions.

These methods have also been incorporated into self-help group treatments as well. Muroff, Steketee, Himle, and Frost (2010) evaluated the benefit of an online CBT-based self-help group for hoarding (n = 106) compared with a wait-list control (n = 155) over five time points (15 months), showing modest benefits, especially for those involved for an extended period. Frost, Pekareva-Kochergina, and Maxner (2011) evaluated a structured in-person 13-week bibliotherapy self-help model for hoarding with two cohorts led by trained undergraduate students, reporting reductions on the SI–R symptoms (18%–27%). Of the first cohort, 41% rated themselves as "much improved" on the CGI. In the second cohort, 72% rated themselves and 73% were rated by clinicians as "much" or "very much improved."

Over the past decade, the development and application of efficacious treatments for hoarding have grown steadily and systematically. Future studies on CBT for hoarding may increase sample sizes, shorten treatment duration, include more follow-up data to assess long-term benefits, use wait-list or controlled comparisons, and address issues of attrition.

FUTURE DIRECTIONS

Although specialized CBT for hoarding has shown promising results, there is much room for continued development and improvement to most effectively treat this multicomponent problem across the life span. A number of additional considerations are essential to the future design, implementation, and testing of hoarding treatments, as we detail in the following paragraphs.

Cultural Diversity

The study of hoarding disorder interventions has been conducted largely in academic institutions in North America, Europe, and Australia. As a result, less is known about how hoarding manifests in diverse cultural groups and in nonindustrialized nations. Understanding the cultural influences on thoughts, behaviors, and emotions related to collecting and saving is critical to assessing and intervening with hoarding appropriately. Recognizing the role of cultural traditions and practices in hoarding symptoms and treatment is helpful; however, it is not advisable to assign meaning based only on these factors.

Older Adults

Treating older adults who hoard requires special sensitivity to possible cognitive and physical declines at this stage of life. Treatment strategies may be adjusted for older adults that experience limitations with executive functioning tasks such as prospective memory (Ayers et al., 2011). Physical limitations (e.g., difficulty bending, lifting) may require accommodations or home assistance to complete sorting and discarding tasks.

Families

Family members of people who hoard are often significantly affected by the problem either because they live with the person who hoards or unexpectedly discover it (e.g., an elderly parent is hospitalized and the adult child visits the home to find the amassed possessions). Family members often try to assess the level of risk and are motivated to assist in the intervention. Supporting families in the use of appropriate communication strategies such as motivational interviewing and evidence-based intervention strategies (e.g., CBT) can be helpful in ensuring that everyone's perspective and desired outcomes are honored.

Clean-Outs

When people who hoard are threatened with severe consequences such as condemnation of a property, eviction from their home, or the end of a relationship with a spouse or adult child, the first impulse is often to engage in a full-scale clean-out of the home. It is well documented that clean-outs often result in the accumulation of possessions again and feelings of mistrust and betrayal in the person who hoards. Instead, a harm-reduction approach (Tompkins & Hartl, 2009) is recommended, followed by clinical treatment, if appropriate.

Collaboration

Addressing the multiple manifestations and comorbidities of hoarding often requires expertise from a range of human services disciplines, including but not limited to mental health, housing, protective services, and the medical and legal professions (Bratiotis et al., 2011). When the person who hoards works with a team of diverse professionals, he or she has increased access to multiple resources and vast expertise, which can reduce the impact of the hoarding problem.

Animal Hoarding

Little is known about animal hoarding. The veterinary and animal welfare communities have characterized animal hoarding and provided guidelines for managing this difficult problem (Patronek, Loar, & Nathanson, 2006). Similarities and differences between animal and object hoarders have recently been illuminated (Frost, Patronek, & Rosenfield, 2011), and this information provides clues for the development of clinical treatment for animal hoarding. Such treatment is still in its infancy.

REFERENCES

Abramowitz, J. S., Foa, E. B., & Franklin, M. E. (2003). Exposure and ritual prevention for obsessive–compulsive disorder: Effects of intensive versus twice-weekly sessions. *Journal of Consulting and Clinical Psychology, 71*, 394–398. doi:10.1037/0022-006X.71.2.394

American Psychiatric Association. (2011). F 02 hoarding disorder. *DSM–V Development*. Retrieved from http://www.dsm5.org/ProposedRevisions/Pages/proposedrevision.aspx?rid=398

American Psychiatric Association. (2013). *Diagnostic and statistical manual of mental disorders* (5th ed.). Washington, DC: Author.

Ayers, C. R., Wehterell, J. L., Golsshan, S., & Saxena, S. (2011). Cognitive-behavioral therapy for geriatric compulsive hoarding. *Behaviour Research and Therapy, 49*, 689–694. doi:10.1016/j.brat.2011.07.002

Bratiotis, C. (2009). *Task force community response to compulsive hoarding cases*. (Doctoral dissertation). Retrieved from ProQuest Dissertations and Theses. (Accession Order Number 3363599)

Bratiotis, C. (2013). Community hoarding task forces: A comparative case study of five task forces in the United States. *Health and Social Care in the Community, 21*, 245–253.

Bratiotis, C., Schmalisch, C. S., & Steketee, G. (2011). *The hoarding handbook: A guide for human service professionals*. New York, NY: Oxford University Press.

Frost, R. O., & Gross, R. C. (1993). The hoarding of possessions. *Behaviour Research and Therapy, 31*, 367–381. doi:10.1016/0005-7967(93)90094-B

Frost, R. O., & Hartl, T. L. (1996). A cognitive-behavioral model of compulsive hoarding. *Behaviour Research and Therapy, 34*, 341–350. doi:10.1016/0005-7967(95)00071-2

Frost, R. O., & Hristova, V. (2011). Assessment of hoarding. *Journal of Clinical Psychology, 67*, 456–466. doi:10.1002/jclp.20790

Frost, R. O., & Hunt, S. (2000). *Brief treatment of compulsive hoarding*. Unpublished manuscript, Smith College, Northampton, MA.

Frost, R. O., Kim, H. J., Morris, C., Bloss, C., Murray-Close, M., & Steketee, G. (1998). Hoarding, compulsive buying and reasons for saving. *Behaviour Research and Therapy, 36,* 657–664. doi:10.1016/S0005-7967(98)00056-4

Frost, R. O., Krause, M. S., & Steketee, G. (1996). Hoarding and obsessive–compulsive symptoms. *Behavior Modification, 20,* 116–132. doi:10.1177/01454455960201006

Frost, R. O., Meagher, B. M., & Riskind, J. H. (2001). Obsessive–compulsive features in pathological lottery and scratch-ticket gamblers. *Journal of Gambling Studies, 17,* 5–19. doi:10.1023/A:1016636214258

Frost, R. O., Patronek, G., & Rosenfield, E. (2011). Comparison of object and animal hoarding. *Depression and Anxiety, 28,* 885–891. doi:10.1002/da.20826

Frost, R. O., Pekareva-Kochergina, A., & Maxner, S. (2011). The effectiveness of a biblio-based support group for hoarding disorder. *Behaviour Research and Therapy, 49,* 628–634. doi:10.1016/j.brat.2011.06.010

Frost, R. O., Steketee, G., & Grisham, J. (2004). Measurement of compulsive hoarding: Saving Inventory-Revised. *Behaviour Research and Therapy, 42,* 1163–1182. doi:10.1016/j.brat.2003.07.006

Frost, R. O., Steketee, G., & Tolin, D. F. (2011). Comorbidity in hoarding disorder. *Depression and Anxiety, 28,* 876–884. doi:10.1002/da.20861

Frost, R., Steketee, G., Tolin, D., & Renaud, D. (2008). Development and validation of the Clutter Image Rating. *Journal of Psychopathology and Behavioral Assessment, 30,* 193–203. doi:10.1007/s10862-007-9068-7

Frost, R. O., Steketee, G., & Williams, L. (2000). Hoarding: A community health problem. *Health & Social Care in the Community, 8,* 229–234. doi:10.1046/j.1365-2524.2000.00245.x

Frost, R. O., Steketee, G., & Williams, L. (2002). Compulsive buying, compulsive hoarding, and obsessive–compulsive disorder. *Behavior Therapy, 33,* 201–214. doi:10.1016/S0005-7894(02)80025-9

Frost, R. O., Steketee, G., Williams, L. F., & Warren, R. (2000). Mood, personality disorder symptoms and disability in obsessive compulsive hoarders: A comparison with clinical and nonclinical controls. *Behaviour Research and Therapy, 38,* 1071–1081. doi:10.1016/S0005-7967(99)00137-0

Frost, R. O., Tolin, D. F., & Maltby, N. (2010). Insight-related challenges in the treatment of hoarding. *Cognitive and Behavioral Practice, 17,* 404–413. doi:10.1016/j.cbpra.2009.07.004

Gilliam, C. M., Norberg, M. M., Villavicencio, A., Morrison, S., Hannan, S. E., & Tolin, D. F. (2011). Group cognitive-behavioral therapy for hoarding disorder: An open trial. *Behaviour Research and Therapy, 49,* 802–807. doi:10.1016/j.brat.2011.08.008

Grisham, J. R., Frost, R. O., Steketee, G., Kim, H. J., & Hood, S. (2006). Age of onset of compulsive hoarding. *Journal of Anxiety Disorders, 20,* 675–686. doi:10.1016/j.janxdis.2005.07.004

Iervolino, A. C., Perroud, N., Fullana, M. A., Guipponi, M., Cherkas, L., Collier, D. A., & Mataix-Cols, D. (2009). Prevalence and heritability of compulsive hoarding: A twin study. *The American Journal of Psychiatry, 166,* 1156–1161. doi:10.1176/appi.ajp.2009.08121789

Mataix-Cols, D., Frost, R. O., Pertusa, A., Clark, L. A., Saxena, S., Leckman, J. F., . . . Wilhelm, S. (2010). Hoarding disorder: A new diagnosis for *DSM–V? Depression and Anxiety, 27,* 556–572. doi:10.1002/da.20693

Meunier, S. A., Tolin, D. F., Frost, R. O., Steketee, G., & Brady, R. E. (2006, March). *Prevalence of hoarding symptoms across the anxiety disorders.* Paper presented at the Annual Meeting of the Anxiety Disorders Association of America, Miami, FL.

Miller, W. R., & Rollnick, S. (2002). *Motivational interviewing: Preparing people for change* (2nd ed.). New York, NY: Guilford Press.

Mueller, A., Mitchell, J. E., Crosby, R. D., Glaesmer, H., & Zwaan, M. (2009). The prevalence of compulsive hoarding and its association with compulsive buying in a German population-based sample. *Behaviour Research and Therapy, 47,* 705–709. doi:10.1016/j.brat.2009.04.005

Muroff, J., Steketee, G., Bratiotis, C., & Ross, A. (2012). Group cognitive and behavioral therapy and bibliotherapy for hoarding: A pilot trial. *Depression and Anxiety, 29,* 597–604.

Muroff, J., Steketee, G., & Frost, R. (2009, November). *Cognitive behavioral treatment delivered via Webcam.* Paper presented at the Association for Behavioral and Cognitive Therapies Convention, New York, NY.

Muroff, J., Steketee, G., Himle, J., & Frost, R. (2010). Delivery of Internet treatment for compulsive hoarding (D.I.T.C.H.). *Behaviour Research and Therapy, 48,* 79–85. doi:10.1016/j.brat.2009.09.006

Muroff, J., Steketee, G., Rasmussen, J., Gibson, A., Bratiotis, C., & Sorrentino, C. (2009). Group cognitive and behavioral treatment for compulsive hoarding: A preliminary trial. *Depression and Anxiety, 26,* 634–640. doi:10.1002/da.20591

Patronek, G. J., Loar, L., & Nathanson, J. N. (2006). *Animal hoarding: Structuring interdisciplinary responses to help people, animals and communities at risk.* Paper Presented at the Hoarding of Animals Research Consortium, Boston, MA.

Pertusa, A., Frost, R. O., Fullana, M. A., Samuels, J., Steketee, G., Tolin, D., . . . Mataix-Cols, D. (2010). Refining the diagnostic boundaries of compulsive hoarding: A critical review. *Clinical Psychology Review, 30,* 371–386. doi:10.1016/j.cpr.2010.01.007

Rasmussen, J. L., Steketee, G., Frost, R. O., & Tolin, D. L. (2013). *Assessing squalor in compulsive hoarding. The Home Environment Index.* Manuscript submitted for publication.

Samuels, J., Bienvenu, O. J., 3rd, Riddle, M. A., Cullen, B. A., Grados, M. A., Liang K. Y., . . . Nestadt, G. (2002). Hoarding in obsessive compulsive disorder: Results from a case-control study. *Behaviour Research and Therapy, 40,* 517–528. doi:10.1016/S0005-7967(01)00026-2

Samuels, J. F., Bienvenu, O. J., Grados, M. A., Cullen, B., Riddle, M. A., Liang, K. Y., . . . Nestadt, G. (2008). Prevalence and correlates of hoarding behavior in a community-based sample. *Behaviour Research and Therapy, 46,* 836–844. doi:10.1016/j.brat.2008.04.004

Saxena, S. (2008). Recent advances in compulsive hoarding. *Current Psychiatry Reports, 10,* 297–303. doi:10.1007/s11920-008-0048-8

Seedat, S., & Stein, D. J. (2002). Hoarding in obsessive–compulsive disorder and related disorders: A preliminary report of 15 cases. *Psychiatry Clinical Neuroscience, 56,* 17–23. Steketee, G., Frost, R., & Kyrios, M. (2003). Cognitive aspects of compulsive hoarding. *Cognitive Therapy and Research, 27,* 463–479.

Steketee, G., Frost, R., & Kyrios, M. (2003). Cognitive aspects of compulsive hoarding. *Cognitive Therapy and Research, 27,* 463–479. doi:10.1023/A:1025428631552

Steketee, G., & Frost, R. O. (2007a). *Compulsive hoarding and acquiring: A Therapist Guide.* New York, NY: Oxford University Press.

Steketee, G., & Frost, R. O. (2007b). *Compulsive hoarding and acquiring: Workbook.* New York, NY: Oxford University Press.

Steketee, G., Frost, R. O., Tolin, D. F., Rasmussen, J., & Brown, T. A. (2010). Waitlist-controlled trial of cognitive behavior therapy for hoarding disorder. *Depression and Anxiety, 27,* 476–484. doi:10.1002/da.20673

Tolin, D. F., Frost, R., Steketee, G., & Fitch, K. (2008). Family burden of compulsive hoarding: Results of an Internet survey. *Behaviour Research and Therapy, 46,* 334–344. doi:10.1016/j.brat.2007.12.008

Tolin, D. F., Frost, R. O., & Steketee, G. (2007a). *Buried in treasures: Help for compulsive hoarding.* New York, NY: Oxford University Press.

Tolin, D. F., Frost, R. O., & Steketee, G. (2007b). An open trial of cognitive–behavioral therapy for compulsive hoarding. *Behaviour Research and Therapy, 45,* 1461–1470. doi:10.1016/j.brat.2007.01.001

Tolin, D. F., Frost, R. O., & Steketee, G. (2010). A brief interview for assessing compulsive hoarding: The Hoarding Rating Scale. *Psychiatry Research, 178,* 147–152. doi:10.1016/j.psychres.2009.05.001

Tolin, D. F., Frost, R. O., Steketee, G., Gray, K. D., & Fitch, K. E. (2008). The economic and social burden of compulsive hoarding. *Psychiatry Research, 160,* 200–211. doi:10.1016/j.psychres.2007.08.008

Tompkins, M. A., & Hartl, T. L. (2009). *Digging out: Helping your loved one manage clutter, hoarding, and compulsive acquiring.* Oakland, CA: New Harbinger.

Turner, K., Steketee, G., & Nauth, L. (2010). Treating elders with compulsive hoarding: A pilot program. *Cognitive and Behavioral Practice, 17,* 449–457. doi:10.1016/j.cbpra.2010.04.001

7

BODY DYSMORPHIC DISORDER

ANDREA S. HARTMANN, AARON J. BLASHILL,
JENNIFER L. GREENBERG, AND SABINE WILHELM

SYMPTOMS OF BODY DYSMORPHIC DISORDER

Body dysmorphic disorder (BDD) is characterized by a preoccupation with an imagined or slight defect in appearance. Appearance-related concerns can involve any body area; however, the concern is usually focused on the face and head (Phillips, 2005a). Individuals might be preoccupied with perceived flaws of their skin (scars, wrinkles, pores, acne), hair (balding or thinning, excessive hair, symmetry), and/or nose (too large or disproportionate). It is not uncommon for individuals to be concerned with several body parts; over time, the number of body parts can increase or the focus can shift (Phillips, 2005a), with an average number of six to seven areas of concern

The writing of this chapter was supported in part by a fellowship awarded to Dr. Andrea S. Hartmann by the Swiss National Science Foundation (Grant PBSKP1_134330/1) and a grant awarded to Dr. Aaron J. Blashill by the Harvard University Center for AIDS Research, National Institutes of Health/National Institute of Allergies and Infectious Diseases (Grant 5P30AI060354-08).

http://dx.doi.org/10.1037/14323-008
Obsessive–Compulsive Disorder and Its Spectrum: A Life-Span Approach, Eric A. Storch and Dean McKay (Editors)
Copyright © 2014 by the American Psychological Association. All rights reserved.

over the course of the disorder (Phillips, Grant, Siniscalchi, Stout, & Price, 2005). These concerns are often obsessive in nature; they consume significant time and are difficult to resist and control. In some patients, insight is poor, and thus they may have difficulty realizing that they actually look normal. Some patients also have ideas or delusions of reference (i.e., they are convinced that others are taking special notice of them and their perceived flaw; Phillips, 2004). The degree of insight often varies across the course of the disorder; therefore, it has been suggested that delusional and nondelusional BDD reflect one disorder with a continuum of insight (Phillips, 2004).

Most patients also engage in repetitive, compulsive behaviors as a means to temporarily alleviate the distress associated with the appearance-related concerns and intrusive thoughts (Phillips, 2005a). These include comparing their appearance with that of others, seeking reassurance, checking their appearance in mirrors or other reflective surfaces, camouflaging the perceived flaw with clothing or makeup, excessive grooming (hair combing, shaving), tanning, and skin picking. The behaviors are compulsive; thus, patients feel driven to perform them and find them difficult to control. However, they provide only short-term relief and maintain the disorder in the long term. Some of the behaviors even worsen the condition because patients may injure themselves while attempting to fix the flaw (e.g., a patient might cause skin damage by using a razor blade to fix acne; Veale, Boocock, et al., 1996). Prevalence of cosmetic procedures is also high; however, such procedures can worsen BDD (Crerand, Menard, & Phillips, 2010). To avoid negative appearance evaluations by others as well as an exacerbation of appearance-related thoughts, patients may avoid daily activities (e.g., school, work, and social interactions), as well as occasions in which they or others would be increasingly aware of the perceived flaw, such as looking at mirrors, shopping, swimming, and sex. Avoidance can become so severe that a patient is housebound (Phillips, Menard, Fay, & Pagano, 2005).

Muscle dysmorphia (MD) is characterized as a pathological preoccupation that one's body is not sufficiently lean and muscular (H. G. Pope, Gruber, Choi, Olivardia, & Phillips, 1997) and tends to disproportionately affect males (Olivardia, 2007). Core symptoms of MD-BDD include compulsive weight-lifting, rigid adherence to workout and dietary schedules, use of performance-enhancing substances, body and mirror checking, and avoidance of situations in which one's body is exposed or endurance of these situations with great distress (Olivardia, 2007). This clinical phenomenon is considered a subtype of BDD, and there is some evidence that individuals with MD-BDD are more severely ill, with greater number of diagnoses of eating disorders and substance use, as well as a greater number of past suicide attempts and worse quality of life than those with other, non-muscle-related forms of BDD (C. G. Pope et al., 2005). Although there are a number of similarities between

MD-BDD and other forms of BDD, the symptomatology just outlined reveals important differences. For instance, dietary and exercise rigidity and use of anabolic-androgenic steroids are not typically seen in other variants of BDD. Among men with BDD, roughly 25% meet criteria for MD-BDD (C. G. Pope et al., 2005).

DIAGNOSTIC CRITERIA

In the *Diagnostic and Statistical Manual of Mental Disorders—Fifth Edition* (*DSM–5;* American Psychiatric Association, 2013), BDD is placed in the Obsessive–Compulsive Related Disorders category (Anxiety, Obsessive–Compulsive Spectrum, Posttraumatic, and Dissociative Disorders Work Group, 2012; Phillips et al., 2010). The current criteria for the disorder include muscle dysmorphia as a specifier. Furthermore, as a result of extant research, in the *DSM–5*, the delusional and the nondelusional variants of BDD have been combined into a single disorder with insight being a specifier, and the delusional variant has been removed from the psychosis section.

EPIDEMIOLOGY

Recent epidemiological studies revealed a prevalence rate for BDD of 1.8% in Germany (Buhlmann et al., 2010) and 2.4% in the United States (Koran, Abujaoude, Large, & Sepre, 2008). A much higher prevalence can be found in clinical and medical populations (e.g., psychiatric inpatients with other diagnosed mental disorders, patients in dermatology and in reconstructive/cosmetic surgery; Conroy et al., 2008; Crerand, Sarwer, & Magee, 2004; Sarwer & Crerand, 2008). Prevalence rates might be slightly higher in females (Phillips & Diaz, 1997). Men and women with BDD appear to share more similarities than differences; however, the genders differ somewhat with respect to the specific body parts concerned. No differences in prevalence rates have been noted cross-culturally (e.g., Bohne, Keuthen, Wilhelm, Deckersbach, & Jenike, 2002). However, ethnicity may influence body dissatisfaction and symptom manifestation (e.g., body part of concern, repetitive behaviors; e.g., Marques, LeBlanc, et al., 2011).

Studies indicate a typical age of onset of BDD in late childhood, with the mean age of onset of 16.4 (*SD* = 7.0) and a mode of 13 years (Phillips, Menard, Fay, & Weisberg, 2005). BDD has a chronic course if not treated (Phillips, Pinto, Menard, et al., 2007). A prospective study corroborated this finding, indicating that BDD was chronic over the course of 1 year in 91% of 161 individuals (Phillips, Pagano, Menard, et al., 2006).

ASSOCIATED FEATURES AND COMORBIDITY

Individuals with BDD, in particular, those suffering from a delusional form, exhibit much lower self-esteem, quality of life, and level of functioning than the U.S. general population (Phillips, 2000). Suicidal ideation and rates of attempted suicide are high in BDD compared with U.S. norms but also compared with other mental disorders, with 80% lifetime suicidal ideation and 24% to 28% having attempted suicide—an estimated 6 to 23 times higher than rates reported for the U.S. population. Preliminary findings also indicate that the completed suicide rate is markedly high (Phillips, 2007). Comorbidity is common; the most commonly diagnosed comorbid Axis I disorders in BDD are major depressive disorder, social anxiety disorder, obsessive–compulsive disorder (OCD), substance abuse disorder, and eating disorders, in particular, anorexia nervosa (Gunstad & Phillips, 2003; Phillips, Menard, et al., 2005; Ruffolo, Phillips, Menard, Fay, & Weisberg, 2006). With regard to personality disorders, avoidant, obsessive–compulsive, paranoid, and dependent are most commonly diagnosed with BDD (Neziroglu, McKay, Todaro, & Yaryura-Tobias, 1996).

COGNITIVE–BEHAVIORAL MODEL OF BDD

A biopsychosocial framework underlies the cognitive–behavioral model of BDD, and thus the disorder evolves as an interaction of biological, psychological, and sociocultural factors (e.g., Wilhelm, Buhlmann, Hayward, Greenberg, & Dimaite, 2010; Wilhelm & Neziroglu, 2002). The response of BDD to pharmacological treatment provides support for the role of neurobiological factors, such as a serotonergic dysregulation, in its development (Phillips & Hollander, 2008). Results from pharmacological studies also suggest that dopamine may, in combination with serotonin, play a role in the etiology of BDD, particularly in its delusional form (e.g., Phillips, 2005b, 2005c). There is also preliminary evidence for specific characteristics in genetic, neurobiological, and immunological factors in BDD (e.g., Feusner et al., 2009, 2010; Hounie et al., 2004; Phillips et al., 2003; Rauch et al., 2003).

Psychological influences in BDD include personality, affective, perceptive, and cognitive factors. A particularly salient trait is perfectionism, which can lead to unrealistic standards. This trait combined with an increased fear of disapproval may facilitate the development of BDD (Buhlmann, Etcoff, & Wilhelm, 2008). Recent studies have also shown distinctive biases in perception of attractiveness. For example, individuals with BDD are likely to underestimate their own physical appearance but also to overrate attractiveness in others in general (Buhlmann et al., 2008). Additionally, persons with BDD tend to adopt an internal focus, which leads to a determination of body image and self-esteem based exclusively on the body parts they are most concerned with. This in turn produces maladaptive beliefs about their appearance, such as conditional love based on attractiveness (Buhlmann, Teachman, & Kathmann, 2011; Buhlmann, Teachman, Naumann, Fehlinger, & Rief, 2009). In addition to these beliefs about attractiveness, patients with BDD frequently have automatic thoughts that other people are negatively evaluating their appearance (Wilhelm et al., 2010). When walking into a room, a patient who is worried about her hair might think, "Everyone is staring at me and thinking about how ugly my hair is." Patients may also be more likely to place a greater level of importance on their appearance and interpret minor appearance concerns as major personal flaws (e.g., "If my hair is a mess, people won't like me"), as well as confusing physical attractiveness with well-being in general (e.g., "If my hair is a mess, I will be unhappy for the rest of my life"; Wilhelm et al., 2010). These dysfunctional thoughts lead to negative emotions (e.g., anxiety, shame, sadness) that patients try to neutralize with ritualistic behaviors (e.g., mirror checking) or avoidance of trigger situations (e.g., going to a party). Avoidance and rituals temporarily decrease negative emotions. However, in the long run, these behaviors negatively reinforce BDD-related thoughts, feelings, and behaviors (Wilhelm et al., 2010). Furthermore, people with BDD selectively direct their attention to their perceived appearance flaws and other BDD-related threat cues (Buhlmann, McNally, Wilhelm & Florin, 2002; Stangier, Adam-Schwebe, Muller, & Wolter, 2008). Additionally, they are more likely to negatively interpret ambiguous body-related and social scenarios (Buhlmann, Wilhelm, et al., 2002) and more often misidentify pictures of facial expressions as angry or contemptuous (Buhlmann, Etcoff, & Wilhelm, 2006).

Sociocultural factors primarily include messages of the beauty ideal spread via the media and the internalization thereof. Additionally, excessive appearance-based reinforcement such as teasing (or excessive appearance-based praise) can contribute to the development and maintenance of BDD (Buhlmann, Cook, Fama, & Wilhelm, 2007). Cultural backgrounds in which the importance of appearance is emphasized can also inflate beliefs about the importance of physical attractiveness (e.g., the United States, where advertising and technology promulgate notions of the "perfect" physical appearance; Neziroglu, Khemlani-Patel, & Veale, 2008; Wilhelm et al., 2013). Regarding sexual orientation, members of sexual minorities endorsed more BDD symptoms than their heterosexual counterparts (Boroughs, Krawczyk, & Thompson, 2010).

TREATMENT

Despite the considerable burden and distress associated with BDD, only a small number of individuals with the disorder seek psychological or psychiatric treatment. Logistic and financial concerns, stigma, shame, and skepticism about treatment preclude treatment seeking (Buhlmann, 2011; Marques, Weingarden, Leblanc, & Wilhelm, 2011). When individuals with BDD do seek treatment, they often seek surgical, dermatological, or other nonpsychiatric interventions (Conrado et al., 2010; Lai, Lee, Yeh, & Chen, 2010), although these types of treatment do not appear effective for BDD (Sarwer & Crerand, 2008).

Empirical Support for Efficacy and Effectiveness of Treatment

A current Cochrane review and the guideline of the National Institute for Health and Clinical Excellence (NICE) recommend cognitive behavior therapy (CBT), serotonin reuptake inhibitors (SRIs), or a combination of these as the preferred treatments for BDD (Ipser, Sander, & Stein, 2009; NICE, 2009). The SRIs clomipramine, fluvoxamine, fluoxetine, citalopram, and escitalopram have proven to be effective for 53% to 73% of patients (for an overview, see Phillips & Hollander, 2008). As in OCD, the dosage is usually higher than in depression, and response is slower, more gradual, and appears over several months (Phillips & Hollander, 2008). Studies also suggest that after trials with different SRIs at an optimal dose showing inadequate responses, clinicians may consider augmentation with neuroleptics even though their effectiveness has not been demonstrated adequately and universally (e.g., Phillips, 2005b, 2005c). For more in-depth information on pharmacological treatment of OCD spectrum disorders, see Chapter 12, this volume.

There is considerable evidence for the effectiveness of CBT in adults with BDD. Two randomized controlled trials with wait-list control groups showed favorable outcomes for both an individual (Veale, Gourney, et al., 1996) and a group CBT intervention (Rosen, Reiter, & Orosan, 1995), supported by findings from open trials and case series (McKay, 1999; McKay et al., 1997; Neziroglu et al., 1996; Wilhelm, Otto, Lohr, & Deckersbach, 1999). A recent study corroborated these findings, indicating that a newly developed modular CBT delivered over 18 to 22 weeks significantly improved BDD and related symptoms at posttreatment and at 3- and 6-month follow-up (Wilhelm, Phillips, Fama, Greenberg, & Steketee, 2011).

Components of CBT

In the following sections, we describe components of CBT with patients in an individual setting. We comment on practical aspects of implementing the techniques and on special aspects of implementation in adolescents. We conclude with a case example.

Psychoeducation

The first treatment component in CBT for BDD is psychoeducation. In a first step, the therapist provides some general information about BDD, such as typical symptoms and prevalence rates. In a second step, the components of the CBT treatment for BDD are summarized, and evidence supporting the treatment is discussed. In a third step, therapist and patient develop an individualized model of BDD based on the patient's specific symptoms as well as the general cognitive–behavioral model of BDD (Veale, Gournay et al., 1996; Wilhelm et al., 2013). On the basis of this individualized model, CBT techniques can be derived in a next step. Also, therapist and patient will refer back to the model during the course of treatment as a method of tailoring intervention strategies.

Psychoeducation can also be used to explain the structure of treatment sessions. Each session typically begins with a check of mood and BDD symptoms, followed by a review of the homework assigned in the last session. Homework is important because it assists with the transfer of behavior change to real-life settings and allows for the consolidation of newly learned behaviors. Homework can include monitoring thoughts about appearance, exposure to feared situations, and reduction of ritualistic behaviors. After completing the homework review, the agenda for the session is covered; for example, a particular exposure exercise is planned. This will usually take up about 75% of the total session time. The last part of the session is dedicated to assigning the new homework and providing an opportunity for the patient to give feedback on the session and treatment in general (Wilhelm et al., 2013).

Cognitive Restructuring

The central aim of cognitive restructuring is to identify, evaluate, and subsequently modify negative thoughts and beliefs the patient has about his appearance and the importance of appearance. The patient learns to evaluate whether her beliefs are realistic and/or helpful, and if not, to generate more accurate alternative thoughts (Wilhelm et al., 2013).

To familiarize patients with the concept of cognitive restructuring, the therapist can introduce thought distortions that are common in BDD, such as all or nothing thinking ("I am either beautiful or monstrous, hideous, and ugly"). In the next step, the patient is taught to monitor her negative and automatic appearance-related thoughts inside and outside the session ("I broke out, which makes my face look absolutely hideous") in order to identify such cognitive distortions. A helpful strategy is to use a "thought record." The patient is asked to complete the record whenever she feels distressed. The record captures information on the triggering event and the negative automatic thought. Additionally, patients might find it helpful to use Socratic questioning in situations in which they feel particularly distressed or that they are avoiding ("Why do I always feel so stressed out about my appearance when I go to a party with my boyfriend?" "Perhaps I am worried that no one will like me because of my bad skin"). In a next step, the therapist can assist the patient in evaluating and modifying these thoughts. On the one hand, the patient can evaluate the validity of the maladaptive thought ("Is there any evidence that no one likes me because of my bad skin?"). On the other hand, it can also be effective to evaluate the usefulness of the thought ("Does it help me to think I can only have a good time if I do not break out anymore?"). Together, with the therapist, the pros and cons of holding onto the appearance-related thoughts can be examined and weighed ("It is beneficial to hold onto the thought because it helps me feel in control; on the other hand, I cannot enjoy myself anymore when going out"; Wilhelm et al., 2013).

The therapist might also use cognitive methods, such as the pie chart technique or role playing. In the pie chart technique, the therapist draws a pie, and patient and therapist identify together slices of the pie that represent areas of life other than attractiveness that have an impact on self-esteem or are important for the person (e.g., being a good parent, having a successful career).

After having established cognitive restructuring of automatic negative thoughts, therapists can use Socratic questioning to explore core beliefs relating to appearance concerns (Wilhelm et al., 2013). Such core beliefs might include, "I'm unlovable" or "I'm a failure." Core beliefs can be explored using the downward arrow technique. For example, if the thought is "People will think that my skin is too bad," using the downward arrow technique, the therapist would ask, "What would it mean if . . . " over and over again, like a broken record. So the therapist might start by asking, "What would it mean if people noticed your skin looks bad?" and wait for the patient to answer. Then the therapist keeps asking questions (e.g., "What would it mean if people would not like you?") until the core belief is reached (e.g., "If people notice my bad skin, they won't like me, and this means that I am not lovable"). As with other maladaptive thoughts, the validity of core beliefs can be examined through cognitive restructuring as well as behavioral experiments.

Behavioral Experiments

Behavioral experiments can complement cognitive restructuring because both techniques help to teach patients to objectively evaluate the accuracy of appearance-related beliefs. Exposure and response prevention exercises are often set up as behavioral experiments to help patients test their negative predictions. The first step in conducting a behavioral experiment is the therapist and patient specifying the hypotheses that warrant testing (e.g., "Do people really stare at my ugly skin and face when I am walking around in a store?"). Then the experiment is designed, feared consequences are explored and rated with regard to the likelihood of their occurrence, and subsequently the experiment is carried out. This can be done with the therapist or as homework between sessions. After completing the experiment, the patient records what the outcome was, whether the predictions came true, and what he or she learned from the experiment (Wilhelm, 2006).

Exposure and Response (Ritual) Prevention

One of the core strategies in the CBT treatment of BDD is exposure and response prevention (e.g., Wilhelm et al., 2013). In the first step toward an exposure exercise, the therapist and patient develop a list of situations that the patient typically avoids and arrange them into a hierarchy with regard to the extent of avoidance and the amount of anxiety associated with it (using Subjective Units of Distress Scale [SUDS] ratings ranging from 0 to 100). Ideally, eight to 10 situations would be generated across the spectrum of the SUDS ratings. Common exposure situations would include walking around in public without wearing specific camouflaging items of clothing, leaving the house without wearing makeup, or going to the beach.

Exposures begin with situations at the lower end of the SUDS scale. It is important to stay in the situation long enough to let the anxiety decrease significantly (distress rating of 25 or lower). Usually, habituation occurs after an initial increase in anxiety when entering the situation. After a successful exposure, the patient and therapist move on to the next higher rated situation. It is crucial that a patient practice exposure repeatedly and frequently, which will lead to a quicker habituation over time. Additionally, it is essential for the patient not to attempt to distract herself from the anxiety experienced during the exposure because the experience of anxiety together with the experience of its reduction is important for relearning to occur. The patient should also be encouraged to use ritual prevention skills during exposures. Therefore, it is necessary to thoroughly assess a patient's rituals (e.g., camouflaging) and avoidance behaviors (e.g., avoiding social functions) related to BDD symptoms. On the basis of this assessment, patient and therapist can set specific goals with regard to ritual prevention as homework. The ultimate goal is the elimination of all BDD rituals; however, often it is too difficult to give up all BDD rituals right at the beginning, and the therapist might encourage the patient to take some interim steps. Such interim steps can focus either on delaying response (e.g., waiting several minutes before checking the mirror) or reducing rituals (e.g., wearing only one camouflaging clothing item instead of two), with the eventual goal of eliminating these behaviors altogether (Wilhelm et al., 2013).

Other CBT Techniques Incorporated in the Treatment of BDD

Additional CBT techniques that therapists may use in the treatment of BDD are mirror retraining, habit reversal, relapse prevention, and booster sessions. Mirror retraining might be included in the treatment plan if patients have established a dysfunctional behavior regarding mirrors, such as avoiding them or checking them over and over again as a form of ritualistic behavior. It is also a valuable treatment component if patients show selective attention toward particular body parts that they perceive as ugly instead of engaging in more global (holistic) information processing. Such behaviors may maintain negative thoughts and feelings about appearance (Wilhelm et al., 2013).

Important aspects to consider before beginning mirror retraining, also called mindfulness or perceptual retraining, are purchasing a mirror that is large enough to reflect the entire face or body, having a well-lit area to perform the training, and standing 1 foot away if looking at the face and 2 to 3 feet (i.e., arm's length) if looking at the body. If this setup is too anxiety-provoking for the patient, lighting may be initially dimmed and distance to the mirror might be expanded and gradually changed.

The patient is asked to examine different body parts (from head to toe) and to describe them in as much detail as possible in an objective, nonevaluative fashion. The therapist also teaches the patient to perceive her body with all senses. Individuals with BDD tend to use negative and judgmental language about their appearance (e.g., "I have disgusting frog eyes"). During mirror retraining, they learn to use more objective language to describe themselves (e.g., "My eyes are hazel"). The detailed, neutral, and nonjudgmental description of themselves eventually leads them to practice a less distorted manner of perceiving their own body as well as to engage in healthier mirror-related behaviors (i.e., not avoiding the mirror entirely, not getting too close to the mirror). It is essential that the therapist assist patients in eliminating ritualistic behaviors they may typically use in front of the mirror, such as grooming or touching certain body parts (e.g., elimination of skin picking).

As Veale and Neziroglu (2010) described, feedback to patients through video, photos, or through face and body masks to create an offprint of the face or body part can also be valuable supplements to the mirror retraining exercises. Perceptual and attentional retraining can also be useful in everyday life in which the patient selectively focuses on aspects of his and others' appearance (e.g., in class or at a party). It might be helpful for patients to train to shift their focus outward, such as toward a conversation in which they are engaged, as opposed to focusing on their or others' appearance (Wilhelm et al., 2013).

Habit reversal is used primarily for compulsive behaviors such as skin picking, hair plucking, and body touching (Veale & Neziroglu, 2010; Wilhelm, et al., 2013). The patient starts by describing the behavior in as much detail as possible in a diary to increase awareness of the behavior (length and situation in which it occurs). In a second step, a competing response is introduced, and thus another behavior is performed that is incompatible with the original behavior, such as clenching a fist or squeezing an object, for example, if the patient feels the need to pull his hair.

The last sessions are focused on relapse prevention. The aim here is to review and consolidate CBT skills and plan for the maintenance of gains. It is important to plan ahead so that the patient with BDD can cope effectively with situations that are typically challenging (going on a date or a job interview). Recommendations for the patient include being his own therapist by setting a weekly time to review treatment strategies, to set upcoming goals related to BDD treatment (planning an exposure exercise on his own), and to incorporate new activities in his life to fill the gap left by the reduction of BDD symptoms. Additionally, patient and therapist may arrange for booster sessions after the treatment has concluded. These sessions can be used to refresh the patient's BDD-specific CBT skills, to boost prevention skills, and to problem solve around difficult situations (Wilhelm et al., 2013).

Practical Aspects in Implementation and Potential Difficulties

Once a patient has found appropriate treatment, other difficulties may arise, such as low motivation, ambivalence about treatment of comorbid depression, and suicidality. Lack of motivation and ambivalence about psychiatric treatment may stem from poor insight and can pose a challenge to the therapy. If the patient is convinced that her problems should be fixed via cosmetic techniques rather than by an alteration of her self-perception or body image, the therapist should initially focus on increasing motivation through motivational interviewing techniques. Motivational strategies for BDD are based on the principles of Miller and Rollnick (2002) and have been adapted by Wilhelm and colleagues (2013) for disorder-specific use. The assessment of possible barriers to change, such as lack of insight into appearance-based concerns or desire for surgical or dermatological interventions, can help anticipate the need for motivational strategies during the course of treatment. In BDD, motivational strategies are used in a nonjudgmental, collaborative way to guide the patient to explore her willingness and readiness to change with regard to her appearance concerns (Wilhelm et al., 2013). In a first step, the therapist tries to empathize with the patient's body image–related distress instead of directly and immediately questioning the validity of the beliefs ("I see that you really suffer because you are so worried about the way you look. Let's try to reduce this distress"). Another technique used is nonjudgmental Socratic questioning in which pros and cons of change are explored ("What might be the advantages of trying this CBT treatment for BDD?"). The therapist can also guide the patient to discover the discrepancy between BDD symptoms and her goals ("What should your life look like 10 years from now?"). In particular, with patients with low insight, it might be worthwhile to address the usefulness of beliefs instead of the validity (e.g., "Are your beliefs preventing you from participating in activities you enjoy?").

Motivational strategies might be necessary not only at the beginning of but also later on in treatment (e.g., for getting started with exposures). Lack of motivation and ambivalence may also originate from the distress or discomfort associated with CBT components itself because the treatment requires patients to deliberately confront avoided situations and to test deeply held beliefs. Interventions can be made more acceptable to patients by starting with exposure to less anxiety-provoking situations or with components of cognitive therapy. This allows for early mastery, which leads to increased confidence when engaging in more difficult situations. Patients who refuse exposure may still benefit from cognitive therapy focusing on restructuring dysfunctional appearance-related thoughts.

Comorbid depression can interfere with comprehension of in-session skills and completion of homework due to symptoms such as lack of energy and concentration difficulties. If depressive symptoms are significant and/or interfering with treatment focused on BDD, it is recommended that depression be targeted directly via activity scheduling and cognitive restructuring of depressive beliefs. Additionally, the therapist might recommend adjunctive pharmacotherapy. Throughout treatment, the therapist should regularly monitor each patient via self-report instruments and clinician-based assessment for suicidal ideation, intent, and plans. If there is acute suicidality, a higher level of care may become necessary, for example, full or partial hospitalization (Wilhelm et al., 2013).

Specific Considerations for Implementation in Adolescents

A recent review on the clinical features of BDD in adolescents and adults indicated that the features of the disorder appear largely similar across age groups (Phillips, Didie, et al., 2006). Diagnostic criteria in the fourth edition of the *DSM* were the same for adolescents as for adults (American Psychiatric Association, 2000), and given the paucity of adolescent research, no age-specific revisions were made in *DSM–5* (Phillips et al., 2010).

Reports of CBT for youth with BDD are limited to a small number of case studies (Aldea, Storch, & Geffken, 2009; Greenberg et al., 2010, Horowitz, Gorfinkle, Lewis, & Phillips, 2002; Sobanski & Schmidt, 2000). CBT for adolescents differs from that for adults in that it must take into account age and developmentally appropriate tasks and transitions, the involvement of the parents and school, and potential skill deficits (for an overview, see Greenberg et al., 2010). For example, some researchers had parents assist in their children's treatment by providing psychoeducation about BDD, advising parents to reduce accommodation of rituals (e.g., offering reassurance, not buying beauty products) and to help maintain adolescents' motivation for treatment (e.g., rewarding their children for homework compliance and for participating in non-BDD activities). Parental involvement will vary depending on the adolescent's developmental stage and individual goals for therapy; however, it is important to help the adolescent develop autonomy. It is also essential to clarify issues of confidentiality at the beginning of the treatment when working with youth.

Because it is often the parents initiating therapy, adolescents' motivation for treatment may be particularly low. It may therefore be worthwhile to spend initial sessions getting to know the adolescent's interests. Because youth may have less insight into their disorder than adults and may lack metacognitive abilities, motivational interviewing strategies may be advisable. In addition to BDD-specific components of treatment, adolescent transitions and tasks need to be addressed, such as autonomy from family and peer or romantic affiliations, because they may be adversely affected by BDD (Greenberg et al., 2010; Phillips & Rogers, 2011).

In a case report series of 33 patients, a majority of adolescent patients had clinically significant improvement in BDD with SRIs but no improvement with non-SRI medications (Albertini, Phillips, & Guevremont, 1996). However, the use of SRIs has not yet been systematically examined in adolescents with BDD.

A CASE EXAMPLE

Alex, a 36-year-old man, presented with concerns about aging. He was obsessed with his "leathery" skin and dry, thinning hair. He constantly worried about what others thought about his appearance. Despite his anxiety, Alex worked as a lawyer; however, he avoided speaking in weekly conference meetings, dreaded client meetings, and constantly felt others were judging him as worthless and incompetent because he looked like "such a freak." Alex's appearance concerns led him to repeatedly check the mirror and compare himself with other men in the office or on television. He spent hundreds of dollars each month on facial creams and hair products. He avoided getting his haircut and would never be seen in public without wearing a baseball hat. His anxiety prevented him from going out after work with colleagues. He would ask his wife for reassurance about his looks up to 20 times per day, but nothing she said could allay his concerns. Taking his sons to karate class was out of the question because he was convinced they were embarrassed to be seen with such an ugly dad. When Alex sought treatment, he was severely depressed and had considered suicide; he was convinced that his wife was on the verge of leaving him because he had "really let himself go."

Alex participated in 22 sessions of CBT for BDD over 24 weeks and received booster sessions 1 and 3 months after acute treatment ended. Early sessions focused on providing Alex with education about BDD and understanding what had led to the development and maintenance of his BDD symptoms. Alex was ashamed about his BDD, and despite frequent requests for reassurance, he never spoke directly of his appearance concerns to his wife for fear that she would think of him as inadequate or weak and leave him. Alex agreed to have his wife come in for a family session; the therapist answered questions and provided information to his wife about BDD and ways to support Alex rather than accommodating BDD rituals. Alex was surprised by his wife's positive response; they continued to work as a team throughout treatment. The core treatment focused on helping Alex to evaluate his negative appearance-related beliefs and gradually reenter avoided situations (e.g., work events, getting a haircut). At the same time, Alex also learned to decrease his ritualistic behavior (e.g., reassurance seeking, mirror checking, purchasing and applying skin and hair products). The therapist taught Alex mindfulness and perceptual retraining (e.g., mirror retraining) to help him learn to "see the big picture" and use objective, nonjudgmental terms when describing his appearance. The therapist also helped Alex to identify and increase positive, valued activities that BDD had interfered with, such as playing piano, photography, and playing cards with friends. The final sessions were spent identifying and planning for future challenges (e.g., his brother's wedding, family vacation). By the end of treatment, Alex's BDD symptoms had been significantly reduced. Although Alex still experienced some negative beliefs about his appearance, they were less frequent, not as intense, and less meaningful to him. As his symptoms improved, he was able to apply for a promotion at work. He no longer avoided social invitations, and by the end of treatment, he was going out on a date night with his wife and having lunch with colleagues on a weekly basis.

CONCLUSION

BDD is a common, underdiagnosed disorder that is associated with severe psychopathology, impairment, and dysfunction. BDD patients often look for interventions that can "fix" their appearance, such as cosmetic surgery or dermatological treatment, rather than psychological or psychiatric treatment. However, as research indicates, state-of-the-art treatments for BDD include CBT, pharmacological treatment with SRIs, or a combination thereof. The components of CBT for BDD generally include psychoeducation, cognitive restructuring of appearance-related thoughts and beliefs, behavioral experiments, exposure with response prevention, and relapse prevention. Additional components may include mirror retraining, attentional retraining such as shifting the focus outward enabling to see the big picture, and habit reversal. Motivational interviewing techniques may play an important role not only in fostering insight but also in quelling the initial increase of anxiety during treatment that may result in lower treatment motivation. Additionally, depressive symptoms may need to be specifically targeted during or in advance of BDD treatment with CBT techniques or SRIs. Because BDD usually first manifests in adolescence, treatment development and testing are critical for this age group. Suggestions for CBT for adolescent BDD consist of parent involvement and taking into account age-appropriate tasks and transitions in the development of treatment materials (e.g., language, graphics), topics, and rewards.

Whenever a treatment plan for BDD is designed, a combination of available research, clinical expertise, and the individual needs of the patient must be considered. Given the heterogeneity of symptoms, a modular approach (i.e., Wilhelm et al., 2013) is desirable because the treatment can easily be individualized and focused on the most salient issues for the patient. A thorough and comprehensive assessment is required before treatment planning. Directions for future treatment research are clearly set. There is a need for dismantling randomized controlled trials, including the direct comparison of CBT and SRIs as well as their combination. Various approaches to augmenting pharmacotherapy with SRIs should be tested. For CBT, randomized controlled trials are needed to determine the optimal length and number of sessions, implementation in a group or individual setting, and the effectiveness of different treatment components (e.g., cognitive and behavioral domains). Additionally, broader samples need to be included such as different gender and race/ethnicity, patients with delusional BDD, and different levels of severity. In a next step, generalizability of these findings should be tested for different subtypes such as muscle dysmorphia.

It would also be worthwhile to examine the effectiveness of treatment approaches other than CBT and SRIs because CBT and SRIs do not work for all patients, and not all patients are amenable to such approaches. There is preliminary evidence for the effectiveness of acceptance and commitment therapy for disorders related to BDD, such as OCD and anxiety disorders (Dalrymple & Herbert, 2007; Forman, Herbert, Moitra, Yeomans, & Geller, 2007; Twohig, Hayes, & Masuda, 2006) and people with chronic skin-picking disorders (Twohig et al., 2006), as well as for mindfulness-based strategies in BDD (Wilhelm et al., 2011). A recent study revealed that inference-based therapy might be a valuable treatment for BDD (Taillon, O'Connor, Dupuis, & Lavoie, 2013). Interference-based therapy is a cognitive intervention that has been developed for and has been proven successful in OCD with high-overvalued ideation (O'Connor et al., 2005); obsessions are characterized as idiosyncratic inferences arrived at through inductive reasoning processes, leading to obsessional doubts.

In sum, future research should focus on elucidating the mechanisms underlying CBT and pharmacological treatment, the differential diagnosis and treatment indication for subtypes of BDD such as muscle dysmorphia, the development of new treatment strategies (in particular, with regard to treatment for youth), and the augmentation of current pharmacological treatment with other agents in refractory cases. In addition, identifying shared core mechanisms of psychopathology and response to treatment across disorders may help to inform targeted treatment components.

REFERENCES

Albertini, R. S., Phillips, K. A., & Guevremont, D. (1996). Body dysmorphic disorder. *Journal of the American Academy of Child & Adolescent Psychiatry, 35*, 1425–1426. doi:10.1097/00004583-199611000-00010

Aldea, M., Storch, E., & Geffken, G. (2009). Intensive cognitive-behavioral therapy for adolescents with body dysmorphic disorder. *Clinical Case Studies, 8*, 113–121. doi:10.1177/1534650109332485

American Psychiatric Association. (2000). *Diagnostic and statistical manual of mental disorders* (4th ed., text revision). Washington, DC: Author.

American Psychiatric Association. (2013). *Diagnostic and statistical manual of mental disorders* (5th ed.). Washington, DC: Author.

Anxiety, Obsessive–Compulsive Spectrum, Posttraumatic, and Dissociative Disorders Work Group, American Psychiatric Association. (2012). *Provisional criteria for obsessive–compulsive and related disorders*. Retrieved from http://www.dsm5.org/ProposedRevision/Pages/proposedrevision.aspx?rid=11)

Bohne, A., Keuthen, N. J., Wilhelm, S., Deckersbach, T., & Jenike, M. A. (2002). Prevalence of symptoms of body dysmorphic disorder and its correlates: A cross-cultural comparison. *Psychosomatics, 43*, 486–490. doi:10.1176/appi.psy.43.6.486

Boroughs, M. S., Krawczyk, R., & Thompson, J. K. (2010). Body dysmorphic disorder among diverse racial/ethnic and sexual orientation groups: Prevalence estimates and associated factors. *Sex Roles, 63*, 725–737. doi:10.1007/s11199-010-9831-1

Buhlmann, U. (2011). Treatment barriers for individuals with body dysmorphic disorder: An internet survey. *Journal of Nervous and Mental Disease, 199*, 268–271. doi:10.1097/NMD.0b013e31821245ce

Buhlmann, U., Cook, L., Fama, J., & Wilhelm, S. (2007). Perceived teasing experiences in body dysmorphic disorder. *Body Image, 4*, 381–385. doi:10.1016/j.bodyim.2007.06.004

Buhlmann, U., Etcoff, N. L., & Wilhelm, S. (2006). Emotion recognition bias for contempt and anger in body dysmorphic disorder. *Journal of Psychiatric Research, 40*, 105–111. doi:10.1016/j.jpsychires.2005.03.006

Buhlmann, U., Etcoff, N. L., & Wilhelm, S. (2008). Facial attractiveness ratings and perfectionism in body dysmorphic disorder and obsessive-compulsive disorder. *Journal of Anxiety Disorders, 22*, 540–547. doi:10.1016/j.janxdis.2007.05.004

Buhlmann, U., Gläsmer, H., Mewes, R., Fama, J. M., Wilhelm, S., Brähler, E., & Rief, W. (2010). Updates on the prevalence of body dysmorphic disorder: A population-based survey. *Psychiatry Research, 178*, 171–175. doi:10.1016/j.psychres.2009.05.002

Buhlmann, U., McNally, R. J., Wilhelm, S., & Florin, I. (2002). Selective processing of emotional information in body dysmorphic disorder. *Journal of Anxiety Disorders, 16*, 289–298. doi:10.1016/S0887-6185(02)00100-7

Buhlmann, U., Teachman, B. A., & Kathmann, N. (2011). Evaluating implicit attractiveness beliefs in body dysmorphic disorder using the Go/No-go Association Task. *Journal of Behavior Therapy and Experimental Psychiatry, 42*, 192–197. doi:10.1016/j.jbtep.2010.10.003

Buhlmann, U., Teachman, B. A., Naumann, E., Fehlinger, T., & Rief, W. (2009). The meaning of beauty: Implicit and explicit self-esteem and attractiveness beliefs in body dysmorphic disorder. *Journal of Anxiety Disorders, 23*, 694–702. doi:10.1016/j.janxdis.2009.02.008

Buhlmann, U., Wilhelm, S., McNally, R. J., Tuschen-Caffier, B., Baer, L., & Jenike, M. A. (2002). Interpretive biases for ambiguous information in body dysmorphic disorder. *CNS Spectrums, 7*, 435–436.

Conrado, L. A., Hounie, A. G., Diniz, J. B., Fossaluza, V., Torres, A. R., & Miguel, E. C. (2010). Body dysmorphic disorder among dermatologic patients: Prevalence and clinical features. *Journal of the American Academy of Dermatology, 63*, 235–243. doi:10.1016/j.jaad.2009.09.017

Conroy, M., Menard, W., Fleming-Ives, K., Modha, P., Cerullo, H., & Phillips, K. A. (2008). Prevalence and clinical characteristics of body dysmorphic disorder in an adult inpatient setting. *General Hospital Psychiatry, 30*, 67–72. doi:10.1016/j.genhosppsych.2007.09.004

Crerand, C. E., Menard, W., & Phillips, K. A. (2010). Surgical and minimally invasive cosmetic procedures among persons with body dysmorphic disorder. *Annals of Plastic Surgery, 65*, 11–16. doi:10.1097/SAP.0b013e3181bba08f

Crerand, C. E., Sarwer, D. B., Magee, L., Gibbons, L. M., Lowe, M. R., Bartlett, S. P., . . . Whitaker, L. A. (2004). Rate of body dysmorphic disorder among patients seeking facial cosmetic procedures. *Psychiatric Annals, 34*, 958–965.

Dalrymple, K. L., & Herbert, J. D. (2007). Acceptance and commitment therapy for generalized social anxiety disorder: A pilot study. *Behavior Modification, 31*, 543–568. doi:10.1177/0145445507302037

Feusner, J. D., Moody, T., Hembacher, E., Townsend, J., McKinley, M., Moller, H., & Bookheimer, S. (2010). Abnormalities of visual processing and frontostriatal systems in body dysmorphic disorder. *Archives of General Psychiatry, 67*, 197–205. doi:10.1001/archgenpsychiatry.2009.190

Feusner, J. D., Townsend, J., Bystritsky, A., McKinley, M., Moller, H., & Bookheimer, S. (2009). Regional brain volumes and symptom severity in body dysmorphic disorder. *Psychiatry Research: Neuroimaging, 172*, 161–167. doi:10.1016/j.pscychresns.2008.12.003

Forman, E. M., Herbert, J. D., Moitra, E., Yeomans, P. D., & Geller, P. A. (2007). A randomized controlled effectiveness trial of acceptance and commitment therapy and cognitive therapy for anxiety and depression. *Behavior Modification, 31*, 772–799. doi:10.1177/0145445507302202

Greenberg, J. L., Markowitz, S., Petronko, M. R., Taylor, C. E., Wilhelm, S., & Wilson, G. T. (2010). Cognitive-behavioral therapy for adolescent body dysmorphic disorder. *Cognitive and Behavioral Practice, 17*, 248–258. doi:10.1016/j.cbpra.2010.02.002

Gunstad, J., & Phillips, K. A. (2003). Axis I comorbidity in body dysmorphic disorder. *Comprehensive Psychiatry, 44*, 270–276. doi:10.1016/S0010-440X(03)00088-9

Horowitz, K., Gorfinkle, K., Lewis, O., & Phillips, K. A. (2002). Body dysmorphic disorder in an adolescent girl. *Journal of the American Academy of Child & Adolescent Psychiatry, 41*, 1503–1509. doi:10.1097/00004583-200212000-00023

Hounie, A. G., Pauls, D. L., Mercadante, M. T., Rosario-Campos, M. C., Shavitt, R. G., de Mathis, M. A., . . . Miguel, E. C. (2004). Obsessive–compulsive spectrum disorders in rheumatic fever with and without Sydenham's chorea. *The Journal of Clinical Psychiatry, 65*, 994–999. doi:10.4088/JCP.v65n0717

Ipser, J. C., Sander, C., & Stein, D. J. (2009). Pharmacotherapy and psychotherapy for body dysmorphic disorder. *Cochrane Database of Systematic Reviews, 1*, CD005332.

Koran, L. M., Abujaoude, E., Large, M. D., & Serpe, R. T. (2008). The prevalence of body dysmorphic disorder in the United States adult population. *CNS Spectrums, 13*, 316–322.

Lai, C. S., Lee, S. S., Yeh, Y. C., & Chen, C. S. (2010). Body dysmorphic disorder in patients with cosmetic surgery. *The Kaohsiung Journal of Medical Sciences, 26*, 478–482. doi:10.1016/S1607-551X(10)70075-9

Marques, L., LeBlanc, N., Weingarden, H., Greenberg, J. L., Traeger, L. N., Keshaviah, A., & Wilhelm, S. (2011). Body dysmorphic symptoms: Phenomenology and ethnicity. *Body Image, 8*, 163–167. doi:10.1016/j.bodyim.2010.12.006

Marques, L., Weingarden, H. M., Leblanc, N. J., & Wilhelm, S. (2011). Treatment utilization and barriers to treatment engagement among people with body dysmorphic symptoms. *Journal of Psychosomatic Research, 70,* 286–293. doi:10.1016/j.jpsychores.2010.10.002

McKay, D. (1999). Two-year follow-up of behavioral treatment and maintenance for body dysmorphic disorder. *Behavior Modification, 23,* 620–629. doi:10.1177/0145445599234006

McKay, D., Todaro, J., Neziroglu, F., Campisi, T., Moritz, E. K., & Yaryura-Tobias, J. A. (1997). Body dysmorphic disorder: A preliminary evaluation of treatment and maintenance using exposure with response prevention. *Behaviour Research and Therapy, 35,* 67–70. doi:10.1016/S0005-7967(96)00082-4

Miller, W., & Rollnick, S. (2002). *Motivational interviewing: Preparing people for change* (2nd ed.). New York, NY: Guilford Press.

National Institute for Health and Clinical Excellence. (2009). *Obsessive–compulsive disorder: Core interventions in the treatment of obsessive–compulsive disorder and body dysmorphic disorder.* Leicester, England: British Psychological Society.

Neziroglu, F., Khemlani-Patel, S., & Veale, D. (2008). Social learning theory and cognitive behavioral models of body dysmorphic disorder. *Body Image, 5,* 28–38.

Neziroglu, F., McKay, D., Todaro, J., & Yaryura-Tobias, J. (1996). Effects of cognitive behavior therapy on persons with body dysmorphic disorder and comorbid axis II diagnoses. *Behavior Therapy, 27,* 67–77. doi:10.1016/S0005-7894(96)80036-0

O'Connor, K. P., Aardema, F., Bouthillier, D., Fournier, S., Guay, S., Robillard, S., . . . Pitre, D. (2005). Evaluation of an inference-based approach to treating obsessive–compulsive disorder. *Cognitive Behaviour Therapy, 34,* 148–163. doi:10.1080/16506070510041211

Olivardia, R. (2007). Muscle dysmorphia: Characteristics, assessment, and treatment. In J. Thompson & G. Cafri (Eds.), *The muscular ideal: Psychological, social, and medical perspectives* (pp. 123–139). Washington, DC: American Psychological Association. doi:10.1037/11581-006

Phillips, K. A. (2000). Quality of life for patients with body dysmorphic disorder. *Journal of Nervous and Mental Disease, 188,* 170–175. doi:10.1097/00005053-200003000-00007

Phillips, K. A. (2004). Psychosis in body dysmorphic disorder. *Journal of Psychiatric Research, 38,* 63–72. doi:10.1016/S0022-3956(03)00098-0

Phillips, K. A. (2005a). *The broken mirror.* Oxford, England: Oxford University Press.

Phillips, K. A. (2005b). Olanzapine augmentation of fluoxetine in body dysmorphic disorder. *The American Journal of Psychiatry, 162,* 1022–1023. doi:10.1176/appi.ajp.162.5.1022-a

Phillips, K. A. (2005c). Placebo-controlled study of pimozide augmentation of fluoxetine in body dysmorphic disorder. *The American Journal of Psychiatry, 162,* 377–379. doi:10.1176/appi.ajp.162.2.377

Phillips, K. A. (2007). Suicidality in body dysmorphic disorder. *Primary Psychiatry*, *14*, 58–66.

Phillips, K. A., & Diaz, S. F. (1997). Gender differences in body dysmorphic disorder. *Journal of Nervous and Mental Disease*, *185*, 570–577. doi:10.1097/00005053-199709000-00006

Phillips, K. A., Didie, E. R., Menard, W., Pagano, M. E., Fay, C., & Weisberg, R. B. (2006). Clinical features of body dysmorphic disorder in adolescents and adults. *Psychiatry Research*, *141*, 305–314. doi:10.1016/j.psychres.2005.09.014

Phillips, K. A., Grant, J. E., Siniscalchi, J. M., Stout, R. L., & Price, L. H. (2005). A retrospective follow-up study of body dysmorphic disorder. *Comprehensive Psychiatry*, *46*, 315–321.

Phillips, K. A., & Hollander, E. (2008). Treating body dysmorphic disorder with medication: evidence, misconceptions, and a suggested approach. *Body Image*, *5*, 13–27. doi:10.1016/j.bodyim.2007.12.003

Phillips, K. A., Menard, W., Fay, C., & Pagano, M. E. (2005). Psychosocial functioning and quality of life in body dysmorphic disorder. *Comprehensive Psychiatry*, *46*, 254–260. doi:10.1016/j.comppsych.2004.10.004

Phillips, K. A., Menard, W., Fay, C., & Weisberg, R. (2005). Demographic characteristics, phenomenology, comorbidity, and family history in 200 individuals with body dysmorphic disorder. *Psychosomatics*, *46*, 317–325. doi:10.1176/appi.psy.46.4.317

Phillips, K. A., Pagano, M. E., Menard, W., & Stout, R. L. (2006). A 12-month follow-up study of the course of body dysmorphic disorder. *The American Journal of Psychiatry*, *163*, 907–912. doi:10.1176/appi.ajp.163.5.907

Phillips, K. A., Pinto, A., Menard, W., Eisen, J. L., Mancebo, M., & Rasmussen, S. A. (2007). Obsessive–compulsive disorder vs. body dysmorphic disorder: A comparison study of two possibly related disorders. *Depression and Anxiety*, *24*, 399–409. doi:10.1002/da.20232

Phillips, K. A., Richter, M. A., Tharmalingam, S., King, N. A., Jeffers, C., Menard, W., & Kennedy, J. L. (2003, September). *The 5HTTLPR and GABA-A-gamma-2 genes may be implicated in body dysmorphic disorder*. Paper presented at the World Congress of Psychiatric Genetics. Quebec City, Canada.

Phillips, K. A., & Rogers, J. (2011). Cognitive-behavioral therapy for youth with body dysmorphic disorder: Current status and future directions. *Child and Adolescent Psychiatric Clinics of North America*, *20*(2), 287–304. doi:10.1016/j.chc.2011.01.004

Phillips, K. A., Wilhelm, S., Koran, L. M., Didie, E. R., Fallon, B. A., Feusner, J., & Stein, D. J. (2010). Body dysmorphic disorder: Some key issues for *DSM–V*. *Depression and Anxiety*, *27*, 573–591. doi:10.1002/da.20709

Pope, C. G., Pope, H. G., Menard, W., Fay, C., Olivardia, R., & Phillips, K. A. (2005). Clinical features of muscle dysmorphia among males with body dysmorphic disorder. *Body Image*, *2*, 395–400. doi:10.1016/j.bodyim.2005.09.001

Pope, H. G., Jr., Gruber, A. J., Choi, P., Olivardia, R., & Phillips, K. A. (1997). Muscle dysmorphia. An underrecognized form of body dysmorphic disorder. *Psychosomatics: Journal of Consultation and Liaison Psychiatry, 38*, 548–557. doi:10.1016/S0033-3182(97)71400-2

Rauch, S. L., Phillips, K. A., Segal, E., Makris, N., Shin, L. M., Whalen, P. J., . . . Kennedy, D. N. (2003). A preliminary morphometric magnetic resonance imaging study of regional brain volumes in body dysmorphic disorder. *Psychiatry Research: Neuroimaging, 122*, 13–19. doi:10.1016/S0925-4927(02)00117-8

Rosen, J. C., Reiter, J., & Orosan, P. (1995). Cognitive-behavioral body image therapy for body dysmorphic disorder. *Journal of Consulting and Clinical Psychology, 63*, 263–269. doi:10.1037/0022-006X.63.2.263

Ruffolo, J. S., Phillips, K. A., Menard, W., Fay, C., & Weisberg, R. B. (2006). Comorbidity of body dysmorphic disorder and eating disorders: Severity of psychopathology and body image disturbance. *International Journal of Eating Disorders, 39*, 11–19. doi:10.1002/eat.20219

Sarwer, D. B., & Crerand, C. E. (2008). Body dysmorphic disorder and appearance enhancing medical treatments. *Body Image, 5*, 50–58. doi:10.1016/j.bodyim.2007.08.003

Sobanski, E., & Schmidt, M. H. (2000). "Everybody looks at my pubic bone"—a case report of an adolescent patient with body dysmorphic disorder. *Acta Psychiatrica Scandinavica, 101*, 80–82. doi:10.1034/j.1600-0447.2000.101001080.x

Stangier, U., Adam-Schwebe, S., Muller, T., & Wolter, M. (2008). Discrimination of facial appearance stimuli in body dysmorphic disorder. *Journal of Abnormal Psychology, 117*, 435–443. doi:10.1037/0021-843X.117.2.435

Taillon, A., O'Connor, K., Dupuis, G., & Lavoie, M. (2013). Inference-based therapy for body dysmorphic disorder. *Clinical Psychology and Psychotherapy, 20*, 67–76. doi:10.1002/cpp.767.

Twohig, M. P., Hayes, S. C., & Masuda, A. (2006). Increasing willingness to experience obsessions: Acceptance and commitment therapy as a treatment for obsessive–compulsive disorder. *Behavior Therapy, 37*, 3–13. doi:10.1016/j.beth.2005.02.001

Veale, D., Boocock, A., Gournay, K., Dryden, W., Shah, F., Willson, R., & Walburn, J. (1996). Body dysmorphic disorder. A survey of fifty cases. *The British Journal of Psychiatry, 169*, 196–201. doi:10.1192/bjp.169.2.196

Veale, D., Gournay, K., & Dryden, W. (1996). Body dysmorphic disorder: A cognitive behavioural model and pilot randomized controlled trial. *Behaviour Research and Therapy, 34*, 717–729. doi:10.1016/0005-7967(96)00025-3

Veale, D., & Neziroglu, F. (2010). *Body dysmorphic disorder a treatment manual.* Chichester, England: Wiley. doi:10.1002/9780470684610

Wilhelm, S. (2006). *Feeling good about the way you look. A program for overcoming body image problems.* New York, NY: Guilford Press.

Wilhelm, S., Buhlmann, U., Hayward, L., Greenberg, J., & Dimaite, R. (2010). A cognitive-behavioral treatment approach for body dysmorphic disorder. *Cognitive and Behavioral Practice, 17*, 241–247. doi:10.1016/j.cbpra.2010.02.001

Wilhelm, S., & Neziroglu, F. (2002). Cognitive theory of body dysmorphic disorder. In R.O. Frost & G. Sketee (Eds.), *Cognitive approaches to its sessions and compulsions: Theory, assessment, and treatment* (pp. 203–214). Amsterdam, the Netherlands: Pergamon.

Wilhelm, S., Otto, M. W., Lohr, B., & Deckersbach, T. (1999). Cognitive behavior group therapy for body dysmorphic disorder: A case series. *Behaviour Research and Therapy, 37*, 71–75. doi:10.1016/S0005-7967(98)00109-0

Wilhelm, S., Phillips, K., Fama, J., Greenberg, J., & Steketee, G. (2011). Modular cognitive behavioral therapy for body dysmorphic disorder. *Behavior Therapy, 42*, 624–633. doi:10.1016/j.beth.2011.02.002

Wilhelm, S., Phillips, K., & Steketee, G. (2013). *A cognitive-behavioral treatment manual for body dysmorphic disorder.* New York, NY: Guilford Press.

8

HAIR PULLING, SKIN PICKING, AND OTHER BODY-FOCUSED REPETITIVE BEHAVIORS

IVAR SNORRASON AND DOUGLAS W. WOODS

Clinical observations and the emerging empirical literature suggest a relatedness between various habitual behaviors directed toward the body (Snorrason, Belleau, & Woods, 2012; Sulkowski et al., 2011). These habits have collectively been referred to as *body-focused repetitive behaviors* (BFRBs) and include hair pulling, skin picking, nail biting, and cheek or lip biting (Teng, Woods, Twohig, & Marcks, 2002). Benign forms of BFRBs are common in the general population (Hansen, Tishelman, Hawkins, & Doepke, 1990; Woods, Miltenberger, & Flach, 1996), but studies show that a small minority of individuals experience significant distress and disability because of these behaviors (Joubert, 1993; Sarkhel, Praharaj, & Akhtar, 2011; Tucker, Woods, Flessner, Franklin, & Franklin, 2011; Woods, Wetterneck, & Flessner, 2006). Pathological hair pulling (trichotillomania) and skin picking (excoriation disorder) have distinct diagnostic criteria in the *Diagnostic and Statistical Manual of Mental Disorders* (fifth edition;

http://dx.doi.org/10.1037/14323-009
Obsessive–Compulsive Disorder and Its Spectrum: A Life-Span Approach, Eric A. Storch and Dean McKay (Editors)
Copyright © 2014 by the American Psychological Association. All rights reserved.

DSM–5 and are classified under *obsessive–compulsive and related disorders*. Other pathological BFRBs do not have specific criteria but can be diagnosed as *other specified obsessive–compulsive and related disorders* (American Psychiatric Association, 2013).

In this chapter, we describe the clinical characteristics of these problems. We also discuss cognitive–behavioral treatments of BFRBs and briefly review the literature on their efficacy.

HAIR PULLING

Individuals with hair-pulling disorder (HPD; trichotillomania) repeatedly pluck out hairs from the scalp, eyebrows, eyelids, pubic areas, legs, or anywhere on the body (Woods, Flessner, et al., 2006). Many patients engage in a variety of habitual behaviors before and after pulling (e.g., searching for the perfect hair to pull and scrutinizing or eating the hair afterward; Mansueto, Townsley-Stemberger, Thomas, & Golomb, 1997). Typically, hair pulling and pre–post pulling activities produce pleasurable feelings or regulate negative affective states, such as boredom or anxiety (Diefenbach, Tolin, Meunier, & Worhunsky, 2008). Because patients sometimes report no reflective awareness of the behavior, it has been suggested that HPD consists of at least two styles of pulling (Flessner, Woods, et al., 2008). An *automatic* style that involves pulling without reflective awareness, typically during sedentary activities in which the attention is absorbed (e.g., reading, watching TV), and a *focused* style that involves pulling with full awareness, usually in response to some internal state, such as an urge or negative affect.

Adverse consequences of HPD include hair thinning, bald spots, carpal tunnel syndrome, low self-esteem, relationship problems, social avoidance, and disruption in work or academic functioning (Diefenbach, Tolin, Hannan, Crocetto, & Worhunsky, 2005; Woods, Flessner, et al., 2006). A small minority of patients eat the pulled hairs, which may cause a life-threatening complication if the hairs clog the digestive tract. The *DSM–5* criteria require hair pulling to cause noticeable hair loss, significant distress or functional impairment and exclude hair pulling due to a medical problem or the use of drugs (American Psychiatric Association, 2013). The criteria also require that the individual experience increasing arousal or tension just before the pulling, and gratification or relief while pulling. However, because a substantial minority of patients (approximately 20%) do not report preceding arousal and subsequent relief or gratification, these items were not included in the *DSM–5* criteria for HPD (Stein et al., 2010).

It is estimated that 0.6% of college students meet strict *DSM* criteria for HPD, and 2.5% report problematic hair pulling without associated relief or gratification (Christenson, Pyle, & Mitchell, 1991). A large majority of patients who seek treatment for HPD are female (> 90%), but it is unclear to what extent this reflects the greater tendency among females to seek help (Snorrason, Belleau, et al., 2012). HPD is typically chronic with waxing and waning severity. The most common age at onset is early adolescence, but the disorder frequently occurs in early childhood. It has been proposed that early-onset cases represent a distinct subtype that is less chronic and more likely to resolve without treatment (Swedo, Leonard, Lenane, & Rettwe, 1992). However, this has yet to been investigated empirically with longitudinal data (Park, Rahman, Murphy, & Storch, 2012).

SKIN PICKING

The phenomenology of skin-picking disorder (SPD) is strikingly similar to that of HPD (Snorrason, Belleau, et al., 2012). Many patients engage in pre- and postpicking behaviors. Patients commonly stroke the skin to find imperfections to pick, and many will manipulate the product afterward (rolling it between the fingers, chewing on it, eating it; Snorrason, Smari, & Olafsson, 2011; Wilhelm et al., 1999). Skin-picking episodes are typically associated with gratification, pleasure, and reduction in negative affective states, such as boredom, tension, and anxiety (Snorrason et al., 2010; Wilhelm et al, 1999). Like hair pulling, skin picking often occurs without reflective awareness, and similar automatic and focused picking styles have been proposed (Walther, Flessner, Conelea, & Woods, 2009). Individuals with SPD report a range of medical and psychosocial complications caused by the behavior, including infections, skin damage, and, in severe cases, permanent disfigurement (Odlaug & Grant, 2008; Wilhelm et al., 1999). Damage to the skin and the inability to control the behavior may lead to significant emotional distress (Keuthen et al., 2001), and some patients report occupational and economic disruption due to the disorder (Flessner & Woods, 2006; Tucker, Woods, Flessner, Franklin, & Franklin, 2011). The *DSM–5* diagnostic criteria (American Psychiatric Association, 2013) defines SPD as recurrent skin picking that results in skin lesions, emotional distress or functional impairment, and is not exclusively due to the use of drugs, a medical condition (e.g., dermatological illness), or other psychiatric disorders (e.g., body dysmorphic disorder).

Prevalence estimates suggest that 2.2% of college students (Bohne, Wilhelm, Keuthen, Baer, & Jenike, 2002) and 1.4% of adults in the general population meet criteria for SPD (Keuthen, Rothbaum, et al., 2010). Most SPD patients (75%–94%) in clinical populations are female (Snorrason, Belleau, et al., 2012), and the most common age of SPD onset is in the adolescent years. SPD may also have onset in childhood, but distinct childhood-onset SPD has not been reported in the literature (Snorrason, Belleau, et al., 2012).

NAIL BITING

Benign nail biting is common (Hansen et al., 1990), but individuals with problematic nail biting (onychophagia) will engage in the behavior more often and more excessively than other people. Sufferers will repeatedly bite the nails far beyond the edge of the fingertips, leaving the nail bed exposed. Most chronic nail biters typically bite the nails on all 10 fingers equally, without preference for a specific finger. Sometimes individuals will inspect the nails they have bitten, play with them, chew on them, or eat them (Billig, 1941; Snorrason, Ingolfsdottir, et al., 2012). Nail biting commonly occurs when the individual is bored, anxious, tense, frustrated, or concentrating (Teng, Woods, Marcks, & Twohig, 2004; Tröster, 1994; Williams, Rose, & Chisholm, 2007). Experimental evidence suggests the behavior regulates physiological arousal (Wells, Haines, Williams, & Brain, 1999). Nail biting can also occur automatically without awareness of the act, typically when the attention is absorbed (Leung, & Rogson, 1990; Snorrason, Ingolfsdottir, et al., 2012). This suggests that it may be meaningful to talk of automatic and focused nail biting style, similar to hair pulling and skin picking. Chronic nail biting can lead to a variety of complications including dental problems, infections, damaged nails, elimination of nail beds, and tissue damage on the fingers (Mostaghimi, 2012). The habit may also decrease self-esteem and cause distress due to the inability to control the behavior or the unattractive appearance of the fingers (Hansen et al., 1990; Joubert, 1993). To the best of our knowledge, reliable prevalence estimates of problematic nail biting have not been reported. Also, little is known about gender ratio and course of the disorder.

CHEEK AND LIP BITING

Cheek and lip biting is the habit of chewing the inside of the mouth (*morsicatio buccarum*), lips (*morsicatio labiorum*), or the tip of the tongue (*morsicatio linguarum*). A variant of this behavior is sucking (not biting) the inside of the cheek or lip (Hjorting-Hansen, & Holst, 1970). Survey data in healthy populations suggest that a mild form of the behavior is common (Woods et al., 1996). A large dental survey (van Wyk, Staz, & Farman, 1977) showed that the prevalence of lesions indicative of cheek and lip biting was significantly higher among students in government reform schools than among students in ordinary state schools, leading the authors to speculate that stress plays a role in the behavior. The survey also demonstrated that many individuals engage in this behavior without reflective awareness of it. Others have speculated that environments requiring concentration and focus predispose people to cheek and lip biting (Sewerin, 1971). Empirical evidence consistent with this view comes from a study showing that youth are more likely to engage in cheek and lip biting in situations characterized by "concentration/demand" (Tröster, 1994).

To the best of our knowledge, no systematic study has been conducted on a problematic form of cheek and lip biting, but several case studies have described individuals experiencing significant distress and disability due to this habit (e.g., Hjorting-Hansen, & Holst, 1970; Jones, Swearer, & Friman, 1997). For example, Sarkhel and colleagues (2011) reported a case of a 41-year-old man with a 20-year history of a cheek-biting habit and no comorbid psychiatric disorder other than habitual nail biting. The patient reported sudden urges to bite the skin inside his cheeks. He would nibble at the skin for few minutes, and then bite of a small chunk of the skin, resulting in a sense of relief. The patient would not be satisfied until he visually inspected the skin piece and rolled it between the fingers. The behavior frequently resulted in bleeding, swelling, and ulcerations inside the cheeks to the point that he had to restrict himself to a liquid diet.

OTHER BFRBS

In addition to the BFRBs described earlier (i.e., hair pulling, skin picking, nail biting, and cheek and lip biting), several other problematic habit behaviors may be construed as BFRBs. Studies show that chronic nose picking (*rhinotilexomania*) can become a problem (Jefferson & Thompson, 1995) and may be related to other BFRBs (Stein et al., 2008). Chronic thumb sucking can also be problematic and often co-occurs with other BFRBs, including nail biting (Ooki, 2005) and hair pulling (Friman, & Hove, 1987). Cases of problematic hair twirling have been reported, and this behavior may be related to HPD (Deaver, Miltenberger, & Stricker, 2001). Other behaviors possibly related to HPD are compulsively picking at the hair, breaking off hair ends (e.g., split ends), or cutting the hair with the fingernails (*trichocryptomania* or *trichorrexomania*; Pereira, 2004). Also, several case studies have described patients who repeatedly pick or pull at the nails (*onychotillomania*) with the fingers or implements, often resulting in damage to the nails or the surrounding skin (e.g., Inglese, Haley, & Elewski, 2004). Finally, case reports have described individuals with a problematic habit of gnawing or biting their skin (*dermatophagia* or *dermatodaxia*; Mitropoulos & Norton, 2005).

RELATION AMONG BFRBS

A growing body of research shows that BFRBs tend to co-occur (Snorrason, Belleau, et al., 2012; Snorrason, Ricketts, et al., 2012; Stein et al., 2008). In addition, studies have shown that BFRBs share substantial similarities in core phenomenological features. Most BFRBs involve removing parts of the body (i.e., the skin, hair, or nails) with the teeth, fingers, or implements, and all BFRBs typically include somewhat ritualized habit behavior surrounding the act (e.g., pre and post hair-pulling behaviors). All BFRBs can be construed as a soothing behavior, and evidence suggests they provide pleasurable feelings and regulate high and low arousal states, such as anxiety or boredom (Diefenbach et al., 2008; Snorrason et al., 2010; Wells et al., 1999). Another characteristic shared by different BFRBs is that they tend to occur automatically or when the attention is absorbed, perhaps suggesting a common attention-regulation mechanism. Finally, research indicates a potential familial and genetic link between BFRBs. Preliminary evidence shows that first-degree relatives of HPD patients have an increased risk for SPD, and relatives of SPD patients are at a heightened risk for HPD (Snorrason, Belleau, et al., 2012). Twin studies have shown a shared heritability factor between thumb sucking and nail biting (Ooki, 2005), and possibly between hair pulling and skin picking (Snorrason, Belleau, et al., 2012). Moreover, a study in a large obsessive–compulsive disorder sample identified a common genetic component among problematic skin picking, hair pulling, and nail biting (Bienvenu et al., 2009). Despite these promising findings, much more research is needed to understand the nature and the extent of the relationship between BFRBs.

ASSESSMENT OF BFRBS

Currently, clinician-administered diagnostic interviews for HPD (Diefenbach, Tolin, Crocetto, Maltby, & Hannan, 2005) and SPD (Odlaug & Grant, 2008) are available, as well as a clinician-rated interview for severity and impairment of hair pulling (Swedo et al., 1989) and nail biting (Leonard, Lenane, Swedo, Rettew, & Rapoport, 1991). However, no interview measures have been designed for other BFRBs. The habit questionnaire is a self-report scale that assesses the frequency and impairment associated with a range of

BFRBs, including hair pulling, hair twirling, nail biting, thumb sucking, skin biting, skin picking, and cheek/lip biting. The scale has moderate test–retest reliability over 1 week among college students (Teng et al., 2002) but no additional psychometric information is available.

Psychometrically sound self-report scales assessing current symptom severity have been developed for children (Tolin et al., 2008) and adults with HPD (Keuthen et al., 2007) and adults with SPD (Snorrason, Olafsson, et al., 2012). Self-report scales assessing automatic and focused pulling and picking styles have been developed for children (Flessner et al., 2007) and adults with HPD (Flessner, Woods, et al., 2008) and adults with SPD (Walther et al., 2009). Instruments assessing automatic and focused styles in other BFRBs have not been developed (McGuire et al., 2012).

Assessment of BFRBs may also involve direct examination of the skin, hair, or nails. For example, dentists can identify distinct lesions of the cheek and lip indicative of cheek and lip biting, which can become helpful in diagnosing the problem when a patient is unaware of or denies it (Hjorting-Hansen, & Holst, 1970; Sewerin, 1971). Also, dermatological examination of skin damage, hair loss, or damage on the nails or surrounding areas may be necessary to confirm diagnosis of BFRBs or provide further information about impairment (Mostaghimi, 2012). The collection of physical traces of BFRBs may be useful in tracking treatment outcome. Clients may be asked to save and count the hairs they pull (Rothbaum & Ninan, 1994), or photographs can be taken of bold spots, skin damage, or fingernail damage (Teng et al., 2006). In one case report, cheek and lip biting was assessed by having the client wipe a bloodstain into a handkerchief every time he bit his cheek or lip. At each session, the therapist would count the bloodstains to assess the frequency of the behavior (Jones et al., 1997).

In addition to establishing a diagnosis and obtaining an index of severity or impairment, it can be imperative to conduct a thorough functional assessment of BFRBs when implementing cognitive behavior therapy (discussed next). Functional assessment involves obtaining an accurate and detailed description of the behavior and its antecedents and consequences, through interview, self-report, or direct observation. Mansueto, Golomb, Thomas, and Stemberger (1999) provided a useful framework for conducting a functional interview for HPD (and other BFRBs).

COGNITIVE BEHAVIOR THERAPY

Broadly speaking, cognitive–behavioral techniques for BFRBs can be divided into two categories. The first category involves techniques directly aimed at preventing BFRBs from occurring or stopping the behavior once it has started. These techniques include stimulus control and habit reversal training (HRT). In the second category are strategies aimed at managing internal states (e.g., urge, anxiety) thought to contribute to the development and maintenance of the habit. These techniques include acceptance and commitment therapy (ACT), dialectical behavior therapy (DBT), and cognitive therapy (CT). Here we describe the treatment strategies in both categories and briefly review research examining their efficacy.

Strategies Aimed at Preventing or Stopping BFRBs: Stimulus Control and HRT

The most extensively studied treatments for BFRBs are HRT and stimulus control. These techniques are typically implemented together and frequently require only two or three sessions, although subsequent sessions are often necessary to review and modify the procedures as therapy progresses.

Stimulus Control

This technique is based on a behavioral model of BFRBs that assumes various contextual cues become associated with the habit behavior through classical conditioning (Mansueto et al., 1997). For example, an individual with HPD may tend to pull hair in the bathroom, during certain periods of the day or when feeling stressed. Over time, features of the context (e.g., the bathroom mirror, negative affective state) acquire the ability to trigger or exacerbate the behavior. The aim of stimulus control is to reduce or eliminate such triggers from the client's environment. Triggers vary between individuals, and it is important to conduct a thorough functional assessment of the behavior to design appropriate stimulus control interventions.

Common cues for BFRBs are visual and tactile features of the target (the skin, nails, or hair), some type of activity (e.g., watching TV), or certain posture or body position (e.g., sitting with the hand close to the head). After the client's triggers have been identified, the therapist may recommend avoiding high-risk situations or eliminating or modifying the triggering stimuli. For example, the patient may be encouraged to cover mirrors in the bathroom and avoid watching TV in a certain room or chair. Also, as noted previously, studies show that various internal states (e.g., urges, boredom, anxiety) may evoke BFRBs (Diefenbach et al., 2008; Snorrason et al., 2010; Williams et al., 2007). In such cases, the client may be advised to avoid or alter (if possible) situations that produce these internal states. Moreover, interventions directly aimed at managing negative emotions or aversive internal states may be a valuable addition to treatment (see below).

In addition to managing triggers of the behavior, another aim of stimulus control is to introduce factors that make it harder for the client to perform the habit. This may include asking an individual with nail biting to wear gloves during certain high-risk situations or asking a client with cheek or lip biting to wear an oral screen between the teeth and the chin (Hjorting-Hansen & Holst, 1970).

Finally, stimulus control can be used to eliminate or reduce reinforcing consequences of the behavior. For example, an HPD client reporting a reinforcing sensation when stroking hair against the lips may be asked to wear a lipstick (if doing so attenuates the sensation). Note that the same stimulus control intervention can serve different functions for different patients (e.g., glove wearing can be used either to increase effort or to attenuate reinforcing qualities of the behavior). Alternatively, the therapist may make the BFRBs less desirable by introducing activities that provide similar reinforcing stimulation as the BFRB. For example, if a client is prone to tactile stimulation during picking or pulling episodes, she may benefit from learning to get such stimulation in other ways, such as playing with a koosh ball.

HRT

HRT involves teaching the client to engage in an incompatible behavior as soon as she recognizes the habit behavior is about to occur (Azrin & Nunn, 1973). HRT typically has three components: awareness training, competing response training, and social support. Awareness training involves having the client provide a detailed description of the behavior as well as its antecedents and consequences. On the basis of this description, the client and the therapist identify warning signs, which can cue the client that the behavior is about to occur. These warning signs can be certain motor behaviors performed before the habit (e.g., hand starts to move toward the head), certain internal states (e.g., an urge), or high-risk situations (e.g., sitting in a chair with the hand close to the head). After the client has described the behavior in detail and defined common warning signs, he is trained to identify occurrences of both in session. To further enhance the client's awareness, a self-monitoring task is assigned as homework (i.e., the client is asked to monitor and document occurrence of the BFRB).

When the client has learned to become aware of the behavior and warning signs, competing response training is implemented. This involves teaching the client to perform a specific behavior for at least 1 minute (i.e., a competing response) contingent on the habit or its warning signs. The competing response needs to be physically incompatible with the BFRB, such that the client cannot perform the habit when doing the competing response. At the same time, the competing response should be easy to implement and socially appropriate. For example, an individual with hair pulling may be taught to lightly clench her fist every time she gets an urge to pull hair.

The third component of HRT is social support. The purpose of social support is to have a person close to the client (e.g., a parent, romantic partner, roommate) provide reinforcement for applying the techniques taught in treatment. The support person is asked to gently remind the client to perform the competing response and praise her when she does remember.

Strategies Aimed at Internal States: ACT, DBT, and CT

Researchers and clinicians have attempted to augment HRT and stimulus control with techniques that focus on managing internal states, such as urges, impulses, dysfunctional cognitions, and negative affect. Three types of augmentation therapy have been examined: ACT, DBT, and CT. Cognitive therapy is based on the traditional cognitive model that assumes faulty cognitions maintain psychiatric symptoms. Thus, the aim of the treatment is correcting or rectifying faulty cognitions. On the other hand, ACT (and to some extent DBT) is based on the view that it is not the internal events (e.g., cognitions, urges) themselves that are the problem but the individual's struggle with them. Instead of trying to change or control internal events directly, the intervention focuses on the relationship the individual has with them. ACT emphasizes acceptance of internal states and aims to reduce the literal meaning of language and cognitions in the service of minimizing their impact on behavior. All three augmentation treatments were developed for HPD, but they may apply to other BFRBs.

ACT

In ACT, the client is taught to accept internal states (e.g., urges) without reacting to or trying to control them (e.g., by engaging in BFRBs) and, at the same time, to engage in behaviors that are consistent with her personal values and goals (Hayes, Strosahl, & Wilson, 1999). Woods and colleagues (Twohig & Woods, 2004; Woods & Twohig, 2008; Woods, Wetterneck, et al., 2006) developed a 10-session ACT-enhanced HRT for HPD. The first two sessions include psychoeducation, functional assessment, stimulus control, and HRT. ACT components start at Session 3, when the client and the therapist clarify the client's values and life goals and discuss how efforts to control urges to pull can stand in the way of pursuing them. Session 4 continues with the same theme, and the client is asked to list strategies she has used in the past to try controlling urges to pull and other triggering cognitive or emotional stimuli. This is followed by discussion of the effectiveness of these strategies. The main goal of the session is to demonstrate that attempts to control internal states are ultimately ineffective and are potentially problematic (e.g., they distract from pursuing life goals). In Session 5, metaphors and exercises are used to demonstrate further that attempts to control or suppress internal states are ineffective. Also, the concept of acceptance is introduced, and the client is asked to consider the benefit of accepting (rather than controlling) internal states (e.g., urges, cognitions, emotions). Sessions 6 and 7 include several exercises and metaphors designed to demonstrate that internal states are responses that can simply be observed and are not literal truths that necessarily dictate behavior (i.e., cognitive defusion exercises). In Sessions 8 and 9, the client is given an opportunity to review and practice the material learned in previous sessions. The 10th and final session provides an opportunity to reexamine material learned in the treatment. The session also includes relapse prevention strategies, such as discussion of the difference between lapse and relapse.

DBT

DBT was designed to help clients learn to better tolerate stress, regulate emotions, and deal with impulsiveness (Linehan, 1993). The treatment uses mindfulness- and acceptance-based strategies to indirectly change the individual's relation with internal events such as emotions and urges. Keuthen and colleagues developed a DBT-enhanced HRT protocol for HPD (Keuthen, Rothbaum, et al., 2010; Keuthen et al., 2011). The treatment consists of 11 weekly sessions and four booster sessions that are implemented 2, 4, 8, and 12 weeks after treatment. The first session includes psychoeducation, motivational interviewing (to enhance the motivation to break the habit), functional assessment, and self-monitoring. Competing response training and stimulus control are implemented in the second session. Sessions 3 through 5 focus on mindfulness training to enhance early awareness of hair pulling and urges. Sessions 6 through 8 consist of emotion regulation training including progressive muscle relaxation and acceptance-based strategies such as "urge surfing" (i.e., the client is asked to observe the urge increase and decrease in a detached mindful manner without acting on it). In Sessions 9 and 10, the client is taught stress-tolerance skills that allow her to refocus attention away from uncomfortable internal states such as pain, emotions, and urges. To better tolerate such states, the client may be taught to use distraction (e.g., engaging in a hobby), self-soothing (e.g., listening to music), or "improve the moment" methods (e.g., use imagery to create a scene that is different from the current physical situation). Session 11, which is the final session of the general treatment, includes relapse prevention techniques such as discussion of the differences between lapse and relapse and identification of possible solutions for high-risk situations. As noted earlier, Sessions 12 through 15 are booster sessions implemented between 2 and 12 weeks after treatment. These sessions focus on relapse prevention and review of material previously covered in the treatment.

Cognitive Therapy

Dysfunctional cognitions may be associated with BFRBs. For example, individuals with HPD often have distorted cognitions about hairs (e.g., "gray hairs are bad and need to be pulled out") that may play a role in maintaining the behavior. Some authors have therefore used CT as an adjunct to HRT and stimulus control in the treatment of HPD (Franklin, Edson, Ledley, & Cahill, 2011; Lerner, Franklin, Meadows, Hembree, & Foa, 1998) and SPD (Schuck, Keijsers, & Rinck, 2011). The package developed by Lerner et al. (1998) consists of nine weekly sessions. The first session involves functional assessment and introduction to self-monitoring (awareness training). Session 2 focuses on HRT and stimulus control and Sessions 3 and 4 on relaxation training (i.e., deep muscle relaxation techniques). Sessions 5 through 9 include the following cognitive techniques: (a) thought stopping, (b) cognitive restructuring (e.g., using Socratic questioning to help client challenge dysfunctional thinking about hair pulling), (c) guided self-dialogue (e.g., helping patient replace a dysfunctional self-dialogue with one that is more adaptive), (d) covert modeling (patient is asked to imagining herself dealing with stress effectively without pulling), and (e) relapse prevention (e.g., prepare the client for setbacks and differentiate between "lapses" and "relapses").

Efficacy of Cognitive–Behavioral Treatments of BFRBs

Adults

A meta-analysis of four randomized controlled trials (RCTs) showed that treatments involving HRT and stimulus control are more effective than control conditions in reducing hair pulling (Bloch et al., 2007). RCT evidence also suggest that the combination of HRT and stimulus control is more effective than control conditions in reducing skin picking (Schuck et al., 2011; Teng et al., 2006), nail biting (Flessner et al., 2005; Twohig, Woods, Marcks, & Teng, 2003), and oral habits such as cheek and lip biting (Azrin, Nunn, & Frantz-Renshaw, 1982). Furthermore, findings from RCTs suggest that HRT and stimulus control delivered in group format may benefit individuals with hair pulling (Diefenbach et al., 2006) and nail biting (Azrin, Nunn, & Frantz, 1980a).

Azrin and colleagues reported that individuals with hair pulling (Azrin et al., 1980b) and oral habits (Azrin et al., 1982) showed excellent gains that were maintained 22 months after treatment. Azrin et al. (1980a) also showed that individuals with nail biting showed good gain maintenance at 5-month follow-up. However, these studies only reported maintenance for those individuals available for follow-up, and recent studies that used a more stringent assessment of maintenance indicate that relapse is common among HPD patients (Keijsers et al., 2006; Keuthen et al., 1998, 2001).

Adding treatment techniques aimed at internal states (e.g., DBT, ACT, CT) may improve long-term outcome (Keuthen et al., 2011). A few studies have examined the efficacy of HRT and stimulus control in combination with such techniques at the end of treatment and at 2- or 3-month follow-up. Woods, Wetterneck, et al. (2006) found that ACT-enhanced HRT was more effective than wait list in reducing hair pulling, and the treatment gains were mostly maintained 3 months later. Similarly, Keuthen and colleagues (Keuthen, Rothbaum, et al., 2010; Keuthen et al., 2011) found that DBT-enhanced HRT was effective in reducing hair pulling and, with booster sessions, produced acceptable gain maintenance at 3-month follow-up. Finally, Schuck et al. (2011) found CT-enhanced HRT to be more effective than wait list in reducing skin picking both at posttreatment and at 2-month follow-up. Although these findings are promising, additional studies are needed to examine whether these interventions prevent relapse for longer than 3 months.

Children and Adolescents

A recent meta-analysis showed that combined HRT and stimulus control is more effective than control conditions in reducing thumb sucking, nail biting, and oral habits such as cheek and lip biting in children and adolescents (four RCTs; Bate, Malouff, Thorsteinsson, & Bhullar, 2011). Furthermore, Franklin and colleagues (2011) conducted an RCT showing that CT-enhanced HRT was more effective than minimum attention control in reducing hair pulling in children and adolescents. To the best of our knowledge, no study has examined treatment of skin picking in youth. To date, most studies have implemented individualized treatment for children and adolescents with BFRBs; however, one RCT showed that HRT and stimulus control for parents of children with thumb sucking was superior to a control condition (Christensen & Sanders, 1987).

Azrin and colleagues reported that reductions in thumb sucking (Azrin, Nunn, & Frantz-Renshaw, 1980) and oral habits in children (Azrin et al., 1982) were maintained up to 22 months after HRT. Also, de L. Horne and Wilkinson (1980) found a low relapse rate at 2-month follow-up among children receiving HRT for nail biting. Again, it should be noted that these studies only reported on patients who were available for follow-up. Also, no study has examined long-term maintenance among children with HPD, and it remains to be seen if they relapse less than adults with HPD.

FUTURE RESEARCH

Evidence suggests that combined HRT and stimulus control is an effective treatment for BFRBs. Some authors have attempted to determine the essential components, but limited empirical data exist. Few early studies suggested that awareness training alone may be sufficient to reduce nail biting and hair pulling (e.g., Ladouceur, 1979). However, it may be wise to always include the competing response training because theoretical accounts assume it is an important mechanism of change in treatment, and the effectiveness of awareness training alone may be transient (Miltenberger, Fuqua, & Woods, 1998). Flessner and colleagues (2005) found that the social support component of HRT did not add to the effectiveness of the treatment among adult nail biters; however, it is unclear whether this is true of other BFRBs or whether the same findings hold for children.

As noted earlier, several authors have augmented combined HRT and stimulus control with ACT, DBT, or CT. Even though RCTs show that these treatment packages are effective, no study has examined whether, or to what extent, these interventions add to the effectiveness of HRT and stimulus control, either at posttreatment or in extended follow-up phases.

Another important avenue for research is matching different components to client characteristics. For example, it has been suggested that different CBT techniques may suit automatic and focused styles differently (Flessner, Woods, et al., 2008; Walther et al., 2009). HRT and stimulus control may be especially effective in dealing with the automatic style, and strategies aimed at internal states (i.e., CT, ACT, and DBT) may be effective in managing the focused style. However, research has yet to examine this possibility, and most patients endorse both styles (Flessner, Conelea, et al., 2008). We therefore recommend including both components until empirical data are collected.

Future researchers may also want to investigate predictors of outcome. Preliminary studies show that complete abstinence after HRT and stimulus control predicts good long-term outcome (Keijsers et al., 2006); therefore, it may be helpful to encourage patients to stop the habit completely or continue treatment until complete abstinence is obtained. Also, clinical experience suggests that relapse often occurs when individuals stop applying the techniques they learned in treatment (e.g., the competing response). Thus, booster sessions may be helpful to some patients. Another potential predictor of good outcome is treatment compliance, suggesting that it is imperative to form a good therapeutic alliance and establish motivation early in treatment.

REFERENCES

American Psychiatric Association. (2000). *Diagnostic and statistical manual of mental disorders* (4th ed., text revision). Washington, DC: Author.

American Psychiatric Association. (2013). *Diagnostic and statistical manual of mental disorders* (5th ed.). Washington, DC: Author.

Azrin, N. H., & Nunn, R. G. (1973). Habit-reversal: A method of eliminating nervous habits and tics. *Behaviour Research and Therapy, 11,* 619–628. doi:10.1016/0005-7967(73)90119-8

Azrin, N. H., Nunn, R. G., & Frantz, S. E. (1980a). Habit reversal vs. negative practice treatment of nailbiting. *Behaviour Research and Therapy, 18,* 281–285. doi:10.1016/0005-7967(80)90086-8

Azrin, N. H., Nunn, R. G., & Frantz, S. E. (1980b). Treatment of hair pulling (trichotillomania): A comparative study of habit reversal and negative practice training. *Behaviour Research and Therapy, 18,* 281–285. doi:10.1016/0005-7967(80)90086-8

Azrin, N. H., Nunn, R. G., & Frantz-Renshaw, S. E. (1980). Habit reversal treatment of thumbsucking. *Behaviour Research and Therapy, 18,* 395–399. doi:10.1016/0005-7967(80)90004-2

Azrin, N. H., Nunn, R. G., & Frantz-Renshaw, S. E. (1982). Habit reversal vs. negative practice treatment of self-destructive oral habits (self-biting, chewing or licking of the lips, cheeks, tongue or palate). *Journal of Behavior Therapy and Experimental Psychiatry, 13,* 49–54. doi:10.1016/0005-7916(82)90035-0

Bate, K. S., Malouff, J. M., Thorsteinsson, E. T., & Bhullar, N. (2011). The efficacy of habit reversal therapy for tics, habit disorders, and stuttering: A meta-analytic review. *Clinical Psychology Review, 31,* 865–871. doi:10.1016/j.cpr.2011.03.013

Bienvenu, O. J., Wang, Y., Shugart, Y. Y., Welch, J. M., Grados, M. A., Fyer, A. J., . . . Nestadt, G. (2009). *Sapap3* and pathological grooming in humans: Results from the OCD collaborative genetics study. *American Journal of Medical Genetics: Part B. Neuropsychiatric Genetics, 150B,* 710–720. doi:10.1002/ajmg.b.30897

Billig, A. L. (1941). Fingernail biting: Its incipiency, incidence, and amelioration. *Genetic Psychology Monographs, 24,* 123–218.

Bloch, M. H., Landeros-Weisenberger, A., Dombrowski, P., Kelmendi, B., Wegner, R., Nudel, J., . . . Coric, V. (2007). Systematic review: Pharmacological and behavioral treatment for trichotillomania. *Biological Psychiatry, 62,* 839–846. doi:10.1016/j.biopsych.2007.05.019

Bohne, A., Wilhelm, S., Keuthen, N. J., Baer, L., & Jenike, M. A. (2002). Skin picking in German students: Prevalence, phenomenology, and associated characteristics. *Behavior Modification, 26,* 320–339. doi:10.1177/0145445502026003002

Christensen, A. P., & Sanders, M. R. (1987). Habit reversal and differential reinforcement of other behavior in the treatment of thumb-sucking: An analysis of generalization and side-effects. *Journal of Child Psychology and Psychiatry, and Allied Disciplines, 28*, 281–295. doi:10.1111/j.1469-7610.1987.tb00211.x

Christenson, G. A., Pyle, R. L., & Mitchell, J. E. (1991). Estimated lifetime prevalence of trichotillomania in college students. *The Journal of Clinical Psychiatry, 52*, 415–417.

Deaver, C. M., Miltenberger, R. G., & Stricker, J. M. (2001). Functional analysis and treatment of hair twirling in a young child. *Journal of Applied Behavior Analysis, 34*, 535–538. doi:10.1901/jaba.2001.34-535

de L. Horne, D. J., & Wilkinson, J. (1980). Habit reversal treatment for fingernail biting. *Behaviour Research and Therapy, 18*, 287–291. doi:10.1016/0005-7967(80)90087-X

Diefenbach, G. J., Tolin, D. F., Crocetto, J., Maltby, N., & Hannan, S. (2005). Assessment of trichotillomania: A psychometric evaluation of hair-pulling scales. *Journal of Psychopathology and Behavioral Assessment, 27*, 169–178. doi:10.1007/s10862-005-0633-7

Diefenbach, G. J., Tolin, D. F., Hannan, S., Crocetto, J., & Worhunsky, P. (2005). Trichotillomania: Impact on psychosocial functioning and quality of life. *Behaviour Research and Therapy, 43*, 869–884. doi:10.1016/j.brat.2004.06.010

Diefenbach, G. J., Tolin, D. F., Hannan, S., Maltby, N., & Crocetto, J. (2006). Group treatment for trichotillomania: Behavior therapy versus supportive therapy. *Behavior Therapy, 37*, 353–363. doi:10.1016/j.beth.2006.01.006

Diefenbach, G. J., Tolin, D. F., Meunier, S., & Worhunsky, P. (2008). Emotion regulation and trichotillomania: A comparison of clinical and nonclinical hair pulling. *Journal of Behavior Therapy and Experimental Psychiatry, 39*, 32–41. doi:10.1016/j.jbtep.2006.09.002

Flessner, C. A., Conelea, C. A., Woods, D. W., Franklin, M. E., Keuthen, N. J., & Cashin, S. E. (2008). Styles of pulling in trichotillomania: Exploring the differences in symptom severity, phenomenology, and functional impact. *Behaviour Research and Therapy, 46*, 345–357. doi:10.1016/j.brat.2007.12.009

Flessner, C. A., Miltenberger, R. G., Egemo, K., Kelso, P., Jostad, C., Johnson, B., . . . Neighbors, C. (2005). An evaluation of the social support component of simplified habit reversal. *Behavior Therapy, 36*, 35–42. doi:10.1016/S0005-7894(05)80052-8

Flessner, C. A., & Woods, D. W. (2006). Phenomenological characteristics, social problems, and the economic impact associated with chronic skin picking. *Behavior Modification, 30*, 944–963. doi:10.1177/0145445506294083

Flessner, C. A., Woods, D. W., Franklin, M. E., Cashin, S. E., Keuthen, N. J., & the Trichotillomania Learning Center—Scientific Advisory Board. (2008). The Milwaukee Inventory for Subtypes of Trichotillomania—Adult Version (MIST–A): Development of an instrument for the assessment of "focused" and "automatic" hair pulling. *Journal of Psychopathology and Behavioral Assessment, 30,* 20–30. doi:10.1007/s10862-007-9073-x

Flessner, C. A., Woods, D. W., Franklin, M. E., Keuthen, N. J., Piacentini, J., . . . Moore, P. S. (2007). The Milwaukee inventory for styles of trichotillomania-child version (MIST-C): Initial development and psychometric properties. *Behavior Modification, 31,* 896–918. doi:10.1177/0145445507302521

Franklin, M. E., Edson, A. L., Ledley, D. A., & Cahill, S. P. (2011). Behavior therapy for pediatric trichotillomania: A randomized controlled trial. *Journal of the American Academy of Child & Adolescent Psychiatry, 50,* 763–771. doi:10.1016/j.jaac.2011.05.009

Friman, P. C., & Hove, G. (1987). Apparent covariation between child habit disorders: Effects of successful treatment for thumb sucking on untargeted chronic hair pulling. *Journal of Applied Behavior Analysis, 20,* 421–425. doi:10.1901/jaba.1987.20-421

Hansen, D. J., Tishelman, A. C., Hawkins, R. P., & Doepke, K. J. (1990). Habits with potential as disorders: Prevalence, severity, and other characteristics among college students. *Behavior Modification, 14,* 66–80. doi:10.1177/01454455900141005

Hayes, S. C., Strosahl, K. D., & Wilson, K. G. (1999). *Acceptance and commitment therapy: An experiential approach to behavior change.* New York, NY: The Guilford Press.

Hjorting-Hansen, E., & Holst, E. (1970). Morsicato mucosae oris and suction oris: An analysis of oral mucosal changes due to biting and sucking habits. *Scandinavian Journal of Dental Research, 78,* 492–499.

Inglese, M., Haley, H. R., & Elewski, B. E. (2004). Onychotillomania: 2 case reports. *Cutis, 73,* 171–174.

Jefferson, J. W., & Thompson, T. D. (1995). Rhinotillexomania: Psychiatric disorder or habit? *The Journal of Clinical Psychiatry, 56,* 56–59.

Jones, K. M., Swearer, S. M., & Friman, P. C. (1997). Relax and try this instead: Abbreviated habit reversal for maladaptive self-biting. *Journal of Applied Behavior Analysis, 30,* 697–699. doi:10.1901/jaba.1997.30-697

Joubert, C. E. (1993). Relationship of self-esteem, manifest anxiety, and obsessive–compulsiveness to personal habits. *Psychological Reports, 73,* 579–583. doi:10.2466/pr0.1993.73.2.579

Keijsers, G. P., van Minnen, A., Hoogduin, C. A., Klaassen, B. N., Hendriks, M. J., & Tanis-Jacobs, J. (2006). Behavioural treatment of trichotillomania: Two-year follow-up results. *Behaviour Research and Therapy, 44,* 359–370. doi:10.1016/j.brat.2005.03.004

Keuthen, N. J., Flessner, C. A., Woods, D. W., Franklin, M. E., Stein, D. J., Cashin, S. W., & The Trichotillomania Learning Center—Scientific Advisory Board. (2007). Factor analysis of the Massachusetts general hospital hairpulling scale. *Journal of Psychosomatic Research, 62,* 707–709. doi:10.1016/j.jpsychores.2006.12.003

Keuthen, N. J., Fraim, C., Deckersbach, T., Dougherty, L., Baer, L., & Jenicke, M. A. (2001). Longitudinal follow-up of naturalistic treatment outcome in patients with trichotillomania. *The Journal of Clinical Psychiatry, 62,* 101–107. doi:10.4088/JCP.v62n0205

Keuthen, N. J., Koran, L. M., Aboujaoude, E., Large, M. D., & Serpe, R. T. (2010). The prevalence of pathological skin picking in US adults. *Comprehensive Psychiatry, 51,* 183–186. doi:10.1016/j.comppsych.2009.04.003

Keuthen, N. J., O'Sullivan, P., Goodchild, P., Rodriguez, D., Jenike, M. A., & Baer, L. (1998). Retrospective review of treatment outcome for 63 patients with trichotillomania. *The American Journal of Psychiatry, 155,* 560–561.

Keuthen, N. J., Rothbaum, B. O., Falkenstein, M. J., Meunier, S., Timpano, K. R., Timpano, K. R., . . . Welch, S. S. (2011). DBT-enhanced habit reversal treatment for trichotillomania: 3- and 6-month follow-up results. *Depression and Anxiety, 28,* 310–313. doi:10.1002/da.20778

Keuthen, N. J., Rothbaum, B. O., Welch, S. S., Taylor, C., Falkenstein, M., Heekin, M., . . . Jenike, M. A. (2010). Pilot trial of dialectical behavior therapy-enhanced habit reversal for trichotillomania. *Depression and Anxiety, 27,* 953–959. doi:10.1002/da.20732

Ladouceur, R. (1979). Habit reversal treatment: Learning an incompatible response or increasing the subject's awareness? *Behaviour Research and Therapy, 17,* 313–316. doi:10.1016/0005-7967(79)90003-2

Leonard, H. L., Lenane, M. C., Swedo, S. E., Rettew, D. C., & Rapoport, J. L. (1991). A double-blind comparison of clomipramine and desipramine treatment of severe onychophagia (nail biting). *Archives of General Psychiatry, 48,* 821–827. doi:10.1001/archpsyc.1991.01810330045007

Lerner, J., Franklin, M. E., Meadows, E. A., Hembree, E., & Foa, E. B. (1998). Effectiveness of a cognitive behavioral treatment program for trichotillomania: An uncontrolled evaluation. *Behavior Therapy, 29,* 157–171. doi:10.1016/S0005-7894(98)80036-1

Leung, A. K. C., & Rogson, W. L. M. (1990). Nailbiting. *Clinical Pediatrics, 29,* 690–692.

Linehan, M. M. (1993). *Cognitive-behavioral treatment of borderline personality disorder.* New York, NY: Guilford Press.

Mansueto, C. S., Golomb, R. G., Thomas, A. M., & Stemberger, R. M. T. (1999). A comprehensive model for behavioral treatment of trichotillomania. *Cognitive and Behavioral Practice, 6,* 23–43. doi:10.1016/S1077-7229(99)80038-8

Mansueto, C. S., Townsley-Stemberger, R. M., Thomas, A., & Golomb, R. (1997). Trichotillomania: A comprehensive behavioral model. *Clinical Psychology Review, 17,* 567–577. doi:10.1016/S0272-7358(97)00028-7

Massler, M., & Malone, A. J. (1950). Nail biting: A review. *American Journal of Orthodontics, 36,* 351–367. doi:10.1016/0002-9416(50)90075-3

McGuire, J. F., Kugler, B. B., Park, J. M., Horng, B., Lewin, A. B., Murphy, T. K., & Storch, E. A. (2012). Evidence-based assessment of compulsive skin picking, chronic tic disorders and trichotillomania in children. *Child Psychiatry & Human Development, 43*, 855–883. doi:10.1007/s10578-012-0300-7

Miltenberger, R. G., Fuqua, R. W., & Woods, D. W. (1998). Applying behavior analysis to clinical problems: Review and analysis of habit reversal. *Journal of Applied Behavior Analysis, 31*, 447–469. doi:10.1901/jaba.1998.31-447

Mitropoulos, P., & Norton, S. A. (2005). Dermatophagia or dermatodaxia? *Journal of the American Academy of Dermatology, 53*, 365. doi:10.1016/j.jaad.2005.04.021

Mostaghimi, L. (2012). Dermatological assessment of hair pulling, skin picking and nail biting. In J. E. Grant, D. J. Stein, W. D. Woods, & N. J. Keuthen (Eds.), *Trichotillomania, skin picking and other body-focused repetitive behaviors* (pp. 97–112). Washington, DC: American Psychiatric Publishing.

Odlaug, B. L., & Grant, J. E. (2008). Clinical characteristics and medical complications of pathologic skin picking. *General Hospital Psychiatry, 30*, 61–66. doi:10.1016/j.genhosppsych.2007.07.009

Ooki, S. (2005). Genetic and environmental influences on finger-sucking and nail-biting in Japanese twin children. *Twin Research and Human Genetics, 8*, 320–327. doi:10.1375/twin.8.4.320

Park, J. M., Rahman, O., Murphy, T. K., & Storch, E. A. (2012). Early childhood trichotillomania: Initial considerations on phenomenology, treatment, and future directions. *Infant Mental Health Journal, 33*, 163–172. doi:10.1002/imhj.21317

Pereira, J. M. (2004). Compulsive trichoses. *Anais Brasileiros de Dermatologia, 79*, 609–618. doi:10.1590/S0365-05962004000500012

Rothbaum, B. O., & Ninan, P. T. (1994). The assessment of trichotillomania. *Behaviour Research and Therapy, 32*, 651–662. doi:10.1016/0005-7967(94)90022-1

Sarkhel, S., Praharaj, S. K., & Akhtar, S. (2011). Cheek-biting disorder: Another stereotypic movement disorder? *Journal of Anxiety Disorders, 25*, 1085–1086. doi:10.1016/j.janxdis.2011.07.006

Schuck, K., Keijsers, G. P., & Rinck, M. (2011). The effects of brief cognitive-behaviour therapy for pathological skin picking: A randomized comparison to wait-list control. *Behaviour Research and Therapy, 49*, 11–17. doi:10.1016/j.brat.2010.09.005

Sewerin, I. (1971). A clinical and epidemiologic study: Morsicatio buccarum/labiorum. *European Journal of Oral Sciences, 79*, 73–80.

Snorrason, I., Belleau, E. L., & Woods, D. W. (2012). How related are hair pulling disorder (trichotillomania) and skin picking disorder? A review of evidence for comorbidity, similarities and shared etiology. *Clinical Psychology Review, 32*, 618–629. doi:10.1016/j.cpr.2012.05.008

Snorrason, I., Ingolfsdottir, H., Ran, D., Olafsson, R. P., Hansdottir, I., & Woods, D. W. (2012, November). *Body-focused repetitive behaviors: Co-occurrence, similarities and shared family history*. Poster presented at the 46th Annual Convention of Association for Behavioral and Cognitive Therapies, National Harbor, MD.

Snorrason, I., Olafsson, R. P., Flessner, C. A., Keuthen, N. J., Franklin, M. E., & Woods, D. W. (2012). Skin Picking Scale—Revised: Factor structure and psychometric properties. *Journal of Obsessive–Compulsive and Related Disorders, 1*, 133–137. doi:10.1016/j.jocrd.2012.03.001

Snorrason, I., Ricketts, E. J., Flessner, C. A., Franklin, M. E., Stein, D. J., & Woods, D. W. (2012). Skin picking disorder is associated with other body-focused repetitive behaviors: Findings from an Internet study. *Annals of Clinical Psychiatry, 24*, 292–299.

Snorrason, I., Smari, J., & Olafsson, R. P. (2010). Emotion regulation in pathological skin picking: Findings from a non-treatment seeking sample. *Journal of Behavior Therapy and Experimental Psychiatry, 41*, 238–245. doi:10.1016/j.jbtep.2010.01.009

Snorrason, I., Smari, J., & Olafsson, R. P. (2011). Motor inhibition, reflection impulsivity and trait impulsivity in pathological skin picking. *Behavior Therapy, 42*, 521–532. doi:10.1016/j.beth.2010.12.002

Stein, D. J., Flessner, C. A., Franklin, M., Keuthen, N. J., Lochner, C., & Woods, D. W. (2008). Is trichotillomania a stereotypic movement disorder? An analysis of body focused repetitive behaviors in people with hair pulling. *Annals of Clinical Psychiatry, 20*, 194–198. doi:10.1080/10401230802435625

Stein, D. J., Grant, J. E., Franklin, M. E., Keuthen, N., Lochner, C., Singer, H. S., & Woods, D. W. (2010). Trichotillomania (hair pulling disorder), skin picking disorder, and stereotypic movement disorder: Toward DSM–V. *Depression and Anxiety, 27*, 611–626. doi:10.1002/da.20700

Sulkowski, M. L., Mancil, T. L., Jordan, C., Reid, A., Chakoff, E., & Storch, E. A. (2011). Validation of a classification system of obsessive–compulsive spectrum disorder symptoms in a non-clinical sample. *Psychiatry Research, 188*, 65–70. doi:10.1016/j.psychres.2011.01.015

Swedo, S. E., Leonard, H. L., Lenane, M. C., & Rettwe, D. C. (1992). Trichotillomania a profile of the disorder from infancy through adulthood. *International Pediatrics, 7*, 144–150.

Swedo, S. E., Leonard, H. L., Rapoport, J. L., Lenane, M. C., Goldberger, B. A., & Cheslow, B. A. (1989). A double-blind comparison of clomipramine and desipramine in the treatment of trichotillomania (hair pulling). *The New England Journal of Medicine, 321*, 497–501. doi:10.1056/NEJM198908243210803

Teng, E. J., Woods, D. W., Marcks, B. S., & Twohig, M. P. (2004). Body-focused repetitive behaviors: The proximal and distal effects of affective variables on behavioral expression. *Journal of Psychopathology and Behavioral Assessment, 26*, 55–64. doi:10.1023/B:JOBA.0000007456.24198.e4

Teng, E. J., Woods, D. W., & Twohig, M. P. (2006). Habit reversal as a treatment for chronic skin picking. *Behavior Modification, 30,* 411–422. doi:10.1177/0145445504265707

Teng, E. J., Woods, D. W., Twohig, M. P., & Marcks, B. A. (2002). Body-focused repetitive behavior problems: Prevalence in a nonreferred population and differences in perceived somatic activity. *Behavior Modification, 26,* 340–360. doi:10.1177/0145445502026003003

Tolin, D. F., Diefenbach, G. J., Flessner, C. A., Franklin, M. E., Keuthen, N. J., Moore, P., & The Trichotillomania Learning Center Scientific Advisory Board. (2008). The trichotillomania scale for children: Development and validation. *Child Psychiatry and Human Development, 39,* 331–349. doi:10.1007/s10578-007-0092-3

Tröster, H. (1994). Prevalence and function of stereotyped behaviors in nonhandicapped children in residential care. *Journal of Abnormal Psychology, 22,* 79–97. doi:10.1007/BF02169257

Tucker, B. T., Woods, D. W., Flessner, C. A., Franklin, S. A., & Franklin, M. E. (2011). The skin picking impact project: Phenomenology, interference, and treatment utilization of pathological skin picking in a population based sample. *Journal of Anxiety Disorders, 25,* 88–95. doi:10.1016/j.janxdis.2010.08.007

Twohig, M. P., & Woods, D. W. (2004). A preliminary investigation of acceptance and commitment therapy and habit reversal as a treatment for trichotillomania. *Behavior Therapy, 35,* 803–820. doi:10.1016/S0005-7894(04)80021-2

Twohig, M. P., Woods, D. W., Marcks, B. A., & Teng, E. J. (2003). Evaluating the efficacy of habit reversal: Comparison with a placebo control. *The Journal of Clinical Psychiatry, 64,* 40–48. doi:10.4088/JCP.v64n0109

Van Wyk, C. W., Staz, J., & Farman, A. G. (1977). The chewing lesion of the cheeks and lips: Its features and prevalence among a selected group of adolescents. *Journal of Dentistry, 5,* 193–199. doi:10.1016/0300-5712(77)90003-3

Walther, M. R., Flessner, C. A., Conelea, C. A., & Woods, D. W. (2009). The Milwaukee inventory for the dimensions of adult skin picking (MIDAS): Initial development and psychometric properties. *Journal of Behavior Therapy and Experimental Psychiatry, 40,* 127–135. doi:10.1016/j.jbtep.2008.07.002

Wells, J. H., Haines, J., Williams, C. L., & Brain, K. L. (1999). The self-mutilative nature of severe onychophagia: A comparison with self-cutting. *Canadian Journal of Psychiatry, 44,* 40–47.

Wilhelm, S., Keuthen, N. J., Deckersbach, T., Engelhard, I. M., Forker, A. E., Bear, L., . . . Jenike, M. A. (1999). Self-injurious skin picking: Clinical characteristics and comorbidity. *The Journal of Clinical Psychiatry, 60,* 454–459. doi:10.4088/JCP.v60n0707

Williams, T. I., Rose, R., & Chisholm, S. (2007). What is the function of nail biting: An analog assessment study. *Behaviour Research and Therapy, 45,* 989–995. doi:10.1016/j.brat.2006.07.013

Woods, D. W., Flessner, C. A., Franklin, M. E., Keuthen, N. J., Goodwin, R. D., Stein, D. J., & the Trichotillomania Learning Center—Scientific Advisory Board. (2006). The trichotillomania impact project (TIP): Exploring phenomenology, functional impairment, and treatment utilization. *The Journal of Clinical Psychiatry, 67,* 1877–1888. doi:10.4088/JCP.v67n1207

Woods, D. W., Miltenberger, R. G., & Flach, A. D. (1996). Habits, tics, and stuttering: Prevalence and relation to anxiety and somatic awareness. *Behavior Modification, 20,* 216–225. doi:10.1177/01454455960202005

Woods, D. W., & Twohig, M. P. (2008). *Trichotillomania: An ACT-enhanced behavior therapy approach. Therapist guide.* Oxford, England: Oxford University Press.

Woods, D. W., Wetterneck, C. T., & Flessner, C. A. (2006). A controlled evaluation of acceptance and commitment therapy plus habit reversal for trichotillomania. *Behaviour Research and Therapy, 44,* 639–656. doi:10.1016/j.brat.2005.05.006

9

TOURETTE'S DISORDER AND TICS

MICHAEL B. HIMLE AND LORAN P. HAYES

Tic disorders are a class of neuropsychiatric disorders, characterized by involuntary movements and vocalizations (i.e., tics). Although tics are caused by neurobiological dysfunction, recent research has shown that they are influenced by environmental (i.e., behavioral) factors.

The purpose of this chapter is to provide an overview of recent advancements in the understanding and treatment of tics. We begin with an overview of tics and tic disorders, including their classification, prevalence, developmental course, comorbidity, and functional outcomes. We then present recent advancements in how tic disorders are conceptualized, with an emphasis on an integrative behavioral model. We conclude by describing how the integrative behavioral model has been translated into an efficacious comprehensive behavioral treatment approach for managing tic disorders.

http://dx.doi.org/10.1037/14323-010
Obsessive–Compulsive Disorder and Its Spectrum: A Life-Span Approach, Eric A. Storch and Dean McKay (Editors)
Copyright © 2014 by the American Psychological Association. All rights reserved.

185

DEFINITION AND CLASSIFICATION OF TICS
AND TIC DISORDERS

Tics are defined as "sudden, rapid, recurrent, nonrhythmic motor movements or vocalizations" (American Psychiatric Association, 2013). There are four primary tic disorders that are differentiated by the number, type, and duration of tics present (American Psychiatric Association, 2013). *Persistent (chronic) motor tic disorder* and *vocal tic disorder* involve the presence of single or multiple motor *or* vocal tics but not both, that may wax and wane in frequency but have persisted for at least 1 year since first tic onset. *Tourette's disorder* (commonly referred to as *Tourette syndrome* [TS][1]) is generally considered the most severe of the tic disorders and involves the presence of multiple motor *and* one or more vocal tic(s) (although not necessarily concurrently) that may wax and wane in frequency but have persisted for at least 1 year since first tic onset. *Transient tic disorder,* generally considered the most benign of the tic disorders, involves single or multiple tics that have been present for less than 1 year since first tic onset.

Tics are categorized as either *motor* or *vocal* and further categorized as either *simple* or *complex* (Leckman, King, & Cohen, 1999). Simple tics are discrete, rapid, meaningless movements or sounds (or both), whereas complex tics are orchestrated and often mimic purposeful expressions, behavior, or speech. Examples of common simple motor tics include eye blinking, head jerking, facial grimacing, shoulder shrugging, and brief movements of the torso or extremities. Examples of simple vocal tics include throat clearing, coughing, sniffing, and other brief sounds that are performed out of context and carry no meaning. Examples of complex motor tics include hand gestures, facial expressions, patterned touching or tapping, and orchestrated combinations of simple motor tics. Complex vocal tics may include orchestrated patterns of simple vocal tics, or more purposeful syllables, words, or phrases. These vocalizations may be neutral (words or phrases illogical in the present context), or they may be specialized vocalizations such as echolalia (repeating sounds or words heard from others or in the environment), palilalia (repetition of one's own vocalizations), or coprolalia (unwanted utterance of swear words or vulgar phrases). Although coprolalia has been highlighted in popular media as a hallmark symptom of TS, it is relatively rare (Leckman et al., 1999). Because of their purposeful appearance, complex tics are often difficult to distinguish from comparable volitional actions or symptoms of related disorders, such as the compulsions that characterize obsessive–compulsive disorder (OCD; Mansueto, 2005).

---

[1]To avoid confusion among acronyms, throughout this chapter we use TS to refer specifically to Tourette disorder or syndrome; CTD to refer to the general class of chronic tic disorders, including chronic motor or vocal tic disorder and Tourette disorder; and *tics* to refer to the specific symptoms.

PREMONITORY URGES

In addition to the tics, most individuals with chronic tic disorder (CTD) report somatic sensations that precede certain tics. These sensations have been referred to as *premonitory urges* (e.g., Leckman, Walker, & Cohen, 1993). Premonitory urges are often described as sensations of energy, burning, itching, or a general sense that something is "just not right." They are usually localized to the area of the tic (Leckman et al., 1993). Most patients who experience premonitory urges describe them as aversive signals of an upcoming tic that increase in intensity, especially upon attempts to suppress the tic, until the tic is performed (Kwak, Vuong, & Jankovic, 2003). In fact, many report that their tics are semivolitional responses that are performed to reduce the urge such that if there were no urge, there would be no tic (Kwak et al., 2003; Leckman et al., 1993). Although the exact nature of the underlying urge–tic mechanism(s) remains unknown, the premonitory urge has become central to conceptual models attempting to understand the development and maintenance of CTD.

PREVALENCE, DEVELOPMENT, AND COURSE

Prevalence estimates for tics and CTD vary considerably based on definition, sample characteristics, and ascertainment methods. Simple transient tics have been shown to be relatively common in school-age children (5%–15%; Zohar et al., 1992), whereas chronic tics affect approximately .5% to 3% of children and adolescents (Robertson, 2008). CTDs show a male preponderance with a ratio of approximately 4 to 1 (e.g., Freeman et al., 2000).

The hereditary nature of tic disorders is well documented. Family studies of TS show that tics co-occur in children and families at a rate of 20% to 40%, and concordance rates in twin studies show much higher rates in monozygotic twins (approximately 50% for TS and 75% for tics) compared with dizygotic twins (approximately 10% for TS and 23% for tics; Leary, Reimschisel, & Singer, 2007).

Tics typically emerge around the ages of 4 to 6, usually beginning with simple facial tics (Bloch & Leckman, 2009). In those for whom the disorder becomes chronic, tics generally progress from face to torso to limbs, increasing in frequency, complexity, and severity over time. In TS, motor tics usually emerge before vocal tics (Leckman et al., 1999). Tics typically wax and wane in frequency and severity over time, peaking in late childhood and declining in severity through adolescence and early adulthood. By adulthood, most CTD patients report significant reduction in tic severity (Bloch & Leckman, 2009). Although rare, adult-onset tics have been reported (Chouinard & Ford,

2000), and in rare cases, sudden onset of tics in childhood has been observed following streptococcal infections (Leonard & Swedo, 2001).

In addition to natural waxing and waning, most individuals report that their tics and premonitory urges fluctuate in response to environmental and contextual cues (Leckman et al., 1993). The impact of specific contextual factors on tics is idiosyncratic; however, several studies have shown that stressful events, anxiety, emotional trauma, fatigue, and social activities exacerbate tics (O'Connor, Brisebois, Brault, Robillard, & Loiselle, 2003; Silva, Munoz, Barickman, & Friedhoff, 1995).

COMORBIDITY

Individuals with a tic disorder are at greater risk for a number of psychiatric comorbidities. In fact, large studies have shown that "pure" TS is rare (10%–12% of TS cases), and multiple comorbidities are the norm (Freeman et al., 2000). The most prevalent co-occurring conditions are attention-deficit/hyperactivity disorder (ADHD, 40-50%) and OCD (30% to 40%). Because of the high co-occurrence of these conditions, TS, ADHD, and OCD occurring together is commonly referred to as the *Tourette triad* (Freeman et al., 2000). Tic disorders are also associated with increased risk for learning problems, sleep problems, mood and anxiety disorders, and anger and impulse control problems (for a review, see Freeman et al., 2000).

As noted earlier, it is often difficult to distinguish complex tics from symptoms of comorbid conditions. Some complex tics, such as touching, tapping, and repeating, may be phenotypically similar to the compulsions seen in OCD. Tics of this nature, however, usually present with an urge to perform the behavior or a sense that something "just doesn't feel right" unless the behavior is performed. Compulsions, on the other hand, are typically associated with anxiety and a feared outcome if the compulsion is not performed. Similarly, frequent tics, especially those of the eyes, head, or face, may make it difficult for a person to concentrate and thus may present as inattention or hyperactivity. Distinguishing between tics and symptoms of co-occurring conditions can be difficult but is crucial for formulating a treatment plan.

FUNCTIONAL OUTCOMES AND IMPAIRMENT

Many individuals with tics report problems with social, educational, and occupational functioning and diminished quality of life (QOL). Research has shown that individuals with tics are viewed as less socially acceptable by their peers, have more difficulties making and keeping friends, are often ridiculed or rejected by peers, and are more socially withdrawn and less popular (Woods, Marcks, & Flessner, 2007). Studies have also shown CTD to have a negative impact on family functioning and increase family stress (Champion, Fulton, & Shady, 1988; Hubka, Fulton, Shady, Champion, & Wand, 1988). Occupational difficulties have also been reported. Shady, Broder, Staley, Furer, and Papadopolos (1995) surveyed a sample of adults with tics and found that more than half reported that tics affected their career choice, and 20% to 30% reported that they had been fired or denied a promotion because of their tics. Other studies have found increased rates of unemployment and lower income in TS samples compared with the general population (Elstner, Selai, Trimble, & Robertson, 2001). Finally, studies with both children and adults have found that TS is associated with reduced quality of life compared with healthy control subjects (Elstner et al., 2001; Storch et al., 2007).

Although tics often remit by adulthood, several tic-specific variables have predicted poor health-related outcomes in adulthood. Cavanna, David, Orth, and Robertson (2012) found that increased tic severity in childhood predicted the overall health-related QOL. The presence of premonitory urges and a family history of TS also predict overall negative QOL. However, although tics themselves may be functionally impairing in some cases, comorbid diagnoses also contribute to functional impairment (Wand, Matzow, Shady, Furer, & Staley, 1993).

BIOLOGICAL MODELS AND PHARMACOTHERAPY

It is well established that tics are the result of neurobiological dysfunction. Although the specific mechanisms remain unknown, evidence implicates disruption of cortico-striato-thalamo-cortical (CSTC) pathways (see Leary et al., 2007). The organization of the CSTC circuitry consists of a complex collection of cortical and subcortical connections between various structures of the basal ganglia and the cerebral cortex (especially frontal areas), via projections through the thalamus (Alexander, DeLong, & Strick, 1986). These largely parallel neuronal pathways are believed to subserve various functions, including motor inhibition, executive functioning, and emotion regulation (for reviews, see Singer & Minzer, 2003, and Alexander et al., 1986). The various convergent and divergent connections within CSTC pathways have led some to argue that CTD and common comorbid conditions (e.g., ADHD, OCD) make up a spectrum of basal ganglia disorders that manifest differently depending on the specific circuit(s) involved (Osmon & Smerz, 2005). Dopaminergic projections are abundant in these pathways, and neuroimaging studies suggest that abnormal dopamine utilization is involved in the production of tics (see Leary et al., 2007).

On the basis of the neurobiological conceptualization of CTD, pharmacotherapy is the most commonly prescribed intervention. Traditional antipsychotics (e.g., haloperidol, pimozide), atypical antipsychotics (e.g., risperidone, olanzapine, ziprasidone), and alpha-adrenergic agonists (e.g., clonidine, guanfacine) are the most commonly used (Scahill et al., 2006). Antipsychotics directly block or lower the action of dopamine via various presynaptic and postsynaptic actions, and thus their tic suppressing effect is consistent with findings suggesting dysregulation of dopamine in the etiology of tics. Traditional antipsychotics have been shown to be the most effective for reducing tics (approximately 50%–60% reduction; Sallee, Nesbitt, Jackson, Sine, & Sethuraman, 1997) but are associated with an adverse side effect profile, which limits their use, except in severe cases. Atypical antipsychotics are generally less effective (approximately 25%–35% tic reduction, Scahill et al., 2006) but are better tolerated and thus more commonly used. Alpha-adrenergic agonists function to directly lower central noradrenergic activity, which has indirect effects on serotonergic and dopaminergic neurotransmission (Carpenter, Leckman, Scahill, & McDougle, 1999). Although alpha-adrenergic receptor agonists are better tolerated than neuroleptics and are moderately effective for treating ADHD symptoms, they are generally less effective than neuroleptics for reducing tics (Gilbert, 2006). A recent placebo-controlled trial (Jankovic, Jimenez-Shahed, & Brown, 2010) also showed promise for topiramate (a broad-spectrum antiepileptic) in the treatment of tics (54% reduction), but the mechanism of action is unclear. Overall, research supports the use of medication to treat tics, but response is idiosyncratic and incomplete, and side effects limit the use of the most effective agents. Furthermore, because comorbidity is common in CTD, many children are prescribed a complex multidrug regimen that needs to be carefully monitored.

HABIT MODEL AND HABIT REVERSAL TRAINING

In 1973, Azrin and Nunn outlined a behavioral model that likened tics to other problematic habitual behaviors (e.g., hair pulling, nail biting, skin picking), which they referred to as "nervous habits." The habit model proposes that tics begin as normal reflexive reactions to stress or physical/emotional trauma which serve to protect the individual by preventing, diminishing, or alleviating the aversive state inflicted by the trauma (e.g., by reducing muscle tension). According to the model, such behavior would typically be inhibited by personal or social awareness of its peculiarity or by its inherent inconvenience. However, if the tic is incorporated into normal ongoing behavior (i.e., through behavioral chaining), it is unlikely to be inhibited and may be strengthened through automatic and social reinforcement. As a result of these conditioning processes, the habit becomes overlearned (automatic) and is performed outside of the individual's awareness. Over time, internal (automatic, e.g., tension reduction) and external (social, e.g., attention and sympathy) reinforcement contingencies further shape the behavior.

On the basis of this habit model, Azrin and Nunn (1973) developed habit reversal training (HRT) as a treatment for tics and other nervous habits. HRT is a collection of behavioral techniques designed to reduce tics by increasing awareness of discrete occurrences of the tic and then interrupting the tic so that is no longer part of a normal chain of behavior. The original HRT procedure used four primary techniques: (a) awareness training (AT), (b) competing response training (CRT), (c) habit control motivation, and (d) generalization. The purpose of AT was to teach the individual to recognize each instance of the behavior. After awareness was achieved, CRT taught the individual to engage in a response that was directly incompatible with the performance of the habit (i.e., competing response [CR]) to break the behavioral chain. Motivational techniques were used to enhance compliance with the procedure. Finally, to encourage generalization, clients were instructed to imagine using the CR in high-risk situations and were assigned to publicly demonstrate their ability to control their tics with the CR to extinguish social reinforcement. Later iterations of HRT added relaxation training (RT) with the goal of teaching an individual to become more aware of bodily sensations (e.g., muscle tension, pretic sensations) and then engage in targeted relaxation of the muscles involved in the tic.

HRT has garnered strong empirical support as an effective intervention for tics. A recent review concluded that HRT meets criteria for a "well-established treatment" according to guidelines outlined by the American Psychological Association's Task Force on Promotion and Dissemination of Psychological Procedures (Cook & Blacher, 2007). In addition to several studies that have demonstrated the efficacy of HRT using tightly controlled small N designs (for a review, see Himle, Woods, Piacentini, & Walkup, 2006), randomized controlled trials (RCTs) have shown HRT to be more effective than wait-list control (Azrin & Peterson, 1990) and supportive psychotherapy (Deckersbach, Rauch, Buhlman, & Wilhelm, 2006; Wilhelm et al., 2003). Although these studies vary in their sample size and methodology, they have consistently shown strong response in the HRT group, with tic reduction ranging from 35% to 92% and generally good maintenance of treatment gains for up to 12 months. A recent meta-analysis that included five RCTs for HRT found an overall strong effect size for HRT ($d = 0.78$) for treating tics (Bate, Malouff, Thorsteinsson, & Bhullar, 2011). Additional evidence for HRT comes from two large RCTs evaluating a comprehensive behavioral treatment package (i.e., comprehensive behavioral intervention for tics [CBIT]), which is reviewed later in this chapter.

Over the past few decades, various iterations and combinations of HRT have been tested. Miltenberger, Fuqua, and McKinley (1985) evaluated the original HRT procedure and a simplified HRT (SHRT) protocol involving only AT and CRT. They found that both protocols were efficacious, suggesting that AT and CRT may be the most important HRT ingredients. Other studies have suggested that AT alone may be effective for reducing tics (Billings, 1978; Wright & Miltenberger, 1987), but these studies were conducted with single participants, raising questions of generalizability. Researchers have also examined the effectiveness of the RT component of HRT with mixed results. Bergin, Waranch, Brown, Carson, and Singer (1998) randomly assigned 23 children and adolescents with TS to receive either RT or a minimal attention control condition and found no differences between the groups, suggesting that RT is not an effective stand-alone treatment for tics. Other studies, however, have found that RT can reduce tics in the short term, suggesting that it may have clinical benefit for managing tics, especially during periods of stress, anxiety, or arousal (Canavan & Powell, 1981; Thomas, Abrams, & Johnson, 1971).

TENSION REDUCTION MODEL AND EXPOSURE WITH RESPONSE PREVENTION

Another behavioral model that has been proposed is the tension reduction model (TRM; Evers & van de Wetering, 1994). Like other behavioral models, the TRM emphasizes reinforcement (i.e., learning) processes as a mechanism through which some tics develop and are maintained. However, in contrast to other models reviewed in this chapter, the TRM focuses less on social reinforcement contingencies and more on automatic (internal) negative reinforcement as the most important process. The model is based on research showing that some individuals with tics experience aversive premonitory urges that "build up" before tics (or upon attempts to suppress tics) and that are temporarily alleviated by performance of the tic (Leckman, Walker, & Cohen, 1993). The TRM suggests that there is a functional relationship between premonitory sensations and tics such that the tic is strengthened (although not caused) by temporary relief from an aversive internal sensation (i.e., negative automatic reinforcement).

Several observational findings support the role of urge reduction in the maintenance of tics. Leckman et al. (1993) found that 92% reported that their tics were partially or wholly voluntary responses performed to eliminate a premonitory urge. In a similar study, Kwak et al. (2003) found that 92% of patients reported premonitory urges, 74% reported intensification of the urge if prevented from ticcing, 72% reported relief of premonitory sensations following a tic, and 68% described their tics as a voluntary (or semivoluntary) response to the urge. There is experimental evidence to support the urge reduction model as well. Himle et al. (2007) used an A-B-A-B reversal design to record tic frequency and self-reported premonitory urge ratings under conditions of suppression and free-to-tic conditions. The study found that most children who were able to suppress their tics reported increased premonitory urges during suppression.

On the basis of the TRM, Verdellen Keijsers, Cath, and Hoogduin (2004) adapted exposure with response prevention (ERP) as a treatment for motor and vocal tics. ERP is a well-established treatment for OCD in which the individual is taught to confront fear-inducing stimuli (i.e., experience anxiety) while inhibiting compulsions (for a review, see Abramowitz, 1996). Applied to TS, ERP involves exposing the individual to the aversive premonitory urge while preventing the occurrence of the tic. Theoretically, if an individual prevents himself or herself from performing the tic, the urge will habituate, and the tic will no longer produce relief and thus will be reduced. Preliminary research on ERP for TS has shown promise. Hoogduin, Verdellen, and Cath (1997) treated four individuals with TS using ERP and found that tics were significantly reduced for three of the participants. All three responders reported a reduction in the urge to tic during the session. Verdellen et al. (2004) randomly assigned individuals to either ERP or HRT and found both treatments were effective. These studies provide preliminary support for ERP as a viable treatment for tics; however, more research is needed to understand the mechanism through which ERP is effective. For example, the tension reduction model acknowledges that not all tics are associated with premonitory urges, but it is unclear whether only tics, not associated urges, were targeted for ERP treatment.

OPERANT MODEL AND FUNCTION-BASED TREATMENT

The basis for the operant model is that tics can become conditioned to specific contextual cues and thus fluctuate in response to internal and external stimuli (antecedents) and social reactions (e.g., reinforcement and punishment consequences). Several of the studies described earlier showing that tics and premonitory urges fluctuate in response to contextual cues provide indirect support for this model (Leckman et al., 1993). Additional evidence comes from studies demonstrating the impact of operant reinforcement and punishment consequences on tics. Some research has shown that tics can be worsened by contingent attention. For example, Watson and Sterling (1998) demonstrated that a child's vocal tic occurred more frequently at the dinner table, particularly when a parent provided attention following the tic. When the parents were instructed to stop attending to the tic, it was greatly reduced.

The impact of social reinforcement on tics has been demonstrated in other studies as well (Lahey, McNees, & McNees, 1973).

Laboratory research has also demonstrated that operant contingencies can reduce tics presumably by reinforcing an active suppression strategy. Woods and Himle (2004) observed children when they were asked to suppress tics (voluntary suppression) with and without token reinforcers for short tic-free periods (reinforced suppression). Reinforced suppression resulted in a 76% reduction in tics from baseline levels compared with 10% reduction during voluntary suppression, suggesting that tic suppression can be motivated by operant contingencies, perhaps explaining some of the contextual variation that is common to tic disorders.

Although the operant model has not resulted in a formal treatment for tics per se, it does suggest that antecedent and consequence variables should be considered as part of any behavioral intervention. For example, an individual's tics may be more common at school or work, at home immediately after school or work, or while doing homework, for example. A thorough analysis of these contexts might suggest relatively simple environmental modifications that could reduce tics. Likewise, the tics may produce social outcomes that influence tics in the short term, such as parents or peers confronting the person about tics, teasing, requests for the individual to leave the area, or getting out of completing a task or assignment. Outcomes that are hypothesized to worsen tics can be targeted for intervention. For example, the aforementioned study by Watson and Sterling (1998) demonstrated that removing tic-contingent attention significantly reduced the child's vocal tic.

COMPREHENSIVE BEHAVIORAL INTERVENTION FOR TICS

CBIT is based on an integrative behavioral model (see Woods et al., 2008) that draws upon each of the aforementioned models of TS. The underlying assumption of this model is that tics have a biological basis, but once they are performed, they are shaped through learning processes. In other words, the biology and environment interact to produce individual tic presentations. When referring to *environment*, the integrative model considers two types of variables: *antecedents* and *consequences*. Antecedents are contextual variables that precede tics and function to make tics better or worse. Consequences are outcomes that occur after tics (i.e., contingent on tics) that make tics more or less likely to recur. Antecedents and consequences are often linked such that antecedents (e.g., a quiet movie theater) predict the likely consequence(s) that will follow performance of a tic (e.g., shushing from the crowd). The functional relationship between the two allows either variable to influence tics depending on whether the consequence serves to reinforce (increase) or punish (decrease) tic performance.

The integrative model also assumes that antecedents and consequences can be either *internal* or *external* to the individual. Examples of internal antecedents include premonitory sensations, mood states, or specific thoughts. External antecedents include particular settings, people, or activities. Internal consequences typically include alterations in internal states such as reduction in the urge (reinforcement) or pain (punishment). External consequences include tic-contingent attention or disruption in ongoing activities or tasks. Real-world contingencies are complex and often are not recognized by the individual; nonetheless, they can have an impact on their tics.

On the basis of this model, researchers from the Tourette Syndrome Association's Behavioral Sciences Consortium (with support from the National Institutes of Health) developed and tested CBIT (Woods et al., 2008). CBIT combines HRT with psychoeducation, self-monitoring, RT, and a collection of function-based techniques to address both internal and external contextual variables believed to be exacerbating and maintaining tics. The rationale and techniques for each of the CBIT components are described next.

Nuts and Bolts of CBIT

CBIT is typically delivered in 60- to 90-minute sessions taking place weekly for 10 to 12 weeks and targeting one tic per session, although the treatment allows flexibility to meet individual clients' needs. The primary components of CBIT are psychoeducation, RT, HRT, and function-based intervention, with the latter two generally considered the most important therapeutic ingredients (Woods et al., 2008). In addition, adjunctive techniques such as inconvenience reviews and reinforcement programs are used to enhance motivation. Self-monitoring is used to track treatment progress and to aid in AT (as described subsequently). Of course, as with all effective psychosocial interventions, the treatment must be delivered within a supportive therapeutic context, and at least one study has found that patient–therapist working alliance is related to maintenance of treatment gains (Himle et al., 2012).

CBIT begins with psychoeducation about tics and associated conditions. The purpose of psychoeducation is to alleviate stigma and blame by helping the patient and family better understand the cause, course, and nature of tic disorders. In addition, psychoeducation addresses commonly held misbeliefs about behavioral interventions for tics and helps set the stage for using a behavioral intervention to address a disorder with a biological cause. Most clinicians are likely to find that some of their clients have been told (or have read) that their tics are uncontrollable and may have even been warned about negative side effects of behavioral interventions, such as symptom substitution (replacing one tic with another) and worsening of tics following attempts at suppression (the rebound effect). In such cases, the client will understandably find the idea of CBIT to be puzzling and may even find it to be in direct conflict with recommendations from other health care providers (Burd & Kerbeshian, 1987). Psychoeducation can help address this by dispelling myths about negative side effects of CBIT (Woods et al., 2008) and by clearly outlining the integrative model, which emphasizes the interplay between the underlying biological cause of tics, the effects of the day-to-day environment, and learning processes.

Function-based techniques are used to identify and address contextual variables that exacerbate tics (e.g., settings, specific activities) and to modify social contingencies that may be worsening tics (e.g., attention, tic-related talk). The rationale is that if tic-exacerbating variables are systematically assessed and manipulated, tics will decrease (Woods et al., 2008). Function-based intervention begins with a semistructured functional assessment interview. On a tic-by-tic basis, the clinician interviews the client and family about situations in which particular tics are more frequent, making careful note of both antecedents (e.g., settings, people present) and consequences (e.g., reactions). Between sessions, clients are asked to monitor for fluctuations in tic frequency or severity, paying particular attention to relevant variables associated with exacerbations. The clinician then uses this information to collaboratively develop function-based treatment strategies to reduce or eliminate tic-exacerbating antecedents and alter tic-exacerbating consequences.

The following examples illustrate how function-based procedures work. If the functional assessment indicates that a child's tics are worsened by abrupt or unanticipated transition between a preferred activity and a less preferred activity, such as from television time to homework after school (antecedent), the child may be given an after-school activity schedule or advance notice of upcoming transitions, or the schedule may be altered to ease the transition (e.g., television time followed by a break followed by homework). If the function-based intervention indicates that the child's tics are exacerbated by social reactions such as teasing from a peer or sibling, then the clinician might work with the family, teacher, and child to reduce teasing through peer education or direct intervention with the sibling.

RT strategies, including progressive muscle relaxation and diaphragmatic breathing, are also included in the CBIT treatment package. Consistent with a function-based approach, RT can reduce overall levels of anxiety and stress, which have been shown in several studies to be associated with tic exacerbation in many individuals. In addition, RT can have the added benefit of helping the client become more aware of bodily sensations (e.g., muscle tension, pretic sensations) and so is a useful adjunct to HRT.

The final component of CBIT is HRT. As noted earlier, HRT involves three specific techniques: AT, CRT, and social support. On the basis of the habit and tension-reduction models, the purposes of HRT are to (a) help the individual become more aware of each occurrence of a tic (and early tic warning signs); (b) interrupt the tic using a tic-incompatible response to break the behavioral chain; and (c) facilitate habituation of the premonitory urge, thereby breaking the urge-reduction (negative reinforcement) cycle.

The first step in HRT is AT. The purpose of AT is to teach an individual to detect each instance of a tic so that he or she can engage in a CR. There are four primary awareness techniques: response description, response detection, identifying early warning signs, and situational awareness. In response description, the therapist uses Socratic questioning and guidance to help the client develop detailed descriptions of the movements and premonitory sensations involved in the tic. For example, what might initially be described by the client as a "head jerk" might rather be defined as "an energy sensation building in the back of the neck followed by a slight forward movement of the chin toward the sternum that is immediately followed by backward thrusting of the head toward the left shoulder, creating a snapping sound in the right ear, and terminating with an immediate return of the head to upright resting position and termination of the pretic sensation." In essence, the tic is described as a behavioral chain with each of the specific sensations and movements constituting links. Such detailed descriptions are created to help the patient focus on the muscles and movements involved in the tic so that he or she will be better able to recognize the earliest warning signs of the tic as well as to teach the patient to recognize each tic occurrence. After the tic has been thoroughly described, the therapist works with the client to help him or her reliably detect each instance of the tic (response detection). Initially, the therapist observes the client and informs him or her when a tic is observed. The ultimate goal is to teach the client to self-detect each occurrence without the therapist's assistance. As AT progresses, the client is encouraged to recognize the earliest warning signs such that he or she detects tics immediately, or even before their occurrence. Finally, the client is assigned to self-monitor his or her tics at regular times and to identify contextual variables that are associated with high- or low- tic occurrence (situational awareness).

After AT has been mastered, the client is taught to use a CR to interrupt or prevent tics by engaging in a behavior designed to suppress or interrupt the tic. A CR typically involves tensing muscles antagonistic to those involved in the tic and holding the CR for at least 1 minute or until the premonitory urge dissipates, whichever is longer. Although it is often most practical to use a CR that is directly antagonistic to the tic, some research suggests that the contingent use of the CR immediately on detecting pretic sensations or initial links in the tic chain is more important than the specific topography of the CR. In addition to being incompatible with the tic, the CR should be less socially conspicuous than the tic, capable of being held for 1 to 3 minutes, and should be a behavior that can be performed across most contexts and activities without interfering with normal ongoing behavior such as walking, driving, schoolwork, or conversing.

The final component of HRT is social support. In most cases, a social support person (typically a parent or spouse) is recruited to prompt the use of the CR and to reinforce its correct use. In addition to providing reinforcement for mastery of HRT, prompting use of the CR can enhance awareness.

Evidence for CBIT

Evidence for the efficacy of CBIT comes from two parallel multisite RCTs (child and adult) comparing CBIT to an active psychoeducation and supportive therapy (PST) control. In the child CBIT trial (Piacentini et al., 2010), children with CTD ($N = 126$) were randomly assigned to receive either CBIT or PST. Results showed that 53% of children receiving CBIT demonstrated a clinically significant improvement in symptoms compared with 19% in PST with a mean 31% reduction in tic severity after CBIT treatment. In the adult trial (Wilhelm et al., 2012; $N = 122$) 38% of participants showed a clinically significant response compared with 6.4% in the control group with a mean tic reduction of 26% after CBIT treatment. In both trials, treatment gains were generally maintained at 6 months posttreatment. Importantly, the between-group effect sizes reported in the CBIT trials ($d = 0.68$ and $d = 0.57$ for the child and adult trials, respectively) were similar to the effect sizes reported in various drug trials for CTD (Scahill et al., 2006) but without any of the commonly associated side effects. Furthermore, at 6 months posttreatment, responders in the child trial showed decreased anxiety, disruptive behavior, and family strain and improved social functioning (Woods et al., 2011).

CONCLUSIONS AND FUTURE DIRECTIONS

The past quarter century has witnessed exciting new advancements in the understanding and treatment of CTD. Research has helped to better understand the role of environmental and contextual variables on tics, which in turn has led to the development and testing of effective behavioral interventions. However, despite the strong empirical evidence that behavioral interventions are effective for reducing tics in both children and adults, there are still barriers to effective clinical care for CTD, and more research is needed in several areas.

To start, many children do not get diagnosed at an early age, which delays treatment. Given the relatively high percentage of children who show transient tics at some point in their lives, identifying those who are likely to develop CTD should be a primary focus of future research, and the results may guide early intervention efforts.

Second, CTD is a complex clinical condition that often involves more than tics. Individuals with CTD are at increased risk for problems in social, family, academic, and occupational functioning. In addition, comorbid conditions are common and often contribute to more impairment than the tics. Clinicians often find themselves struggling to decide which symptoms to address first and how. Although most of this chapter has focused on effective treatments to reduce tics, clinical care for CTD necessitates a comprehensive approach. It is beyond the scope of this chapter to review the various pharmacological and psychosocial approaches for treating the myriad conditions that commonly co-occur with CTD, but empirically based interventions are available for the treatment of OCD, ADHD, mood and anxiety problems, disruptive behavior, and others (see Woods, Piacentini, & Walkup, 2007). More research is needed to test these interventions in children with CTD and to better understand how to treat CTD using a comprehensive, hierarchical approach for addressing tics, associated functioning, and common comorbid conditions.

Third, although it is clear that behavioral interventions are effective for some children, not all children respond, and many show only moderate benefit, emphasizing the need for continued treatment development and testing. Studies examining mediators and moderators of treatment outcome are needed.

Finally, many individuals with CTD do not have access to empirically supported behavioral treatments due to a variety of barriers (Woods, Conelea, & Himle, 2010). Although there are exciting new advancements in this area (Himle et al., 2012), future research to address barriers and improve dissemination is an important next step.

REFERENCES

Abramowitz, J. S. (1996). Variants of exposure and response prevention in the treatment of obsessive–compulsive disorder: A meta-analysis. *Behavior Therapy, 27,* 583–600. doi:10.1016/S0005-7894(96)80045-1

Alexander, G. E., DeLong, M. R., & Strick, P. L. (1986). Parallel organization of functionally segregated circuits linking basal ganglia and cortex. *Annual Review of Neuroscience, 9,* 357–381. doi:10.1146/annurev.ne.09.030186.002041

American Psychiatric Association. (2013). *Diagnostic and statistical manual of mental disorders* (5th ed.). Washington, DC: Author.

Azrin, N. H., & Nunn, R. G. (1973). Habit-reversal: A method of eliminating nervous habits and tics. *Behaviour Research and Therapy, 11*, 619–628. doi:10.1016/0005-7967(73)90119-8

Azrin, N. H., & Peterson, A. L. (1990). Treatment of Tourette syndrome by habit reversal: A wait-list control group comparison. *Behavior Therapy, 21*, 305–318. doi:10.1016/S0005-7894(05)80333-8

Bate, K. S., Malouff, J. M., Thorsteinsson, E. T., & Bhullar, N. (2011). The efficacy of habit reversal therapy for tics, habit disorders, and stuttering: A meta-analytic review. *Clinical Psychology Review, 31*, 865–871. doi:10.1016/j.cpr.2011.03.013

Bergin, A., Waranch, H. R., Brown, J., Carson, K., & Singer, H. S. (1998). Relaxation therapy in Tourette syndrome: A pilot study. *Pediatric Neurology, 18*, 136–142. doi:10.1016/S0887-8994(97)00200-2

Billings, A. (1978). Self-monitoring in the treatment of tics: A single-subject analysis. *Journal of Behavior Therapy and Experimental Psychiatry, 9*, 339–342. doi:10.1016/0005-7916(78)90010-1

Bloch, M. H., & Leckman, J. F. (2009). Clinical course of Tourette syndrome. *Journal of Psychosomatic Research, 67*, 497–501. doi:10.1016/j.jpsychores.2009.09.002

Burd, L., & Kerbeshian, J. (1987). Treatment-generated problems associated with behavior modification in Tourette disorder. *Developmental Medicine and Child Neurology, 29*, 831–833.

Canavan, A. G. M., & Powell, G. E. (1981). The efficacy of several treatments of Gilles de la Tourette syndrome as assessed in a single case. *Behaviour Research and Therapy, 19*, 549–556. doi:10.1016/0005-7967(81)90083-8

Carpenter, L. L., Leckman, J. F., Scahill, L., & McDougle, C. J. (1999). Pharmacological and other somatic approaches to treatment. In J. F. Leckman & D. J. Cohen (Eds.), *Tourette's syndrome—Tics, obsessions, compulsions: Developmental psychopathology and clinical care* (pp. 370–398). New York, NY: Wiley.

Cavanna, A.E., David, K., Orth, M., & Robertson, M.M. (2012). Predictors during childhood of future health-related quality of life in adults with Gilles de la Tourette syndrome. *European Journal of Pediatric Neurology.* doi:10.1016/j.ejpn.2012.02.004.

Champion, L. M., Fulton, W. A., & Shady, G. A. (1988). Tourette syndrome and social functioning in a Canadian population. *Neuroscience and Biobehavioral Reviews, 12*, 255–257. doi:10.1016/S0149-7634(88)80054-X

Chouinard, S., & Ford, B. (2000). Adult onset tic disorders. *Journal of Neurology, Neurosurgery, and Psychiatry, 68*, 738–743. doi:10.1136/jnnp.68.6.738

Cook, C. R., & Blacher, J. (2007). Evidence-based psychosocial treatments for tic disorders. *Clinical Psychology: Science and Practice, 14*, 252–267. doi:10.1111/j.1468-2850.2007.00085.x

Deckersbach, T., Rauch, S., Buhlman, U., & Wilhelm, S. (2006). Habit reversal versus supportive psychotherapy in Tourette's disorder: A randomized trial and predictors of treatment response. *Behaviour Research and Therapy, 44*, 1079–1090. doi:10.1016/j.brat.2005.08.007

Elstner, K., Selai, C. E., Trimble, M. R., & Robertson, M. M. (2001). Quality of life of patients with Gilles de la Tourette's syndrome. *Acta Psychiatrica Scandinavica*, *103*, 52–59. doi:10.1034/j.1600-0447.2001.00147.x

Evers, R. A. F., & van de Wetering, B. J. M. (1994). A treatment model for motor tics based on specific tension-reduction technique. *Journal of Behavior Therapy and Experimental Psychiatry*, *25*, 255–260. doi:10.1016/0005-7916(94)90026-4

Freeman, R. D., Fast, D. K., Burd, L., Kerbeshian, J., Robertson, M. M., & Sandor, P. (2000). An international perspective on Tourette syndrome: Selected findings from 3500 individuals in 22 countries. *Developmental Medicine & Child Neurology*, *42*, 436–447. doi:10.1017/S0012162200000839

Gilbert, D. (2006). Treatment of children and adolescents with tics and Tourette syndrome. *Journal of Child Neurology*, *21*, 690–700. doi:10.1177/08830738 0602100804 01

Himle, M. B., Freitag, M., Walther, M., Franklin, S., Ely, L., & Woods, D. W. (2012). A randomized pilot trial comparing videoconference versus face-to-face delivery of behavior therapy for childhood tic disorders. *Behaviour Research and Therapy*, *51*, 571–579. doi:10.1016/j.brat.2012.05.009

Himle, M. B., Woods, D. W., Conelea, C. A., Bauer, C. C., & Rice, K. A. (2007). Investigating the effects of tic suppression on premonitory urge ratings in children and adolescents with Tourette's syndrome. *Behaviour Research and Therapy*, *45*, 2964–2976. doi:10.1016/j.brat.2007.08.007

Himle, M. B., Woods, D. W., Piacentini, J., & Walkup, J. (2006). A brief review of habit reversal training for Tourette syndrome. *Journal of Child Neurology*, *21*, 719–725. doi:10.1177/08830738060210080101

Hoogduin, K., Verdellen, C., & Cath, D. (1997). Exposure and response prevention in the treatment of Gilles de la Tourette's syndrome: Four case studies. *Clinical Psychology & Psychotherapy*, *4*, 125–135. doi:10.1002/(SICI)1099-0879(199706)4:2<125::AID-CPP125>3.0.CO;2-Z

Hubka, G. B., Fulton, W. A., Shady, G. A., Champion, L. M., & Wand, R. (1988). Tourette syndrome: Impact on Canadian family functioning. *Neuroscience and Biobehavioral Reviews*, *12*, 259–261. doi:10.1016/S0149-7634(88)80055-1

Jankovic, J., Jimenez-Shahed, J., & Brown, L. W. (2010). A randomised, double-blind, placebo-controlled study of topiramate in the treatment of Tourette syndrome. *Journal of Neurology, Neurosurgery, & Psychiatry*, *81*, 70–73. doi:10.1136/jnnp.2009.185348

Kwak, C., Vuong, K. D., & Jankovic, J. (2003). Premonitory sensory phenomenon in Tourette's syndrome. *Movement Disorders*, *18*, 1530–1533. doi:10.1002/mds.10618

Lahey, B. B., McNees, M. P., & McNees, M. C. (1973). Control of an obscene "verbal tic" through time out in an elementary classroom. *Journal of Applied Behavior Analysis*, *6*, 101–104. doi:10.1901/jaba.1973.6-101

Leary, J., Reimschisel, T., & Singer, H. (2007). Genetic and neurobiological bases for Tourette syndrome. In D. W. Woods, J. C. Piacentini, & J. T. Walkup

(Eds.), *Treating Tourette syndrome and tic disorders* (pp. 58–84). New York, NY: Guilford Press.

Leckman, J. F., King, R. A., & Cohen, D. J. (1999). Tics and tic disorders. In J. F. Leckman & D. J. Cohen (Eds.), *Tourette's syndrome—tics, obsessions, compulsions: Developmental psychopathology and clinical care* (pp. 23–42). New York, NY: Wiley.

Leckman, J. F., Walker, D. E., & Cohen, D. J. (1993). Premonitory urges in Tourette's syndrome. *The American Journal of Psychiatry, 150,* 98–102.

Leonard, H. L., & Swedo, S. E. (2001). Paediatric autoimmune neuropsychiatric disorders associated with streptococcal infection (PANDAS). *International Journal of Neuropsychopharmacology, 4,* 191–198. doi:10.1017/S1461145701002371

Mansueto, C. S. (2005). Tic or compulsion? It's Tourettic OCD. *Behavior Modification, 29,* 784–799. doi:10.1177/0145445505279261

Miltenberger, R. G., Fuqua, R. W., & McKinley, T. (1985). Habit reversal with muscle tics: Replication and component analysis. *Behavior Therapy, 16,* 39–50. doi:10.1016/S0005-7894(85)80054-X

O'Connor, K., Brisebois, H., Brault, M., Robillard, S., & Loiselle, J. (2003). Behavioral activity associated with onset in chronic tic and habit disorder. *Behaviour Research and Therapy, 41,* 241–249. doi:10.1016/S0005-7967(02)00051-7

Osmon, D. C., & Smerz, J. M. (2005). Neuropsychological evaluation in the diagnosis and treatment of Tourette's syndrome. *Behavior Modification, 29,* 746–783. doi:10.1177/0145445505279380

Piacentini, J., Woods, D. W., Scahill, L. D., Wilhelm, S., Peterson, A., Chang, S., . . . Walkup, J. T. (2010). Behavior therapy for children with Tourette syndrome: A randomized controlled trial. *JAMA, 303,* 1929–1937. doi:10.1001/jama.2010.607

Robertson, M. M. (2008). The prevalence and epidemiology of Gilles de la Tourette syndrome: Part 1: The epidemiological and prevalence studies. *Journal of Psychosomatic Research, 65,* 461–472. doi:10.1016/j.jpsychores.2008.03.006

Sallee, F. R., Nesbitt, L., Jackson, C., Sine, L., & Sethuraman, G. (1997). Relative efficacy of haloperidol and pimozide in children and adolescents with Tourette's disorder. *The American Journal of Psychiatry, 154,* 1057–1062.

Scahill, L., Erenberg, G., Berlin, C. M., Budman, C., Coffey, B. J., Jankovic, J., . . . Walkup, J. (2006). Contemporary assessment and pharmacotherapy of Tourette syndrome. *NeruoRX, 3,* 192–206. doi:10.1016/j.nurx.2006.01.009

Shady, G., Broder, R., Staley, D., Furer, P., & Papadopolos, R. B. (1995). Tourette syndrome and employment: Descriptors, predictors, and problems. *Psychiatric Rehabilitation Journal, 19,* 35–42. doi:10.1037/h0095462

Silva, R. R., Munoz, D. M., Barickman, J., & Friedhoff, A. J. (1995). Environmental factors and related fluctuation of symptoms in children and adolescents with Tourette's disorder. *Journal of Child Psychology and Psychiatry, & Allied Disciplines, 36,* 305–312. doi:10.1111/j.1469-7610.1995.tb01826.x

Singer, H. S., & Minzer, K. (2003). Neurobiology of Tourette's syndrome: Concepts of neuroanatomic localization and neurochemical abnormalities. *Brain & Development, 25*(Suppl. 1), S70–S84. doi:10.1016/S0387-7604(03)90012-X

Storch, E. A., Lack, C. W., Simons, L. E., Goodman, W. K., Murphy, T. K., & Geffken, G. R. (2007). A measure of functional impairment in youth with tics. *Journal of Pediatric Psychology, 32*, 950–959. doi:10.1093/jpepsy/jsm034

Thomas, E. J., Abrams, K. S., & Johnson, J. B. (1971). Self-monitoring and reciprocal inhibition in the modification of multiple tics of Gilles de la Tourette syndrome. *Journal of Behavior Therapy and Experimental Psychiatry, 2*, 159–171. doi:10.1016/0005-7916(71)90054-1

Verdellen, C. W. J., Keijsers, G. P. J., Cath, D. C., & Hoogduin, C. A. L. (2004). Exposure with response prevention versus habit reversal in Tourette's syndrome: A controlled study. *Behaviour Research and Therapy, 42*, 501–511. doi:10.1016/S0005-7967(03)00154-2

Wand, R. R., Matazow, G. S., Shady, G. A., Furer, P., & Staley, D. (1993). Tourette's syndrome: Associated symptoms and most disabling features. *Neuroscience and Biobehavioral Reviews, 17*, 271–275. doi:10.1016/S0149-7634(05)80010-7

Watson, T. S., & Sterling, H. E. (1998). Brief functional analysis and treatment of a vocal tic. *Journal of Applied Behavior Analysis, 31*, 471–474. doi:10.1901/jaba.1998.31-471

Wilhelm, S., Deckersbach, T., Coffey, B. J., Bohne, A., Peterson, A. L., & Baer, L. (2003). Habit reversal versus supportive psychotherapy for Tourette's disorder: A randomized controlled trial. *The American Journal of Psychiatry, 160*, 1175–1177. doi:10.1176/appi.ajp.160.6.1175

Wilhelm, S., Peterson, A. L., Piacentini, J., Woods, D. W., Deckersbach, T., Sukhodolsky, D. G., . . . Scahill, L. (2012). Randomized trial of behavior therapy for adults with Tourette syndrome. *Archives of General Psychiatry, 69*, 795–803. doi:10.1001/archgenpsychiatry.2011.1528

Woods, D. W., Conelea, C. A., & Himle, M. B. (2010). Behavior therapy for Tourette's disorder: Utilization in a community sample and an emerging area of practice. *Professional Psychology: Research and Practice, 41*, 518–525. doi:10.1037/a0021709

Woods, D. W., & Himle, M. B. (2004). Creating tic suppression: Comparing the effects of verbal instruction to differential reinforcement. *Journal of Applied Behavior Analysis, 37*, 417–420. doi:10.1901/jaba.2004.37-417

Woods, D. W., Marcks, B. A., & Flessner, C. A. (2007). Management of social and occupational difficulties in persons with Tourette syndrome. In D. W. Woods, J. C. Piacentini, & J. T. Walkup (Eds.), *Treating Tourette syndrome and tic disorders* (pp. 265–277). New York, NY: Guilford Press.

Woods, D. W., Piacentini, J. C., Chang, S. W., Deckersbach, T., Ginsburg, G. S., Peterson, A. L., & Wilhelm, S. (2008). *Managing Tourette syndrome: A behavioral intervention for children and adults: Therapist guide.* New York, NY: Oxford University Press.

Woods, D. W., Piacentini, J. C., Scahill, L., Peterson, A. L., Wilhelm, S., Chang, S., . . . Walkup, J. T. (2011). Behavior therapy for tics in children: Acute and long-term effects on psychiatric and psychosocial functioning. *Journal of Child Neurology, 26,* 858–865. doi:10.1177/0883073810397046

Woods, D. W., Piacentini, J. P., & Walkup, J. T. (2007). *Treating Tourette syndrome and tic disorders: A guide for practitioners.* New York, NY: Guilford Press.

Wright, K. M., & Miltenberger, R. (1987). Awareness training in the treatment of head and facial tics. *Journal of Behavior Therapy and Experimental Psychiatry, 18,* 269–274. doi:10.1016/0005-7916(87)90010-3

Zohar, A. H., Ratzoni, G., Pauls, D. L., Apter, A., Bleich, A., . . . Cohen, D. J. (1992). An epidemiological study of obsessive–compulsive disorder and related disorders in Israeli adolescents. *Journal of the American Academy of Child & Adolescent Psychiatry, 31,* 1057–1061. doi:10.1097/00004583-199211000-00010

10

HEALTH ANXIETY

HEATHER D. HADJISTAVROPOULOS, NICOLE M. ALBERTS,
AND GORDON J. G. ASMUNDSON

In this chapter, we begin by describing the case of Iris, a patient who experienced severe health anxiety (some details have been modified to protect patient privacy). We then briefly describe the epidemiology of health anxiety, highlighting research on the origins and maintenance of the problem. The primary focus of this chapter is on the assessment and treatment of severe health anxiety using a cognitive-behavioral framework.

IRIS

At the time of assessment, Iris was a 46-year-old married mother of one son (age 16).[1] She had suffered from severe health anxiety for more than 25 years. In the 2 years preceding the psychological assessment, she reported

http://dx.doi.org/10.1037/14323-011
Obsessive–Compulsive Disorder and Its Spectrum: A Life-Span Approach, Eric A. Storch and Dean McKay (Editors)
Copyright © 2014 by the American Psychological Association. All rights reserved.

[1]Certain details of this case have been altered to protect patient confidentiality.

being particularly preoccupied with the idea that she had undiagnosed breast cancer. She shared that she had feared other diseases in the past, including thyroid cancer, brain cancer, ovarian cancer, and stomach cancer. Iris recalled the exact day that she became preoccupied with breast cancer. She reported that one day in the shower when washing her breasts, she noticed a red spot on her right breast. She indicated that thereafter she became preoccupied with lumps in her breasts. She reported engaging in repeated daily checking of her breasts, most commonly checking her breasts each time she went to the washroom. She also reported spending time on the Internet each day (ranging from 15 minutes to several hours) checking for information on the signs and symptoms of breast cancer. She described visiting her physician on a monthly basis, each time having her physician examine her breasts. She had undergone several mammograms and had several times requested that her physician conduct a biopsy. Her physician repeatedly reassured her that this was not necessary. Despite this reassurance, Iris remained concerned that she had breast cancer. She reported being "immobilized" by her worry. Because of her preoccupation, she reported that her relationships with her son and husband had deteriorated. She tearfully said that they did not take her health concerns seriously and often teased her about her fears. She described difficulties maintaining her household (e.g., cooking meals, cleaning) because of the amount of time she engaged in checking, and she shared that this was a source of stress in her relationships with her son and husband. Iris expressed an interest in finding part-time employment as a sales clerk (a position she held before the birth of her son) but reported having no energy or time to pursue this interest. She had never received psychological services in the past. She reluctantly agreed to seek cognitive–behavioral treatment after considerable pressure from her family physician.

DIAGNOSTIC CONSIDERATIONS

It should be evident from reading the case of Iris that she was experiencing severe health anxiety. *Health anxiety* refers to a dimensional construct characterized by a lack of concern about one's health at one end of the continuum and excessive anxiety about health on the other (Asmundson, Taylor, & Cox, 2001). Sometimes this health anxiety is so severe that the individual may meet diagnostic criteria for a mental disorder.

Using the *Diagnostic and Statistical Manual of Mental Disorders, Fourth Edition, Text Revision* (*DSM–IV–TR*; American Psychiatric Association, 2000), Iris was actually given a diagnosis of hypochondriasis. In the *DSM–IV–TR*, this diagnosis was given to individuals who were preoccupied with fears of having a serious disease based on misinterpretation of bodily symptoms and who continued to be fearful even after receiving reassurance that no medical problem was present. In addition, for a diagnosis of hypochondriasis, the health anxiety had to create significant distress or disability, last at least 6 months, and not be attributable to another mental disorder (American Psychiatric Association, 2000).

The DSM–IV–TR was recently revised, and hypochondriasis was actually eliminated in fifth edition of the DSM (DSM–5); it was replaced with two related diagnoses: somatic symptom disorder and illness anxiety disorder (American Psychiatric Association, 2013). Changes were made because of concern that there was an overemphasis in the DSM–IV–TR on the presence of medically unexplained symptoms, which cannot always be reliably determined (American Psychiatric Association, 2013). The DSM–5 notes that "it is not appropriate to give an individual a mental disorder diagnosis solely because a medical cause cannot be demonstrated"; instead diagnosis should be based on the presence and not the absence of symptoms (American Psychiatric Association, 2013, p. 309).

In the DSM–5, a diagnosis of somatic symptom disorder is given to individuals who report on a persistent basis (a) "one or more somatic symptoms that are distressing and or result in significant disruption of daily life" and (b) "excessive thoughts, feelings, and behaviors related to these somatic symptoms or associated health concerns" (e.g., health anxiety; American Psychiatric Association, 2013, p. 311). In contrast, a diagnosis of illness anxiety disorder is given to individuals who do not report significant somatic symptoms or, if they are present, report only mild somatic symptoms. Despite having no somatic symptoms, those with illness anxiety disorder describe their preoccupation with having or acquiring a serious illness, high levels of anxiety about health, and either excessive health behavior or maladaptive avoidance.

Per the DSM–5, Iris would be given a diagnosis of illness anxiety disorder because she had minimal somatic symptoms. Her health anxiety was specifically focused on misinterpretation of normal breast fatty tissue and fibrous connective tissue that gives the breast its size and shape. Consistent with a diagnosis of illness anxiety disorder, however, she was preoccupied with having breast cancer, had a high level of health anxiety, and was performing excessive health-related behaviors; in addition, this preoccupation was present for more than 6 months. Given that the DSM was only recently revised, most research available at this time is on individuals with hypochondriasis or individuals who have elevated health anxiety but have not been specifically diagnosed with hypochondriasis. It is this research and literature that is reviewed here.

EPIDEMIOLOGY

Creed and Barsky (2004) conducted a systematic review of the literature to identify the prevalence of hypochondriasis in population-based and primary care samples (e.g., general practice, internal medicine practice). They reported that in four population-based studies, the prevalence of hypochondriasis varied from 0.02% to 7.77%, and in seven primary care samples, the prevalence of hypochondriasis ranged from 0.8% to 8.5%. There was considerable variability in these studies in terms of how a diagnosis of hypochondriasis was made. Only one population-based study examined the prevalence of a DSM (fourth edition; DSM–IV) diagnosis of hypochondriasis (Noyes, Happel, & Yagla, 1999). In that study, the authors compared first-degree relatives of reference individuals with or without a diagnosis of hypochondriasis and found that, regardless of the family history, hypochondriasis was present in 7.7% of relatives (Noyes et al., 1999). In terms of primary care samples, only one study examined the prevalence of a DSM–IV diagnosis of hypochondriasis. In this study, using a large sample ($N = 1,456$) of primary care users diagnosed by structured interview, the prevalence of hypochondriasis was 3.4% (Escobar et al., 1998).

As one would expect, having elevated health anxiety without meeting criteria for hypochondriasis is more common than hypochondriasis itself. Tyrer et al. (2011) studied health anxiety in 28,991 patients attending medical clinics within hospitals in the United Kingdom. The prevalence of significant health anxiety was substantial, with neurology (24.7%) having the highest prevalence followed by respiratory medicine (20.9%), gastroenterology (19.5%), cardiology (19.1%), and endocrinology (17.5%).

Little research has examined the age of onset of health anxiety. Although it is commonly assumed that health anxiety is more common among older adults who have more medical concerns, there is no solid research evidence to suggest that health anxiety increases with age (Barsky, Frank, Cleary, Wyshak, & Klerman, 1991). In fact, there is some research to suggest that when older adults experience few health problems, their risk of health anxiety is lower than among younger adults (Bourgault-Fagnou & Hadjistavropoulos, 2009).

olde Hartman et al. (2009) conducted a systematic review of the course of hypochondriasis and estimated that 50% to 70% of patients with hypochondriasis do not recover. They also reported that poorer course was associated with a greater number of somatic symptoms (olde Hartman et al., 2009). In terms of comorbidity, hypochondriasis has been associated with chronic pain (Fishbain, Lewis, Gao, Cole, & Steele Rosomoff, 2009), irritable bowel syndrome, chronic fatigue syndrome, as well as with a recurrent and lifetime diagnosis of anxiety, depressive, and somatoform disorders (Faravelli et al., 1997; Noyes et al., 1999).

In addition to creating distress for the individual, research shows that hypochondriasis is associated with increased disability (Looper & Kirmayer, 2001; Noyes et al., 1999) and a greater probability of being off work (Barsky, Wyshak, Klerman, & Latham, 1990). It is also associated with increased medical services utilization (Noyes et al., 1999). This is problematic not only from a financial perspective in terms of the burden on our health care system but also because it increases the risk that individuals will undergo unnecessary invasive diagnostic and treatment procedures (Abramowitz & Braddock, 2008).

ORIGINS AND MAINTENANCE

What causes severe health anxiety to develop? Unfortunately, the answer to that question is far from complete. In terms of genetics, there has been limited research to date on the heritability of health anxiety. One study that specifically examined the concordance rates of hypochondriasis in monozygotic versus dizygotic twins did not find a difference in rates. This study, however, was based on a small sample size (35 twin pairs) and thus cannot be seen as definitive (Torgersen, 1986). Other researchers have not examined health anxiety directly but have examined variables that are associated with health anxiety. Genetic factors, for instance, have been found to explain about 30% of the variation in somatization scores (Gillespie, Zhu, Heath, Hickie, & Martin, 2000) and about 45% of the variance in anxiety sensitivity (Stein, Jang, & Livesley, 1999).

Although other models have been proposed (e.g., psychodynamic), the cognitive–behavioral model of health anxiety has been predominant in understanding health anxiety over the past several decades (Warwick & Salkovskis, 1990). According to this model, learning is central to the development of health anxiety and results in individuals developing dysfunctional beliefs about health and illness; the model holds that that the degree of health anxiety experienced is a function of dysfunctional beliefs about the severity of illness, personal vulnerability to illness, inability to cope with illness, and the inadequacy of resources for dealing with illness. Recent research has indicated that these beliefs are present among those with high levels of health anxiety (Hadjistavropoulos et al., 2012).

According to the cognitive–behavioral model, dysfunctional beliefs about health and illness are largely the product of an individual's past experiences with illness. For example, someone who develops a serious illness as a child and is exposed to various negative events as a result (e.g., frequent hospital visits, procedures) may develop a belief that all illnesses are awful and that medical resources are of little benefit. Although many individuals with high levels of health anxiety may have had a serious illness themselves or witnessed illness in someone close to them, it has been noted that these experiences alone cannot adequately account for the development of dysfunctional beliefs about health and illness (Abramowitz & Braddock, 2008). In regard to this issue, anxiety sensitivity has been shown to mediate the relationship between young adults' beliefs associated with health anxiety and their retrospectively reported learning experiences in childhood and adolescence (Watt & Stewart, 2000). The transmission of illness-related information via observational learning as well as relevant information sources (e.g., media) may also influence the development of erroneous beliefs (Abramowitz & Braddock, 2008). Once erroneous beliefs are triggered, they are proposed to result in the misinterpretation of benign (harmless) bodily sensations and changes, leading to increased anxiety.

The model also proposes that a number of cognitive and behavioral factors serve to maintain health anxiety once it has developed. More specifically, people with excessive health anxiety tend to be overly attentive to information related to illness and tend to actively seek evidence that would validate their beliefs while discounting information that would disconfirm them. They also tend to interpret illness-related information in a catastrophic and personally threatening manner. In terms of behavioral factors, individuals may engage in checking and reassurance seeking in an attempt to gain absolute certainty about their health status. However, these attempts often lead to obtaining distressing information, which further triggers health anxiety. Avoidance and safety-seeking behaviors may also be used to reduce distress in the short term. These behaviors, unfortunately, prevent the disconfirmation of erroneous beliefs about health and illness and may also lead to further preoccupation with the feared illness.

It has also been proposed that interpersonal factors such as attachment may be involved in the development and maintenance of health anxiety. More specifically, the interpersonal model of health anxiety (Stuart & Noyes, 1999) proposes that negative parenting styles and aversive early experiences predispose individuals to developing an insecure attachment style and a focus on bodily sensations. Reassurance seeking behaviors are thus viewed as behaviors that allow individuals to seek emotional and interpersonal support from others, which acts to alleviate attachment insecurity. In support of the interpersonal model, researchers have found that higher levels of health anxiety are associated with insecure compared with secure attachment among patients in a general medical clinic (Noyes et al., 2003).

It appears that the cognitive–behavioral and interpersonal models may be more complementary than contradictory. For example, our own research found that attachment anxiety and dysfunctional health beliefs regarding the likelihood of illness and difficulty coping with illness were statistically significant predictors of health anxiety among emerging adults who had a parent diagnosed with a serious medical illness (Alberts & Hadjistavropoulos, in press). Further research on the complementary nature of these models is warranted.

ASSESSMENT

Various authors have published books on the topic of health anxiety (e.g., Abramowitz & Braddock, 2008; Furer, Walker, & Stein, 2007; Taylor & Asmundson, 2004). These books each provide valuable information on the assessment of health anxiety. In this chapter, we focus on the standard process we follow in the assessment of health anxiety but urge the interested reader to examine these books for additional details. Typically, the first step we take when working with individuals with health anxiety is to conduct an interview to help establish whether a diagnosis of somatic symptom disorder or illness anxiety disorder is appropriate as well as whether there are any other comorbid disorders. Our next step is to gather information to understand the idiosyncratic presentation of health anxiety. Specifically, this interview explores the patient's specific emotions, thoughts, images, behaviors and somatic sensations. We begin the interview by asking patients about the physical concerns they experience, because patients characteristically view their anxiety as rooted in physical health problems rather than problems related to problematic emotions, thoughts, and behaviors. From a somatic perspective, we inquire about bodily sensations or changes that they have experienced, including those related to medical conditions or anxiety (e.g., racing heart, fatigue).

We explore not only the presence of anxiety but also the presence of other emotions, such as anger and depression, and how these emotions are interconnected. We are particularly interested in thoughts about the severity of illness, vulnerability to illness, ability to cope with illness, and perceptions of medical care. We also explore whether patients believe that there is a possibility that the bodily sensations or changes they experience might be due to normal bodily processes (e.g., arousal, anxiety). The extent to which patients are aware of their thoughts and attempt to resist these thoughts is also explored.

We gather information that will help us understand the behaviors that the individual both avoids and engages in as means of coping with health anxiety. This involves asking questions about settings or events they avoid to reduce health anxiety (e.g., hospitals, television shows) as well as whether patients engage in bodily checking and reassurance seeking from family, friends, health care providers, and the media. Although health anxiety is not consistently related to health behaviors, such as dieting and exercise (e.g., Pugh & Hadjistavropoulos, 2011), we inquire about these behaviors. Furthermore, we explore the extent to which the individual may engage in safety behaviors (e.g., staying close to the phone, carrying medication).

Following an understanding of the idiosyncratic presentation, we inquire about the intensity, frequency, duration, triggers, and course of the concerns. Additionally, we delve into the impact the problem has on the individual's self-image, mood, and interpersonal and daily functioning. We also examine the potential origins of the problems, as well as medical and mental health history. To conclude, to transition into treatment, we ask patients about their motivation and expectations for treatment.

Essential to the assessment process following the interview is consultation with the patient's medical providers. During this consultation, it is important to learn about any medical conditions the patient may have, the medical testing that has been conducted to investigate the patient's current health concerns, and the patient's response to such testing. For example, did the patient appear to be reassured by lack of negative findings on tests or ask for additional medical testing? This consultation can also be used to assess how medical providers are responding to the patient's problems (e.g., any restrictions on testing) and to determine medical provider knowledge and openness to psychological treatment.

We find several instruments helpful when working with patients who have health anxiety. Our preference is to use the Short Health Anxiety Inventory (SHAI; Salkovskis, Rimes, Warwick, & Clark, 2002) to assess health anxiety at the beginning and end of treatment. We recently conducted a review of this measure and found considerable evidence across studies in support of its psychometric properties (Alberts et al., 2013). This measure consists of 14 items assessing health anxiety and an additional four items assessing perceived negative consequences of being ill. Each item of the SHAI consists of a group of four statements; individuals select the statement that best reflects their feelings over the past 6 months (or 1 week if used on a weekly basis). Items are weighted 0 to 3 and are summed to obtain a total score on the 18 items ranging from 0 to 54. Past research shows that patients with hypochondriasis have an average score of 34.18 ($SD = 9.78$) on the 18 items (Muse, McManus, Hackmann, Williams, & Williams, 2010), patients with OCD have an average of score of 15.43 ($SD = 12.87$; Deacon & Abramowitz, 2008), and individuals in the general population have an average score of 12.48 ($SD = 6.79$; Wheaton, Berman, Franklin, & Abramowitz, 2010).

Another measure that we find helpful to directly monitor health anxiety is the Whiteley Index (WI; Pilowsky, 1967). Respondents answer yes or no to 14 questions on the WI. Researchers have determined that a cutoff score of 8 provides optimal sensitivity and specificity for determining cases with and without hypochondriasis (Hiller, Leibbrand, Rief, & Fichter, 2002). The

WI's psychometric properties are well established (Speckens, Van Hemert, Spinhoven, & Bolk, 1996).

To further explore cognitions, we recently developed the Health Cognitions Questionnaire (Hadjistavropoulos et al., 2012) to assess four core beliefs involved in the development of health anxiety, including (a) likelihood of illness, (b) awfulness of illness, (c) difficulty coping with illness, and (d) medical service inadequacy. Respondents rate 20 statements on a 5-point scale that ranges from 1 (*strongly disagree*) to 5 (*strongly agree*). Initial investigations of the HCQ provided evidence for good factorial, predictive, and discriminant validity (Hadjistavropoulos et al., 2012).

Absent in the literature are psychometrically sound measures of health anxious behaviors. As such, we find it useful to identify behaviors that are specific to the patient and have him or her rate these behaviors on Likert type scales ranging from 0 to 10, with 10 indicating that the patient feels that the behavior was performed to an extreme degree and 0 indicating that the patient did not perform the behavior at all. Additional measures often administered as part of the assessment process include the Somatic Symptom Inventory (Barsky, Wyshak, & Klerman, 1986a, 1986b), the Anxiety Sensitivity Index—3 (Taylor et al., 2007), and the Body Vigilance Scale (Schmidt, Lerew, & Trakowski, 1997).

TREATMENT

By far the most common and empirically supported approach to treating health anxiety is individually delivered cognitive behavior therapy (CBT); thus, we focus on this approach here. Evidence supports both the efficacy (Barsky & Ahern, 2004; Greeven et al., 2007; Seivewright et al., 2008; Warwick, Clark, Cobb, & Salkovskis, 1996) and effectiveness (Wattar et al., 2005) of individual CBT. Treatment results in reductions in health anxiety and associated problems such as generalized anxiety, depression, social function, and health service consultations, with results maintained over a 1-year period (e.g., Seivewright et al., 2008). Examination of the findings using meta-analysis suggests that CBT produces moderate to large effect sizes across studies (Taylor, Asmundson, & Coons, 2005). Furthermore, CBT has been found to be efficacious for treating health anxiety when delivered in cost-efficient ways, such as online (Hedman et al., 2011) and in group treatment (Avia et al., 1996; Sorensen, Birket-Smith, Wattar, Buemann, & Salkovskis, 2011) formats. There is additional evidence that when delivered in component parts, both cognitive therapy and exposure plus response prevention are efficacious on their own in reducing health anxiety (Visser & Bouman, 2001). There is also support for a variant of CBT—namely, mindfulness-based cognitive therapy (Lovas & Barsky, 2010)—and for psychoeducation based on CBT principles (Buwalda, Bouman, & van Duijn, 2008). The interested reader should also be aware that other approaches are available, with varying degrees of evidence to support their efficacy. These include medication (e.g., paroxetine; Greeven et al., 2007), behavioral stress management (Clark et al., 1998), group psychoeducation based on a problem-solving approach (Buwalda, Bouman, & van Duijn, 2007), and short-term psychodynamic psychotherapy (Sorensen et al., 2011).

CBT for health anxiety is commonly brief, varying from six to 16 sessions, with sessions ranging from 1 hour to 90 minutes in length. It can be described as present-focused and mechanistic in that the goal is to identify the essential components of the problem as it exists in the present and target these areas. Patients also take an active role in sessions and complete homework between sessions. Collaborative empiricism is used, which means that the therapist and patient take a scientific view of the problem by formulating and testing hypotheses in and outside of the therapy sessions.

CBT varies to some extent across the studies we have described. The following represent the core components of CBT for health anxiety: (a) psychoeducation about the development and maintenance of health anxiety, and the relationships among cognitive, behavioral, physiological, and affective components; (b) encouraging patients to identify, challenge, and replace maladaptive negative thoughts about illness; (c) formulation of behavioral experiments to test automatic versus alternative cognitions; (d) exposure to health-related fears or situations that have been avoided by the patient (e.g., through narratives related to their anxious thoughts about illness); and (e) response prevention of checking, body vigilance, and reassurance seeking.

As noted earlier, several recent books written for clinicians are devoted to health anxiety (Abramowitz & Braddock, 2008; Furer et al., 2007; Taylor & Asmundson, 2004). These authors often recommend additional components to the treatment of health anxiety. These include behavioral stress management (e.g., identifying stressors, identifying reactions to stress, training in stress management strategies such as relaxation, problem solving, time management; Taylor & Asmundson, 2004), addressing fear of death as well as satisfaction and enjoyment of life (Furer et al., 2007), attention to mood management and illness and sick-role behaviors (Barsky & Ahern, 2004), and mindfulness (Wattar et al., 2005).

Psychoeducation begins by helping patients understand the relationship between catastrophic thinking and emotional reactions. Information is shared regarding how specific thoughts lead to health anxiety, which then results in selective attention to bodily sensations or changes and behaviors (e.g., avoidance, reassurance seeking, checking) that serve to increase health anxiety. To further illustrate this point, it is often helpful to have patients monitor their worries, physical sensations, thoughts, and behaviors so that they can better understand the components of health anxiety. We also spend time discussing factors that may have contributed to the onset of health anxiety, such as learning experiences. In Iris's case, she shared how her father was a physician and that she recalled him frequently speaking about individuals who unexpectedly developed cancer.

Providing written materials on health anxiety is beneficial as a component of homework and can assist patients in viewing their response to physical sensations as problematic rather than seeing the sensations or changes themselves as problematic. In other words, it is important for the patient to view the worry, preoccupation, and illness behaviors as creating difficulties instead of focusing on an undiagnosed medical condition. At this stage of treatment, it is critical to convey to patients that the bodily sensations and changes they are concerned about are "not all in their head"; that is, what they are experiencing is real but not necessarily best explained by a diagnosable medical condition. The aim is to educate patients about the many sources and explanations for the perturbations they experience (e.g., homeostasis, shifts in daily routine, minor medical conditions) as well as about the effects of paying excessive attention to benign bodily sensations and changes. A critical component of Iris's education on health anxiety was learning about how her tendency to monitor and check her breasts resulted in increased rather than decreased worry about her breasts. Iris also learned how her excessive focus on her breasts caused her to notice minute changes that most would not notice and that, in turn, led to increased anxiety. Likewise, Iris learned that constant palpation could lead to swelling in her breasts and exacerbated anxiety as a result.

We follow this component of therapy with a focus on inaccurate thoughts and beliefs. We often use a patient's self-monitoring forms and information gained during the assessment to identify the specific thoughts that are associated with anxiety. This process typically begins by having patients examine the evidence for and against their thoughts and exploring whether after this process they are able to formulate and accept an alternative thought. With Iris, a core thought she held was that the lumps in her breasts must be a sign of cancer. Once she was able to identify and challenge this thought, she was able to replace it with the alternative thought that "the lumps in my breast are normal, and poking and prodding my breasts makes them tender." A further thought she worked on was the belief that she would not be able to cope with having breast cancer. In this case, we had Iris fully consider how she would respond if she were diagnosed with breast cancer. Through therapy, Iris acknowledged that, although the process of diagnosis and treatment would be difficult, she would be able to adequately cope with this situation.

Following cognitive restructuring, we use behavioural experiments to help patients discover how behaviors maintain rather than decrease health anxiety and to test problematic thoughts. For example, Iris held the belief that if she kept a thought record related to health anxiety, her worries would intensify. We thus formulated a behavioral experiment, where she kept a thought record and monitored the impact of this on her health anxiety. In contrast to her hypothesis, her health anxiety did not increase.

We follow this with the use of exposure with response prevention. This involves making a hierarchy with patients of the stimuli and thoughts that they tend to avoid. The hierarchy is ordered from lowest to highest, and we gradually have patients expose themselves to the stimuli that they avoid, while asking them to avoid the responses they typically use to manage anxiety (e.g., repeated checking of body, seeking reassurance). We commonly start with imaginal exposure (e.g., having patients imagine the feared stimulus) and follow this with in vivo exposure (e.g., exposure to disease-related objects or situations that are harmless yet anxiety provoking). Increasingly, we are incorporating interoceptive exposure into treatment of health anxiety (Taylor & Asmundson, 2004). This involves inducing feared bodily sensations (e.g., heart palpitations, shortness of breath).

To illustrate, once we generated an initial list of situations and stimuli that provoked Iris's health anxiety (i.e., the fear hierarchy), she assigned a numerical rating of subjective units of discomfort score (SUDS) for each item. The SUDS scale ranges from 0 (*no distress*) to 100 (*maximal distress*). Iris began exposure by imagining herself watching several television shows that involved women with cancer and then by imagining herself going to the palliative care ward at the local hospital. She initially assigned a SUDS of 50 to these situations. Following the typical pattern of habituation, Iris's discomfort immediately increased to 70 but then gradually declined as time passed. She rerated her SUDS as 10 at the end of both imaginal exposures. At the top of the hierarchy, Iris visited the palliative care ward (initially rated as 100). Again, her discomfort initially increased but then reduced as she remained exposed to these situations. We did not spend any sessions conducting interoceptive exposure because Iris did not appear to fear any particular body sensations.

CLINICAL PRACTICE CHALLENGES

This review may give the impression that working with patients such as Iris is relatively straightforward and without challenges. This can certainly be the case, but quite often, there are challenges to treatment. Taylor, Asmundson, and Coons (2005) highlighted a number of factors that are associated with a poor prognosis, including (a) longer duration of health anxiety, (b) severe symptoms, (c) strongly held beliefs, (d) personality disorders,

(e) comorbid general medical conditions, (f) presence of secondary gains that reinforce health anxiety, and (g) presence of stressful life events. Their review of the literature suggested that age is an ambiguous prognostic indicator, with some reporting that outcomes are better when individuals present at young ages, and others reporting that age is unrelated to outcome. In our own experience, we have found that, first and foremost, it is important to have a comprehensive understanding of the medical condition(s) that the patient fears. Lack of this understanding limits one's ability to assist and can be a substantial barrier to building the therapeutic alliance. Second, more often than not, the role of psychoeducation cannot be overemphasized. Because patients are often focused on physical sensations and changes and associated medical explanations, they can have difficulty discussing emotional or social difficulties. Many health care providers also require education about the role of psychology in the treatment of health anxiety. In these cases, it is helpful to work with providers to determine what constitutes necessary information and to minimize provision of unnecessary (and health-anxiety reinforcing) reassurance. General recommendations to share with providers include (a) listening so that the patient feels understood, (b) answering specific questions about fears, (c) using simple terminology and clear explanations, and (d) providing consistent statements. If willing, clinical health psychologists can review medical feedback that is provided to patients, identifying areas where the health care communication could be improved.

Smaller yet nonetheless important challenges may arise when working with patients whose health-anxiety concerns are more straightforward. With Iris, one particular challenge was helping her find an appropriate balance between having no concern about her health and excessive worry, which also meant finding an appropriate balance in her behaviors. For example, questions that often came up included the following: How many times should I check for moles or lumps? If I experience an unexplained bodily symptom, how long should I leave it before I see the doctor to have it checked out? With respect to the latter question, we used the "wait for 2 weeks" approach (Furer et al., 2007), which assumes that most symptoms such as pain and colds disappear on their own in 2 weeks and do not require medical attention. If the symptoms persist beyond this period, then it is reasonable to see a physician. Iris was also encouraged to speak with her family physician regarding other general guidelines in this area as well as the current guidelines regarding the frequency of breast self-exams and mammograms. Near the end of treatment, we observed that Iris looked to her therapist for answers regarding what would be considered normal versus abnormal health behaviors. In response, she was encouraged to generate these answers on her own, with minimal assistance from her therapist. This was done to help Iris "become her own therapist," and in turn, help ease treatment termination.

FUTURE DIRECTIONS IN HEALTH ANXIETY

Our understanding of health anxiety is far from complete. With the publication of the *DSM–5* (American Psychiatric Association, 2013), it will be important to examine the epidemiology, etiology, and treatment of individuals diagnosed with illness anxiety disorder or somatic symptom disorder. With respect to the origins of health anxiety, there is a need for more sophisticated studies that allow for multivariate analysis of health anxiety that considers biological and psychosocial determinants. Given that our population is rapidly becoming ethnically diverse and older, we also need to develop conceptual models and treatment programs that are sensitive to these groups. It is also apparent that there is still much to be learned about health anxiety across the life span. For example, relatively little is known about the course and clinical presentation of health anxiety among children, adolescents, and older adults.

With increased evidence supporting psychosocial interventions to improve health anxiety, additional attention needs to be given to knowledge translation. There is significant room for improvement in the extent to which patients and medical providers embrace psychological treatment of health anxiety. This means that there is a need to focus on ensuring research is appropriately disseminated and effectively translated into practice. A further important direction that will facilitate knowledge translation is the study of the cost-effectiveness of treating health anxiety. Preliminary research has been conducted in this area (Hedman et al., 2010) and suggests that, when individuals participate in group CBT, medical and nonmedical costs are substantially lowered.

Finally, it is important to note that there are enormous opportunities to better use technology to advance the treatment of health anxiety. Preliminary studies support the delivery of CBT online (Hedman et al., 2011), but there is substantial work to be done to translate this knowledge into everyday practice. Furthermore, we still have much to learn about the benefits and potential perils of self-help chat rooms, computerized assessment, computer-based adherence strategies (e.g., e-mail), and interactive computer programs.

Iris experienced a significant decrease in her health anxiety over the course of 15 sessions of CBT. Her low mood also improved substantially. She no longer met diagnostic criteria for hypochondriasis by the end of treatment. Moreover, she observed significant improvements in her social functioning as she was able to establish more meaningful interactions with her son and husband. With her health anxiety no longer prominent, Iris indicated that she felt ready to reenter the workforce and later submitted her resume to several potential employers, ultimately securing a part-time job at a bookstore.

REFERENCES

Abramowitz, J. S., & Braddock, A. E. (2008). *Psychological treatment of health anxiety and hypochondriasis: A biopsychosocial approach.* Ashland, OH: Hogrefe & Huber.

Alberts, N. M., & Hadjistavropoulos, H. D. (in press). Parental illness, attachment dimensions and health beliefs: Testing the cognitive-behavioural and interpersonal models of health anxiety. *Anxiety, Stress & Coping.*

Alberts, N. M., Hadjistavropoulos, H. D., Jones, S. L., & Sharpe, D. (2013). The Short Health Anxiety Inventory: A systematic review and meta-analysis. *Journal of Anxiety Disorders, 27,* 68–78. doi:10.1016/j.janxdis.2012.10.009

American Psychiatric Association. (2000). *Diagnostic and statistical manual of mental disorders* (4th ed., text revision). Washington, DC: Author.

American Psychiatric Association. (2013). *Diagnostic and statistical manual of mental disorders* (5th ed.). Washington, DC: Author.

Asmundson, G. J., Taylor, S., & Cox, B. J. (Eds.). (2001). *Health anxiety: Clinical and research perspectives on hypochondriasis and related conditions.* New York, NY: Wiley.

Avia, M. D., Ruiz, M., Olivares, M., Crespo, M., Guisado, A. B., Sánchez, A., & Varela, A. (1996). The meaning of psychological symptoms: Effectiveness of a group intervention with hypochondriacal patients. *Behaviour Research and Therapy, 34,* 23–31. doi:10.1016/0005-7967(95)00052-Y

Barsky, A. J., & Ahern, D. K. (2004). Cognitive behavior therapy for hypochondriasis: A randomized controlled trial. *JAMA, 291,* 1464–1470. doi:10.1001/jama.291.12.1464

Barsky, A. J., Frank, C. B., Cleary, P. D., Wyshak, G., & Klerman, G. (1991). The relation between hypochondriasis and age. *The American Journal of Psychiatry, 148,* 923–928.

Barsky, A. J., Wyshak, G., & Klerman, G. L. (1986a). Hypochondriasis: An evaluation of the *DSM–III* criteria in medical outpatients. *Archives of General Psychiatry, 43,* 493–500. doi:10.1001/archpsyc.1986.01800050099013

Barsky, A. J., Wyshak, G., & Klerman, G. L. (1986b). Medical and psychiatric determinants of outpatient medical utilization. *Medical Care, 24,* 548–560. doi:10.1097/00005650-198606000-00009

Barsky, A. J., Wyshak, G., Klerman, G., & Latham, K. (1990). The prevalence of hypochondriasis in medical outpatients. *Social Psychiatry and Psychiatric Epidemiology, 25,* 89–94.

Bourgault-Fagnou, M. D., & Hadjistavropoulos, H. D. (2009). Understanding health anxiety among community dwelling seniors with varying degrees of frailty. *Aging & Mental Health, 13,* 226–237. doi:10.1080/13607860802380664

Buwalda, F. M., Bouman, T., & van Duijn, M. A. (2007). Psychoeducation for hypochondriasis: A comparison of a cognitive-behavioural approach and a problem-solving approach. *Behaviour Research and Therapy, 45,* 887–899. doi:10.1016/j.brat.2006.08.004

Buwalda, F. M., Bouman, T. K., & van Duijn, M. A. (2008). The effect of a psycho-educational course on hypochondriacal metacognition. *Cognitive Therapy and Research, 32,* 689–701. doi:10.1007/s10608-007-9176-4

Clark, D. M., Salkovskis, P. M., Hackmann, A., Wells, A., Fennell, M., Ludgate, J., . . . Gelder, M. (1998). Two psychological treatments for hypochondriasis: A randomised controlled trial. *The British Journal of Psychiatry, 173,* 218–225. doi:10.1192/bjp.173.3.218

Creed, F., & Barsky, A. (2004). A systematic review of the epidemiology of somatisation disorder. *Journal of Psychosomatic Research, 56,* 391–408.

Deacon, B., & Abramowitz, J. S. (2008). Is hypochondriasis related to obsessive compulsive-disorder, panic disorder, or both? An empirical evaluation. *Journal of Cognitive Psychotherapy, 22,* 115–127. doi:10.1891/0889-8391.22.2.115

Escobar, J. I., Gara, M., Waitzkin, H., Silver, R. C., Holman, A., & Compton, W. (1998). *DSM–IV* hypochondriasis in primary care. *General Hospital Psychiatry, 20,* 155–159. doi:10.1016/S0163-8343(98)00018-8

Faravelli, C., Salvatori, S., Galassi, F., Aiazzi, L., Drei, C., & Cabras, P. (1997). Epidemiology of somatoform disorders: A community survey in Florence. *Social Psychiatry and Psychiatric Epidemiology, 32,* 24–29. doi:10.1007/BF00800664

Fishbain, D. A., Lewis, J. E., Gao, J., Cole, B., & Steele Rosomoff, R. (2009). Is chronic pain associated with somatization/hypochondriasis? An evidence-based structured review. *Pain Practice, 9,* 449–467. doi:10.1111/j.1533-2500.2009.00309.x

Furer, P., Walker, J. R., & Stein, M. B. (2007). *Treating health anxiety and fear of death: A practitioner's guide.* New York, NY: Springer Science + Business Media.

Gillespie, N. A., Zhu, G., Heath, A., Hickie, I., & Martin, N. (2000). The genetic aetiology of somatic distress. *Psychological Medicine: A Journal of Research in Psychiatry and the Allied Sciences, 30,* 1051–1061.

Greeven, A., van Balkom, A. J., Visser, S., Merkelbach, J. W., van Rood, Y. R., van Dyck, R., . . . Spinhoven, P. (2007). Cognitive behavior therapy and paroxetine in the treatment of hypochondriasis: A randomized controlled trial. *The American Journal of Psychiatry, 164,* 91–99. doi:10.1176/appi.ajp.164.1.91

Hadjistavropoulos, H. D., Janzen, J. A., Kehler, M. D., Leclerc, J. A., Sharpe, D., & Bourgault-Fagnou, M. D. (2012). Core cognitions related to health anxiety in self-reported medical and non-medical samples. *Journal of Behavioral Medicine, 35,* 167–178.

Hedman, E., Andersson, G., Andersson, E., Ljotsson, B., Ruck, C., Asmundson, G. J., & Lindefors, N. (2011). Internet-based cognitive-behavioural therapy for severe health anxiety: Randomised controlled trial. *The British Journal of Psychiatry, 198,* 230–236. doi:10.1192/bjp.bp.110.086843

Hedman, E., Ljotsson, B., Andersson, E., Ruck, C., Andersson, G., & Lindefors, N. (2010). Effectiveness and cost offset analysis of group CBT for hypochondriasis delivered in a psychiatric setting: An open trial. *Cognitive Behaviour Therapy, 39,* 239–250. doi:10.1080/16506073.2010.496460

Hiller, W., Leibbrand, R., Rief, W., & Fichter, M. M. (2002). Predictors of course and outcome in hypochondriasis after cognitive-behavioral treatment. *Psychotherapy and Psychosomatics, 71*, 318–325. doi:10.1159/000065990

Looper, K. J., & Kirmayer, L. J. (2001). Hypochondriacal concerns in a community population. *Psychological Medicine: A Journal of Research in Psychiatry and the Allied Sciences, 31*, 577–584.

Lovas, D. A., & Barsky, A. J. (2010). Mindfulness-based cognitive therapy for hypochondriasis, or severe health anxiety: A pilot study. *Journal of Anxiety Disorders, 24*, 931–935. doi:10.1016/j.janxdis.2010.06.019

Muse, K., McManus, F., Hackmann, A., Williams, M., & Williams, M. (2010). Intrusive imagery in severe health anxiety: Prevalence, nature and links with memories and maintenance cycles. *Behaviour Research and Therapy, 48*, 792–798. doi:10.1016/j.brat.2010.05.008

Noyes, R., Happel, R. L., & Yagla, S. J. (1999). Correlates of hypochondriasis in a nonclinical population. *Psychosomatics: Journal of Consultation Liaison Psychiatry, 40*, 461–469. doi:10.1016/S0033-3182(99)71183-7

Noyes, R., Stuart, S. P., Langbehn, D. R., Happel, R. L., Longley, S. L., Muller, B. A., & Yagla, S. J. (2003). Test of an interpersonal model of hypochondriasis. *Psychosomatic Medicine, 65*, 292–300. doi:10.1097/01.PSY.0000058377.50240.64

olde Hartman, T. C., Borghuis, M. S., Lucassen, P. L., van de Laar, F. A., Speckens, A. E., & van Weel, C. (2009). Medically unexplained symptoms, somatisation disorder and hypochondriasis: Course and prognosis. A systematic review. *Journal of Psychosomatic Research, 66*, 363–377. doi:10.1016/j.jpsychores.2008.09.018

Pilowsky, I. (1967). Dimensions of hypochondriasis. *The British Journal of Psychiatry, 113*, 89–93. doi:10.1192/bjp.113.494.89

Pugh, N. E., & Hadjistavropoulos, H. D. (2011). Is anxiety about health associated with desire to exercise, physical activity, and exercise dependence? *Personality and Individual Differences, 51*, 1059–1062. doi:10.1016/j.paid.2011.08.025

Salkovskis, P. M., Rimes, K., Warwick, H., & Clark, D. (2002). The Health Anxiety Inventory: Development and validation of scales for the measurement of health anxiety and hypochondriasis. *Psychological Medicine: A Journal of Research in Psychiatry and the Allied Sciences, 32*, 843–853.

Schmidt, N. B., Lerew, D. R., & Trakowski, J. H. (1997). Body vigilance in panic disorder: Evaluating attention to bodily perturbations. *Journal of Consulting and Clinical Psychology, 65*, 214–220. doi:10.1037/0022-006X.65.2.214

Seivewright, H., Green, J., Salkovskis, P., Barrett, B., Nur, U., & Tyrer, P. (2008). Cognitive-behavioural therapy for health anxiety in a genitourinary medicine clinic: Randomised controlled trial. *The British Journal of Psychiatry, 193*, 332–337. doi:10.1192/bjp.bp.108.052936

Sorensen, P., Birket-Smith, M., Wattar, U., Buemann, I., & Salkovskis, P. (2011). A randomized clinical trial of cognitive behavioural therapy versus short-term psychodynamic psychotherapy versus no intervention for patients with hypochondriasis. *Psychological Medicine, 41*, 431–441.

Speckens, A. E., Van Hemert, A., Spinhoven, P., & Bolk, J. (1996). The diagnostic and prognostic significance of the Whitely Index, the Illness Attitudes Scales and the Somatosensory Amplification Scale. *Psychological Medicine, 26,* 1085–1090.

Stein, M. B., Jang, K. L., & Livesley, W. (1999). Heritability of anxiety sensitivity: A twin study. *The American Journal of Psychiatry, 156,* 246–251.

Stuart, S., & Noyes, R. (1999). Attachment and interpersonal communication in somatization. *Psychosomatics, 40,* 34–43. doi:10.1016/S0033-3182(99)71269-7

Taylor, S., Asmundson, G. J., & Coons, M. J. (2005). Current directions in the treatment of hypochondriasis. *Journal of Cognitive Psychotherapy, 19,* 285–304. doi:10.1891/jcop.2005.19.3.285

Taylor, S., & Asmundson, G. J. G. (2004). *Treating health anxiety: A cognitive-behavioral approach.* New York, NY: Guilford Press.

Taylor, S., Zvolensky, M., Cox, B., Deacon, B., Heimberg, R., & Ledley, D. R. (2007). Robust dimensions of anxiety sensitivity: Development and initial validation of the Anxiety Sensitivity Index—3 (ASI–3). *Psychological Assessment, 19,* 176–188. doi:10.1037/1040-3590.19.2.176

Torgersen, S. (1986). Genetics of somatoform disorders. *Archives of General Psychiatry, 43,* 502–505. doi:10.1001/archpsyc.1986.01800050108014

Tyrer, P., Cooper, S., Crawford, M., Dupont, S., Green, J., Murphy, D., . . . Tyrer, H. (2011). Prevalence of health anxiety problems in medical clinics. *Journal of Psychosomatic Research, 71,* 392–394.

Visser, S., & Bouman, T. K. (2001). The treatment of hypochondriasis: Exposure plus response prevention vs cognitive therapy. *Behaviour Research and Therapy, 39,* 423–442. doi:10.1016/S0005-7967(00)00022-X

Warwick, H. M., Clark, D. M., Cobb, A. M., & Salkovskis, P. M. (1996). A controlled trail of cognitive-behavioural treatment of hypochondriasis. *The British Journal of Psychiatry, 169,* 189–195. doi:10.1192/bjp.169.2.189

Warwick, H. M., & Salkovskis, P. M. (1990). Hypochondriasis. *Behaviour Research and Therapy, 28,* 105–117. doi:10.1016/0005-7967(90)90023-C

Watt, M. C., & Stewart, S. H. (2000). Anxiety sensitivity mediates the relationship between childhood learning experiences and elevated hypochondriacal concerns in young adulthood. *Journal of Psychosomatic Research, 49,* 107–118. doi:10.1016/S0022-3999(00)00097-0

Wattar, U., Sorensen, P., Buemann, I., Birket-Smith, M., Salkovskis, P. M., Albertsen, M., & Strange, S. (2005). Outcome of cognitive-behavioural treatment for health anxiety (hypochondriasis) in a routine clinical setting. *Behavioural and Cognitive Psychotherapy, 33,* 165–175. doi:10.1017/S1352465804002000

Wheaton, M. G., Berman, N. C., Franklin, J. C., & Abramowitz, J. S. (2010). Health anxiety: Latent structure and associations with anxiety-related psychological processes in a student sample. *Journal of Psychopathology and Behavioral Assessment, 32,* 565–574. doi:10.1007/s10862-010-9179-4

II

COMORBIDITIES

11

DEPRESSION IN THE OBSESSIVE–COMPULSIVE SPECTRUM

JONATHAN S. ABRAMOWITZ AND SHANNON M. BLAKEY

This chapter begins with a description of the presentation of depressive symptoms in obsessive–compulsive disorder (OCD) and related problems. We then describe the effects of depression on the treatment for these problems as well as various approaches to improving outcome for patients with comorbid OCD and depression.

Depression is a psychological state characterized by a chronically sad mood (e.g., feeling empty or hopeless) that is often associated with anhedonia—the diminished capacity to experience pleasure or interest in activities that are typically enjoyed. The following other signs and symptoms are also often present: reduced appetite and weight loss (or, in some cases, weight gain), insomnia or hypersomnia, psychomotor agitation or retardation, fatigue, feelings of guilt, diminished concentration, and recurrent thoughts of death. Although depression is observed within the context of many psychological syndromes, as well as in nonclinical individuals, a person meets criteria for a

http://dx.doi.org/10.1037/14323-012
Obsessive–Compulsive Disorder and Its Spectrum: A Life-Span Approach, Eric A. Storch and Dean McKay (Editors)
Copyright © 2014 by the American Psychological Association. All rights reserved.

major depressive episode if the aforementioned symptoms persist for at least a 2-week period and interfere with daily functioning (American Psychiatric Association, 2013). Major depressive disorder (MDD) is defined by the occurrence of one or more major depressive episodes at any point during one's lifetime (American Psychiatric Association, 2013). Dysthymia, a similarly chronic form of depression, involves a chronically depressed mood and reduced interest but does not grossly disable the person's daily functioning (American Psychiatric Association, 2013).

Depressive symptoms are often observed in individuals with OCD spectrum conditions,[1] which is not surprising given that anxiety is a main feature of OCD and also the single best predictor of the development of clinically severe depressive symptoms (Hranov, 2007). Depression also ranks as the most commonly co-occurring problem among anxiety diagnoses (Kessler, Stang, & Wittchen, 1998), affecting up to 90% of people with anxiety disorders (Gorman, 1996). We next review the rates of comorbid depression across the OCD spectrum.

OCD

Table 11.1 shows the rates of MDD among adult OCD samples. Across seven countries, the lifetime prevalence ranged from 12.4% to 60.3%. In the United States, researchers found a lifetime comorbidity rate of 54.1% and a concurrent comorbidity rate of 36% (e.g., Nestadt et al., 2001). Studies on the temporal nature of this comorbidity have long found that in most (but not all) instances, OCD symptoms predate the depressive symptoms (Bellodi, Scioto, Diaferia, Ronchi, & Smiraldi, 1992; Demal, Lenz, Mayrhofer, Zapotoczky, & Zitterl, 1993). This suggests that the mood disturbance often occurs as a response to the distress and functional impairment associated with obsessions and compulsions, as described earlier.

Patients with OCD and depression also show an earlier age of OCD onset and more severe symptoms compared with OCD sufferers who are not depressed (e.g., Abramowitz, Storch, Keeley, & Cordell, 2007). Depressive symptoms are also more strongly associated with the severity of obsessions than with compulsions (Ricciardi & McNally, 1995) and may be specifically associated with sexual and religious obsessions (Hasler et al., 2005). Finally,

---

[1]Considerable disagreement exists, on both conceptual and empirical grounds, regarding what constitutes an OC-related disorder. In this chapter, we define an OCD spectrum disorder as one involving (a) anxiety-provoking intrusive thoughts and (b) safety behaviors, avoidance, and "compulsive" rituals performed to reduce anxiety (e.g., Storch, Abramowitz, & Goodman, 2008). When this definition is used, body dysmorphic disorder and hypochondriasis, along with OCD, fit within the OCD spectrum category (Abramowitz & Deacon, 2005).

TABLE 11.1
Rates of Lifetime Major Depressive Disorder in Samples of Adult Patients With Obsessive–Compulsive Disorder

Study	*DSM* edition	*N*	% Comorbidity
Antony et al. (1998)	IV	87	24
Yaryura-Tobias et al. (1996)	III–R	391	29
Crino & Andrews (1996)	III–R	108	50
Ricciardi & McNally (1995)	III–R	125	21
Andrews et al. (2002)	IV	641	17
Nestadt et al. (2001)	IV	80	54
Sanderson et al. (1990)	III–R	12	33

Note. *DSM* = *Diagnostic and Statistical Manual of Mental Disorders.*

relative to nondepressed patients with OCD, those with depression more strongly believe that their intrusive obsessional thoughts are significant and meaningful (Abramowitz et al., 2007).

BODY DYSMORPHIC DISORDER

Body dysmorphic disorder (BDD) involves excessive preoccupation with an imagined defect in appearance that causes subjective distress and interference with functioning (American Psychiatric Association, 2013). Examples include perceived flaws in the size or shape of the face, skin, hair, and muscles. The preoccupations often lead to anxiety-reducing behaviors, such as mirror gazing (or mirror avoidance), camouflaging the perceived defect with makeup or clothing, or performing other checking and grooming behaviors. Some people with BDD also undergo cosmetic surgeries to correct the flaw (Veale, 2000).

MDD is the primary comorbid condition among individuals with BDD (Gunstad & Phillips, 2003) with rates ranging from 36% to 87% in adult samples (see Table 11.2). Although there are instances in which MDD arises before the onset of BDD symptoms, depression generally presents after the development of BDD, supporting theoretical speculations that the distress and dissatisfaction associated with body image preoccupation in BDD leads to depressive symptoms (Phillips, 1999). Indeed, this is not surprising: Feelings associated with BDD (i.e., beliefs that one is unattractive) are similar to core dysfunctional beliefs characteristic of MDD.

Compared with BDD without depression, BDD with comorbid MDD is associated with more severe BDD symptoms, increased anxiety and personality disorder comorbidity, and decreased quality of life (Phillips, Didie, & Menard, 2007). Comorbid BDD and MDD diagnoses are also associated

TABLE 11.2
Rates of Lifetime Major Depressive Disorder in Samples of Adult Patients
With Body Dysmorphic Disorder

Study	*DSM* edition	*N*	% Comorbidity
Hollander et al. (1993)	III–R	50	68
Veale et al. (1996)	III–R	50	36
Perugi et al. (1997)	III–R	58	41
Zimmerman & Mattia (1998)	IV	16	69
Gunstad & Philips (2003)	IV	293	76
Phillips et al. (2007)	IV	178	74
Phillips et al. (2007)	IV	45	87

Note. DSM = Diagnostic and Statistical Manual of Mental Disorders.

with an earlier age of onset of depression (midadolescence vs. mid-20s) and more chronic depression (Nierenberg et al., 2002). Thus, a comorbid MDD and BDD diagnosis may forecast exacerbated psychiatric symptoms and more complicated treatment.

HYPOCHONDRIASIS

Hypochondriasis (HC; termed *health anxiety* in *DSM–5*) involves a persistent fear or belief that one has a serious disease (e.g., cancer), resulting in distress and functional impairment as well as urges to seek reassurance of good health from medical professionals (and other sources), avoidance of health cues, and taking unreasonable preventative measures (American Psychiatric Association, 2013). Although these behaviors might provide an immediate relief from anxiety, they ultimately maintain HC symptoms (Warwick & Salkovskis, 1990).

HC is frequently comorbid with other psychiatric disorders, with MDD being among the most common (Creed & Barsky, 2004). Table 11.3 shows the rates of MDD in patients diagnosed with HC. As can be seen, a majority of adults with HC experience MDD at some point in their lifetime. It is also worth noting that patients with MDD frequently present with somatic symptoms, a reverse pattern that has clinical implications for patients' prognosis and treatment (see Kirmayer & Robbins, 1991). As with OCD and BDD, HC symptoms tend to temporally precede the onset of MDD (Noyes et al., 1994).

Compared with nondepressed HC patients, most patients with comorbid MDD and HC experience more chronic and persistent HC symptoms, especially disease fears (Barsky, Wyshak, & Klerman, 1992; Creed & Barsky, 2004; Noyes et al., 1994). Additionally, those with comorbid MDD and HC have greater overall functional impairment and endorse more depressive symptoms than those with HC in the absence of MDD (Noyes et al., 1994).

TABLE 11.3
Rates of Major Depressive Disorder in Samples of Adult Patients With Hypochondriasis

Study	*DSM* edition	*N*	% Comorbidity	
Hiller et al. (2005)	IV	46	72	Lifetime
Bach et al. (1996)	III–R	37	68	Lifetime
Barsky et al. (1992)	III–R	42	43	Lifetime
			33	Current
Noyes et al. (1994)	III–R	50	28	Current
Escobar et al. (1998)	IV	49	84	Unspecified

Note. DSM = Diagnostic and Statistical Manual of Mental Disorders.

PREDICTORS OF DEPRESSIVE SYMPTOMS IN OC SPECTRUM DISORDERS

Limited data exist on predictors of depressive symptoms in OCD spectrum disorders. Ricciardi and McNally (1995) found that depression was associated with more severe obsessional symptoms but not with compulsive rituals. Later studies revealed that depression was particularly strongly associated with the presence of obsessional intrusions concerning sexual and religious themes (Hasler et al., 2005). Moreover, relative to nondepressed patients with OCD, those with MDD showed more severe cognitive distortions (i.e., the tendency to misinterpret the significance of obsessional thoughts) and poorer insight into the senselessness of obsessions and rituals. Thus, the presence of depression is associated not only with greater overall OCD symptom severity but also with certain presentations of this highly heterogeneous condition.

TREATMENT

Outcome

There are two empirically supported approaches to the treatment of OCD and related disorders: cognitive–behavioral psychological treatment and pharmacotherapy. Effective psychological treatment for OCD, BDD, and HC emphasizes psychoeducation, exposure and response prevention (ERP), and cognitive restructuring (e.g., Abramowitz, Deacon, & Whiteside, 2011; Taylor & Asmundson, 2004). Yet these techniques require considerable work and practice, and ERP involves deliberately confronting one's fears without accompanying rituals or avoidance. Individuals suffering with depression, however, might lack the willpower to complete such challenging work and fall prey to dysfunctional self-defeating beliefs (e.g., "I don't deserve to get better"). Although cognitive behavior therapy (CBT) is effective in reducing OC and related symptoms, the cognitive, physiological, behavioral, and affective symptoms of depression can interfere with the effects of this treatment. The most effective pharmacological treatments for OCD, BDD, and HC are the serotonin reuptake inhibitor (SRI) medications. Next, we turn to a review of the pharmacological and cognitive-behavioral treatment outcome literature with respect to comorbid MDD in OCD and BDD. There are currently no treatment data on comorbid depression in HC.

OCD

Studies with OCD patients consistently show that in addition to reducing OCD symptoms, CBT and SRIs are associated with improvement in depressive symptoms, yielding large pre- to posttreatment effects (e.g., Eddy, Dutra, Bradley, & Westen, 2004; Franklin et al., 2000). Two studies with OCD patients receiving CBT, primarily involving ERP, have examined the effects of comorbid MDD on treatment response. Abramowitz and Foa (2000) compared outcome for 15 depressed OCD patients with that for 33 nondepressed OCD patients following 15 sessions of this treatment. Although immediate and long-term improvement was observed in both groups (respectively, 87.9% and 73.3% showed at least a 30% reduction in OCD symptoms at posttest), at posttreatment and at follow-up, the depressed patients had more severe symptoms. Steketee, Chambless, and Tran (2001) examined 63 patients with OCD who had received CBT, nine of whom had MDD. Among treatment completers, the presence of MDD significantly predicted poorer outcome on measures of OCD symptoms. Although clinical observations suggest that patients with OCD and depression require higher doses of SRIs than do nondepressed patients with OCD, empirical findings demonstrating an attenuated response to pharmacotherapy among comorbid patients are lacking (e.g., Fineberg & Craig, 2010).

BDD

Williams, Hadjistavropoulos, and Sharpe (2006) conducted a meta-analysis to examine the relative effectiveness of pharmacological and psychological (CBT and behavioral) therapies in 13 studies of patients with BDD and comorbid MDD. They found that each treatment approach was associated with large effect sizes for improvement in both BDD and MDD symptoms. When these effects were compared meta-analytically, however, CBT was significantly more effective in reducing both BDD and comorbid MDD symptoms than was pharmacotherapy. These findings suggest that although both

SRIs and psychological treatments are effective for comorbid BDD and MDD, CBT provides a greater and more inclusive benefit (Williams et al., 2006).

Why Does Depression Attenuate Treatment Outcome?

A number of factors might contribute to depression interfering with treatment outcome, especially where CBT for OCD and related disorders is concerned (for a review, see Keeley, Storch, Merlo, & Geffken, 2008). For example, depressed individuals can show decreased compliance with treatment instructions. Yet, to be effective, CBT requires that the patient repeatedly practice the treatment techniques (e.g., confronting feared stimuli and remaining exposed until anxiety subsides on its own). Individuals who are depressed might not be able to properly comply with these demanding instructions if they perceive themselves as more helpless (Seligman, 1975), less deserving of a happy life, or if they hold low expectations of improvement (Bandura, 1977). Depressed patients might also have psychomotor retardation, which would attenuate their ability to do the work required to improve.

With respect to medication, patients with depression have reduced hope and optimism, depleting medications of their nonspecific (i.e., placebo) effects. They might also attribute any treatment gains to external or circumstantial sources and therefore evidence less improvement and more relapses than nondepressed patients. In the remainder of this chapter, we discuss possible approaches to managing patients with OCD and related disorders with depression.

TREATMENT APPROACHES TO ADDRESS COMORBID DEPRESSION

For the most part, research on the treatment of OCD and related disorders has focused on more or less "straightforward" or "clean" presentations of these problems (e.g., Foa et al., 2005). Less attention has been paid to complex cases, such as those involving comorbid depression. Yet, as we have discussed, a great many individuals with OCD and related disorders present with complexities of one sort or another—comorbid depression being among the most common.

As mentioned, exposure—repeated and prolonged confrontation with feared stimuli—along with help refraining from subtle and overt avoidance and safety-seeking behaviors (i.e., response prevention) is the centerpiece of CBT for OCD, BDD, and HC (Abramowitz et al., 2011). Someone with contamination obsessions, for example, is helped to confront sources of feared germs (e.g., public bathrooms) while simultaneously refraining from any avoidance or anxiety-reducing behavior (e.g., hand washing). Exposure-based CBT can be highly effective for OCD, BDD, and HC, producing an average of 60% to 70% reduction in fear, avoidance, and the use of safety behaviors (Abramowitz et al., 2011). A drawback of this approach, however, is that patients must confront their fear-evoking stimuli and resist urges to immediately reduce anxiety via escape or avoidance. Because exposure therapy requires compliance with these somewhat demanding procedures, some patients either refuse this form of therapy or terminate prematurely. Moreover, exposure therapy is highly focused on alleviating anxiety and fear and does not directly address comorbid problems such as depression.

Cognitive conceptualizations of OCD (e.g., Clark, 2004), BDD (e.g., Veale & Neziroglu, 2010), and HC (e.g., Taylor & Asmundson, 2004) have led to the inclusion of cognitive therapy (CT) strategies along with exposure in many treatment protocols (e.g., Abramowitz & Braddock, 2008). In CT, a number of verbal and skill-development techniques are used to (a) educate patients about the nature of anxiety and how pathological anxiety is maintained and (b) help patients correct dysfunctional beliefs and automatic thoughts that lead directly to anxiety and fear (e.g., misinterpretations of benign physical sensations). For example, someone with BDD would be helped to recognize that others are unlikely to notice or judge her based on the imagined defect in appearance. In addition to verbally challenging dysfunctional thinking patterns, patients test out the validity of these (and corrected) beliefs using real-life "experiments" (that are similar to exposure exercises), such as walking through a shopping mall without concealing an imagined facial defect. The efficacy of CT is suggested by numerous outcome studies, yet CT does not appear to be as effective as exposure-based therapy for OCD and related conditions (Abramowitz et al., 2011).

Treatment protocols developed for OCD, BDD, and HC have not routinely addressed the common comorbid depressive symptoms that are known to present challenges. There are, however, a few possible ways in which CBT could be implemented to address comorbid depression. These are described below, along with the theoretical and practical considerations relevant to each.

Combining Antidepressant Medication and CBT

Antidepressant medications, such as the SRIs, are the most widely used treatments for both depression and OCD related disorders (e.g., Schatzberg & Nemeroff, 2009). Thus, intuitively, the use of these agents should improve outcomes for patients suffering from both types of these problems comorbidly. Few studies, however, have addressed whether antidepressants offer an advantage over exposure-based CBT, specifically for comorbid samples, and the existing studies have numerous methodological difficulties, limiting the conclusions that can be drawn. The OCD literature provides the best examples of such studies. In one investigation with OCD patients, Marks et al. (1980) found that clomipramine helped severe depression and OCD symptoms more than did placebo. However, the comparison included only five patients on clomipramine and five on placebo, and the statistical analysis was conducted at the 4-week point in treatment, which may not have been enough time for clomipramine to yield full benefit in all patients.

In another study, Foa, Kozak, Steketee, and McCarthy (1992) examined whether using imipramine before CBT would facilitate improvement in OCD symptoms once CBT began. In their prospective study, mildly and severely depressed patients with OCD received either pill placebo or imipramine for 6 weeks before CBT. Results indicated that although imipramine improved the symptoms of depression, it did not potentiate the effects of CBT on OCD symptoms. Abramowitz, Franklin, Kozak, Street, and Foa (2000) also included a comparison between severely depressed OCD patients who either were or were not using SRI medications during CBT. No differences between groups were reported, although the small size of the severely depressed group in that study ($n = 11$) limits the generalizability of this finding. To date, there is little compelling evidence that medication potentiates the effects of CBT with severely depressed anxiety patients.

One explanation for this conclusion is that because SRI medications are the most widely used therapy for anxiety, patients with anxiety disorders have often already tried these agents before presenting for psychological treatment. Thus, many patients with depression and an anxiety disorder in treatment studies might have been "medication resistant," thus putting a ceiling on the effects of medications. It is also possible that newer medications (including newer SRIs) will be more helpful as adjunctive treatment strategies but have yet to be examined in this population. Nevertheless, because the average improvement with SRI medication is somewhat modest (approximately 20%–40%), there is a need to consider nonmedication strategies for augmenting psychological treatment for patients with comorbid depression and anxiety disorders.

Adding CT for Depression

CT is a useful intervention for all OCD-related disorders and for depression. Indeed, CT yields high responder rates, few adverse effects, and good durability of gains in depressed patients (e.g., Elkin et al., 1989). CT for depression involves identifying and challenging overly negative beliefs about oneself, the world, and the future that lead to overly negative and biased interpretations of events, giving rise to feelings of extreme hopelessness, helplessness, and personal failure. It also includes the use of behavioral activation in which the patient increases his or her engagement with other people and in activities he or she finds enjoyable. This helps reinforce behavior that is the opposite of depressive behavior. Numerous studies report significant and lasting improvement in dysphoric mood and other MDD symptoms following CT (Dobson, 1989). Typically, 50% to 70% of MDD patients who complete CT no longer meet criteria for MDD at posttreatment, and only 20% to 30% show significant relapse at follow-up (Craighead, Evans, & Robins, 1992).

Another reason CT is a good choice to use in the treatment of patients with OCD and related disorders who also suffer from comorbid depression is efficiency: That is, the conceptual approach and implementation of CT as used for depression (e.g., identifying and challenging beliefs) are largely similar to those used in CT for OCD, BDD, and HC, although the content of the dysfunctional beliefs that are targeted is different. For example, cognitive restructuring can be used to modify dysfunctional cognitions relevant to intrusive thoughts (e.g., "thinking about molesting a child is as morally wrong as actually molesting the child"), as well as those relevant to depression (e.g., "everyone else has a better life than I do"). Thus, patients could learn to make use of the same skills to reduce both anxiety and depressive symptoms.

Engaging in CT to reduce depressive symptoms before beginning exposure techniques might alleviate some depressive symptoms and help patients with OCD and related conditions increase motivation and compliance with difficult exposure therapy assignments. Engaging in CT before, or concomitantly with, serotonergic medication use might also increase hopefulness about this treatment, helping patients tap into any psychological effects of using these medications. Unfortunately, however, no systematic evaluations of such treatment programs have been conducted, although we are currently conducting a study on the use of CT and exposure therapy for patients with OCD and comorbid depression.

CONCLUSIONS AND FUTURE DIRECTIONS

To date, the following can be said about the influence of comorbid depression on OCD spectrum disorders such as BDD and HC: (a) At least half of all patients with OCD-related disorders also suffer from depressive symptoms or meet criteria for a unipolar mood disorder; (b) in most instances, depressive symptoms emerge following the onset of OC symptoms, and perhaps in response to the distress and functional impairment associated with these symptoms; and (c) the presence of comorbid depression hinders outcome of both CBT and SRIs, which are the most effective treatments for OC-related disorders. The precise mechanisms for how depression hinders treatment outcome, however, are not completely understood.

Although it intuitively seems that adding CT for depression to exposure-based CBT for OC spectrum disorders would be the best approach to managing this pattern of comorbidity, important questions need to be answered to determine the clinical effectiveness and cost-effectiveness of this approach. It will, for example, be necessary to determine whether such a treatment package is more effective than exposure therapy, CT, or SRI medication alone or that it is superior to the combination of psychological treatment and medication in this population. We await this next phase of treatment development for OCD and related disorders.

REFERENCES

Abramowitz, J. S., & Braddock, A. E. (2008). *Psychological treatment of health anxiety and hypochondriasis*. Cambridge, MA: Hogrefe & Huber.

Abramowitz, J. S., & Deacon, B. J. (2005). Obsessive–compulsive disorder: Essential phenomenology and overlap with other anxiety disorders. In J. S. Abramowitz & A. C. Houts (Eds.), *Concepts and controversies in obsessive–compulsive disorder* (pp. 119–149). New York, NY: Springer.

Abramowitz, J. S., Deacon, B. J., & Whiteside, S. P. (2011). *Exposure therapy for anxiety: Principles and practice*. New York, NY: Guilford Press.

Abramowitz, J. S., & Foa, E. B. (2000). Does comorbid major depressive disorder influence outcome or exposure and response prevention for OCD? *Behavior Therapy, 31*, 795–800. doi:10.1016/S0005-7894(00)80045-3

Abramowitz, J. S., Franklin, M. E., Kozak, M. J., Street, G. P., & Foa, E. B. (2000). The effects of pretreatment depression on cognitive-behavioral treatment outcome in OCD clinic patients. *Behavior Therapy, 31*, 517–528.

Abramowitz, J. S., Storch, E. A., Keeley, M., & Cordell, E. (2007). Obsessive–compulsive disorder with comorbid major depressive disorder: What is the role of cognitive factors? *Behaviour Research and Therapy, 45*, 2257–2267. doi:10.1016/j.brat.2007.04.003

American Psychiatric Association. (2000). *Diagnostic and statistical manual of mental disorders* (4th ed., text revision). Washington, DC: Author.

American Psychiatric Association. (2013). *Diagnostic and statistical manual of mental disorders* (5th ed.). Washington, DC: Author.

Antony, M., Downie, F., & Swinson, R. (1998). Diagnostic issues and epidemiology in obsessive–compulsive disorder. In R. P. Swinson, M. M. Antony, S. Rachman, M. A. Richter (Eds.), *Obsessive–compulsive disorder: Theory, research, and treatment* (pp. 3–32). New York, NY: Guilford Press.

Bach, M., Nutzinger, D. O., & Hartl, L. (1996). Comorbidity of anxiety disorders and hypochondriasis considering different diagnostic systems. *Comprehensive Psychiatry, 37*, 62–67.

Bandura, A. (1977). Self-efficacy: Toward a unifying theory of behavioral change. *Psychological Review, 84*, 191–215. doi:10.1037/0033-295X.84.2.191

Barsky, A. J., Wyshak, G., & Klerman, G. L. (1992). Psychiatric comorbidity in DSM–III–R hypochondriasis. *Archives of General Psychiatry, 49*, 101–108. doi:10.1001/archpsyc.1992.01820020021003

Bellodi, L., Scioto, G., Diaferia, G., Ronchi, P., & Smiraldi, E. (1992). Psychiatric disorders in families of patients with obsessive–compulsive disorder. *Psychiatry Research, 42*, 111–120. doi:10.1016/0165-1781(92)90075-E

Clark, D. A. (2004). *Cognitive-behavioral therapy for OCD*. New York, NY: Guilford Press.

Craighead, W., Evans, D., & Robins, C. (1992). Unipolar depression. In S. M. Turner, K. S. Calhoun, & H. Adams (Eds.), *Handbook of clinical behavior therapy* (2nd ed., pp. 99–116). New York, NY: Wiley.

Creed, F., & Barsky, A. (2004). A systematic review of the epidemiology of somatization disorder and hypochondriasis. *Journal of Psychosomatic Research, 56*, 391–408. doi:10.1016/S0022-3999(03)00622-6

Crino, R., & Andrews, G. (1996). Obsessive–compulsive disorder and Axis I comorbidity. *Journal of Anxiety Disorders, 10*, 37–46.

Demal, U., Lenz, G., Mayrhofer, A., Zapotoczky, H.-G., & Zitterl, W. (1993). Obsessive–compulsive disorder and depression. A retrospective study on course and interaction. *Psychopathology, 26*, 145–150. doi:10.1159/000284814

Dobson, K. S. (1989). A meta-analysis of the efficacy of cognitive therapy for depression. *Journal of Consulting and Clinical Psychology, 57*, 414–419. doi:10.1037/0022-006X.57.3.414

Eddy, K. T., Dutra, L., Bradley, R., & Westen, D. (2004). A multidimensional meta-analysis of psychotherapy and pharmacotherapy for obsessive–compulsive disorder. *Clinical Psychology Review, 24*, 1011–1030. doi:10.1016/j.cpr.2004.08.004

Elkin, I., Shea, M., Watkins, J. T., Imber, S., Sotsky, S., Collins, J., . . . Parloff, M. (1989). National Institute of Mental Health Treatment of Depression Collaborative Research program: General effectiveness of treatments. *Archives of General Psychiatry, 46*, 971–982. doi:10.1001/archpsyc.1989.01810110013002

Escobar, J. I., Gara, M., Waitzkin, H., Silver, R. C., Holman, A., & Compton, W. (1998). *DSM–IV* hypochondriasis in primary care. *General Hospital Psychiatry, 20*, 155–159.

Fineberg, N., & Craig, K. J. (2010). Pharmacotherapy for obsessive–compulsive disorder. In D. Stein, E. Hollander, & B. Rothbaum (Eds.), *Textbook of anxiety disorders* (2nd ed., pp. 311–338). Washington, DC: American Psychiatric Publishing.

Foa, E. B., Kozak, M. J., Steketee, G., & McCarthy, P. (1992). Treatment of depressive and obsessive–compulsive symptoms in OCD by imipramine and behavior therapy.

British Journal of Clinical Psychology, 31, 279–292. doi:10.1111/j.2044-8260.1992. tb00995.x

Foa, E. B., Liebowitz, M. R., Kozak, M. J., Davies, S., Campeas, R., Franklin, M. E., . . . Tu, X. (2005). Randomized, placebo-controlled trial of exposure and ritual prevention, clomipramine, and their combination in the treatment of obsessive–compulsive disorder. *The American Journal of Psychiatry, 162*, 151–161. doi:10.1176/appi.ajp.162.1.151

Gorman, J. M. (1996–1997). Comorbid depression and anxiety spectrum disorders. *Depression and Anxiety, 4*, 160–168. doi:10.1002/(SICI)1520-6394(1996)4:4< 160::AID-DA2>3.0.CO;2-J

Gunstad, J., & Phillips, K. A. (2003). Axis I comorbidity in body dysmorphic disorder. *Comprehensive Psychiatry, 44*, 270–276. doi:10.1016/S0010-440X(03)00088-9

Hasler, G., LaSalle-Ricci, V. H., Ronquillo, J. G., Crawley, S. A., Cochran, L. W., Kazuba, D., . . . Murphy, D. L. (2005). Obsessive–compulsive disorder symptom dimensions show specific relationships to psychiatric comorbidity. *Psychiatry Research, 135*, 121–132. doi:10.1016/j.psychres.2005.03.003

Hiller, W., Leibbrand, R., Rief, W., & Fichter, M. M. Differentiating hypochondriasis from panic disorder. *Journal of Anxiety Disorders, 19*, 29–49.

Hollander, E., Cohen, L., & Simeon, D. (1993). Body dysmorphic disorder. *Psychiatric Annals, 23*, 359–364.

Hranov, L. G. (2007). Comorbid anxiety and depression: Illumination of a controversy. *International Journal of Psychiatry in Clinical Practice, 11*, 171–189. doi:10.1080/13651500601127180

Keeley, M. L., Storch, E. A., Merlo, L. J., & Geffken, G. R. (2008). Clinical predictors of response to cognitive-behavioral therapy for obsessive–compulsive disorder. *Clinical Psychology Review, 28*, 118–130. doi:10.1016/j.cpr.2007.04.003

Kessler, R. C., Stang, P. E., & Wittchen, H. U. (1998). Lifetime panic–depression comorbidity in the National Comorbidity Survey. *Archives of General Psychiatry, 55*, 801–808. doi:10.1001/archpsyc.55.9.801

Kirmayer, L. J., & Robbins, J. M. (1991). Three forms of somatization in primary care: Prevalence, co-occurrence, and sociodemographic characteristics. *Journal of Nervous and Mental Disease, 179*, 647–655. doi:10.1097/00005053-199111000-00001

Marks, I. M., Stern, R. S., Mawson, D., Cobb, J., & McDonald, R. (1980). Clomipramine and exposure for obsessive–compulsive rituals. *The British Journal of Psychiatry, 136*, 1–25. doi:10.1192/bjp.136.1.1

Nestadt, G., Samuels, J, Riddle, M. A., Liang, K. Y., Bienvenu, O. J., Hoehn-Saric, R., . . . Cullen, B. et al. (2001). Relationship between obsessive–compulsive disorder and anxiety and affective disorders: Results from the Johns Hopkins OCD Family Study. *Psychological Medicine, 31*, 481–487. doi:10.1017/ S0033291701003579

Nierenberg, A. A., Phillips, K. A., Petersen, T. J., Kelly, K. E., Alpert, J. E., Worthington, J. J., . . . Fava, M. (2002). Body dysmorphic disorder in outpatients with major depression. *Journal of Affective Disorders, 69,* 141–148. doi:10.1016/S0165-0327 (01)00304-4

Noyes, R., Kathol, R. G., Fisher, M. M., Phillips, B. M., Suelzer, M. T., & Woodman, C. L. (1994). Psychiatric comorbidity among patients with hypochondriasis. *General Hospital Psychiatry, 16,* 78–87. doi:10.1016/0163-8343(94)90049-3

Perugi, G., Akiskal, H.S., Pfanner, C., Presta, S., Gemignani, A., Milanfranchi, A., . . . Cassano, G.B. (1997). The clinical impact of bipolar and unipolar affective comorbidity on obsessive–compulsive disorder. *Journal of Affective Disorders, 46,* 15–23.

Phillips, K. A. (1999). Body dysmorphic disorder and depression: Theoretical considerations and treatment strategies. *Psychiatric Quarterly, 70,* 313–331. doi:10.1023/A:1022090200057

Phillips, K. A., Didie, E. R., & Menard, W. (2007). Clinical features and correlates of major depressive disorder in individuals with body dysmorphic disorder. *Journal of Affective Disorders, 97,* 129–135. doi:10.1016/j.jad.2006.06.006

Ricciardi, J., & McNally, R. J. (1995). Depressed mood is related to obsessions but not compulsions in obsessive–compulsive disorder. *Journal of Anxiety Disorders, 9,* 249–256. doi:10.1016/0887-6185(95)00006-A

Sanderson, W., Beck, A., & Beck, J. (1990). Syndrome comorbidity in patients with major depression or dysthymia: Prevalence and temporal relationships. *American Journal of Psychiatry, 47,* 1025–1028.

Schatzberg, A. F., & Nemeroff, C. B. (Eds.). (2009). *Textbook of psychopharmacology* (4th ed.). Washington, DC: American Psychiatric Publishing. doi:10.1176/appi.books.9781585623860

Seligman, M. E. P. (1975). *Helplessness.* San Francisco, CA: Freeman.

Steketee, G., Chambless, D. L., & Tran, G. Q. (2001). Effects of Axis I and II comorbidity on behavior therapy outcome for obsessive–compulsive disorder and agoraphobia. *Comprehensive Psychiatry, 42,* 76–86. doi:10.1053/comp.2001.19746

Storch, E. A., Abramowitz, J., & Goodman, W. K. (2008). Where does obsessive–compulsive disorder belong in *DSM–V? Depression and Anxiety, 25,* 336–347.

Taylor, S., & Asmundson, G. J. G. (2004). *Treating health anxiety: A cognitive-behavioral approach.* New York, NY: Guilford Press.

Veale, D. (2000). Outcome of cosmetic surgery and "DIY" surgery in patients with body dysmorphic disorder. *Psychiatric Bulletin, 24,* 218–220. doi:10.1192/pb.24.6.218

Veale, D., Babcock, A., Gournay, K., Dryden, W., Shah, F., Wilson, R., & Walburn, J. (1996). Body dysmorphic disorder: A survey of 50 cases. *British Journal of Psychiatry, 169,* 196–201.

Veale, D., & Neziroglu, F. (2010). *Body dysmorphic disorder: A treatment manual.* Oxford, NY: Wiley-Blackwell. doi:10.1002/9780470684610

Warwick, H. M. C., & Salkovskis, P. M. (1990). Hypochondriasis. *Behaviour Research and Therapy, 28*, 105–117. doi:10.1016/0005-7967(90)90023-C

Williams, J., Hadjistavropoulos, T., & Sharpe, D. (2006). A meta-analysis of psychological and pharmacological treatments for body dysmorphic disorder. *Behaviour Research and Therapy, 44*, 99–111. doi:10.1016/j.brat.2004.12.006

Yaryuba-Tobias, J., Todaro, J., Gunes, M., McKay, D., Stockman, R., & Neziroglu, F. (1996, December). *Comorbidity versus continuum of Axis I disorders in OCD*. Paper presented at the meeting of the Association for Advancement of Behavior Therapy, New York, NY.

Zimmerman, M., & Mattia, J. (1998). Body dysmorphic disorder in psychiatric outpatients: Recognition, prevalence, comorbidity, demographic, and clinical correlates. *Comprehensive Psychiatry, 39*, 265–270.

12

SUICIDAL AND NONSUICIDAL SELF-INJURY IN THE OBSESSIVE–COMPULSIVE SPECTRUM

MARGARET S. ANDOVER AND BLAIR W. MORRIS

Both suicidal and nonsuicidal self-injury are alarmingly prevalent in clinical and nonclinical samples. Suicide is the 11th leading cause of death in the United States and the second leading cause of death for individuals ages 25 to 34 years (Centers for Disease Control and Prevention, 2007). Suicide attempts occur more frequently than suicide deaths; there are approximately 25 suicide attempts for each suicide death (Goldsmith, Pellmar, Kleinman, & Bunney, 2002). Nearly 3% of a nationally representative sample of individuals ages 15 to 54 years reported a suicide attempt. Nearly 4% reported having a suicide plan, and 13.5% reported suicidal ideation (Kessler, Borges, & Walters, 1999; Nock & Kessler, 2006). Although the emotional and economic consequences of attempted suicide alone merit attention for this significant public health problem, a history of suicide attempts has been shown to be the strongest predictor of future suicidal behavior (Joiner et al., 2005), reinforcing the need for identification and clinical intervention.

http://dx.doi.org/10.1037/14323-013
Obsessive–Compulsive Disorder and Its Spectrum: A Life-Span Approach, Eric A. Storch and Dean McKay (Editors)
Copyright © 2014 by the American Psychological Association. All rights reserved.

241

Nonsuicidal self-injury (NSSI) refers to the direct or deliberate destruction of one's own body tissue in the absence of suicidal intent. It includes behaviors such as cutting, scratching, skin picking, interfering with wound healing, and carving words, designs, or symbols into the skin. Research indicates that 21% to 45% of clinical samples report a history of NSSI (Andover & Gibb, 2010; Briere & Gil, 1998; Nijman et al., 1999; Zlotnick, Mattia, & Zimmerman, 1999). The behavior is especially prevalent among young adults and adolescents (Jacobson & Gould, 2007), with up to 40% of adolescent inpatients reporting a history of the behavior (Rodham & Hawton, 2009). NSSI also occurs frequently in the community (Andover, Pepper, Ryabchenko, Orrico, & Gibb, 2005; Hooley, Ho, Slater, & Lockshin, 2010; Klonsky, Oltmanns, & Turkheimer, 2003; Whitlock, Eckenrode, & Silverman, 2006). Studies have shown that up to 38% of young adults engage in NSSI at least once in their lifetimes (Gratz, Conrad, & Roemer, 2002). NSSI is repetitive and chronic (Briere & Gil, 1998; Muehlenkamp, 2005; Suyemoto, 1998); 18% of young adults report having engaged in NSSI more than 10 times, and 10% report having engaged in NSSI more than 100 times (Gratz et al., 2002). Emotion regulation is the most commonly reported function of NSSI (Klonsky, 2007), suggesting that NSSI is most often performed with the intent to alleviate negative emotions. However, NSSI is associated with significant negative consequences, such as physical injury, scarring, social stigma, guilt, shame, and social isolation (Gratz, 2003). NSSI behaviors are likely to increase in risk or lethality over time, including more severe injuries and possible death (Briere & Gil, 1998; Joiner, 2005; Stanley, Gameroff, Venezia, & Mann, 2001; Stellrecht et al., 2006). These factors highlight the importance of identifying and treating NSSI.

Attempted suicide and NSSI are significant clinical and public health problems that are often reported among individuals with anxiety disorders, including obsessive–compulsive disorder (OCD). Therefore, the purpose of this chapter is to review the current literature on the associations of suicide and NSSI with OCD and obsessive–compulsive spectrum disorders (OCSDs).

SUICIDE AND OCD

Little research on suicidal thoughts and behaviors among individuals with OCD exists. This may be because individuals with OCD are considered to be at particularly low risk for suicide on the basis of early reports of low prevalence of suicide deaths within the disorder (Goodwin, Guze, & Robins, 1969). However, more recent research indicates that a significant percentage of patients with anxiety disorders experience suicidal ideation and attempt suicide (Simeon & Hollander, 2006). Specifically, recent prevalence rates suggest that suicidality is more common in OCD than previously thought. Nearly 30% of individuals with a history of attempted suicide and 8% of those reporting suicidal ideation meet diagnostic criteria for OCD specifically (Kessler, Berglund, Borges, Nock, & Wang, 2005). Although prevalence rates vary, researchers have reported that suicide attempts are more common among individuals with OCD than among the general population. Some studies have shown that between 7% and 15% of individuals diagnosed with OCD report a history of attempted suicide (Alonso et al., 2010; Hollander et al., 1996; Sareen et al., 2005; Torres et al., 2007, 2011). However, other studies have reported even higher rates of attempted suicide among individuals with OCD. Between 10% and 25% of individuals with OCD endorse a history of attempted suicide (Angst et al., 2004; Torres et al., 2006, 2007, 2011). Rates of suicidal ideation among individuals with OCD are even higher. Approximately 60% of individuals with OCD report suicidal ideation in their lifetimes (Kamath, Reddy, & Kandavel, 2007; Torres et al., 2006, 2007, 2011), and up to 28% of patients with OCD report current suicidal ideation (Kamath et al., 2007; Torres et al., 2011).

Compared with individuals with other psychiatric diagnoses, patients diagnosed with OCD report similar levels of suicidal ideation, suicide threats, and suicide gestures (Apter et al., 2003). However, individuals with OCD are significantly less likely to attempt suicide than patients with other psychiatric diagnoses (Apter et al., 2003). Despite that finding, they report more suicidality than individuals without a psychiatric disorder (Hollander et al., 1996; Shoval, Zalsman, Sher, Apter, & Weizman, 2006). The high rate of suicide attempts among individuals with OCD warrants clinical attention.

Although individuals with primary OCD may be less likely to attempt suicide than those with other psychiatric disorders, comorbid OCD may increase the risk of attempted suicide among persons with an additional psychiatric disorder. Psychiatric patients with comorbid OCD report a significantly higher rate of attempted suicide than individuals with other psychiatric disorders; this finding is independent of other psychiatric disorders that have been linked with attempted suicide, such as major depressive disorder and agoraphobia (Hollander et al., 1996). Similar findings were reported among patients with bipolar disorder; 70% of those with comorbid OCD reported a history of suicide attempts, whereas 56% of patients with another comorbid anxiety disorder and 35% of patients with no anxiety comorbidity endorsed a suicide attempt history (Magalhães, Kapczinski, & Kapczinski, 2010). Similarly, individuals with clinical or subclinical OCD and a comorbid anxiety and/or bipolar disorder were up to 10 times more likely to report a suicide attempt than those with clinical or subclinical OCD alone (Angst et al., 2005). These findings suggest that although patients with OCD alone may be less likely to report a history of suicide attempts than other psychiatric patients, those with comorbid OCD may actually be more likely to attempt suicide.

Some researchers have specifically investigated the association between depression and suicidal behavior among individuals with OCD, yielding mixed, and potentially controversial, findings. Consistent with research on suicide, Kamath et al. (2007) found depression and hopelessness to be associated with suicidal behavior in individuals diagnosed with OCD, and Torres et al. (2007) found severity of depressive symptoms among individuals with OCD to be associated with past and current suicidal ideation and history of suicide attempts. However, other researchers have reported a negative correlation between depression and suicidal ideation among individuals with OCD. Specifically, Apter and colleagues (2003) found that suicidal ideation increased as levels of depressive symptoms decreased, leading the authors to suggest that depressive symptoms may be a protective factor against suicidal behavior among individuals with OCD. This finding is counterintuitive, given that individuals with comorbid major depression and OCD report more severe psychopathology, including increased obsessive–compulsive (OC) symptoms, depression, and anxiety (e.g., Quarantini et al., 2011). Further research is necessary to interpret Apter and colleagues' (2003) finding.

Individuals with OCD are more likely to report a suicide attempt than individuals without a psychiatric disorder (Hollander et al., 1996; Shoval et al., 2006), and OCD is associated with increased risk of suicidal ideation and suicide attempts over time (Kamath et al., 2007; Sareen et al., 2005). Findings are mixed regarding the association between OCD severity and suicidality. Although Kamath and colleagues (2007) found that the severity of OCD symptoms was higher among individuals with histories of suicidal ideation and suicide attempts, they did not find OCD symptom severity to be a significant risk factor for suicidality. However, Balci and Sevincok (2010) and Torres et al. (2007) did find that OCD severity significantly predicted suicidal ideation in their sample. Furthermore, severity of obsessions was found to be associated with lifetime and current suicidal ideation, and severity of compulsions was associated with current suicidal ideation (Torres et al., 2007). Regardless of OCD severity, assessment of suicide risk is important; Angst et al. (2004) found that subclinical OCD is also associated with increased suicide risk.

Researchers have begun to investigate demographic and clinical factors that are associated with increased risk of suicidal thoughts and behaviors among individuals with OCD. Alonso et al. (2010) found that being unmarried, having higher levels of depression at baseline, and having a comorbid diagnosis of either a current or past affective disorder significantly predicted the incidence of suicidal behaviors among individuals with OCD over a 6-year follow-up period. Specific characteristics of OCD are also associated with suicidality. Specifically, symmetry and ordering obsessions were associated with incidence of suicidality over a 6-year follow-up period (Alonso et al., 2010), and religious obsessions and reassurance seeking and repeating compulsions were higher among OCD patients with a suicide attempt history than without (Kamath et al., 2007). The similar suicide risk between symmetry and ordering obsessions and religious obsessions is noteworthy because research suggests that religious obsessions may be more difficult to treat than symmetry and ordering obsessions (Rufer, Fricke, Moritz, Kloss, & Hand, 2006). An individual's response to treatment for OCD may also be associated with suicidal behavior; research has shown that individuals with suicidal behaviors are more likely than those without to have had an initial response to treatment, followed by a relapse of OCD symptoms (Alonso et al., 2010). Use of antidepressants in the treatment of OCD does not appear to increase the risk of suicidal ideation or behaviors (Beasley et al., 1992; Bridge et al., 2007).

The OC spectrum includes disorders of impulsivity and compulsivity, which are thought to be associated through deficits in behavior regulation and through similar features, including repetitive thoughts and behaviors and similar response to treatment (Abramowitz, Storch, McKay, Taylor, & Asmundson, 2009; Hollander & Rosen, 2000; McKay & Neziroglu, 2009; Phillips et al., 2010). Disorders that comprise OCSDs include OCD, body dysmorphic disorder (BDD), trichotillomania, compulsive hoarding, and hypochondriasis. Research on the association between suicide and OCSDs is scant, with the exception of the limited body of research on suicidality and BDD. Researchers have reported high rates of suicidal thoughts and behaviors among patients with BDD. Nearly 80% of patients with BDD report suicidal ideation during their lifetimes, and nearly 30% report a history of attempted suicide (Phillips, 2007; Phillips et al., 2005). More than half report suicidal ideation in the past year, and 2.6% report a suicide attempt in the past year (Phillips & Menard, 2006). Among BDD patients with a history of suicidal thoughts or behaviors, more than 75% report that BDD was the primary reason for their suicidal ideation, and half report that BDD was the primary reason for their suicide attempt (Phillips et al., 2005). Researchers are beginning to examine the factors associated with increased suicidality in BDD. Witte, Didie, Menard, and Phillips (2012) investigated whether the physically painful behaviors performed by individuals with BDD increased the acquired capability for suicide, a necessary factor for lethal suicidal behavior as posed by Joiner et al. (2005). They found that BDD-related restricted food intake was associated with suicide attempts but not suicidal ideation, suggesting a possible mechanism for the association between suicidal behaviors and this specific OCSD.

Research has shown that NSSI does not occur exclusively in the context of a psychiatric disorder and does not alone indicate existing psychopathology. In fact, the behavior can occur across psychiatric disorders (Briere & Gil, 1998; Nock, 2009; Nock, Joiner, Gordon, Lloyd-Richardson, & Prinstein, 2006; Zlotnick et al., 1999). A significant number of individuals who engage in NSSI meet criteria for an anxiety disorder (e.g., Jacobson, Muehlenkamp, Miller, & Turner, 2008; Nock et al., 2006), and increased levels of anxiety have been found among individuals with a history of NSSI (e.g., Andover et al., 2005; Bennum & Phil, 1983; Klonsky et al., 2003; Penn, Esposito, Schaeffer, Fritz, & Spirito, 2003; Ross & Heath, 2002). However, few researchers have investigated the relationship between NSSI and OCD, and even fewer have investigated the association between NSSI and OCSDs. To the best of our knowledge, only one study has specifically investigated NSSI among individuals with OCD. Garrison et al. (1993) found that among a community sample of adolescents, individuals diagnosed with OCD were almost 5.3 times more likely to engage in NSSI than those without OCD, suggesting a link between the disorders.

Little research has been conducted on the association between NSSI and OCSDs; existing research focuses on NSSI's association with BDD and trichotillomania. Among a sample of patients with borderline personality disorder, those with BDD reported significantly more episodes of NSSI and NSSI of a longer duration than those without BDD (Semiz et al., 2008). Research on the association between NSSI and trichotillomania is complex because trichotillomania is thought by some to represent a form of NSSI (Favazza, 1998). Stanley, Winchel, Molcho, Simeon, and Stanley (1992) proposed that trichotillomania and NSSI exist on a self-harm continuum, with trichotillomania at the less severe and suicidal behavior at the more severe ends. Considering NSSI an OCSD, Lochner and colleagues (2005) suggested that NSSI and trichotillomania represent two distinct dimensions of OCSDs (impulsivity and reward deficiency, respectively). One study to date has investigated self-injury among individuals with trichotillomania. Simeon, Cohen, Stein, Schmeidler, and Spadaccini (1997) reported that more than half of their sample of individuals with trichotillomania engaged in self-injury. Comorbid self-injury and trichotillomania was associated with more severe depressive symptoms and histories of suicidality, suggesting that a history of both behaviors is associated with greater psychopathology than trichotillomania alone.

Although the association between NSSI and OCD has received little attention, researchers have investigated a specific method of NSSI, self-injurious skin picking. Also called psychogenic excoriation, pathological skin picking, or compulsive skin picking, this method of NSSI involves excessive scratching, picking, digging or gouging of the skin that leads to tissue damage associated with significant distress or impairment (Arnold, Auchenbach, & McElroy, 2001; Grant, Odlaug, & Won Kim, 2010; Hayes, Storch, & Berlanga, 2009). Tissue damage from skin picking can be severe; in a sample of individuals who engaged in skin picking, number of visible lesions ranged from few to more than 100, and the majority reported scarring from their injuries. More than 60% reported infections, and 45% reported "deep craters" as a result of their skin picking (Wilhelm et al., 1999). Like NSSI, skin picking results in shame and social isolation. Nearly 60% of Wilhelm et al.'s (1999) sample reported that they avoided social situations because of their skin picking and appearance, and more than 80% reported using clothing or cosmetics to cover scars and lesions. Rates of skin picking have ranged from 1.4% to 5.4% of community samples (Hayes et al., 2009; Keuthen et al., 2000; Keuthen, Koran, Aboujaoude, Large, & Serpe, 2010) and 11.8% of adolescent psychiatric samples (Grant, Williams & Potenza, 2007). Although self-injurious skin picking may be performed automatically, it is often used to lessen feelings of tension, anxiety, and frustration, with the individual reporting relief upon completion of the act (Arnold et al., 1998; Deckersbach, Wilhelm, & Keuthen, 2003; Stein, Hutt, Spitz, & Hollander, 1993), making the behavior consistent with other methods of NSSI.

Although the association between OCD and NSSI has been little investigated, there has been more research on the association between OCD and self-injurious skin picking by comparison. Approximately half of individuals with self-injurious skin picking met criteria for an OCD diagnosis (Çalikuşu, Yücel, Polat, & Baykal, 2003; Wilhelm et al., 1999). Self-injurious skin picking is prevalent among individuals with OCD; more than 15% of individuals with OCD report self-injurious skin picking (Lovato et al., 2012). Research has shown that self-injurious skin picking is significantly greater among individuals with OCD than among those without OCD (Cullen et al., 2001). Furthermore, body-focused repetitive behaviors, which often include self-injurious skin picking, trichotillomania, and severe nail biting (Stein et al., 2007; Teng, Woods, Twohig, & Marcks, 2002), are more common among individuals with OCD than individuals with either social anxiety disorder or panic disorder (Lochner & Stein, 2010). However, individuals with a history of skin picking are also significantly more likely to have other Axis I diagnoses, such as BDD or recurrent major depression (Cullen et al., 2001), suggesting that the behavior does not occur exclusively within the context of OCD.

Research has indicated several similarities between NSSI and OC characteristics. For example, some individuals who skin pick report obsessions about skin irregularities or preoccupations with smooth skin and skin pick in response to these thoughts (Arnold et al., 2001). In addition, self-injurious skin picking is often repetitive and ritualistic, as are compulsions in OCD (Stein et al., 1993). Research suggests that there may also be similarities between the functions of NSSI and compulsive behaviors. Although NSSI may be performed for automatic or social reinforcement (Nock & Prinstein, 2004, 2005), emotion regulation (i.e., automatic negative reinforcement) is the most commonly reported function of NSSI (e.g., Klonsky, 2007), suggesting that NSSI is most often performed with the intent to alleviate negative emotions. Automatic negative reinforcement is thought to be the primary means by which NSSI is maintained; those who engage in the behavior experience a relief of tension and negative emotional states (Nock & Prinstein, 2004). Self-injurious skin picking, the focus of much research regarding OCD, is used to reduce feelings of tension, anxiety, and frustration, and individuals often report relief after skin picking (Arnold et al., 1998; Deckersbach et al., 2003; Stein et al., 1993). Compulsions are similarly performed to reduce or eliminate the distress associated with obsessions (Abramowitz, McKay, & Taylor, 2008). Compulsions are frequently performed automatically with the goal of decreasing distress or anxiety, although this may differ based on the type of compulsion (Starcevic et al., 2011). Some compulsions are performed with the goal of preventing a negative outcome, which would be less consistent with the functions of NSSI.

Similarities between NSSI and OCD, as well as the association between NSSI and impulsivity (Glenn & Klonsky, 2010; Herpertz, Sass, & Favazza, 1997; Herpertz, Steinmeyer, Marx, Oidtmann, & Sass, 1995; Janis & Nock, 2009), have led some researchers to consider the behavior as part of the OC spectrum (Hollander & Rosen, 2000; Lochner et al., 2005; Lochner & Stein, 2010; Stein et al., 2010; see also McKay & Andover, 2012). Arnold et al. (2001) proposed diagnostic criteria for psychogenic excoriation, noting three subtypes of self-injurious skin picking: impulsive, compulsive, and mixed impulsive and compulsive. The authors suggested that impulsive self-injurious skin picking serves to reduce feelings of tension and may be associated with an experience of pleasure or arousal. It is performed with little awareness or resistance, and individuals have little insight into the irrational nature of the behavior or its potential negative consequences. Compulsive self-injurious skin picking, in contrast, is performed in an effort to avoid anxiety or in reaction to an obsession. Unlike impulsive skin picking, compulsive skin picking is performed with full awareness and may be associated with some degree of attempted resistance on the part of the individual engaging the behavior. The authors proposed that individuals engaging in compulsive skin picking have some insight into the irrational and harmful nature of the behavior.

Although Arnold et al.'s (2001) proposal focused on self-injurious skin picking, compulsivity is evident in the habitual and repetitive nature of NSSI (Simeon, Stein, & Hollander, 1995), whereas pleasurable feelings and lack of control associated with the behavior are suggestive of impulsivity (Wilhelm et al., 1999). Therefore, impulsive and compulsive subtypes have been proposed for NSSI more broadly. As conceptualized by Favazza and Simeon (1995), impulsive NSSI is episodic, is triggered by external events, and includes behaviors such as cutting or burning. Compulsive NSSI, however, is repetitive and habitual, with attempts to resist the behavior, and includes behaviors such as skin picking and hair pulling. Although impulsive and compulsive subtypes of NSSI have been theorized, they have not yet been formally assessed or applied to NSSI research. However, some research on NSSI has been consistent with these theorized subtypes. Specifically, Croyle and Waltz (2007) compared mildly injurious NSSI (i.e., self-injurious skin picking, severe nail biting) with moderately injurious NSSI (i.e., cutting, carving, hitting, burning) on several clinical factors. The researchers reported that although both mildly and moderately injurious NSSI were associated with some OC characteristics (i.e., impulsivity, rumination, and precision), moderately injurious NSSI was more strongly associated with impulsivity than mildly injurious NSSI. Although these findings do not confirm the concept of impulsive and compulsive subtypes of NSSI, they do suggest that additional research in this area is warranted.

Although research supports an association between OCD and NSSI, specifically self-injurious skin picking, researchers have also provided support for OCD and NSSI as separate disorders. Self-injurious skin picking is associated with OCD, but individuals with self-injurious skin picking also report other comorbid diagnoses, including BDD (32%), major depression (26%), dysthymia (23%), bulimia nervosa (19%), and generalized anxiety disorder (16%; Wilhelm et al., 1999). Grant et al. (2010) compared clinical characteristics and psychiatric comorbidities in two groups: individuals with a diagnosis of OCD alone and individuals with a history of skin picking alone. The researchers found that individuals with OCD were more likely to have comorbid diagnoses of BDD than those with skin picking, whereas individuals with skin picking reported higher rates of trichotillomania and compulsive nail biting. Researchers have suggested that body-focused repetitive behaviors, which can include self-injurious skin picking, have more in common with disorders of impulse control than with OCD (Keuthen, Bohne, Himle, & Woods, 2005). Grant et al. (2010) also found that individuals with OCD reported spending significantly more time on OCD-related thoughts and behaviors that those with self-injurious skin picking alone. Consistent with these findings, Hollander, Braun, and Simeon (2008) suggested that only a mild association exists between self-injurious skin picking and OC-related disorders (OCRDs). Whereas compulsions aim to neutralize obsessions and associated distress in OCD (Wilhelm et al., 1999), the primary function of NSSI is to regulate emotions (Nock & Prinstein, 2004), suggesting that the behaviors may be performed for different reasons. McKay and Andover (2012) reviewed the evidence for and against the inclusion of NSSI as an OCRD, concluding that although the similarities between NSSI and OCRDs merits further investigation, research indicates that NSSI should be conceptualized as distinct from OCRDs. The clinical differences and the lack of overlap in comorbid disorders (e.g., Grant et al., 2010; Hollander et al., 2008; McKay & Andover, 2012) suggest that OCD and skin picking may be associated but should be conceptualized as distinct constructs.

TREATMENT AND CLINICAL IMPLICATIONS

Individuals with OCD report more suicidality than those without a psychiatric diagnosis (e.g., Hollander et al., 1996; Shoval et al., 2006), and suicidal thoughts and behaviors have been associated with BDD, a specific OCRD (e.g., Phillips, 2007). Similarly, increased rates of NSSI have been found for adolescents with versus without OCD (Garrison et al., 1993), and a specific type of NSSI, skin picking, has been suggested as an OCRD (i.e., Stein et al., 2010). Therefore, clinicians working with individuals with OCD or OCRDs should be especially vigilant for self-injurious behaviors. Clinicians should assess for a history of and current suicidal and nonsuicidal thoughts and behaviors (i.e., Andover, Morris, Schatten, & Kelly, 2013; Walsh, 2007), and the self-injurious behaviors should be addressed directly in psychotherapy. Although a review of treatments for self-injurious behaviors is beyond the scope of this chapter, several promising or effective interventions have been identified for the prevention of self-injury, including cognitive behavior therapy, dialectical behavior therapy, and interpersonal therapy (for a review, see Comtois & Linehan, 2006). Interventions need not require inpatient treatment; Comtois and Linehan (2006) stated that outpatient treatment for self-injury may in fact be more efficacious. A successful intervention would also address the potential for treatment noncompliance because this has been shown to be an important factor in several trials focused on the prevention of suicidal behaviors (i.e., Comtois & Linehan, 2006).

CONCLUSION

Research on the association between OCD and self-injurious behaviors, including attempted suicide and NSSI, has been limited. However, existing research suggests that the area merits further consideration. Although individuals with OCD may attempt suicide at a lower rate than individuals with other psychiatric disorders, the rates are much higher than those found among community samples. Suicide is a significant problem among individuals with OCD, and research is necessary to identify risk factors for suicide in OCD and to better understand the role of OCD in the association between psychiatric comorbidity and suicide. Similarly, little research has investigated the association between NSSI and OCD. However, the research on a specific method of NSSI, self-injurious skin picking, suggests that an association does exist. The nature of the behavior has led to the inclusion of a skin-picking disorder diagnosis (called excoriation disorder) under OCRDs in the fifth edition of the *Diagnostic and Statistical Manual of Mental Disorders* (American Psychiatric Association, 2010, 2013; Stein et al., 2010). Although others have argued that the current evidence does not support this classification (McKay & Andover, 2012), future research is necessary to better understand the similarities and differences between NSSI and OCD, as well as the utility of conceptualizing NSSI as part of the OC spectrum. Clinically, the high prevalence of suicidality, including suicidal ideation and attempted suicide, and NSSI among individuals with OCD mandates the need for specific assessment of self-injury in this population.

REFERENCES

Abramowitz, J. S., McKay, D., & Taylor, S. (2008). *Obsessive–compulsive disorder: Subtypes and spectrum conditions.* Amsterdam, the Netherlands: Elsevier.

Abramowitz, J. S., Storch, E. A., McKay, D., Taylor, S., & Asmundson, G. J. (2009). The obsessive–compulsive spectrum: A critical review. In D. Mckay, J. S. Abramowitz, S. Taylor, & G. J. Asmundson (Eds.), *Current perspectives on the anxiety disorders: Implications for DSM–V and beyond* (pp. 329–352). New York, NY: Springer.

Alonso, P., Segalàs, C., Real, E., Pertusa, A., Labad, J., Jiménez-Murcia, S., . . . Menchón, J. M. (2010). Suicide in patients treated for obsessive–compulsive disorder: A prospective follow-up study. *Journal of Affective Disorders, 124,* 300–308. doi:10.1016/j.jad.2009.12.001

American Psychiatric Association. (2010). *DSM–5 development: F 04 Skin Picking Disorder.* Retrieved from http://www.dsm5.org/ProposedRevision/Pages/proposedrevision.aspx?rid=401

American Psychiatric Association. (2013). *Diagnostic and statistical manual of mental disorders* (5th ed.). Washington, DC: Author.

Andover, M. S., & Gibb, B. E. (2010). Non-suicidal self-injury, attempted suicide, and suicidal intent among psychiatric inpatients. *Psychiatry Research, 178,* 101–105. doi:10.1016/j.psychres.2010.03.019

Andover, M. S., Morris, B. W., Schatten, H. T., & Kelly, C. A. (2013). Assessment of suicidal and non-suicidal self-injury in anxiety disorders (pp. 119–138). In

D. McKay & E. Storch (Eds.), *Handbook of assessing variants and complications in anxiety disorders*. New York, NY: Springer. doi:10.1007/978-1-4614-6452-5_9

Andover, M. S., Pepper, C. M., Ryabchenko, K. A., Orrico, E. G., & Gibb, B. E. (2005). Self-mutilation and symptoms of depression, anxiety, and borderline personality disorder. *Suicide and Life-Threatening Behavior, 35*, 581–591. doi:10.1521/suli.2005.35.5.581

Angst, J., Gamma, A., Endrass, J., Goodwin, R., Ajdacic, V., Eich, D., & Rössler, W. (2004). Obsessive–compulsive severity spectrum in the community: Prevalence, comorbidity, and course. *European Archives of Psychiatry and Clinical Neuroscience, 254*, 156–164. doi:10.1007/s00406-004-0459-4

Angst, J., Gamma, A., Endrass, J., Hantouche, E., Goodwin, R., Ajdacic, V., . . . Rössler, W. (2005). Obsessive–compulsive syndromes and disorders: Significance of comorbidity with bipolar and anxiety syndromes. *European Archives of Psychiatry and Clinical Neuroscience, 255*, 65–71. doi:10.1007/s00406-005-0576-8

Apter, A., Horesh, N., Gothelf, D., Zalsman, G., Erlich, Z., Soreni, N., & Weizman, A. (2003). Depression and suicidal behavior in adolescent inpatients with obsessive–compulsive disorder. *Journal of Affective Disorders, 75*, 181–189. doi:10.1016/S0165-0327(02)00038-1

Arnold, L. M., Auchenbach, M. B., & McElroy, S. L. (2001). Psychogenic excoriation: Clinical features, proposed diagnostic criteria, epidemiology and approaches to treatment. *CNS Drugs, 15*, 351–359. doi:10.2165/00023210-200115050-00002

Arnold, L. M., McElroy, S. L., Mutasim, D. F., Dwight, M. M., Lamerson, C. L., & Morris, E. M. (1998). Characteristics of 34 adults with psychogenic excoriation. *The Journal of Clinical Psychiatry, 59*, 509–514. doi:10.4088/JCP.v59n1003

Balci, V., & Sevincok, L. (2010). Suicidal ideation in patients with obsessive–compulsive disorder. *Psychiatry Research, 175*, 104–108. doi:10.1016/j.psychres.2009.03.012

Beasley, C. M., Potvin, J. H., Masica, D. N., Wheadon, D. E., Dornseif, B. E., & Genduso, L. A. (1992). Fluoxetine: No association with suicidality in obsessive–compulsive disorder. *Journal of Affective Disorders, 24*, 1–10. doi:10.1016/0165-0327(92)90054-A

Bennum, I., & Phil, M. (1983). Depression and hostility in self-mutilation. *Suicide and Life-Threatening Behavior, 13*, 71–84.

Bridge, J. A., Iyengar, S., Salary, C. B., Barbe, R. P., Birmaher, B., Pincus, H. A., . . . Brent, D. A. (2007). Clinical response and risk for reported suicidal ideation and suicide attempts in pediatric antidepressant treatment: A meta-analysis of randomized controlled trials. *JAMA, 297*, 1683–1696. doi:10.1001/jama.297.15.1683

Briere, J., & Gil, E. (1998). Self-mutilation in clinical and general population samples: Prevalence, correlates, and functions. *American Journal of Orthopsychiatry, 68*, 609–620. doi:10.1037/h0080369

Çalikuşu, C., Yücel, B., Polat, A., & Baykal, C. (2003). The relation of psychogenic excoriation with psychiatric disorders: A comparative study. *Comprehensive Psychiatry, 44*, 256–261. doi:10.1016/S0010-440X(03)00041-5

Centers for Disease Control and Prevention, National Center for Injury Prevention and Control. (2007). *Web-based Injury Statistics Query and Reporting System (WISQARS)*. Retrieved from http://www.cdc.gov/ncipc/wisqars

Comtois, K. A., & Linehan, M. M. (2006). Psychosocial treatments of suicidal behaviors: A practice-friendly review. *Journal of Clinical Psychology, 62*, 161–170. doi:10.1002/jclp.20220

Croyle, K. L., & Waltz, J. (2007). Subclinical self-harm: Range of behaviors, extent, and associated characteristics. *American Journal of Orthopsychiatry, 77*, 332–342. doi:10.1037/0002-9432.77.2.332

Cullen, B. A., Samuels, J. F., Bienvenu, O. J., Grados, M., Hoehn-Saric, R., Hahn, J., & Nestadt, G. (2001). The relationship of pathologic skin picking to obsessive–compulsive disorder. *Journal of Nervous and Mental Disease, 189*, 193–195. doi:10.1097/00005053-200103000-00010

Deckersbach, T., Wilhelm, S., & Keuthen, N. (2003). Self-injurious skin picking: Clinical characteristics, assessment methods, and treatment modalities. *Brief Treatment and Crisis Intervention, 3*, 249–260. doi:10.1093/brief-treatment/mhg018

Favazza, A. R. (1998). The coming of age of self-mutilation. *Journal of Nervous and Mental Disease, 186*, 259–268. doi:10.1097/00005053-199805000-00001

Favazza, A. R., & Simeon, D. (1995). Self-mutilation. In E. Hollander & D. J. Stein (Eds.), *Impulsivity and aggression* (pp. 185–200). Oxford, England: Wiley.

Garrison, C. Z., Addy, C. L., McKeown, R. E., Cuffe, S. P., Jackson, K. L., & Waller, J. L. (1993). Nonsuicidal physically self-damaging acts in adolescents. *Journal of Child and Family Studies, 2*, 339–352. doi:10.1007/BF01321230

Glenn, C. R., & Klonsky, E. D. (2010). A multimethod analysis of impulsivity in non-suicidal self-injury. *Personality Disorders: Theory, Research, and Treatment, 1*, 67–75. doi:10.1037/a0017427

Goldsmith, S. K., Pellmar, T. C., Kleinman, A. M., & Bunney, W. E. (2002). *Reducing suicide: A national imperative*. Washington, DC: National Academy Press.

Goodwin, D. W., Guze, S. B., & Robins, E. (1969). Follow-up studies in obsessional neurosis. *Archives of General Psychiatry, 20*, 182–187. doi:10.1001/archpsyc.1969.01740140054006

Grant, J. E., Odlaug, B. L., & Won Kim, S. (2010). A clinical comparison of pathologic skin picking and obsessive–compulsive disorder. *Comprehensive Psychiatry, 51*, 347–352. doi:10.1016/j.comppsych.2009.10.006

Grant, J. E., Williams, K. A., & Potenza, M. N. (2007). Impulse-control disorders in adolescent psychiatric inpatients: Co-occurring disorders and sex differences. *The Journal of Clinical Psychiatry, 68*, 1584–1592. doi:10.4088/JCP.v68n1018

Gratz, K. L. (2003). Risk factors for and functions of deliberate self-harm: An empirical and conceptual review. *Clinical Psychology: Science and Practice, 10*, 192–205. doi:10.1093/clipsy.bpg022

Gratz, K. L., Conrad, S. D., & Roemer, L. (2002). Risk factors for deliberate self-harm among college students. *American Journal of Orthopsychiatry, 72*, 128–140. doi:10.1037/0002-9432.72.1.128

Hayes, S. L., Storch, E. A., & Berlanga, L. (2009). Skin picking behaviors: An examination of the prevalence and severity in a community sample. *Journal of Anxiety Disorders, 23*, 314–319. doi:10.1016/j.janxdis.2009.01.008

Herpertz, S., Sass, H., & Favazza, A. R. (1997). Impulsivity in self-mutilative behavior: Psychometric and biological findings. *Journal of Psychiatric Research, 31*, 451–465. doi:10.1016/S0022-3956(97)00004-6

Herpertz, S., Steinmeyer,, S. M., Marx, D., Oidtmann, A., & Sass, H. (1995). The significance of aggression and impulsivity for self-mutilative behavior. *Pharmacopsychiatry, 28*, 64–72. doi: 10.1055/s-2007-979622

Hollander, E., Braun, A., & Simeon, D. (2008). Should OCD leave the anxiety disorders in *DSM–V?* The case for obsessive compulsive–related disorders. *Depression and Anxiety, 25*, 317–329. doi:10.1002/da.20500

Hollander, E., Greenwald, S., Neville, D., Johnson, J., Hornig, C. D., & Weissman, M. M. (1996). Uncomplicated and comorbid obsessive–compulsive disorder in an epidemiologic sample. *Depression and Anxiety, 4*, 111–119. doi:10.1002/(SICI)1520-6394(1996)4:3<111::AID-DA3>3.0.CO;2-J

Hollander, E., & Rosen, J. (2000). Obsessive–compulsive spectrum disorders: A review. In M. Maj, N. Sartorius, A. Okasha, & J. Zohar (Eds.), *Obsessive–compulsive disorder* (pp. 203–252). Chichester, England: Wiley. doi:10.1002/0470846496.ch5

Hooley, J. M., Ho, D. T., Slater, J., & Lockshin, A. (2010). Pain perception in nonsuicidal self-injury: A laboratory investigation. *Personality Disorders: Theory, Research, and Treatment, 1*, 170–179. doi:10.1037/a0020106

Jacobson, C. M., & Gould, M. (2007). The epidemiology and phenomenology of nonsuicidal self-injurious behavior among adolescents: A critical review of the literature. *Archives of Suicide Research, 11*, 129–147. doi:10.1080/13811110701247602

Jacobson, C. M., Muehlenkamp, J. J., Miller, A. L., & Turner, J. B. (2008). Psychiatric impairment among adolescents engaging in different types of deliberate self-harm. *Journal of Clinical Child & Adolescent Psychology, 37*, 363–375. doi:10.1080/15374410801955771

Janis, I. B., & Nock, M. K. (2009). Are self-injurers impulsive? Results from two behavioral laboratory studies. *Psychiatry Research, 169*, 261–267. doi:10.1016/j.psychres.2008.06.041

Joiner, T. (2005). *Why people die by suicide.* Cambridge, MA: Harvard University Press.

Joiner, T. E., Conwell, Y., Fitzpatrick, K. K., Witte, T. K., Schimdt, N. B., Berlim, M. T., . . . Rudd, M. D. (2005). Four studies on how past and current suicidality relate even when "everything but the kitchen sink" is covaried. *Journal of Abnormal Psychology, 114,* 291–303. doi:10.1037/0021-843X.114.2.291

Kamath, P., Reddy, Y. C. J., & Kandavel, T. (2007). Suicidal behavior in obsessive–compulsive disorder. *The Journal of Clinical Psychiatry, 68,* 1741–1750. doi: 10.4088/JCP.v68n1114

Kessler, R. C., Berglund, P., Borges, G., Nock, M., & Wang, P. S. (2005). Trends in suicide ideation, plans, gestures, and attempts in the United States, 1990–1992 to 2001–2003. *JAMA, 293,* 2487–2495. doi:10.1001/jama.293.20.2487

Kessler, R. C., Borges, G., & Walters, E. E. (1999). Prevalence and risk factors for lifetime suicide attempts in the national comorbidity survey. *Archives of General Psychiatry, 56,* 617–626. doi:10.1001/archpsyc.56.7.617

Keuthen, N. J., Bohne, A., Himle, M., & Woods, D. W. (2005). Advances in the conceptualization and treatment of body-focused repetitive behaviors. In B. E. Ling (Ed.), *Obsessive compulsive disorder research* (pp. 1–29). Hauppauge, NY: Nova Biomedical Books.

Keuthen, N. J., Deckersbach, T., Wilhelm, S., Hale, E., Fraim, C., Baer, L., & Jenike, M. A. (2000). Repetitive skin-picking in a student population and comparison with a sample of self-injurious skin-pickers. *Psychosomatics, 41,* 210–215. doi:10.1176/appi.psy.41.3.210

Keuthen, N. J., Koran, L. M., Aboujaoude, E., Large, M. D., & Serpe, R. T. (2010). The prevalence of pathologic skin picking in US adults. *Comprehensive Psychiatry, 51,* 183–186. doi:10.1016/j.comppsych.2009.04.003

Klonsky, E. D. (2007). The functions of deliberate self-injury: A review of the evidence. *Clinical Psychology Review, 27,* 226–239. doi:10.1016/j.cpr.2006.08.002

Klonsky, E. D., Oltmanns, T. F., & Turkheimer, E. (2003). Deliberate self-harm in a nonclinical population: Prevalence and psychological correlates. *The American Journal of Psychiatry, 160,* 1501–1508. doi:10.1176/appi.ajp.160.8.1501

Lochner, C., Hemmings, S. M., Kinnear, C. J., Niehaus, D. J., Nel, D. G., Corfield, V. A., . . . Stein, D. J. (2005). Cluster analysis of obsessive–compulsive spectrum disorders in patients with obsessive–compulsive disorder: Clinical and genetic correlates. *Comprehensive Psychiatry, 46,* 14–19. doi:10.1016/j.comppsych.2004.07.020

Lochner, C., & Stein, D. J. (2010). Obsessive–compulsive spectrum disorders in obsessive compulsive–disorder and other anxiety disorders. *Psychopathology, 43,* 389–396. doi:10.1159/000321070

Lovato, L., Arzeno Ferrao, Y., Stein, D. J., Shavitt, R. G., Fontenelle, L. F., & Vivan, A. . . . Cordioli, A. V. (2012). Skin picking and trichotillomania in adults with obsessive–compulsive disorder. *Comprehensive Psychiatry, 53,* 562–568.

Magalhães, P. V. S., Kapczinski, N. S., & Kapczinski, F. (2010). Correlates and impact of obsessive–compulsive comorbidity in bipolar disorder. *Comprehensive Psychiatry, 51,* 353–356. doi:10.1016/j.comppsych.2009.11.001

McKay, D., & Andover, M. (2012). Should nonsuicidal self-injury be a putative obsessive–compulsive-related condition? A critical appraisal. *Behavior Modification, 36*, 3–17. doi:10.1177/0145445511417707

McKay, D., & Neziroglu, F. (2009). Methodological issues in the obsessive–compulsive spectrum. *Psychiatry Research, 170*, 61–65. doi:10.1016/j.psychres.2009.01.004

Muehlenkamp, J. J. (2005). Self-injurious behavior as a separate clinical syndrome. *American Journal of Orthopsychiatry, 75*, 324–333. doi:10.1037/0002-9432.75.2.324

Nijman, H. L., Dautzenberg, M., Merckelbach, H. L., Jung, P., Wessel, I., & del Campo, J. A. (1999). Self-mutilating behaviour of psychiatric inpatients. *European Psychiatry, 14*, 4–10. doi:10.1016/S0924-9338(99)80709-3

Nock, M. K. (2009). Why do people hurt themselves? New insights into the nature and functions of self-injury. *Current Directions in Psychological Science, 18*, 78-83. doi:10.1111/j.1467-8721.2009.01613.x

Nock, M. K., Joiner, T. E., Jr., Gordon, K. H., Lloyd-Richardson, E., & Prinstein, M. J. (2006). Non-suicidal self-injury among adolescents: Diagnostic correlates and relation to suicide attempts. *Psychiatry Research, 144*, 65–72. doi:10.1016/j.psychres.2006.05.010

Nock, M. K., & Kessler, R. C. (2006). Prevalence of and risk factors for suicide attempts versus suicide gestures: Analysis of the National Comorbidity Survey. *Journal of Abnormal Psychology, 115*, 616–623. doi:10.1037/0021-843X.115.3.616

Nock, M. K., & Prinstein, M. J. (2004). A functional approach to the assessment of self- mutilative behavior. *Journal of Consulting and Clinical Psychology, 72*, 885–890. doi:10.1037/0022-006X.72.5.885

Nock, M. K., & Prinstein, M. J. (2005). Contextual features and behavioral functions of self-mutilation among adolescents. *Journal of Abnormal Psychology, 114*, 140–146. doi:10.1037/0021-843X.114.1.140

Penn, J. V., Esposito, C. L., Schaeffer, L. E., Fritz, G. K., & Spirito, A. (2003). Suicide attempts and self-mutilative behavior in a juvenile correctional facility. *Journal of the American Academy of Child & Adolescent Psychiatry, 42*, 762–769. doi:10.1097/01.CHI.0000046869.56865.46

Phillips, K. A. (2007). Suicidality in body dysmorphic disorder. *Primary Psychiatry, 14*, 58–66.

Phillips, K. A., Coles, M. E., Menard, W., Yen, S., Fay, C., & Weisberg, R. B. (2005). Suicidal ideation and suicide attempts in body dysmorphic disorder. *The Journal of Clinical Psychiatry, 66*, 717–725. doi:10.4088/JCP.v66n0607

Phillips, K. A., & Menard, W. (2006). Suicidality in body dysmorphic disorder: A prospective study. *The American Journal of Psychiatry, 163*, 1280–1282. doi:10.1176/appi.ajp.163.7.1280

Phillips, K. A., Stein, D. J., Rauch, S. L., Hollander, E., Fallon, B. A., Barsky, A., . . . Leckman, J. (2010). Should an obsessive–compulsive spectrum grouping of disorders be included in *DSM–V? Depression and Anxiety, 27,* 528–555. doi:10.1002/da.20705

Quarantini, L. C., Torres, A. R., Sampaio, A. S., Fossaluza, V., de Mathis, M. A., do Rosário, Fontenelle, L. F., . . . Koenen, K. C. (2011). Comorbid major depression in obsessive–compulsive disorder patients. *Comprehensive Psychiatry, 52,* 386–393. doi:10.1016/j.comppsych.2010.09.006

Rodham, K., & Hawton, K. (2009). Epidemiology and phenomenology of nonsuicidal self-injury. In M. K. Nock (Ed.), *Understanding nonsuicidal self-injury: Origins, assessment, and treatment* (pp. 37–62). Washington, DC: American Psychological Association. doi:10.1037/11875-003

Ross, S., & Heath, N. (2002). A study of the frequency of self-mutilation in a community sample of adolescents. *Journal of Youth and Adolescence, 31,* 67–77. doi:10.1023/A:1014089117419

Rufer, M., Fricke, S., Moritz, S., Kloss, M., & Hand, I. (2006). Symptom dimensions in obsessive–compulsive disorder: Prediction of cognitive-behavior therapy outcome. *Acta Psychiatrica Scandinavica, 113,* 440–446. doi:10.1111/j.1600-0447.2005.00682.x

Sareen, J., Cox, B. J., Afifi, T. O., de Graaf, R., Asmundson, G. J. G., ten Have, M., & Stein, M. B. (2005). Anxiety disorders and risk for suicidal ideation and suicide attempts: A population-based longitudinal study of adults. *Archives of General Psychiatry, 62,* 1249–1257. doi:10.1001/archpsyc.62.11.1249

Semiz, U., Basoglu, C., Cetin, M., Ebrinc, S., Uzun, O., & Ergun, B. (2008). Body dysmorphic disorder in patients with borderline personality disorder: Prevalence, clinical characteristics, and role of childhood trauma. *Acta Neuropsychiatrica, 20,* 33–40. doi:10.1111/j.1601-5215.2007.00231.x

Shoval, G., Zalsman, G., Sher, L., Apter, A., & Weizman, A. (2006). Clinical characteristics of inpatient adolescents with severe obsessive–compulsive disorder. *Depression and Anxiety, 23,* 62–70. doi:10.1002/da.20135

Simeon, D., Cohen, L. J., Stein, D. J., Schmeidler, J., & Spadaccini, E. (1997). Comorbid self-injurious behaviors in 71 female hair-pullers: A survey study. *Journal of Nervous and Mental Disease, 185,* 117–119. doi:10.1097/00005053-199702000-00009

Simeon, D., & Hollander, E. (2006). Anxiety Disorders. In R. I. Simon & R. E. Hales (Eds.), *Textbook of suicide assessment and management* (pp. 313–327). Washington, DC: American Psychiatric Publishing.

Simeon, D., Stein, D. J., & Hollander, E. (1995). Depersonalization disorder and self-injurious behavior. *The Journal of Clinical Psychiatry, 56,* 36–39.

Stanley, B., Gameroff, M. J., Venezia, M., & Mann, J. J. (2001). Are suicide attempters who self-mutilate a unique population? *The American Journal of Psychiatry, 158,* 427–432. doi:10.1176/appi.ajp.158.3.427

Stanley, B., Winchel, R., Molcho, A., Simeon, D., & Stanley, M. (1992). Suicide and the self-harm continuum: Phenomenological and biochemical evidence. *International Review of Psychiatry, 4,* 149–155. doi:10.3109/09540269209066312

Starcevic, V., Berle, D., Brakoulias, V., Sammut, P., Moses, K., Milicevic, D., & Hannan, A. (2011). Functions of compulsions in obsessive–compulsive disorder. *Australian and New Zealand Journal of Psychiatry, 45,* 449–457. doi:10.3109/00048674.2011.567243

Stein, D. J., Garner, J. P., Keuthen, N. J., Frankin, M. E., Walkup, J. T., & Woods, D. W. (2007). Trichotillomania, stereotypic movement disorder, and related disorders. *Current Psychiatry Reports, 9,* 301–302. doi:10.1007/s11920-007-0036-4

Stein, D. J., Grant, J. E., Franklin, M. E., Keuthen, N., Lochner, C., Singer, H. S., & Woods, D. W. (2010). Trichotillomania (hair pulling disorder), skin picking disorder, and stereotypic movement disorder: Toward *DSM–V. Depression and Anxiety, 27,* 611–626. doi:10.1002/da.20700

Stein, D. J., Hutt, C. S., Spitz, J. L., & Hollander, E. (1993). Compulsive picking and obsessive–compulsive disorder. *Psychosomatics, 34,* 177–181. doi:10.1016/S0033-3182(93)71911-8

Stellrecht, N. E., Gordon, K. H., Van Orden, K., Witte, T. K., Wingate, L. R., Cukrowicz, K. C., & Joiner, T. E., Jr. (2006). Clinical applications of the interpersonal-psychological theory of attempted and completed suicide. *Journal of Clinical Psychology, 62,* 211–222. doi:10.1002/jclp.20224

Suyemoto, K. L. (1998). The functions of self-mutilation. *Clinical Psychology Review, 18,* 531–554. doi:10.1016/S0272-7358(97)00105-0

Teng, E. J., Woods, D. W., Twohig, M. P., & Marcks, B. A. (2002). Body-focused repetitive behavior problems: Prevalence in a nonreferred population and differences in perceived somatic activity. *Behavior Modification, 26,* 340–360. doi:10.1177/0145445502026003003

Torres, A. R., de Abreu Ramos-Cerqueira, A. T. A., Torresan, R. C., de Souza Domingues, M. S., . . . Guimarães, A. B. (2007). Prevalence and associated factors for suicidal ideation and behaviors in obsessive–compulsive disorder. *CNS Spectrums, 12,* 771–778.

Torres, A. R., Prince, M. J., Bebbington, P. E., Bhugra, D., Brugha, T. S., Farrell, M., . . . Singleton, N. (2006). Obsessive–compulsive disorder: Prevalence, comorbidity, impact, and help-seeking in the British National Psychiatric Morbidity Survey of 2000. *The American Journal of Psychiatry, 163,* 1978–1985. doi:10.1176/appi.ajp.163.11.1978

Torres, A. R., Ramos-Cerqueira, A. T., Ferrão, Y. A., Fontenelle, L. F., do Rosário, M. C., & Miguel, E. C. (2011). Suicidality in obsessive–compulsive disorder: Prevalence and relation to symptom dimensions and comorbid conditions. *The Journal of Clinical Psychiatry, 72,* 17–26. doi:10.4088/JCP.09m05651blu

Walsh, B. (2007). Clinical assessment of self-injury: A practical guide. *Journal of Clinical Psychology, 63,* 1057–1068. doi: 10.1002/jclp.20413

Witte, T. K., Didie, E. R., Menard, W., & Phillips, K. A. (2012). The relationship between body dysmorphic disorder behaviors and the acquired capability for suicide. *Suicide and Life-Threatening Behaviors, 42,* 318–331. doi: 10.1111/j.1943-278X.2012.00093.x

Whitlock, J., Eckenrode, J., & Silverman, D. (2006). Self-injurious behaviors in a college population. *Pediatrics, 117*, 1939–1948. doi:10.1542/peds.2005-2543

Wilhelm, S., Keuthen, N. J., Deckersbach, T., Engelhard, I. M., Forker, A. E., Baer, L., & Jenike, M. A. (1999). Self-injurious skin picking: Clinical characteristics and comorbidity. *The Journal of Clinical Psychiatry, 60*, 454–459. doi:10.4088/JCP.v60n0707

Zlotnick, C., Mattia, J. I., & Zimmerman, M. (1999). Clinical correlates of self-mutilation in a sample of general psychiatric patients. *Journal of Nervous and Mental Disease, 187*, 296–301. doi:10.1097/00005053-199905000-00005

13

RESTRICTED REPETITIVE BEHAVIORS: CONNECTIONS BETWEEN AUTISM SPECTRUM AND OBSESSIVE–COMPULSIVE SPECTRUM DISORDERS

SUNDAY M. FRANCIS, SOO-JEONG KIM, AND SUMA JACOB

There is growing evidence demonstrating that autism spectrum disorders (ASDs) and obsessive–compulsive spectrum disorders (OCSDs) are both heterogeneous, related, spectrum disorders that can have devastating effects on individuals and families. Obsessive–compulsive disorder (OCD) is a neuropsychiatric disorder characterized by obsessions, compulsions, or both. *Obsessions* are clinically significant intrusive thoughts, impulses, or images that can cause marked anxiety and distress. *Compulsions* are defined as ritualistic and rigid behaviors performed often to alleviate obsession or anxiety (American Psychiatric Association, 2000). OCD has a worldwide prevalence of 1% to 3% and is equally represented in males and females.

We are particularly grateful to Mark H. Lewis for his careful review, expertise, and suggestions for this chapter. We are also thankful to David Simpson for his assistance in reviewing the clinical content and flow of the chapter. Thanks to Angela Sagar as well for her discussion of treatment options. We thank Jonathan Kim for his help with the tables and double checking the references. S. J. and S. F. were supported in part by the National Institutes of Health (grant NIH-K23MH082121 and its supplement). S. J. K. was supported in part by Grants NIH-R03MH083673 and K23MH082883.

http://dx.doi.org/10.1037/14323-014
Obsessive–Compulsive Disorder and Its Spectrum: A Life-Span Approach, Eric A. Storch and Dean McKay (Editors)
Copyright © 2014 by the American Psychological Association. All rights reserved.

ASD is an increasingly identified disability, which is devastating to the individuals and their families. The lifetime cost to society for a person with autism is reported to be nearly $4 million (Hines et al., 2008; Järbrink & Knapp, 2001). ASD is a relatively common, chronic, highly heritable group of neurodevelopmental disorders with rare variants and interactions among susceptibility alleles (Bailey et al., 1995; Veenstra-VanderWeele, Christian, & Cook, 2004). The current estimated prevalence of ASD is one in 88 (Gürkan & Hagerman, 2012), and it is 3 to 4 times more likely to occur in males than females (Chakrabarti & Fombonne, 2005). ASD is characterized by qualitative impairments in reciprocal social interaction and communication and the presence of repetitive behaviors (American Psychiatric Association, 2013). According to the *Diagnostic and Statistical Manual of Mental Disorders* (5th ed.; *DSM-5*; American Psychiatric Association, 2013), ASD is conceptualized as a single autism spectrum disorder with specifiers of strengths and weaknesses.

Both of these disorders are heterogeneous and complex in nature and have genetic components. Additionally, ASD and OCD share a common and central symptom: restricted repetitive behavior (RRB). Currently, literature reflects a bias in autism research, with few studies devoted to RRB pathogenesis research versus other aspects of autism, such as social and language impairments (Lewis & Bodfish, 1998; Lewis, Tanimura, Lee, & Bodfish, 2007).

RRB describes a heterogeneous group of maladaptive behaviors observed in various neurodevelopmental disorders that may or may not have an identifiable genetic defect, for example, Prader–Willi syndrome (PWS) and tic disorder. RRB overlaps with the phenotype of OCD and remains one of the core features of ASD even within current diagnostic frameworks (Frith & Done, 1990; Snow, Lecavalier, & Houts, 2009). Many forms of repetitive behavior are exhibited in ASD, including lining up objects, narrow restricted interests, intolerance to changes in routine, peculiar fascination with odd objects or parts of objects, and arm flapping (Lewis & Kim, 2009; Rutter, 1985). It has been reported that, in comparing observed behaviors of individuals with autism with those of individuals with OCD, individuals with autism perform more hoarding; ordering; touching, tapping, rubbing; and self-injurious behavior (SIB), whereas individuals with OCD display more cleaning, checking, and counting behaviors (McDougle et al., 1995). However, when controlled for intellectual ability, high-functioning adults with autism have similar frequencies of obsessive–compulsive (OC) symptoms as adults with a primary diagnosis of OCD (Russell, Mataix-Cols, Anson, & Murphy, 2005). The Autism Diagnostic Interview—Revised (ADI–R; Lord, Rutter, & Le Couteur, 1994), considered the gold standard for clinical research diagnosis, revealed that two of the three factor domains in ASD were related to RRB: inflexible language and behavior factor and repetitive sensorimotor behavior factor (Georgiades et al., 2007). Using the ADI–R, Cuccaro et al. (2003) also found two factors related to ASD; however, they were insistence on sameness and repetitive sensorimotor behavior factors. These data support the significant role RRB plays in ASD. Like autism, RRB can have a significant functional impact on the affected individuals and their caregivers. The more time occupied by OC and repetitive behaviors, the less time individuals spend exploring their environment (Pierce & Courchesne, 2001) and having normal interactions with their surroundings. This may lead to missed learning opportunities during critical cognitive and neurobiological periods of development (Lam & Aman, 2007; Pierce & Courchesne, 2001; Scahill et al., 2006).

Although RRB can be pathological in many central nervous system and developmental disorders, one must also realize that RRB is common in normative development (Evans, Elliott, & Packard, 1997; Thelen, 1980). During early development, children perform a variety of repetitive motor, compulsive, and ritualistic behaviors (Leekam et al., 2007). These intense, restricted interests can appear before the age of 2 years, be relatively long lasting, and be performed in different contexts (DeLoache, Simcock, & Macari, 2007). At the peak (age 2 years), approximately 40% of the infant's time is directed toward performing these repetitive, rhythmical behaviors (Thelen, 1979). In preschoolers, the repetitive behaviors take on more complexity and are characterized by rigidity; this rigidity may take the form of strict likes and dislikes, ritualization of daily activities, and compulsive ordering and arranging until some subjective criterion of "just right" is met (Evans et al., 1997).

Despite the significance of RRB within and outside of normative development, researchers are just beginning to explore the underlying neurobiological mechanisms of these behaviors. In this chapter, we examine RRB associated with ASD, first by exploring how RRB is defined and characterized within the framework of ASD. Next, we examine different neurobiological models used to induce and study RRB. The chapter also explores two theoretical models believed to play a role in RRB. Treatment is briefly discussed in closing.

DEFINING RRB WITHIN THE FRAMEWORK OF ASD AND OTHER DISORDERS

ASD and RRB

Similar to ASD, RRB is a heterogeneous and complex set of behaviors. This inherent complexity makes getting to the root cause of RRB complicated. Sometimes viewed as "extreme" habits (Graybiel, 2008), the transition from habit to pathological behavior is a valuable time window, providing insight into the underlying biological and environmental factors that mediate the transition and persistence of repetitive behaviors. Although little is known about this developmental time course, increased frequency and duration of repetitive sensory motor behavior has been observed in children with ASD (ages 18–24 months) compared with intellectually challenged and typically developing control participants (Watt, Wetherby, Barber, & Morgan, 2008).

Although RRB is inherently variable, tools have been developed to characterize and quantify specific types of repetitive behaviors. Under broad categorization, repetitive behaviors fall into two groups: *higher order* and *lower order* behaviors. Higher order behaviors are characterized as repetitive cognitive behavior and lower order behaviors as repetitive sensorimotor behavior (Autism Genome Project Consortium, 2006; Lewis & Bodfish, 1998; Rutter, 1985). Lower order behaviors include stereotyped body movements, repetitive manipulation of objects, and SIB, whereas obsession, compulsion, ritualistic behavior, sameness behavior, and restricted interests are often conceptualized as higher order repetitive behaviors. A clinical tool that delves deeper into the characterization, presence, and severity of RRB is the Repetitive Behavior Scale—Revised (RBS–R; Bodfish, Symons, Parker, & Lewis, 2000). This scale is empirically derived, standardized, psychometrically sound, and specifically tailored to study various repetitive behaviors in individuals with developmental disorders such as ASD (Bodfish et al., 1995, 2000; Cuccaro et al., 2003). The RBS–R is a 43-item form with the following five factors (see Figure 13.1): (a) compulsive behaviors, (b) ritualistic and sameness behaviors, (c) restricted behaviors, (d) stereotyped behaviors, and (e) SIBs (Cuccaro et al., 2007; Mirenda et al., 2010). *Compulsive behaviors* are defined as behaviors repeated and performed according to rules or involving the need to do things "just so." *Ritualistic and sameness behaviors* are characterized by the performance of daily life activities in a similar manner. Sameness behaviors are defined as resistance to change. *Restricted behaviors* are characterized by a limited range of focus, interest, or activity. *Stereotyped behaviors* or *stereotypies* are apparently purposeless movements or actions repeated in a similar manner. *SIBs* are repeated movements or actions that cause or have the potential to cause redness, bruising, or other bodily injury (Lam, 2004). The reliability, stability, and validity of the RBS–R have been demonstrated in large samples of young children, adolescents, and adults with autism and other developmental disorders (Flores et al., 2011).

No single factor of RRB has been strictly associated with ASD, leading to the question of whether there are there specific sensory, motor, or cognitive abnormalities that co-occur with RRB that could provide insight into the pathophysiology of RRB and ASD. For example, the sensory domain theory of RRB pathophysiology hypothesizes that these behaviors modulate increased or decreased levels of stimulation resulting from abnormal sensory processing. Although abnormal sensory processing in individuals with autism has been

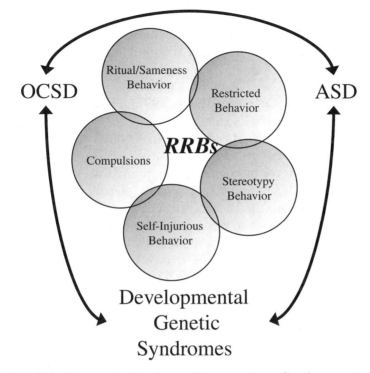

OCSD

ASD

Ritual/Sameness Behavior

Restricted Behavior

RRBs

Compulsions

Stereotypy Behavior

Self-Injurious Behavior

Developmental
Genetic
Syndromes

Figure 13.1. This diagram depicts the continuous nature of autism spectrum disorders (ASD), obsessive–compulsive spectrum disorders (OCSD), and other developmental genetic syndromes and the overlapping nature of restricted repetitive behaviors (RRBs) in these disorders. The RRB selected are the five factors validated in the Repetitive Behavior Scale—Revised (Bodfish, et al., 2000; Lam & Aman, 2007).

reported for decades (Gabriels et al., 2008; Lovaas, Newsom, & Hickman, 1987; Minshew & Goldstein, 1998), this association is still inconclusive. The works reviewed in Rogers and Ozonoff (2005) found no difference in the sensory symptoms between ASD and other developmental disorders. However, Chen, Rodgers, and McConachie (2009) found that children with autism and severe sensory processing deficits had more RRB. The research by Chen et al. was further supported by the findings of Gal, Dyck, and Passmore (2009). Motor deficits have also been associated with RRB in ASD; these impairments include clumsiness, poor motor coordination, postural instability, and poor performance on standardized tests of motor functioning (M. L. Bauman, 1992; Hallett et al., 1993; Molloy, Dietrich, & Bhattacharya, 2003). However, a clear, established relationship between these impairments and ASD has not been established.

Abnormalities in the cognitive domain, specifically, executive function, may also contribute to RRB or its severity in ASD. *Executive function* is a group of processes involved in the planning and execution of goal-directed behavior (O'Hearn, Asato, Ordaz, & Luna, 2008; M. Turner, 1997). Impairments in this group of processes center on flexibility and inhibition of prepotent responses (O'Hearn et al., 2008; Ozonoff, Pennington, & Rogers, 1991). These deficits in cognition have often been observed in individuals with autism, regardless of intellectual capability (Ozonoff & Strayer, 1997). These deficits are consistent with the higher order behavior category.

In another experiment, Lopez, Lincoln, Ozonoff, and Lai (2005) positively correlated the severity of RRB in autism with cognitive inflexibility, controlling for the level of cognitive function. However, there has been research that has failed to find this association. Therefore, this link has not been clearly established (Geurts, Corbett, & Solomon, 2009). Another cognitive deficit theory focuses on weak central coherence. This has also proven inconclusive with supporting data in typically developing children (Evans et al., 2001) but weak or no association in children with ASD (Chen et al., 2009; South, Ozonoff, & McMahon, 2007).

GENETIC SYNDROMES AND RRB

As shown in Table 13.1, genetically characterized disorders often have RRB associated with their symptomatology. Given the heterogeneity of RRB and its presence in many varying disorders, it is likely that there are numerous complex neurobiological mechanisms underlying the behaviors. As the chapter continues, several neurobiological models of RRB are presented. Two of the neurobiological systems implicated in repetitive behavior are glutamate and dopamine (DA). The neural circuitry theorized to be involved in RRB associated with ASD includes the basal ganglia and the cortical-basal ganglia circuit. The chapter also explores the depth of knowledge and understanding that animal studies and models of RRB have and continue to provide.

NEUROBIOLOGY OF RRB

Because there are different types of repetitive behaviors (i.e., SIBs, stereotyped behaviors, and ritualistic and sameness behaviors) and these behaviors manifest in myriad disorders, several questions arise: Are different neurobiological mechanisms giving rise to the various forms of RRB? More specifically, do individuals with ASD or OCD have a unique pattern of these behaviors, implying specialized pathophysiology? Given the heterogeneity of the psychiatric disorder, ASD better fits a model with multiple or more than one genetic variant to contribute to the full syndrome of autism (Geschwind,

TABLE 13.1
Examples of Genetic Disorders With Restricted Repetitive Behavior (RRB)

Disorder	Description
Fragile X syndrome	*Cause:* single trinucleotide gene sequence (CGG) expansion in the *FMR-1* gene (Brzustowicz et al., 1993; Zang et al., 2009) *Associated RRB:* hand flapping, tidying up, lining up, restricted conversation, echolalia, preference for routines, just right behaviors, repetitive phrases, and restricted interests (Moss, Oliver, Arron, Burbidge, & Berg, 2009)
Prader–Willi syndrome	*Cause:* Absence of paternally expressed genes in the 15q11–q13 region (Cassidy & Driscoll, 2009; Veltman, Craig, & Bolton, 2005) *Associated RRB:* hoarding, ordering/arranging, concerns with symmetry and exactness, rewriting, need to tell/know/ask, and skin picking (Bittel & Butler, 2005; Dykens, Leckman, & Cassidy, 1996; Dykens & Shah, 2003)
Angelman syndrome	*Cause:* absence of maternally expressed genes in the 15q11–q13 region (Lossie et al., 2001; Veltman, et al., 2005) *Associated RRB:* stereotypic hand flapping and fascination with water (Clarke & Marston, 2000)
Rett syndrome	*Cause:* mutations in the *MECP2* gene (Xq28) *Associated RRB:* mouthing and wringing (Ben Zeev Ghidoni, 2007)

2007; Veenstra-VanderWeele et al., 2004). This is also likely for RRB as a phenomenological construct, given the heterogeneous nature of the encompassed behaviors. This section investigates these questions and ideas, adding insight and knowledge to an ongoing query.

Animal Models

There are four main categories of RRB animal models: (a) nongenomic causes, (b) inbred mouse strains, (c) pharmacological agents, and (d) restricted environments and experience (Lewis et al., 2007). These models have allowed us to manipulate and control RRB in a way not possible in human studies.

Nongenomic Factors in Animals

Nongenomic factors of RRB have been explored using animal models. Examples of nongenomic factors are chemical treatment, viral infection, and lesioning. The appearance or increase in repetitive behaviors has been observed in various animals using different methodologies. In nonhuman primates, early damage to the amygdala, hippocampus, and adjacent temporal cortex have led to stereotypies (Bachevalier & Loveland, 2006). This is evident in work by Bauman and colleagues, who noted that a specific pattern of repetitive behaviors emerged after 1 year in infant macaques after lesioning the amygdala or hippocampus (M. D. Bauman, Toscano, Babineau, Mason, & Amaral, 2008). This developmental effect was similar to rodent work showing delayed effects from similar lesions on frontal lobes and subcortical dopamine function (Lipska, Jaskiw, Chrapusta, Karoum, & Weinberger, 1992). Additional rodent work has used valproic acid and viral infection. Embryonic rats (Day 12) were exposed to valproic acid, which increased the frequency of stereotypy (Ingram, Peckham, Tisdale, & Rodier, 2000; Schneider & Przewlocki, 2005), and spontaneous stereotypies arose after intracerebral inoculation of newborn rats with Borna disease virus (Hornig, Weissenbock, Horscroft, & Lipkin, 1999). An experiment performed by Martin and colleagues exposed pregnant nonhuman primates to immunoglobulin G (Martin et al., 2008). The immunoglobulin G was purified from serum collected from women with a minimum of two children with ASD. The offspring of the rhesus displayed whole body stereotypies, which were observed up to 6 months after weaning. This type of exposure has been implicated in other RRB disorders, such as compulsive and tic disorders.

Inbred Mouse Strains and RRB

Several mutant mouse models exhibiting different repetitive behavior phenotypes are utilized in RRB research. Inbred mouse strains, such as C58/J and BTBR, have been used in the study of ASD because of their variety of autismlike traits. These traits include stereotypy, as observed in the C58/J strain as jumping and back-flipping (Moy, Nadler, Poe, et al., 2008; Moy, Nadler, Young, et al., 2008). However, the traits can be more cognitive in nature. C58/J mice also have reduced exploratory behavior. BTBR, another strain increasingly used as an animal model of autism, display spontaneous repetitive behavior (usually excessive grooming), low sociability, and insistence on sameness behaviors (Amodeo, Jones, Sweeney, & Ragozzino, 2012; McFarlane et al., 2008; Yang et al., 2012). The *Gabrb3* homozygous knockout mouse has a deletion in the area that codes for the beta three subunit of the gamma-aminobutyric acid (GABA)A receptor. Deletions in this area have been linked with PWS, a disorder described earlier with repetitive behaviors such as hoarding and skin picking. Some of the repetitive behaviors exhibited in these mice fall under the stereotype factor and include intense tail chasing or circling (DeLorey et al., 1998; Homanics et al., 1997). Another model exhibiting stereotypies is the RS mouse model, Mecp2(308/Y), which expresses truncated MECP2 protein. RS is caused by mutations in the *Mecp2* gene. These mice display repetitive forelimb movements similar to hand movements noted in RS (Moretti, Bouwknecht, Teague, Paylor, & Zoghbi, 2005; Shahbazian et al., 2002). Similarly, a mouse model exhibiting the SIB factor is the *Sapap3* knockout (Welch et al., 2007). Of interest in this model is the expression of the SAPAP3 protein, which is specific to striatal glutamatergic synapses in this mouse. This gene, *SAPAP3*, found on human chromosome 1, has been shown to have deleterious mutations and single nucleotide polymorphisms associations linked to the putative OCSDs that share overlapping phenomenological and neurobiological features with OCD (Chez et al., 2007; Peca, Ting, & Feng, 2011).

Drug-Induced RRB

Research on drug-induced repetitive behavior in animals has provided scientists with most of the neurobiologically based information of repetitive motor behavior. By injecting the DA agonist apomorphine or DA into the striatum, stereotyped behaviors were induced in rats; this and other experiments helped establish a critical role for the basal ganglia in RRB (A. M. Ernst & Smelik, 1966). These results were further strengthened by work performed in the 1990s. Interstriatal administration of N-methyl-D-aspartate (NMDA) induced stereotyped behavior (Karler, Bedingfield, Thai, & Calder, 1997), and administration into the frontal cortex of bicuculline or sulpiride enhanced the motor effects of amphetamine, while intracortical infusion of DA or GABA agonists decreased amphetamine induced stereotyped behavior (Karler, Calder, Thai, & Bedingfield, 1998; Kiyatkin & Rebec, 1999). These findings and others have provided data and reasoning for the use of pharmacologically induced repetitive behavior studies and the role of basal ganglia in the production of RRB.

Experience and Environment Restriction

At first glance, animal models focused on repetitive behavior induced by restricted environment or experience may not seem relevant to autism or childhood OCD, but symptom manifestation early in development may decrease experience-dependent learning and development through marked social, communicative, and adaptive behavioral deficits. This has been observed in the occurrence of repetitive behavior in children in restricted environments (e.g., orphanage), which is similar to RRB observed in captive animals (e.g., zoo, laboratory) and animals subjected to early social deprivation (Mason & Rushen, 2006; Würbel, 2001). These behaviors can be species specific, but regardless of species, all the repetitive behaviors last through the majority of the animal's life (Bachmann, Audige, & Stauffacher, 2003; Goodwin, Davidson, & Harris, 2002; Presti, Powell, & Lewis, 2002; Presti, Watson, Kennedy, Yang, & Lewis, 2004).

Sameness Behaviors in Animals

Unlike replicating stereotyped motor behaviors in animals, researchers have found it quite difficult to produce animal models of cognitive flexibility or resistance to change. Several paradigms measuring these behaviors in animals include response extinction, reversal learning, and intra- and extra-dimensional set shifting (Colacicco, Welzl, Lipp, & Würbel, 2002). Given the overlapping nature of repetitive behaviors, it is not surprising that sameness behavior has been linked to RRB-related stereotypies. Recent research has shown that repetitive motor behaviors are inversely correlated with measures of cognitive flexibility. This has been observed in several species, including voles, bears, and parrots (Garner & Mason, 2002; Garner, Meehan, & Mench, 2003; Vickery & Mason, 2005). Tanimura, Yang, and Lewis (2008) used a reversal learning paradigm to examine RRB. Deer mice were trained to navigate a T-maze turning either right or left to find a reward at the end of the arm. After learning, the reinforced arm was switched. Deficits in the task were correlated with high levels of stereotypy. These researchers also noted an inverse relationship between an enriched environment and stereotypy and a positive correlation between an enriched environment and cognitive flexibility in the form of reversal learning. This experiment and others using animals to research cognitive flexibility have proven invaluable to understanding higher order behaviors, which are quite central to RRB in ASD and other developmental genetically influenced disorders, including childhood OCD.

Neurobiology

Imaging ASD-Related RRB

Imaging has proven to be an extremely useful tool in the exploration of the brain and behavior. In 2008, Thakkar et al. used functional magnetic resonance imaging (fMRI) to study RRB in patients with ASD, using an antisaccade task. They noted that high-functioning individuals with ASD had increased activity in the anterior cingulate cortex (ACC) for correct trials and higher error rates in the antisaccade condition. They also observed that higher ADI–R repetitive behavior scores were linked to ACC activity—specifically, that stereotype behavior scores, more than sameness behavior scores, were associated with ACC activity during correct trials. These results corresponded to similar results in patients with OCD. In the same year, another experiment highlighting the influence of ACC in RRB was performed. Shafritz, Dichter, Baranek, and Belger (2008) studied high-functioning individuals with ASD and cognitive flexibility, using response and set shifting. They compared these individuals with control participants and found that subjects with ASD showed deficits in response shifting.

During these trials, the affected group had decreased activation in the frontal, striatal, and parietal areas. Also, RRB severity was negatively correlated with ACC and posterior parietal areas. Another fMRI experiment used a visuomotor coordination task to assess activity in the caudate and cortex (K. C. Turner, Frost, Linsenbardt, McIlroy, & Muller, 2006). The findings indicated that ASD subjects have atypical connectivity patterns between these two areas compared with control participants.

Other imaging studies measured anatomic differences versus differences in activity levels or activation pattern. Studying regional gray matter volume, Rojas et al. (2006) found increased volume in the right caudate of patients with ASD after controlling for age and overall gray matter volume. Another group of researchers found an association with the frontal lobe and vermis volume (Pierce & Courchesne, 2001). The frontal lobe volume in young children with autism was positively correlated with repetitive behavior displayed during an exploratory task. They also found a negative correlation between repetitive behavior and cerebellar vermis volume. Using the ADI–R, Sears et al. (1999) found a negative association between caudate volume and difficulties with minor changes in routine, compulsions and rituals, and complex mannerisms. Hollander et al. (2000) also focused on the caudate and found a positive correlation between right caudate volumes and sameness behavior. This experiment also revealed that individuals with ASD had greater right caudate volume as well. In two additional studies, Kates, Lanham, and Singer (2005) and O'Sullivan et al. (1997) examined the possible roles of basal ganglia in RRB. Kates et al. compared boys with stereotypies with no other known developmental or neurological disorder with matched control participants. After controlling for total white matter volume, they observed lower frontal white matter volume in the affected group, whereas caudate volumes were similar for both groups. O'Sullivan et al. looked at individuals with trichotillomania. Their MRI study noted alterations in putamen volume for these individuals.

Cortical-Basal Ganglia Circuitry and RRB

The role the basal ganglia play in ASD and RRB is not confined to its structural borders but also involves the cortico-striato-thalamo-cortical circuit. Although not specifically focused on ASD-associated RRB, a positron emission tomography experiment performed by Horwitz, Rumsey, Grady, and Rapoport (1988) noted differences in the activity patterns of the cortico-basal ganglia circuit between ASD and control participants. They noted lower correlations between the thalamus and caudate with frontal and parietal areas in ASD subjects. Other studies have examined RRB associated with other disorders. For example, others have studied individuals with Tourette syndrome. The Berardelli group observed abnormal cortico-basal ganglia activation and increased cortical excitability in Tourette syndrome subjects utilizing fMRI and magnetic stimulation (Berardelli, Curra, Fabbrini, Gilio, & Manfredi, 2003). Bloch, Leckman, Zhu, and Peterson (2005) noted that the volume of the caudate predicted the severity of tic and OC symptoms in early adulthood. Finally, Peterson et al. (1998) described the activity of the prefrontal cortex, thalamus, and basal ganglia as inversely correlated with tic severity during tic suppression.

The cortico-striato-thalamo-cortical circuit has been implicated across disorders with RRB as a core symptom. It has been proposed that this circuit is organized into multiple, parallel loops that are functionally and anatomically distinct but clearly interact (Alexander, DeLong, & Strick, 1986; Langen, Durston, Kas, van Engeland, & Staal, 2011). As many as five loops have been suggested, but we focused on three: (a) sensorimotor, (b) associative, and (c) limbic. It is hypothesized that abnormal activity or damage to a particular loop may give rise to different RRBs and that the individual behaviors may have anatomically distinct forms. The sensorimotor loop is involved with the production of stereotypies. The associative loop, also called the prefrontal loop, is involved with inappropriate repetition of a goal. This is related to impulsivity and rigidity issues in RRB. The third loop, the limbic loop, is associated with the obsessive and compulsive aspects of RRB. This is viewed as the motivational component of behavioral control (reviewed in Langen et al., 2011).

Neuroadaptation and Learning Within RRB

Given autism's early onset, it would be wise to assume that the development and persistence of repetitive behaviors in autism involve long-term, experience-dependent striatal plasticity. The study of dynamic neuro-adaptation and plasticity in RRB arises from research in habit formation or habit learning (see Figure 13.2). This area of research has led to the concept of repetitive behaviors being perceived as "extreme" habits (Graybiel, 2008). Like RRB, habits have both cognitive and motor components. Also similar to RRB, once triggered, habits proceed to completion without conscious cognitive control or clear contingency. Often studied as procedural learning, habit formation involves changes in the cortico-basal ganglia circuitry. A key area of interest is the state of the system when goal-directed behavior changes to habit (reviewed in Graybiel, 2008). The following studies endeavored to get closer and closer to this point of transition. Nelson and Killcross (2006) found that a model of DA-dependent striatal plasticity accelerates habit formation. Canales and Graybiel (2000) noted long-term changes in cells and increased repetitive behavior after repeated, intermittent drug exposure.

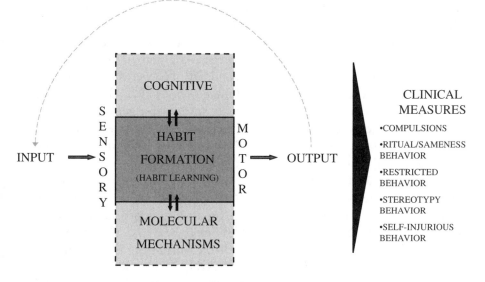

Figure 13.2. A schematic displaying the formation of habits and how they lead to the clinical measures defined by the Repetitive Behavior Scale-Revised (RBS–R; (Bodfish, et al., 2000; Lam & Aman, 2007).

THEORIES

The Glutamate Models

Glutamate is the primary excitatory neurotransmitter in the central nervous system. As such, abnormalities within the system have been linked to a number of psychiatric and neurological disorders—schizophrenia, bipolar disorder, depression, OCD, epilepsy, stroke, and amyotrophic lateral sclerosis. Glutamate plays a role in fast synaptic transmissions, as well as other complex signal processes. The neurotransmitter also has a role in development, learning, memory, neuronal proliferation, response to injury, and cell survival during early development (reviewed in Luján, Shigemoto, & Lopez-Bendito, 2005). It is important to note that glutamate levels increase steeply during the first year of life (M. E. Kornhuber, Kornhuber, Retz, & Riederer, 1993) and NMDA-sensitive binding sites reach maximum levels between ages 1 and 2 years (J. Kornhuber, Mack-Burkhardt, Konradi, Fritze, & Riederer, 1989; J. Kornhuber, Mack-Burkhardt, Kornhuber, & Riederer, 1989), which is the period when the first signs of autism typically begin to manifest. Indeed, increased levels of mRNAs for glutamate transporter and receptor genes (Purcell, Jeon, Zimmerman, Blue, & Pevsner, 2001) and an increased plasma concentration of glutamate in both child and adult autism patients

(Moreno-Fuenmayor, Borjas, Arrieta, Valera, & Socorro-Candanoza, 1996; Shinohe et al., 2006) have been reported.

In studying the glutamate system, scientists have also researched glutamate receptors and transporters. Between 2002 and 2005, the glutamate receptor subunit genes GRIK2, GRIA2, and GRIN2A were found to be associated with autism (Barnby et al., 2005; Ramanathan et al., 2004; Shuang et al., 2004). Additionally, in 2007, a glutamate transporter gene, SLC1A2, was identified as one of several genes centered under the highest linkage peak in the completed Autism Genome Project scan (Szatmari et al., 2007). Also during this time period, pharmacological studies revealed the beneficial effects of the glutamate receptor antagonists amantadine and memantine in individuals with autism (King et al., 2001; Owley et al., 2006). Using deer mice, Presti and colleagues reported that striatal injections of MK-801 and NMDA antagonist could block stereotypies (Presti, Mikes, & Lewis, 2003; Presti, Watson, et al., 2004). Considering the potential role of glutamate in OCD, the substantial overlap in symptomology between OCD and the repetitive behaviors in autism, and the pharmacologic data in autism, it is plausible that abnormal glutamate neurotransmission may play a role in RRB associated with ASD (Lewis et al., 2007; Presti, Gibney, & Lewis, 2004).

The Serotonin Model

The 5-HT system, including receptors and transporters, draw significant attention in the field of autism. Two findings driving this focus are reports of hyperserotonemia in individuals with autism and the beneficial effects of selective serotonin reuptake inhibitors (SSRIs) in the treatment of repetitive behaviors. Additionally, depletion of tryptophan, a 5-HT precursor, worsens repetitive behaviors in adult autism patients (McDougle et al., 1996), and 5-HT1D agonist–induced growth hormone response was positively correlated with baseline compulsion scores in individuals with autism (Hollander et al., 2000). In the area of 5-HT transporters, links to autism have been found through SLC6A4 and polymorphisms in 5-HTTLPR (International Molecular Genetic Study of Autism Consortium, 2001; Sutcliffe et al., 2005; Yonan et al., 2003). This association with SLC6A4 came from a family-based association study performed by Sutcliffe et al. (2005) that noted a link between novel variants in SLC6A4 and compulsive behavior. In the same gene, Brune et al. (2006) observed an association with the 5-HTTLR long/long genotype and stereotype behaviors. Although there is strong support for a serotonergic role in ASD and RRB, it is not conclusive and may play a role in OC behaviors that are distressing to the individual. King et al. (2009) administered citalopram or placebo to children with ASD for 12 weeks.

Using the Children's Yale–Brown Obsessive Compulsive Scale (CY–BOCS; Scahill et al., 2006) as an outcome measure, they found no reduction in total scores between the placebo and SSRI groups.

The DA Model

Another neurochemical pathway with possible involvement in the production of autism-related RRB is DA. The importance of DA in RRB can be observed through Lesch–Nyhan syndrome (LNS). Deficiencies in the basal ganglia dopaminergic system have been found in patients with LNS (Lloyd et al., 1981). The disorder, characterized by severe SIB, has been shown to be X-linked and occurs mainly in boys. The repetitive injurious behaviors in LNS have also been linked to DA, and the severe behavior of these patients has been associated with fewer dopaminergic nerve terminals and cell bodies (M. Ernst et al., 1996). Pharmacological studies have also linked repetitive behaviors and the DA system. Administration of DA agonist or repeated administration of a DA uptake inhibitor–induced self-injurious and stereotyped behaviors (Lewis & Baumeister, 1982; Sivam, 1995). Other links between RRB and DA system genes include catechol-O-methyltransferase (*COMT*) and DA transporter (*DAT*) genes. *COMT* is related to schizophrenia, another disorder with RRB, whereas *DAT* knockout mice show greater invariance in complex fixed action patterns, a possible connection to repetitive behaviors (Berridge, Aldridge, Houchard, & Zhuang, 2005). Overall, these studies noted an association between RRB and DA. However, RRB associated with autism has not been linked directly to DA system genes. Because of the role of DA in the basal ganglia and the importance of the basal ganglia in RRB production within and outside of autism, researchers continue to explore the possible involvement of DA in ASD-associated RRB.

TREATMENT

An extensive discussion of the treatment for RRB associated with ASD or ASD comorbid with OCD is beyond the scope of this chapter. Here we briefly discuss recent treatments; for more details, see recent reviews such as McPheeters et al. (2011) and Gürkan and Hagerman (2012). Antipsychotics are a class of drug used to treat psychotic and mood disorders; however, within ASD, two antipsychotics have been shown to improve challenging behaviors (i.e., irritability and aggression) and SIB. These substances, which act primarily on the 5-HT and DA systems, have also been shown to improve RRB. Most treatment studies focus on the social and behavioral deficits caused by ASD, but RRB is often used as a secondary outcome measure. Risperidone,

one of the antipsychotics used in the treatment of ASD, has significantly decreased RRB characterized by the Aberrant Behavior Checklist—Community (ABC–C; Aman, Burrow, & Wolford, 1995) stereotypy subscale and CY–BOCS. Treatment studies with aripiprazole, another antipsychotic, have also shown improvement in RRB characterized by ABC–C and CY–BOCS. Additionally, an improvement in repetitive speech as measured by the ABC–C inappropriate speech subscale has been observed. Because of the adverse effects of these drugs, they have been limited to patients with severe impairment or at high risk of injury. These reported adverse effects include weight gain, extrapyramidal symptoms (i.e., tremor, dyskinesia, rigidity), increased prolactin levels with no clinical events reported, and some drowsiness or sedation.

The SSRIs citalopram, escitalopram, and fluoxetine are used primarily to treat behavioral components of ASD. The results have been mixed, with the citalopram and escitalopram studies reviewed in McPheeters et al. (2011) and Myers (2010) showing no effects. In a study of citalopram and escitalopram conducted in 2005, Owley et al. observed improvements in RRB in children and adolescents with pervasive developmental disorder not otherwise specified. Fluoxetine studies reviewed in McPheeters et al. reported improvement in CY–BOCS scores. No adverse effects were reported with fluoxetine, but increased energy and disinhibition, decreased sleep, diarrhea, and dry or itchy skin were reported with citalopram.

Two drugs, reviewed in the Gürkan and Hagerman (2012) fragile X review, that affect the glutamate system are arbaclofen and memantine, but studies are preliminary with small samples. An unpublished open-label study using arbaclofen showed a positive effect on the primary and secondary measure of children with autism. This has led to a multisite clinical trial for children and young adults with autism (ClinicalTrials.gov Identifier: NCT01288716). Memantine was also used in a long-term open-label study by Chez et al. (2007). This group noted an improvement in language function, social behavior, and self-stimulatory stereotypic behaviors in children with autism and pervasive developmental disorder not otherwise specified.

The overall consensus is that lower order RRB (skin picking, stereotypy) seems resistant to any treatment, whereas higher order RRB (similar to OCD) and insistence on sameness that may stem from anxiety appear responsive to pharmacologic treatment. It is also suggested that drug treatment be used in conjunction with cognitive behavior therapy. In rare and severe cases, some individuals respond to neurosurgical procedures, such as deep brain stimulation. Future research will clarify how effective drug and cognitive behavior therapy treatment is for higher order RRB (similar to OCD) in ASD or subsets of ASD patients.

CONCLUSION

RRB refers to a broad class of responses characterized by their repetition, inflexibility, and frequent lack of obvious function. They are a shared phenomenology commonly occurring across a number of clinical disorders such as ASD, OCSDs, and a range of syndromes including PWS, tic, and Lowe syndrome (Bittel & Butler, 2005; Dykens & Shah, 2003; Moss et al., 2009). The repetitive behaviors often observed in individuals with ASD include but are not limited to insistence on sameness; compulsions, rituals, and routines; narrow and circumscribed interests; stereotyped motor movements; and repetitive SIBs (Lewis & Bodfish, 1998; M. Turner, 1999). As scientists continue to study the occurrence of RRB in ASD, OCSDs, and other developmental genetic syndromes, researchers realize that the neurobiology behind these behaviors are dimensional versus categorical in nature. Viewing repetitive behaviors as overlapping and continuous can change our approach to identifying and understanding the pathophysiological mechanisms behind RRB.

REFERENCES

Alexander, G. E., DeLong, M. R., & Strick, P. L. (1986). Parallel organization of functionally segregated circuits linking basal ganglia and cortex. *Annual Review of Neuroscience, 9*, 357–381. doi:10.1146/annurev.ne.09.030186.002041

Aman, M. G., Burrow, W. H., & Wolford, P.L. (1995). The Aberrant Behavior Checklist–Community: Factor validity and effect of subject variables for adults in group homes. *American Journal of Mental Retardation, 100*, 283–292.

American Psychiatric Association. (2000). *Diagnostic and statistical manual of mental disorders* (4th ed., text revision). Washington, DC: Author.

American Psychiatric Association. (2013). *Diagnostic and statistical manual of mental disorders* (5th ed.). Washington, DC: Author.

Amodeo, D. A., Jones, J. H., Sweeney, J. A., & Ragozzino, M. E. (2012). Differences in BTBR T+ tf/J and C57BL/6J mice on probabilistic reversal learning and stereotyped behaviors. *Behavioural Brain Research, 227*, 64–72. doi:10.1016/j.bbr.2011.10.032

Autism Genome Project Consortium, Szatmari, P., Paterson, A. D., Zwaigenbaum, L., Roberts, W., Brian, J., . . . Meyer, K. J. (2007). Mapping autism risk loci using genetic linkage and chromosomal rearrangements [corrected in *Nature Genetics* (2007), *39*, 1285]. *Nature Genetics, 39*, 319–328. doi:10.1038/ng1985

Bachevalier, J., & Loveland, K. A. (2006). The orbitofrontal-amygdala circuit and self-regulation of social-emotional behavior in autism. *Neuroscience and Biobehavioral Reviews, 30*, 97–117. doi:10.1016/j.neubiorev.2005.07.002

Bachmann, I., Audige, L., & Stauffacher, M. (2003). Risk factors associated with behavioural disorders of crib-biting, weaving and box-walking in Swiss horses. *Equine Veterinary Journal, 35,* 158–163. doi:10.2746/042516403776114216

Bailey, A., Le Couteur, A., Gottesman, I., Bolton, P., Simonoff, E., Yuzda, E., & Rutter, M. (1995). Autism as a strongly genetic disorder: Evidence from a British twin study. *Psychological Medicine, 25,* 63–77. doi:10.1017/S0033291700028099

Barnby, G., Abbott, A., Sykes, N., Morris, A., Weeks, D. E., Mott, R. . . . International Molecular Genetics Study of Autism Consortium. (2005). Candidate-gene screening and association analysis at the autism-susceptibility locus on chromosome 16p: Evidence of association at GRIN2A and ABAT. *American Journal of Human Genetics, 76,* 950–966. doi:10.1086/430454

Bauman, M. D., Toscano, J. E., Babineau, B. A., Mason, W. A., & Amaral, D. G. (2008). Emergence of stereotypies in juvenile monkeys (*Macaca mulatta*) with neonatal amygdala or hippocampus lesions. *Behavioral Neuroscience, 122,* 1005–1015. doi:10.1037/a0012600

Bauman, M. L. (1992). Motor dysfunction in autism. In A. B. Joseph & R. R. Young (Eds.), *Movement disorders in neurology and psychiatry* (pp. 660–663). Boston, MA: Blackwell.

Ben Zeev Ghidoni, B. (2007). Rett syndrome. *Child and Adolescent Psychiatric Clinics of North America, 16,* 723–743. doi:10.1016/j.chc.2007.03.004

Berardelli, A., Curra, A., Fabbrini, G., Gilio, F., & Manfredi, M. (2003). Pathophysiology of tics and Tourette syndrome. *Journal of Neurology, 250,* 781–787. doi:10.1007/s00415-003-1102-4

Berridge, K. C., Aldridge, J. W., Houchard, K. R., & Zhuang, X. (2005). Sequential super-stereotypy of an instinctive fixed action pattern in hyper-dopaminergic mutant mice: A model of obsessive compulsive disorder and Tourette's. *BMC Biology, 3,* 4. doi:10.1186/1741-7007-3-4

Bittel, D. C., & Butler, M. G. (2005). Prader–Willi syndrome: Clinical genetics, cytogenetics and molecular biology. *Expert Reviews in Molecular Medicine, 7,* 1–20. doi:10.1017/S1462399405009531

Bloch, M. H., Leckman, J. F., Zhu, H., & Peterson, B. S. (2005). Caudate volumes in childhood predict symptom severity in adults with Tourette syndrome. *Neurology, 65,* 1253–1258. doi:10.1212/01.wnl.0000180957.98702.69

Bodfish, J. W., Crawford, T. W., Powell, S. B., Parker, D. E., Golden, R. N., & Lewis, M. H. (1995). Compulsions in adults with mental retardation: Prevalence, phenomenology, and comorbidity with stereotypy and self-injury. *American Journal on Mental Retardation, 100,* 183–192.

Bodfish, J. W., Symons, F. J., Parker, D. E., & Lewis, M. H. (2000). Varieties of repetitive behavior in autism: Comparisons to mental retardation. *Journal of Autism and Developmental Disorders, 30,* 237–243. doi:10.1023/A:1005596502855

Brune, C. W., Kim, S. J., Salt, J., Leventhal, B. L., Lord, C., & Cook, E. H., Jr. (2006). 5-HTTLPR genotype-specific phenotype in children and adolescents with autism. *The American Journal of Psychiatry, 163,* 2148–2156. doi:10.1176/appi.ajp.163.12.2148

Brzustowicz, L. M., Merette, C., Xie, X., Townsend, L., Gilliam, T. C., & Ott, J. (1993). Molecular and statistical approaches to the detection and correction of errors in genotype databases. *American Journal of Human Genetics, 53,* 1137–1145.

Canales, J. J., & Graybiel, A. M. (2000). Patterns of gene expression and behavior induced by chronic dopamine treatments. *Annals of Neurology, 47*(4, Suppl. 1), S53–S59.

Cassidy, S. B., & Driscoll, D. J. (2009). Prader–Willi syndrome. *European Journal of Human Genetics, 17,* 3–13. doi:10.1038/ejhg.2008.165

Chakrabarti, S., & Fombonne, E. (2005). Pervasive developmental disorders in preschool children: Confirmation of high prevalence. *The American Journal of Psychiatry, 162,* 1133–1141. doi:10.1176/appi.ajp.162.6.1133

Chen, Y. H., Rodgers, J., & McConachie, H. (2009). Restricted and repetitive behaviours, sensory processing and cognitive style in children with autism spectrum disorders. *Journal of Autism and Developmental Disorders, 39,* 635–642.

Chez, M. G., Burton, Q., Dowling, T., Chang, M., Khanna, P., & Kramer, C. (2007). Memantine as adjunctive therapy in children diagnosed with autistic spectrum disorders: An observation of initial clinical response and maintenance tolerability. *Journal of Child Neurology, 22,* 574–579. doi:10.1177/0883073807302611

Clarke, D. J., & Marston, G. (2000). Problem behaviors associated with 15q- Angelman syndrome. *American Journal on Mental Retardation, 105,* 25–31. doi:10.1352/0895-8017(2000)105<0025:PBAWQA>2.0.CO;2

Colacicco, G., Welzl, H., Lipp, H. P., & Würbel, H. (2002). Attentional set-shifting in mice: Modification of a rat paradigm, and evidence for strain-dependent variation. *Behavioural Brain Research, 132,* 95–102. doi:10.1016/S0166-4328(01)00391-6

Cuccaro, M. L., Nations, L., Brinkley, J., Abramson, R. K., Wright, H. H., Hall, A., . . . Pericak-Vance, M. A. (2007). A comparison of repetitive behaviors in Asperger's disorder and high functioning autism. *Child Psychiatry and Human Development, 37,* 347–360. doi:10.1007/s10578-007-0052-y

Cuccaro, M. L., Shao, Y., Grubber, J., Slifer, M., Wolpert, C. M., Donnelly, S. L., . . . Pericak-Vance, M. A. (2003). Factor analysis of restricted and repetitive behaviors in autism using the Autism Diagnostic Interview—R. *Child Psychiatry and Human Development, 34,* 3–17. doi:10.1023/A:1025321707947

DeLoache, J. S., Simcock, G., & Macari, S. (2007). Planes, trains, automobiles—and tea sets: Extremely intense interests in very young children. *Developmental Psychology, 43,* 1579–1586. doi:10.1037/0012-1649.43.6.1579

DeLorey, T. M., Handforth, A., Anagnostaras, S. G., Homanics, G. E., Minassian, B. A., Asatourian A., . . . Olsen, R. W. (1998). Mice lacking the beta3 subunit of the GABAA receptor have the epilepsy phenotype and many of the behavioral characteristics of Angelman syndrome. *The Journal of Neuroscience, 18,* 8505–8514.

Dykens, E., & Shah, B. (2003). Psychiatric disorders in Prader–Willi syndrome: Epidemiology and management. *CNS Drugs, 17,* 167–178. doi:10.2165/00023210-200317030-00003

Dykens, E. M., Leckman, J. F., & Cassidy, S. B. (1996). Obsessions and compulsions in Prader–Willi syndrome. *Journal of Child Psychology and Psychiatry, 37,* 995–1002. doi:10.1111/j.1469-7610.1996.tb01496.x

Ernst, A. M., & Smelik, P. G. (1966). Site of action of dopamine and apomorphine on compulsive gnawing behaviour in rats. *Experientia, 22,* 837–838. doi:10.1007/BF01897450

Ernst, M., Zametkin, A. J., Matochik, J. A., Pascualvaca, D., Jons, P. H., Hardy, K., . . . Cohen, R. M. (1996). Presynaptic dopaminergic deficits in Lesch–Nyhan disease. *The New England Journal of Medicine, 334,* 1568–1572. doi:10.1056/NEJM199606133342403

Evans, D. W., Elliott, J. M., & Packard, M. G. (2001). Visual organization and perceptual closure are related to compulsive-like behavior in typically developing children. *Merrill-Palmer Quarterly, 47,* 323–335. doi:10.1353/mpq.2001.0014

Evans, D. W., Leckman, J. F., Carter, A., Reznick, J. S., Henshaw, D., King, R. A., & Pauls, D. (1997). Ritual, habit, and perfectionism: The prevalence and development of compulsive-like behavior in normal young children. *Child Development, 68,* 58–68. doi:10.2307/1131925

Flores, C. G., Valcante, G., Guter, S., Zaytoun, A., Wray, E., Bell, L., . . . Kim, S. J. (2011). Repetitive behavior profiles: Consistency across autism spectrum disorder cohorts and divergence from Prader–Willi syndrome. *Journal of Neurodevelopmental Disorders, 3,* 316–324. doi:10.1007/s11689-011-9094-3

Frith, D. D., & Done, D. J. (1990). Stereotyped behaviour in madness and in health. In S. J. Cooper & C. T. Dourish (Eds.), *Neurobiology of stereotyped behaviour* (pp. 232–259). Oxford, England: Clarendon Press.

Gabriels, R. L., Agnew, J. A., Miller, L. J., Gralla, J., Pan, Z., Goldson, E., . . . Hooks, E. (2008). Is there a relationship between restricted, repetitive, stereotyped behaviors and interests and abnormal sensory response in children with autism spectrum disorders? *Research in Autism Spectrum Disorders, 2,* 660–670. doi:10.1016/j.rasd.2008.02.002

Gal, E., Dyck, M. J., & Passmore, A. (2009). The relationship between stereotyped movements and self-injurious behavior in children with developmental or sensory disabilities. *Research in Developmental Disabilities, 30,* 342–352. doi:10.1016/j.ridd.2008.06.003

Garner, J. P., & Mason, G. J. (2002). Evidence for a relationship between cage stereotypies and behavioural disinhibition in laboratory rodents. *Behavioural Brain Research, 136,* 83–92. doi:10.1016/S0166-4328(02)00111-0

Garner, J. P., Meehan, C. L., & Mench, J. A. (2003). Stereotypies in caged parrots, schizophrenia and autism: Evidence for a common mechanism. *Behavioural Brain Research, 145,* 125–134. doi:10.1016/S0166-4328(03)00115-3

Georgiades, S., Szatmari, P., Zwaigenbaum, L., Duku, E., Bryson, S., Roberts, W., . . . Mahoney, W. (2007). Structure of the autism symptom phenotype: A proposed multidimensional model. *Journal of the American Academy of Child & Adolescent Psychiatry, 46*, 188–196. doi:10.1097/01.chi.0000242236.90763.7f

Geschwind, D. (2007). Autism: Searching for coherence. *Biological Psychiatry, 62*, 949–950. doi:10.1016/j.biopsych.2007.09.001

Geurts, H. M., Corbett, B., & Solomon, M. (2009). The paradox of cognitive flexibility in autism. *Trends in Cognitive Sciences, 13*, 74–82. doi:10.1016/j.tics.2008.11.006

Goodwin, D., Davidson, H. P., & Harris, P. (2002). Foraging enrichment for stabled horses: Effects on behaviour and selection. *Equine Veterinary Journal, 34*, 686–691. doi:10.2746/042516402776250450

Graybiel, A. M. (2008). Habits, rituals, and the evaluative brain. *Annual Review of Neuroscience, 31*, 359–387. doi:10.1146/annurev.neuro.29.051605.112851

Gürkan, C. K., & Hagerman, R. J. (2012). Targeted treatments in autism and fragile X syndrome. *Research in Autism Spectrum Disorders, 6*, 1311–1320. doi:10.1016/j.rasd.2012.05.007

Hallett, M., Lebiedowska, M. K., Thomas, S. L., Stanhope, S. J., Denckla, M. B., & Rumsey, J. (1993). Locomotion of autistic adults. *Archives of Neurology, 50*, 1304–1308. doi:10.1001/archneur.1993.00540120019007

Hines, R. M., Wu, L., Hines, D. J., Steenland, H., Mansour, S., Dahlhaus, R., . . . El-Husseini, A. (2008). Synaptic imbalance, stereotypies, and impaired social interactions in mice with altered neuroligin 2 expression. *The Journal of Neuroscience, 28*, 6055–6067. doi:10.1523/JNEUROSCI.0032-08.2008

Hollander, E., Novotny, S., Allen, A., Aronowitz, B., Cartwright, C., & Decaria, C. (2000). The relationship between repetitive behaviors and growth hormone response to sumatriptan challenge in adult autistic disorder. *Neuropsychopharmacology, 22*, 163–167. doi:10.1016/S0893-133X(99)00121-9

Homanics, G. E., DeLorey, T. M., Firestone, L. L., Quinlan, J. J., Handforth, A., Harrison, N. L., . . . Olsen, R. W. (1997). Mice devoid of gamma-aminobutyrate type A receptor beta3 subunit have epilepsy, cleft palate, and hypersensitive behavior. *Proceedings of the National Academy of Sciences of the United States of America, 94*, 4143–4148. doi:10.1073/pnas.94.8.4143

Hornig, M., Weissenbock, H., Horscroft, N., & Lipkin, W. I. (1999). An infection-based model of neurodevelopmental damage. *Proceedings of the National Academy of Sciences of the United States of America, 96*, 12102–12107. doi:10.1073/pnas.96.21.12102

Horwitz, B., Rumsey, J. M., Grady, C. L., & Rapoport, S. I. (1988). The cerebral metabolic landscape in autism. Intercorrelations of regional glucose utilization. *Archives of Neurology, 45*, 749–755. doi:10.1001/archneur.1988.00520310055018

Ingram, J. L., Peckham, S. M., Tisdale, B., & Rodier, P. M. (2000). Prenatal exposure of rats to valproic acid reproduces the cerebellar anomalies associated with autism. *Neurotoxicology and Teratology, 22,* 319–324. doi:10.1016/S0892-0362(99)00083-5

International Molecular Genetic Study of Autism Consortium. (2001). A genomewide screen for autism: Strong evidence for linkage to chromosomes 2q, 7q, and 16p. *American Journal of Human Genetics, 69,* 570–581. doi:10.1086/323264

Järbrink, K., & Knapp, M. (2001). The economic impact of autism in Britain. *Autism, 5,* 7–22. doi:10.1177/1362361301005001002

Karler, R., Bedingfield, J. B., Thai, D. K., & Calder, L. D. (1997). The role of the frontal cortex in the mouse in behavioral sensitization to amphetamine. *Brain Research, 757,* 228–235. doi:10.1016/S0006-8993(97)00221-7

Karler, R., Calder, L. D., Thai, D. K., & Bedingfield, J. B. (1998). The role of dopamine in the mouse frontal cortex: A new hypothesis of behavioral sensitization to amphetamine and cocaine. *Pharmacology, Biochemistry and Behavior, 61,* 435–443. doi:10.1016/S0091-3057(98)00133-6

Kates, W. R., Lanham, D. C., & Singer, H. S. (2005). Frontal white matter reductions in healthy males with complex stereotypies. *Pediatric Neurology, 32,* 109–112. doi:10.1016/j.pediatrneurol.2004.09.005

King, B. H., Hollander, E., Sikich, L., McCracken, J. T., Scahill, L., Bregman, J. D., . . . Ritz, L. (2009). Lack of efficacy of citalopram in children with autism spectrum disorders and high levels of repetitive behavior: Citalopram ineffective in children with autism. *Archives of General Psychiatry, 66,* 583–590. doi:10.1001/archgenpsychiatry.2009.30

King, B. H., Wright, D. M., Handen, B. L., Sikich, L., Zimmerman, A. W., McMahon, W., . . . Cook, E. H., Jr. (2001). Double-blind, placebo-controlled study of amantadine hydrochloride in the treatment of children with autistic disorder. *Journal of the American Academy of Child & Adolescent Psychiatry, 40,* 658–665. doi:10.1097/00004583-200106000-00010

Kiyatkin, E. A., & Rebec, G. V. (1999). Striatal neuronal activity and responsiveness to dopamine and glutamate after selective blockade of D1 and D2 dopamine receptors in freely moving rats. *The Journal of Neuroscience, 19,* 3594–3609.

Kornhuber, J., Mack-Burkhardt, F., Konradi, C., Fritze, J., & Riederer, P. (1989). Effect of antemortem and postmortem factors on [3H]MK-801 binding in the human brain: Transient elevation during early childhood. *Life Sciences, 45,* 745–749. doi:10.1016/0024-3205(89)90094-5

Kornhuber, J., Mack-Burkhardt, F., Kornhuber, M. E., & Riederer, P. (1989). [3H] MK-801 binding sites in post-mortem human frontal cortex. *European Journal of Pharmacology, 162,* 483–490. doi:10.1016/0014-2999(89)90339-7

Kornhuber, M. E., Kornhuber, J., Retz, W., & Riederer, P. (1993). L-glutamate and L-aspartate concentrations in the developing and aging human putamen tissue. *Journal of Neural Transmission, 93,* 145–150. doi:10.1007/BF01245343

Lam, K. S. (2004). *The Repetitive Behavior Scale—Revised: Independent validation and the effects of subject variables.* (Unpublished doctoral dissertation). Ohio State University, Columbus [osu1085670074].

Lam, K. S., & Aman, M. G. (2007). The Repetitive Behavior Scale—Revised: Independent validation in individuals with autism spectrum disorders. *Journal of Autism and Developmental Disorders, 37*, 855–866. doi:10.1007/s10803-006-0213-z

Langen, M., Durston, S., Kas, M. J., van Engeland, H., & Staal, W. G. (2011). The neurobiology of repetitive behavior: . . . and men. *Neuroscience and Biobehavioral Reviews, 35*, 356–365. doi:10.1016/j.neubiorev.2010.02.005

Leekam, S., Tandos, J., McConachie, H., Meins, E., Parkinson, K., Wright, C., . . . Le Couteur, A. (2007). Repetitive behaviours in typically developing 2-year-olds. *Journal of Child Psychology and Psychiatry, 48*, 1131–1138. doi:10.1111/j.1469-7610.2007.01778.x

Lewis, M. H., & Baumeister, A. A. (1982). Stereotyped mannerisms in mentally retarded persons: Animal models and theoretical analyses. In N. R. Ellis (Ed.), *International review of research in mental retardation* (Vol. 11, pp. 123–161). New York, NY: Academic Press. doi:10.1016/S0074-7750(08)60291-8

Lewis, M. H., & Bodfish, J. W. (1998). Repetitive behavior disorders in autism. *Mental Retardation and Developmental Disabilities Research Reviews, 4*, 80–89. doi:10.1002/(SICI)1098-2779(1998)4:2<80::AID-MRDD4>3.0.CO;2-0

Lewis, M. H., & Kim, S. J. (2009). The pathophysiology of restricted repetitive behavior. *Journal of Neurodevelopmental Disorders, 1*, 114–132. doi:10.1007/s11689-009-9019-6

Lewis, M. H., Tanimura, Y., Lee, L. W., & Bodfish, J. W. (2007). Animal models of restricted repetitive behavior in autism. *Behavioural Brain Research, 176*, 66–74. doi:10.1016/j.bbr.2006.08.023

Lipska, B. K., Jaskiw, G. E., Chrapusta, S., Karoum, F., & Weinberger, D. R. (1992). Ibotenic acid lesion of the ventral hippocampus differentially affects dopamine and its metabolites in the nucleus accumbens and prefrontal cortex in the rat. *Brain Research, 585*, 1–6. doi:10.1016/0006-8993(92)91184-G

Lloyd, K. G., Hornykiewicz, O., Davidson, L., Shannak, K., Farley, I., Goldstein, M., . . . Fox, I. H. (1981). Biochemical evidence of dysfunction of brain neurotransmitters in the Lesch–Nyhan syndrome. *The New England Journal of Medicine, 305*, 1106–1111. doi:10.1056/NEJM198111053051902

Lopez, B. R., Lincoln, A. J., Ozonoff, S., & Lai, Z. (2005). Examining the relationship between executive functions and restricted, repetitive symptoms of autistic disorder. *Journal of Autism and Developmental Disorders, 35*, 445–460. doi:10.1007/s10803-005-5035-x

Lord, C., Rutter, M., & Le Couteur, A. (1994). Autism Diagnostic Interview—Revised: A revised version of a diagnostic interview for caregivers of individuals with possible pervasive developmental disorders. *Journal of Autism and Developmental Disorders, 24*, 659–685. doi:10.1007/BF02172145

Lossie, A. C., Whitney, M. M., Amidon, D., Dong, H. J., Chen, P., Theriaque, D., . . . Driscoll, D. J. (2001). Distinct phenotypes distinguish the molecular classes of Angelman syndrome. *Journal of Medical Genetics, 38*, 834–845. doi:10.1136/jmg.38.12.834

Lovaas, I., Newsom, C., & Hickman, C. (1987). Self-stimulatory behavior and perceptual reinforcement. *Journal of Applied Behavior Analysis, 20,* 45–68. doi:10.1901/jaba.1987.20-45

Luján, R., Shigemoto, R., & Lopez-Bendito, G. (2005). Glutamate and GABA receptor signalling in the developing brain. *Neuroscience, 130,* 567–580. doi:10.1016/j.neuroscience.2004.09.042

Martin, L. A., Ashwood, P., Braunschweig, D., Cabanlit, M., Van de Water, J., & Amaral, D. G. (2008). Stereotypies and hyperactivity in rhesus monkeys exposed to IgG from mothers of children with autism. *Brain, Behavior, and Immunity, 22,* 806–816. doi:10.1016/j.bbi.2007.12.007

Mason, G., & Rushen, J. (Eds.). (2006). *Stereotypies in captive animals: Fundamentals and implications for welfare* (2nd ed.). Wallingford, England: CAB International. doi:10.1079/9780851990040.0000

McDougle, C. J., Kresch, L. E., Goodman, W. K., Naylor, S. T., Volkmar, F., & Price, L. H. (1995). A case–controlled study of repetitive thoughts and behavior in adults with autistic disorder and obsessive–compulsive disorder. *The American Journal of Psychiatry, 152,* 772–777.

McDougle, C. J., Naylor, S. T., Cohen, D. J., Aghajanian, G. K., Heninger, G. R., & Price, L. H. (1996). Effects of tryptophan depletion in drug-free adults with autistic disorder. *Archives of General Psychiatry, 53,* 993–1000. doi:10.1001/archpsyc.1996.01830110029004

McFarlane, H. G., Kusek, G. K., Yang, M., Phoenix, J. L., Bolivar, V. J., & Crawley, J. N. (2008). Autism-like behavioral phenotypes in BTBR T+tf/J mice. *Genes, Brain & Behavior, 7,* 152–163. doi:10.1111/j.1601-183X.2007.00330.x

McPheeters, M. L., Warren, Z., Sathe, N., Bruzek, J. L., Krishnaswami, S., Jerome, R. N., & Veenstra-Vanderweele, J. (2011). A systematic review of medical treatments for children with autism spectrum disorders. *Pediatrics, 127,* e1312–e1321. doi:10.1542/peds.2011-0427

Minshew, N. J., & Goldstein, G. (1998). Autism as a disorder of complex information processing. *Mental Retardation and Developmental Disabilities Research Reviews, 4,* 129–136. doi:10.1002/(SICI)1098-2779(1998)4:2<129::AID-MRDD10>3.0.CO;2-X

Mirenda, P., Smith, I. M., Vaillancourt, T., Georgiades, S., Duku, E., Szatmari, P., . . . Zwaigenbaum, L; Pathways in ASD Study Team. (2010). Validating the Repetitive Behavior Scale—Revised in young children with autism spectrum disorder. *Journal of Autism and Developmental Disorders, 40,* 1521–1530. doi:10.1007/s10803-010-1012-0

Molloy, C. A., Dietrich, K. N., & Bhattacharya, A. (2003). Postural stability in children with autism spectrum disorder. *Journal of Autism and Developmental Disorders, 33,* 643–652. doi:10.1023/B:JADD.0000006001.00667.4c

Moreno-Fuenmayor, H., Borjas, L., Arrieta, A., Valera, V., & Socorro-Candanoza, L. (1996). Plasma excitatory amino acids in autism. *Investigación Clínica, 37,* 113–128.

Moretti, P., Bouwknecht, J. A., Teague, R., Paylor, R., & Zoghbi, H. Y. (2005). Abnormalities of social interactions and home-cage behavior in a mouse model of Rett syndrome. *Human Molecular Genetics, 14*, 205–220. doi:10.1093/hmg/ddi016

Moss, J., Oliver, C., Arron, K., Burbidge, C., & Berg, K. (2009). The prevalence and phenomenology of repetitive behavior in genetic syndromes. *Journal of Autism and Developmental Disorders, 39*, 572–588. doi:10.1007/s10803-008-0655-6

Moy, S. S., Nadler, J. J., Poe, M. D., Nonneman, R. J., Young, N. B., Koller, B. H., . . . Bodfish, J. W. (2008). Development of a mouse test for repetitive, restricted behaviors: Relevance to autism. *Behavioural Brain Research, 188*, 178–194. doi:10.1016/j.bbr.2007.10.029

Moy, S. S., Nadler, J. J., Young, N. B., Nonneman, R. J., Segall, S. K., Andrade, G. M., . . . Magnuson, T. R. (2008). Social approach and repetitive behavior in eleven inbred mouse strains. *Behavioural Brain Research, 191*, 118–129. doi:10.1016/j.bbr.2008.03.015

Myers, S. M. (2010). Citalopram not effective for repetitive behaviour in autistic spectrum disorders. *Evidence-Based Mental Health, 13*, 22. doi:10.1136/ebmh.13.1.22

Nelson, A., & Killcross, S. (2006). Amphetamine exposure enhances habit formation. *The Journal of Neuroscience, 26*, 3805–3812. doi:10.1523/JNEUROSCI.4305-05.2006

O'Hearn, K., Asato, M., Ordaz, S., & Luna, B. (2008). Neurodevelopment and executive function in autism. *Development and Psychopathology, 20*, 1103–1132. doi:10.1017/S0954579408000527

O'Sullivan, R. L., Rauch, S. L., Breiter, H. C., Grachev, I. D., Baer, L., Kennedy, D. N., . . . Jenike, M. A. (1997). Reduced basal ganglia volumes in trichotillomania measured via morphometric magnetic resonance imaging. *Biological Psychiatry, 42*, 39–45. doi:10.1016/S0006-3223(96)00297-1

Owley, T., Salt, J., Guter, S., Grieve, A., Walton, L., Ayuyao, N., . . . Cook, E. H., Jr. (2006). A prospective, open-label trial of memantine in the treatment of cognitive, behavioral, and memory dysfunction in pervasive developmental disorders. *Journal of Child and Adolescent Psychopharmacology, 16*, 517–524. doi:10.1089/cap.2006.16.517

Owley, T., Walton, L., Salt, J., Guter, S. J., Jr., Winnega, M., Leventhal, B. L., & Cook, E. H., Jr. (2005). An open-label trial of escitalopram in pervasive developmental disorders. *Journal of the American Academy of Child & Adolescent Psychiatry, 44*, 343–348. doi:10.1097/01.chi.0000153229.80215.a0

Ozonoff, S., Pennington, B. F., & Rogers, S. J. (1991). Executive function deficits in high-functioning autistic individuals: Relationship to theory of mind. *Journal of Child Psychology and Psychiatry, 32*, 1081–1105. doi:10.1111/j.1469-7610.1991.tb00351.x

Ozonoff, S., & Strayer, D. L. (1997). Inhibitory function in nonretarded children with autism. *Journal of Autism and Developmental Disorders, 27*, 59–77. doi:10.1023/A:1025821222046

Peca, J., Ting, J., & Feng, G. (2011). SnapShot: Autism and the synapse. *Cell, 147,* 706–706.e1. doi:10.1016/j.cell.2011.10.015

Peterson, B. S., Skudlarski, P., Anderson, A. W., Zhang, H., Gatenby, J. C., Lacadie, C. M., . . . Gore, J. C. (1998). A functional magnetic resonance imaging study of tic suppression in Tourette syndrome. *Archives of General Psychiatry, 55,* 326–333. doi:10.1001/archpsyc.55.4.326

Pierce, K., & Courchesne, E. (2001). Evidence for a cerebellar role in reduced exploration and stereotyped behavior in autism. *Biological Psychiatry, 49,* 655–664. doi:10.1016/S0006-3223(00)01008-8

Presti, M. F., Gibney, B. C., & Lewis, M. H. (2004). Effects of intrastriatal administration of selective dopaminergic ligands on spontaneous stereotypy in mice. *Physiology & Behavior, 80,* 433–439. doi:10.1016/j.physbeh.2003.09.008

Presti, M. F., Mikes, H. M., & Lewis, M. H. (2003). Selective blockade of spontaneous motor stereotypy via intrastriatal pharmacological manipulation. *Pharmacology, Biochemistry and Behavior, 74,* 833–839. doi:10.1016/S0091-3057(02)01081-X

Presti, M. F., Powell, S. B., & Lewis, M. H. (2002). Dissociation between spontaneously emitted and apomorphine-induced stereotypy in *Peromyscus maniculatus bairdii. Physiology & Behavior, 75,* 347–353. doi:10.1016/S0031-9384(02)00641-8

Presti, M. F., Watson, C. J., Kennedy, R. T., Yang, M., & Lewis, M. H. (2004). Behavior-related alterations of striatal neurochemistry in a mouse model of stereotyped movement disorder. *Pharmacology, Biochemistry and Behavior, 77,* 501–507. doi:10.1016/j.pbb.2003.12.004

Purcell, A. E., Jeon, O. H., Zimmerman, A. W., Blue, M. E., & Pevsner, J. (2001). Postmortem brain abnormalities of the glutamate neurotransmitter system in autism. *Neurology, 57,* 1618–1628. doi:10.1212/WNL.57.9.1618

Ramanathan, S., Woodroffe, A., Flodman, P. L., Mays, L. Z., Hanouni, M., Modahl, C. B., . . . Smith, M. (2004). A case of autism with an interstitial deletion on 4q leading to hemizygosity for genes encoding for glutamine and glycine neurotransmitter receptor sub-units (AMPA 2, GLRA3, GLRB) and neuropeptide receptors NPY1R, NPY5R. *BMC Medical Genetics, 5,* 10. doi:10.1186/1471-2350-5-10

Rogers, S. J., & Ozonoff, S. (2005). Annotation: What do we know about sensory dysfunction in autism? A critical review of the empirical evidence. *Journal of Child Psychology and Psychiatry, 46,* 1255–1268. doi:10.1111/j.1469-7610.2005.01431.x

Rojas, D. C., Peterson, E., Winterrowd, E., Reite, M. L., Rogers, S. J., & Tregellas, J. R. (2006). Regional gray matter volumetric changes in autism associated with social and repetitive behavior symptoms. *BMC Psychiatry, 6,* 56. doi:10.1186/1471-244X-6-56

Russell, A. J., Mataix-Cols, D., Anson, M., & Murphy, D. G. (2005). Obsessions and compulsions in Asperger syndrome and high-functioning autism. *The British Journal of Psychiatry, 186,* 525–528. doi:10.1192/bjp.186.6.525

Rutter, M. (1985). The treatment of autistic children. *Journal of Child Psychology and Psychiatry, 26,* 193–214. doi:10.1111/j.1469-7610.1985.tb02260.x

Scahill, L., McDougle, C. J., Williams, S. K., Dimitropoulos, A., Aman, M. G., McCracken, J. T., . . . Vitiello, B.; Research Units on Pediatric Psychopharmacology Autism Network. (2006). Children's Yale–Brown Obsessive Compulsive Scale modified for pervasive developmental disorders. *Journal of the American Academy of Child & Adolescent Psychiatry, 45*, 1114–1123. doi:10.1097/01. chi.0000220854.79144.e7

Schneider, T., & Przewlocki, R. (2005). Behavioral alterations in rats prenatally exposed to valproic acid: Animal model of autism. *Neuropsychopharmacology, 30*, 80–89. doi:10.1038/sj.npp.1300518

Sears, L. L., Vest, C., Mohamed, S., Bailey, J., Ranson, B. J., & Piven, J. (1999). An MRI study of the basal ganglia in autism. *Progress in Neuro-Psychopharmacology & Biological Psychiatry, 23*, 613–624. doi:10.1016/S0278-5846(99)00020-2

Shafritz, K. M., Dichter, G. S., Baranek, G. T., & Belger, A. (2008). The neural circuitry mediating shifts in behavioral response and cognitive set in autism. *Biological Psychiatry, 63*, 974–980. doi:10.1016/j.biopsych.2007.06.028

Shahbazian, M., Young, J., Yuva-Paylor, L., Spencer, C., Antalffy, B., Noebels, J. L., . . . Zoghbi, H. (2002). Mice with truncated MeCP2 recapitulate many Rett syndrome features and display hyperacetylation of histone H3. *Neuron, 35*, 243–254. doi:10.1016/S0896-6273(02)00768-7

Shinohe, A., Hashimoto, K., Nakamura, K., Tsujii, M., Iwata, Y., Tsuchiya, K. J., . . . Mori, N. (2006). Increased serum levels of glutamate in adult patients with autism. *Progress in Neuro-Psychopharmacology & Biological Psychiatry, 30*, 1472–1477. doi:10.1016/j.pnpbp.2006.06.013

Shuang, M., Liu, J., Jia, M. X., Yang, J. Z., Wu, S. P., Xiao, H. G., . . . Zhang, D. (2004). Family-based association study between autism and glutamate receptor 6 gene in Chinese Han trios. *American Journal of Medical Genetics. Part B, Neuropsychiatric Genetics, 131*, 48–50. doi:10.1002/ajmg.b.30025

Sivam, S. P. (1995). GBR-12909-induced self-injurious behavior: Role of dopamine. *Brain Research, 690*, 259–263. doi:10.1016/0006-8993(95)00604-O

Snow, A. V., Lecavalier, L., & Houts, C. (2009). The structure of the Autism Diagnostic Interview—Revised: Diagnostic and phenotypic implications. *Journal of Child Psychology and Psychiatry, 50*, 734–742. doi:10.1111/j.1469-7610.2008.02018.x

South, M., Ozonoff, S., & McMahon, W. M. (2007). The relationship between executive functioning, central coherence, and repetitive behaviors in the high-functioning autism spectrum. *Autism, 11*, 437–451. doi:10.1177/1362361 307079606

Sutcliffe, J. S., Delahanty, R. J., Prasad, H. C., McCauley, J. L., Han, Q., Jiang, L., . . . Blakely, R. D. (2005). Allelic heterogeneity at the serotonin transporter locus (SLC6A4) confers susceptibility to autism and rigid-compulsive behaviors. *American Journal of Human Genetics, 77*, 265–279. doi:10.1086/432648

Szatmari, P., Georgiades, S., Bryson, S., Zwaigenbaum, L., Roberts, W., Mahoney, W., . . . Tuff, L. (2006). Investigating the structure of the restricted, repetitive behaviours and interests domain of autism. *Journal of Child Psychology and Psychiatry, 47*, 582–590. doi:10.1111/j.1469-7610.2005.01537.x

Tanimura, Y., Yang, M. C., & Lewis, M. H. (2008). Procedural learning and cognitive flexibility in a mouse model of restricted, repetitive behaviour. *Behavioural Brain Research, 189*, 250–256. doi:10.1016/j.bbr.2008.01.001

Thakkar, K. N., Polli, F. E., Joseph, R. M., Tuch, D. S., Hadjikhani, N., Barton, J. J. S., & Manoach, D. S. (2008). Response monitoring, repetitive behaviour and anterior cingulate abnormalities in autism spectrum disorders (ASD). *Brain: A Journal of Neurology, 131*, 2464–2478. doi:10.1093/brain/awn099

Thelen, E. (1979). Rhythmical stereotypies in normal human infants. *Animal Behaviour, 27*, 699–715. doi:10.1016/0003-3472(79)90006-X

Thelen, E. (1980). Determinants of amounts of stereotyped behavior in normal human infants. *Ethology and Sociobiology, 1*, 141–150. doi:10.1016/0162-3095(80)90004-7

Turner, K. C., Frost, L., Linsenbardt, D., McIlroy, J. R., & Muller, R. A. (2006). Atypically diffuse functional connectivity between caudate nuclei and cerebral cortex in autism. *Behavioral and Brain Functions, 2*, 34. doi:10.1186/1744-9081-2-34

Turner, M. (1997). Towards an executive dysfunction account of repetitive behaviour in autism. In J. Russell (Ed.), *Autism as an executive disorder* (pp. 57–100). New York, NY: Oxford University Press.

Turner, M. (1999). Annotation: Repetitive behaviour in autism: A review of psychological research. *Journal of Child Psychology and Psychiatry, 40*, 839–849. doi:10.1111/1469-7610.00502

Veenstra-VanderWeele, J., Christian, S. L., & Cook, E. H., Jr. (2004). Autism as a paradigmatic complex genetic disorder. *Annual Review of Genomics and Human Genetics, 5*, 379–405. doi:10.1146/annurev.genom.5.061903.180050

Veltman, M. W., Craig, E. E., & Bolton, P. F. (2005). Autism spectrum disorders in Prader–Willi and Angelman syndromes: A systematic review. *Psychiatric Genetics, 15*, 243–254. doi:10.1097/00041444-200512000-00006

Vickery, S. S., & Mason, G. J. (2005). Behavioral persistence in captive bears: Response to Criswell and Galbreath. *Ursus, 16*, 274–279. doi:10.2192/1537-6176(2005)016[0274:BPICBA]2.0.CO;2

Watt, N., Wetherby, A. M., Barber, A., & Morgan, L. (2008). Repetitive and stereotyped behaviors in children with autism spectrum disorders in the second year of life. *Journal of Autism and Developmental Disorders, 38*, 1518–1533. doi:10.1007/s10803-007-0532-8

Welch, J. M., Lu, J., Rodriguiz, R. M., Trotta, N. C., Peca, J., Ding, J. D., . . . Feng, G. (2007). Cortico-striatal synaptic defects and OCD-like behaviours in *Sapap3*-mutant mice. *Nature, 448*, 894–900. doi:10.1038/nature06104

Würbel, H. (2001). Ideal homes? Housing effects on rodent brain and behaviour. *Trends in Neurosciences, 24*, 207–211. doi:10.1016/S0166-2236(00)01718-5

Yang, M., Abrams, D. N., Zhang, J. Y., Weber, M. D., Katz, A. M., Clarke, A. M. . . . Crawley, J. N. (2012). Low sociability in BTBR T+tf/J mice is independent of partner strain. *Physiology & Behavior, 107,* 649–662. doi:10.1016/j.physbeh. 2011.12.025

Yonan, A. L., Alarcon, M., Cheng, R., Magnusson, P. K., Spence, S. J., Palmer, A. A. . . . Gilliam, T. C. (2003). A genomewide screen of 345 families for autism-susceptibility loci. *American Journal of Human Genetics, 73,* 886–897. doi:10.1086/378778

Zang, J. B., Nosyreva, E. D., Spencer, C. M., Volk, L. J., Musunuru, K., Zhong, R., . . . Darnell, R. B. (2009). A mouse model of the human fragile X syndrome I304N mutation. *PLOS Genetics, 5,* e1000758. doi:10.1371/journal.pgen.1000758

III

PHARMACOLOGICAL TREATMENT

14

PHARMACOTHERAPY FOR OBSESSIVE–COMPULSIVE AND RELATED DISORDERS AMONG CHILDREN AND ADOLESCENTS

S. EVELYN STEWART AND ANDREA C. STACHON

Obsessive–compulsive disorder (OCD) is a common neuropsychiatric illness; its onset is often in childhood (Busatto et al., 2001). This disorder has been listed among the 10 most disabling illnesses by the World Health Organization (Murray & Lopez, 1997) and as the most frequently serious anxiety disorder (Kessler, Chiu, Demler, Merikangas, & Walters, 2005). Yet many children and adolescents with OCD wait years before an appropriate diagnosis is made. Lifetime prevalence rates in youth range between 1% and 3%, and the gross majority of those identified from community studies report being previously undiagnosed and untreated. Obsessive–compulsive spectrum disorders (OCSDs) in the differential diagnosis of OCD include tic disorders, trichotillomania (TTM), hypochondriasis, body dysmorphic disorder (BDD), and body-focused repetitive behaviors (BFRB). The failure of prompt identification for these disorders may be attributable to insufficient specialized OCD-related training among clinicians. This is unfortunate because a more chronic and debilitating course is characteristic of cases that are left untreated

http://dx.doi.org/10.1037/14323-015
Obsessive–Compulsive Disorder and Its Spectrum: A Life-Span Approach, Eric A. Storch and Dean McKay (Editors)
Copyright © 2014 by the American Psychological Association. All rights reserved.

(Micali et al., 2010; Stewart et al., 2004). A better understanding of OCD and OCSDs by mental health professionals is imperative in order to reduce the gap between symptom onset and diagnosis, and to promote early intervention.

This chapter reviews the management of OCD and OCSDs in children and adolescents (i.e., below the age of 18 years) by providing a summary of current, empirically supported pharmacological strategies as well as newer but less well-studied approaches. These approaches should be used as a guide in addition to clinical practice parameters, but they are not meant to replace clinical judgment in the management of OCD and OCSDs. Much of the research is from the adult pharmacotherapy literature; the research on pediatric pharmacotherapy for OCD, particularly with regard to aug-mentation (i.e., adding a medication that is not considered a standard drug for OCD to increase response), is modest at present. Therefore, until fur-ther research is available, practitioners must be judicious in using these agents with children and adolescents.

MEDICATION-RELATED ASSESSMENT OF PEDIATRIC OCD AND OCSDs

Pediatric OCD and OCSDs should be considered in the differential diagnosis of all youth with anxiety or repetitive behaviors. A systematic assessment approach is recommended to establish therapeutic rapport, ensure safety, and define appropriate treatment goals and settings. The assessment should confirm the presence and functional impact of OCD, OCSDs and their comorbidities, and details of past treatment trials. Collateral histories are highly valuable because obsessive–compulsive symptoms are often mini-mized as a result of related guilt, shame, or poor insight. Several structured instruments are beneficial at initial and follow-up assessments. These include the Children's Yale–Brown Obsessive Compulsive Scale (CY-BOCS) and Checklist (CY-BOCS-CL; Scahill et al., 1997) to define target treatment symptoms. Four overlapping OCD symptom dimensions that appear to be stable across development include (a) cleaning/contamination, (b) symmetry/ordering/repeating, (c) checking and sexual/religious/somatic/aggressive obsessions, and (d) hoarding symptoms (Stewart et al., 2007). Useful mea-sures of insight, patient functioning, and family functioning include the Brown Assessment of Beliefs Scale—Modified for Children (BABS–C; Storch, Larson, et al., 2010), the Child Obsessive–Compulsive Impact Scale—Revised (COIS–R; Piacentini, Peris, Bergman, Chang, & Jaffer, 2007), and the OCD Family Functioning (OFF) Scale (Stewart et al., 2011), respectively.

Clarifying diagnoses is important given the symptomatic overlap and frequent comorbidity of OCD and OCSDs with other psychiatric illnesses. Figure 14.1 depicts an algorithm to assist with this differential diagnostic

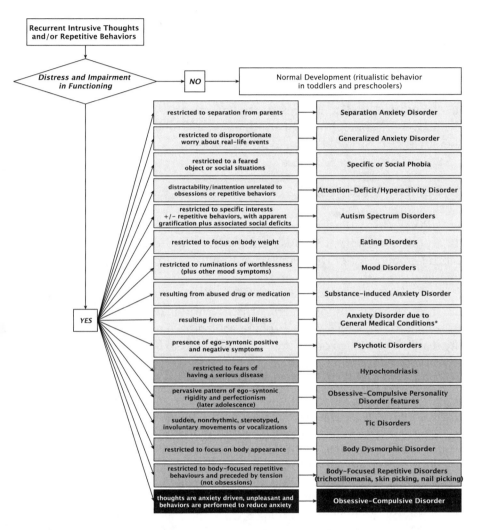

Figure 14.1. Differential diagnosis of pediatric Obsessive–Compulsive Spectrum Disorders. *Includes genetic syndromes that are often diagnosed in childhood: Prader–Willi syndrome (compulsive eating); Lesch–Nyhan syndrome (self-injury repetitive behavior); Smith–Magenis syndrome (self-injury repetitive behavior, skin picking); Cornelia de Lange syndrome (Obsessive–compulsive self-injurious behavior, self-scratching, excessive grooming including hand licking and hair stroking).

process. A diagnosis of pediatric autoimmune neuropsychiatric disorder associated with streptococcus (PANDAS)—diagnostic criteria first defined by Swedo and colleagues in 1998 (Swedo et al., 1998) and recently reviewed by the same group (Swedo, Leckman, & Rose, 2012) with the terminology changed because of nonstreptococcus causes of sudden-onset OCD to pediatric acute-onset neuropsychiatric syndrome (PANS)—should be considered in cases with abrupt onset and severity exacerbations following infections, with potential collection of a throat culture and serologic immune markers. The presence of OCD comorbidities dictates the need for their specific treatment but also predicts poorer treatment response to medications (Geller, Biederman, Stewart, Mullin, Farrell, et al., 2003) and cognitive–behavioral therapy (CBT; Storch, Lewin, Geffken, Morgan, & Murphy, 2010).

GENERAL PRINCIPLES OF PEDIATRIC OCD MANAGEMENT

Psychoeducation for the patient and family with respect to OCD, family accommodation, prognosis, and evidence-based treatment options is a central component of the management plan. Referral to reputable, informative websites such as those hosted by the International Obsessive–Compulsive Disorder Foundation (http://www.ocfoundation.org/ocdinkids) or the Anxiety Disorders Association of America (http://www.adaa.org) may be beneficial. Although this chapter focuses on pharmacological treatment of pediatric OCD, the reader is reminded of the important roles of CBT and family involvement in its management.

As reflected by OCD treatment guidelines, serotonin reuptake inhibitors (SRI) and CBT are the first-line treatments of choice, either together or separately (American Academy of Child and Adolescent Psychiatry [AACAP], 2012). An SRI acts as a reuptake inhibitor for the serotonin neurotransmitter (5-hydroxytryptamine, commonly abbreviated as 5-HT) by blocking the action of the serotonin transporter, which leads to increased extracellular concentrations in the brain (thus increasing serotonergic neurotransmission). Proven SRIs in OCD treatment include two classes of antidepressants: selective serotonin reuptake inhibitors (SSRIs) and the tricyclics (the only effective one of which for pediatric OCD is clomipramine) (Swedo et al., 1989). It is of interest that placebo response rates are significantly lower among children and adolescents affected by OCD (31%) versus youth affected by depression (50%; Cohen et al., 2008).

Initiating Treatment With CBT Alone

Given the proven efficacy of CBT and the potential emergence of medication-related side effects, it is preferable to begin treatment with

CBT alone for those with mild and moderate illness (CY-BOCS total score between 8 and 23; AACAP, 2012). This may also be preferred by families who are hesitant about medication use and by adolescents who are pregnant or nursing. Response predictors to this approach include good insight, fewer externalizing symptoms, and lower OCD severity, impairment, and family accommodation (Garcia et al., 2010).

Initiating Treatment With SRI Medication Alone

Despite the proven efficacy of CBT, there are clinical situations when use of a medication alone should be considered, including those characterized by (a) poor functioning, (b) low motivation, (c) limited insight, and (d) poor family organizational/communication skills. An initial medication trial alone, followed later by CBT, may also be preferred with overwhelmingly severe pediatric OCD (CY-BOCS total score > 23) and with comorbid depression, psychotic symptoms, or severe attention-deficit/hyperactivity disorder that interferes with CBT engagement. This treatment approach may also be useful for adolescents with predominant hoarding symptoms, who tend to lack insight to motivate engagement in CBT alone (Jakubovski et al., 2011) and who respond less well to SRIs alone (Masi et al., 2009). The most frequent reason for beginning with a medication alone, however, is lack of access to an OCD-experienced, CBT-trained clinician.

Initiating Treatment With CBT and SRI Medication Combination

For severe cases (CY-BOCS total score > 23) and for many moderately severe pediatric OCD cases (CY-BOCS total score between 16 and 22), an initial combined approach is recommended (AACAP, 2012). This should be strongly considered with (a) an OCD family history (because CBT alone works less well with this group; Garcia et al., 2010); (b) comorbid tics (because SRIs alone work less well with this group); and (c) psychiatric comorbidities interfering with but not entirely precluding CBT motivation (e.g., generalized anxiety disorder, eating disorders).

COMPARING CBT, MEDICATION, AND COMBINED APPROACHES FOR PEDIATRIC OCD

The decision of whether to initiate pediatric OCD treatment with CBT alone, medication alone, or their combination should be guided by factors including the individual patient variables described above, family preference, treatment accessibility, and also the available evidence-based data comparing these modalities. Results of all pediatric OCD medication randomized controlled trials (RCTs) are described in Table 14.1; meta-analyses combining results of medication and CBT trials are described in Tables 14.2 and 14.3. Both the parents and the youth with OCD should be actively involved in medication selection because this may contribute to treatment adherence, motivation, and satisfaction.

The first major study on OCD treatment (Pediatric OCD Treatment Study, or POTS; Pediatric OCD Treatment Study [POTS] Team, 2004) and a subsequent Cochrane collaborative review (O'Kearney, Anstey, & von Sanden, 2006) similarly concluded that use of CBT alone and use of an SRI alone are equally superior to placebo in reducing pediatric OCD severity. However, it should be noted that side effects (including stomachache, nausea, diarrhea, decreased appetite, enuresis, and motor overactivity) were identified in 5% of patients being treated with sertraline in the POTS, limiting interpretation of findings for CBT alone. A later meta-analysis of pediatric OCD RCTs found a better response to CBT alone than to SRIs alone (Watson & Rees, 2008). Comparisons of a combined CBT and SRI approach versus either modality alone have yielded inconsistent results. Although the POTS reported that a combination of CBT and an SRI was superior to either alone, a second Cochrane review reported that the combination was superior only to SRIs alone (O'Kearney, 2007; O'Kearney et al., 2006). Nonetheless, overwhelming evidence supports that SRIs alone, CBT alone, and the CBT–SRI treatment combination are all superior to placebo in pediatric OCD treatment (POTS Team, 2004). A full discussion with both patients and parents regarding the evidence for each treatment modality followed by informed consent and assent is always recommended before beginning treatment.

PHARMACOLOGICAL TREATMENT OF PEDIATRIC OCD

Once the decision has been made to initiate a medication trial, a decision regarding which medication to use first must be made. Subsequent to starting a pharmacological agent, clinical judgments regarding its effectiveness will guide dose increases, medication switches, and augmentation (addition of a medication that is not considered a standard drug for OCD to increase response), in addition to maintenance strategies. Details are provided below.

Selecting and Starting an Initial Medication

An SSRI should be the first choice in pharmacologic OCD management. SRI medications that are currently approved by the U.S. Food and

TABLE 14.1
Obsessive–Compulsive Disorder (OCD) Medications, Dosages, and Adverse Effects

Drug generic name	Drug trade name	Starting dose range in mg/day for adolescents (children)	Target dose range in mg/day for adolescents (children)	Adverse effects
		First-line OCD agents		
SSRIs				Common: insomnia, anxiety, gastrointestinal symptoms, sexual dysfunction, dizziness, sedation, behavioral activation
Citalopram[a]	Celexa	10–20 (2.5–10)	40 (10–40)	Rare: rash, headache, suicidal ideation/behavior, manic switch, increased bleeding time
Escitalopram	Lexapro	5 (5)	20 (10–20)	
Fluoxetine	Prozac	10–20 (2.5–10)	80 (10–80)	
Fluvoxamine	Luvox	25–50 (12.5–25)	300 (50–300)	
Paroxetine	Paxil	10 (2.5–10)	60 (10–60)	
Sertraline	Zoloft	25–50 (12.5–25)	200 (50–200)	
Tricyclics				Common: dry mouth, constipation, dizziness, postural hypotension, sexual, weight gain, tremor, sedation, hyperhidrosis
Clompiramine	Anafranil	25 (6.25–25)	250 (50–200)	Rare: EKG changes, seizures
		Second-line augmenting agents		
Atypical antipsychotics[b]				Common: weight gain, dizziness, sedation, constipation, dry mouth
Risperidone	Risperdal	0.25–0.5 (0.125–0.25)[c]	0.5–3	Rare: hyperglycemia, elevated prolactin, extrapyramidal symptoms, EKG change.
Olanzapine	Zyprexa	2.5 (1.25)	2.5–10[c]	
Quetiapine	Seroquel	25[d]	25–500 [d]	
Aripiprazole	Abilify	2	2–10	

Note. EKG = electrocardiogram; RCT = randomized controlled trial. [a]QT prolongation risk at > 40 mg/day. [b]Based on adult RCT data; no OCD RCT data available for children/adolescents; risperidone is the only atypical demonstrating efficacy in two adult OCD meta-analyses. [c]Once daily or divided twice daily. [d]Divided twice daily. From "Assessment and Medication Management of Paediatric Obsessive-Compulsive Disorder," by S. E. Stewart, D. Hezel, and A. C. Stachon, Drugs, 72, p. 888. Copyright 2012 by Springer. Adapted with permission.

TABLE 14.2
Studies and Meta-Analyses of Pediatric Obsessive–Compulsive Disorder (OCD) Treatment

Variable		Geller, Biederman, Stewart, Mullin, Martin, et al. (2003)	POTS Team (2004)	Watson & Rees (2008)	O'Kearney (2007)
Trials (n/type)		12 RCTs (Med only)	1 RCT	13 RCTs 15 comparisons: (10 Med + 5 CBT)	8 RCTs and quasi-RCTs 12 comparisons: (4 Med + 8 CBT/BT)
Total sample (N)		1,044	117	1,177	343
Age (years)		19 or under	7–17	19 or under	4–18
Response rate ES (CI)	Med	0.46 (0.37–0.55)	0.67	0.48 (0.36–0.61)	
	CBT	—	0.97	1.45 (0.68–2.22)	
	COMB		1.4	—	
	Summary	30%–40% reduction in OCD symptoms	COMB > CBT = Med > PBO		COMB = CBT, COMB > Med, CBT = Med
Remission rate % (CI)	Med	—	21.4 (10–40)	—	
	CBT	—	39.3 (24–58)	—	
	COMB	—	53.6 (36–70)	—	
	PBO	—	3.6 (0–19)	—	
	Summary		COMB = CBT > Med = PBO	—	COMB = CBT > Med

Note. BT = behavioral therapy; CBT = cognitive behavioral therapy; CI = confidence interval; COMB = combined cognitive–behavioral therapy and medication treatment; ES = effect size; Med = medication; PBO = placebo; POTS = pediatric OCD treatment study; RCT = randomized controlled trial.

TABLE 14.3
Pharmacologic Randomized Controlled Trials in Pediatric Obsessive–Compulsive Disorder (OCD)

First author	Year	Medication (daily dose)	Sample (N)	Comparison (design)	Effective
POTS Team	2004	Sertraline (25–200 mg)	28 + 28	CBT + sertra-line; CBT (parallel)	Yes
Geller	2004	Paroxetine (10–50 mg)	98 + 105	PBO (parallel)	Yes
Geller, Biederman, Stewart, Mullin, Farrell, et al.	2003	Paroxetine (10–60 mg)	95 + 98	PBO (withdrawal)	Yes
Liebowitz	2002	Fluoxetine (20–80 mg)	21 + 22	PBO (parallel)	Yes
Geller	2001	Fluoxetine (20–60 mg)	71 + 32	PBO (parallel)	Yes
Riddle	2001	Fluvoxamine (50–200 mg)	57 + 63	PBO (parallel)	Yes
March	1998	Sertraline (25–200 mg)	92 + 95	PBO (parallel)	Yes
Riddle	1992	Fluoxetine (20 mg)	7 + 6	PBO (cross-over)	Mixed
DeVeaugh-Geiss	1992	Clomipramine (75–200 mg)	31 + 29	PBO (parallel)	Yes
Leonard	1991	Clomipramine (50–225 mg)	11 + 9	Desipramine (50–250mg) (substitution)	Yes
March	1990	Clomipramine (50–200 mg)	8 + 8	PBO (parallel)	No
Leonard	1989	Clomipramine (25–250 mg)	23	Desipramine (25–250mg)	Yes
Flament	1985	Clomipramine (50–200 mg)	19 + 19	PBO (cross-over)	Yes

Note. CBT = cognitive–behavioral therapy; PBO = placebo; POTS = Pediatric OCD Treatment Study.

Drug Administration (FDA) for OCD treatment include clomipramine (for ages 10 and above), paroxetine (in adults only), and fluoxetine (in those older than 7 years), sertraline (in those older than 6 years), and fluvoxamine (in patients older than 8 years). Although neither citalopram nor escitalopram is FDA approved for OCD, adult RCTs have confirmed their efficacy (Alaghband-Rad & Hakimshooshtary, 2009). SSRIs indicated for the treatment of OCD have similar effectiveness for the treatment of OCD, as demonstrated by pediatric (Geller, Biederman, Stewart, Mullin, Martin, et al., 2003) and adult OCD studies (Soomro, Altman, Rajagopal, & Oakley-Browne, 2008). Therefore, helpful factors in SSRI selection include family preferences, family SSRI response history, medication interaction profiles, and applicable FDA warnings. Risks that may be associated with the use of nonapproved agents may include OCD nonresponse, adverse effects, and interactions with other medications taken by the patient.

Treatment Algorithm

A suggested pharmacological management approach for pediatric OCD is outlined in Figure 14.2. Medication trials should begin at a low dose with subsequent increases every 2 to 3 weeks to allow for observed treatment response. Recommended doses for OCD treatment are typically higher than are those for depression (Table 14.1), as supported by an adult OCD meta-analysis demonstrating improved efficacy with increased dose (Bloch, McGuire, Landeros-Weisenberger, Leckman, & Pittenger, 2010). OCD symptom reduction is more common than full remission, with a typically defined response of a > 25% severity decrease. Prior to making conclusions regarding SRI effectiveness, 10- to 12-week medication trials are necessary. If the initial SSRI is not effective, one or two additional SSRI trials should be attempted prior to use of clomipramine, given its undesirable side effects. If the SSRI was used alone, CBT augmentation should be attempted (Franklin, Sapyta, et al., 2011). Between treatment steps, factors to be considered include compliance, side effects, comorbidities, stressors, and family accommodation.

Second-line medication strategies for pediatric OCD, including SRI replacement (trial with a second drug from the same class) and augmentation, are recommended for individuals experiencing at least moderately severe symptoms despite multiple SRI trials and CBT. These have, unfortunately, been understudied in youth. For example, although venlafaxine and duloxetine are usedalone, their efficacy in OCD has not been well demonstrated. The SRI augmenting agents with the strongest empirical support in OCD treatment are the atypical antipsychotics (second-generation antipsychotics). An adult OCD Cochrane review concluded that quetiapine and risperidone are the only atypical antipsychotics with evidence supporting their efficacy in augmentation (Komossa, Depping, Meyer, Kissling, & Leucht, 2010). No RCTs of atypical antipsychotic have been reported for pediatric OCD, although case series suggest benefits of risperidone (Fitzgerald, Stewart, Tawile, & Rosenberg, 1999; Thomsen, 2004) and aripiprazole (Masi, Pfanner, Millepiedi, & Berloffa, 2010). The typical antipsychotic, haloperidol, has also demonstrated OCD efficacy but only in the presence of comorbid tics (Thomsen, 2004). Atypical antipsychotic trials should precede typical antipsychotic use, given their lower tardive dyskinesia risk. Clonazepam had reported benefit in a pediatric case study (Leonard et al., 1994) but was not supported by adult RCTs (Crockett, Churchill, & Davidson, 2004; Hollander, Kaplan, & Stahl, 2003). The OCD American Academy Child

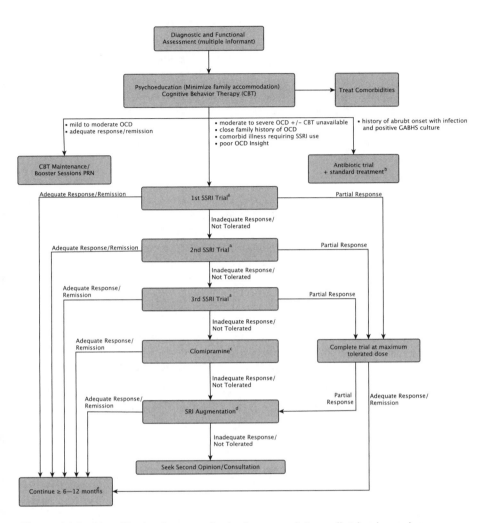

Figure 14.2. Algorithmic pharmacological approach to pediatric obsessive–compulsive disorders (OCD). GABHS = Group A Beta-hemolytic Streptococcal Infections, PRN = As needed, SSRI = selective serotonin reuptake inhibitor. [a]Selection is based on side effect profile, interactions with patient medications, family response history, preferred long half-life if likelihood of missed doses. [b]Monitored for selective serotonin reuptake inhibitor–induced activation. [c]Electrogcardiogram (EKG) indices required: QTc < 450 ms, PR interval < 200 ms, QRS interval < 120 ms, blood pressure (BP) systolic < 140, BP diastolic < 90, heart rate < 130. [d]No randomized controlled trials in pediatric OCD; options include (a) clomipramine low dose (25–75 mg) + fluvoxamine—with monitoring EKG and clomipramine/desmethyl clomipramine serum levels; (b) atypical or typical antipsychotic when comorbid motor tics, poor insight, pervasive developmental disorder symptoms, mood instability—with monitoring weight, fasting lipids, and glucose and EKG; (c) other novel agents such as clonazepam, glutamatergic agents (memantine, riluzole), stimulants, gabapentin, and N-acetyl cysteine. [e]Reassess medication requirement; if discontinuing, gradual decrease over months.

and Adolescent Psychiatry Practice Parameter (AACAP, 2012) also includes a second-line approach of combined low-dose clomipramine and fluvoxamine to optimize the dose:side effect ratio. Glutamate-related medications, including memantine (Hezel, Beattie, & Stewart, 2009), n-acetyl cysteine (Lafleur et al., 2006), and riluzole (Grant, Lougee, Hirschtritt, & Swedo, 2007), have shown promise as augmenting agents. For refractory OCD, intensive residential treatment should also be considered (Björgvinsson et al., 2008; Stewart, Stack, Farrell, Pauls, & Jenike, 2005; Stewart et al., 2009).

Stabilization and Maintenance

Once an effective medication and dose are identified, they should generally be maintained for at least 6 months to 1 year prior to a gradual discontinuation trial. Unfortunately, relapse rates following medication discontinuation are very high. Relapse rates may be attenuated if CBT has been included in treatment (Foa et al., 2005; Simpson et al., 2004). Discontinuation should occur over a period of months. Moreover, for individuals with two to three relapses and moderately severe illness, long-term medication continuation should be considered. Long-term pediatric OCD studies to date suggest that only two fifths of patients have OCD at follow-up, although another fifth continue to have subthreshold symptoms (S. E. Stewart et al., 2004). Risk factors for persistent OCD include female gender, later onset, increased severity, absence of tics, and the presence of oppositional defiant disorder or hoarding symptoms (Bloch et al., 2009).

PHARMACOLOGICAL TREATMENT OF PEDIATRIC OCSDs

Medication management for OCSDs involves distinct but overlapping strategies in comparison with OCD, which are summarized in Table 14.4. No large RCTs regarding medication treatment of youth with OCSDs have been published. It is therefore necessary to treat pediatric OCSDs using the best available evidence from pediatric and adult literature, in addition to clinical judgment.

For youth with mild tic or Tourette disorders, behavioral techniques including "habit reversal" are the most successful interventions. For more severe tics, pharmacotherapy may be advised, including the RCT-proven alpha-2 agonists clonidine and guanfacine (Stewart, Geller, Spender, & Gianini, 2003). Antipsychotics have also been demonstrated as effective, although these should not be used as first-line agents because of potential metabolic and extrapyramidal side effects. Less commonly used medications include tetrabenazine, anticonvulsants, pergolide, and botulin injections

TABLE 14.4
Medication Classes in Pediatric Obsessive–Compulsive Disorder and Obsessive–Compulsive Spectrum Disorders Management

	Serotonin reuptake inhibitors		Alpha agonists	Antipsychotics		Glutamate agents (NMDA related)		Antiepileptic	
	SSRI	CMI	Clonidine	Atypicals	Typicals	N-AC	Memantine	LMG	Topiramate
OCD	✓✓✓	✓✓✓		✓✓ augm	✓✓✓ w tics	✓ augm	✓✓ augm		
TS	X	✓✓	✓✓✓	✓✓✓	✓✓✓				✓✓
TTM	X	✓✓		✓		✓✓			
Hypoch	✓✓	✓							
BFRB	✓✓	✓✓				✓		✓	
BDD	✓✓	✓✓			X				

Note. One check mark indicates effective in nonrandomized study; two check marks indicate effective in adult RCT; three check marks indicate effective in pediatric RCT; letter X signifies ineffective in RCT. Augm = for augmentation; CMI = clomipramine; BDD = body dysmorphic disorder; BFRB = body-focused repetitive behavior; Hypoch, hypochondriasis; LMG = lamotrigine; N-AC = n-acetyl cysteine; NMDA = *N*-methyl-D-aspartic acid; RCT = randomized controlled trial; TS = Tourette Syndrome; TTM = trichotillomania; w tics = with comorbid tics.

(Stewart et al., 2003; Stewart, Jenike, & Keuthen, 2005). For BDD, treatment is guided by adult study findings demonstrating that CBT may be superior to medications (Williams, Hadjistavropoulos, & Sharpe, 2006). Serotonergic antidepressants appear to be more effective than nonserotonergic antidepressants (Hollander et al., 1999) and antipsychotics, which are commonly used for BDD but largely unsupported by research (Uzun & Ozdemir, 2010). For youth with hypochondriasis, SSRI efficacy has been supported by evidence from adult studies (Fallon et al., 2008), and CBT has demonstrated equal efficacy to SSRIs in adult RCTs (Greeven et al., 2007, 2009). For youth with TTM, treatment guidance is also derived from the adult literature. Behavioral therapy (habit reversal) has been demonstrated as superior to placebo in child (Franklin, Edson, Ledley, & Cahill, 2011) and adult RCTs of TTM (Ninan, Rothbaum, Marsteller, Knight, & Eccard, 2000; van Minnen, Hoogduin, Keijsers, Hellenbrand, & Hendriks, 2003). In contrast to findings for OCD and BDD, SSRI use is less well-supported for treatment of TTM (van Minnen et al., 2003), although these may beneficially address comorbid anxiety and depression symptoms. Small clomipramine trials have provided some support for its use in adult TTM (Ninan et al., 2000). Atypical antipsychotics, opioid blockers, and glutamate modulators are also anecdotally considered for treatment use in TTM. With respect to evaluating pharmacotherapy for TTM in youth, RCTs are direly needed.

SIDE EFFECTS AND SAFETY IN PEDIATRIC PSYCHOPHARMACOLOGY

General factors to consider in pharmacologic management of youth include the fact that they are not merely "small adults" in terms of medication absorption, metabolism, and elimination. Dosage is often comparable between adult and child populations, given higher rates of metabolism and elimination among youth. Table 14.1 summarizes OCD medication profiles with their initial and target dose ranges and potential common or rare (but serious) adverse effects among children and adolescents.

In addition to observing for target symptom improvement during drug trials, additional monitoring may be necessary on the basis of the pharmacologic agent being used and specific patient-related variables. Baseline laboratory and clinical evaluations may include measurements for weight, height, abdominal circumference, blood pressure, and pulse. Because weight gain is a common side effect across psychotropic agents, weight, height, and abdominal circumference should be monitored during all medication trials, including SSRIs.

Patient-related variables may influence pharmacologic management. For medically ill patients with OCD, potential drug–drug interactions, ability to metabolize medications, and risk of adverse effects should be considered. Specific medications to either avoid or use with caution among selected medical populations are as follows: SSRIs in patients with coagulopathies or thrombocytopenia; clomipramine and antipsychotics in patients with cardiac or seizure disorders; and atypical antipsychotics in patients with metabolic conditions. In addition, dose sensitivity and "paradoxical" reactions may occur among children with brain injury or intellectual disability.

A risk–benefit analysis of medication use is necessary when treating pregnant or nursing adolescents with OCD because fetal well-being is influenced by maternal health. Current research indicates no increased associated risk for fetal mortality (Wisner et al., 2000) or developmental deficits at 2 to 6 years (Nulman et al., 2002) with prenatal SRI exposure. However, short-term respiratory distress and neonatal adaptation problems commonly occur, and increased risk has been reported for persistent pulmonary hypertension (Ellfolk & Malm, 2010). The specific class of psychotropic agent that has been selected also influences pharmacologic management and safety monitoring. Prior to initiating the tricyclic clomipramine, a personal and family cardiac and seizure history should be obtained in addition to an electrocardiogram (EKG) (for guidelines, see Figure 14.2 caption). EKGs and serum levels of clomipramine and its metabolite should be monitored at baseline, following dosage increases, and annually during maintenance.

Before initiating atypical antipsychotics, a fasting lipid profile, serum glucose levels, and an EKG should be collected. In addition, liver and kidney enzymes, blood pressure, and pulse should also be measured at baseline and as clinically indicated during clomipramine and antipsychotic trials.

No laboratory monitoring is routinely required during SSRI use (although citalopram has been associated with increased EKG QT interval at daily doses higher than 40 mg). Commonly reported SSRI adverse effects across youth and adult samples include insomnia, sedation, gastrointestinal symptoms, dizziness, and sexual dysfunction. Additional side effects to monitor among youth include behavioral activation, SRI-induced mania, and antidepressant-related suicidal thinking or behavior. Behavioral activation frequently occurs in younger children, even after several weeks, and tends to resolve with dose decreases (Murphy, Segarra, Storch, & Goodman, 2008). SRI-induced mania is much less common, often occurring with a family or personal history of bipolar disorder, and should be managed with dose decrease or discontinuation. Last, SRI medications have reportedly been associated with increased suicidal thinking or behavior (but not suicide itself) among youth. A recent meta-analysis of pediatric antidepressant treatment trials investigated 27 RCTs, reporting increased risks for suicidal ideation and attempts (but not completion; Bridge et al., 2007). Importantly, however, the same study concluded that SSRI-induced benefits outweigh the risk of a suicidal event among youth with OCD, and others have noted that SSRIs should not be unduly avoided (American College of Neuropsychopharmacology, 2006). Moreover, newly emergent evidence challenges the notion that antidepressants such as fluoxetine are associated with increased suicidal risk in youth (Gibbons, Brown, Hur, Davis, & Mann, 2012). Nonetheless, close monitoring for emotional and behavioral changes is advised, especially in the initial weeks of treatment.

SUMMARY

Pediatric OCD and OCSDs are common, yet underrecognized and undertreated. Differentiating OCD from OCSDs is important, given their overlapping but distinct treatment approaches. Pediatric OCD is highly treatable via SRI medications, including SSRIs and clomipramine. SRI medications are most effective for symptom improvement and relapse prevention when used concurrently with CBT. SSRI use in pediatric populations requires special clinical monitoring for potentially emergent side effects such as behavioral activation and suicidal ideation. For severe treatment refractory illness, evidence from adult OCD research supports SRI augmenting agents, including some atypical antipsychotics and glutamatergic agents. Clomipramine and atypical antipsychotic use requires laboratory monitoring. Large RCTs regarding medication treatment of pediatric OCSDs are lacking; therefore treatment decisions should be made using best current evidence from pediatric and adult literature, in addition to clinical judgment. Similarly, additional RCTs regarding medication treatment for pediatric OCD are welcome. Common explanations for failed pediatric OCD medication trials include insufficient dosage and premature discontinuation. In conclusion, accurate diagnosis and appropriate treatment of OCD and OCSDs in children and adolescents are essential for improving prognosis.

REFERENCES

Alaghband-Rad, J., & Hakimshooshtary, M. (2009). A randomized controlled clinical trial of citalopram versus fluoxetine in children and adolescents with obsessive–compulsive disorder (OCD). *European Child & Adolescent Psychiatry, 18*, 131–135. doi:10.1007/s00787-007-0634-z

American Academy of Child and Adolescent Psychiatry (AACAP). (2012). Practice parameter for the assessment and treatment of children and adolescents with obsessive–compulsive disorder. *Journal of the American Academy of Child and Adolescent Psychiatry, 51*, 98–113. doi:10.1016/j.jaac.2011.09.019

American College of Neuropsychopharmacology. (2006). ACNP releases final task force report on antidepressants and suicidality among adolescents. *Psychiatric Services, 57,* 283. doi:10.1176/appi.ps.57.2.283

Björgvinsson, T., Wetterneck, C. T., Powell, D. M., Chasson, G. S., Webb, S. A., Hart, J., . . . Stanley, M. A. (2008). Treatment outcome for adolescent obsessive–compulsive disorder in a specialized hospital setting. *Journal of Psychiatric Practice, 14,* 137–145. doi:10.1097/01.pra.0000320112.36648.3e

Bloch, M. H., Craiglow, B. G., Landeros-Weisenberger, A., Dombrowski, P. A., Panza, K. E., Peterson, B. S., & Leckman, J. F. (2009). Predictors of early adult outcomes in pediatric-onset obsessive–compulsive disorder. *Pediatrics, 124,* 1085–1093. doi:10.1542/peds.2009-0015

Bloch, M. H., McGuire, J., Landeros-Weisenberger, A., Leckman, J. F., & Pittenger, C. (2010). Meta-analysis of the dose–response relationship of SSRI in obsessive–compulsive disorder. *Molecular Psychiatry, 15,* 850–855. doi:10.1038/mp.2009.50

Bridge, J. A., Iyengar, S., Salary, C. B., Barbe, R. P., Birmaher, B., Pincus, H. A., . . . Brent, D. A. (2007). Clinical response and risk for reported suicidal ideation and suicide attempts in pediatric antidepressant treatment: A meta-analysis of randomized controlled trials. *JAMA, 297,* 1683–1696. doi:10.1001/jama.297.15.1683

Busatto, G. F., Buchpiguel, C. A., Zamignani, D. R., Garrido, G. E., Glabus, M. F., Rosario-Campos, M. C., . . . Miguel, E. C. (2001). Regional cerebral blood flow abnormalities in early-onset obsessive–compulsive disorder: An exploratory SPECT study. *Journal of the American Academy of Child & Adolescent Psychiatry, 40,* 347–354. doi:10.1097/00004583-200103000-00015

Cohen, D., Deniau, E., Maturana, A., Tanguy, M. L., Bodeau, N., Labelle, R., . . . Guile, J. M. (2008). Are child and adolescent responses to placebo higher in major depression than in anxiety disorders? A systematic review of placebo-controlled trials. *PLoS ONE, 3*(7), e2632. doi:10.1371/journal.pone.0002632

Crockett, B. A., Churchill, E., & Davidson, J. R. (2004). A double-blind combination study of clonazepam with sertraline in obsessive–compulsive disorder. *Annals of Clinical Psychiatry, 16,* 127–132. doi:10.1080/10401230490486972

DeVeaugh-Geiss, J., Moroz, G., Biederman, J., Cantwell, D., Fontaine, R., Greist, J. H., . . . Landau, P. (1992). Clomipramine hydrochloride in childhood and adolescent obsessive–compulsive disorder—A multicenter trial. *Journal of the American Academy of Child & Adolescent Psychiatry, 31,* 45–49. doi:10.1097/00004583-199201000-00008

Ellfolk, M., & Malm, H. (2010). Risks associated with in utero and lactation exposure to selective serotonin reuptake inhibitors (SSRIs). *Reproductive Toxicology, 30,* 249–260. doi:10.1016/j.reprotox.2010.04.015

Fallon, B. A., Petkova, E., Skritskaya, N., Sanchez-Lacay, A., Schneier, F., Vermes, D., . . . Liebowitz, M. R. (2008). A double-masked, placebo-controlled study of fluoxetine for hypochondriasis. *Journal of Clinical Psychopharmacology, 28,* 638–645. doi:10.1097/JCP.0b013e31818d21cf

Fitzgerald, K. D., Stewart, C. M., Tawile, V., & Rosenberg, D. R. (1999). Risperidone augmentation of serotonin reuptake inhibitor treatment of pediatric obsessive compulsive disorder. *Journal of Child and Adolescent Psychopharmacology*, 9, 115–123. doi:10.1089/cap.1999.9.115

Flament, M. F., Rapoport, J. L., & Kilts, C. (1985). A controlled trial of clomipramine in childhood obsessive compulsive disorder. *Psychopharmacology Bulletin*, 21(1), 150–152.

Foa, E. B., Liebowitz, M. R., Kozak, M. J., Davies, S., Campeas, R., Franklin, M. E., . . . Tu, X. (2005). Randomized, placebo-controlled trial of exposure and ritual prevention, clomipramine, and their combination in the treatment of obsessive–compulsive disorder. *The American Journal of Psychiatry*, 162, 151–161. doi:10.1176/appi.ajp.162.1.151

Franklin, M. E., Edson, A. L., Ledley, D. A., & Cahill, S. P. (2011). Behavior therapy for pediatric trichotillomania: A randomized controlled trial. *Journal of the American Academy of Child & Adolescent Psychiatry*, 50, 763–771. doi:10.1016/j.jaac.2011.05.009

Franklin, M. E., Sapyta, J., Freeman, J. B., Khanna, M., Compton, S., Almirall, D., . . . March, J. S. (2011). Cognitive behavior therapy augmentation of pharmacotherapy in pediatric obsessive–compulsive disorder: The Pediatric OCD Treatment Study II (POTS II) randomized controlled trial. *JAMA*, 306, 1224–1232. doi:10.1001/jama.2011.1344

Garcia, A. M., Sapyta, J. J., Moore, P. S., Freeman, J. B., Franklin, M. E., March, J. S., & Foa, E. B. (2010). Predictors and moderators of treatment outcome in the Pediatric Obsessive Compulsive Treatment Study (POTS I). *Journal of the American Academy of Child and Adolescent Psychiatry*, 49, 1024–1033. doi:0.1016/j.jaac.2010.06.013

Geller, D. A., Biederman, J., Stewart, S. E., Mullin, B., Farrell, C., Wagner, K. D., . . . Carpenter, D. (2003). Impact of comorbidity on treatment response to paroxetine in pediatric obsessive–compulsive disorder: Is the use of exclusion criteria empirically supported in randomized clinical trials? *Journal of Child and Adolescent Psychopharmacology*, 13(Suppl. 1), S19–S29. doi:10.1089/104454603322126313

Geller, D. A., Biederman, J., Stewart, S. E., Mullin, B., Martin, A., Spencer, T., & Faraone, S. V. (2003). Which SSRI? A meta-analysis of pharmacotherapy trials in pediatric obsessive–compulsive disorder. *The American Journal of Psychiatry*, 160, 1919–1928. doi:10.1176/appi.ajp.160.11.1919

Geller, D. A., Hoog, S. L., Heiligenstein, J. H., Ricardi, R. K., Tamura, R., Kluszynski, S., . . . Team, F. P. O. S. (2001). Fluoxetine treatment for obsessive–compulsive disorder in children and adolescents: A placebo-controlled clinical trial. *Journal of the American Academy of Child & Adolescent Psychiatry*, 40, 773–779.

Geller, D. A., Wagner, K. D., Emslie, G., Murphy, T., Carpenter, D. J., Wetherhold, E., . . . Gardiner, C. (2004). Paroxetine treatment in children and adolescents with obsessive–compulsive disorder: A randomized, multicenter, double-blind, placebo-controlled trial. *Journal of the American Academy of Child & Adolescent Psychiatry, 43*, 1387–1396. doi:10.1097/01.chi.0000138356.29099.f1

Gibbons, R. D., Brown, C. H., Hur, K., Davis, J. M., & Mann, J. J. (2012). Suicidal thoughts and behavior with antidepressant treatment: Reanalysis of the randomized placebo-controlled studies of fluoxetine and venlafaxine. *Archives of General Psychiatry, 69*, 580–587. doi:10.1001/archgenpsychiatry.2011.2048

Grant, P., Lougee, L., Hirschtritt, M., & Swedo, S. E. (2007). An open-label trial of riluzole, a glutamate antagonist, in children with treatment-resistant obsessive–compulsive disorder. *Journal of Child and Adolescent Psychopharmacology, 17*, 761–767. doi:10.1089/cap.2007.0021

Greeven, A., van Balkom, A. J., van der Leeden, R., Merkelbach, J. W., van den Heuvel, O. A., & Spinhoven, P. (2009). Cognitive behavioral therapy versus paroxetine in the treatment of hypochondriasis: an 18-month naturalistic follow-up. *Journal of Behavior Therapy and Experimental Psychiatry, 40*, 487–496. doi:10.1016/j.jbtep.2009.06.005

Greeven, A., van Balkom, A. J., Visser, S., Merkelbach, J. W., van Rood, Y. R., van Dyck, R., . . . Spinhoven, P. (2007). Cognitive behavior therapy and paroxetine in the treatment of hypochondriasis: A randomized controlled trial. *The American Journal of Psychiatry, 164*, 91–99. doi:10.1176/appi.ajp.164.1.91

Hezel, D. M., Beattie, K., & Stewart, S. E. (2009). Memantine as an augmenting agent for severe pediatric OCD. *American Journal of Psychiatry, 166*, 237. doi:10.1176/appi.ajp.2008.08091427

Hollander, E., Allen, A., Kwon, J., Aronowitz, B., Schmeidler, J., Wong, C., & Simeon, D. (1999). Clomipramine vs desipramine crossover trial in body dysmorphic disorder: Selective efficacy of a serotonin reuptake inhibitor in imagined ugliness. *Archives of General Psychiatry, 56*. 1033–1039. doi:10.1001/archpsyc.56.11.1033

Hollander, E., Kaplan, A., & Stahl, S. M. (2003). A double-blind, placebo-controlled trial of clonazepam in obsessive–compulsive disorder. *The World Journal of Biological Psychiatry, 4*(1), 30–34. doi:10.3109/15622970309167908

Jakubovski, E., Pittenger, C., Torres, A. R., Fontenelle, L. F., do Rosario, M. C., Ferrão, Y. A., . . . Bloch, M. H. (2011). Dimensional correlates of poor insight in obsessive–compulsive disorder. *Progress in Neuropsychopharmacology & Biological Psychiatry, 35*, 1677–1681. doi:10.1016/j.pnpbp.2011.05.012

Kessler, R. C., Chiu, W. T., Demler, O., Merikangas, K. R., & Walters, E. E. (2005). Prevalence, severity, and comorbidity of 12-month *DSM–IV* disorders in the National Comorbidity Survey Replication. *Archives of General Psychiatry, 62*, 617–627. doi:10.1001/archpsyc.62.6.617

Komossa, K., Depping, A. M., Meyer, M., Kissling, W., & Leucht, S. (2010). Second-generation antipsychotics for obsessive compulsive disorder. *Cochrane Database of Systematic Reviews* (12):CD008141. doi:10.1002/14651858.CD008141.pub2

Lafleur, D. L., Pittenger, C., Kelmendi, B., Gardner, T., Wasylink, S., Malison, R. T., . . . Coric, V. (2006). N-acetylcysteine augmentation in serotonin reuptake inhibitor refractory obsessive–compulsive disorder. *Psychopharmacology, 184*, 254–256. doi:10.1007/s00213-005-0246-6

Leonard, H. L., Swedo, S. E., Lenane, M. C., Rettew, D. C., Cheslow, D. L., Hamburger, S. D., & Rapoport, J. L. (1991). A double-blind desipramine substitution during long-term clomipramine treatment in children and adolescents with obsessive–compulsive disorder. *Archives of General Psychiatry, 48*, 922–927.

Leonard, H. L., Swedo, S. E., Rapoport, J. L., Koby, E. V., Lenane, M. C., Cheslow, D. L., & Hamburger, S. D. (1989). Treatment of obsessive–compulsive disorder with clomipramine and desipramine in children and adolescents. A double-blind crossover comparison. *Archives of General Psychiatry, 46*, 1088–1092.

Leonard, H. L., Topol, D., Bukstein, O., Hindmarsh, D., Allen, A. J., & Swedo, S. E. (1994). Clonazepam as an augmenting agent in the treatment of childhood-onset obsessive–compulsive disorder. *Journal of the American Academy of Child & Adolescent Psychiatry, 33*, 792–794. doi:10.1097/00004583-199407000-00003

Liebowitz, M. R., Turner, S. M., Piacentini, J., Beidel, D. C., Clarvit, S. R., Davies, S. O., . . . Simpson, H. B. (2002). Fluoxetine in children and adolescents with OCD: A placebo-controlled trial. *Journal of the American Academy of Child & Adolescent Psychiatry, 41*, 1431–1438. doi:10.1097/00004583-200212000-00014

March, J. S., Biederman, J., Wolkow, R., Safferman, A., Mardekian, J., Cook, E. H., . . . Steiner, H. (1998). Sertraline in children and adolescents with obsessive–compulsive disorder: a multicenter randomized controlled trial. *JAMA, 280*, 1752–1756.

March, J. S., Johnston, H., Jefferson, J. W., Kobak, K. A., & Greist, J. H. (1990). Do subtle neurological impairments predict treatment resistance to clomipramine in children and adolescents with obsessive–compulsive disorder? *Journal of Child and Adolescent Psychopharmacology, 1*, 133–140. doi:10.1089/cap.1990.1.133

Masi, G., Millepiedi, S., Perugi, G., Pfanner, C., Berloffa, S., Pari, C., & Mucci, M. (2009). Pharmacotherapy in paediatric obsessive–compulsive disorder: A naturalistic, retrospective study. *CNS Drugs, 23*, 241–252. doi:10.2165/00023210-200923030-00005

Masi, G., Pfanner, C., Millepiedi, S., & Berloffa, S. (2010). Aripiprazole augmentation in 39 adolescents with medication-resistant obsessive–compulsive disorder. *Journal of Clinical Psychopharmacology, 30*, 688–693. doi:10.1097/JCP.0b013e3181fab7b1

Micali, N., Heyman, I., Perez, M., Hilton, K., Nakatani, E., Turner, C., & Mataix-Cols, D. (2010). Long-term outcomes of obsessive–compulsive disorder: Follow-up of 142 children and adolescents. *The British Journal of Psychiatry, 197*, 128–134. doi:10.1192/bjp.bp.109.075317

Murphy, T. K., Segarra, A., Storch, E. A., & Goodman, W. K. (2008). SSRI adverse events: How to monitor and manage. *International Review of Psychiatry, 20*, 203–208. doi:10.1080/09540260801889211

Murray, C. J., & Lopez, A. D. (1997). Global mortality, disability, and the contribution of risk factors: Global Burden of Disease Study. *The Lancet, 349,* 1436–1442. doi:10.1016/S0140-6736(96)07495-8

Ninan, P. T., Rothbaum, B. O., Marsteller, F. A., Knight, B. T., & Eccard, M. B. (2000). A placebo-controlled trial of cognitive–behavioral therapy and clomipramine in trichotillomania. *Journal of Clinical Psychiatry, 61*(1), 47–50. doi:10.4088/JCP.v61n0111

Nulman, I., Rovet, J., Stewart, D. E., Wolpin, J., Pace-Asciak, P., Shuhaiber, S., & Koren, G. (2002). Child development following exposure to tricyclic antidepressants or fluoxetine throughout fetal life: A prospective, controlled study. *The American Journal of Psychiatry, 159,* 1889–1895. doi:10.1176/appi.ajp.159.11.1889

O'Kearney, R. (2007). Benefits of cognitive–behavioural therapy for children and youth with obsessive–compulsive disorder: Re-examination of the evidence. *Austtralian and New Zealand Journal of Psychiatry, 41,* 199–212. doi:10.1080/00048670601172707

O'Kearney, R. T., Anstey, K. J., & von Sanden, C. (2006). Behavioural and cognitive behavioural therapy for obsessive compulsive disorder in children and adolescents. *Cochrane Database of Systematic Reviews,* (4):CD004856. doi:10.1002/14651858.CD004856.pub2

Pediatric OCD Treatment Study (POTS) Team. (2004). Cognitive–behavior therapy, sertraline, and their combination for children and adolescents with obsessive–compulsive disorder: The Pediatric OCD Treatment Study (POTS) randomized controlled trial. *JAMA, 292,* 1969–1976. doi:10.1001/jama.292.16.1969

Piacentini, J., Peris, T. S., Bergman, R. L., Chang, S., & Jaffer, M. (2007). Functional impairment in childhood OCD: Development and psychometrics properties of the Child Obsessive–Compulsive Impact Scale—Revised (COIS–R). *Journal of Clinical Child and Adolescent Psychology, 36,* 645–653. doi:10.1080/15374410701662790

Riddle, M. A., Reeve, E. A., Yaryura-Tobias, J. A., Yang, H. M., Claghorn, J. L., Gaffney, G., . . . Walkup, J. T. (2001). Fluvoxamine for children and adolescents with obsessive–compulsive disorder: A randomized, controlled, multicenter trial. *Journal of the American Academy of Child & Adolescent Psychiatry, 40,* 222–229. doi:10.1097/00004583-200102000-00017

Riddle, M. A., Scahill, L., King, R. A., Hardin, M. T., Anderson, G. M., Ort, S. I., . . . Cohen, D. J. (1992). Double-blind, crossover trial of fluoxetine and placebo in children and adolescents with obsessive–compulsive disorder. *Journal of Clinical Child and Adolescent Psychology, 31,* 1062–1069. doi:10.1097/00004583-199211000-00011

Scahill, L., Riddle, M. A., McSwiggin-Hardin, M., Ort, S. I., King, R. A., Goodman, W. K., . . . Leckman, J. F. (1997). Children's Yale–Brown Obsessive Compulsive Scale: Reliability and validity. *Journal of the American Academy of Child & Adolescent Psychiatry, 36,* 844–852. doi:10.1097/00004583-199706000-00023

Simpson, H. B., Liebowitz, M. R., Foa, E. B., Kozak, M. J., Schmidt, A. B., Rowan, V., . . . Campeas, R. (2004). Post-treatment effects of exposure therapy and clomipramine in obsessive–compulsive disorder. *Depression and Anxiety, 19,* 225–233. doi:10.1002/da.20003

Soomro, G. M., Altman, D., Rajagopal, S., & Oakley-Browne, M. (2008). Selective serotonin re-uptake inhibitors (SSRIs) versus placebo for obsessive compulsive disorder (OCD). *Cochrane Database of Systematic Reviews,* (1):CD001765. doi:10.1002/14651858.CD001765.pub3

Stewart, S. E., Geller, D., Spender, T., & Gianini, L. (2003). Tics and Tourette's disorder: Which therapies, and when to use them [Special issue]. *Journal of Family Practice, 2*(10).

Stewart, S. E., Hezel, D., & Stachon, A. C. (2012). Assessment and medication management of paediatric obsessive–compulsive disorder. *Drugs, 72,* 881–893. doi:10.2165/11632860-000000000-00000

Stewart, S. E., Hu, Y. P., Hezel, D. M., Proujansky, R., Lamstein, A., Walsh, C., . . . Pauls, D. L. (2011). Development and psychometric properties of the OCD Family Functioning (OFF) Scale. *Journal of Family Psychology, 25,* 434–443. doi:10.1037/a0023735

Stewart, S. E., Jenike, M. A., & Keuthen, N. J. (2005). Severe obsessive–compulsive disorder with and without comorbid hair pulling: Comparisons and clinical implications. *Journal of Clinical Psychiatry, 66,* 864–869. doi:10.4088/JCP.v66n0709

Stewart, S. E., Rosario, M. C., Brown, T. A., Carter, A. S., Leckman, J. F., Sukhodolsky, D., . . . Pauls, D. L. (2007). Principal components analysis of obsessive–compulsive disorder symptoms in children and adolescents. *Biological Psychiatry, 61,* 285–291. doi:10.1016/j.biopsych.2006.08.040

Stewart, S. E., Stack, D. E., Farrell, C., Pauls, D. L., & Jenike, M. A. (2005). Effectiveness of intensive residential treatment (IRT) for severe, refractory obsessive–compulsive disorder. *Journal of Psychiatric Research, 39,* 603–609. doi:10.1016/j.jpsychires.2005.01.004

Stewart, S. E., Stack, D. E., Tsilker, S., Alosso, J., Stephansky, M., Hezel, D. M., . . . Jenike, M. A. (2009). Long-term outcome following intensive residential treatment of obsessive–compulsive disorder. *Journal of Psychiatric Research, 43,* 1118–1123. doi:10.1016/j.jpsychires.2009.03.012

Storch, E. A., Larson, M. J., Muroff, J., Caporino, N., Geller, D., Reid, J. M., . . . Murphy, T. K. (2010). Predictors of functional impairment in pediatric obsessive–compulsive disorder. *Journal of Anxiety Disorders, 24,* 275–283. doi:10.1016/j.janxdis.2009.12.004

Storch, E. A., Lewin, A. B., Geffken, G. R., Morgan, J. R., & Murphy, T. K. (2010). The role of comorbid disruptive behavior in the clinical expression of pediatric obsessive–compulsive disorder. *Behaviour Research and Therapy, 48,* 1204–1210. doi:10.1016/j.brat.2010.09.004

Swedo, E., Leckman, J., & Rose, N. (2012). From research subgroup to clinical syndrome: Modifying the PANDAS criteria to describe PANS (Pediatric

Acute-Onset Neuropsychiatric Syndrome). *Pediatrics & Therapeutics*, 2(2). Retrieved from http://intramural.nimh.nih.gov/research/pubs/swedo01.pdf.

Swedo, S. E., Leonard, H. L., Garvey, M., Mittleman, B., Allen, A. J., Perlmutter, S., . . . Dubbert, B. K. (1998). Pediatric autoimmune neuropsychiatric disorders associated with streptococcal infections: Clinical description of the first 50 cases. *The American Journal of Psychiatry*, 155, 264–271.

Swedo, S. E., Schapiro, M. B., Grady, C. L., Cheslow, D. L., Leonard, H. L., Kumar, A., . . . Rapoport, J. L. (1989). Cerebral glucose metabolism in childhood-onset obsessive–compulsive disorder. *Archives of General Psychiatry*, 46, 518–523. doi:10.1001/archpsyc.1989.01810060038007

Thomsen, P. H. (2004). Risperidone augmentation in the treatment of severe adolescent OCD in SSRI-refractory cases: A case-series. *Annals of Clinical Psychiatry*, 16, 201–207. doi:10.1080/10401230490522016

Uzun, O., & Ozdemir, B. (2010). Aripiprazole as an augmentation agent in treatment-resistant body dysmorphic disorder. *Clinical Drug Investigation*, 30, 707–710. doi:10.2165/11536730-000000000-00000

van Minnen, A., Hoogduin, K. A., Keijsers, G. P., Hellenbrand, I., & Hendriks, G. J. (2003). Treatment of trichotillomania with behavioral therapy or fluoxetine: A randomized, waiting-list controlled study. *Archives of General Psychiatry*, 60, 517–522. doi:10.1001/archpsyc.60.5.517

Watson, H. J., & Rees, C. S. (2008). Meta-analysis of randomized, controlled treatment trials for pediatric obsessive–compulsive disorder. *Journal of Child Psychology and Psychiatry*, 49, 489–498. doi:10.1111/j.1469-7610.2007.01875.x

Williams, J., Hadjistavropoulos, T., & Sharpe, D. (2006). A meta-analysis of psychological and pharmacological treatments for body dysmorphic disorder. *Behaviour Research and Therapy*, 44, 99–111. doi:10.1016/j.brat.2004.12.006

Wisner, K. L., Zarin, D. A., Holmboe, E. S., Appelbaum, P. S., Gelenberg, A. J., Leonard, H. L., & Frank, E. (2000). Risk–benefit decision making for treatment of depression during pregnancy. *The American Journal of Psychiatry*, 157, 1933–1940. doi:10.1176/appi.ajp.157.12.1933

15

PHARMACOTHERAPY FOR OBSESSIVE–COMPULSIVE AND RELATED DISORDERS AMONG ADULTS

JON E. GRANT, BRIAN L. ODLAUG, AND LIANA R.N. SCHREIBER

Twenty years ago, Swedo and Leonard (1992) proposed a concept of an obsessive–compulsive spectrum of psychiatric disorders. At that time and since, a wide range of psychiatric and medical disorders have been hypo-thesized to be related to obsessive–compulsive disorder (OCD) and thus, together, to form a family of disorders known as *obsessive–compulsive spectrum disorders*. The grouping of these conditions is based, arguably, on their phenomenological similarities with OCD (i.e., obsessive thinking and/or compulsive behaviors), as well as their having courses of illness, comorbidity and family history patterns, biological abnormalities, and treatment responses similar to those of OCD. The disorders included in the OCD spectrum have fluctuated over time as the growing body of neurobiological, genetic, and treatment research has helped delineate the parameters of this spectrum. Although which disorders to include has been a source of some debate (as has whether to group them together at all; Bienvenu et al., 2000; McElroy, Phillips, & Keck, 1994; Stein, 2000), the spectrum concept

http://dx.doi.org/10.1037/14323-016
Obsessive–Compulsive Disorder and Its Spectrum: A Life-Span Approach, Eric A. Storch and Dean McKay (Editors)
Copyright © 2014 by the American Psychological Association. All rights reserved.

has been valuable for purposes of clinical research and patient care (see the Introduction to this volume). Obsessive–compulsive spectrum disorders have included body dysmorphic disorder, hypochondriasis, trichotillomania, and skin-picking disorder, among others.

In this chapter, the clinical characteristics and pharmacological management of OCD and selected obsessive–compulsive spectrum disorders are reviewed, predominantly for adults (18+ years old): body dysmorphic disorder, hypochondriasis, trichotillomania, and skin-picking disorder. Although many other disorders could have been included, the ones reviewed attest to the progress that has been made regarding pharmacological treatment of these disorders. Exhibit 15.1 lists medications used for OCD and OCD spectrum disorders, indicating generic and trade names of medications.

OBSESSIVE–COMPULSIVE DISORDER

OCD is characterized by obsessions and compulsions. *Obsessions* are recurrent intrusive and unwanted thoughts that the sufferer cannot dispel. Common themes include thoughts that the person may cause harm to others or that harm may befall others; that the person or others are contaminated; or that behaviors, thoughts, or actions are not complete or done properly. Other common themes include the need for order, symmetry, or perfection. The obsessional thoughts are associated with negative affect, usually anxiety, disgust, guilt, or shame. As a response to the feelings generated by the obsessional thoughts, the person may perform compulsions, and performance of the compulsions temporarily decreases the negative affect. The *compulsions* are stereotypic, ritualized behaviors that are either overt (e.g., repetitive checking, washing or cleaning, repetitive rearranging and ordering of objects, reassurance seeking) or covert mental rituals (e.g., counting, praying, magical thinking; Geller et al., 2001). The obsessions and compulsions may occupy many hours of a person's day and cause severe distress and dysfunction socially or occupationally (Rasmussen & Eisen, 1988).

The variety of symptoms in OCD presents a substantial treatment challenge. Factor and cluster analyses have demonstrated four robust and temporally stable symptom dimensions in OCD: contamination obsessions with cleaning compulsions; harm-related aggressive, sexual, and religious obsessions with checking compulsions; symmetry obsessions with arranging and repeating compulsions; and hoarding/saving symptoms (Leckman et al., 1997; Miguel et al., 1995). Individuals with various OCD subtypes present with a range of obsessions and compulsions, experience different co-occurring disorders, may have unique genetic transmission, appear to have distinct but overlapping neuropathologies, and vary in their response to both

EXHIBIT 15.1
List of Medications: Generic to Trade Name

Generic name	Trade name
Antipsychotic medications	
Olanzapine	Zyprexa
Pimozide	Orap
Quetiapine	Seroquel
Risperidone	Risperdal
Antiepileptic medications	
Lamotrigine	Lamictal
Levetiracetam	Keppra
Topimarate	Topamax
Antidepressant medications (SRI, SNRI, tricyclics)	
Amitriptyline	Elavil
Bupropion	Wellbutrin
Citalopram	Celexa
Clomipramine	Anafranil
Desipramine	Norpramin, Pertofrane
Fluvoxamine	Luvox
Fluoxetine	Prozac
Paroxetine	Paxil
Phenelzine	Nardil
Sertraline	Zoloft
Trazodone	Desyrel
Venlafaxine	Effexor
Benzodiazepines	
Clonazepam	Klonopin
Opioid antagonists	
Naltrexone	ReVia
Other medications	
Buspirone	Buspar
Celecoxib	Celebrex
L-triodothyronine	Cytomel, Liothyronine sodium
Lithium carbonate	Eskalith, Lithane, Lithobid
N-acetylcysteine	Mucolysin, Mucomyst
Ondansetron	Zofran

Note. SNRI = serotonin–norepinephrine reuptake inhibitor; SRI = serotonin reuptake inhibitor.

psychosocial and pharmacological treatments (Alonso et al., 2001; Başoğlu, Lelliott, & Marks, 1988; Mataix-Cols et al., 2004). It is therefore possible that certain subtypes of OCD may necessitate different treatment strategies.

Clinical practice guidelines (Baldwin et al., 2005; Canadian Psychiatric Association, 2006; Koran et al., 2007) recommend that initial treatment be selected on the basis of five factors: (a) nature and severity of patient symptoms, (b) comorbid psychiatric and medical conditions, (c) past treatment history, (d) current medications, and (e) patient preferences. In addition, level of impairment, concomitant medications, and availability of treatments also need to be considered when selecting treatment strategies.

Serotonin Reuptake Inhibitors

Two multicenter and eight smaller double-blind, placebo-controlled studies have examined clomipramine in the treatment of adults with OCD (Piccinelli, Pini, Bellantuono, & Wilkinson, 1995). All of these studies confirm the efficacy of clomipramine for OCD. Other serotonin reuptake inhibitors (SRIs)—paroxetine, fluoxetine, sertraline, and fluvoxamine—have also demonstrated significant superiority to placebo in the treatment of OCD (Denys, 2006; Ellingrod, 1998), and a recent review examining 17 studies (3,097 participants) confirmed that SRIs were effective in reducing the symptoms of OCD (Soomro, Altman, Rajagopal, & Oakley-Browne, 2008). On the basis of 13 studies (2,697 participants), the review showed that people receiving SRIs were nearly twice as likely as those receiving placebo to achieve clinical response (defined as a 25% or more reduction in symptoms) (Soomro et al., 2008). A meta-analysis of the relative benefits of the SRIs, however, suggested that clomipramine might have superior efficacy in comparison with the other SRIs (Greist, Jefferson, Kobak, Katzelnick, & Serline 1995), although this has been questioned (Pigott & Seay, 1999). Although the data on dosing and duration are somewhat problematic, an adequate trial of an SRI is generally considered at least 10-weeks duration and that optimal doses of SRIs for OCD generally exceed those used for depression (Montgomery & Zohar, 1999).

Approximately 40% to 60% of OCD patients respond to an SRI, and the mean improvement of symptoms is about 20% to 40% (Jenike, 2004). The probability of full remission of OCD is only about 12% (Eisen et al., 1999). Relapse rates after medication discontinuation are approximately 90% (Pato, Zohar-Kadouch, Zohar, & Murphy, 1988). Although clomipramine has yielded a larger effect size than have the selective serotonin reuptake inhibitors (SSRIs) (Greist et al., 1995), many patients have trouble tolerating the side effects of clomipramine (March, Frances, Carpenter, & Kahn, 1997).

Given these findings, although SRIs are effective in reducing OCD symptoms, studies examining broader measures of outcome (e.g., quality of life, psychosocial functioning) and long-term treatment outcome are needed (Gava et al., 2007). In light of the fact that SRI treatment more often results in partial remission of OCD symptoms than in complete remission, and changes in psychosocial functioning often lag behind symptom reductions, examining quality of life and long-term functioning of individuals with OCD is critical.

SRI Medication in Combination With Cognitive–Behavioral Therapy

Pharmacological treatment and cognitive–behavioral therapy (CBT), which focuses on modifying cognitions and behaviors, have documented evidence as monotherapies as well as a combined treatment strategy. Although the optimal sequence of treatments has not yet been identified, the American Psychiatric Association guidelines (Koran et al., 2007) recommend exposure and response prevention (ERP) monotherapy for individuals who are motivated to cooperate with ERP demands, do not have severe depressive symptoms, or prefer not to take medications. SRI monotherapy is recommended for individuals who are not able to engage in ERP, report a previous response to an SRI, or prefer medication treatments over CBT. A combination of SRI treatment and CBT is recommended for individuals who have other comorbid conditions that could benefit from SSRI treatment (e.g., major depression, generalized anxiety disorder) or who show an unsatisfactory response to monotherapy. Combined treatment is also recommended for individuals who prefer to take medications for the shortest possible time, because there are data from uncontrolled follow-up studies that suggest that CBT may help to prevent or delay relapse when the SRI is discontinued (Biondi & Picardi, 2005; Hembree, Riggs, Kozak, Franklin, & Foa, 2003; Simpson et al., 2004).

Clinical Variables Affecting SRI Response

In adult OCD treatment, age at time of treatment has generally not been found to moderate treatment outcome (Denys, 2006). In contrast, an earlier age at OCD onset and longer duration of OCD were associated with a poorer response to clomipramine and SSRIs (Fineberg & Gale, 2005). Greater baseline severity of OCD and comorbid tics were also associated with poorer response to clomipramine and SSRIs in adults (Fineberg & Gale, 2005; Mataix-Cols, Rauch, Manzo, Jenike, & Baer, 1999). One study found that sexual and religious obsessions were associated with poorer long-term treatment outcome (Alonso et al., 2001), but another study found that sexual obsessions were not associated with differences in response to pharmacotherapy (Grant et al., 2006). Other possible treatment moderators have been examined such as depression, personality traits, insight, and expressed emotion. However, there is not consistent evidence that these variables affect treatment outcome.

Poor insight is generally considered to be a patient's relative lack of understanding of the degree to which his or her obsessions and compulsions are unreasonable or excessive. A variety of terminology has been used to describe this concept, such as overvalued ideation and obsessive–compulsive psychosis (Insel & Akiskal, 1986; Neziroglu, Pinto, Yaryura-Tobias, & McKay,

2004). Poor insight has been associated with more severe OCD, co-occurring depression, and somatic obsessions (Eisen et al., 2001; Matsunaga et al., 2002). Poor-insight OCD patients appear to respond equally well to SRI treatment as do those with good insight (Catapano, Sperandeo, Perris, Lanzaro, & Maj, 2001). The addition of an antipsychotic medication does not appear necessary for the treatment of poor-insight OCD (Shapira et al., 2004).

No study has examined whether the age of the patients results in a differential response to these medications. Therefore, the data regarding medication for OCD should generally apply to elderly patients with OCD as well. Initial doses of the medications, however, should be lower than the recommended starting doses for other adults given that elderly patients generally metabolize the SRIs more slowly than do younger adults.

Augmentation of Serotonin Reuptake Inhibitors

For patients who do not adequately respond to SRIs as monotherapy, the next approach involves augmentation of the SRI. Low-dose dopamine antagonists have the most impressive data for their use with SRIs. Three placebo-controlled studies support the use of risperidone for OCD (Hollander, Baldini, Rossi, et al., 2003; Li et al., 2005; McDougle, Epperson, Pelton, Wasylink, & Price, 2000) and demonstrated efficacy for aripiprazole (Muscatello et al., 2011), but quetiapine (Carey et al., 2005; Denys, de Geus, van Megen, & Westenberg, 2004) and olanzapine (Bystritsky et al., 2004; Shapira et al., 2004) have produced only mixed results.

One study of ondansetron (4 mg) (a serotonin receptor antagonist) augmentation of fluoxetine in 42 adults with OCD found that ondansetron produced significantly greater improvement in OCD symptoms in comparison with placebo (Soltani et al., 2010). Similarly, a double-blind, placebo-controlled study of 23 subjects with treatment-resistant OCD found that once-weekly oral morphine showed significant reduction in OCD symptoms in comparison with placebo (Koran et al., 2005). Finally, on the basis of the hypothesis that OCD is associated with an inflammatory process, celecoxib, a nonsteroidal anti-inflammatory drug that selectively inhibits prostaglandin synthesis, was added to fluoxetine and compared with placebo in a double-blind study. The combination of celecoxib and fluoxetine was significantly more effective in reducing OCD symptoms than was fluoxetine alone (Sayyah, Boostani, Pakseresht, & Malayeri, 2011).

Other augmentation strategies, however, though promising in open-label studies, yielded little benefit or mixed results in double-blind, placebo-controlled studies. Trials of lithium (McDougle, Price, Goodman, Charney, & Heninger, 1991), L-triodothyronine (Pigott et al., 1991), clonazepam (Crockett, Churchill, & Davidson, 2004), buspirone (Grady et al., 1993), and topiramate (Berlin et al., 2011) all speak against the efficacy of these medications in combination with SRIs for OCD. Thus overall, augmentation studies of SRIs have provided mixed-efficacy results for treating OCD, and thus no treatment recommendations can be made.

Other Monotherapies

For patients who do not report any improvement from SRIs, or who cannot tolerate the side effects of an SRI, the next approach is to consider an alternative monotherapy. Inositol, a dietary supplement that is a precursor of the second messenger phosphatidylinositol, has demonstrated superiority to placebo in one double-blind study (Fux, Levine, Aviv, & Belmaker, 1996). Clonazepam has demonstrated mixed results (Hewlett, Vinogradov, & Agras, 1992; Hollander, Kaplan, & Stahl, 2003); venlafaxine failed to demonstrate efficacy in comparison with placebo (Yaryura-Tobias & Neziroglu, 1996); and trazodone resulted in no difference from placebo (Pigott et al., 1992). Although not including a placebo, controlled studies of buspirone versus clomipramine and phenelzine versus clomipramine both demonstrated similar efficacy between the two medications (Pato et al., 1991; Vallejo, Olivares, Marcos, Bulbena, & Menchón, 1992).

Although preliminary studies suggest that several other medications may be beneficial for OCD (e.g., glutamate-modulating agents), these agents currently lack double-blind, placebo-controlled data to support their efficacy. Given that previous trials of medication were often successful in open-label studies and not in placebo-controlled studies, these medications require more rigorous testing.

BODY DYSMORPHIC DISORDER

Most people are dissatisfied with some aspect of their appearance. In fact, more than half of all women and nearly half of all men in the United States are dissatisfied with the way they look (Pope, Phillips, & Olivardia, 2002). For some people, however, the preoccupation with perceived defects in physical appearance is excessive. These patients suffer from body dysmorphic disorder (BDD), a disorder characterized by significant distress, impaired functioning, social withdrawal, and repeated attempts to hide or correct a perceived defect in appearance, which is ruled out if an eating disorder is present (American Psychiatric Association, 2000).

Individuals with BDD are preoccupied with the idea that some aspect, or aspects, of their appearance looks abnormal, unattractive, deformed, disfigured, ugly, hideous, or "not right." Although any body part can be the focus of concern, and most individuals with BDD are preoccupied with numerous body areas, the face or head is commonly the body area that troubles BDD patients, with a focus on skin flaws, defects, blemishes, wrinkles, scars, or supposed acne (Neziroglu & Yaryura-Tobias, 1993). Typical patients are preoccupied with their appearance for several hours each day (Veale et al., 1996) and limit their social interactions, thus becoming isolated. The majority also have ideas of reference, thinking that others notice their imagined defect and react to it with dislike or disgust (Phillips, McElroy, Keck, Pope, & Hudson, 1993).

Nearly all persons with BDD perform repetitive, time-consuming behaviors that focus on examining, improving, being reassured about, or hiding the perceived defect (Grant & Phillips, 2005; Hollander, Cohen, & Simeon, 1993). These behaviors are often described as "compulsive" in the sense that the urge to perform them is strong and difficult to resist. Along with camouflaging with makeup, other behaviors are also common, including dieting, excessive exercising or weightlifting, touching or measuring the body part, tanning, buying excessive amounts of or compulsive shopping for beauty products or clothing, repeated clothes changing, seeking surgery or medical treatment, and using potentially dangerous anabolic steroids to "bulk up" (Phillips, Grant, Siniscalchi, & Albertini, 2001).

Nearly all patients with BDD experience impairment in social and occupational/academic functioning as a result of their appearance concerns. People with BDD also have markedly poor quality of life, and approximately one quarter of patients with BDD are so distressed that they attempt suicide (Grant & Phillips, 2005). However, the severity of the disorder varies, with some people appearing to lead relatively normal lives despite the suffering and interference they experience.

Medication Treatment

Many people with BDD seek and receive surgical and nonpsychiatric medical treatments (e.g., dermatologic) for their perceived appearance flaws. Available data suggest that such treatments are usually ineffective and that appearance concerns usually persist unchanged (Phillips et al., 2001). Although many patients do not report their symptoms to their physician (Grant, Kim, & Crow, 2001), treatment data suggest that pharmacotherapy is often quite beneficial for BDD (Ipser, Sander, & Stein, 2009).

Serotonin Reuptake Inhibitors

SRIs are the best-studied medications for BDD. All SRI studies to date have found that a majority of patients with BDD improve with these medications. A number of early case reports and open-label studies suggested that fluoxetine, citalopram, fluvoxamine, and clomipramine improved BDD symptoms (Brady, Austin, & Lydiard, 1990; Hollander, Liebowitz, Winchel, Klumker, & Klein, 1989; Pallanti & Koran, 1996; Perugi et al., 1996; Phillips & Najjar, 2003).

Two placebo-controlled trials of SRIs have been conducted in BDD. In the first, 29 subjects with BDD were randomized to a 16-week crossover study of clomipramine (mean dose of 138 mg/day) and desipramine (mean dose 147 mg/day). Clomipramine was superior to desipramine in the acute treatment of BDD symptoms (Hollander et al., 1999). In the second placebo-controlled study, 67 subjects with BDD were randomized to either 12 weeks of fluoxetine (mean dose of 78 mg/day) or placebo. Fluoxetine was significantly more effective than placebo for BDD beginning at Week 8. Eighteen (53%) of 34 assigned to fluoxetine and 6 (18%) of 33 assigned to placebo were responders (Phillips, Albertini, & Rasmussen, 2002).

A third controlled study involved the antipsychotic medication pimozide versus placebo augmented with fluoxetine in 28 BDD subjects. Pimozide augmentation of fluoxetine was not more effective than was placebo; 18.2% of the active group and 17.6% of the placebo group were responders (Phillips, 2005).

Although SRIs such as fluoxetine and clomipramine are encouraging treatments for BDD, there is insufficient evidence, with replication by independent investigators, at this time to definitively recommend them as first-line treatments. Larger controlled studies are necessary in order to properly identify efficacious treatments.

Other Monotherapies

There are no double-blind placebo-controlled studies of pharmacotherapies, other than SRIs, in the treatment of BDD. One small open-label trial ($N = 11$) found that venlafaxine significantly improved BDD symptoms in study completers (Allen et al., 2008). In addition, the antiepileptic medication levetiracetam has recently demonstrated promise in reducing BDD symptoms in an open-label study of 17 subjects treated for 12 weeks (mean dose of $2,044.1 \pm 1,065.2$ per day; Phillips & Menard, 2009).

Future research needs to address clinical strategies to improve proper treatment of BDD. The number of placebo-controlled studies for BDD is simply too few, and therefore it is not possible, on the basis of this evidence, to thoroughly understand the variables that effect treatment response (e.g., age of the patient, focus of body concern). More research is also needed to address the pathophysiology of BDD (e.g., by incorporating imaging and genetics). As with any disorder, understanding etiology should allow for more effective treatments.

HYPOCHONDRIASIS

Hypochondriasis is a relatively common and costly disease (Barsky, Ettner, Horksy, & Bates 2001), with a lifetime prevalence of between 1% and 5% of the population (American Psychiatric Association, 2000; Gureje, Ustun, & Simon, 1997). The *Diagnostic and Statistical Manual of Mental Disorders* (5th ed.) categorizes hypochondriasis as a member of the somatic symptoms and related disorders that is characterized by a preoccupation with having a serious illness resulting from misinterpretations of bodily sensations, despite the presence of an actual disease (American Psychiatric Association, 2013). However, some research has proposed that hypochondriasis falls on the spectrum of OCD because of similar phenomenology and symptomology (Barsky, 1992; Neziroglu, McKay, & Yaryura-Tobias, 2000).

Currently, there is a dearth of research investigating effective treatment for hypochondriasis. Several open-label studies have found that SRIs may be helpful in acute treatment of hypochondriasis (Fallon et al., 1993, 2003; Oosterbaan, van Balkom, van Boeijen, de Meij, & van Dyck, 2001).

Few double-blind pharmacological treatment studies have been carried out in a sample of hypochondriacs. Fallon et al. (2008) completed an efficacy trial in a sample of 45 individuals with hypochondriasis who were randomized to receive either placebo or fluoxetine for 12 weeks. Statistical analysis indicated that in comparison with placebo, fluoxetine was well tolerated and moderately effective for treating hypochondriasis (Fallon et al., 2008). Schweitzer, Zafar, Pavlicova, and Fallon (2011) evaluated the efficacy of SSRIs in 46 individuals with hypochondriasis who had participated in one of two SSRI treatment studies (either from an open-label fluvoxamine study or from a double-blind, placebo-controlled fluoxetine trial) that had taken place 4 to 16 years prior. Results indicated that 60% of subjects no longer met hypochondriasis criteria. Three variables that predicted the continued hypochondriasis at follow-up were a longer duration of hypochondriasis prior to treatment, a history of childhood punishment, and not using SSRI during the follow-up period.

One study randomized 112 individuals with hypochondriasis into CBT, paroxetine, or placebo treatment (Greeven et al., 2007). Of the subjects who completed the study, both the CBT and paroxetine treatment groups significantly improved in comparison with the placebo group. Follow-up analysis of data collected from 62 subjects at 18 months posttreatment indicated that the initial treatment effects were maintained at follow-up (Greeven et al., 2009).

Overall, very limited research suggests that SSRIs might be an effective treatment method for individuals struggling with hypochondriasis. More double-blind, controlled, research trials evaluated by independent investigators need to be completed to validate these results. Future research should also assess the efficacy of SRIs in larger sample sizes and evaluate the impact of comorbid psychiatric disorders. Furthermore, additional research is needed to better understand options for those with treatment-resistant hypochondriasis, whose symptoms may be more severe and debilitating as a result of their illness (Hiller, Leibbrand, Rief, & Fichter, 2002).

TRICHOTILLOMANIA (HAIR-PULLING DISORDER)

Trichotillomania is characterized by repetitive hair pulling, leading to noticeable hair loss and resulting in distress and social or occupational impairment. Hair pulling usually begins at a young age, between ages 11 and 13 (Christenson, Mackenzie, Mitchell, & Callies, 1991). Any site may be the focus of pulling, but the scalp is the most common (72.8%), followed by eyebrows (56.4%; Cohen et al., 1995; Woods et al., 2006). Most commonly, individuals pull from one or two sites. Triggers to pull include sensory cues (i.e., hair thickness, length, and location, and physical sensations on scalp), emotional cues (i.e., feeling anxious, bored, tense, or angry), and cognitive cues (i.e., thoughts about hair and appearance, rigid thinking, and cognitive errors; Walther, Ricketts, Conelea, & Woods, 2010).

Psychosocial dysfunction is common in trichotillomania. In a sample of 1,697 individuals with trichotillomania, approximately 49% avoided social situations, such as dating or group activities (Woods et al., 2006). Low self-esteem and social anxiety are also linked with trichotillomania largely because of the resulting alopecia (Diefenbach, Tolin, Hannan, Crocetto, & Worhunsky, 2005; Woods et al., 2006). Distress results both from the need to avoid certain activities because of hair loss and from the individual's inability to control the pulling. The negative self-evaluation and negative affect may serve to perpetuate the problem by prompting additional pulling episodes.

Serotonin Reuptake Inhibitors

Currently, 10 controlled pharmacological studies have been completed for trichotillomania, with seven investigating SRI antidepressants. The earliest trials examined SRIs, such as clomipramine and SSRI fluoxetine, on the basis of the assumption that trichotillomania is related to OCD and that such agents show selective efficacy in the treatment of OCD (Fineberg & Gale, 2005).

The effects of the tricyclic agent clomipramine (50–250 mg/day) on hair pulling were compared with the tricyclic desipramine (50–250 mg/day) in a 10-week double-blind, crossover design, following 2 weeks of single-blind placebo lead-in (Swedo et al., 1989). Clomipramine has predominant effects on serotonin, and desipramine is relatively noradrenergic in its mechanisms. There were 13 female recruits, all of whom completed the study.

Clomipramine produced significant reductions in the severity, frequency, and intensity of hair-pulling episodes.

One trial compared clomipramine with psychotherapy in conjunction with a placebo arm (Ninan, Rothbaum, Marsteller, Knight, & Eccard, 2000). The total sample size was 23, and 16 subjects ($n = 13$ [81.3%] women) completed the trial. Subjects with trichotillomania were randomly assigned to nine weekly sessions of CBT (a combination of habit reversal, stimulus control, and stress management) (seven subjects), clomipramine (up to 250 mg/day; 10 subjects), or placebo pill (six subjects). CBT significantly reduced the severity of trichotillomania symptoms in comparison with clomipramine and placebo over the course of the study, whereas clomipramine and placebo did not differentiate—arguably not surprising given the small sample size. There was no appropriate control for the CBT condition to evaluate specificity of content in moderating outcome.

A meta-analysis (M. H. Bloch et al., 2007) of the treatment responses of the 24 completers in the above-mentioned studies (Ninan et al., 2000; Swedo et al., 1989) revealed a significant treatment effect of clomipramine in comparison with the control conditions. This observation remained significant with a subsequent last observation carried forward sensitivity analysis. As evidenced above, there is good support for the use of clomipramine in the short-term treatment of trichotillomania. The characteristically chronic course of trichotillomania, however, requires evidence for prolonged, sustained improvements. Swedo, Lenane, and Leonard (1993) reported continued benefit at 6 months in the subjects in their initial study of clomipramine, as well as when assessed by phone at a mean of 4.3 years later. A 40% reduction in trichotillomania symptoms was retained. However, many subjects had changed or added medications or had participated in psychotherapy or behavioral therapy (Swedo et al., 1993). Pollard et al. (1991) also reported on the relapse of three of four patients initially treated with clomipramine when followed for 7 to 12 weeks. Taken together, these observations suggest caution in interpreting the long-term treatment potential of medications for trichotillomania on the basis of short-term treatment studies.

Four double-blind, placebo-controlled studies using fluoxetine for trichotillomania have produced mixed results. An 18-week, double-blind, cross-over trial (6 weeks on each agent, with a 5-week washout period between treatment periods) compared fluoxetine with placebo in 21 subjects. Statistical analysis found both the treatment and placebo groups performed similarly on measures of hair-pulling urges, frequency, and severity (Christenson et al., 1991). Similar results were found by Streichenwein and Thornby (1995) in a 31-week, placebo-controlled, randomized, crossover trial with 16 subjects. The treatment and placebo group reported similar reductions in hair pulling. Pigott et al. (1992) completed another randomized, crossover 20-week trial with a 2-week placebo lead-in comparing fluoxetine with clomipramine in 12 subjects. Findings indicated that both fluoxetine and clomipramine performed well, but did not significantly differ from each other on measures of hair pulling. The last study compared fluoxetine with behavioral therapy in 43 individuals with trichotillomania for a 12-week, randomized, wait-list control study. Although 64% and 20% of those in behavioral therapy and the wait-list control group, respectively, reported a clinically significant change in hair pulling, only 9% on fluoxetine reported a significant change. Additionally, in comparison with the fluoxetine group, the wait-list control group experienced a significantly larger decrease in time spent pulling (van Minnen, Hoogduin, Keijsers, Hellenbrand, & Hendriks, 2003).

The utility of the SSRI sertraline in the treatment of trichotillomania was investigated in a 12-week double-blind, placebo-controlled, randomized study that also assigned additional habit reversal therapy to nonresponders (Dougherty, Loh, Jenike, & Keuthen, 2006). Of the 42 subjects initially enrolled in the study, 26 completed the 22-week study, of whom only two received placebo and were thus excluded from further statistical analysis. Therefore the benefit of placebo control was lost. By the end of the study, both the sertraline and the combination treatment groups demonstrated improvement, although the sertraline group was limited to only four subjects. The combined treatment group demonstrated significantly better improvement than did the sertraline group, although the design of the study and the limited number of subjects made the individual contributions to the treatment response in the combined treatment difficult to ascertain.

To better clarify the treatment literature for trichotillomania, M. H. Bloch and colleagues (2007) conducted a meta-analysis of published comparison treatment studies for SSRIs. Four of the studies described above were identified with acceptable methodology, representing a total of 72 completers who had received either fluoxetine or sertraline. No difference was noted between control conditions and treatment with SSRIs. The overall estimated effect size was negligible and favored placebo. A last observation carried forward sensitivity analysis also revealed a lack of statistically significant difference in SSRI treatment in comparison with control conditions. Thus there is little evidence to support the use of SSRIs as monotherapy for trichotillomania. However, SSRIs may still play a role in treating comorbid conditions such as depression, generalized anxiety, and OCD, all of which could play contributing roles in the severity of trichotillomania.

Other Monotherapies

The remaining three placebo-controlled medication studies in trichotillomania have examined naltrexone (an opioid antagonist), olanzapine (an atypical neuroleptic), and N-acetyl cysteine (NAC; a glutamateric agent). Christenson, Crow, and Mackenzie (1994) studied the opiate antagonist naltrexone (50 mg/day) for the treatment of trichotillomania in a random-ized, placebo-controlled, double-blinded study. Seventeen subjects com-pleted the study, but only seven of those who completed it received the active agent. Three of the seven demonstrated more than a 50% reduction in hair-pulling symptoms in comparison with none in the placebo group. The active-treatment group demonstrated a statistically significant improve-ment in symptoms, as measured by the National Institute of Mental Health trichotillomania severity scale, but not on two other measures. There was no statistically significant difference in the reported number of hair-pulling episodes, although improvement was in the expected direction with nal-trexone. Using a 12-week, placebo-controlled design with 35 subjects, Van Ameringen, Mancini, Patterson, Bennett, and Oakman (2010) found that olanzapine, an atypical neuroleptic, significantly improved the severity of trichotillomania in comparison with placebo. Olanzapine was administered in a flexible manner, ranging from an initial dose of 2.5 mg/day to a maximum dose of 20 mg/day during Weeks 8 and 12. The average olanzapine dose at endpoint was 11 mg/day. Eleven of 13 (85%) subjects assigned to olanzapine were considered responders in comparison with only two of 12 (17%) in the placebo group. Significant improvement in hair-pulling symptoms was noted.

The largest study to date in trichotillomania used NAC, a glutamatergic agent, in 50 subjects in a 12-week, placebo-controlled study (Grant, Odlaug, & Kim, 2009). Glutamate is concentrated in the extracellular regions of the nucleus accumbens, and glutamatergic dysfunction in this region has been proposed to be associated with repetitive behaviors, including those in OCD (Chakrabarty, Bhattacharyya, Christopher, & Khanna, 2005). In a follow-up to some initially promising responses of trichotillomania to the glutamate modulator NAC (Odlaug & Grant, 2007), Grant and colleagues (2009) conducted a 12-week randomized, double-blind, placebo-controlled trial of NAC in 50 subjects with trichotillomania. NAC was given in a dose of 1,200 mg/day for the first 6 weeks and increased to 2,400 mg/day if subjects had not experienced complete cessation of hair pulling during the preceding 3 weeks. Fifty-six percent of the active-treatment group were rated as "much" or "very much" improved in comparison with only 16% of those on placebo. The NAC group also demonstrated a statistically significant 41% symptom reduction on the primary symptom outcome measure, the Massachusetts General Hospital—Hair Pulling Scale (Keuthen et al., 1995). Significant improvement was noted after 9 weeks of treatment.

Overall, data regarding pharmacological treatment of trichotillomania are incomplete. No studies have been successfully replicated to make a well-supported judgment about treatment efficacy. Inadequate sample sizes limit the statistical power of these studies, and short (8–12 weeks) follow-up periods make it difficult to assess long-term efficacy of these treatments. Furthermore, no studies have specifically investigated how comorbid conditions or other clinical variables (e.g., age, gender) affect treatment. Despite these limitations, several medications have shown promise in treating trichotillomania and should be explored further. NAC, clomipramine, and olanzapine may be beneficial for individuals suffering from trichotillomania, but data regarding SSRIs do not support their use. No study analyzed the effects of age on treatment response. Without this information, medication options for adolescents and the elderly with trichotillomania should follow the evidence from general adult studies, although side effects and drug interactions may differ for both age groups. Further research is needed before clear recommendations can be made regarding pharmacotherapeutic interventions.

SKIN-PICKING DISORDER

Skin-picking disorder (SPD) is characterized by repetitive and compulsive picking of skin, which causes tissue damage. Many individuals with SPD begin picking at the onset of a dermatological condition such as acne, but the picking continues even after the dermatological condition clears. Individuals with SPD spend a significant amount of time each day picking their skin, with many reporting that the picking behavior constitutes several hours each day (Grant, Odlaug, & Kim, 2007). Because of the amount of time spent picking, individuals report missing or being late for work, school, or social activities (Flessner & Woods, 2006).

Although the face is the most commonly reported site of picking, other areas such as the hands, fingers, torso, arms, and legs are also common targets (Odlaug & Grant, 2008). A study of 60 individuals with SPD reported that subjects picked from an average of 4.5 sites (Odlaug & Grant, 2008). Many individuals report having a primary body area for picking but may pick at other areas of the body in order to allow the most significantly excoriated areas to heal (Bohne, Wilhelm, Keuthen, Baer, & Jenike, 2002; Odlaug & Grant, 2008). Although most people pick at areas they can reach with their fingers, many report using knives, tweezers, pins, and other objects to pick (Grant, Odlaug, & Kim, 2007; Neziroglu, Rabinowitz, Breytman, & Jacofsky, 2008).

Picking may result in significant tissue damage and often leads to medical complications such as localized infections and septicemia (Neziroglu et al., 2008; Odlaug & Grant, 2008). The repetitive, excoriative nature of picking may even warrant skin grafting and, in severe cases, has resulted in the development of an epidural abscess and paralysis. Studies have shown that patients avoid treatment-seeking behavior either because of social embarrassment

(Wilhelm et al., 1999) or because of a belief that their condition is untreatable (Grant, Odlaug, & Potenza, 2007).

Selective Serotonin Reuptake Inhibitors

There have been four double-blind placebo-controlled pharmacological studies in SPD, three of which used an SSRI. Fluoxetine (20–80 mg/day) was evaluated in 21 adults (16 [76.2%] women) with SPD in a 10-week double-blind placebo-controlled study (Simeon et al., 1997). There were four non-completers, yielding group sizes of six fluoxetine subjects and 11 placebo subjects. In both the completer and intent-to-treat analyses, fluoxetine showed superiority on a visual analogue scale outcome measure in comparison with placebo. On clinical global improvement, the completer analysis yielded a significant benefit of active versus placebo treatment, whereas this comparison did not reach significance in the intent-to-treat analysis.

M. R. Bloch, Elliott, Thompson, and Koran (2001) also examined fluoxetine (20–60 mg/day) in women with SPD, who first had received 6 weeks of open-label active treatment. The initial treatment responders (eight of 15 subjects) were then randomized, double blind, to fluoxetine or placebo for a further 6 weeks. Responders assigned to placebo (four subjects) showed symptom worsening over time, whereas responders assigned to active treatment (four subjects) showed sustained response; the comparison of percentage change from baseline to end point between placebo and active treatment was significant.

Forty-five subjects with SPD (32 [71.1%] women) were randomized to receive an alternative SSRI, fixed-dose citalopram (20 mg/day; 23 subjects) or placebo (22 subjects) in a 4-week double-blind parallel design (Arbabi et al., 2008). There were 20 subjects who completed citalopram and 20 who completed placebo. Both citalopram and placebo were associated with significant improvements on symptom and quality-of-life measures, and the citalopram group showed significantly greater improvements over placebo (these appeared to be according to intent-to-treat analyses, though this was not made explicit). No significant differences, however, were observed between groups in terms of visual analogue scale scores.

Other Monotherapies

On the basis of a promising open-label study, Grant, Odlaug, and Kim (2007) undertook a double-blind placebo-controlled trial with lamotrigine in 35 people with SPD (29 [82.9%] women; Grant, Odlaug, Chamberlain, & Kim, 2010). There were 25 who completed treatment, with 12 randomized to lamotrigine and 13 to placebo. Active and placebo treatment did not significantly differentiate from each other on primary outcome measures. Interestingly, patients assigned to active treatment who showed relatively impaired baseline cognitive function (set shifting and response inhibition) exhibited the most treatment response. The authors suggested that the lamotrigine response in SPD may unmask relevant neurobiological heterogeneity underpinning the disorder.

Other monotherapies lack double-blind placebo-controlled data. Opioid antagonists, such as naltrexone (Arnold, Auchenbach, & McElroy, 2001), and glutamatergic agents, such as NAC (Odlaug & Grant, 2007), have demonstrated benefit but only in case reports.

In terms of pharmacotherapy for SPD, fluoxetine may be considered as a treatment with full evidence of efficacy, though one of the positive placebo-referenced trials tested relapse prevention in a more limited subsample of fluoxetine responders. There was also limited positive evidence to support citalopram. There was one negative double-blind study of lamotrigine that may have been underpowered ($N = 35$), but an open-label study was positive, suggesting ambiguity. The data are simply too limited to understand how various clinical variables (e.g., age, gender, picking severity) may affect treatment response.

CONCLUSION

The pharmacological evidence for the treatment of OCD strongly supports the use of SRIs. Although more limited, early data suggest a similar treatment approach for BDD and hypochondriasis. The other OCD spectrum disorders, such as trichotillomania and SPD, however, have produced more tenuous or mixed results regarding these medications. In fact, data suggest that trichotillomania may respond more robustly to non-SRI monotherapies.

Results from double-blind pharmacotherapy studies in OCD spectrum disorders leave the clinician and researcher with more questions than answers. Although SRIs are beneficial for OCD, do they in fact target a core pathology or do they help in an indirect fashion? Can treatment response in one disorder be meaningful for the treatment of a related disorder, and if so, how? Is it possible that some people with OCD have more in common neurobiologically with some people with trichotillomania than they do with other individuals with OCD? More research into family history, comorbidity, genetics, neuroimaging, and treatment response may all be means by which this complexity can be better understood.

REFERENCES

Allen, A., Hadley, S. J., Kaplan, A., Simeon, D., Friedberg, J., Priday, L., . . . Hollander, E. (2008). An open-label trial of venlafaxine in body dysmorphic disorder. *CNS Spectrums, 13*(2), 138–144.

Alonso, P., Menchon, J. M., Pifarre, J., Mataix-Cols, D., Torres, L., Salgado, P., & Vallejo, J. (2001). Long-term follow-up and predictors of clinical outcome in obsessive–compulsive patients treated with serotonin reuptake inhibitors and behavioral therapy. *The Journal of Clinical Psychiatry, 62,* 535–540. doi:10.4088/JCP.v62n07a06

American Psychiatric Association. (2000). *Diagnostic and statistical manual of mental disorders* (4th ed,, text rev.). Washington, DC: Author.

American Psychiatric Association. (2013). *Diagnostic and statistical manual of mental disorders* (5th ed.). Washington, DC: Author.

Arbabi, M., Farina, V., Balighi, K., Mohammadi, M. R., Nejati-Safa, A. A., Yazdchi, K., . . . Darvish, F. (2008). Efficacy of citalopram in treatment of pathological skin picking: A randomized double blind placebo controlled trial. *Acta Medica Iranica, 46,* 367–372.

Arnold, L. M., Auchenbach, M. B., & McElroy, S. L. (2001). Psychogenic excoriation: Clinical features, proposed diagnostic criteria, epidemiology and approaches to treatment. *CNS Drugs, 15,* 351–359. doi:10.2165/00023210-200115050-00002

Baldwin, D. S., Anderson, I. M., Nutt, D. J., Bandelow, B., Bond, A., Davidson, J. R. T., . . . Wittchen, H.-U. (2005). Evidence-based guidelines for the pharmacological treatment of anxiety disorders: Recommendations from the British Association for Psychopharmacology. *Journal of Psychopharmacology, 19,* 567–596. doi:10.1177/0269881105059253

Barsky, A. J. (1992). Hypochondriasis and obsessive–compulsive disorder. *Psychiatric Clinics of North America, 15,* 791–801.

Başoğlu, M., Lelliott, P. T., & Marks, I. M. (1988). Patterns and predictors of improvement in obsessive–compulsive disorder. *Journal of Anxiety Disorders, 2,* 299–317. doi:10.1016/0887-6185(88)90026-6

Berlin, H. A., Koran, L. M., Jenike, M. A., Shapira, N. A., Chaplin, W., Pallanti, S., & Hollander, E. (2011). Double-blind, placebo-controlled trial of topiramate augmentation in treatment-resistant obsessive–compulsive disorder. *The Journal of Clinical Psychiatry, 72,* 716–721. doi:10.4088/JCP.09m05266gre

Bienvenu, O. J., Samuels, J. F., Riddle, M. A., Hoehn-Saric, R., Liang, K.-Y., Cullen, B. A. M., . . . Nestadt, G. (2000). The relationship of obsessive–compulsive disorder to possible spectrum disorders: Results from a family study. *Biological Psychiatry, 48,* 287–293. doi:10.1016/S0006-3223(00)00831-3

Biondi, M., & Picardi, A. (2005). Increased maintenance of obsessive–compulsive disorder remission after integrated serotonergic treatment and cognitive psychotherapy compared with medication alone. *Psychotherapy and Psychosomatics, 74*, 123–128. doi:10.1159/000083172

Bloch, M. H., Landeros-Weisenberger, A., Dombrowski, P., Kelmendi, B., Wegner, R., Nudel, J., . . . Coric, V. (2007). Systematic review: Pharmacological and behavioral treatment for trichotillomania. *Biological Psychiatry, 62*, 839–846. doi:10.1016/j.biopsych.2007.05.019

Bloch, M. R., Elliott, M., Thompson, H., & Koran, L. M. (2001). Fluoxetine in pathologic skin-picking: Open-label and double-blind results. *Psychosomatics, 42*, 314–319. doi:10.1176/appi.psy.42.4.314

Bohne, A., Wilhelm, S., Keuthen, N. J., Baer, L., & Jenike, M. A. (2002). Skin picking in German students. Prevalence, phenomenology, and associated characteristics. *Behavior Modification, 26*, 320–339. doi:10.1177/0145445502026003002

Brady, K. T., Austin, L., & Lydiard, R. B. (1990). Body dysmorphic disorder: The relationship to obsessive–compulsive disorder. *Journal of Nervous and Mental Disease, 178*, 538–540.

Bystritsky, A., Ackerman, D. L., Rosen, R. M., Vapnik, T., Gorbis, E., Maidment, K. M., & Saxena, S. (2004). Augmentation of serotonin reuptake inhibitors in refractory obsessive–compulsive disorder using adjunctive olanzapine: A placebo-controlled trial. *The Journal of Clinical Psychiatry, 65*, 565–568. doi: 10.4088/JCP.v65n0418

Canadian Psychiatric Association. (2006). Clinical practice guidelines: Management of anxiety disorders. Obsessive–compulsive disorder. *Canadian Journal of Psychiatry, 51*(Suppl. 2), 43S–50S.

Carey, P. D., Vythilingum, B., Seedat, S., Muller, J. E., van Ameringen, M., & Stein, D. J. (2005). Quetiapine augmentation of SRIs in treatment refractory obsessive–compulsive disorder: A double-blind, randomized, placebo-controlled study. *BMC Psychiatry, 5*, 44. doi:10.1186/1471-244X-5-5

Catapano, F., Sperandeo, R., Perris, F., Lanzaro, M., & Maj, M. (2001). Insight and resistance in patients with obsessive–compulsive disorder. *Psychopathology, 34*(2), 62–68. doi:10.1159/000049282

Chakrabarty, K., Bhattacharyya, S., Christopher, R., & Khanna, S. (2005). Glutamatergic dysfunction in OCD. *Neuropsychopharmacology, 30*, 1735–1740. doi: 10.1038/sj.npp.1300733

Christenson, G. A., Crow, J. C., & Mackenzie, T. B. (1994). *A placebo-controlled double-blind study of naltrexone for trichotillomania* [Abstract]. New research program and abstracts presented at the 150th Annual Meeting of the American Psychiatric Association. Philadelphia, PA.

Christenson, G. A., Mackenzie, T. B., Mitchell, J. E., & Callies, A. L. (1991). A placebo-controlled, double-blind crossover study of fluoxetine in trichotillomania. *The American Journal of Psychiatry, 148*, 1566–1571.

Cohen, L. J., Stein, D. J., Simeon, D., Spadaccini, E., Rosen, J., Aronowitz, B., & Hollander, E. (1995). Clinical profile, comorbidity, and treatment history in 123 hair pullers: A survey study. *Journal of Clinical Psychiatry, 56*, 319–326.

Crockett, B. A., Churchill, E., & Davidson, J. R. (2004). A double-blind combination study of clonazepam with sertraline in obsessive–compulsive disorder. *Annals of Clinical Psychiatry, 16*, 127–132. doi:10.1080/10401230490486972

Denys, D. (2006). Pharmacotherapy of obsessive–compulsive disorder and obsessive–compulsive spectrum disorders. *Psychiatric Clinics of North America, 29*, 553–584. doi:10.1016/j.psc.2006.02.013

Denys, D., de Geus, F., van Megen, H. J., & Westenberg, H. G. (2004). A double-blind, randomized, placebo controlled trial of quetiapine addition in patients with obsessive–compulsive disorder refractory to serotonin reuptake inhibitors. *The Journal of Clinical Psychiatry, 65*, 1040–1048. doi:10.4088/JCP.v65n0803

Diefenbach, G. J., Tolin, D. F., Hannan, S., Crocetto, J., & Worhunsky, P. (2005). Trichotillomania: Impact on psychosocial functioning and quality of life. *Behaviour Research and Therapy, 43*, 869–884. doi:10.1016/j.brat.2004.06.010

Dougherty, D. D., Loh, R., Jenike, M. A., & Keuthen, N. J. (2006). Single modality versus dual modality treatment for trichotillomania: Sertraline, behavioral therapy or both? *The Journal of Clinical Psychiatry, 67*, 1086–1092. doi:10.4088/JCP.v67n0711

Eisen, J. L., Goodman, W. K., Keller, M. B., Warshaw, M. G., DeMarco, L. M., Luce, D. D., & Rasmussen, S. A. (1999). Patterns of remission and relapse in obsessive–compulsive disorder: A 2-year prospective study. *The Journal of Clinical Psychiatry, 60*, 346–351. doi:10.4088/JCP.v60n0514

Eisen, J. L., Rasmussen, S. A., Phillips, K. A., Price, L. H., Davidson, J., Lydiard, R. B., . . . Piggott, T. (2001). Insight and treatment outcome in obsessive–compulsive disorder. *Comprehensive Psychiatry, 42*, 494–497. doi:10.1053/comp.2001.27898

Ellingrod, V. L. (1998). Pharmacotherapy of primary obsessive–compulsive disorder: Review of the literature. *Pharmacotherapy, 18*, 936–960.

Fallon, B. A., Liebowitz, M. R., Salmán, E., Schneier, F. R., Jusino, C., Hollander, E., & Klein, D. F. (1993). Fluoxetine for hypochondriacal patients without major depression. *Journal of Clinical Psychopharmacology, 13*, 438–441. doi:10.1097/00004714-199312000-00010

Fallon, B. A., Petkova, E., Skritskaya, N., Sanchez-Lacay, A., Schneier, F., Vermes, D., . . . Liebowitz, M. R. (2008). A double-masked, placebo-controlled study of fluoxetine for hypchondriasis. *Journal of Clinical Psychopharmacology, 28*, 638–645. doi:10.1097/JCP.0b013e31818d21cf

Fallon, B. A., Qureshi, A. I., Schneier, F. R., Sanchez-Lacay, A., Vermes, D., Feinstein, R., . . . Liebowitz, M. R. (2003). An open trial of fluvoxamine for hypochondriasis. *Psychosomatics, 44*, 298–303. doi:10.1176/appi.psy.44.4.298

Fineberg, N. A., & Gale, T. M. (2005). Evidence-based pharmacotherapy of obsessive–compulsive disorder. *The International Journal of Neuropsychopharmacology, 8*, 107–129. doi:10.1017/S1461145704004675

Flessner, C. A., & Woods, D. W. (2006). Phenomenological characteristics, social problems, and the economic impact associated with chronic skin picking. *Behavior Modification*, *30*, 944–963. doi:10.1177/0145445506294083

Fux, M., Levine, J., Aviv, A., & Belmaker, R. H. (1996). Insitol treatment of obsessive–compulsive disorder. *The American Journal of Psychiatry*, *153*, 1219–1221.

Gava, I., Barbui, C., Aguglia, E., Carlino, D., Churchill, R., De Vanna, M., & McGuire, H. F. (2007). Psychological treatments versus treatment as usual for obsessive compulsive disorder (OCD). *Cochrane Database of Systematic Reviews*, *18*(2), CD005333.

Geller, D. A., Biederman, J., Faraone, S., Agranat, A., Cradock, K., Hagermoser, L., . . . Coffey, B. J. (2001). Developmental aspects of obsessive compulsive disorder: Findings in children, adolescent, and adults. *Journal of Nervous and Mental Disease*, *189*, 471–477. doi:10.1097/00005053-200107000-00009

Grady, T. A., Pigott, T. A., L'Heureux, F., Hill, J. L., Bernstein, S. E., & Murphy, D. L. (1993). Double-blind study of adjuvant buspirone for fluoxetine-treated patients with obsessive–compulsive disorder. *The American Journal of Psychiatry*, *150*, 819–821.

Grant, J. E., Kim, S. W., & Crow, S. J. (2001). Prevalence and clinical features of body dysmorphic disorder in adolescent and adult psychiatric inpatients. *Journal of Clinical Psychiatry*, *62*, 517–522. doi:10.4088/JCP.v62n07a03

Grant, J. E., Odlaug, B. L., Chamberlain, S. R., & Kim, S. W. (2010). A double-blind, placebo-controlled trial of lamotrigine for pathological skin picking: Treatment efficacy and neurocognitive predictors of response. *Journal of Clinical Psychopharmacology*, *30*, 396–403. doi:10.1097/JCP.0b013e3181e617a1

Grant, J. E., Odlaug, B. L., & Kim, S. W. (2007). Lamotrigine treatment of pathologic skin picking: An open-label study. *The Journal of Clinical Psychiatry*, *68*, 1384–1391. doi:10.4088/JCP.v68n0909

Grant, J. E., Odlaug, B. L., & Kim, S. W. (2009). N-acetylcysteine, a glutamate modulator, in the treatment of trichotillomania: A double-blind, placebo-controlled study. *Archives of General Psychiatry*, *66*, 756–763. doi:10.1001/archgenpsychiatry.2009.60

Grant, J. E., Odlaug, B. L., & Potenza, M. N. (2007). Addicted to hair pulling? How an alternative model of trichotillomania may improve treatment outcome. *Harvard Review of Psychiatry*, *15*, 80–85. doi:10.1080/10673220701298407

Grant, J. E., & Phillips, K. A. (2005). Recognizing and treating body dysmorphic disorder. *Annals of Clinical Psychiatry*, *17*, 205–210. doi:10.1080/10401230500295313

Grant, J. E., Pinto, A., Gunnip, M., Mancebo, M. C., Eisen, J. L., & Rasmussen, S. A. (2006). Sexual obsessions and clinical correlates in adults with obsessive–compulsive disorder. *Comprehensive Psychiatry*, *47*, 325–329. doi:10.1016/j.comppsych.2006.01.007

Greeven, A., van Balkom, A. J., van der Leeden, R., Merkelbach, J. W., ven den Heuvel, O. A., & Spinhoven, P. (2009). Cognitive behavioral therapy versus paroxetine in the treatment of hypchondriasis: An 18-month naturalistic follow-up. *Journal of Behavior Therapy and Experimental Psychiatry, 40*, 487–496. doi:10.1016/j.jbtep.2009.06.005

Greeven, A., van Balkom, A. J., Visser, S., Merkelbach, J. W., van Rood, Y. R., van Dyck, R., . . . Spinhoven, P. (2007). Cognitive behavior therapy and paroxetine in the treatment of hypochondriasis: A randomized controlled trial. *The American Journal of Psychiatry, 164*, 91–99. doi:10.1176/appi.ajp.164.1.91

Greist, J. H., Jefferson, J. W., Kobak, K. A., Katzelnick, D. J., & Serline, R. C. (1995). Efficacy and tolerability of serotonin transport inhibitors in obsessive–compulsive disorder. A meta-analysis. *Archives of General Psychiatry, 52*, 53–60. doi:10.1001/archpsyc.1995.03950130053006

Hembree, E. A., Riggs, D. S., Kozak, M. J., Franklin, M. E., & Foa, E. B. (2003). Long-term efficacy of exposure and ritual prevention therapy and serotonergic medications for obsessive–compulsive disorder. *CNS Spectrums, 8*, 363–371.

Hewlett, W. A., Vinogradov, S., & Agras, W. S. (1992). Clomipramine, clonazepam, and clonidine treatment of obsessive–compulsive disorder. *Journal of Clinical Psychopharmacology, 12*, 420–430. doi:10.1097/00004714-199212000-00008

Hiller, W., Leibbrand, R., Rief, W., & Fichter, M. M. (2002). Predictors of course and outcome in hypochondriasis after cognitive–behavioral treatment. *Psychotherapy and Psychosomatics, 71*, 318–325. doi:10.1159/000065990

Hollander, E., Allen, A., Kwon, J., Aronowitz, B., Schmeidler, J., Wong, C., & Simeon, D. (1999). Clomipramine vs. desipramine crossover trial in body dysmorphic disorder: Selective efficacy of serotonin reuptake inhibitor in imagined ugliness. *Archives of General Psychiatry, 56*, 1033–1039. doi:10.1001/archpsyc.56.11.1033

Hollander, E., Baldini Rossi, N., Sood, E., & Pallanti, S. (2003). Risperidone augmentation in treatment-resistant obsessive–compulsive disorder: A double-blind, placebo-controlled study. *The International Journal of Neuropsychopharmacology, 6*, 397–401. doi:10.1017/S1461145703003730

Hollander, E., Cohen, L. J., & Simeon, D. (1993). Body dysmorphic disorder. *Psychiatric Annals, 23*, 359–364.

Hollander, E., Kaplan, A., & Stahl, S. M. (2003). A double-blind, placebo-controlled trial of clonazepam in obsessive–compulsive disorder. *The World Journal of Biological Psychiatry, 4*(1), 30–34. doi:10.3109/15622970309167908

Hollander, E., Liebowitz, M., Winchel, R., Klumker, A., & Klein, D. (1989). Treatment of body-dysmorphic disorder with serotonin reuptake blockers. *The American Journal of Psychiatry, 146*, 768–770.

Insel, T. R., & Akiskal, H. S. (1986). Obsessive–compulsive disorder with psychotic features: A phenomenologic analysis. *The American Journal of Psychiatry, 143*, 1527–1533.

Ipser, J. C., Sander, C., & Stein, D. J. (2009). Pharmacotherapy and psychotherapy for body dysmorphic disorder. *Cochrane Database of Systematic Reviews, 21*(1), CD005332.

Jenike, M. A. (2004). Clinical practice. Obsessive–compulsive disorder. *The New England Journal of Medicine, 350,* 259–265. doi:10.1056/NEJMcp031002

Keuthen, N. J., Ricciardi, J. N., Shera, D., Savage, C. R., Borgmann, A. S., Jenike, M. A., & Baer, L. (1995). The Massachusetts General Hospital (MGH) hairpulling scale, I: development and factor analyses. *Psychotherapy and Psychosomatics, 64,* 141–145.

Koran, L. M., Aboujaoude, E., Bullock, K. D., Franz, B., Gamel, N., & Elliott, M. (2005). Double-blind treatment with oral morphine in treatment-resistant obsessive–compulsive disorder. *The Journal of Clinical Psychiatry, 66,* 353–359. doi:10.4088/JCP.v66n0312

Koran, L. M., Hanna, G. L., Hollander, E., Nestadt, G., Simpson, H. B., & American Psychiatric Association. (2007). Practice guideline for the treatment of patients with obsessive–compulsive disorder. *The American Journal of Psychiatry, 164*(7, Suppl.), 5–53.

Leckman, J. F., Grice, D. E., Boardman, J., Zhang, H., Vitale, A., Bondi, C., . . . Pauls, D. L. (1997). Symptoms of obsessive–compulsive disorder. *The American Journal of Psychiatry, 154,* 911–917.

Li, X., May, R. S., Tolbert, L. C., Jackson, W. T., Flournoy, J. M., & Baxter, L. R. (2005). Risperidone and haloperidol augmentation of serotonin reuptake inhibitors in refractory obsessive–compulsive disorder: A crossover study. *The Journal of Clinical Psychiatry, 66,* 736–743. doi:10.4088/JCP.v66n0610

March, J. S., Frances, A., Carpenter, D., & Kahn, D. A. (1997). The Expert Consensus Guideline Series: Treatment of obsessive–compulsive disorder [Special issue]. *The Journal of Clinical Psychiatry, 58*(Suppl. 4).

Mataix-Cols, D., Rauch, S. L., Manzo, P. A., Jenike, M. A., & Baer, L. (1999). Use of factor-analyzed symptom dimensions to predict outcome with serotonin reuptake inhibitors and placebo in the treatment of obsessive–compulsive disorder. *The American Journal of Psychiatry, 156,* 1409–1416.

Mataix-Cols, D., Wooderson, S., Lawrence, N., Brammer, M. J., Speckens, A., & Phillips, M. L. (2004). Distinct neural correlates of washing, checking, and hoarding symptom dimensions in obsessive–compulsive disorder. *Archives of General Psychiatry, 61,* 564–576. doi:10.1001/archpsyc.61.6.564

Matsunaga, H., Kiriike, N., Matsui, T., Oya, K., Iwasaki, Y., Koshimune, K., . . . Stein, D. J. (2002). Obsessive–compulsive disorder with poor insight. *Comprehensive Psychiatry, 43,* 150–157. doi:10.1053/comp.2002.30798

McDougle, C. J., Epperson, C. N., Pelton, G. H., Wasylink, S., & Price, L. H. (2000). A double-blind, placebo-controlled study of risperidone addition in serotonin reuptake inhibitor-refractory obsessive–compulsive disorder. *Archives of General Psychiatry, 57,* 794–801. doi:10.1001/archpsyc.57.8.794

McDougle, C. J., Price, L. H., Goodman, W. K., Charney, D. S., & Heninger, G. R. (1991). A controlled trial of lithium augmentation in fluvoxamine-refractory obsessive–compulsive disorder: Lack of efficacy. *Journal of Clinical Psychopharmacology, 11*, 175–184. doi:10.1097/00004714-199106000-00005

McElroy, S. L., Phillips, K. A., & Keck, P. E., Jr. (1994). Obsessive compulsive spectrum disorders. *The Journal of Clinical Psychiatry, 55*(Suppl.), 33–51.

Miguel, E. C., Coffey, B. J., Baer, L., Savage, C. R., Rauch, S. L., & Jenike, M. A. (1995). Phenomenology of intentional repetitive behaviors in obsessive–compulsive disorder and Tourette's disorder. *The Journal of Clinical Psychiatry, 56*, 246–255.

Montgomery, S., & Zohar, J. (1999). *Obsessive compulsive disorder.* London, England: Martin Dunitz.

Muscatello, M. R., Bruno, A., Pandolfo, G., Micò, U., Scimeca, G., Romeo, V. M., . . . Zoccali, R. A. (2011). Effect of aripiprazole augmentation of serotonin reuptake inhibitors or clomipramine in treatment-resistant obsessive–compulsive disorder: A double-blind, placebo-controlled study. *Journal of Clinical Psychopharmacology, 31*, 174–179.

Neziroglu, F., McKay, D., & Yaryura-Tobias, J. A. (2000). Overlapping and distinctive features of hypochondriasis and obsessive–compulsive disorder. *Journal of Anxiety Disorders, 14*, 603–614. doi:10.1016/S0887-6185(00)00053-0

Neziroglu, F., Pinto, A., Yaryura-Tobias, J. A., & McKay, D. (2004). Overvalued ideation as a predictor of fluvoxamine response in patients with obsessive–compulsive disorder. *Psychiatry Research, 125*, 53–60. doi:10.1016/j.psychres.2003.10.001

Neziroglu, F., Rabinowitz, D., Breytman, A., & Jacofsky, M. (2008). Skin picking phenomenology and severity comparison. *Primary Care Companion to the Journal of Clinical Psychiatry, 10*, 306–312. doi:10.4088/PCC.v10n0406

Neziroglu, F., & Yaryura-Tobias, J. A. (1993). Body dysmorphic disorder: Phenomenology and case descriptions. *Behavioural Psychotherapy, 21*, 27–36. doi:10.1017/S0141347300017778

Ninan, P. T., Rothbaum, B. O., Marsteller, F. A., Knight, B. T., & Eccard, M. B. (2000). A placebo-controlled trial of cognitive–behavioral therapy and clomipramine in trichotillomania. *The Journal of Clinical Psychiatry, 61*(1), 47–50. doi:10.4088/JCP.v61n0111

Odlaug, B. L., & Grant, J. E. (2007). N-acetyl cysteine in the treatment of grooming disorder. *Journal of Clinical Psychopharmacology, 27*, 227–229. doi:10.1097/01.jcp.0000264976.86990.00

Odlaug, B. L., & Grant, J. E. (2008). Clinical characteristics and medical complications of pathologic skin picking. *General Hospital Psychiatry, 30*(1), 61–66. doi:10.1016/j.genhosppsych.2007.07.009

Oosterbaan, D. B., van Balkom, A. J., van Boeijen, C. A., de Meij, T. G., & van Dyck, R. (2001). An open study of paroxetine in hypochondriasis. *Progress in Neuro-*

Psychopharmacology & Biological Psychiatry, 25, 1023–1033. doi:10.1016/S0278-5846(01)00177-4

Pallanti, S., & Koran, L. M. (1996). Intravenous, pulse-loaded clomipramine in body dysmorphic disorder: Two case reports. *CNS Spectrums, 1,* 54–57.

Pato, M. T., Pigott, T. A., Hill, J. A., Grover, G. N., Bernstein, S., & Murphy, D. L. (1991). Controlled comparison of buspirone and clomipramine in obsessive–compulsive disorder. *The American Journal of Psychiatry, 148,* 127–129.

Perugi, G., Giannotti, D., DiVaio, S., Frare, F., Saettoni, M., & Cassano, G. B. (1996). Fluvoxamine in the treatment of body dysmorphic disorder (dysmorphophobia). *International Clinical Psychopharmacology, 11,* 247–254. doi:10.1097/00004850-199612000-00006

Phillips, K. A. (2005). Olanzapine augmentation of fluoxetine in body dysmorphic disorder. *The American Journal of Psychiatry, 162,* 1022–1023. doi:10.1176/appi.ajp.162.5.1022-a

Phillips, K. A., Albertini, R. S., & Rasmussen, S. A. (2002). A randomized placebo-controlled trial of fluoxetine in body dysmorphic disorder. *Archives of General Psychiatry, 59,* 381–388. doi:10.1001/archpsyc.59.4.381

Phillips, K. A., Grant, J. E., Siniscalchi, J., & Albertini, R. S. (2001). Surgical and nonpsychiatric medical treatment of patients with body dysmorphic disorder. *Psychosomatics, 42,* 504–510. doi:10.1176/appi.psy.42.6.504

Phillips, K. A., McElroy, S. L., Keck, P. E., Jr., Pope, H. G., & Hudson, J. L. (1993). Body dysmorphic disorder: 30 cases of imagined ugliness. *The American Journal of Psychiatry, 150,* 302–308.

Phillips, K. A., & Menard, W. (2009). A prospective pilot study of levetiracetam for body dysmorphic disorder. *CNS Spectrums, 14,* 252–260.

Piccinelli, M., Pini, S., Bellantuono, C., & Wilkinson, G. (1995). Efficacy of drug treatment in obsessive–compulsive disorder. A meta-analytic review. *The British Journal of Psychiatry, 166,* 424–443. doi:10.1192/bjp.166.4.424

Pigott, T. A., L'Heureux, F., Hill, J. L., Bihari, K., Bernstein, S. E., & Murphy, D. L. (1992). A double-blind study of adjuvant buspirone hydrochloride in clomipramine-treated patients with obsessive–compulsive disorder. *Journal of Clinical Psychopharmacology, 12*(1), 11–18. doi:10.1097/00004714-199202000-00003

Pigott, T. A., Pato, M. T., L'Heureux, F., Hill, J. L., Grover, G. N., Bernstein, S. E., & Murphy, D. L. (1991). A controlled comparison of adjuvant lithium carbonate or thyroid hormone in clomipramine-treated patients with obsessive–compulsive disorder. *Journal of Clinical Psychopharmacology, 11,* 242–248. doi:10.1097/00004714-199108000-00004

Pigott, T. A., & Seay, S. M. (1999). A review of the efficacy of selective serotonin reuptake inhibitors in obsessive–compulsive disorder. *The Journal of Clinical Psychiatry, 60,* 101–106. doi:10.4088/JCP.v60n0206

Pollard, C. A., Ibe, I. O., Krojanker, D. N., Kitchen, A. D., Bronson, S. S., & Flynn, T. M. (1991). Clomipramine treatment of trichotillomania: A follow-up report on four cases. *The Journal of Clinical Psychiatry, 52,* 128–130.

Pope, H. G., Phillips, K. A., & Olivardia, R. (2002). *The Adonis complex: How to identify, treat, and prevent body obsession in men and boys.* New York, NY: The Free Press.

Rasmussen, S. A., & Eisen, J. L. (1988). Clinical and epidemiologic findings of significance to neuropharmacologic trials in OCD. *Psychopharmacology Bulletin, 24,* 466–470.

Sayyah, M., Boostani, H., Pakseresht, S., & Malayeri, A. (2011). A preliminary randomized double-blind clinical trial on the efficacy of celecoxib as an adjunct in the treatment of obsessive–compulsive disorder. *Psychiatry Research, 189,* 403–406. doi:10.1016/j.psychres.2011.01.019

Schweitzer, P. J., Zafar, U., Pavlicova, M., & Fallon, B. A. (2011). Long-term follow-up of hypochondriasis after selective serotonin reuptake inhibitor treatment. *Journal of Clinical Psychopharmacology, 31,* 365–368. doi:10.1097/JCP.0b013e31821896c3

Shapira, N. A., Ward, H. E., Mandoki, M., Murphy, T. K., Yang, M. C., Biler, P., & Goodman, W. K. (2004). A double-blind, placebo-controlled trial of olanzapine addition in fluoxetine-refractory obsessive–compulsive disorder. *Biological Psychiatry, 55,* 553–555. doi:10.1016/j.biopsych.2003.11.010

Simeon, D., Stein, D. J., Gross, S., Islam, N., Schmeidler, J., & Hollander, E. (1997). A double-blind trial of fluoxetine in pathological skin picking. *The Journal of Clinical Psychiatry, 58,* 341–347. doi:10.4088/JCP.v58n0802

Simpson, H. B., Liebowitz, M. R., Foa, E. B., Kozak, M. J., Schmidt, A. B., Rowan, V., . . . Campeas, R. (2004). Post-treatment effects of exposure therapy and clomipramine in obsessive–compulsive disorder. *Depression and Anxiety, 19,* 225–233. doi:10.1002/da.20003

Soltani, F., Sayyah, M., Feizy, F., Malayeri, A., Siahpoosh, A., & Motlagh, I. (2010). A double-blind, placebo-controlled pilot study of ondansetron for patients with obsessive–compulsive disorder. *Human Psychopharmacology, 25,* 509–513. doi:10.1002/hup.1145

Soomro, G. M., Altman, D., Rajagopal, S., & Oakley-Browne, M. (2008). Selective serotonin re-uptake inhibitors versus placebo for obsessive compulsive disorder. *Cochrane Database of Systematic Reviews, 23*(1), CD001765.

Stein, D. J. (2000). Neurobiology of obsessive–compulsive spectrum disorders. *Biological Psychiatry, 47,* 296–304. doi:10.1016/S0006-3223(99)00271-1

Streichenwein, S. M., & Thornby, J. I. (1995). A long-term, double-blind, placebo-controlled crossover trial of the efficacy of fluoxetine for trichotillomania. *The American Journal of Psychiatry, 152,* 1192–1196.

Swedo, S. E., Lenane, M. C., & Leonard, H. L. (1993). Long-term treatment of trichotillomania (hair pulling). *The New England Journal of Medicine, 329,* 141–142. doi:10.1056/NEJM199307083290220

Swedo, S. E., & Leonard, H. L. (1992). Trichotillomania. An obsessive compulsive spectrum disorder? *Psychiatric Clinics of North America, 15*, 777–790.

Swedo, S. E., Leonard, H. L., Rapoport, J. L., Lenane, M. C., Goldberger, E. L., & Cheslow, D. L. (1989). A double-blind comparison of clomipramine and desipramine in the treatment of trichotillomania. *The New England Journal of Medicine, 321*, 497–501. doi:10.1056/NEJM198908243210803

Vallejo, J., Olivares, J., Marcos, T., Bulbena, A., & Menchón, J. M. (1992). Clomipramine versus phenelzine in obsessive–compulsive disorder. *The British Journal of Psychiatry, 161*, 665–670. doi:10.1192/bjp.161.5.665

Van Ameringen, M., Mancini, C., Patterson, B., Bennett, M., & Oakman, J. (2010). A randomized, double-blind, placebo-controlled trial of olanzapine in the treatment of trichotillomania. *The Journal of Clinical Psychiatry, 71*, 1336–1343. doi:10.4088/JCP.09m05114gre

van Minnen, A., Hoogduin, K. A., Keijsers, G. P., Hellenbrand, I., & Hendriks, G. J. (2003). Treatment of trichotillomania with behavioral therapy or fluoxetine: A randomized waiting-list controlled study. *Archives of General Psychiatry, 60*, 517–522. doi:10.1001/archpsyc.60.5.517

Veale, D., Boocock, A., Gourney, K., Dryden, W., Shah, F., Willon, R., & Walburn, J. (1996). Body dysmorphic disorder: A survey of fifty cases. *The British Journal of Psychiatry, 169*, 196–201. doi:10.1192/bjp.169.2.196

Walther, M. R., Ricketts, E. J., Conelea, C. A., & Woods, D. W. (2010). Recent advances in the understanding and treatment of trichotillomania. *Journal of Cognitive Psychotherapy, 24*, 46–64. doi:10.1891/0889-8391.24.1.46

Wilhelm, S., Keuthen, N. J., Deckersbach, T., Engelhard, I. M., Forker, A. E., Baer, L., . . . Jenike, M. A. (1999). Self-injurious skin picking: Clinical characteristics and comorbidity. *The Journal of Clinical Psychiatry, 60*, 454–459. doi:10.4088/JCP.v60n0707

Woods, D. W., Flessner, C. A., Franklin, M. E., Keuthen, N. J., Goodwin, R. D., Stein, D. J., Walther, M. R., & Trichotillomania Learning Center-Scientific Advisory Board. (2006). The Trichotillomania Impact Project: Exploring phenomenology, functional impairment, and treatment utilization. *The Journal of Clinical Psychiatry, 67*, 1877–1888. doi:10.4088/JCP.v67n1207

Yaryura-Tobias, J. A., & Neziroglu, F. A. (1996). Venlafaxine in obsessive–compulsive disorder. *Archives of General Psychiatry, 53*, 653–654. doi:10.1001/archpsyc.1996.01830070103016

IV

NEUROSCIENTIFIC SUPPORT FOR THE OBSESSIVE–COMPULSIVE SPECTRUM

16

TWIN STUDIES OF THE GENETIC AND ENVIRONMENTAL ETIOLOGY OF OBSESSIVE–COMPULSIVE AND RELATED PHENOMENA

STEVEN TAYLOR

Obsessive–compulsive (OC) symptoms and OC-related phenomena are likely to have a complex biopsychosocial etiology (Abramowitz, Taylor, & McKay, 2009; Taylor, 2011a, 2011b). Behavioral–genetic (twin) studies are a promising means of understanding the etiology of OC and related phenomena. Contemporary behavioral–genetic (twin) studies apply structural equation modeling of data from pairs of monozygotic (MZ) and dizygotic (DZ) twins. This methodology has been used to estimate the importance of additive genetic effects (A), nonadditive genetic effects (D), shared environment (C), and non-shared environment (E).

Additive genetic effects are those in which the probability of occurrence, or severity, of a given phenotype (e.g., symptom, disorder) is influenced by

From "Etiology of Obsessions and Compulsions: A Meta-Analysis and Narrative Review of Twin Studies," by S. Taylor, *Clinical Psychology Review, 31*, pp. 1361–1372. Copyright 2011 Elsevier. Adapted with permission.

http://dx.doi.org/10.1037/14323-017
Obsessive–Compulsive Disorder and Its Spectrum: A Life-Span Approach, Eric A. Storch and Dean McKay (Editors)
Copyright © 2014 by the American Psychological Association. All rights reserved.

many genes, which additively combine in their effects. Nonadditive genetic effects include epistatic effects (gene–gene interactions) and dominance effects. Shared environment includes experiences shared by both members of a twin pair, such as the experience of being raised by parents who exhibit particular parenting styles, such as a tendency to be critical and overcontrolling. Such parental influences have been emphasized in contemporary cognitive–behavioral models of obsessions and compulsions (e.g., Clark, 2004; Frost & Steketee, 2002; Salkovskis, Shafran, Rachman, & Freeston, 1999). Nonshared environment includes experiences that are not shared by members of a twin pair, such as a stressful life event experienced by one twin but not his or her cotwin. In twin studies, nonshared environment also includes error variance, which can be minimized by using psychometrically sound measures and by using structural equation modeling methods that explicitly model error variance (Taylor, Jang, & Asmundson, 2010).

In twin studies, structural equation modeling is used to estimate unknown parameters (A, C, D, and E) from known parameters (within-pair correlations of MZ and DZ twin pairs and sample sizes). To solve simultaneous equations, it is necessary to have a greater number of known than unknown parameters. Accordingly, it is possible to separately test an ACE model (i.e., a model consisting of A, C, and E) or an ADE model (consisting of A, D, and E), but C and D cannot be estimated simultaneously. Here, A, C, D, and E represent the proportions of phenotypic variance (e.g., variance in OC symptom scores) that can be attributed to these forms of genetic and environmental influence. Within-pair MZ and DZ correlations form the basis of computing the values of the ACE and ADE models (e.g., correlations of OC symptom scores for the individuals forming each twin pair). Monozygotic twins share 100% of their segregating genes, whereas DZ twins share approximately 50%. In general, larger MZ than DZ within-pair correlations for a given variable indicate the presence of genetic effects because the greater MZ similarity is attributed to the twofold-greater genetic similarity of MZ twins over DZ twins.

In addition to estimating the variance due to various genetic and environmental components, twin studies can be used to investigate whether two or more clinical phenomena (e.g., checking, hoarding) are etiologically related to one another. Twin studies can also yield useful information for guiding molecular genetic research, such as information about whether a given phenotype (e.g., the diagnostic category of OC disorder [OCD], the total score on a global measure of OC symptoms) is etiologically homogeneous or heterogeneous. Replication failure in molecular genetic research is a common problem, and such studies are more likely to be fruitful when they focus on etiologically homogeneous phenomena (Taylor, 2011b). Accordingly, twin studies can yield information about etiologically homogeneous phenotypes, which can be used for molecular genetic analyses.

In the following sections of this chapter, we (a) summarize the meta-analytic findings of twin studies; (b) review whether the twin findings generalize across levels of symptom severity; (c) investigate whether the importance of genetic and environmental components differs across OC symptom subtypes; (d) review the evidence for gene–environment interactions; (e) review the etiological relationship of OC symptoms with other symptoms, traits, and disorders; and (f) describe our empirically based biopsychosocial model of OC symptoms.

META-ANALYSIS OF TWIN STUDIES

Taylor (2011b) recently conducted the first meta-analysis of twin studies of OC symptoms. Each variance component (A, C, and E for the ACE model, and A, D, and E for the ADE model) was treated as an effect size and separately meta-analyzed. Fourteen twin studies yielding 37 samples were included in the meta-analysis. All were studies of twins recruited from the community and used either OC symptom severity assessments or diagnostic assessments of OCD. Some samples included in the meta-analysis were overlapping, that is, samples of people assessed over time, coming from two longitudinal research programs. One was the Netherlands Twin Registry, consisting of samples from van Grootheest et al. (2008) and van Grootheest, Cath, Hottenga, Beekman, and Boomsma (2009), and another was all samples from Hudziak et al. (2004) except for their 9-year-old male and female samples, the latter coming from a different (U.S.) twin registry. The other set of overlapping samples was from a British longitudinal study (Bolton, Rijsdijk, O'Connor, Perrin, & Eley, 2007; Eley et al., 2003). Overlapping samples were included in the meta-analysis to maximize statistical power. Effects of sample overlap were investigated by rerunning the meta-analysis in which the effect sizes within each set of overlapping samples were averaged. That is, the two sets of overlapping samples yielded three sets of mean results (Dutch males, Dutch females, and British males and females), which when added to the other, nonoverlapping samples, yielded a total of 17 samples. Studies used either dimensional measures of global OC symptom severity or used the diagnosis of OCD as the unit of analysis.

Table 16.1 summarizes the meta-analytic results for the ACE and ADE models. For both models the mean A and E effects were statistically significant, with A accounting for 37% to 41% of variance, and E accounting for 50% to 52% of variance. These estimates varied only slightly across models (ACE vs. ADE) and samples (all samples vs. nonoverlapping samples). C effects were marginally significant only for the overall set of samples, but substantively C accounted for only a small proportion of variance (5% to 6%).

TABLE 16.1
Summary of Meta-Analytic Findings: Mean Variances
(and Their 99th Percentile Confidence Intervals)

Model	Mean proportions of explained variance		
ACE	A	C	E
All samples	**.405**	**.052**	**.509**
	(.349–.460)	(.005–.101)	(.492–.526)
Nonoverlapping samples	**.384**	.058	**.522**
	(.302–.462)	(.000–.128)	(.497–.548)
ADE	A	D	E
All samples	**.386**	.097	**.495**
	(.290–.479)	(.000–.195)	(.479–.511)
Nonoverlapping samples	**.370**	.091	**.508**
	(.228–.474)	(.000–.237)	(.484–.533)

Note. A = additive genetic factors; C = shared environment; E = nonshared environment; D = nonadditive genetic factors. Statistically significant means are in boldface type.

None of the individual studies in the meta-analysis obtained significant C effects; all confidence intervals overlapped with zero (Taylor, 2011b). It was only with the large pooled sample used in the meta-analysis that it was possible to detect marginally statistically significant but small C effects. Table 16.1 further shows that D effects were nonsignificant, accounting for 9% to 10% of variance. D effects may have become significant with greater statistical power. But even if a larger sample had been available, it appears that D effects would have been small, at best accounting for only a small fraction of phenotypic variance.

There was statistically significant across-sample heterogeneity of effect sizes for each of ACE and ADE models, for both the overall and nonoverlapping samples, that is, heterogeneity attributable to variation in true effect sizes (i.e., in excess of that attributable to random error). Subgroup analyses and meta-regressions were conducted in an effort to identify the sources of heterogeneity in effect sizes. The initial set of analyses concerned methodological factors, including type of symptom rating scale, its reliability (as gauged by Cronbach's α), language of assessment, and whether the assessment was a symptom severity rating or diagnostic assessment. None of these variables significantly predicted the effect sizes of A, C, D, or E. Biological sex was consistently unrelated to the magnitude of A, D, C, or E. Age was unrelated to A, C, and D effects, but was significantly related to E. The latter significantly increased as a function of age at assessment (Taylor, 2011b). People with early-onset OCD, compared with their late onset counterparts, have a greater prevalence of OCD among their first-degree relatives (Taylor, 2011a). Accordingly, it may be that the importance of genetic and environmental influences on OC symptoms varies as a function of the age of onset of OC symptoms or OCD. This remains to be investigated.

In summary, the meta-analytic results indicated the following: (a) A and E, but not C and D, accounted for a significant amount of variance in OC symptoms (in terms of mean effect sizes); (b) there was significant heterogeneity of effect sizes, suggesting that the effects of A, C, D, and E might significantly vary with methodological variables or variables defining subpopulations; (c) heterogeneity in effect size for E could be at least partly accounted for in terms of age; (d) none of the variables available for inclusion in the meta-analysis were able to account for the heterogeneity in A, C, or D effects—an issue for further investigation; and (e) effect sizes obtained from studies using diagnostic measures of OCD (Bolton et al., 2007; Tambs et al., 2009) were not significantly different from those based on OC symptom measures.

GENERALIZATION OF FINDINGS ACROSS LEVELS OF SYMPTOM SEVERITY

The meta-analysis suggested that effect sizes from OC symptom rating scales were no different from effect sizes from OCD diagnostic ratings, with A and E being most important. Results of a participant stratification analysis by Taylor, Jang, et al. (2010) were consistent with this finding. The magnitude of A and E effects did not differ when results for the overall community-based twin sample were compared with results from participants with relatively high scores on measures of OC symptoms (i.e., OC symptom severity scores above the 50th percentile of the sample). However, further research is needed to determine whether very severe OCD is influenced by the same sets of genetic and environmental factors that play a role in mild OC symptoms.

OC SYMPTOM SUBTYPES

Two twin studies conducted a comprehensive evaluation of the importance of genetic and environmental factors for each of the major, empirically defined, subtypes of OC symptoms (Iervolino, Rijsdijk, Cherkas, Fullana, & Mataix-Cols, 2011; Taylor, Jang, et al., 2010). The results, based on the same measure of symptoms (the revised Obsessive–Compulsive Inventory; Foa et al., 2002), were remarkably consistent across studies. Figure 16.1 summarizes the results in terms of weighted mean effect sizes. Only weighted means were computed, rather than a full meta-analysis, because only two relevant studies were available.

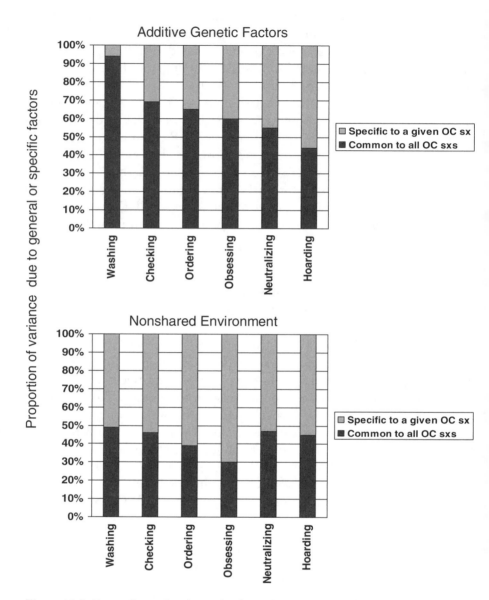

Figure 16.1. Proportions of variance in obsessive–compulsive (OC) symptom (sx) scores due to general (across all OC symptoms) or symptom-specific etiologic factors. The upper panel shows the relative importance of general and specific additive genetic factors, and the lower panel shows the relative importance of general and specific nonshared environmental factors. Results were based on the weighted values (weighted by sample size) from Taylor, Jang, et al. (2010) and Iervolino et al. (2011). From "Etiology of Obsessions and Compulsions: A Meta-Analysis and Narrative Review of Twin Studies," by S. Taylor, *Clinical Psychology Review, 31,* p. 1369. Copyright 2011 Elsevier. Reprinted with permission.

The results show that washing, and to a lesser extent other OC symptoms, was strongly shaped by etiologic factors common to all other OC symptoms. Hoarding symptoms were among those that had the least etiologic resemblance with other OC symptoms. This is consistent with the new disorder in the *Diagnostic and Statistical Manual of Mental Disorders* (5th ed.; American Psychiatric Association, 2013), hoarding disorder, which is said to fall within the spectrum of OC-related disorders (Pertusa et al., 2010). Hoarding disorder is thought to be etiologically related to, but distinct from, other OC-related phenomena. This conjecture is supported by the etiologic results summarized in Figure 16.1. That is, hoarding symptoms do have genetic and environmental variance in common with other OC symptoms, but hoarding tended to have a greater proportion of symptom-specific genetic and environmental variance.

GENE–ENVIRONMENT INTERACTIONS

Taylor, Jang, et al. (2010) found evidence of gene–environment interactions; that is, A-by-E interactions significantly predicted variance in OC symptoms above and beyond variance due to A and E main effects. Thus, the effects of A and E identified in the meta-analysis can be partitioned into main effects and an interaction. Such results were obtained for each of the OC symptom subtypes described in Figure 16.2.

ETIOLOGICAL RELATIONSHIP WITH OTHER SYMPTOMS, TRAITS, AND DISORDERS

Table 16.2 shows the proportions of genetic and nonshared environmental variance of OC symptoms or disorder shared with other non-OC symptoms, traits, or disorders. Cohen's (1988) classification scheme was used to facilitate the interpretation of findings, for which large effects are defined by $r \geq .50$ (i.e., $\geq 25\%$ shared variance) and medium (moderate) effect sizes are defined by $r \geq .30$ ($\geq 9\%$ shared variance). Large and medium effects are flagged in Table 16.2. The table shows that OC symptoms had a medium or large amount of shared genetic variance with many different forms of psychopathology, but comparatively less overlapping environmental variance. The genetic findings are consistent with studies of other forms of psychopathology in which general (pleiotropic) genetic factors have been identified, playing a role in many different kinds of psychopathology (Haworth & Plomin, 2010).

Table 16.2 shows that OC symptoms and negative emotionality had a large amount of shared genetic variance, with a weighted mean of 37%

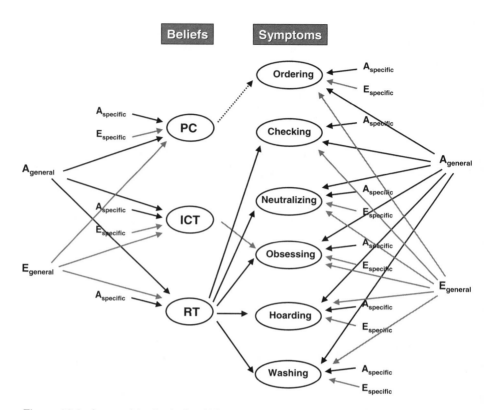

Figure 16.2. An empirically derived biopsychosocial model of obsessive–compulsive (OC) symptoms, based on twin research, in which additive genetic effects, nonshared environment, and dysfunctional beliefs influence OC symptoms. Here, belief-specific and general genetic factors ($A_{specific}$, $A_{general}$) and belief-specific and general environmental factors ($E_{specific}$, $E_{general}$) influence dysfunctional beliefs, which in turn influence OC symptoms. The latter symptoms are also directly influenced by their own set of OC-specific and general genetic factors ($A_{specific}$, $A_{general}$) and environmental factors ($E_{specific}$, $E_{general}$). ICT = overimportance and need to control thoughts; PC = perfectionism and intolerance of uncertainty; RT = inflated responsibility and overestimation of threat; Symptoms = major OC symptoms. Each arrow represents a statistically significant pathway ($p < .001$, based on a Bonferroni correction). From "Etiology of Obsessions and Compulsions: A Meta-Analysis and Narrative Review of Twin Studies," by S. Taylor, *Clinical Psychology Review, 31,* p. 1370. Copyright 2011 Elsevier. Reprinted with permission.

overlapping variance across three studies (Clifford, Murray, & Fulker, 1984; Hur, 2009; Taylor, Jang, et al., 2010). In comparison, OC symptoms and negative emotionality had only a moderate amount of overlapping variance due to environmental effects; weighted mean = 12% overlapping variance. Taylor, Jang, et al. (2010) found that OC symptoms and negative emotionality were influenced by a common genetic factor but arose from different environmental factors. OC symptoms also were shaped by symptom-specific genetic factors.

TABLE 10.2

Proportions of Genetic and Environmental Variance of Obsessive–Compulsive (OC) Symptoms or Disorder Shared With Other Symptoms, Traits, or Disorders

OC variable	Comparison variable	Nature of comparison variable	Study	% overlapping A	% overlapping E
S	Negative emotionality	T	Clifford et al. (1984)	36*	4
S	Negative emotionality	T	Hur (2009)	26*	15†
S	Negative emotionality	T	Taylor, Jang, et al. (2010)	65*	17†
S	Traits of OC personality disorder	T	Taylor et al. (2011)	32*	13†
S	Symptoms of general distress	S	Eley et al. (2003)	7	2
S	Separation anxiety	S	Eley et al. (2003)	1	1
S	Phobic anxiety	S	Eley et al. (2003)	3	2
S	Shyness/inhibition	S	Eley et al. (2003)	35*	7
S	Major depressive disorder	S	Lahey et al. (2011)	25*	2
S	Generalized anxiety disorder	S	Lahey et al. (2011)	23†	2
S	Social anxiety disorder	S	Lahey et al. (2011)	10†	2
S	Specific phobia	S	Lahey et al. (2011)	22†	1
S	Agoraphobia	S	Lahey et al. (2011)	29*	<1
S	Separation anxiety disorder	S	Lahey et al. (2011)	46*	3
S	Conduct disorder	S	Lahey et al. (2011)	4	1
S	Inattentiveness	S	Lahey et al. (2011)	9†	1
S	Hyperactivity/impulsivity	S	Lahey et al. (2011)	19†	<1
S	Oppositional-defiant disorder	S	Lahey et al. (2011)	8	1
S	Interpersonal sensitivity	S/T	Fagnani et al. (2011)	98*	19†
S	Paranoid ideation	S/T	Fagnani et al. (2011)	79*	13†
S	Psychoticism (schizotypal features)	S/T	Fagnani et al. (2011)	69*	26*
Dx	Any anxiety disorder other than OCD	Dx	Bolton et al. (2007)	7	<1
Dx	Any tic disorder	Dx	Bolton et al. (2007)	9†	2

Note. A = additive genetic factors; E = nonshared environment; Dx = lifetime diagnosis; S = current symptoms; T = trait variable; S/T = Fagnani et al. (2011) regarded these as symptoms, although they could be equally regarded as personality traits; OCD = obsessive–compulsive disorder; Dx = lifetime diagnosis. From "Etiology of Obsessions and Compulsions: A Meta-Analysis and Narrative Review of Twin Studies," by S. Taylor, *Clinical Psychology Review, 31,* p. 1370. Copyright 2011 Elsevier. Adapted with permission.
*Large effects (≥ 25% overlapping variance). †Medium effects (≥ 9% overlapping variance).

Similar findings were reported by Lahey, Van Hulle, Singh, Waldman, and Rathouz (2011).

Table 16.2 also shows that OC symptoms and OC personality traits had a large amount of shared genetic variance but only a moderate amount of overlapping environmental variance. Taylor, Asmundson, and Jang (2011) found that OC symptoms and OC personality traits had a common genetic influence but differed in their environmental influences.

Table 16.2 further indicates that OC symptoms had a large amount of overlapping genetic variance with symptoms of social anxiety or interpersonal discomfort (i.e., shyness/inhibition, interpersonal sensitivity), and with symptoms of agoraphobia, separation anxiety, and major depressive disorder. OC symptoms or disorder had a moderate amount of overlapping genetic variance with many other measures of anxiety-related psychopathology, with tic disorders, and with features of attention-deficit/hyperactivity disorder (i.e., inattentiveness, hyperactivity/impulsivity). The amount of overlapping environmental variance with these variables was largely trivial, being mostly less than 2% (Table 16.2).

In terms of the relationship between OC symptom and psychotic features, the findings of Fagnani et al. (2011) merit particular consideration because the proportion of shared variance in this study tended to be much higher than the proportions reported in most of the other studies in Table 16.2. Those authors, using data from a community sample, claimed that three of their scales (interpersonal sensitivity, paranoid ideation, psychoticism) all measured psychotic features and concluded that OC symptoms and psychotic features have common genetic and environmental etiologies. There are several problems with this conclusion. Fagnani et al. used the Symptom Checklist–90, revised (SCL-90; Derogatis, 1975), which is problematic for the purpose of examining the genetic and environmental variance shared between OC symptoms and psychotic symptoms. The SCL-90 scales, developed in the 1970s (before the publication of the *Diagnostic and Statistical Manual of Mental Disorders*, 3rd ed.; American Psychiatric Association, 1980), contain many items that measure general (nonspecific) distress, and so correlations among its scales may be spuriously inflated because they all measure, to some extent, a common variable (general distress) (Taylor, 1995). Fagnani et al. used the SCL-90 interpersonal sensitivity scale as a measure of psychotic features. Inspection of the item content reveals that the scale measures interpersonal discomfort, including fear of negative evaluation. Interpersonal discomfort is a nonspecific feature of many different forms of psychopathology (e.g., anxiety disorders, major depressive disorder, personality disorders, psychotic disorders), and so it cannot be claimed that it specifically measures psychotic symptoms. A further problem concerns the 10-item SCL-90 scale that purportedly measured psychoticism. Half of the items are nonspecific in that they could refer to psychotic symptoms or to features of OCD. For example, the item "Having thoughts about sex that bother you" could refer to sexual obsessions; "The idea that you should be punished for your sins" could refer to scrupulosity obsessions; and "The idea that something serious is wrong with your body" could refer to somatic obsessions. The item "The idea that something is wrong with your mind" could reflect a person's appraisals of the meaning of obsessional thoughts (see Frost & Steketee, 2002). Even the six-item SCL-90 paranoid ideation scale contains items referring to awareness that other people do not share one's ideas (which might be construed as insight into one's obsessions) and that people are negatively judging the person (which may occur if a person with OCD is criticized for engaging in compulsive rituals). Accordingly, the very high proportions of overlapping variance between OC symptoms and so-called psychotic symptoms (Table 16.2) may have been an artifact due to criterion contamination (i.e., the scales measured overlapping symptom domains). Further research, using methodologically rigorous methods, is needed to determine whether OC symptoms are etiologically related to psychotic symptoms.

TOWARD A BIOPSYCHOSOCIAL MODEL OF OC SYMPTOMS

Taylor and Jang (2011) recently evaluated the role of genetic and environmental factors in a broader, biopsychosocial context, in a way that integrates behavioral–genetic models with contemporary cognitive–behavioral models. The latter propose that OC symptoms arise from particular kinds of dysfunctional beliefs, in which the strength of belief influences the development and severity of OC symptoms (Clark, 2004; Frost & Steketee, 2002; Salkovskis et al., 1999). Three intercorrelated sets of beliefs have been theoretically and empirically linked to OC symptoms: (a) perfectionism and intolerance of uncertainty (PC), (b) overimportance of thoughts and the need to control thoughts (ICT), and (c) inflated responsibility and the overestimation of threat (RT) (Obsessive Compulsive Cognitions Working Group, 2005; Taylor, Coles, et al., 2010). PC involves beliefs that mistakes and imperfection are intolerable, along with beliefs that it is necessary and possible to be completely certain that aversive events will not occur. ICT entails beliefs that the mere presence of unwanted thoughts indicates that such thoughts are important or portentous (e.g., the belief that "bad thoughts, even unwanted ones, lead to bad deeds"), along with beliefs that complete control over one's thoughts is necessary and possible. RT includes beliefs that aversive events are quite likely to occur and that one has a duty to prevent such events.

Although there is evidence supporting contemporary cognitive models (Abramowitz et al., 2009), such models are limited in that they ignore the importance of genetic factors and overemphasize the role of shared environment

(Taylor & Jang, 2011). Although it is widely acknowledged that OC symptoms probably have a complex biopsychosocial etiology, to our knowledge there had been no previous attempt to integrate dysfunctional beliefs and genetic factors into a unified, empirically supported model. On the basis of a community sample of MZ and DZ twins who completed measures of dysfunctional beliefs and OC symptoms, we used structural equation modeling to compare three models: (a) the belief causation model, in which genetic and nonshared environmental factors influence beliefs and OC symptoms, and beliefs also influence symptoms; (b) the symptom causation model, which was the same as model (a) except that symptoms cause beliefs; and (c) the belief coeffect model, in which beliefs and OC symptoms are the product of common genetic and environmental factors, and beliefs have no causal influence on symptoms. The belief causation model was the best-fitting model. Beliefs accounted for a mean of 18% of phenotypic variance in OC symptoms. Genetic and environmental factors accounted, respectively, for an additional 36% and 47% of phenotypic variance. The best-fitting model obtained from these analyses appears in Figure 16.2. The model describes an empirically supported integration of cognitive–behavioral and behavioral–genetic approaches. However, it is noteworthy that shared environment was not a significant component of this model and that dysfunctional beliefs accounted for only a small proportion (18%) of the variance in OC symptoms. Although the available findings offer a degree of support for some of the etiologic variables proposed by cognitive–behavioral models (i.e., dysfunctional beliefs but not shared environment), these models are insufficient in part because they neglect the importance of genetic factors.

SUMMARY AND CONCLUSIONS

Findings from this review indicated that additive genetic effects (A) and nonshared environment (E) accounted for most of the variance in OC symptoms. There was evidence of A-by-E interactions, and the importance of E increased with age. Shared environment (C) and nonadditive genetic effects (D) made little or no contribution. The findings did not vary with sex or symptom severity. Results further indicated that OC symptoms are shaped by etiologic factors common to all types of OC symptoms but also have symptom-specific etiologies. OC symptoms are also shaped by very general etiologic factors (e.g., those influencing negative emotionality).

The conclusion that shared environment plays a limited role might seem at odds with studies suggesting that family environment plays an important role in OC symptoms (e.g., van Noppen & Steketee, 2009). The problem with such studies is that they failed to disentangle the effects of genes and shared environment. To illustrate, some studies suggest that parental rearing style and family emotional atmosphere (particularly parental overcontrol and criticism) are correlated with offspring OCD or OC symptom severity and course (van Noppen & Steketee, 2009; Waters & Barrett, 2000). The problem with such studies is that they fail to establish whether the effects are due to parental behavior (shared environment) or parent–child reciprocal interactions (which could reflect gene–environment interactions), or whether the effects are simply due to shared genetic factors (e.g., genes regulating overcontrolling parenting styles might also play a role in offspring OC symptoms). Future research is needed to investigate whether, or how, parenting influences offspring OC symptoms.

OC symptoms have a complex etiologic architecture, which does not appear to be adequately captured by contemporary psychosocial or biological models. Part of the problem is that such models are typically reductionistic, in which the causes of OC symptoms are reduced to explanations based largely on either environmental effects (i.e., learning experiences) or hardwired biological factors (Abramowitz et al., 2009; Taylor, Abramowitz, McKay, & Cuttler, 2011). Cognitive–behavioral models overemphasize environmental variables, particularly shared environment, to the neglect of genetic factors. Contemporary biological models (reviewed by Abramowitz et al., 2009) overemphasize the role of hardwired (inherited) dysregulations in neurobiological circuitry, to the neglect of the role of environmental factors. Few, if any, contemporary models would have predicted, a priori, the complex etiologic architecture identified by twin studies, such as the nature of genetic and environmental factors, their hierarchy of specific and nonspecific etiological influences, and the genetic effects on OC-related dysfunctional beliefs. Twin studies highlight the need for comprehensive biopsychosocial models that are able to account for the etiological complexity revealed by empirical research.

Although twin studies indicate that genetic factors play an important role in OC symptoms, little is known about the specific genes that are involved. There have been many molecular genetic studies of OCD, but there have been a great many replication failures. The nature of E also remains to be elucidated. That is, what kinds of nonshared environmental experiences are most likely to contribute to the development of OC symptoms? A number of studies have found that the onset of OC symptoms is associated with the onset of life stressors, such as job-related difficulties, becoming a new parent, or exposure to traumatic events (Abramowitz, Khandker, Nelson, Deacon, & Rygwall, 2006; Abramowitz, Nelson, Rygwall, & Khandker, 2007; Cromer, Schmidt, & Murphy, 2007; Millet et al., 2004). Further research is required to determine whether these events are causally related to OC symptoms or to OCD. Further research is also needed to better understand how genes and environmental factors interact to shape the development of OC symptoms, and how genes and the environment are moderated by age or other variables in the genesis and course of obsessions and compulsions.

REFERENCES

Abramowitz, J. S., Khandker, M., Nelson, C. A., Deacon, B. J., & Rygwall, R. (2006). The role of cognitive factors in the pathogenesis of obsessive–compulsive symptoms: A prospective study. *Behaviour Research and Therapy, 44,* 1361–1374. doi:10.1016/j.brat.2005.09.011

Abramowitz, J. S., Nelson, C. A., Rygwall, R., & Khandker, M. (2007). The cognitive mediation of obsessive–compulsive symptoms: A longitudinal study. *Journal of Anxiety Disorders, 21,* 91–104. doi:10.1016/j.janxdis.2006.05.003

Abramowitz, J. S., Taylor, S., & McKay, D. (2009). Obsessive–compulsive disorder. *The Lancet, 374,* 491–499. doi:10.1016/S0140-6736(09)60240-3

American Psychiatric Association. (1980). *Diagnostic and statistical manual of mental disorders* (3rd ed.). Washington, DC: Author.

American Psychiatric Association. (2013). *Diagnostic and statistical manual of mental disorders* (5th ed.). Washington, DC: Author.

Bolton, D., Rijsdijk, F., O'Connor, T. G., Perrin, S., & Eley, T. C. (2007). Obsessive–compulsive disorder, tics, and anxiety in 6-year-old twins. *Psychological Medicine, 37,* 39–48. doi:10.1017/S0033291706008816

Clark, D. A. (2004). *Cognitive–behavioral therapy for OCD.* New York, NY: Guilford Press.

Clifford, C. A., Murray, R. M., & Fulker, D. W. (1984). Genetic and environmental influences on obsessional traits and symptoms. *Psychological Medicine, 14,* 791–800. doi:10.1017/S0033291700019760

Cohen, J. (1988). *Statistical power analyses for the behavioral sciences* (2nd ed.). Hillsdale, NJ: Erlbaum.

Cromer, K. R., Schmidt, N. B., & Murphy, D. L. (2007). An investigation of traumatic life events and obsessive–compulsive disorder. *Behaviour Research and Therapy, 45,* 1683–1691. doi:10.1016/j.brat.2006.08.018

Derogatis, L. R. (1975). *SCL-90-R: Administration, scoring and procedures manual II for the revised version and other instruments of the psychopathology rating scale series.* Towson, MD: Clinical Psychometric Research.

Eley, T. C., Bolton, D., O'Connor, T. G., Perrin, S., Smith, P., & Plomin, R. (2003). A twin study of anxiety-related behaviours in pre-school children. *Journal of Child Psychology and Psychiatry and Allied Disciplines, 44,* 945–960. doi:10.1111/1469-7610.00179

Fagnani, C., Bellani, M., Tansella, M., Balestrieri, M., Toccaceli, V., Patriarca, V., . . . Brambilla, P. (2011). Investigation of shared genetic effects for psychotic and obsessive symptoms in young adult twins. *Psychiatry Research, 188,* 276–282. doi:10.1016/j.psychres.2010.12.002

Foa, E. B., Huppert, J. D., Leiberg, S., Langner, R., Kichic, R., Hajcak, G., . . . Salkovskis, P. M. (2002). The Obsessive–Compulsive Inventory: Development and validation of a short version. *Psychological Assessment, 14,* 485–496. doi:10.1037/1040-3590.14.4.485

Frost, R. O., & Steketee, G. (2002). *Cognitive approaches to obsessions and compulsions: Theory, assessment and treatment*. Oxford, England: Elsevier.

Haworth, C. M. A., & Plomin, R. (2010). Quantitative genetics in the era of molecular genetics: Learning abilities and disabilities as an example. *Journal of the American Academy of Child and Adolescent Psychiatry, 49*, 783–793. doi:10.1016/j.jaac.2010.01.026

Hudziak, J. J., van Beijsterveldt, C. E. M., Althoff, R. R., Stanger, C., Rettew, D. C., Nelson, E. C., . . . Boomsma, D. I. (2004). Genetic and environmental contributions to the Child Behavior Checklist Obsessive–Compulsive Scale: A cross-cultural twin study. *Archives of General Psychiatry, 61*, 608–616. doi:10.1001/archpsyc.61.6.608

Hur, Y.-M. (2009). Genetic and environmental covariations among obsessive–compulsive symptoms, neuroticism, and extraversion in South Korean adolescent and young adult twins. *Twin Research and Human Genetics, 12*, 142–148. doi:10.1375/twin.12.2.142

Iervolino, A. C., Rijsdijk, F. V., Cherkas, L., Fullana, M. A., & Mataix-Cols, D. (2011). A multivariate twin study of obsessive–compulsive symptom dimensions. *Archives of General Psychiatry, 68*, 637–644. doi:10.1001/archgenpsychiatry.2011.54

Lahey, B. B., Van Hulle, C. A., Singh, A. L., Waldman, I. D., & Rathouz, P. J. (2011). Higher-order genetic and environmental structure of prevalent forms of child and adolescent psychopathology. *Archives of General Psychiatry, 68*, 181–189. doi:10.1001/archgenpsychiatry.2010.192

Millet, B., Kochman, F., Gallarda, T., Krebs, M. O., Demonfaucon, F., Barrot, I., . . . Hantouche, E. G. (2004). Phenomenological and comorbid features associated in obsessive–compulsive disorder: Influence of age of onset. *Journal of Affective Disorders, 79*, 241–246. doi:10.1016/S0165-0327(02)00351-8

Obsessive Compulsive Cognitions Working Group. (2005). Psychometric validation of the Obsessive Beliefs Questionnaire and the Interpretation of Intrusions Inventory: Part 2. Factor analyses and testing of a brief version. *Behaviour Research and Therapy, 43*, 1527–1542. doi:10.1016/j.brat.2004.07.010

Pertusa, A., Frost, R., Fullana, M., Samuels, J., Steketee, G., Tolin, D., . . . Mataix-Cols, D. (2010). Refining the diagnostic boundaries of compulsive hoarding. *Clinical Psychology Review, 30*, 371–386. doi:10.1016/j.cpr.2010.01.007

Salkovskis, P., Shafran, R., Rachman, S., & Freeston, M. H. (1999). Multiple pathways to inflated responsibility beliefs in obsessional problems: Possible origins and implications for therapy and research. *Behaviour Research and Therapy, 37*, 1055–1072. doi:10.1016/S0005-7967(99)00063-7

Tambs, K., Czajkowsky, N., Røysamb, E., Neale, M., Reichborn-Kjennerud, T., Aggen, S., . . . Kendler, K. S. (2009). Structure of genetic and environmental risk factors for dimensional representations of DSM–IV anxiety disorders. *The British Journal of Psychiatry, 195*, 301–307. doi:10.1192/bjp.bp.108.059485

Taylor, S. (1995). Assessment of obsessions and compulsions: Reliability, validity, and sensitivity to treatment effects. *Clinical Psychology Review, 15*, 261–296. doi:10.1016/0272-7358(95)00015-H

Taylor, S. (2011a). Early versus late onset obsessive–compulsive disorder: Evidence for distinct subtypes. *Clinical Psychology Review, 31*, 1083–1100. doi:10.1016/j.cpr.2011.06.007

Taylor, S. (2011b). Etiology of obsessions and compulsions: A meta-analysis and narrative review of twin studies. *Clinical Psychology Review, 31*, 1361–1372. doi:10.1016/j.cpr.2011.09.008

Taylor, S., Abramowitz, J. S., McKay, D., & Cuttler, C. (2011). Cognitive approaches to understanding obsessive–compulsive and related disorders. In G. Steketee (Ed.), *Oxford handbook of obsessive compulsive and spectrum disorders* (pp. 233–250). New York, NY: Oxford University Press. doi:10.1093/oxfordhb/9780195376210.013.0044

Taylor, S., Asmundson, G. J. G., & Jang, K. L. (2011). Etiology of obsessive–compulsive symptoms and obsessive–compulsive personality traits: Common genes, mostly different environments. *Depression and Anxiety, 28*, 863–869. doi:10.1002/da.20859

Taylor, S., Coles, M. E., Abramowitz, J. S., Wu, K. D., Olatunji, B. O., Timpano, K. R., . . . Tolin, D. F. (2010). How are dysfunctional beliefs related to obsessive–compulsive symptoms? *Journal of Cognitive Psychotherapy, 24*, 165–176. doi:10.1891/0889-8391.24.3.165

Taylor, S., & Jang, K. L. (2011). Biopsychosocial etiology of obsessions and compulsions: An integrated behavioral–genetic and cognitive–behavioral analysis. *Journal of Abnormal Psychology, 120*, 174–186. doi:10.1037/a0021403

Taylor, S., Jang, K. L., & Asmundson, G. J. G. (2010). Etiology of obsessions and compulsions: A behavioral–genetic analysis. *Journal of Abnormal Psychology, 119*, 672–682. doi:10.1037/a0021132

van Grootheest, D. S., Bartels, M., van Beijsterveldt, C., Cath, D., Beekman, A., Hudziak, J., . . . Boomsma, D. I. (2008). Genetic and environmental contributions to self-report obsessive–compulsive symptoms in Dutch adolescents at ages 12, 14, and 16. *Journal of the American Academy of Child & Adolescent Psychiatry, 47*, 1182–1188. doi:10.1097/CHI.0b013e3181825abd

van Grootheest, D. S., Cath, D., Hottenga, J. J., Beekman, A. T., & Boomsma, D. I. (2009). Genetic factors underlie stability of obsessive–compulsive symptoms. *Twin Research and Human Genetics, 12*, 411–419. doi:10.1375/twin.12.5.411

Van Noppen, B., & Steketee, G. (2009). Testing a conceptual model of patient and family predictors of obsessive compulsive disorder (OCD) symptoms. *Behaviour Research and Therapy, 47*, 18–25. doi:10.1016/j.brat.2008.10.005

Waters, T. L., & Barrett, P. M. (2000). The role of the family in childhood obsessive–compulsive disorder. *Clinical Child and Family Psychology Review, 3*, 173–184. doi:10.1023/A:1009551325629

17

FUNCTIONAL NEUROIMAGING AND MODELS FOR OBSESSIVE–COMPULSIVE DISORDER AND OBSESSIVE–COMPULSIVE SPECTRUM DISORDERS

KYLE A.B. LAPIDUS, EMILY R. STERN, HEATHER A. BERLIN, AND WAYNE K. GOODMAN

This chapter provides an overview of neuroimaging and cognitive neuroscience research on obsessive–compulsive disorder (OCD) and related disorders. We begin with a discussion of studies in OCD focusing on conflict and error monitoring, motor suppression, and task switching. We continue with a focus on reward and emotional processing in OCD. This is followed by consideration of the role of disgust and fear and the importance of these systems in OCD. Finally, we discuss data from imaging studies in OCD spectrum disorders, focusing on trichotillomania, body dysmorphic disorder, and hoarding.

COGNITIVE NEUROSCIENCE STUDIES IN OCD

For the past several decades, neuroimaging techniques such as functional magnetic resonance imaging (fMRI) and positron emission tomography (PET) have been used to investigate neurocircuit functioning in OCD. Numerous

http://dx.doi.org/10.1037/14323-018
Obsessive–Compulsive Disorder and Its Spectrum: A Life-Span Approach, Eric A. Storch and Dean McKay (Editors)
Copyright © 2014 by the American Psychological Association. All rights reserved.

studies have explored the neural correlates of cognitive and affective processes in OCD, with varying relevance for the symptoms of the disorder. On one end of the spectrum, tasks directly provoking symptoms are clearly relevant for the disorder, yet they do not address whether basic cognitive–affective mechanisms are impaired in the absence of symptom exacerbation. By contrast, the other end of the spectrum examines neural correlates of psychological processes whose impairment is likely secondary to the central dysfunction (or dysfunctions) driving the disorder. In this section, we selectively review neuroimaging studies using tasks that probe basic cognitive–affective processes potentially at the core of OCD, focusing on those constructs for which three or more studies have compared adults with OCD and a control group.

Conflict and Error Monitoring

Probably the most widespread investigation into the cognitive neuroscience of OCD has taken place in the field of conflict monitoring and error detection. This approach is based on the proposal that obsessions are caused by an overactive conflict or error signal, continually telling the patient that "something is wrong," despite evidence to the contrary (Pitman, 1987). In this view, compulsions are behaviors that attempt to reduce this heightened conflict signal or to correct perceived errors. Cognitive conflict is typically studied in tasks in which there is a mismatch between what a subject would automatically do (i.e., a prepotent response) and what is required in the task. In the Stroop task, subjects must make a response according to the font color of a word, in which the word itself is the name of a color that is different from the font color (e.g., the word *blue* written in red font). In this case, the prepotent response is to read the name of the word, yet the task requires a response according to the color of the word, which creates conflict that significantly increases response times in comparison with trials in which the color and word name are the same (MacLeod, 1991). Conflict monitoring in healthy controls implicates dorsal medial frontal regions including anterior cingulate cortex (dACC) and supplemental motor area (SMA) (Botvinick, Braver, Barch, Carter, & Cohen, 2001; Garavan, Ross, Kaufman, & Stein, 2003; Hester, Fassbender, & Garavan, 2004; Ridderinkhof, Ullsperger, Crone, & Nieuwenhuis, 2004), yet results from the many neuroimaging studies investigating this process in OCD do not present a coherent picture. Although some investigations have found hyperactivity of dorsal medial frontal cortex during conflict in OCD (Ursu, Stenger, Shear, Jones, & Carter, 2003; Yücel et al., 2007), other studies have identified reduced activity in this region (K. D. Fitzgerald et al., 2005; Nakao et al., 2005) or no differences between patients and controls (Stern et al., 2011; Viard et al., 2005). Many studies have reported differences between patients and controls during conflict monitoring in several other brain regions, including parietal cortex (Page et al., 2009; van den Heuvel et al., 2005), caudate nucleus (K. D. Fitzgerald et al., 2005; Nakao et al., 2005), ventral/rostral regions of medial frontal cortex (B. J. Harrison et al., 2006; Nabeyama et al., 2008; Yücel et al., 2007), and lateral (Nakao et al., 2005; Page et al., 2009) and medial (van den Heuvel et al., 2005) temporal cortex, but these results are often contradictory (i.e., some finding activations to be greater in OCD than controls, with others finding the opposite effect). At present it is unknown whether these inconsistencies are due to variability in task design and patient characteristics or whether brain mechanisms of conflict monitoring are simply not reliably altered in OCD.

Errors reflect a specific instance of conflict during which the intended or correct response does not match the actual response made by the subject. Similar to conflict monitoring, errors elicit activation in dorsal medial frontal regions including dACC and SMA. More than for conflict monitoring, errors tend to elicit an emotional/motivational reaction related to frustration, disappointment, or fear of punishment and elicit activation in a broad range of brain regions including anterior inferior medial frontal regions, including rostral ACC (rACC) and ventromedial prefrontal cortex (VMPFC) and, less consistently, in bilateral anterior insula (aIns), dorsolateral prefrontal cortex (DLPFC), prefrontal cortex (PFC), ventrolateral prefrontal cortex/ orbitofrontal cortex (OFC), and inferior parietal cortex (S. F. Taylor, Stern, & Gehring, 2007). Rostral ACC/VMPFC, aIns, and OFC have been associated with valuation and emotional/motivational responses (N. A. Harrison, Gray, Gianaros, & Critchley, 2010; Kober et al., 2008; Kringelbach & Rolls, 2004; Lebreton, Jorge, Michel, Thirion, & Pessiglione, 2009); as such, activation of these brain regions to errors may reflect the neural processing of the motivational significance of mistakes, whereas conflict associated with the mismatch between the actual and intended response may be processed in dorsal medial frontal cortex. Support for this notion comes from a study by S. F. Taylor et al. (2006), in which errors associated with a loss of money showed greater activation in rACC/VMPFC than did those involving no motivational consequences, with no effect of error consequence on activity in dorsal medial frontal regions.

OCD patients show an increased neural response to errors in dACC (Maltby, Tolin, Worhunsky, O'Keefe, & Kiehl, 2005; Ursu et al., 2003), rACC (Maltby et al., 2005), and lateral frontal cortex, including OFC and DLPFC (Maltby et al., 2005). K. D. Fitzgerald et al. (2005) found hyperactivity in VMPFC in a small group of patients with OCD, a finding that was replicated in a larger study (E. R. Stern et al., 2011), which also identified hyperactivity of aIns. Despite some variation among the studies, overall these data suggest that OCD patients respond more strongly to errors than do healthy individuals, particularly in ventral frontal and insula regions involved in processing the value or emotional importance of the error. However, it is important to note that these studies examined OCD patients' responses to actual errors (and conflict), whereas the phenotype of the disorder is more consistent with the detection of errors (or conflict) where there are none (or at least where their presence is uncertain). Thus, while hyperactive error responses in OCD may reflect an important characteristic of the disorder related to sensitivity to mistakes, these studies did not directly probe the neural mechanisms associated with the feeling or belief frequently expressed by patients that something is wrong even in the absence of overt errors.

Motor Output Suppression

Unlike conflict- or error-monitoring models of OCD, in which compulsions are often viewed as secondary responses to overactive conflict/error signals, experiments examining the suppression of motor output in OCD are directly relevant for repetitive motor compulsions. Inhibition of motoric output is commonly studied using a go/no-go task (or variant thereof, such as the stop-signal task) during which subjects make button-press responses to frequent stimuli (go trials) and are required to inhibit responses to infrequently presented stimuli (no-go trials). Even though this task inevitably involves conflict monitoring between the frequent go and infrequent no-go trials, these paradigms additionally involve a specific motor suppression component not present in conflict studies. Accordingly, although no-go trials are associated with activation of some of the same regions as for conflict monitoring including dACC and SMA (Aron & Poldrack, 2006; Buchsbaum, Greer, Chang, & Berman, 2005; Garavan, Hester, Murphy, Fassbender, & Kelly, 2006; Garavan, Ross, & Stein, 1999), they also elicit activation in subcortical structures, including thalamus and basal ganglia, as well as predominantly right-hemisphere lateral frontal and inferior parietal regions (Aron & Poldrack, 2006; Buchsbaum et al., 2005; Garavan et al., 1999, 2006; Robbins, 2007). In a meta-analysis, right inferior frontal (IFG) regions have been most consistently associated with no-go trials (Buchsbaum et al., 2005), which has been supported by lesion and brain stimulation studies showing impaired response inhibition after inactivation of this region (Aron, Fletcher, Bullmore, Sahakian, & Robbins, 2003; Chambers et al., 2006).

It may be hypothesized that an OCD deficit in suppressing motor output would be associated with aberrant recruitment of the response suppression network, which would lead to more failed inhibitions on no-go trials. Although this type of analysis has not as of yet been performed, prior studies have compared OCD patients and controls during successful inhibition during which motor output is successfully suppressed on no-go trials. Reduced activity in SMA, right IFG, basal ganglia, and thalamus has been found in OCD patients during correct no-go trials (Page et al., 2009; Roth et al., 2007), which would suggest reduced recruitment of the response suppression network even during inhibition success. However, OCD hyperactivity in caudate nucleus and thalamus (Maltby et al., 2005; Roth et al., 2007)—as well as medial and lateral frontal regions, premotor cortex, middle temporal cortex, posterior cingulate cortex, and cerebellum (Maltby et al., 2005; Page et al., 2009)—has also been reported for successful inhibition, which has been interpreted as compensatory activation (Page et al., 2009). Given the variability of findings and the focus on neural differences during successful inhibitions (as opposed to inhibition failures), further research will be needed to determine whether dysfunction in a network for suppressing motor output is a core mechanism of OCD.

Switching and Cognitive Inflexibility

Another approach to investigating basic mechanisms of OCD has focused on how patients switch attention between two or more different tasks, stimuli, or rewards. Rather than hypothesizing an overactive conflict or error signal or a failure to suppress motor output, these studies are predicated on the notion that OCD patients exhibit an inflexibility that prevents them from shifting away from stimuli that may have at one time been correct or rewarding but are no longer so. As switching deficits need not be limited to the motor domain, impaired switching in OCD may be able to explain the presence of obsessions in addition to compulsions.

Many studies of switching have investigated neural activity associated with shifting attention between features or dimensions of stimuli (cognitive switching tasks). Not surprisingly, in a meta-analysis examining brain regions involved in cognitive switching and motor suppression, overlap between these processes was found in dACC/SMA, IFG, DLPFC, and inferior parietal cortex (Buchsbaum et al., 2005). However, frontoparietal activations were more widespread and bilateral for cognitive switching (Buchsbaum et al., 2005; Robbins, 2007), appearing very similar to a frontoparietal network often described as a being involved in executive functions and task control (Bressler & Menon, 2010; J. D. Power et al., 2011). Studies looking at brain activity in OCD during cognitive switching have found reduced activation in patients in comparison with controls in this frontoparietal network as well as in OFC, caudate nucleus, temporal cortex, and medial parietal regions (Gu et al., 2008; Han et al., 2011; Page et al., 2009). Two studies reported widespread reductions across the cortex and basal ganglia (Gu et al., 2008;

Han et al., 2011), whereas one study found hypoactivations localized to a few regions of lateral frontal and medial parietal cortex (Page et al., 2009). Despite this difference, results were fairly consistent in pointing to cortical hypoactivation in OCD during cognitive switching.

Another type of switching that has been a topic of much research involves reversing stimulus–reward contingencies (so-called affective switching). In reversal tasks, the reward and punishment value of two stimuli switch so that the currently rewarded stimulus is punished and the previously punished stimulus is rewarded. Given the overall similarity between cognitive switching and reversal, it is surprising that evidence from human and animal studies indicates that lateral prefrontal regions involved in cognitive switching are not necessary for reversal of reward–punishment contingencies, which instead relies primarily on OFC (Dias, Robbins, & Roberts, 1996; Fellows & Farah, 2003; Hampshire & Owen, 2006; Robbins, 2007). Studies of reversal in OCD have examined neural activation on trials during which subjects made a reversal error that lead to a successful switch in comparison with errors that did not lead to a successful switch, thereby isolating activity associated with the moment that subjects learn that a switch is required (Chamberlain, Menzies, Hampshire, et al., 2008; Remijnse et al., 2006, 2009). For this comparison, OCD patients exhibit reduced activation in OFC, but similar to results from cognitive switching studies, reductions were also found throughout a frontoparietal network including DLPFC, bilateral insula, and lateral parietal cortex (Chamberlain, Menzies, Hampshire, et al., 2008; Remijnse et al., 2006, 2009). In one study, unaffected relatives of OCD also showed reduced activity in lateral OFC, DLPFC, and lateral parietal cortex during reversal (Chamberlain, Menzies, Hampshire, et al., 2008), suggesting that impaired frontal recruitment during reversal may be an endophenotype of the disorder.

Overall, these data do support the notion that OCD patients show hypoactivation in a variety of cortical regions both during cognitive switching and when reversing reward–punishment contingencies. Despite the dissociation of lateral and orbital frontal involvement in these processes, dysfunctional brain activity in OCD does not appear to be localized to one of these systems. Reduced recruitment of both DLPFC and OFC has been found when patients switch cognitive set as well as when they reverse reward contingencies. However, similar to the concerns discussed for the other approaches, interpretation of results from switching studies is complicated by the fact that neural differences between OCD patients and controls are examined during successful switches (either at the time of the correct switch response or at the time of the error right before a correct switch) rather than for unsuccessful switches, the latter of which would of course be most relevant for the OCD phenotype.

Reward Processing in OCD

It has been suggested that the difficulty exhibited by OCD patients in terminating inappropriate responses is related to a reduced signal of goal attainment or satiety (Szechtman & Woody, 2004). Within this framework, OCD patients continue to engage in compulsive behaviors such as checking, washing, or repeating/ordering because the normal reward signal associated with successfully completing these tasks is not attained. In healthy individuals, rewards elicit activation in a network of brain regions including ventral striatum, thalamus, putamen, hippocampus, anterior insula, medial frontal cortex, and parietal cortex (Liu, Hairston, Schrier, & Fan, 2011), and some studies in OCD have found reduced activation in patients in reward-related regions such as ventral medial frontal cortex during reward feedback in a reversal task (Remijnse et al., 2006, 2009). However, Jung et al. (2011) reported increased activity in cortical and subcortical regions, including putamen and dorsal medial frontal cortex, to monetary gain in OCD patients, with no regions showing reduced activity in patients in comparison with controls. In this same study, in comparison with controls, patients also showed increased activation of ventral striatum and temporal and parietal cortex in response to trials in which they avoided monetary loss. Finally, a recent study found no difference between OCD patients and controls during reward feedback (Figee et al., 2011), although patients did show reduced activation in ventral striatum when anticipating an upcoming trial that could potentially provide reward. Overall, it is not yet clear whether dysfunctional brain responses to reward contribute to reduced feelings of goal attainment during compulsive behavior in OCD; future work may benefit from further investigation of brain responses in successfully avoiding a loss or bad event (as was done by Jung et al., 2011), which may be particularly important for OCD patients, as well as goal attainment or task completion unrelated to monetary outcomes.

Emotional Face Processing in OCD

Given the importance of negative emotion in OCD, it is somewhat surprising that so few studies have directly examined emotional processing in the disorder. It is possible that heightened neural activation in response to emotional stimuli in OCD could lead to the excessive fear and anxiety associated with obsessions. Experiments investigating the functional neuroanatomy of emotion often compare brain activity when viewing facial expressions of various emotions to activity elicited by neutral faces or nonface control tasks (see Phan, Wager, Taylor, & Liberzon, 2002). Studies examining the neural correlates of emotional face processing in OCD have yielded conflicting results. A recent study found hyperactivation in OCD in visual cortex,

DLPFC, posterior thalamus, and limbic regions including amygdala and para-hippocampus when matching either happy or fearful facial expressions, in comparison with matching nonface shapes (Cardoner et al., 2011). There was also an effect of expression valence, such that OCD patients showed greater activation than did control patients in DLPFC and anterior insula for fearful in comparison with happy expressions. However, these findings contrast with an earlier report of reduced amygdala activation in OCD when observing fearful, happy, and neutral faces in comparison with a fixation condition (Cannistraro et al., 2004). Finally, when compared with neutral faces, facial expressions of disgust have been found to elicit greater activity in left OFC but reduced activity in thalamus in OCD, with no differences between patients and control subjects for fearful versus neutral faces (Lawrence et al., 2007). These discrepancies may be due to variability in task design and analyses, and further work is needed to determine whether OCD patients exhibit abnormality in response to other types of emotional stimuli.

Other Tasks and Conclusions

The above summary discusses a nonexhaustive selection of studies that focus on neuroimaging correlates of psychological processes that could potentially underlie the complex symptom presentation of patients with OCD. The most consistent findings from these studies were hyperactivation in response to errors and hypoactivation during switching tasks, with both effects occurring predominantly in the PFC. However, given the limitations concerning the applicability of analyses to the phenomenology of the disorder and inconsistency among studies using the same (or similar) tasks, it is clear that further investigation into the neurocircuitry underlying cognitive-affect dysfunction in OCD is needed. Other approaches investigating habit formation (Rauch et al., 1997; Rauch, Wedig, et al., 2007), loss expectancy (Jung et al., 2011; Ursu & Carter, 2009), decision uncertainty (Stern et al., 2012), image suppression (Koçak, Ozpolat, Atbasoglu, & Cicek, 2011), and working memory (Henseler et al., 2008; Koch et al., 2012; Nakao et al., 2009; van der Wee et al., 2003) have identified alterations in OCD that may also contribute to the phenomenology of the disorder.

OCD AND DISGUST

Contamination (intense, persistent feeling of having been polluted or infected; Rachman, 2004) concerns are the most common themes associated with OCD (Rasmussen & Tsuang, 1986), presenting in up to 50% of people with the disorder (Rachman & Hodgson, 1980; Rasmussen & Eisen,

1992). Intrusive contamination thoughts often lead to excessive sanitizing and disinfecting of the self and the environment, and to avoidance of situations and stimuli largely because of perceptions of being susceptible to disease and infection. Compulsive cleaning is the second most common compulsion of OCD (Rachman, 2004). Studies support the role of disgust in contamination-related OCD (Cisler, Olatunji, & Lohr, 2009; Mancini, Gragnani, & D'Olimpio, 2001; Olatunji, Forsyth, & Cherian, 2007; Olatunji & Sawchuk, 2005; Olatunji, Sawchuk, Arrindell, & Lohr, 2005; Thorpe, Patel, & Simonds, 2003; Tsao & McKay, 2004) and the notion that disgust is distinct from other negative affective states (e.g., anxiety, depression; Mancini et al., 2001; Olatunji, Sawchuk, Lohr, & de Jong, 2004; Tolin, Woods, & Abramowitz, 2006; Wood & Tolin, 2002).

Disgust is an emotion that likely evolved to provide protection, by way of avoidance, from contamination and disease (Izard, 1993); it involves the appraisal of objects and events for their potential role in contamination (Rozin & Fallon, 1987). Some forms of OCD conceivably involve a dysfunction of this appraisal process (Sprengelmeyer et al., 1997; S. R. Woody & Teachman, 2000; S. R. Woody & Tolin, 2002). Feelings of disgust may arise from sensory experiences (e.g., taste, smell) and from more abstract concerns (e.g., those related to aspects of the body or to moral judgments; Rozin, Lowery, Imada, & Haidt, 1999). Accordingly, OCD concerns may be quite concrete (e.g., about germs, bodily secretion, and illness) or more abstract (e.g., religious, ethical, and moral issues).

In terms of the psychosocial aspects of OCD, the disorder may involve a false contamination alarm in which disgust plays a crucial organizing or embodying role at a basic brain level (Stein, Liu, Shapira, & Goodman, 2001). Before the onset of contamination-related OCD, people who are high in disgust sensitivity may avoid objects (e.g., public toilets) and situations (e.g., public gatherings) associated with contamination. Because of limited exposure, those high in disgust sensitivity may be more prone to contamination obsessions and washing compulsions when they come into contact with perceived contaminants (Merckelbach, Dejong, Arntz, & Schouten, 1993). Disgust sensitivity has been shown to positively correlate with OCD and to predict contamination fear.

Intrusive thoughts and avoidance efforts may be associated with feelings of fear; however, disgust may also contribute to the etiology and phenomenology of OCD-related contamination obsessions and washing compulsions (Olatunji et al., 2007; M. L. Phillips, Senior, Fahy, & David, 1998; M. Power & Dalgleish, 1997). In fact, patients with contamination concerns often describe threat-relevant objects as "disgusting" rather than as "frightening" (Sieg & Scholz, 2001; Tolin, Worhunsky, & Maltby, 2004), and after exposure to a disgusting object, cleaning rituals are seen (Rozin & Fallon, 1987).

The distinction between fear/anxiety (i.e., sympathetic activation) and disgust (i.e., parasympathetic activation) in contamination-related OCD is not merely semantic: The two emotions may be represented by different neural circuits (Olatunji & Sawchuk, 2005). Disgust in OCD patients seems to be more resistant to extinction than is fear (Smits, Telch, & Randall, 2002), and functional imaging and patient-based studies have shown that the amygdala is involved in fear recognition (Calder, 2003), whereas the insular cortex and putamen appear to underlie disgust recognition (Calder, Keane, Manes, Antoun, & Young, 2000; Calder, Lawrence, & Young, 2001).

Although OCD is classified as an anxiety disorder, several lines of evidence suggest that the emotion of disgust plays an important role in its pathogenesis and maintenance (M. L. Phillips, Senior, et al., 1998; Schienle, Schafer, Stark, Walter, & Vaitl, 2005a; Stein et al., 2001). There is a strong relationship between the emotion of disgust/disgust sensitivity and obsessive–compulsive symptoms in both clinical and nonclinical populations (Mancini et al., 2001; Muris, Merckelbach, Schmidt, & Tierney, 1999; Olatunji & Sawchuk, 2005; Olatunji et al., 2004; Olatunji, Williams, Lohr, & Sawchuk, 2005; Schienle, Stark, Walter, & Vaitl, 2003; Thorpe et al., 2003; Tsao & McKay, 2004; S. R. Woody & Tolin, 2002). OCD patients have also shown deficits in identification of facial representations of disgust, in comparison with other anxiety disorders (Sprengelmeyer et al., 1997). Furthermore, OCD patients, especially those with contamination fears and washing compulsions, report experiencing intense disgust feelings during symptom provocation (M. L. Phillips et al., 2000; Sieg & Scholz, 2001). People with Huntington's disorder and OCD, both disorders with striatal dysfunction, have shown impairment in the recognition of disgust but not of other basic emotions (Sprengelmeyer et al., 1996).

One of the reasons the sense of taste exists is so that organisms can detect potential nutrients and toxins. The ability to distinguish between appetitive (e.g., sweet) and aversive (e.g., bitter) tastes is critical to survival because taste and expulsion are the last defenses against ingestion of toxins. Primary gustatory cortex includes anterior insula; therefore, it makes sense that the insula is involved in the disgust response. Disgust (measured by perception of and response to facial expressions of disgust and disgust-inducing stimuli) appears to be controlled most notably by the insular cortex and corticostriatothalamocortical circuitry (in particular, the striatum), according to lesion (Calder et al., 2000; Gray, Young, Barker, Curtis, & Gibson, 1997; Sprengelmeyer et al., 1996, 1997) and imaging data (Calder et al., 2001; Heining et al., 2003; Mataix-Cols et al., 2004, 2008; M. L. Phillips et al., 1997; Wicker et al., 2003; Wright, He, Shapira, Goodman, & Liu, 2004). The anterior insula and ventral striatum appear to be key structures in a system mediating the response to disgusting stimuli irrespective of sensory modality (Calder et al., 2001;

Heining et al., 2003; M. L. Phillips, Young, et al., 1998; M. L. Phillips et al., 1997; Shapira et al., 2003; Sprengelmeyer et al., 1996, 1997).

Functional brain imaging studies in healthy subjects show that the insula responds selectively to facial expressions of disgust (M. L. Phillips et al., 1997; Sprengelmeyer, Rausch, Eysel, & Przuntek, 1998) and that viewing disgust-eliciting pictures increases neural activity in the insula and basal ganglia (notably, the caudate and putamen) (Mataix-Cols et al., 2004, 2008; Phan et al., 2004; Shapira et al., 2003; Wicker et al., 2003). Imaging studies that expose subjects to unpleasant odors or tastes have also reported an association between the insula and ventral striatal activation and disgusting stimuli (Heining et al., 2003; Royet, Plailly, Delon-Martin, Kareken, & Segebarth, 2003; Small et al., 1999; Wicker et al., 2003; Zald & Pardo, 2000). In addition, an fMRI study of subjects asked to recall or reexperience an event that evoked disgust found increased activation of the insula and basal ganglia, indicating the involvement of these regions in the interoceptive experience of disgust (D. A. Fitzgerald et al., 2004).

Neuroimaging studies have shown that abnormalities of the same neural regions involved in disgust processing, in particular, the insula cortex and striatum, are also involved in OCD (Berle & Phillips, 2006; M. L. Phillips et al., 2000; Stein et al., 2001). Two recent structural MRI studies found that OCD patients have significantly larger anterior insular cortices bilaterally in comparison with healthy controls (HCs; Nishida et al., 2011; Song et al., 2011). Furthermore, functional imaging studies show that OCD patients with predominantly washing symptoms have increased neural responses to washing-related stimuli (Mataix-Cols et al., 2004; M. L. Phillips et al., 2000) and to disgusting pictures (Schienle et al., 2005a; Shapira et al., 2003) in brain regions implicated in disgust and autonomic response processing, including the anterior insula, ventrolateral PFC, and putamen/globus pallidus (Calder et al., 2001; Critchley, Wiens, Rotshtein, Ohman, & Dolan, 2004; M. L. Phillips et al., 1997, 2004; M. L. Phillips, Young, et al., 1998; Sprengelmeyer et al., 1998). Research has also found that there was greater activation of the insula to disgust-inducing images in OCD patients than in control patients but no difference in brain activation in response to threat-inducing images (Shapira et al., 2003). Furthermore, confrontation with disorder-relevant stimuli (vs. innocuous/disorder irrelevant stimuli) in OCD subjects has been shown to trigger activation of the anterior insula (Schienle et al., 2005a), as well as OFC, anterior cingulate, caudate nucleus, and amygdala (Breiter et al., 1996). Finally, OCD patients with contamination concerns demonstrate activation of the same neural regions with disgust-inducing pictures as with symptom relevant stimuli, most notably the insula (M. L. Phillips et al., 2000). Thus, the neurocircuits involved in disgust processing may be relevant to OCD and, in particular, the contamination subtype.

Disgust Versus Fear-Related Neural Circuits

Disgust and fear are basic emotions that have different elicitors and expressions, and they appear to be mediated by different neurocircuits (Miller, 1997; M. L. Phillips et al., 1997, 2004; M. L. Phillips, Young, et al., 1998; Stein et al., 2001). Studies in healthy people show that insular cortex and the basal ganglia are more frequently activated during disgust processing than during fear processing, and amygdala is more frequently activated in fear processing (Calder et al., 2001; Murphy, Nimmo-Smith, & Lawrence, 2003). Functional MRI experiments (M. L. Phillips et al., 1997, 2004; M. L. Phillips, Young, et al., 1998) support a double dissociation in healthy subjects for whom fearful faces activate the amygdala (confirming other reports; Breiter et al., 1996; Morris et al., 1996) but not the insula, whereas disgust faces activate the anterior insular cortex, medial frontal cortex, right putamen, and thalamus, but not the amygdala (confirmed by others; Anderson, Christoff, Panitz, De Rosa, & Gabrieli, 2003; Sprengelmeyer et al., 1998). However, these differential patterns of activation only occur when the participants are fully aware of the stimuli presented (M. L. Phillips et al., 2004).

Stark et al. (2007) also found that insula activation was associated with disgust ratings and the processing of disgusting scenes, but not fear ratings or the processing of fearful scenes. But both fear- and disgust-inducing scenes activated the amygdala, occipital cortex, and PFC. Disgust-related amygdala activation has repeatedly been found (Britton et al., 2006; D. A. Fitzgerald, Angstadt, Jelsone, Nathan, & Phan, 2006; Schienle et al., 2002, 2006; Schienle, Schafer, Stark, Walter, & Vaitl, 2005b; Stark et al., 2003, 2005, 2007). Furthermore, people with lesions that include the amygdala show reduced startle potentiation to disgust and fearful pictures (Buchanan, Tranel, & Adolphs, 2004). However, Sprengelmeyer et al. (1999) described a patient with bilateral amygdala damage, whose ability to recognize and experience fear was reduced while recognition and experience of disgust were intact. Some of these inconsistencies could be due to interindividual differences in the experience of emotional stimuli and difference in experimental design (Stark et al., 2007). Further research is needed to clarify the role of the amygdala in disgust processing.

Disgust Versus Fear-Related Neural Circuits in OCD Patients

The basic emotions of fear and disgust have clear relevance to the anxiety disorders in general and to OCD in particular (McKay, 2002; M. L. Phillips, Senior, et al., 1998). The amygdala plays a key role in mediating fear and anxiety (Davis, 1997; LeDoux, 1998) and has been implicated in anxiety disorders (Davis & Whalen, 2001; Gorman, Kent, Sullivan, & Coplan,

2000). In contrast, disgust appears to be mediated primarily by the insula and striatum (Adolphs, Tranel, & Damasio, 2003; M. L. Phillips, Senior, et al., 1998; Sprengelmeyer et al., 1998), which have been implicated in OCD in particular (Kim et al., 2001; Rauch & Baxter, 1998; Rauch, Shin, Whalen, & Pitman, 1998; Stein, Arya, Pietrini, Rapoport, & Swedo, 2006).

Using PET, Stein et al. (2006) found that in comparison with controls, OCD had greater activation of the left insula during the disgust-inducing tasks than during the resting tasks. OCD patients, but not control patients, showed greater right lateral OFC activation than rest during the disgust-inducing task. Neural activity of OCD subjects did not differ from controls in the anticipatory anxiety versus resting state, and anxiety ratings, heart rate, and electrodermal activity increased during an anticipatory anxiety task in both groups. Using fMRI, Shapira et al. (2003) found that activation patterns in response to threat-inducing stimuli were similar in OCD and control subjects, but OCD patients had greater activation in the insula and inferior frontal regions in response to disgust-inducing stimuli. Various findings also suggest a role for the ventrolateral PFC in mediating enhanced responses to disgust-related visual stimuli in OCD patients than in control patients (Lawrence et al., 2007; Mataix-Cols et al., 2004; Schienle et al., 2005a; Shapira et al., 2003; Sprengelmeyer et al., 1998).

In contrast to the findings of increased insula activation to disgusting stimuli in OCD patients in comparison with HCs, most findings to date suggest that there is no difference in neural activation between OCD patients and HCs during the processing of threatening/fearful stimuli (Shapira et al., 2003; Stein et al., 2006). However, one study did report increased insula responses in OCD patients to pictures of fearful, as well as disgusting and disorder-relevant, scenes (Schienle et al., 2005a). The increased insular reactivity of OCD patients during all aversive picture conditions might reflect their susceptibility/proneness to experience negative somatic states, which might be a vulnerability factor for OCD.

The profile of amygdala activation in response to facial expressions in OCD distinguishes it from other anxiety disorders, which show exaggerated amygdala activation to threatening faces (Britton et al., 2010). Although exaggerated amygdala activation has been shown in response to OCD-specific stimuli (e.g., disgusting toilets) in some studies of adults with OCD (Adler et al., 2000; Breiter et al., 1996; van den Heuvel et al., 2004), less amygdala activation in response to happy, fearful, and neutral faces (in relation to fixation) has been found in adult (Cannistraro et al., 2004) and pediatric (Britton et al., 2010) OCD subjects, in comparison with HCs. Britton et al. (2010) also found reduced amygdala activation in pediatric OCD patients in response to disgusted faces. So although OCD may be similar to other anxiety disorders with respect to greater amygdala activation during symptom provocation (Breiter et al., 1996), the finding of less amygdala activation to emotional stimuli (facial expressions) may distinguish OCD from other anxiety disorders. Reduced amygdala activation may predict disease onset or be an endophenotype of OCD.

In line with this, in a recent, thorough review of the literature, Fiddick (2011) argued for a distinction between fear-provoking immediate threats and anxiety-provoking potential threats, with the amygdala processing immediate threats and the cingulate cortex (and insular) processing potential threats. This provides support for recent models proposing the existence of a separate potential threat system that is dysfunctional in OCD (Szechtman & Woody, 2004; E. Z. Woody & Szechtman, 2011). However, S. Taylor, McKay, and Abramowitz (2005) pointed out some limitations of this model. In particular, they claimed that proposing a single dysfunctional mechanism to explain OCD is limited and does not account for the heterogeneity and complexity of the disorder.

In summary, findings in OCD patients, particularly those with contamination preoccupation, suggest a specific enhancement in insula and ventrolateral PFC activation in response to symptom-related and disgusting pictures (and some suggest reduced amygdala activation) but no difference in brain activation or decreased amygdala activation (Britton et al., 2010; Cannistraro et al., 2004) or increased insula activation to fearful stimuli, in comparison with HCs (Schienle et al., 2005a).

FUNCTIONAL IMAGING STUDIES IN OCD SPECTRUM DISORDERS

Neuroimaging techniques have also been used to investigate neurocircuit functioning in related OCD spectrum disorders. Unfortunately, many fewer studies have been published involving these disorders. Among these few studies, small sample sizes and failure to correct for multiple comparisons complicate interpretation of the data. In this section, we review the available data from neuroimaging studies probing disorders from the OCD spectrum, including trichotillomania (TTM), body dysmorphic disorder (BDD), and hoarding. Additional putative members of the OCD spectrum such as dermatillomania (skin picking) and onychophagia (nail biting) lack published data and are excluded, as are impulse control disorders, of which only pathological gambling has been explored in published imaging studies.

Trichotillomania

Classified in the *Diagnostic and Statistical Manual of Mental Disorders* (4th ed., text rev.; *DSM–IV–TR*; American Psychiatric Association, 2000) as an impulse control disorder, TTM involves the pathological pulling out of the affected person's own hair. Similar pathological grooming behavior is seen in other related disorders: skin picking (dermatillomania) and nail biting (onychophagia) disorders. Excessive grooming behavior is a salient feature of some putative animal models of OCD (Welch et al., 2007).

There is significant comorbidity between TTM and OCD (Lochner & Stein, 2010; Richter, Summerfeldt, Antony, & Swinson, 2003). Additionally, relatives of OCD patients show high levels of pathological grooming behaviors such as TTM (Bienvenu et al., 2012). Comorbidity, familial commonalities, and phenomenological relationships, including difficulty in suppressing behaviors, have led some to suggest that TTM may be part of the OCD spectrum. Structural imaging studies have yielded inconsistent results, though some have indicated that as with OCD, TTM is associated with alterations in frontostriatal volumes and density (Chamberlain, Menzies, Fineberg, et al., 2008; Keuthen et al., 2007; O'Sullivan et al., 1997; Stein, Coetzer, Lee, Davids, & Bouwer, 1997).

Diffusion tensor imaging has been used to assess connectivity in these circuits. Eighteen subjects with TTM—but without comorbid OCD, other impulse control disorders, or depression—were compared with 19 HCs using MRI (Chamberlain et al., 2010). In this study, the TTM group displayed abnormal reductions in fractional anisotropy (FA) in white matter tracts connecting bilateral anterior cingulate and orbitofrontal cortices. Fractional anisotropy decreases were also noted in presupplementary and left primary somatosensory cortices along with left temporal lobe. Changes in FA did not correlate with disease severity and were independent of prior treatment.

Global brain metabolic rate was found to be increased using PET and 18-F-fluorodeoxyglucose in 10 TTM patients versus 20 HCs (Swedo et al., 1991). In TTM subjects, metabolic rates were significantly elevated in every brain region analyzed. Normalizing each region to total brain metabolic rate identified regions with locally increased metabolism in TTM subjects: right superior parietal and bilateral cerebellum. Additionally, ratios of left caudate to global metabolic activity and right cerebellum to global activity correlated negatively with measures of TTM symptom severity. Cerebellar and left ACC activation correlated with chronic, though not acute, anxiety severity. Although only some regions were found to be important in similar studies in OCD, this study found that clomipramine-related improvement in symptoms was associated with similar changes in TTM subjects, as has been reported in OCD subjects (Swedo et al., 1991). Anterior cingulate and orbitofrontal activity was negatively correlated with symptomatic improvement in response to 5 weeks of clomipramine treatment.

Treatment response to 12 weeks of citalopram was studied in 10 women with TTM (Stein et al., 2002). These subjects underwent single photon emission computed tomography (SPECT) scans before and after treatment while being asked to try to experience hair-pulling urges and were allowed to pull out hair if they wanted. Findings suggested that citalopram treatment leads to decreases in regional brain activity in relation to whole brain activity in posterior–inferior and anterior–superior frontal regions as well as in the right anterior temporal area and left putamen. At baseline, hair-pulling severity correlated negatively with bilateral frontal, left parietal, and left putamen activity. After pharmacotherapy, symptom severity correlated with increases in left frontal, right medial–temporal, and right putamen activity.

Brain activation during implicit sequence learning using the serial reaction time was assessed in 10 TTM and 12 HC female subjects (Rauch, Wright, et al., 2007). No significant differences in reaction time were identified between groups, and both groups were able to learn in this paradigm. Also, activations of right dorsal caudate and left ventral striatum were similar between groups. No between-groups differences were found in any brain region analyzed.

In combination with fMRI, symptom provocation (exposing subjects to imagery and tactile stimuli of hair vs. neutral stimuli of a ball) was used to identify differences in brain activation between children and adolescents with TTM and HC. In a study of seven female subjects with TTM and nine female HCs, both groups showed activation of the inferior temporal and middle occipital gyri and inferior parietal lobule with visual symptom provoking stimuli only (Lee et al., 2010). In contrast to HCs, TTM subjects also displayed activation in the superior temporal gyrus, posterior cingulate, cerebellum, putamen, and insula. When exposed to both visual and tactile symptom provoking stimuli, HC and TTM groups both exhibited activation of the middle occipital gyrus, though HCs displayed further activation of inferior parietal lobule, cuneus, inferior temporal, lingual, and postcentral gyri along with cerebellar activation. The middle temporal gyrus was activated in TTM but not HCs under these conditions.

These studies of TTM suggest structural and functional brain abnormalities that partially resemble those identified in subjects with OCD. Regions frequently identified as important include striatum, particularly putamen, along with insula, orbitotemporal, and cingulate cortex. Interestingly, cerebellar abnormalities have also been identified in several TTM studies.

Body Dysmorphic Disorder

BDD involves a preoccupation with imagined or trivial appearance defects (American Psychiatric Association, 2000). Partly because of phenomenological similarities (e.g., recurrent disturbing thoughts accompanied by repetitive behaviors) between BDD and OCD, they have been viewed as along the so-called OCD spectrum. BDD, along with TTM and hoarding disorder, are listed in the *Diagnostic and Statistical Manual of Mental Disorders* (5th ed.; *DSM–5*; American Psychiatric Association, 2013) in a new category of obsessive–compulsive and related disorders. BDD also shares comorbidities, familial loading, and treatment-response similarities with OCD (K. A. Phillips & Kaye, 2007).

Morphometric comparison between eight BDD and eight HC women indicated increased total cerebral volume, accounted for by an increase in white matter in the BDD group (Rauch et al., 2003). Although no other between-groups volumetric differences were found, the BDD group displayed abnormally left-shifted caudate asymmetry. These results were interpreted as further support for BDD being part of this group of OCD spectrum disorders. Another morphometric study in men found reduced OFC and ACC volumes in BDD in relation to HC subjects (Atmaca et al., 2010). This study failed to find between-groups differences in caudate, but reported data consistent with leftward shift of caudate asymmetry, without reporting laterality. Additionally, this study confirmed the finding of increased white matter in the BDD group. In contrast, a study of both sexes found no difference between BDD and HC subjects in total white matter and caudate laterality (Feusner et al., 2009). Subgroup analysis of only women and subjects without comorbid MDD also failed to replicate the prior findings. Instead, this group found a correlation of BDD symptom severity with left inferior frontal gyrus and right amygdala volumes. Perfusion deficits in parietal and occipital areas of six BDD subjects were suggested by SPECT data from an uncontrolled case series (Carey, Seedat, Warwick, van Heerden, & Stein, 2004). This study did not detect consistent abnormalities in other regions, though increases in basal ganglia perfusion were seen in two of the subjects; the study's findings have not been replicated.

Visual information processing has been examined using fMRI in several studies of BDD. The first published study included 12 BDD and 13 HC subjects (Feusner, Townsend, Bystritsky, & Bookheimer, 2007). In this study of face matching, both groups activated extrastriate visual cortex and fusiform gyrus. In addition, the BDD group showed significantly greater activation of left middle and inferior temporal gyri when high-pass-filtered faces were presented. With low-pass faces, the BDD group activated left infraparietal sulcus and left inferior and superior frontal gyri, along with right precentral and postcentral gyri, right superior and middle frontal gyri, and bilateral dorsal ACC. Without filtering, the BDD group displayed significantly greater activation of left superior temporal gyrus, left inferior frontal gyrus, and left insula. The HC group exhibited no significantly greater activation when given filtered faces, but in the task with unfiltered faces had significantly greater activation of bilateral cuneus and left middle occipital gyrus.

Post hoc analysis revealed significantly greater right amygdala activation in the BDD group when filtered faces were presented. These differences were interpreted to suggest greater and focused attention on details of faces in the BDD group. These face-matching tasks were used in another study that included images of the subjects' own faces. This study included 17 BDD and 16 HC subjects (Feusner et al., 2010). This confirmed the previous finding of extrastriate visual cortex and fusiform gyrus activation in both groups. It also found greater activation of left OFC and bilateral caudate for subjects' own unfiltered faces in the BDD group. When these faces were low-pass filtered, HCs displayed greater left occipital cortex activation. Also, BDD symptom severity correlated with own-face-induced activation of right OFC, right head of caudate, right precentral and postcentral gyri, and right dorsal occipital cortex. In total, these findings suggest frontostriatal hyperactivity in BDD. To assess brain activation with stimuli that do not pertain to symptoms, we used a similar task involving pictures of unfiltered and filtered houses rather than faces. A study using this task in 14 BDD and 14 HC subjects again found similar activations of visual cortex and fusiform areas (Feusner, Hembacher, Moller, & Moody, 2011). No significant activation differences were found between groups with unfiltered images. However, for low-pass-filtered images, the BDD group displayed lower activation of left parahippocampal cortex, left hippocampus, left lingual gyrus, left posterior cingulated, and bilateral precuneus, whereas with high-pass-filtered images, the BDD group displayed greater activation of bilateral frontal pole, left superior frontal gyrus, right anterior cingulate gyrus, and right paracingulate gyrus. These data suggest abnormalities in generalized visual processing in BDD. In addition to these visual processing abnormalities, many of the BDD imaging findings suggest that it may be part of this spectrum. These include cortical striatal and limbic anomalies.

Hoarding

Historically seen strictly as a subtype or symptom dimension of OCD, hoarding—the acquisition of and inability to discard objects seen by others as having little or no value—appears as a distinct disorder in *DSM–5* (Pertusa et al., 2010). This history may have led some previous imaging studies to mix cases of OCD and hoarding disorder. A few have performed analyses on the basis of symptom dimensions, and others have focused explicitly on hoarding.

The only structural study of hoarding found a trend-level association of symptoms with reduced volumes in Brodmann Area 6, including premotor cortex and supplementary motor cortex (Gilbert et al., 2008). The analysis of symptom dimensions was post hoc and included only a few patients, given the total population of OCD subjects ($n = 25$). In a PET study of 45 OCD subjects, 12 of whom had hoarding as their most prominent symptom, and 17 HC subjects, nonhoarding OCD subjects had significantly greater bilateral thalamic metabolism than did either of the other groups (Saxena et al., 2004). Hoarders had significantly lower metabolism in the posterior cingulate gyrus than did HCs. In comparison with OCD subjects without hoarding disorder, hoarders had lower bilateral dACC metabolism, and hoarding severity negatively correlated with metabolism in dACC across all OCD subjects. Yet hoarders displayed higher metabolism in part of the right SMA than did nonhoarders, and activity in this region correlated with hoarding severity.

A symptom provocation study in 17 OCD subjects with mixed symptoms and 17 HCs showed that hoarding provocation induced greater activation of left precentral/superior frontal gyrus, left fusiform gyrus, and right OFC in OCD subjects than in HCs, and HCs displayed greater activation of bilateral visual areas (Mataix-Cols et al., 2004). Hoarding-related anxiety also correlated with activation of left precentral/superior frontal gyrus. Another symptom provocation study in 13 OCD subjects with and 16 without prominent hoarding symptoms along with 21 HCs found that hoarders uniquely activated frontal pole, anterior OFC, and medial frontal gyrus, whereas nonhoarders activated putamen and caudate, and controls activated striatum, left thalamus, and VMPFC, including OFC and anterior ACC (An et al., 2009). The hoarding group exhibited significantly greater activation of the anterior VMPFC and cerebellum than did HCs. The correlation of hoarding-related anxiety with pre- and postcentral gyri activations confirmed findings from prior studies (Mataix-Cols et al., 2004; Saxena et al., 2004). This anxiety inversely correlated with activity in bilateral dorsal prefrontal regions, basal ganglia, temporal cortex, and parieto-occipital regions, further implicating emotional regulation and planning deficits in these patients.

Another study focused on decision making in subjects with hoarding (Tolin, Kiehl, Worhunsky, Book, & Maltby, 2009). Here, 12 subjects with hoarding were compared with 12 HCs while making decisions about whether to keep or discard items that did or did not belong to them. Of note, only two of the hoarding subjects had comorbid OCD. When deciding to discard personal items, hoarders exhibited greater activation of left lateral OFC, left amygdala, left parahippocampal gyrus, and left cerebellum. The increased cingulate activity noted in this study contrasts with earlier reports of decreased cingulate activity in this population, suggesting that decreased activity at rest may be accompanied by excessive activation with provocation.

OFC and ACC abnormalities have been noted in multiple hoarding studies. In addition, as with BDD, pre- and postcentral gyrus abnormalities have been identified. Finally, amygdala and other limbic and prefrontal activation abnormalities have been noted.

In total, these studies suggest partly overlapping but distinct patterns of functional changes in OCD and related spectrum disorders. These illnesses require further study, including replication and evaluation of commonalities and differences. Future research will benefit from focused studies that limit inclusion of comorbidity along with increased diagnostic specificity.

OVERALL CONCLUSIONS

In this chapter, we present a summary of neuroimaging studies in OCD and OC spectrum disorders including TTM, BDD, and hoarding. A review of the cognitive neuroscientific literature to date yields contradictory findings in a variety of studies examining cognitive, motor, and emotional functioning, with the most consistent effects pointing to prefrontal hyperactivation and to errors or hypoactivation during switching in OCD. Some of the difficulty in identifying consistent areas of dysfunction could be due to the wide variety of tasks used in these investigations. The majority of studies focus on cognitive or motor functioning without addressing the importance of anxiety and emotional discomfort in the disorder. However, studies of emotional face processing do not capture the characteristic cognitive and motoric inflexibility shown by patients. It is clear that no one paradigm or approach is likely to explain all the clinical phenomena of this heterogeneous disorder, and future work would benefit from combining the strengths of these many approaches to explore the cognitive neuroscientific study of OCD and its spectrum from a variety of perspectives.

The study of OC spectrum disorders reveals both commonalities and differences between OCD and TTM, BDD, and hoarding. Limited data are currently available on the OC spectrum, and future studies will clarify the neurobiological abnormalities along this putative spectrum. Investigation of this spectrum is likely to prove useful in that it may also provide endophenotypes or specific mechanistic targets for future treatment development.

The neurocircuitry involved in disgust processing has been shown to be relevant to OCD, in particular, contamination-type OCD. More research is needed to better understand the neural mechanisms underlying disgust and the role disgust plays in the pathophysiology of OCD, which will have important implications for rehabilitation. For example, exposure–response therapy could be aimed at desensitizing OCD patients to disgusting stimuli rather than targeting their specific cognitive symptoms. Or deep transcranial magnetic stimulation therapy could be used to modulate OCD patients' increased insula activation to disgusting stimuli. Targeting the neurocircuitry related to disgust processing via pharmacological, cognitive, behavioral, or brain stimulation techniques may produce more effective and rapid treatment results.

REFERENCES

Adler, C. M., McDonough-Ryan, P., Sax, K. W., Holland, S. K., Arndt, S., & Strakowski, S. M. (2000). fMRI of neuronal activation with symptom provocation in unmedicated patients with obsessive compulsive disorder. *Journal of Psychiatric Research, 34*, 317–324. doi:10.1016/S0022-3956(00)00022-4

Adolphs, R., Tranel, D., & Damasio, A. R. (2003). Dissociable neural systems for recognizing emotions. *Brain and Cognition, 52*, 61–69. doi:10.1016/S0278-2626(03)00009-5

American Psychiatric Association. (2000). *Diagnostic and statistical manual of mental disorders* (4th ed., text rev.). Washington, DC: Author.

American Psychiatric Association. (2013). *Diagnostic and statistical manual of mental disorders* (5th ed.). Washington, DC: Author.

An, S. K., Mataix-Cols, D., Lawrence, N. S., Wooderson, S., Giampietro, V., Speckens, A., . . . Phillips, M. L. (2009). To discard or not to discard: The neural basis of hoarding symptoms in obsessive–compulsive disorder. *Molecular Psychiatry, 14*, 318–331. doi:10.1038/sj.mp.4002129

Anderson, A. K., Christoff, K., Panitz, D., De Rosa, E., & Gabrieli, J. D. (2003). Neural correlates of the automatic processing of threat facial signals. *The Journal of Neuroscience, 23*, 5627–5633.

Aron, A. R., Fletcher, P. C., Bullmore, E. T., Sahakian, B. J., & Robbins, T. W. (2003). Stop-signal inhibition disrupted by damage to right inferior frontal gyrus in humans. *Nature Neuroscience, 6*, 115–116. doi:10.1038/nn1003

Aron, A. R., & Poldrack, R. A. (2006). Cortical and subcortical contributions to stop signal response inhibition: Role of the subthalamic nucleus. *The Journal of Neuroscience, 26*, 2424–2433. doi:10.1523/JNEUROSCI.4682-05.2006

Atmaca, M., Bingol, I., Aydin, A., Yildirim, H., Okur, I., Yildirim, M. A., . . . Gurok, M. G. (2010). Brain morphology of patients with body dysmorphic disorder. *Journal of Affective Disorders, 123*(1–3), 258–263. doi:10.1016/j.jad.2009.08.012

Berle, D., & Phillips, E. S. (2006). Disgust and obsessive–compulsive disorder: An update. *Psychiatry, 69*, 228–238.

Bienvenu, O. J., Samuels, J. F., Wuyek, L. A., Liang, K. Y., Wang, Y., Grados, M. A., . . . Nestadt, G. (2012). Is obsessive–compulsive disorder an anxiety disorder, and what, if any, are spectrum conditions? A family study perspective. *Psychological Medicine, 42*(1), 1–13. doi:10.1017/S0033291711000742

Botvinick, M. M., Braver, T. S., Barch, D. M., Carter, C. S., & Cohen, J. D. (2001). Conflict monitoring and cognitive control. *Psychological Review, 108*, 624–652. doi:10.1037/0033-295X.108.3.624

Breiter, H. C., Rauch, S. L., Kwong, K. K., Baker, J. R., Weisskoff, R. M., Kennedy, D. N., . . . Rosen, B. R. (1996). Functional magnetic resonance imaging of symptom provocation in obsessive–compulsive disorder. *Archives of General Psychiatry, 53*, 595–606. doi:10.1001/archpsyc.1996.01830070041008

Bressler, S. L., & Menon, V. (2010). Large-scale brain networks in cognition: Emerging methods and principles. *Trends in Cognitive Sciences, 14,* 277–290. doi:10.1016/j.tics.2010.04.004

Britton, J. C., Phan, K. L., Taylor, S. F., Welsh, R. C., Berridge, K. C., & Liberzon, I. (2006). Neural correlates of social and nonsocial emotions: An fMRI study. *NeuroImage, 31,* 397–409. doi:10.1016/j.neuroimage.2005.11.027

Britton, J. C., Stewart, S. E., Killgore, W. D., Rosso, I. M., Price, L. M., Gold, A. L., . . . Rauch, S. L. (2010). Amygdala activation in response to facial expressions in pediatric obsessive-compulsive disorder. *Depression and Anxiety, 27,* 643–651. doi:10.1002/da.20718

Buchanan, T. W., Tranel, D., & Adolphs, R. (2004). Anteromedial temporal lobe damage blocks startle modulation by fear and disgust. *Behavioral Neuroscience, 118,* 429–437. doi:10.1037/0735-7044.118.2.429

Buchsbaum, B. R., Greer, S., Chang, W. L., & Berman, K. F. (2005). Meta-analysis of neuroimaging studies of the Wisconsin card-sorting task and component processes. *Human Brain Mapping, 25*(1), 35–45. doi:10.1002/hbm.20128

Calder, A. J. (2003). Disgust discussed. *Annals of Neurology, 53,* 427–428. doi:10.1002/ana.10565

Calder, A. J., Keane, J., Manes, F., Antoun, N., & Young, A. W. (2000). Impaired recognition and experience of disgust following brain injury. *Nature Neuroscience, 3,* 1077–1078. doi:10.1038/80586

Calder, A. J., Lawrence, A. D., & Young, A. W. (2001). Neuropsychology of fear and loathing. *Nature Reviews Neuroscience, 2,* 352–363. doi:10.1038/35072584

Cannistraro, P. A., Wright, C. I., Wedig, M. M., Martis, B., Shin, L. M., Wilhelm, S., & Rauch, S. L. (2004). Amygdala responses to human faces in obsessive–compulsive disorder. *Biological Psychiatry, 56,* 916–920. doi:10.1016/j.biopsych.2004.09.029

Cardoner, N., Harrison, B. J., Pujol, J., Soriano-Mas, C., Hernandez-Ribas, R., Lopez-Sola, M., . . . Menchón, J. M. (2011). Enhanced brain responsiveness during active emotional face processing in obsessive compulsive disorder. *The World Journal of Biological Psychiatry, 12,* 349–363. doi:10.3109/15622975.2011.559268

Carey, P., Seedat, S., Warwick, J., van Heerden, B., & Stein, D. J. (2004). SPECT imaging of body dysmorphic disorder. *The Journal of Neuropsychiatry and Clinical Neurosciences, 16,* 357–359. doi:10.1176/appi.neuropsych.16.3.357

Chamberlain, S. R., Hampshire, A., Menzies, L. A., Garyfallidis, E., Grant, J. E., Odlaug, B. L., . . . Sahakian, B. J. (2010). Reduced brain white matter integrity in trichotillomania: A diffusion tensor imaging study. *Archives of General Psychiatry, 67,* 965–971. doi:10.1001/archgenpsychiatry.2010.109

Chamberlain, S. R., Menzies, L. A., Fineberg, N. A., Del Campo, N., Suckling, J., Craig, K., . . . Sahakian, B. J. (2008). Grey matter abnormalities in trichotillomania: Morphometric magnetic resonance imaging study. *The British Journal of Psychiatry, 193,* 216–221. doi:10.1192/bjp.bp.107.048314

Chamberlain, S. R., Menzies, L., Hampshire, A., Suckling, J., Fineberg, N. A., del Campo, N., . . . Sahakian, B. J. (2008). Orbitofrontal dysfunction in patients with obsessive–compulsive disorder and their unaffected relatives. *Science, 321,* 421–422. doi:10.1126/science.1154433

Chambers, C. D., Bellgrove, M. A., Stokes, M. G., Henderson, T. R., Garavan, H., Robertson, I. H., . . . Mattingly, J. B. (2006). Executive "brake failure" following deactivation of human frontal lobe. *Journal of Cognitive Neuroscience, 18,* 444–455.

Cisler, J. M., Olatunji, B. O., & Lohr, J. M. (2009). Disgust, fear, and the anxiety disorders: A critical review. *Clinical Psychology Review, 29*(1), 34–46. doi:10.1016/j.cpr.2008.09.007

Critchley, H. D., Wiens, S., Rotshtein, P., Ohman, A., & Dolan, R. J. (2004). Neural systems supporting interoceptive awareness. *Nature Neuroscience, 7,* 189–195. doi:10.1038/nn1176

Davis, M. (1997). Neurobiology of fear responses: The role of the amygdala. *The Journal of Neuropsychiatry and Clinical Neurosciences, 9,* 382–402.

Davis, M., & Whalen, P. J. (2001). The amygdala: Vigilance and emotion. *Molecular Psychiatry, 6*(1), 13–34. doi:10.1038/sj.mp.4000812

Dias, R., Robbins, T. W., & Roberts, A. C. (1996). Dissociation in prefrontal cortex of affective and attentional shifts. *Nature, 380,* 69–72. doi:10.1038/380069a0

Fellows, L. K., & Farah, M. J. (2003). Ventromedial frontal cortex mediates affective shifting in humans: evidence from a reversal learning paradigm. *Brain: A Journal of Neurology, 126,* 1830–1837.

Feusner, J. D., Hembacher, E., Moller, H., & Moody, T. D. (2011). Abnormalities of object visual processing in body dysmorphic disorder. *Psychological Medicine, 41,* 2385–2397. doi:10.1017/S0033291711000572

Feusner, J. D., Moody, T., Hembacher, E., Townsend, J., McKinley, M., Moller, H., & Bookheimer, S. (2010). Abnormalities of visual processing and frontostriatal systems in body dysmorphic disorder. *Archives of General Psychiatry, 67,* 197–205. doi:10.1001/archgenpsychiatry.2009.190

Feusner, J. D., Townsend, J., Bystritsky, A., & Bookheimer, S. (2007). Visual information processing of faces in body dysmorphic disorder. *Archives of General Psychiatry, 64,* 1417–1425. doi:10.1001/archpsyc.64.12.1417

Feusner, J. D., Townsend, J., Bystritsky, A., McKinley, M., Moller, H., & Bookheimer, S. (2009). Regional brain volumes and symptom severity in body dysmorphic disorder. *Psychiatry Research, 172,* 161–167. doi:10.1016/j.pscychresns.2008.12.003

Fiddick, L. (2011). There is more than the amygdala: Potential threat assessment in the cingulate cortex. *Neuroscience and Biobehavioral Reviews, 35,* 1007–1018. doi:10.1016/j.neubiorev.2010.09.014

Figee, M., Vink, M., de Geus, F., Vulink, N., Veltman, D. J., Westenberg, H., & Denys, D. (2011). Dysfunctional reward circuitry in obsessive–compulsive disorder. *Biological Psychiatry, 69,* 867–874. doi:10.1016/j.biopsych.2010.12.003

Fitzgerald, D. A., Angstadt, M., Jelsone, L. M., Nathan, P. J., & Phan, K. L. (2006). Beyond threat: Amygdala reactivity across multiple expressions of facial affect. *NeuroImage, 30*, 1441–1448. doi:10.1016/j.neuroimage.2005.11.003

Fitzgerald, D. A., Posse, S., Moore, G. J., Tancer, M. E., Nathan, P. J., & Phan, K. L. (2004). Neural correlates of internally-generated disgust via autobiographical recall: A functional magnetic resonance imaging investigation. *Neuroscience Letters, 370*(2–3), 91–96. doi:10.1016/j.neulet.2004.08.007

Fitzgerald, K. D., Welsh, R. C., Gehring, W. J., Abelson, J. L., Himle, J. A., Liberzon, I., & Taylor, S. F. (2005). Error-related hyperactivity of the anterior cingulate cortex in obsessive–compulsive disorder. *Biological Psychiatry, 57*, 287–294. doi:10.1016/j.biopsych.2004.10.038

Garavan, H., Hester, R., Murphy, K., Fassbender, C., & Kelly, C. (2006). Individual differences in the functional neuroanatomy of inhibitory control. *Brain Research, 1105*, 130–142. doi:10.1016/j.brainres.2006.03.029

Garavan, H., Ross, T. J., Kaufman, J., & Stein, E. A. (2003). A midline dissociation between error-processing and response-conflict monitoring. *NeuroImage, 20*, 1132–1139. doi:10.1016/S1053-8119(03)00334-3

Garavan, H., Ross, T. J., & Stein, E. A. (1999). Right hemispheric dominance of inhibitory control: An event-related functional MRI study. *Proceedings of the National Academy of Sciences of the United States of America, 96*, 8301–8306. doi:10.1073/pnas.96.14.8301

Gilbert, A. R., Mataix-Cols, D., Almeida, J. R., Lawrence, N., Nutche, J., Diwadkar, V., . . . Phillips, M. L. (2008). Brain structure and symptom dimension relationships in obsessive–compulsive disorder: A voxel-based morphometry study. *Journal of Affective Disorders, 109*(1–2), 117–126. doi:10.1016/j.jad.2007.12.223

Gorman, J. M., Kent, J. M., Sullivan, G. M., & Coplan, J. D. (2000). Neuroanatomical hypothesis of panic disorder, revised. *The American Journal of Psychiatry, 157*, 493–505. doi:10.1176/appi.ajp.157.4.493

Gray, J. M., Young, A. W., Barker, W. A., Curtis, A., & Gibson, D. (1997). Impaired recognition of disgust in Huntington's disease gene carriers. *Brain: A Journal of Neurology, 120*(Pt. 11), 2029–2038. doi:10.1093/brain/120.11.2029

Gu, B. M., Park, J. Y., Kang, D. H., Lee, S. J., Yoo, S., Jo, H. J., . . . Kwon, J. S. (2008). Neural correlates of cognitive inflexibility during task-switching in obsessive–compulsive disorder. *Brain, 131*, 155–164.

Hampshire, A., & Owen, A. M. (2006). Fractionating attentional control using event-related fMRI. *Cerebral Cortex, 16*, 1679–1689. doi:10.1093/cercor/bhj116

Han, J. Y., Kang, D. H., Gu, B. M., Jung, W. H., Choi, J. S., Choi, C. H., . . . Kwon, J. S. (2011). Altered brain activation in ventral frontal-striatal regions following a 16-week pharmacotherapy in unmedicated obsessive–compulsive disorder. *Journal of Korean Medical Science, 26*, 665–674. doi:10.3346/jkms.2011.26.5.665

Harrison, B. J., Yucel, M., Shaw, M., Kyrios, M., Maruff, P., Brewer, W. J., . . . Pantelis, C. (2006). Evaluating brain activity in obsessive–compulsive disorder: Preliminary insights from a multivariate analysis. *Psychiatry Research, 147*(2–3), 227–231. doi:10.1016/j.pscychresns.2006.03.002

Harrison, N. A., Gray, M. A., Gianaros, P. J., & Critchley, H. D. (2010). The embodiment of emotional feelings in the brain. *The Journal of Neuroscience, 30,* 12878–12884. doi:10.1523/JNEUROSCI.1725-10.2010

Heining, M., Young, A. W., Ioannou, G., Andrew, C. M., Brammer, M. J., Gray, J. A., . . . Phillips, M. L. (2003). Disgusting smells activate human anterior insula and ventral striatum. *Annals of the New York Academy of Sciences, 1000,* 380–384. doi:10.1196/annals.1280.035

Henseler, I., Gruber, O., Kraft, S., Krick, C., Reith, W., & Falkai, P. (2008). Compensatory hyperactivations as markers of latent working memory dysfunctions in patients with obsessive–compulsive disorder: An fMRI study. *Journal of Psychiatry & Neuroscience, 33,* 209–215.

Hester, R., Fassbender, C., & Garavan, H. (2004). Individual differences in error processing: A review and reanalysis of three event-related fMRI studies using the GO/NOGO task. *Cerebral Cortex, 14,* 986–994. doi:10.1093/cercor/bhh059

Izard, C. E. (1993). *Organizational and motivational functions of discrete emotions.* New York, NY: Guilford Press.

Jung, W. H., Kang, D. H., Han, J. Y., Jang, J. H., Gu, B. M., Choi, J. S., . . . Kwon, J. S. (2011). Aberrant ventral striatal responses during incentive processing in unmedicated patients with obsessive–compulsive disorder. *Acta Psychiatrica Scandinavica, 123,* 376–386. doi:10.1111/j.1600-0447.2010.01659.x

Keuthen, N. J., Makris, N., Schlerf, J. E., Martis, B., Savage, C. R., McMullin, K., . . . Rauch, S. L. (2007). Evidence for reduced cerebellar volumes in trichotillomania. *Biological Psychiatry, 61,* 374–381. doi:10.1016/j.biopsych.2006.06.013

Kim, J. J., Lee, M. C., Kim, J., Kim, I. Y., Kim, S. I., Han, M. H., . . . Kwon, J. S. (2001). Grey matter abnormalities in obsessive–compulsive disorder: Statistical parametric mapping of segmented magnetic resonance images. *The British Journal of Psychiatry, 179,* 330–334. doi:10.1192/bjp.179.4.330

Kober, H., Barrett, L. F., Joseph, J., Bliss-Moreau, E., Lindquist, K., & Wager, T. D. (2008). Functional grouping and cortical–subcortical interactions in emotion: A meta-analysis of neuroimaging studies. *NeuroImage, 42,* 998–1031. doi:10.1016/j.neuroimage.2008.03.059

Koçak, O. M., Ozpolat, A. Y., Atbasoglu, C., & Cicek, M. (2011). Cognitive control of a simple mental image in patients with obsessive–compulsive disorder. *Brain and Cognition, 76,* 390–399. doi:10.1016/j.bandc.2011.03.020

Koch, K., Wagner, G., Schachtzabel, C., Peikert, G., Schultz, C. C., Sauer, H., & Schlösser, R. G. (2012). Aberrant anterior cingulate activation in obsessive–compulsive disorder is related to task complexity. *Neuropsychologia, 50,* 958–964. doi:10.1016/j.neuropsychologia.2012.02.002

Kringelbach, M. L., & Rolls, E. T. (2004). The functional neuroanatomy of the human orbitofrontal cortex: Evidence from neuroimaging and neuropsychology. *Progress in Neurobiology, 72,* 341–372. doi:10.1016/j.pneurobio.2004.03.006

Lawrence, N. S., An, S. K., Mataix-Cols, D., Ruths, F., Speckens, A., & Phillips, M. L. (2007). Neural responses to facial expressions of disgust but not fear are modulated by washing symptoms in OCD. *Biological Psychiatry, 61*, 1072–1080. doi:10.1016/j.biopsych.2006.06.033

Lebreton, M., Jorge, S., Michel, V., Thirion, B., & Pessiglione, M. (2009). An automatic valuation system in the human brain: Evidence from functional neuroimaging. *Neuron, 64*, 431–439. doi:10.1016/j.neuron.2009.09.040

LeDoux, J. (1998). Fear and the brain: Where have we been, and where are we going? *Biological Psychiatry, 44*, 1229–1238. doi:10.1016/S0006-3223(98)00282-0

Lee, J. A., Kim, C. K., Jahng, G. H., Hwang, L. K., Cho, Y. W., Kim, Y. J., . . . Bahn, G. H. (2010). A pilot study of brain activation in children with trichotillomania during a visual–tactile symptom provocation task: A functional magnetic resonance imaging study. *Progress in Neuro-Psychopharmacology & Biological Psychiatry, 34*, 1250–1258. doi:10.1016/j.pnpbp.2010.06.031

Liu, X., Hairston, J., Schrier, M., & Fan, J. (2011). Common and distinct networks underlying reward valence and processing stages: A meta-analysis of functional neuroimaging studies. *Neuroscience and Biobehavioral Reviews, 35*, 1219–1236. doi:10.1016/j.neubiorev.2010.12.012

Lochner, C., & Stein, D. J. (2010). Obsessive–compulsive spectrum disorders in obsessive–compulsive disorder and other anxiety disorders. *Psychopathology, 43*, 389–396. doi:10.1159/000321070

MacLeod, C. M. (1991). Half a century of research on the Stroop effect: An integrative review. *Psychological Bulletin, 109*, 163–203. doi:10.1037/0033-2909.109.2.163

Maltby, N., Tolin, D. F., Worhunsky, P., O'Keefe, T. M., & Kiehl, K. A. (2005). Dysfunctional action monitoring hyperactivates frontal-striatal circuits in obsessive–compulsive disorder: An event-related fMRI study. *NeuroImage, 24*, 495–503. doi:10.1016/j.neuroimage.2004.08.041

Mancini, F., Gragnani, A., & D'Olimpio, F. (2001). The connection between disgust and obsessions and compulsions in a non-clinical sample. *Personality and Individual Differences, 31*, 1173–1180. doi:10.1016/S0191-8869(00)00215-4

Mataix-Cols, D., An, S. K., Lawrence, N. S., Caseras, X., Speckens, A., Giampietro, V., . . . Phillips, M. L. (2008). Individual differences in disgust sensitivity modulate neural responses to aversive/disgusting stimuli. *European Journal of Neuroscience, 27*, 3050–3058. doi:10.1111/j.1460-9568.2008.06311.x

Mataix-Cols, D., Wooderson, S., Lawrence, N., Brammer, M. J., Speckens, A., & Phillips, M. L. (2004). Distinct neural correlates of washing, checking, and hoarding symptom dimensions in obsessive–compulsive disorder. *Archives of General Psychiatry, 61*, 564–576. doi:10.1001/archpsyc.61.6.564

McKay, D. (2002). Introduction to the special issue: The role of disgust in anxiety disorders. *Journal of Anxiety Disorders, 16*, 475–476. doi:10.1016/S0887-6185(02)00166-4

Merckelbach, H., Dejong, P. J., Arntz, A., & Schouten, E. (1993). The role of evaluative learning and disgust sensitivity in the etiology and treatment of spider phobia. *Advances in Behaviour Research & Therapy, 15*, 243–255. doi:10.1016/0146-6402(93)90011-P

Miller, W. I. (1997). *The anatomy of disgust.* Cambridge, MA: Harvard University Press.

Morris, J. S., Frith, C. D., Perrett, D. I., Rowland, D., Young, A. W., Calder, A. J., & Dolan, R. J. (1996). A differential neural response in the human amygdala to fearful and happy facial expressions. *Nature, 383,* 812–815. doi:10.1038/383812a0

Muris, P., Merckelbach, H., Schmidt, H., & Tierney, S. (1999). Disgust sensitivity, trait anxiety and anxiety disorders symptoms in normal children. *Behaviour Research and Therapy, 37,* 953–961. doi:10.1016/S0005-7967(99)00045-5

Murphy, F. C., Nimmo-Smith, I., & Lawrence, A. D. (2003). Functional neuroanatomy of emotions: A meta-analysis. *Cognitive, Affective & Behavioral Neuroscience, 3,* 207–233. doi:10.3758/CABN.3.3.207

Nabeyama, M., Nakagawa, A., Yoshiura, T., Nakao, T., Nakatani, E., Togao, O., . . . Kanba, S. (2008). Functional MRI study of brain activation alterations in patients with obsessive–compulsive disorder after symptom improvement. *Psychiatry Research, 163,* 236–247. doi:10.1016/j.pscychresns.2007.11.001

Nakao, T., Nakagawa, A., Nakatani, E., Nabeyama, M., Sanematsu, H., Yoshiura, T., . . . Tomita, M. (2009). Working memory dysfunction in obsessive–compulsive disorder: A neuropsychological and functional MRI study. *Journal of Psychiatric Research, 43,* 784–791. doi:10.1016/j.jpsychires.2008.10.013

Nakao, T., Nakagawa, A., Yoshiura, T., Nakatani, E., Nabeyama, M., Yoshizato, C., . . . Kawamoto, M. (2005). A functional MRI comparison of patients with obsessive–compulsive disorder and normal controls during a Chinese character Stroop task. *Psychiatry Research, 139,* 101–114. doi:10.1016/j.pscychresns.2004.12.004

Nishida, S., Narumoto, J., Sakai, Y., Matsuoka, T., Nakamae, T., Yamada, K., . . . Fukui, K. (2011). Anterior insular volume is larger in patients with obsessive–compulsive disorder. *Progress in Neuro-Psychopharmacology & Biological Psychiatry, 35,* 997–1001. doi:10.1016/j.pnpbp.2011.01.022

Olatunji, B. O., Forsyth, J. P., & Cherian, A. (2007). Evaluative differential conditioning of disgust: A sticky form of relational learning that is resistant to extinction. *Journal of Anxiety Disorders, 21,* 820–834. doi:10.1016/j.janxdis.2006.11.004

Olatunji, B. O., & Sawchuk, C. N. (2005). Disgust: Characteristic features, social manifestations, and clinical implications. *Journal of Social and Clinical Psychology, 24,* 932–962. doi:10.1521/jscp.2005.24.7.932

Olatunji, B. O., Sawchuk, C. N., Arrindell, W. A., & Lohr, J. M. (2005). Disgust sensitivity as a mediator of the sex differences in contamination fears. *Personality and Individual Differences, 38,* 713–722. doi:10.1016/j.paid.2004.05.025

Olatunji, B. O., Sawchuk, C. N., Lohr, J. M., & de Jong, P. J. (2004). Disgust domains in the prediction of contamination fear. *Behaviour Research and Therapy, 42,* 93–104. doi:10.1016/S0005-7967(03)00102-5

Olatunji, B. O., Williams, N. L., Lohr, J. M., & Sawchuk, C. N. (2005). The structure of disgust: Domain specificity in relation to contamination ideation and excessive washing. *Behaviour Research and Therapy, 43,* 1069–1086. doi:10.1016/j.brat.2004.08.002

O'Sullivan, R. L., Rauch, S. L., Breiter, H. C., Grachev, I. D., Baer, L., Kennedy, D. N., . . . Jenike, M. A. (1997). Reduced basal ganglia volumes in trichotillomania measured via morphometric magnetic resonance imaging. *Biological Psychiatry, 42*(1), 39–45. doi:10.1016/S0006-3223(96)00297-1

Page, L. A., Rubia, K., Deeley, Q., Daly, E., Toal, F., Mataix-Cols, D., . . . Murphy, D. G. (2009). A functional magnetic resonance imaging study of inhibitory control in obsessive–compulsive disorder. *Psychiatry Research, 174,* 202–209. doi:10.1016/j.pscychresns.2009.05.002

Pertusa, A., Frost, R. O., Fullana, M. A., Samuels, J., Steketee, G., Tolin, D., . . . Mataix-Cols, D. (2010). Refining the diagnostic boundaries of compulsive hoarding: A critical review. *Clinical Psychology Review, 30,* 371–386. doi:10.1016/j.cpr.2010.01.007

Phan, K. L., Fitzgerald, D. A., Gao, K., Moore, G. J., Tancer, M. E., & Posse, S. (2004). Real-time fMRI of cortico-limbic brain activity during emotional processing. *NeuroReport, 15,* 527–532. doi:10.1097/00001756-200403010-00029

Phan, K. L., Wager, T., Taylor, S. F., & Liberzon, I. (2002). Functional neuroanatomy of emotion: A meta-analysis of emotion activation studies in PET and fMRI. *NeuroImage, 16,* 331–348. doi:10.1006/nimg.2002.1087

Phillips, K. A., & Kaye, W. H. (2007). The relationship of body dysmorphic disorder and eating disorders to obsessive–compulsive disorder. *CNS Spectrums, 12,* 347–358.

Phillips, M. L., Marks, I. M., Senior, C., Lythgoe, D., O'Dwyer, A. M., Meehan, O., . . . McGuire, P. K. (2000). A differential neural response in obsessive–compulsive disorder patients with washing compared with checking symptoms to disgust. *Psychological Medicine, 30,* 1037–1050. doi:10.1017/S0033291799002652

Phillips, M. L., Senior, C., Fahy, T., & David, A. S. (1998). Disgust—The forgotten emotion of psychiatry. *The British Journal of Psychiatry, 172,* 373–375. doi:10.1192/bjp.172.5.373

Phillips, M. L., Williams, L. M., Heining, M., Herba, C. M., Russell, T., Andrew, C., . . . Gray, J. A. (2004). Differential neural responses to overt and covert presentations of facial expressions of fear and disgust. *NeuroImage, 21,* 1484–1496. doi:10.1016/j.neuroimage.2003.12.013

Phillips, M. L., Young, A. W., Scott, S. K., Calder, A. J., Andrew, C., Giampietro, V., . . . Gray, J. A. (1998). Neural responses to facial and vocal expressions of fear and disgust. *Proceedings of the Royal Society B: Biological Sciences, 265,* 1809–1817. doi:10.1098/rspb.1998.0506

Phillips, M. L., Young, A. W., Senior, C., Brammer, M., Andrew, C., Calder, A. J., . . . David, A. S. (1997). A specific neural substrate for perceiving facial expressions of disgust. *Nature, 389*, 495–498. doi:10.1038/39051

Pitman, R. K. (1987). A cybernetic model of obsessive–compulsive psychopathology. *Comprehensive Psychiatry, 28*, 334–343. doi:10.1016/0010-440X(87)90070-8

Power, J. D., Cohen, A. L., Nelson, S. M., Wig, G. S., Barnes, K. A., Church, J. A., ... Petersen, S. E. (2011). Functional network organization of the human brain. *Neuron, 72*, 665–678. doi:10.1016/j.neuron.2011.09.006

Power, M., & Dalgleish, T. (1997). *Cognition and emotion: from order to disorder*. East Sussex, England: Psychology Press.

Rachman, S. (2004). Fear of contamination. *Behaviour Research and Therapy, 42*, 1227–1255. doi:10.1016/j.brat.2003.10.009

Rachman, S., & Hodgson, R. J. (1980). *Obsessions and compulsions*. Englewood Cliffs, NJ: Prentice-Hall.

Rasmussen, S. A., & Eisen, J. L. (1992). The epidemiology and clinical features of obsessive compulsive disorder. *Psychiatric Clinics of North America, 15*, 743–758.

Rasmussen, S. A., & Tsuang, M. T. (1986). Clinical characteristics and family history in *DSM–III* obsessive–compulsive disorder. *The American Journal of Psychiatry, 143*, 317–322.

Rauch, S. L., & Baxter, L. R., Jr. (1998). *Neuroimaging in obsessive–compulsive disorder and related disorders*. St. Louis, MO: Mosby.

Rauch, S. L., Phillips, K. A., Segal, E., Makris, N., Shin, L. M., Whalen, P. J., . . . Kennedy, D. N. (2003). A preliminary morphometric magnetic resonance imaging study of regional brain volumes in body dysmorphic disorder. *Psychiatry Research, 122*, 13–19. doi:10.1016/S0925-4927(02)00117-8

Rauch, S. L., Savage, C. R., Alpert, N. M., Dougherty, D., Kendrick, A., Curran, T., . . . Jenike, M. A. (1997). Probing striatal function in obsessive–compulsive disorder: A PET study of implicit sequence learning. *The Journal of Neuropsychiatry and Clinical Neurosciences, 9*, 568–573.

Rauch, S. L., Shin, L. M., Whalen, P. J., & Pitman, R. K. (1998). Neuroimaging and the neuroanatomy of posttraumatic stress disorder. *CNS Spectrums, 3*, 31–41.

Rauch, S. L., Wedig, M. M., Wright, C. I., Martis, B., McMullin, K. G., Shin, L. M., . . . Wilhelm, S. (2007). Functional magnetic resonance imaging study of regional brain activation during implicit sequence learning in obsessive–compulsive disorder. *Biological Psychiatry, 61*, 330–336. doi:10.1016/j.biopsych.2005.12.012

Rauch, S. L., Wright, C. I., Savage, C. R., Martis, B., McMullin, K. G., Wedig, M. M., . . . Keuthen, N. J. (2007). Brain activation during implicit sequence learning in individuals with trichotillomania. *Psychiatry Research, 154*, 233–240. doi:10.1016/j.pscychresns.2006.09.002

Remijnse, P. L., Nielen, M. M., van Balkom, A. J., Cath, D. C., van Oppen, P., Uylings, H. B., & Veltman, D. J. (2006). Reduced orbitofrontal-striatal activity on a reversal learning task in obsessive–compulsive disorder. *Archives of General Psychiatry, 63,* 1225–1236. doi:10.1001/archpsyc.63.11.1225

Remijnse, P. L., Nielen, M. M., van Balkom, A. J., Hendriks, G. J., Hoogendijk, W. J., Uylings, H. B., . . . Veltman, D. J. (2009). Differential frontal-striatal and paralimbic activity during reversal learning in major depressive disorder and obsessive–compulsive disorder. *Psychological Medicine, 39,* 1503–1518. doi:10.1017/S0033291708005072

Richter, M. A., Summerfeldt, L. J., Antony, M. M., & Swinson, R. P. (2003). Obsessive–compulsive spectrum conditions in obsessive-compulsive disorder and other anxiety disorders. *Depression and Anxiety, 18,* 118–127. doi:10.1002/da.10126

Ridderinkhof, K. R., Ullsperger, M., Crone, E. A., & Nieuwenhuis, S. (2004). The role of the medial frontal cortex in cognitive control. *Science, 306,* 443–447. doi:10.1126/science.1100301

Robbins, T. W. (2007). Shifting and stopping: Fronto-striatal substrates, neurochemical modulation and clinical implications. *Philosophical Transactions of the Royal Society of London: Series B. Biological Sciences, 362,* 917–932. doi:10.1098/rstb.2007.2097

Roth, R. M., Saykin, A. J., Flashman, L. A., Pixley, H. S., West, J. D., & Mamourian, A. C. (2007). Event-related functional magnetic resonance imaging of response inhibition in obsessive–compulsive disorder. *Biological Psychiatry, 62,* 901–909. doi:10.1016/j.biopsych.2006.12.007

Royet, J. P., Plailly, J., Delon-Martin, C., Kareken, D. A., & Segebarth, C. (2003). fMRI of emotional responses to odors: Influence of hedonic valence and judgment, handedness, and gender. *NeuroImage, 20,* 713–728. doi:10.1016/S1053-8119(03)00388-4

Rozin, P., & Fallon, A. E. (1987). A perspective on disgust. *Psychological Review, 94*(1), 23–41. doi:10.1037/0033-295X.94.1.23

Rozin, P., Lowery, L., Imada, S., & Haidt, J. (1999). The CAD triad hypothesis: A mapping between three moral emotions (contempt, anger, disgust) and three moral codes (community, autonomy, divinity). *Journal of Personality and Social Psychology, 76,* 574–586. doi:10.1037/0022-3514.76.4.574

Saxena, S., Brody, A. L., Maidment, K. M., Smith, E. C., Zohrabi, N., Katz, E., & Baxter, L. R., Jr. (2004). Cerebral glucose metabolism in obsessive-compulsive hoarding. *The American Journal of Psychiatry, 161,* 1038–1048. doi:10.1176/appi.ajp.161.6.1038

Schienle, A., Schafer, A., Hermann, A., Walter, B., Stark, R., & Vaitl, D. (2006). fMRI responses to pictures of mutilation and contamination. *Neuroscience Letters, 393*(2–3), 174–178. doi:10.1016/j.neulet.2005.09.072

Schienle, A., Schafer, A., Stark, R., Walter, B., & Vaitl, D. (2005a). Neural responses of OCD patients towards disorder-relevant, generally disgust-inducing and fear-inducing pictures. *International Journal of Psychophysiology, 57*(1), 69–77. doi:10.1016/j.ijpsycho.2004.12.013

Schienle, A., Schafer, A., Stark, R., Walter, B., & Vaitl, D. (2005b). Relationship between disgust sensitivity, trait anxiety and brain activity during disgust induction. *Neuropsychobiology, 51*(2), 86–92. doi:10.1159/000084165

Schienle, A., Stark, R., Walter, B., Blecker, C., Ott, U., Kirsch, P., . . . Vaitl, D. (2002). The insula is not specifically involved in disgust processing: An fMRI study. *Neuroreport, 13*, 2023–2026. doi:10.1097/00001756-200211150-00006

Schienle, A., Stark, R., Walter, B., & Vaitl, D. (2003). The connection between disgust sensitivity and blood related fears, faintness symptoms and obsessive–compulsiveness in a non-clinical sample. *Anxiety, Stress, and Coping, 16*, 185–193.

Shapira, N. A., Liu, Y., He, A. G., Bradley, M. M., Lessig, M. C., James, G. A., . . . Goodman, W. K. (2003). Brain activation by disgust-inducing pictures in obsessive–compulsive disorder. *Biological Psychiatry, 54*, 751–756. doi:10.1016/S0006-3223(03)00003-9

Sieg, J., & Scholz, O. B. (2001). Subjective emotional and physical experience during compulsive washing and checking. *Verhaltenstherapie, 11*, 288–296. doi:10.1159/000056672

Small, D. M., Zald, D. H., Jones-Gotman, M., Zatorre, R. J., Pardo, J. V., Frey, S., & Petrides, M. (1999). Human cortical gustatory areas: A review of functional neuroimaging data. *Neuroreport, 10*(1), 7–14. doi:10.1097/00001756-199901180-00002

Smits, J. A., Telch, M. J., & Randall, P. K. (2002). An examination of the decline in fear and disgust during exposure-based treatment. *Behaviour Research and Therapy, 40*, 1243–1253. doi:10.1016/S0005-7967(01)00094-8

Song, A., Jung, W. H., Jang, J. H., Kim, E., Shim, G., Park, H. Y., . . . Kwon, J. S. (2011). Disproportionate alterations in the anterior and posterior insular cortices in obsessive–compulsive disorder. *PLoS ONE, 6*(7), e22361. doi:10.1371/journal.pone.0022361

Sprengelmeyer, R., Rausch, M., Eysel, U. T., & Przuntek, H. (1998). Neural structures associated with recognition of facial expressions of basic emotions. *Proceedings of the Royal Society B: Biological Sciences, 265*, 1927–1931. doi:10.1098/rspb.1998.0522

Sprengelmeyer, R., Young, A. W., Calder, A. J., Karnat, A., Lange, H., Homberg, V., . . . Rowland, D. (1996). Loss of disgust. Perception of faces and emotions in Huntington's disease. *Brain: A Journal of Neurology, 119*(Pt. 5), 1647–1665. doi:10.1093/brain/119.5.1647

Sprengelmeyer, R., Young, A. W., Pundt, I., Sprengelmeyer, A., Calder, A. J., Berrios, G., . . . Przuntek, H. (1997). Disgust implicated in obsessive–compulsive disorder. *Proceedings of the Royal Society B: Biological Sciences, 264*, 1767–1773. doi:10.1098/rspb.1997.0245

Sprengelmeyer, R., Young, A. W., Schroeder, U., Grossenbacher, P. G., Federlein, J., Buttner, T., & Przuntek, H. (1999). Knowing no fear. *Proceedings of the Royal Society B: Biological Sciences, 266*, 2451–2456. doi:10.1098/rspb.1999.0945

Stark, R., Schienle, A., Sarlo, M., Palomba, D., Walter, B., & Vaitl, D. (2005). Influences of disgust sensitivity on hemodynamic responses towards a disgust-inducing film clip. *International Journal of Psychophysiology, 57*, 61–67. doi:10.1016/j.ijpsycho.2005.01.010

Stark, R., Schienle, A., Walter, B., Kirsch, P., Sammer, G., Ott, U., . . . Vaitl, D. (2003). Hemodynamic responses to fear and disgust-inducing pictures: An fMRI study. *International Journal of Psychophysiology, 50*, 225–234. doi:10.1016/S0167-8760(03)00169-7

Stark, R., Zimmermann, M., Kagerer, S., Schienle, A., Walter, B., Weygandt, M., & Vaitl, D. (2007). Hemodynamic brain correlates of disgust and fear ratings. *NeuroImage, 37*, 663–673. doi:10.1016/j.neuroimage.2007.05.005

Stein, D. J., Arya, M., Pietrini, P., Rapoport, J. L., & Swedo, S. E. (2006). Neurocircuitry of disgust and anxiety in obsessive–compulsive disorder: A positron emission tomography study. *Metabolic Brain Disease, 21*, 267–277. doi:10.1007/s11011-006-9021-6

Stein, D. J., Coetzer, R., Lee, M., Davids, B., & Bouwer, C. (1997). Magnetic resonance brain imaging in women with obsessive–compulsive disorder and trichotillomania. *Psychiatry Research, 74*, 177–182. doi:10.1016/S0925-4927(97)00010-3

Stein, D. J., Liu, Y., Shapira, N. A., & Goodman, W. K. (2001). The psychobiology of obsessive–compulsive disorder: How important is the role of disgust? *Current Psychiatry Reports, 3*, 281–287. doi:10.1007/s11920-001-0020-3

Stein, D. J., van Heerden, B., Hugo, C., van Kradenburg, J., Warwick, J., Zungu-Dirwayi, N., & Seedat, S. (2002). Functional brain imaging and pharmacotherapy in trichotillomania. Single photon emission computed tomography before and after treatment with the selective serotonin reuptake inhibitor citalopram. *Progress in Neuro-Psychopharmacology & Biological Psychiatry, 26*, 885–890. doi:10.1016/S0278-5846(01)00334-7

Stern, E. R., Welsh, R. C., Fitzgerald, K. D., Gehring, W. J., Lister, J. J., Himle, J. A., . . . Taylor, S. F. (2011). Hyperactive error responses and altered connectivity in ventromedial and frontoinsular cortices in obsessive–compulsive disorder. *Biological Psychiatry, 69*, 583–591. doi:10.1016/j.biopsych.2010.09.048

Stern, E. R., Welsh, R. C., Gonzalez, R., Fitzgerald, K. D., Abelson, J. L., & Taylor, S. F. (2012). Subjective uncertainty and limbic hyperactivation in obsessive–compulsive disorder. *Human Brain Mapping*. Advance online publication. doi:10.1002/hbm.22038

Swedo, S. E., Rapoport, J. L., Leonard, H. L., Schapiro, M. B., Rapoport, S. I., & Grady, C. L. (1991). Regional cerebral glucose metabolism of women with trichotillomania. *Archives of General Psychiatry, 48*, 828–833. doi:10.1001/archpsyc.1991.01810330052008

Szechtman, H., & Woody, E. (2004). Obsessive–compulsive disorder as a disturbance of security motivation. *Psychological Review, 111*, 111–127. doi:10.1037/0033-295X.111.1.111

Taylor, S., McKay, D., & Abramowitz, J. S. (2005). Is obsessive–compulsive disorder a disturbance of security motivation? Comment on Szechtman and Woody (2004). *Psychological Review, 112,* 650–657. doi:10.1037/0033-295X.112.3.650

Taylor, S. F., Martis, B., Fitzgerald, K. D., Welsh, R. C., Abelson, J. L., Liberzon, I., . . . Gehring, W. J. (2006). Medial frontal cortex activity and loss-related responses to errors. *The Journal of Neuroscience, 26,* 4063–4070. doi:10.1523/JNEUROSCI.4709-05.2006

Taylor, S. F., Stern, E. R., & Gehring, W. J. (2007). Neural systems for error monitoring: Recent findings and theoretical perspectives. *The Neuroscientist, 13,* 160–172. doi:10.1177/1073858406298184

Thorpe, S. J., Patel, S. P., & Simonds, L. M. (2003). The relationship between disgust sensitivity, anxiety and obsessions. *Behaviour Research and Therapy, 41,* 1397–1409. doi:10.1016/S0005-7967(03)00058-5

Tolin, D. F., Kiehl, K. A., Worhunsky, P., Book, G. A., & Maltby, N. (2009). An exploratory study of the neural mechanisms of decision making in compulsive hoarding. *Psychological Medicine, 39,* 325–336. doi:10.1017/S0033291708003371

Tolin, D. F., Woods, C. M., & Abramowitz, J. S. (2006). Disgust sensitivity and obsessive–compulsive symptoms in a non-clinical sample. *Journal of Behavior Therapy and Experimental Psychiatry, 37,* 30–40. doi:10.1016/j.jbtep.2005.09.003

Tolin, D. F., Worhunsky, P., & Maltby, N. (2004). Sympathetic magic in contamination-related OCD. *Journal of Behavior Therapy and Experimental Psychiatry, 35,* 193–205. doi:10.1016/j.jbtep.2004.04.009

Tsao, S. D., & McKay, D. (2004). Behavioral avoidance tests and disgust in contamination fears: Distinctions from trait anxiety. *Behaviour Research and Therapy, 42,* 207–216. doi:10.1016/S0005-7967(03)00119-0

Ursu, S., & Carter, C. S. (2009). An initial investigation of the orbitofrontal cortex hyperactivity in obsessive–compulsive disorder: Exaggerated representations of anticipated aversive events? *Neuropsychologia, 47,* 2145–2148. doi:10.1016/j.neuropsychologia.2009.03.018

Ursu, S., Stenger, V. A., Shear, M. K., Jones, M. R., & Carter, C. S. (2003). Overactive action monitoring in obsessive–compulsive disorder: Evidence from functional magnetic resonance imaging. *Psychological Science, 14,* 347–353. doi:10.1111/1467-9280.24411

van den Heuvel, O. A., Veltman, D. J., Groenewegen, H. J., Dolan, R. J., Cath, D. C., Boellaard, R., . . . van Dyck, R. (2004). Amygdala activity in obsessive–compulsive disorder with contamination fear: A study with oxygen-15 water positron emission tomography. *Psychiatry Research, 132,* 225–237. doi:10.1016/j.pscychresns.2004.06.007

van den Heuvel, O. A., Veltman, D. J., Groenewegen, H. J., Witter, M. P., Merkelbach, I., Cath, D. C., . . . van Dyck, R. (2005). Disorder-specific neuroanatomical correlates of attentional bias in obsessive–compulsive disorder, panic disorder, and hypochondriasis. *Archives of General Psychiatry, 62,* 922–933. doi:10.1001/archpsyc.62.8.922

van der Wee, N. J. A., Ramsey, N. F., Jansma, J. M., Denys, D. A., van Megen, H. J. G. M., Westenberg, H. M. G., & Kahn, R. S. (2003). Spatial working memory deficits in obsessive compulsive disorder are associated with excessive engagement of the medial frontal cortex. *NeuroImage, 20,* 2271–2280. doi:10.1016/j.neuroimage.2003.05.001

Viard, A., Flament, M. F., Artiges, E., Dehaene, S., Naccache, L., Cohen, D., . . . Martinot, J. L. (2005). Cognitive control in childhood-onset obsessive–compulsive disorder: A functional MRI study. *Psychological Medicine, 35,* 1007–1017. doi:10.1017/S0033291704004295

Welch, J. M., Lu, J., Rodriguiz, R. M., Trotta, N. C., Peca, J., Ding, J. D., . . . Feng, G. (2007). Cortico-striatal synaptic defects and OCD-like behaviours in *Sapap3*-mutant mice. *Nature, 448,* 894–900. doi:10.1038/nature06104

Wicker, B., Keysers, C., Plailly, J., Royet, J. P., Gallese, V., & Rizzolatti, G. (2003). Both of us disgusted in *my* insula: The common neural basis of seeing and feeling disgust. *Neuron, 40,* 655–664. doi:10.1016/S0896-6273(03)00679-2

Woody, E. Z., & Szechtman, H. (2011). Adaptation to potential threat: The evolution, neurobiology, and psychopathology of the security motivation system. *Neuroscience and Biobehavioral Reviews, 35,* 1019–1033. doi:10.1016/j.neubiorev.2010.08.003

Woody, S. R., & Teachman, B. A. (2000). Intersection of disgust and fear: Normative and pathological views. *Clinical Psychology: Science and Practice, 7,* 291–311. doi:10.1093/clipsy.7.3.291

Woody, S. R., & Tolin, D. F. (2002). The relationship between disgust sensitivity and avoidant behavior: Studies of clinical and nonclinical samples. *Journal of Anxiety Disorders, 16,* 543–559. doi:10.1016/S0887-6185(02)00173-1

Wright, P., He, G., Shapira, N. A., Goodman, W. K., & Liu, Y. (2004). Disgust and the insula: fMRI responses to pictures of mutilation and contamination. *NeuroReport, 15,* 2347–2351. doi:10.1097/00001756-200410250-00009

Yücel, M., Harrison, B. J., Wood, S. J., Fornito, A., Wellard, R. M., Pujol, J., . . . Pantelis, C. (2007). Functional and biochemical alterations of the medial frontal cortex in obsessive–compulsive disorder. *Archives of General Psychiatry, 64,* 946–955. doi:10.1001/archpsyc.64.8.946

Zald, D. H., & Pardo, J. V. (2000). Functional neuroimaging of the olfactory system in humans. *International Journal of Psychophysiology, 36,* 165–181. doi:10.1016/S0167-8760(99)00110-5

INDEX

Cognitive coping, 45–46
Cognitive development, CBT and, 74–76
Cognitive distortions, 229
Cognitive features of OCD, 14–16
Cognitive functioning
    affect of declining, on ERP, 103
    declining, and late-onset OCD, 98
    identifying problems with, 122
    and RRB, 266
Cognitive inflexibility, 367–368
Cognitive restructuring
    in BDD treatment, 147–148
    in CBT for pediatric OCD, 46
    in CT for depression, 234
    in hoarding treatment, 109
Cognitive switching, 367–368
Cognitive techniques, in CBT, 71–72
Cognitive therapy (CT)
    as alternative to ERP, 4
    for BFRBs, 174, 175
    for comorbid depression, 233–234
    ERP vs., 25–26
    for hoarding disorder, 109–110, 125–127, 129
    for OCD, 22–23
    and poor insight, 88–89
Cohen, L. J., 246
Cohen-Mansfield, J., 105
COIS–R (Child Obsessive–Compulsive Impact Scale—Revised), 294
Collaboration, of multiple agencies, 136
Comorbidity
    and BDD, 144
    and geriatric hoarding, 107
    and hoarding disorder, 118–119
    and NSSI, 249
    and pediatric OCD (ages 5-8), 60, 64–65
    and pediatric OCD (ages 7-17), 39–40
    and response to ERP, 26
    of SPD, 247
    and tic disorders, 188
Competing response (CR), 197–198
Competing response training (CRT), 171–172, 191, 192
Complex tics, 186

Comprehensive behavioral intervention (CBIT), 194–198
Compulsions
    arranging, 18
    in BDD, 142
    checking, 17
    cleaning, 17
    common, in young children, 60–61
    and depressive symptoms, 226
    ERP for treatment of, 26
    as feature of OCD, 17–18
    functionally related to obsessions, 63
    habit reversal for treating, 151
    mental rituals as, 18
    ordering, 18
    repeating, 17–18
    in SPD, 248
    washing, 17
Compulsions by proxy, 18
Compulsive behaviors, 264
Compulsive subtype, of NSSI, 248–249
Computer-guided interventions, 28
COMT (catechol-O-methyltransferase) gene, 275
Comtois, K. A., 250
Conflict monitoring, 364–366
Consequences (term), 194–196
Contamination fears, 14, 370–371
Continuum technique, 24
Coons, M. J., 216–217
Coping strategies, 132
Coprolalia, 186
Core beliefs
    about appearance, and BDD, 148
    uncovering, with CT, 126
Cortex, 271
Cortico-striato-thalmo-cortical (CSTC) pathways, 189, 271, 272, 372
Cosmetic surgery, 146, 151
Cottraux, J., 98
CR (competing response), 197–198
Creed, F., 208
Crow, J. C., 330
Croyle, K. L., 249
CRT. See Competing response training
CSTC pathways. See Cortico-striato-thalmo-cortical pathways
CT. See Cognitive therapy

Dopamine transporter (DAT) gene, 275
Dorsal medial frontal cortex, 364, 365, 369
Downward Arrow (technique), 126, 132, 148
Drug-induced RRB, 269
DSM–5. *See Diagnostic and Statistical Manual of Mental Disorders*
DSM–IV–TR. *See Diagnostic and Statistical Manual of Mental Disorders, Fourth edition, Text Revision*
Duloxetine, 302
Dyck, M. J., 265
Dysfunctional beliefs, 209–210
DZ (dizygotic) twins, 347

Early-childhood-onset OCD, 60
Early-onset OCD, 350
Early warning signs, 197
Echolalia, 186
Effexor, 319
Elavil, 319
Eley, T. C., 355
Elliot, M., 332
Emery, G., 23
Emotional face processing, 369–370
Emotional Reasoning (term), 126
Emotion regulation, 242, 248
Emotion regulation training, 173
Emotions, and hoarding disorder, 122
Encouragement, from parents, 70
Environmental factors
    in animal models of RRB, 269
    and tic disorders, 188, 194
Epidemiology
    of BDD, 143
    of health anxiety, 208–209
    of pediatric OCD (ages 7-17), 38
ERP. *See* Exposure and response prevention
Error monitoring, 364–366
Escitalopram, 276, 299, 301
Eskalith, 319
Ethnicity, and BDD, 143
Etiology, of pediatric OCD, 61–62
"Etiology of Obsessions and Compulsions" (S. Taylor), 352, 354, 355
Excoriation disorder, 246–247. *See also* Skin picking disorder

Executive functioning
    and ASD, 266
    deficits in, and CBT, 109
    and geriatric hoarding, 107
    identifying problems with, 122
    and RRB, 265–266
Exposure and response prevention (ERP)
    for adult OCD, 21–22
    for BDD, 149–150
    in CBT for health anxiety, 216
    in CBT for pediatric OCD, 47–50
    CT as alternative to, 4
    CT vs., 25–26
    with elderly patients, 101
    explaining, to children, 45
    in family-based CBT, 70–71
    for hoarding disorder, 119, 129–131
    introduction of, 4
    and physical health, 102–103
    and SRIs, 321
    for tic disorders, 193
Exposure hierarchy, 21, 129
External antecedents, 195
External consequences, 195
Externalizing behaviors, 39–40
Externalizing symptoms, 85
External stimuli, 193

FA. *See* Family accommodation
Fagnani, C., 355, 356
Fallon, B. A., 326
Family accommodation (FA)
    of pediatric OCD (ages 7-17), 41
    reducing, in response prevention plan, 50–51
    and treatment outcomes, 84–86
Family Accommodation Scale, 43
Family-based CBT, 66–74
Family disruptions, 40–41
Family functioning
    and CTD, 189
    effect of hoarding on, 118
    impaired due to pediatric OCD, 60
    OCD exacerbated by, 86–87
Family members
    in CBT, 27, 104
    in OCD rituals, 61
    of patients with hoarding disorders, 136

Leckman, J. F., 192, 272
Lenane, M. C., 39, 328
Leonard, H. L., 39, 301, 317, 328
Lerner, J., 174
Lesch–Nyhan syndrome (LNS), 275
Levetiracetam, 319
Lewis, M. H., 270
Lexapro, 299
Liebowitz, M. R., 301
Limbic loop, 272
Limbic regions, 369–370, 381
Lincoln, A. J., 266
Linehan, M. M., 250
Liothyronine sodium, 319
Lip biting, 166–167
Lithane, 319
Lithium carbonate, 319
Lithobid, 319
LMG, 305
LNS (Lesch–Nyhan syndrome), 275
Lochner, C., 246
Lopez, B. R., 266
Lower order RRB, 264, 276
L-tridothyronine, 319
Luvox, 299, 319

Mackenzie, T. B., 330
Mackin, R. S., 107
Magical thinking, 23
Mail, management of, 129
Major depression, 26
Major depressive disorder (MDD). *See also* Depression
    and BDD, 227–228, 230–231
    and CT, 234
    defined, 226
    and HC, 228–229
    and increased cognitive distortions, 229
    and OCD, 226–227, 230
Maladaptive beliefs, 15–16, 145
Maladaptive cognitions
    and BFRBs, 174
    identifying and challenging, 23–25
    in patients with BDD, 148
Maladaptive thoughts, 215
Mancini, C., 330
Mansueto, C. S., 169
March, J. S., 44, 47, 301

Marks, I. M., 233
Martin, A., 300
Martin, L. A., 268
Marx, M. S., 105
Massachusetts General Hospital—Hair Pulling Scale, 330
Maxner, S., 135
McCarthy, P., 233
McConachie, H., 265
McKay, D., 250, 376
McKinley, T., 192
McNally, R. J., 229
McPheeters, M. L., 276
MD (muscle dysmorphia), 142–143
MDD. *See* Major depressive disorder
Mecp2 gene, 268
Mecp2(308/Y) mice, 268–269
Medial frontal cortex, 365
Medical tests, and medication, 307
Medication. *See also specific medications*
    anticonvulsants, 304
    antidepressant, 232–233, 319
    antiepileptics, 305, 319
    antipsychotics. *See* Antipsychotics
    benzodiazepines, 319
    and CBT, 232–233
    for hoarding, 107–108
    for hoarding disorder, 119
    interactions between, 101
    medical tests before administering, 307
    neuroleptics, 146, 190
    with or without CBT, 297–298
    for pediatric OCD (ages 7-17), 43
    and pregnancy, 307
    selecting and starting, 298, 301–302
    SRIs. *See* Serotonin reuptake inhibitors
    SSRIs. *See* Selective serotonin reuptake inhibitors
    treatment algorithm for, 302–304
    tricyclics, 296
Medication-related assessment, 294–296
Memantine, 174, 276, 304, 305
Menard, W., 245
Mental rituals, 18
Meyer, V., 4
MI. *See* Motivational interviewing
Miller, W., 124, 151

Riluzole, 304
Risk assessment, 107
Risk factors, for suicidality, 244–245
Risperdal, 299, 319
Risperidone, 275–276, 299, 302, 319, 322
Ritualistic behaviors, 264
Rituals
   in BDD, 145
   BFRBs as, 168
   difficulty in identifying, 75
   mental, 18
   and mirror retraining, 150
   physical, 42
   preventing, in ERP, 47, 149–150
   verbal, 42
   in young children, 75
Robertson, M. M., 189
Rodgers, J., 265
Rogers, S. J., 265
Rojas, D. C., 271
Rollnick, S., 124, 151
RRBs. *See* Restricted repetitive behaviors
RS (Rett syndrome), 267–269
RT. *See* Relaxation training
Rumsey, J. M., 271

Sameness behaviors, 264, 270
SAPAP3 protein, 269
Sarkhel, S., 167
Saving Cognitions Inventory (SCI), 120
Savings Inventory—Revised (SI–R), 106, 108, 118, 120, 134, 135
Scaffolding, 70
Schizophrenia
   and COMT, 275
   hoarding symptoms with, 105
   and OCD symptoms, 87
Schmeidler, J., 246
Schuck, K., 175
Schweitzer, P. J., 326
SCI (Saving Cognitions Inventory), 120
SCL-90 (Symptom Checklist–90), 356–357
Scrupulosity obsessions, 15
Sears, L. L., 271

Selective serotonin reuptake inhibitors (SSRIs), 299, 305
   for ASD, 276
   for OCD, 4
   for PANDAS, 38, 39
   for pediatric OCD, 296
   for repetitive behaviors, 274
   for SPD, 332
Self-efficacy, 124, 133
Self-help interventions, 28
Self-injurious behaviors (SIBs), 264, 269
Self-injury, 241–251
   future research on OCD and, 250–251
   NSSI and OCD, 246–250
   suicide and OCD, 242–246
   treatment for OCD and, 250
Self-monitoring, 23
Self-report measures, 20, 169
Sensorimotor loop (CSTC pathway), 272
Sensory domain theory, 264
Seroquel, 299, 319
Serotonin, 144
Serotonin model, of BDD, 274–275
Serotonin reuptake inhibitors (SRIs), 305
   for BDD, 146, 324–325
   for depression with OCD, 233
   for hoarding disorder, 119
   and MDD, 230
   for OCD, 320–323
   for pediatric OCD, 296
   for TTM, 327–329
Sertraline, 299, 319, 329
Sevincok, L., 244
Sexual orientation, BDD and, 145
Shady, G., 189
Shafritz, K. M., 270–271
SHAI (Short Health Anxiety Inventory), 212
Shalev, I., 44
Shapira, N. A., 375
Shared environment (C), 347–348
Sharpe, D., 230
Short Health Anxiety Inventory (SHAI), 212
SHRT (simplified habit reversal training), 192
SIBs (self-injurious behaviors), 264, 269

Simeon, D., 246, 249

Simple tics, 186

Simplified habit reversal training (SHRT), 192

Singer, H. S., 271

Singh, A. L., 356

Single photon emission computed tomography (SPECT), 377–378

Sinoff, G., 98

SI–R. *See* Savings Inventory—Revised

Situational awareness, 197

Skills training, 127–129

Skin picking disorder (SPD)
    as BFRBs, 165–166
    comorbidity of, 247
    as NSSI, 246–247
    and OCD, 247–248
    pharmacotherapy for, 331–333
    subtypes of, 248

SLC1A2 gene, 274

SLC6A4, 274

SMA (supplemental motor area), 364–367, 380

Social deprivation, 269

Social functioning, 40, 60, 188–189

Social reinforcement, 193–194

Social support, 172, 198

Socratic questioning
    in BDD treatment, 148, 152
    as cognitive strategy, 132
    in hoarding disorder treatment, 127
    and responsibility pie charts, 24–25

Somatic obsessions, 14

Somatic symptom disorder, 207

Somatic Symptom Inventory, 213

Spadaccini, E., 246

SPD. *See* Skin picking disorder

SPECT (single photon emission computed tomography), 377–378

Sprengelmeyer, R., 374

SRI-induced mania, 307

SRIs. *See* Serotonin reuptake inhibitors

SSRIs. *See* Selective serotonin reuptake inhibitors

Staley, D., 189

Stanley, B., 246

Stanley, M., 246

Stark, R., 374

Stein, D. J., 246, 375

Steketee, G., 119, 134, 135, 230, 233

Stemberger, R. M. T., 169

Stereotyped behaviors, 264, 267–268, 270

Sterling, H. E., 193, 194

Stewart, S. E., 300, 301

Stimulus control (technique), 170–171, 174–175

Street, G. P., 233

Streichenwein, S. M., 328

Streptococcal infection, 187–188

Stressors, OCD symptoms exacerbated by, 104

Stress-tolerance skills, 173

Striatal area, 271

Stroop task, 364

Subcortical structures, 366, 369

Subjective Units of Distress Scale (SUDS), 21, 149, 216

Suicidality
    and BDD, 144, 245
    increased by medication, 307–308
    and OCD, 242–246
    prevalence of, 241

Sulcus, 379

Sulpiride, 269

Supplemental motor area (SMA), 364–367, 380

Sutcliffe, J. S., 274

Swedo, S. E., 39, 296, 317, 328

Symmetry obsessions, 14, 245

Symptom Checklist–90 (SCL-90), 356–357

Symptoms, externalizing, 85

TAF (thought–action fusion), 15–16, 45–46

Taking Another Perspective (technique), 127

Taking the Opposite Perspective (technique), 127

Tanimura, Y., 270

Task List form, 128

Taste, sense of, 372

Taylor, S., 216–217, 349, 352–357, 376

Taylor, S. F., 365

Teachman, B. A., 98–99

Temporal cortex, 267–268, 365, 369, 377, 381

ABOUT THE EDITORS

Eric A. Storch, PhD, is a professor and All Children's Hospital Guild Endowed Chair in the Departments of Pediatrics, Psychiatry and Behavioral Neurosciences, and Psychology at the University of South Florida. He has published more than 325 peer-reviewed journal articles and book chapters, and has edited or coedited six books dealing with treatment of complex cases in children, obsessive–compulsive disorder (OCD), and childhood anxiety. He has received grant funding for his work in OCD, related disorders, and anxiety from the National Institutes of Health, Centers for Disease Control and Prevention, Agency for Healthcare Research and Quality, International OCD Foundation, Tourette Syndrome Association, and National Alliance for Research on Schizophrenia and Affective Disorders. He directs the cognitive–behavioral therapy component at the University of South Florida OCD Program and is highly regarded for his treatment of pediatric and adult OCD patients.

Dean McKay, PhD, ABPP, is a professor in the Department of Psychology at Fordham University. He serves on the editorial boards of *Behaviour Research and Therapy, Behavior Modification, Behavior Therapy,* and the *Journal of Anxiety*

Disorders and is editor-in-chief of *Journal of Cognitive Psychotherapy*. Dr. McKay is the 2013–2014 president of the Association for Behavioral and Cognitive Therapies. He has published more than 130 journal articles and book chapters and has given more than 150 conference presentations. He is board certified in behavioral and clinical psychology by the American Board of Professional Psychology and is a fellow of the American Board of Behavioral Psychology and the Academy of Clinical Psychology. He is also a fellow of the American Psychological Society. Dr. McKay has edited or coedited eight books dealing with treatment of complex cases in children and adults, OCD, disgust in psychopathology, and research methodology. His research has focused primarily on OCD, body dysmorphic disorder, and hypochondriasis and their link to OCD as well as the role of disgust in psychopathology. Dr. McKay is also director and founder of the Institute for Cognitive Behavior Therapy and Research, a private treatment and research center in Westchester County, New York.

616.8584
S88 41

LINCOLN CHRISTIAN UNIVERSITY

3 4711 00224 7221